Garfield

FAT CAT 3-PACK

VOLUME 18

Garfield
FAT CAT 3-PACK
VOLUME 18

BY
JIM DAVIS

BALLANTINE BOOKS · NEW YORK

2016 Ballantine Books Trade Paperback Edition

Based on the Garfield® characters created by Jim Davis

Published in the United States by Ballantine Books, an imprint of Random House,
a division of Penguin Random House LLC, New York.

GARFIELD LARD OF THE JUNGLE, GARFIELD BRINGS HOME THE BACON, and GARFIELD GETS IN A PICKLE
were each published separately by Ballantine Books, an imprint of Random House, a division of Penguin
Random House LLC, New York, in 2011, 2012, and 2012 respectively.

ISBN 978-0-399-59440-3

Printed in China on acid-free paper

randomhousebooks.com

9 8 7 6

Garfield
LARD OF THE JUNGLE

BY JIM DAVIS

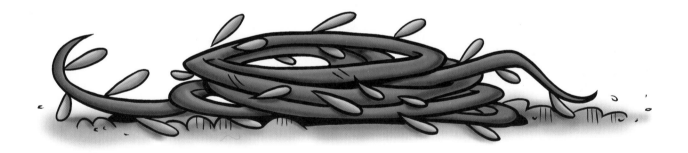

Ballantine Books • New York

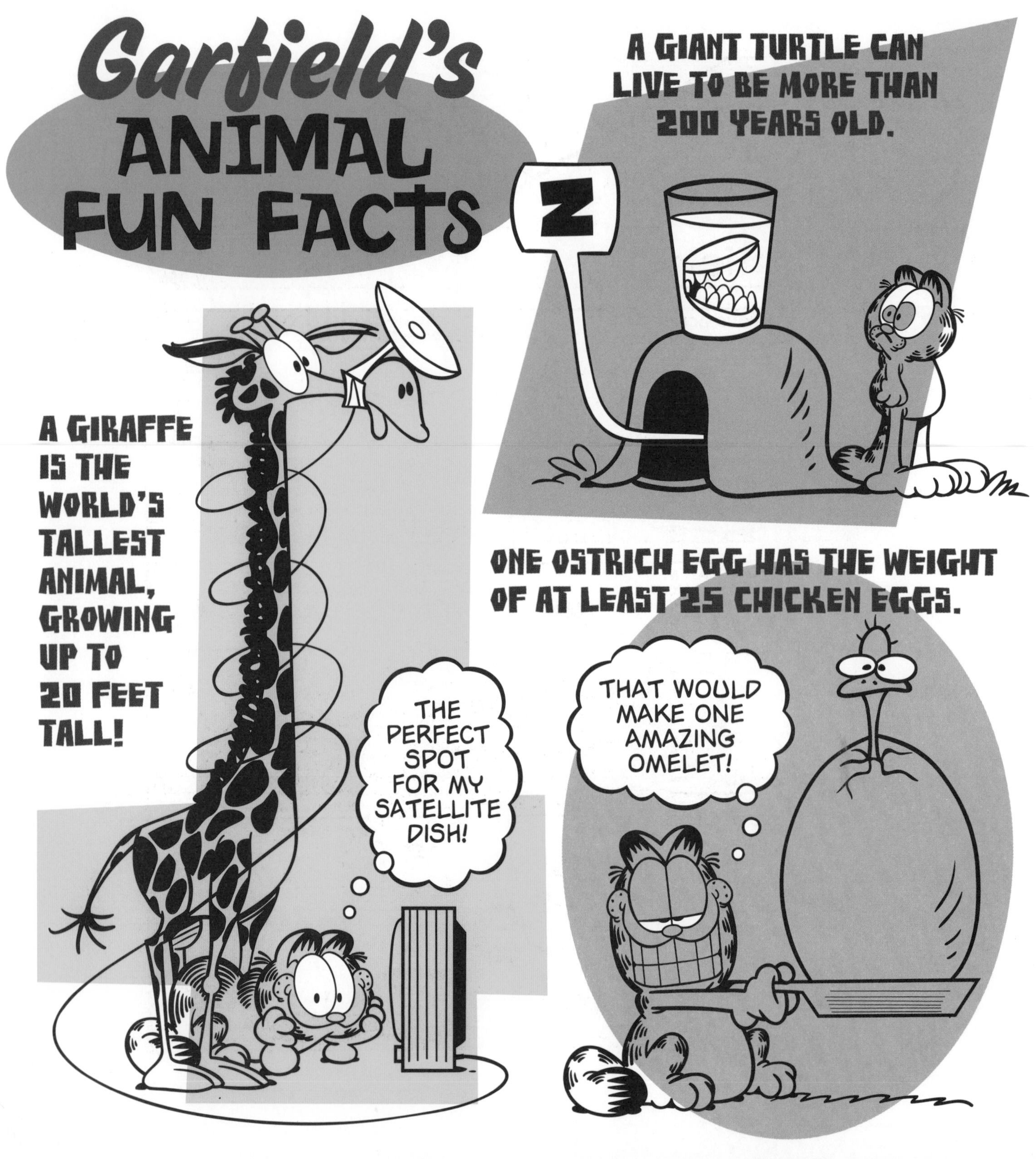
Garfield's ANIMAL FUN FACTS
A GIANT TURTLE CAN LIVE TO BE MORE THAN 200 YEARS OLD.
Z
A GIRAFFE IS THE WORLD'S TALLEST ANIMAL, GROWING UP TO 20 FEET TALL!
THE PERFECT SPOT FOR MY SATELLITE DISH!
ONE OSTRICH EGG HAS THE WEIGHT OF AT LEAST 25 CHICKEN EGGS.
THAT WOULD MAKE ONE AMAZING OMELET!

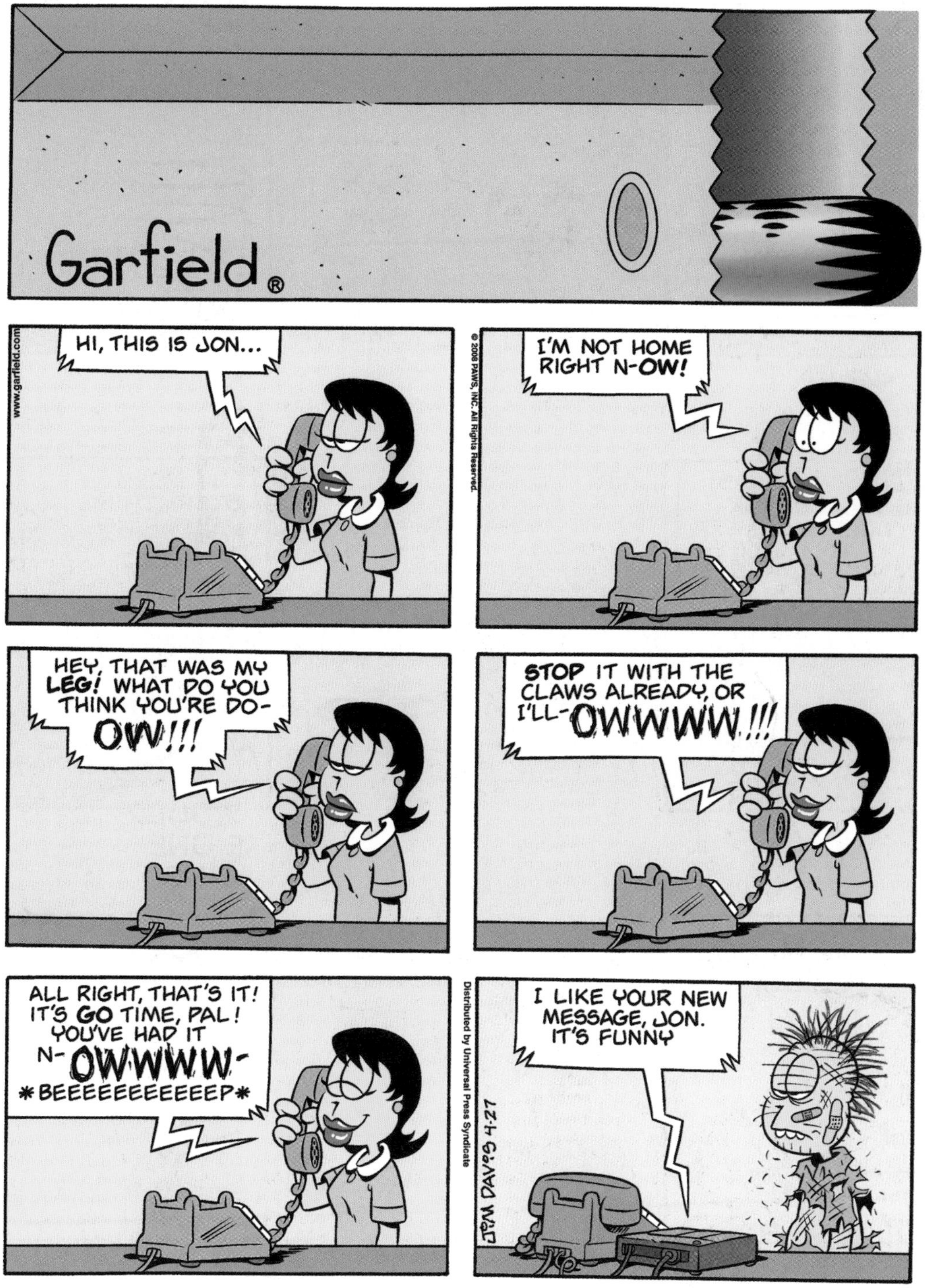
Garfield®
www.garfield.com
HI, THIS IS JON...
© 2008 PAWS, INC. All Rights Reserved.
I'M NOT HOME RIGHT N-OW!
HEY, THAT WAS MY LEG! WHAT DO YOU THINK YOU'RE DO- OW!!!
STOP IT WITH THE CLAWS ALREADY, OR I'LL- OWWWW!!!
ALL RIGHT, THAT'S IT! IT'S GO TIME, PAL! YOU'VE HAD IT N- OWWWW- *BEEEEEEEEEEEP*
Distributed by Universal Press Syndicate
JPM DAVIS 4-27
I LIKE YOUR NEW MESSAGE, JON. IT'S FUNNY

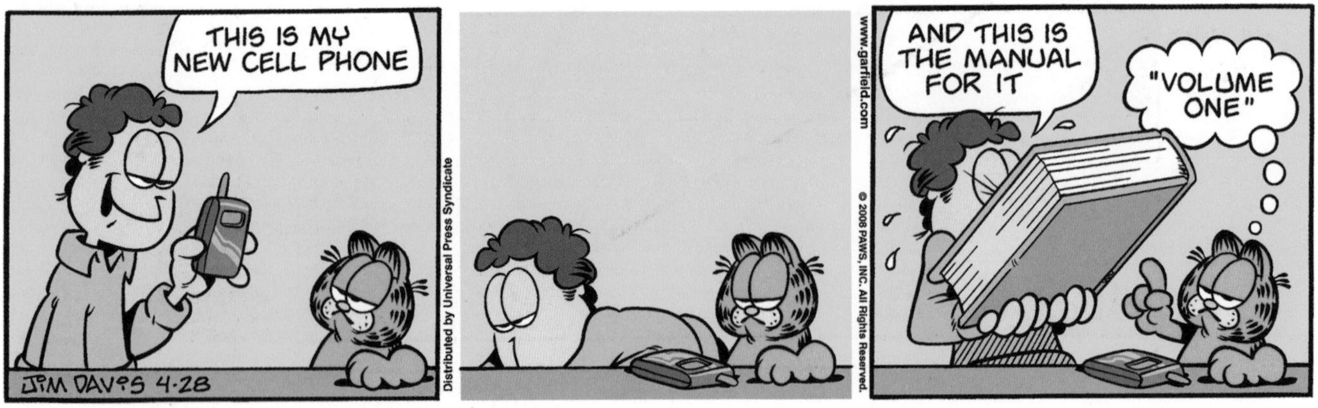
THIS IS MY NEW CELL PHONE
JIM DAVIS 4·28
Distributed by Universal Press Syndicate
www.garfield.com
© 2008 PAWS, INC. All Rights Reserved.
AND THIS IS THE MANUAL FOR IT
"VOLUME ONE"

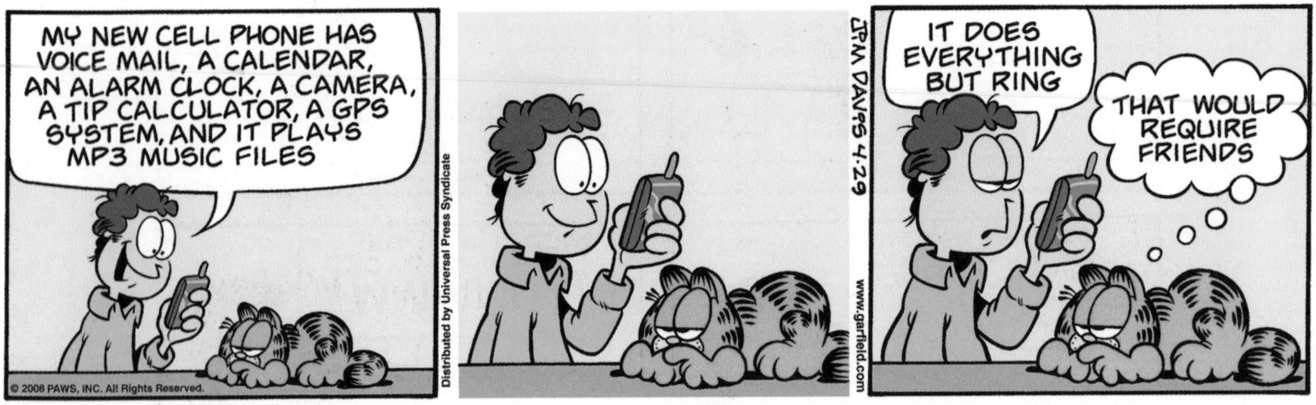
MY NEW CELL PHONE HAS VOICE MAIL, A CALENDAR, AN ALARM CLOCK, A CAMERA, A TIP CALCULATOR, A GPS SYSTEM, AND IT PLAYS MP3 MUSIC FILES
© 2008 PAWS, INC. All Rights Reserved.
Distributed by Universal Press Syndicate
JIM DAVIS 4·29
www.garfield.com
IT DOES EVERYTHING BUT RING
THAT WOULD REQUIRE FRIENDS

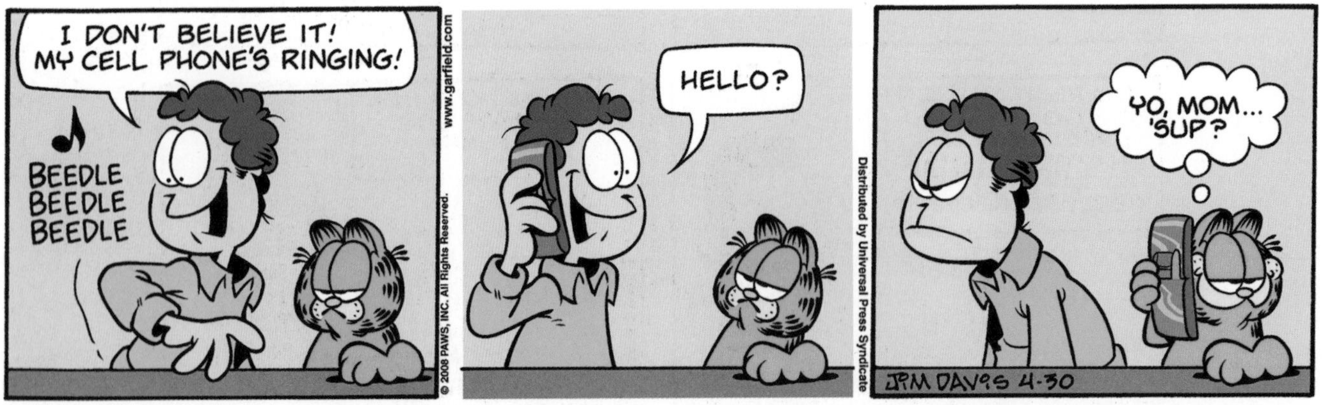
I DON'T BELIEVE IT! MY CELL PHONE'S RINGING!
BEEDLE BEEDLE BEEDLE
www.garfield.com
© 2008 PAWS, INC. All Rights Reserved.
HELLO?
Distributed by Universal Press Syndicate
YO, MOM... 'SUP?
JIM DAVIS 4-30

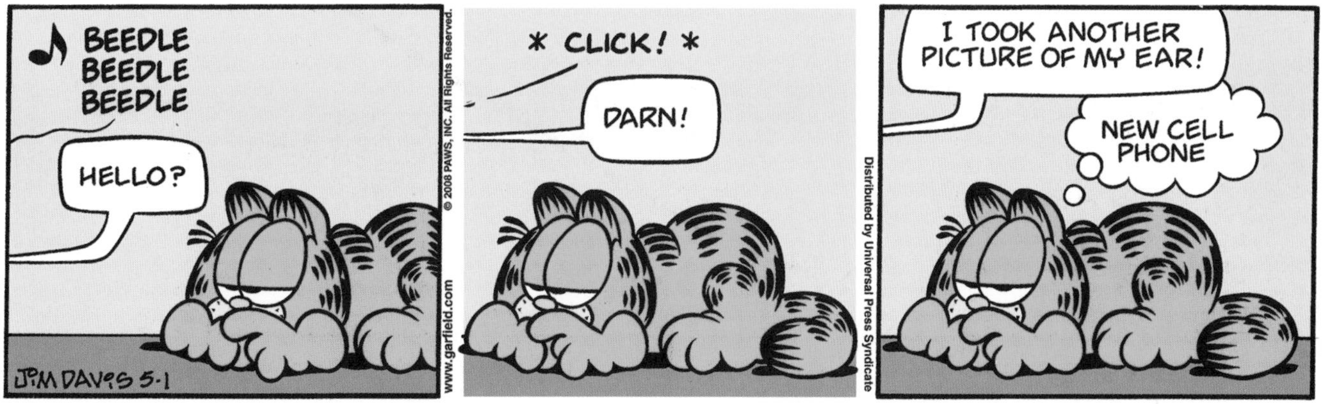
BEEDLE BEEDLE BEEDLE
HELLO?
* CLICK! *
DARN!
I TOOK ANOTHER PICTURE OF MY EAR!
NEW CELL PHONE
JIM DAVIS 5-1
© 2008 PAWS, INC. All Rights Reserved.
www.garfield.com
Distributed by Universal Press Syndicate

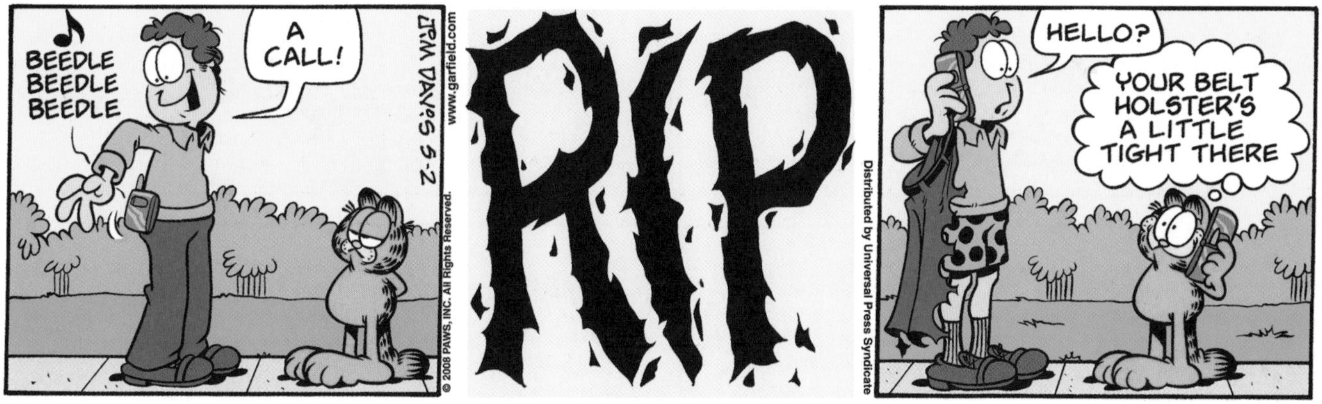
BEEDLE BEEDLE BEEDLE
A CALL!
JIM DAVIS 5-2
RIP
HELLO?
YOUR BELT HOLSTER'S A LITTLE TIGHT THERE
© 2008 PAWS, INC. All Rights Reserved.
www.garfield.com
Distributed by Universal Press Syndicate

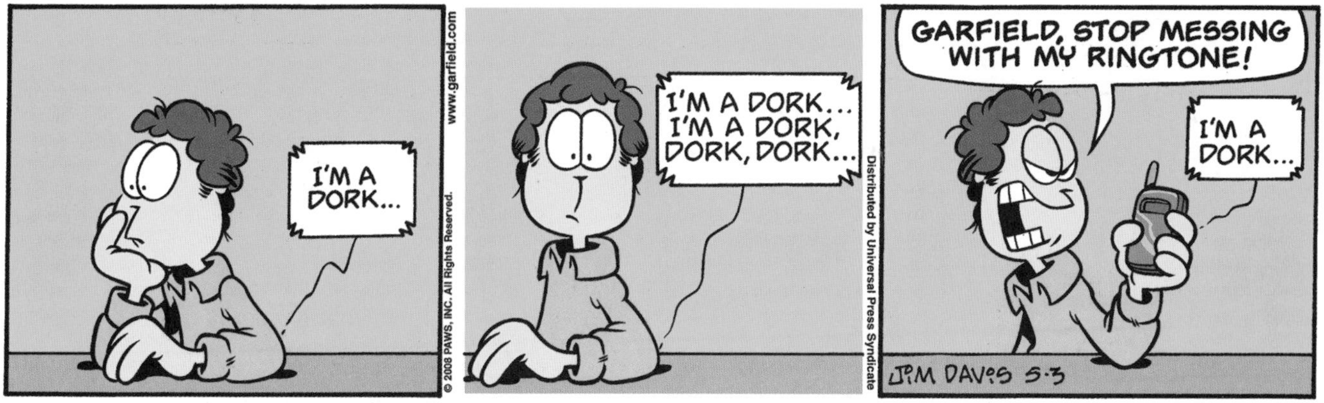
I'M A DORK...
I'M A DORK... I'M A DORK, DORK, DORK...
GARFIELD, STOP MESSING WITH MY RINGTONE!
I'M A DORK...
JIM DAVIS 5-3
© 2008 PAWS, INC. All Rights Reserved.
www.garfield.com
Distributed by Universal Press Syndicate

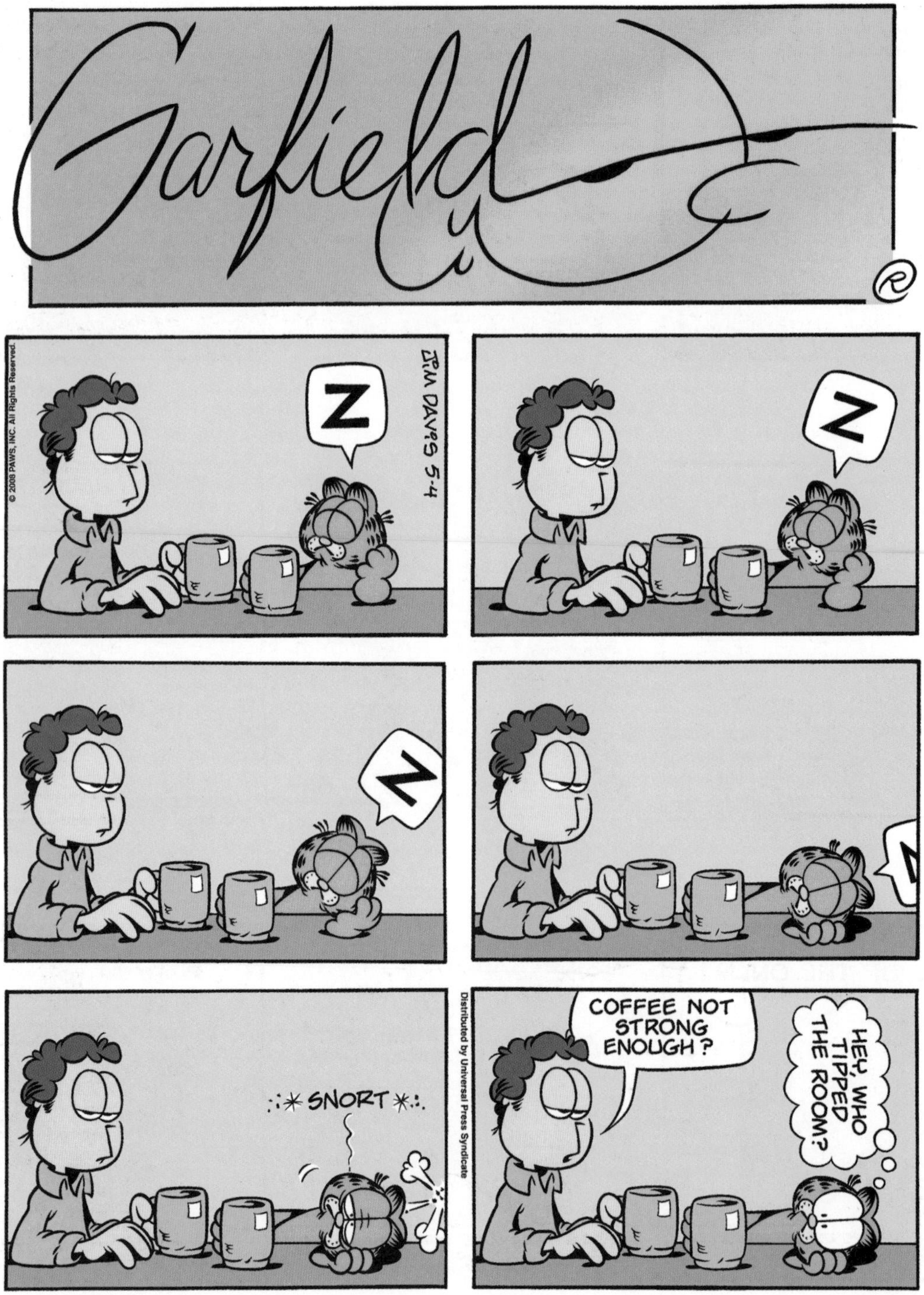
Garfield
© 2008 PAWS, INC. All Rights Reserved.
JIM DAVIS 5-4
Z
Z
Z
Distributed by Universal Press Syndicate
SNORT
COFFEE NOT STRONG ENOUGH?
HEY, WHO TIPPED THE ROOM?

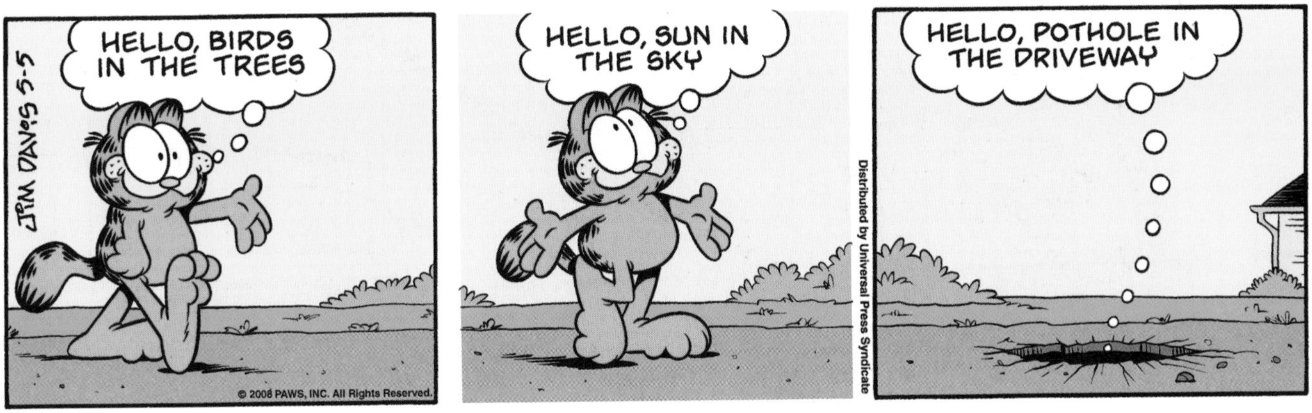
JIM DAVIS 5-5
HELLO, BIRDS IN THE TREES
HELLO, SUN IN THE SKY
HELLO, POTHOLE IN THE DRIVEWAY
© 2008 PAWS, INC. All Rights Reserved.
Distributed by Universal Press Syndicate

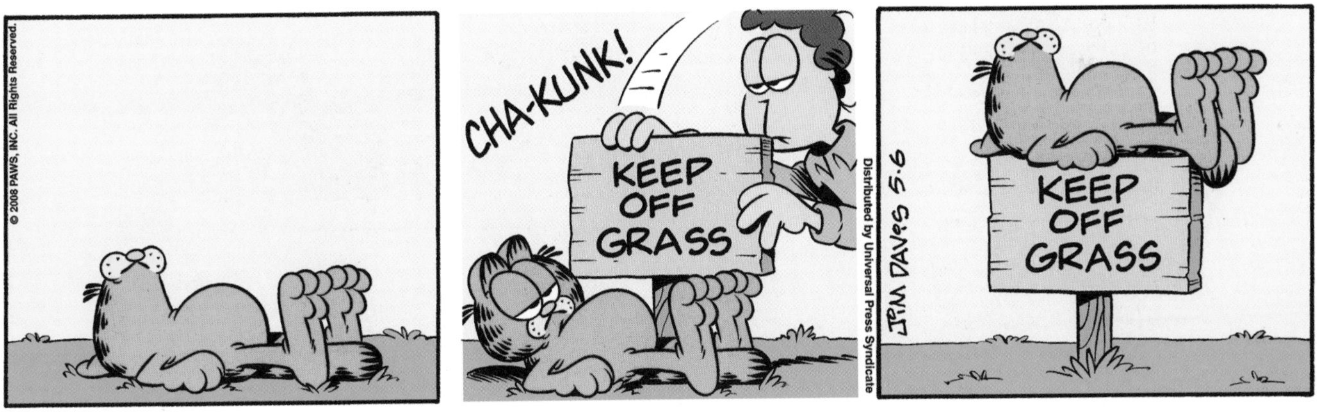
© 2008 PAWS, INC. All Rights Reserved.
CHA-KUNK!
KEEP OFF GRASS
Distributed by Universal Press Syndicate
JIM DAVIS 5-6
KEEP OFF GRASS

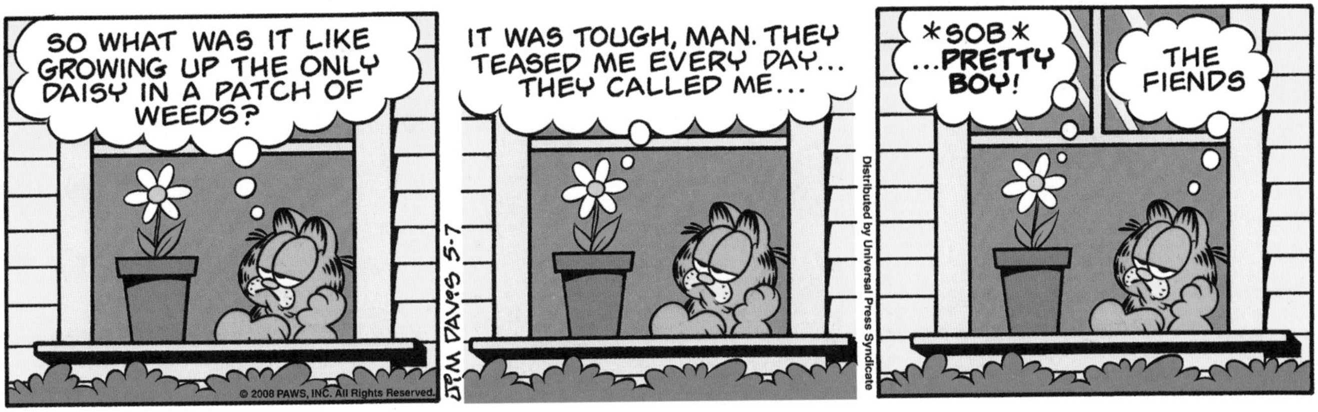
SO WHAT WAS IT LIKE GROWING UP THE ONLY DAISY IN A PATCH OF WEEDS?
© 2008 PAWS, INC. All Rights Reserved.
JIM DAVIS 5-7
IT WAS TOUGH, MAN. THEY TEASED ME EVERY DAY... THEY CALLED ME...
Distributed by Universal Press Syndicate
SOB ...PRETTY BOY!
THE FIENDS

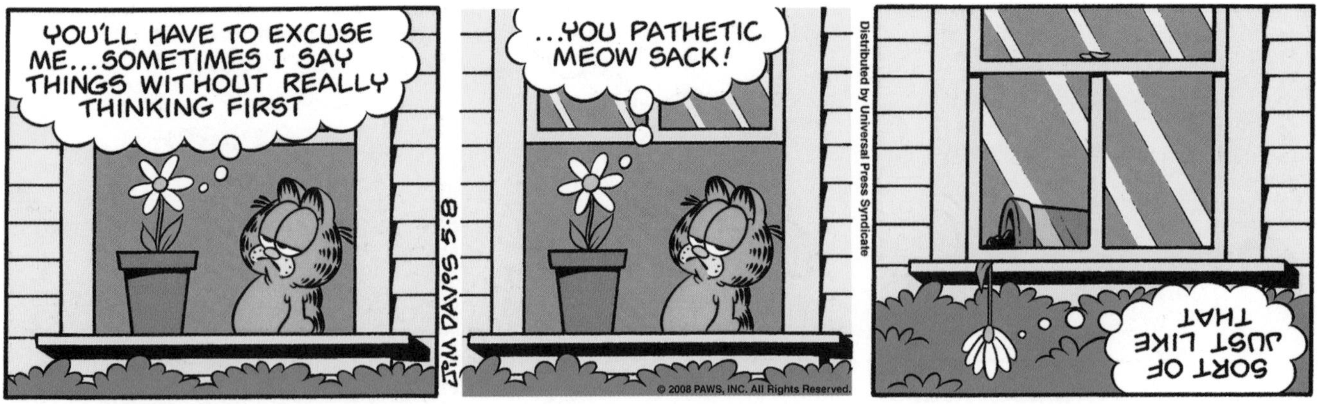
YOU'LL HAVE TO EXCUSE ME...SOMETIMES I SAY THINGS WITHOUT REALLY THINKING FIRST
JIM DAVIS 5-8
...YOU PATHETIC MEOW SACK!
© 2008 PAWS, INC. All Rights Reserved.
Distributed by Universal Press Syndicate
SORT OF JUST LIKE THAT

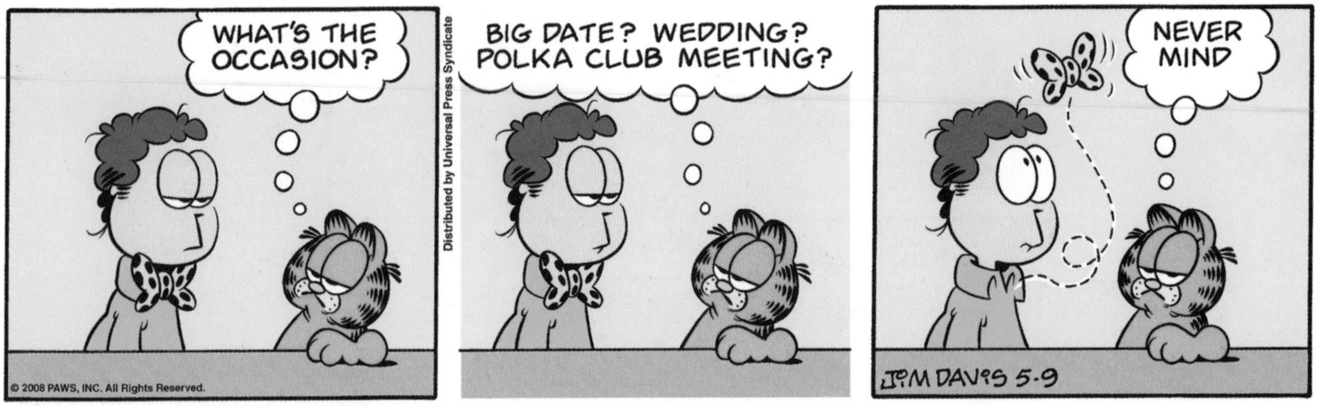
WHAT'S THE OCCASION?
© 2008 PAWS, INC. All Rights Reserved.
Distributed by Universal Press Syndicate
BIG DATE? WEDDING? POLKA CLUB MEETING?
NEVER MIND
JIM DAVIS 5-9

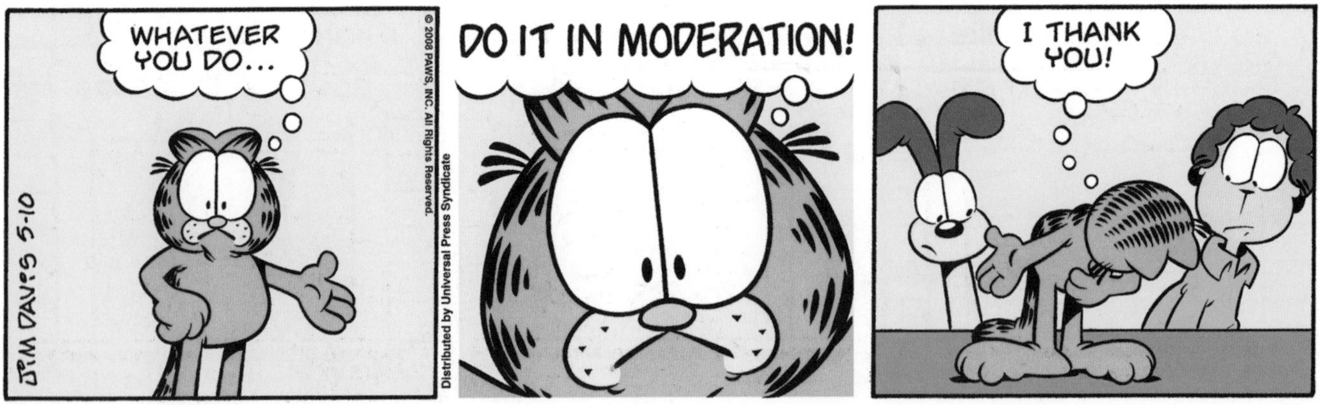
WHATEVER YOU DO...
JIM DAVIS 5-10
© 2008 PAWS, INC. All Rights Reserved.
Distributed by Universal Press Syndicate
DO IT IN MODERATION!
I THANK YOU!

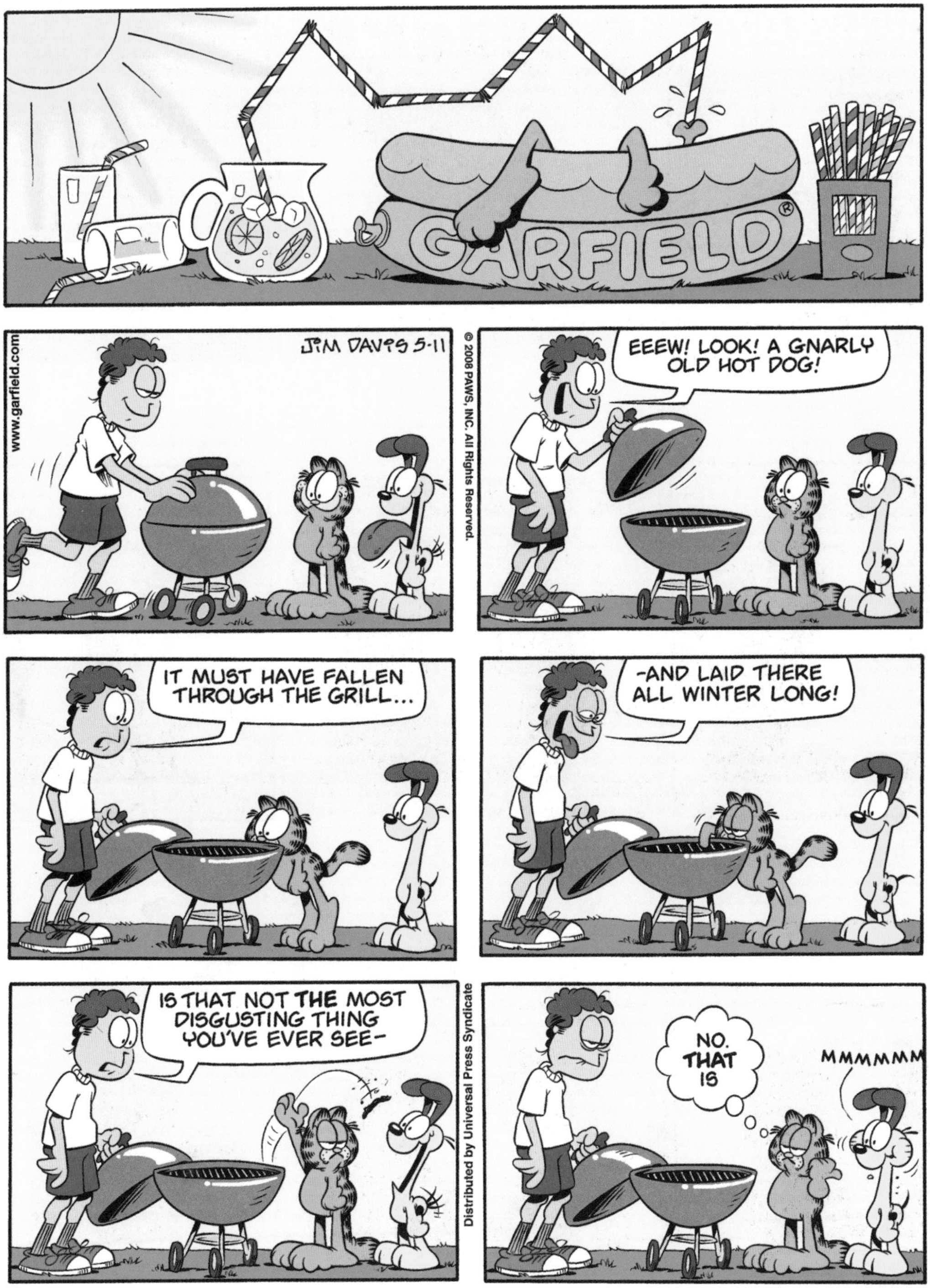
GARFIELD®
JIM DAVIS 5-11
www.garfield.com
© 2008 PAWS, INC. All Rights Reserved.
EEEW! LOOK! A GNARLY OLD HOT DOG!
IT MUST HAVE FALLEN THROUGH THE GRILL...
-AND LAID THERE ALL WINTER LONG!
IS THAT NOT **THE** MOST DISGUSTING THING YOU'VE EVER SEE-
Distributed by Universal Press Syndicate
NO. **THAT** IS
MMMMMM

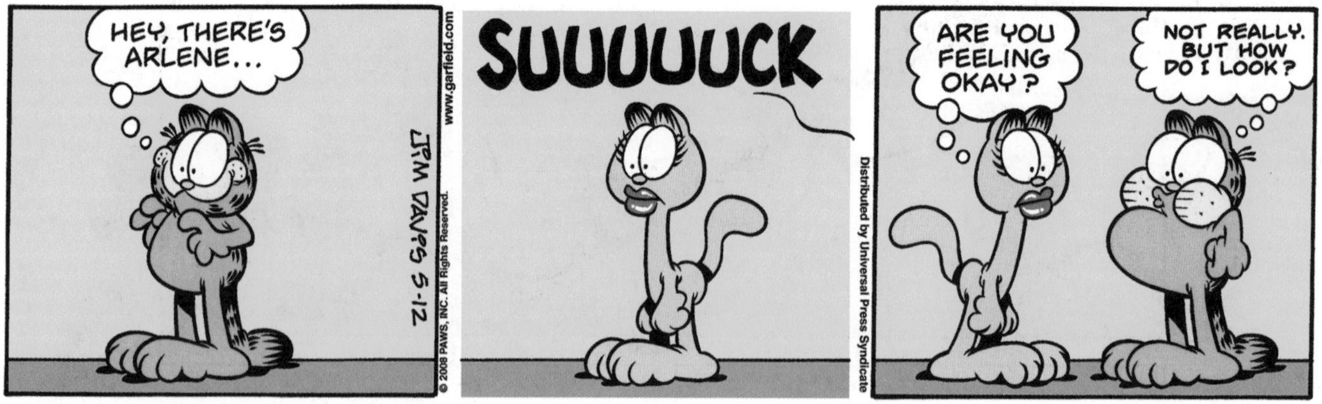
HEY, THERE'S ARLENE...
JPM DAVIS 5-12
© 2008 PAWS, INC. All Rights Reserved.
www.garfield.com
SUUUUUCK
Distributed by Universal Press Syndicate
ARE YOU FEELING OKAY?
NOT REALLY. BUT HOW DO I LOOK?

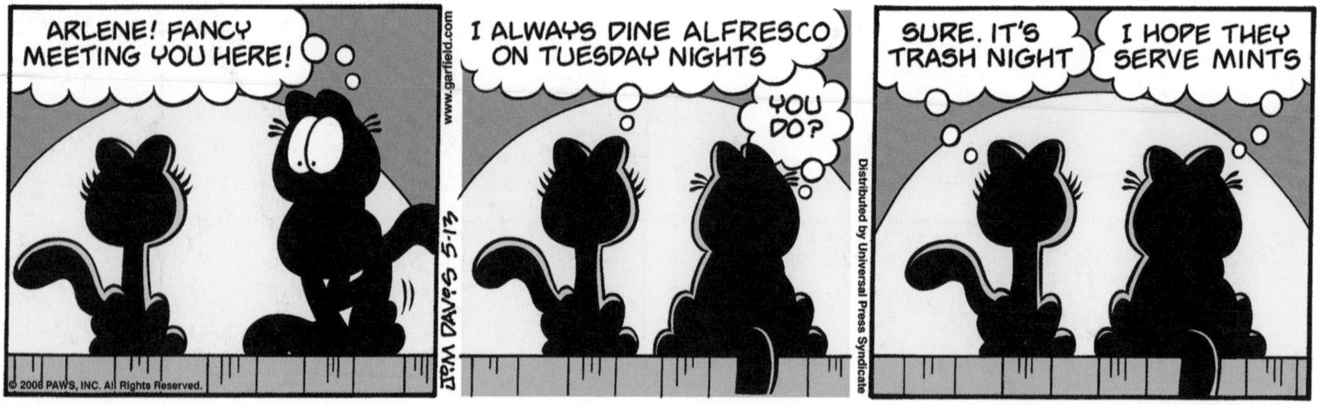
ARLENE! FANCY MEETING YOU HERE!
© 2008 PAWS, INC. All Rights Reserved.
JPM DAVIS 5-13
www.garfield.com
I ALWAYS DINE ALFRESCO ON TUESDAY NIGHTS
YOU DO?
Distributed by Universal Press Syndicate
SURE. IT'S TRASH NIGHT
I HOPE THEY SERVE MINTS

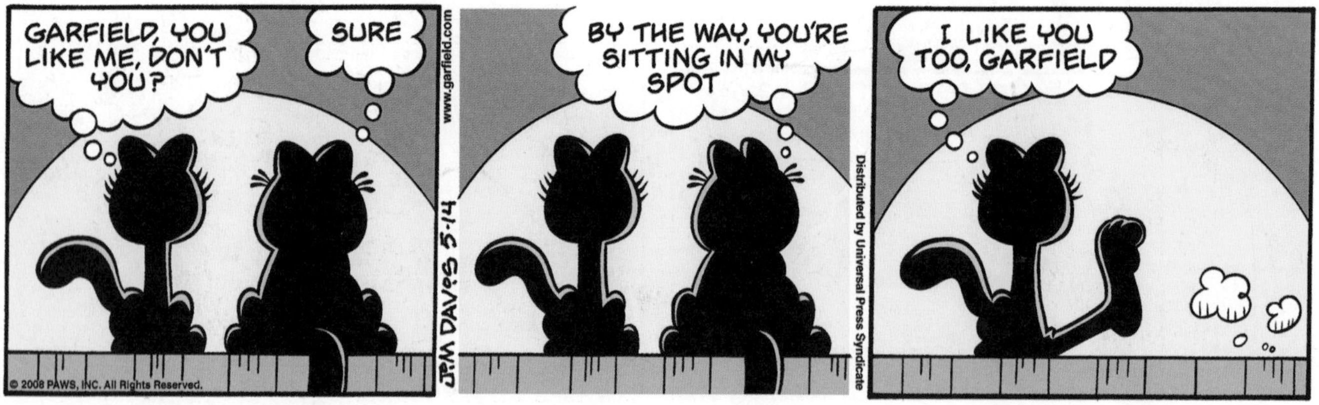
GARFIELD, YOU LIKE ME, DON'T YOU?
SURE
© 2008 PAWS, INC. All Rights Reserved.
JPM DAVIS 5-14
www.garfield.com
BY THE WAY, YOU'RE SITTING IN MY SPOT
Distributed by Universal Press Syndicate
I LIKE YOU TOO, GARFIELD

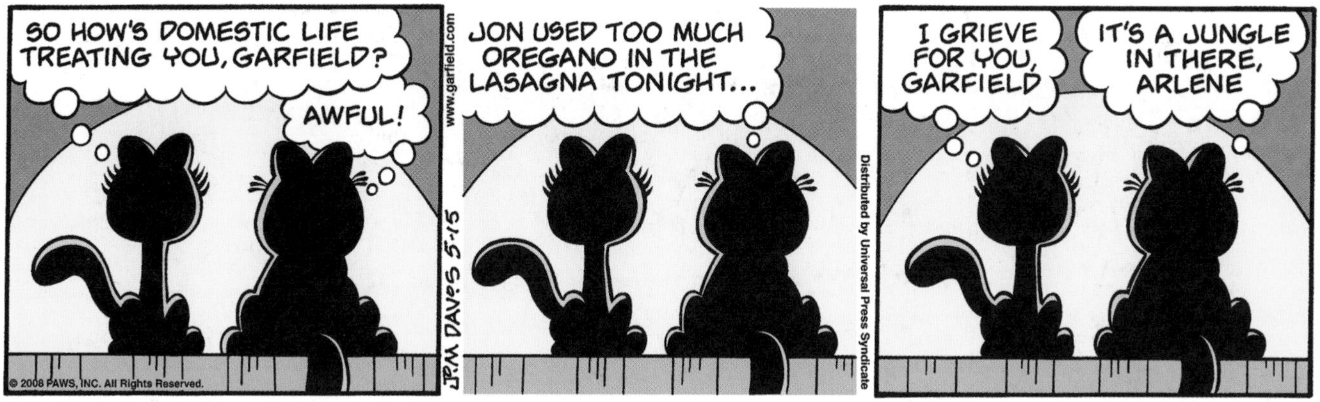
SO HOW'S DOMESTIC LIFE TREATING YOU, GARFIELD?
AWFUL!
JON USED TOO MUCH OREGANO IN THE LASAGNA TONIGHT...
I GRIEVE FOR YOU, GARFIELD
IT'S A JUNGLE IN THERE, ARLENE
© 2008 PAWS, INC. All Rights Reserved.
www.garfield.com
JPM DAVIS 5-15
Distributed by Universal Press Syndicate

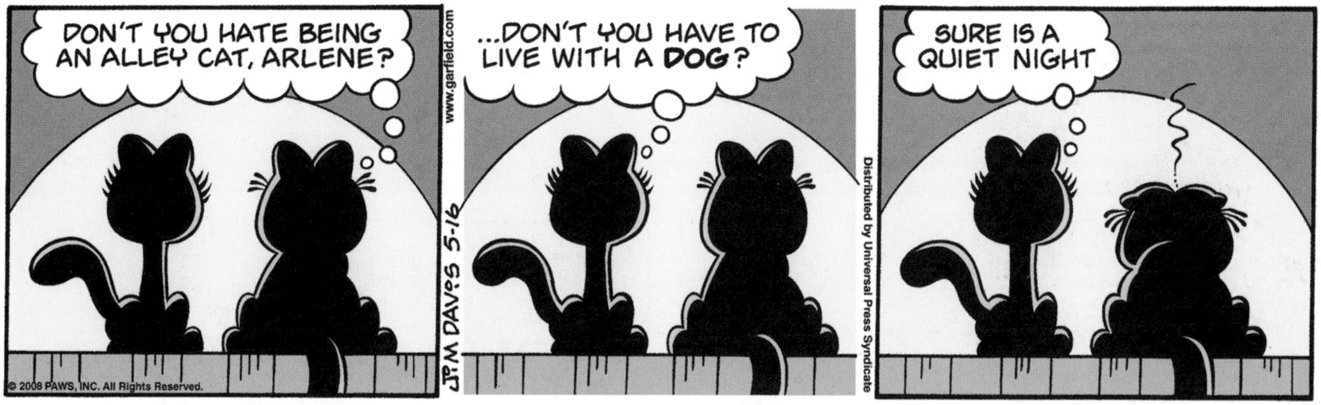
DON'T YOU HATE BEING AN ALLEY CAT, ARLENE?
...DON'T YOU HAVE TO LIVE WITH A **DOG**?
SURE IS A QUIET NIGHT
© 2008 PAWS, INC. All Rights Reserved.
www.garfield.com
JPM DAVIS 5-16
Distributed by Universal Press Syndicate

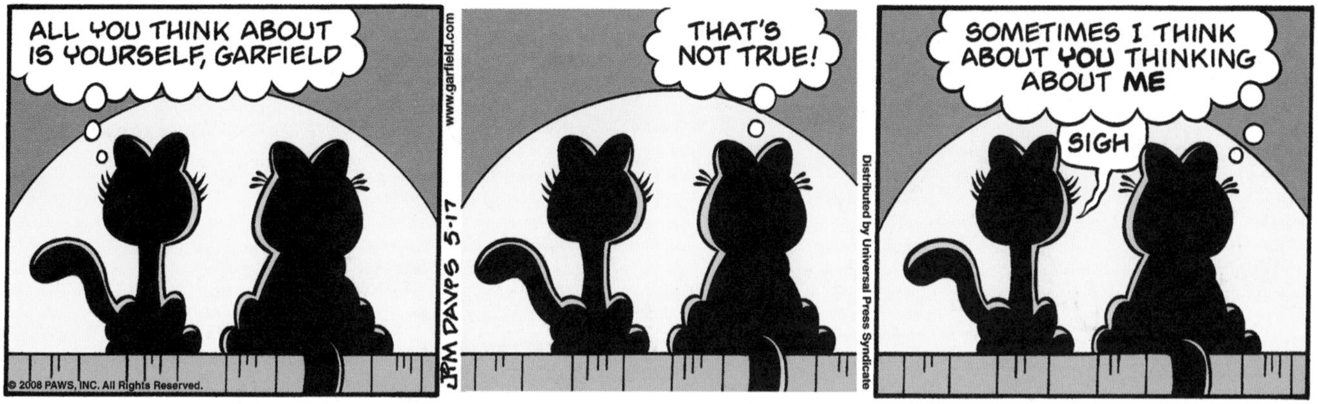
ALL YOU THINK ABOUT IS YOURSELF, GARFIELD
THAT'S NOT TRUE!
SOMETIMES I THINK ABOUT **YOU** THINKING ABOUT **ME**
SIGH
© 2008 PAWS, INC. All Rights Reserved.
www.garfield.com
JPM DAVIS 5-17
Distributed by Universal Press Syndicate

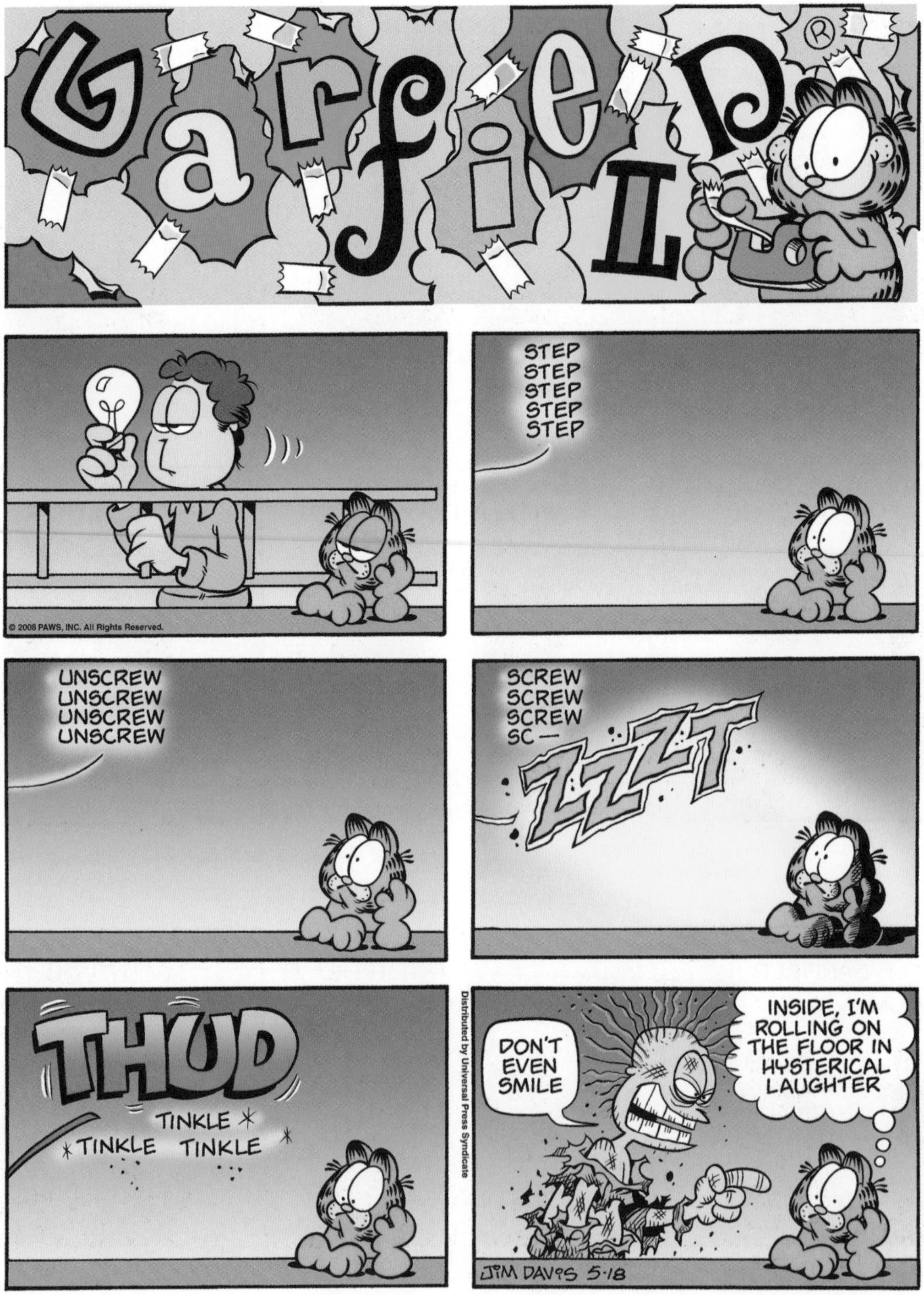
Garfield®
© 2008 PAWS, INC. All Rights Reserved.
STEP STEP STEP STEP STEP
UNSCREW UNSCREW UNSCREW UNSCREW
SCREW SCREW SCREW SC—
ZZZT
THUD
TINKLE TINKLE TINKLE
Distributed by Universal Press Syndicate
DON'T EVEN SMILE
INSIDE, I'M ROLLING ON THE FLOOR IN HYSTERICAL LAUGHTER
JIM DAVIS 5-18

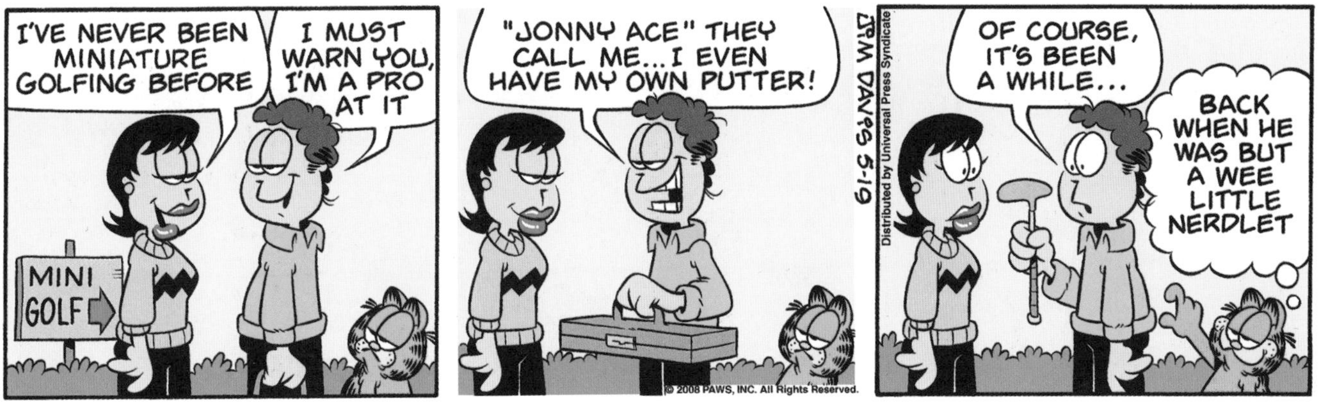
I'VE NEVER BEEN MINIATURE GOLFING BEFORE
I MUST WARN YOU, I'M A PRO AT IT
MINI GOLF
"JONNY ACE" THEY CALL ME... I EVEN HAVE MY OWN PUTTER!
JPM DAVPS 5-19
© 2008 PAWS, INC. All Rights Reserved.
Distributed by Universal Press Syndicate
OF COURSE, IT'S BEEN A WHILE...
BACK WHEN HE WAS BUT A WEE LITTLE NERDLET

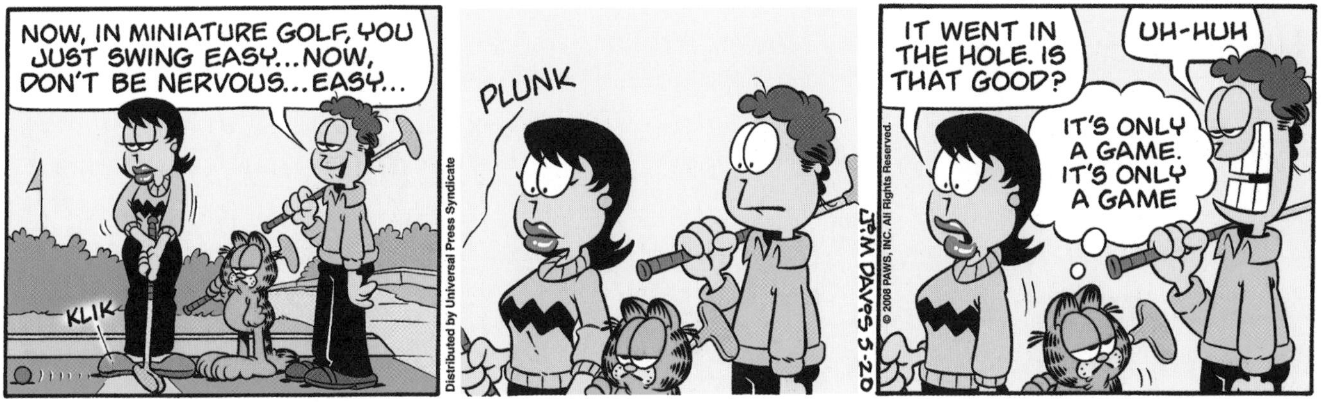
NOW, IN MINIATURE GOLF, YOU JUST SWING EASY...NOW, DON'T BE NERVOUS...EASY...
KLIK
Distributed by Universal Press Syndicate
PLUNK
JPM DAVPS 5-20
© 2008 PAWS, INC. All Rights Reserved.
IT WENT IN THE HOLE. IS THAT GOOD?
UH-HUH
IT'S ONLY A GAME. IT'S ONLY A GAME

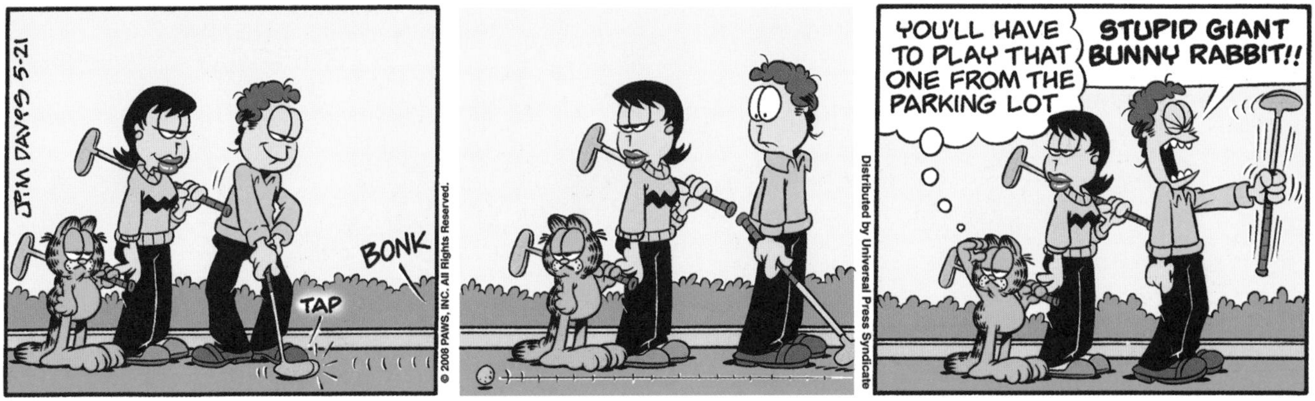
JPM DAVPS 5-21
TAP
BONK
© 2008 PAWS, INC. All Rights Reserved.
Distributed by Universal Press Syndicate
YOU'LL HAVE TO PLAY THAT ONE FROM THE PARKING LOT
STUPID GIANT BUNNY RABBIT!!

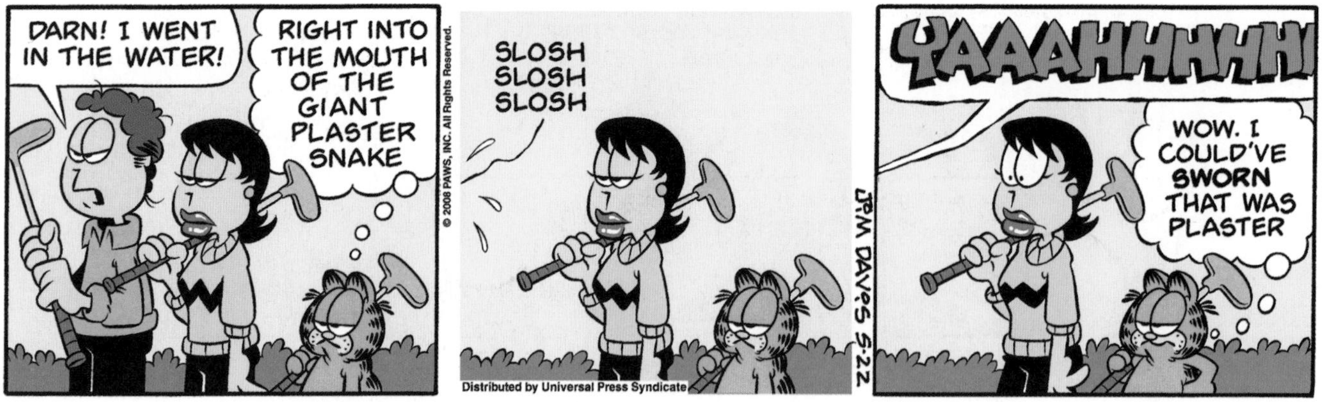
DARN! I WENT IN THE WATER!
RIGHT INTO THE MOUTH OF THE GIANT PLASTER SNAKE
© 2008 PAWS, INC. All Rights Reserved.
SLOSH SLOSH SLOSH
Distributed by Universal Press Syndicate
JPM DAVIS 5-22
YAAAHHHHH!
WOW. I COULD'VE **SWORN** THAT WAS PLASTER

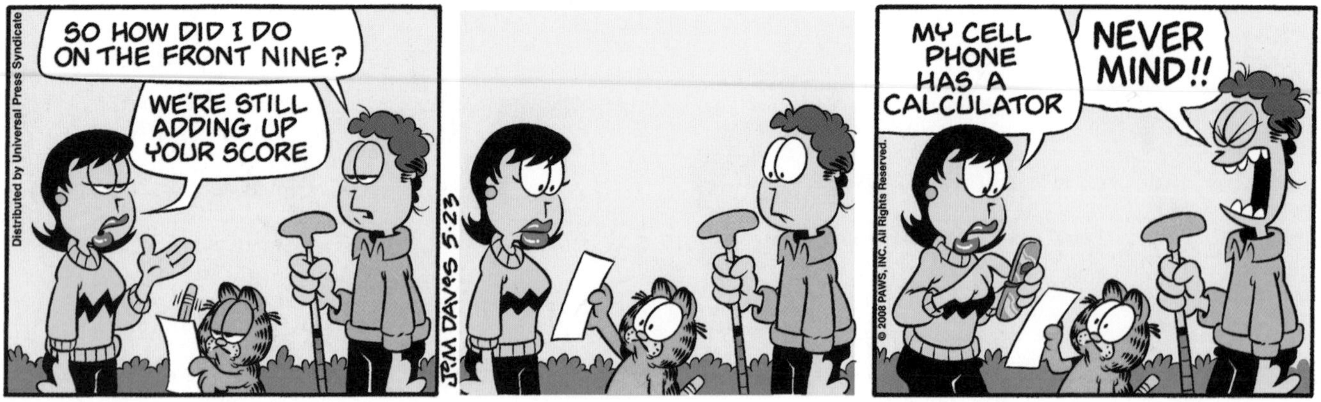
Distributed by Universal Press Syndicate
SO HOW DID I DO ON THE FRONT NINE?
WE'RE STILL ADDING UP YOUR SCORE
JPM DAVIS 5-23
© 2008 PAWS, INC. All Rights Reserved.
MY CELL PHONE HAS A CALCULATOR
NEVER MIND!!

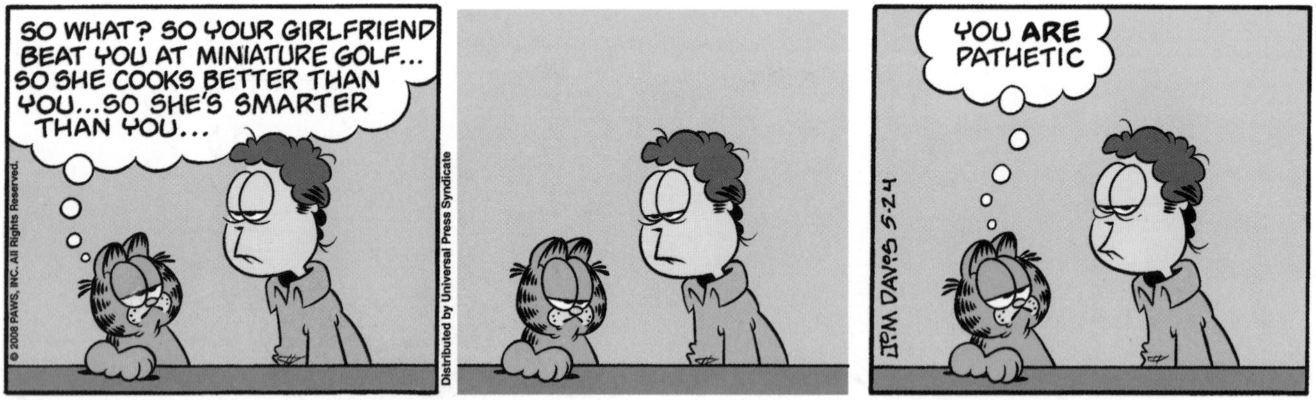
SO WHAT? SO YOUR GIRLFRIEND BEAT YOU AT MINIATURE GOLF... SO SHE COOKS BETTER THAN YOU...SO SHE'S SMARTER THAN YOU...
© 2008 PAWS, INC. All Rights Reserved.
Distributed by Universal Press Syndicate
JPM DAVIS 5-24
YOU **ARE** PATHETIC

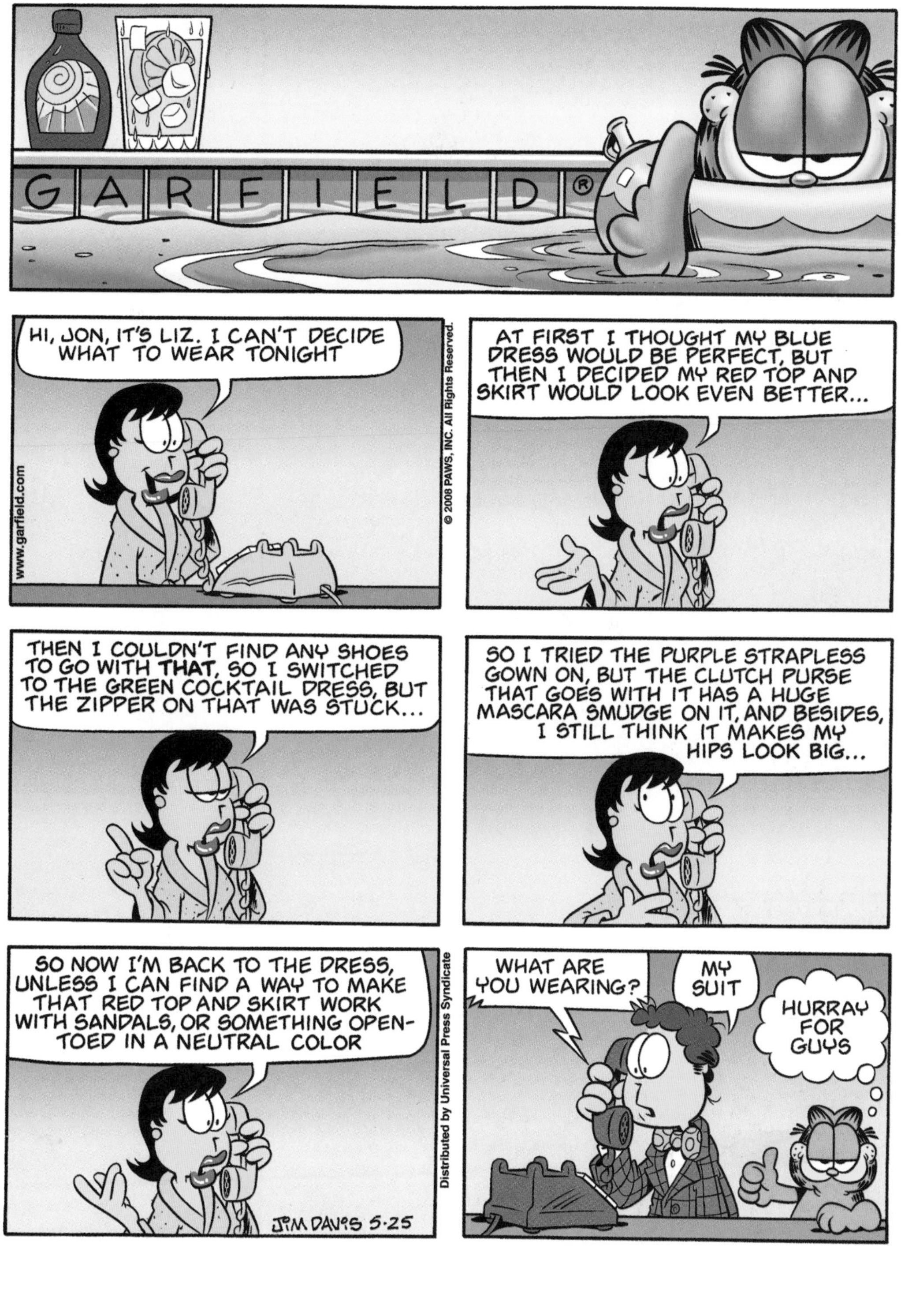
GARFIELD®
HI, JON, IT'S LIZ. I CAN'T DECIDE WHAT TO WEAR TONIGHT
www.garfield.com
© 2008 PAWS, INC. All Rights Reserved.
AT FIRST I THOUGHT MY BLUE DRESS WOULD BE PERFECT, BUT THEN I DECIDED MY RED TOP AND SKIRT WOULD LOOK EVEN BETTER...
THEN I COULDN'T FIND ANY SHOES TO GO WITH **THAT**, SO I SWITCHED TO THE GREEN COCKTAIL DRESS, BUT THE ZIPPER ON THAT WAS STUCK...
SO I TRIED THE PURPLE STRAPLESS GOWN ON, BUT THE CLUTCH PURSE THAT GOES WITH IT HAS A HUGE MASCARA SMUDGE ON IT, AND BESIDES, I STILL THINK IT MAKES MY HIPS LOOK BIG...
SO NOW I'M BACK TO THE DRESS, UNLESS I CAN FIND A WAY TO MAKE THAT RED TOP AND SKIRT WORK WITH SANDALS, OR SOMETHING OPEN-TOED IN A NEUTRAL COLOR
JIM DAVIS 5-25
Distributed by Universal Press Syndicate
WHAT ARE YOU WEARING?
MY SUIT
HURRAY FOR GUYS

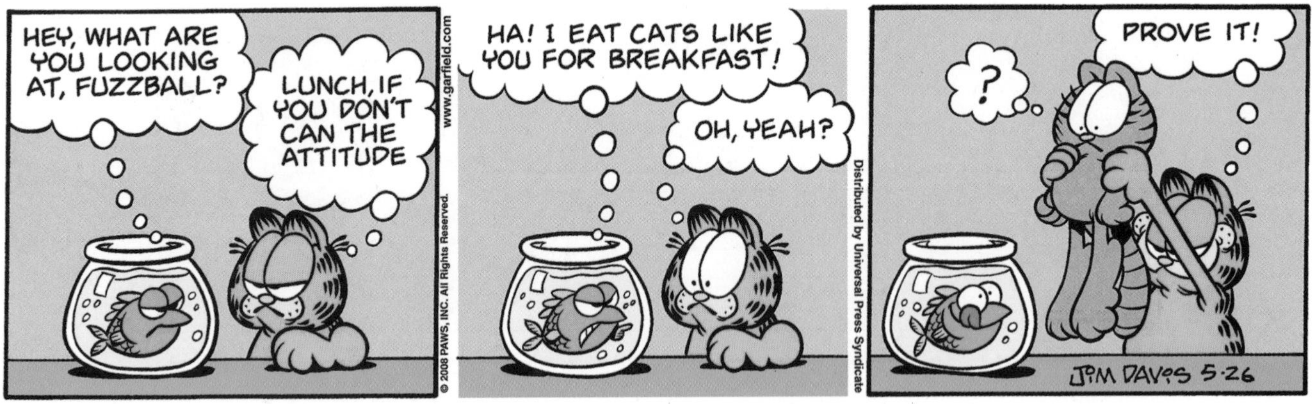
HEY, WHAT ARE YOU LOOKING AT, FUZZBALL?
LUNCH, IF YOU DON'T CAN THE ATTITUDE
© 2008 PAWS, INC. All Rights Reserved. www.garfield.com
HA! I EAT CATS LIKE YOU FOR BREAKFAST!
OH, YEAH?
Distributed by Universal Press Syndicate
?
PROVE IT!
JIM DAVIS 5·26

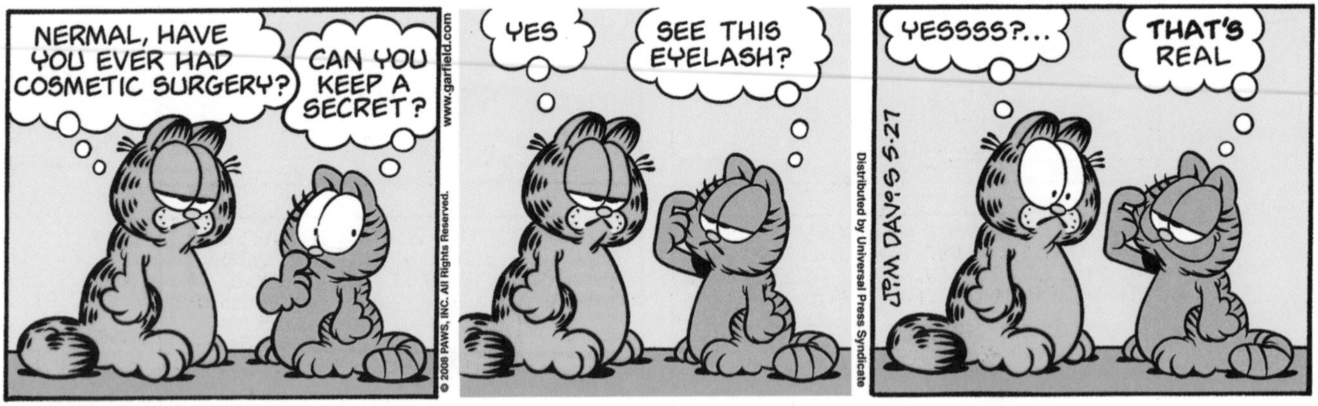
NERMAL, HAVE YOU EVER HAD COSMETIC SURGERY?
CAN YOU KEEP A SECRET?
© 2008 PAWS, INC. All Rights Reserved. www.garfield.com
YES
SEE THIS EYELASH?
Distributed by Universal Press Syndicate
JIM DAVIS 5·27
YESSSS?...
THAT'S REAL

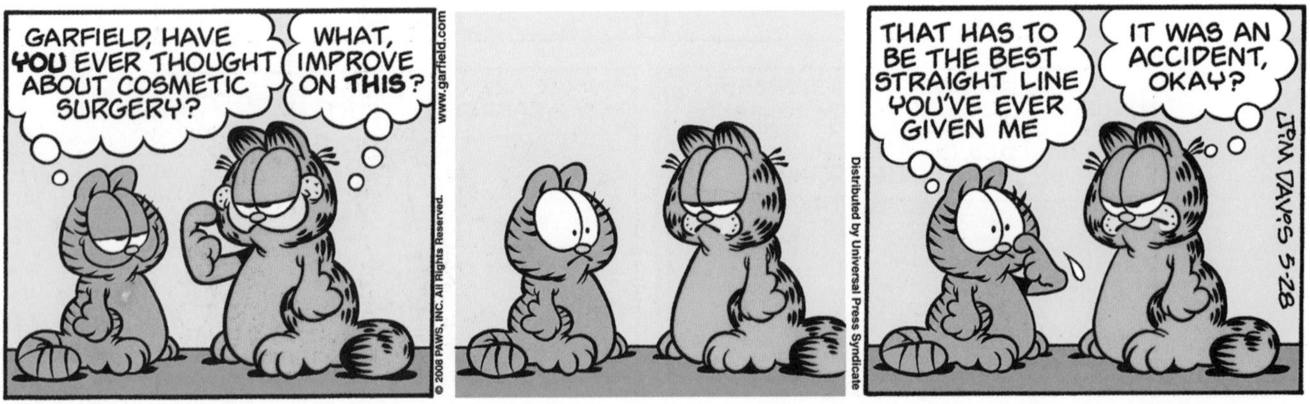
GARFIELD, HAVE **YOU** EVER THOUGHT ABOUT COSMETIC SURGERY?
WHAT, IMPROVE ON **THIS**?
© 2008 PAWS, INC. All Rights Reserved. www.garfield.com
Distributed by Universal Press Syndicate
THAT HAS TO BE THE BEST STRAIGHT LINE YOU'VE EVER GIVEN ME
IT WAS AN ACCIDENT, OKAY?
JIM DAVIS 5·28

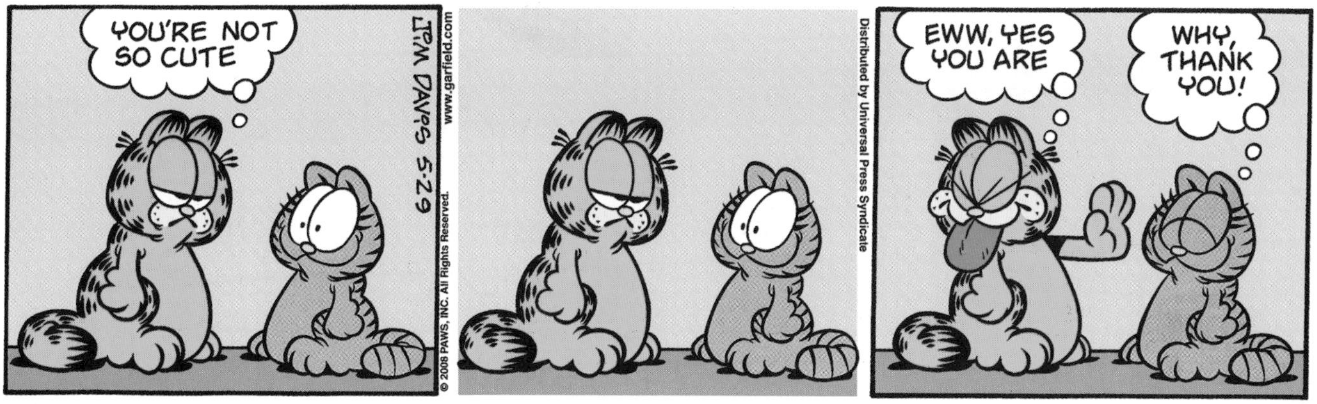
YOU'RE NOT SO CUTE
JIM DAVIS 5·29
© 2008 PAWS, INC. All Rights Reserved.
www.garfield.com
Distributed by Universal Press Syndicate
EWW, YES YOU ARE
WHY, THANK YOU!

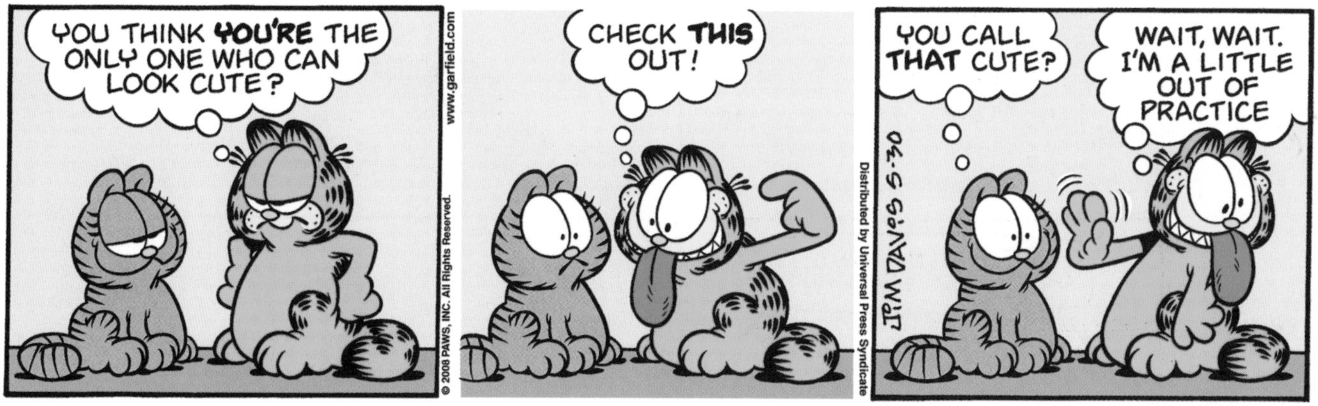
YOU THINK **YOU'RE** THE ONLY ONE WHO CAN LOOK CUTE?
© 2008 PAWS, INC. All Rights Reserved.
www.garfield.com
CHECK **THIS** OUT!
Distributed by Universal Press Syndicate
JIM DAVIS 5·30
YOU CALL **THAT** CUTE?
WAIT, WAIT. I'M A LITTLE OUT OF PRACTICE

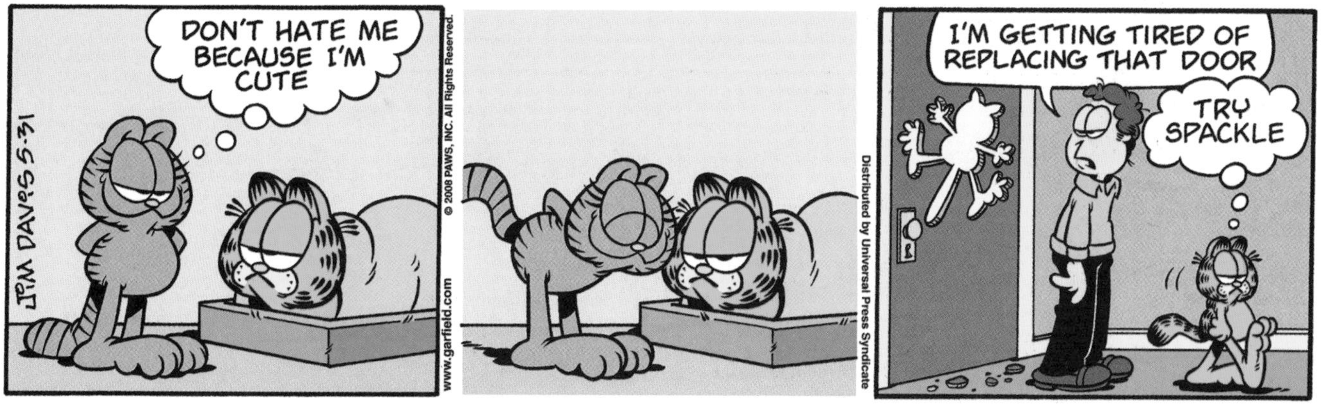
JIM DAVIS 5·31
DON'T HATE ME BECAUSE I'M CUTE
www.garfield.com
© 2008 PAWS, INC. All Rights Reserved.
Distributed by Universal Press Syndicate
I'M GETTING TIRED OF REPLACING THAT DOOR
TRY SPACKLE

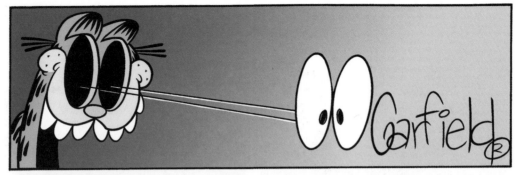

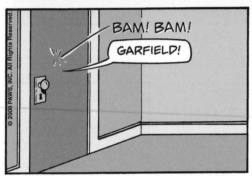

Garfield
© 2008 PAWS, INC. All Rights Reserved.
BAM! BAM!
GARFIELD!
BAM! BAM! BAM!
GARFIELD, OPEN THE DOOR!
GARFIELD!! MY ARMS ARE FULL OF GROCERIES!
JIM DAVIS 6-1
WELL! IT'S ABOUT
Distributed by Universal Press Syndicate
...TIME
OOOH, COOKIES!

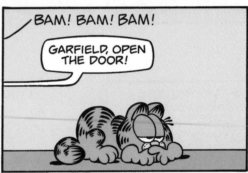

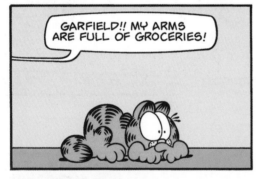

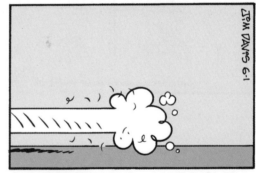

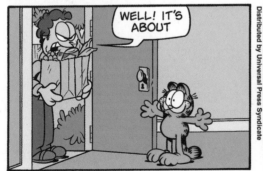

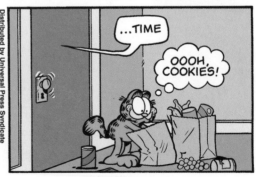

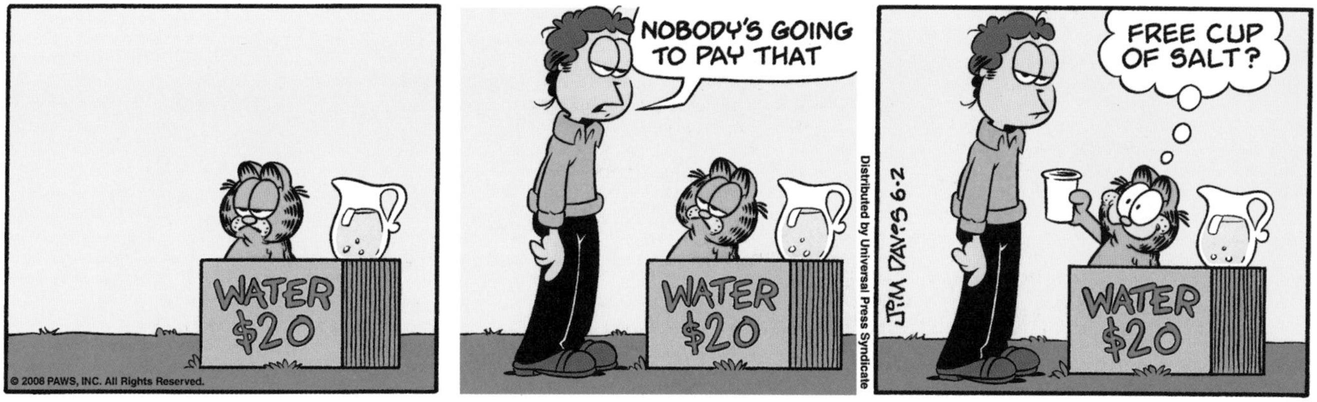
WATER $20
© 2008 PAWS, INC. All Rights Reserved.
NOBODY'S GOING TO PAY THAT
WATER $20
Distributed by Universal Press Syndicate
JIM DAVIS 6-2
FREE CUP OF SALT?
WATER $20

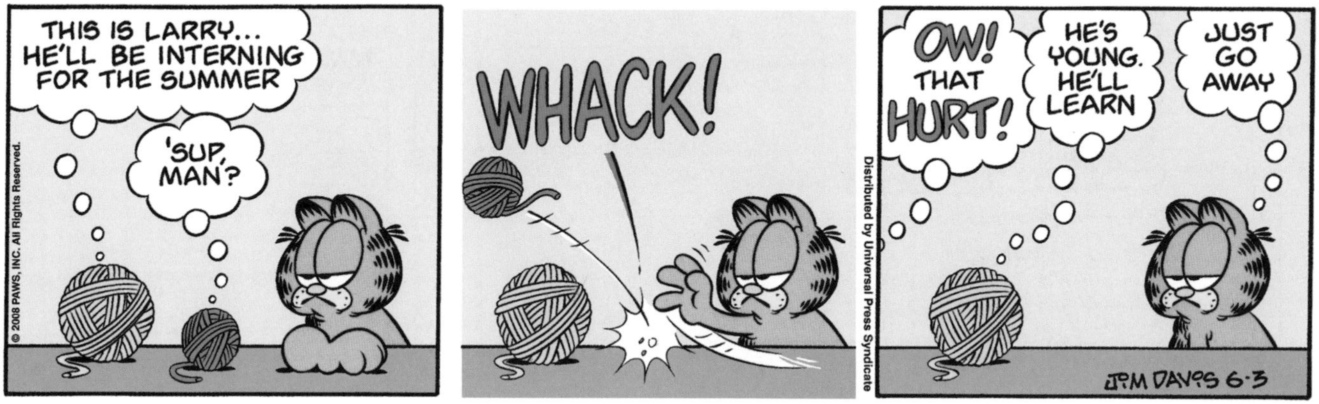
THIS IS LARRY... HE'LL BE INTERNING FOR THE SUMMER
'SUP, MAN?
© 2008 PAWS, INC. All Rights Reserved.
WHACK!
Distributed by Universal Press Syndicate
OW! THAT HURT!
HE'S YOUNG. HE'LL LEARN
JUST GO AWAY
JIM DAVIS 6-3

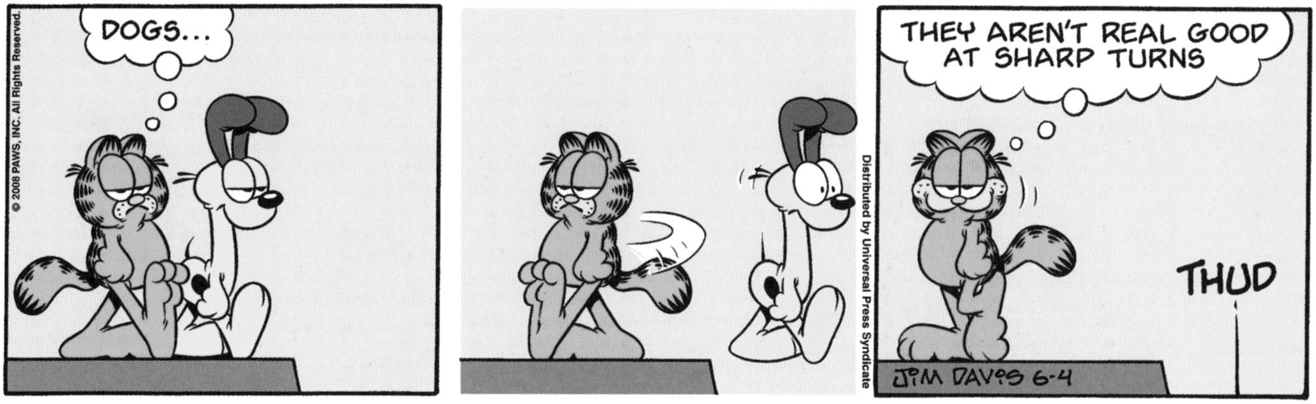
DOGS...
© 2008 PAWS, INC. All Rights Reserved.
Distributed by Universal Press Syndicate
THEY AREN'T REAL GOOD AT SHARP TURNS
THUD
JIM DAVIS 6-4

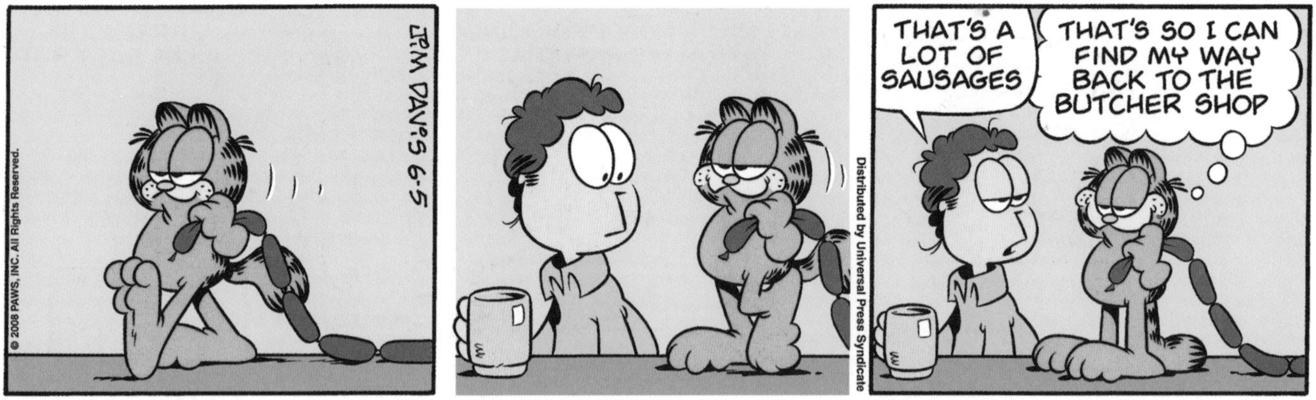
JIM DAVIS 6-5
© 2008 PAWS, INC. All Rights Reserved.
THAT'S A LOT OF SAUSAGES
THAT'S SO I CAN FIND MY WAY BACK TO THE BUTCHER SHOP
Distributed by Universal Press Syndicate

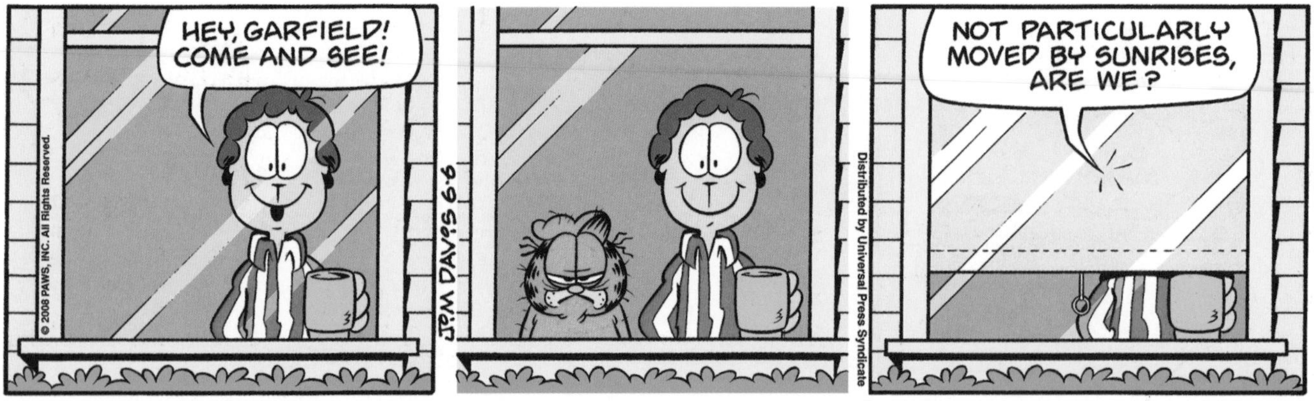
HEY, GARFIELD! COME AND SEE!
© 2008 PAWS, INC. All Rights Reserved.
JIM DAVIS 6-6
NOT PARTICULARLY MOVED BY SUNRISES, ARE WE?
Distributed by Universal Press Syndicate

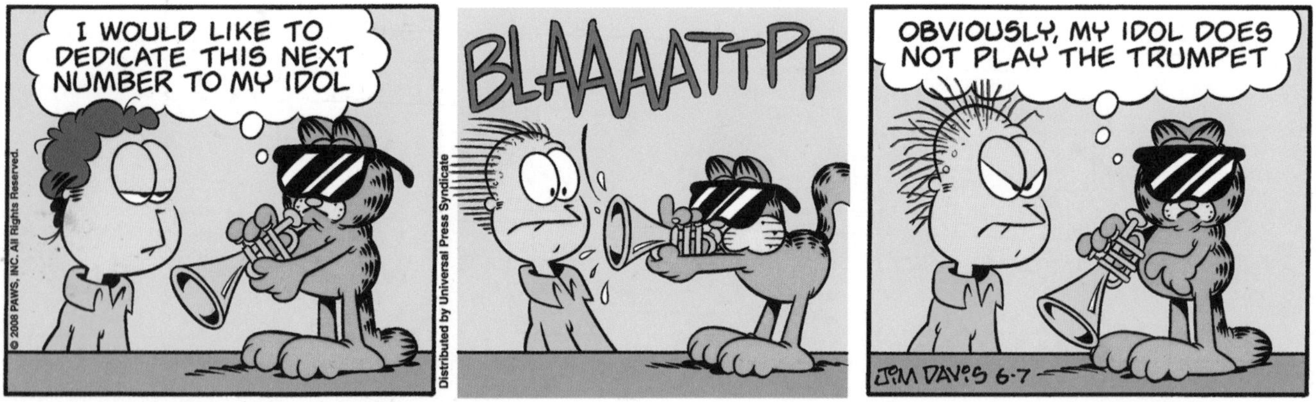
I WOULD LIKE TO DEDICATE THIS NEXT NUMBER TO MY IDOL
© 2008 PAWS, INC. All Rights Reserved.
BLAAAAATTPP
Distributed by Universal Press Syndicate
OBVIOUSLY, MY IDOL DOES NOT PLAY THE TRUMPET
JIM DAVIS 6-7

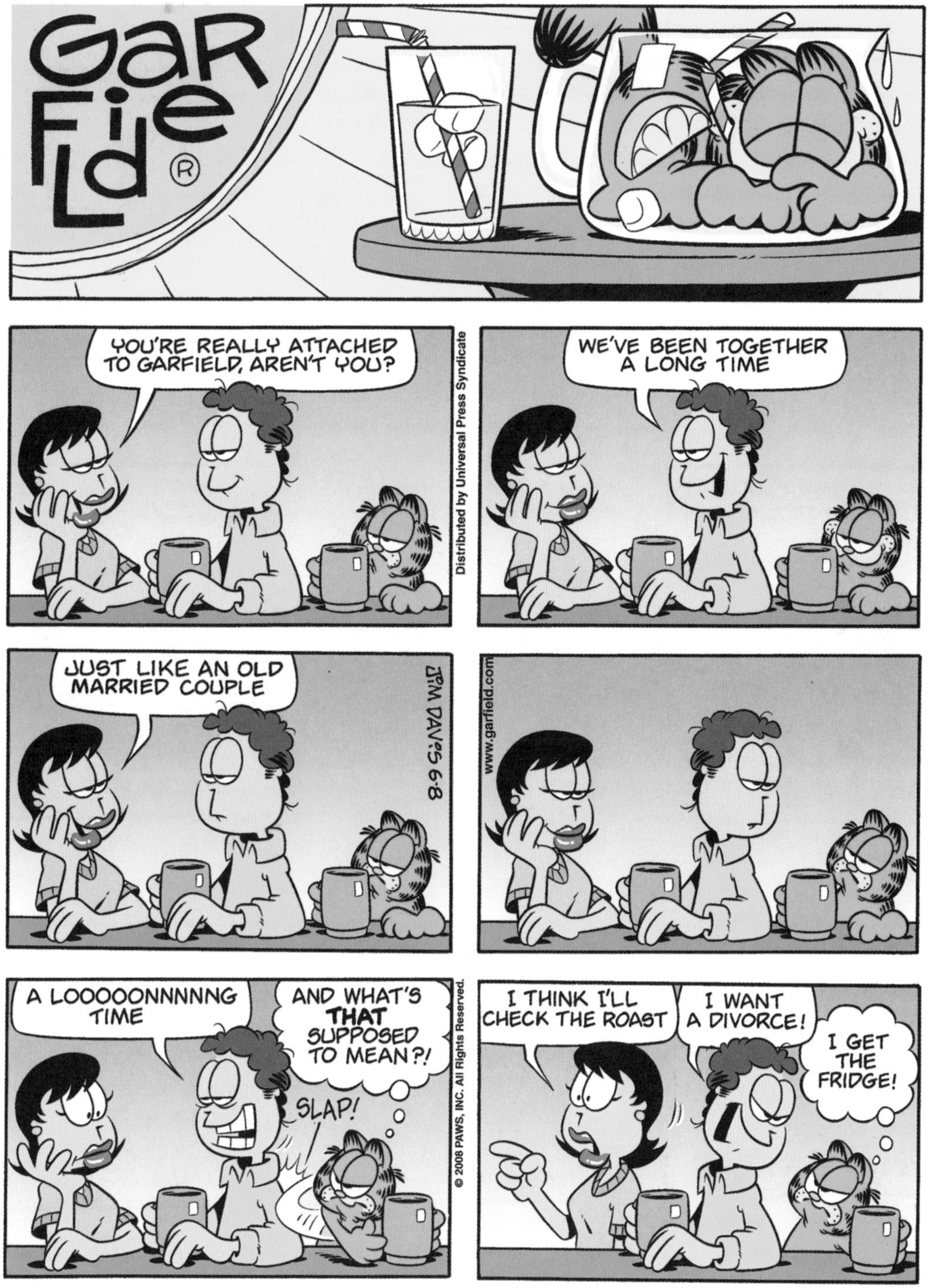
GARFIELD ®
YOU'RE REALLY ATTACHED TO GARFIELD, AREN'T YOU?
Distributed by Universal Press Syndicate
WE'VE BEEN TOGETHER A LONG TIME
JUST LIKE AN OLD MARRIED COUPLE
JIM DAVIS 6-8
www.garfield.com
A LOOOOONNNNNG TIME
AND WHAT'S **THAT** SUPPOSED TO MEAN?!
SLAP!
© 2008 PAWS, INC. All Rights Reserved.
I THINK I'LL CHECK THE ROAST
I WANT A DIVORCE!
I GET THE FRIDGE!

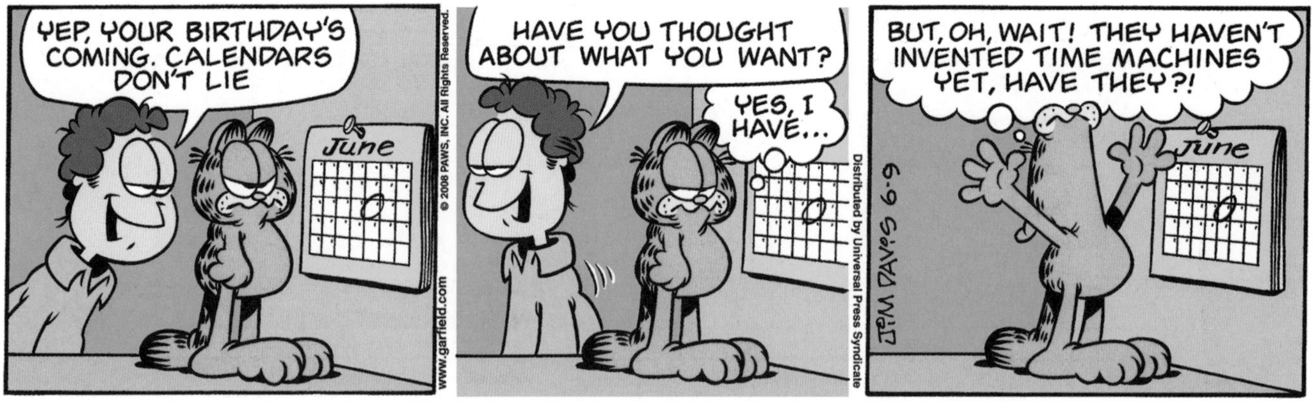
YEP, YOUR BIRTHDAY'S COMING. CALENDARS DON'T LIE
June
© 2008 PAWS, INC. All Rights Reserved.
www.garfield.com
HAVE YOU THOUGHT ABOUT WHAT YOU WANT?
YES, I HAVE...
Distributed by Universal Press Syndicate
BUT, OH, WAIT! THEY HAVEN'T INVENTED TIME MACHINES YET, HAVE THEY?!
JIM DAVIS 6-9

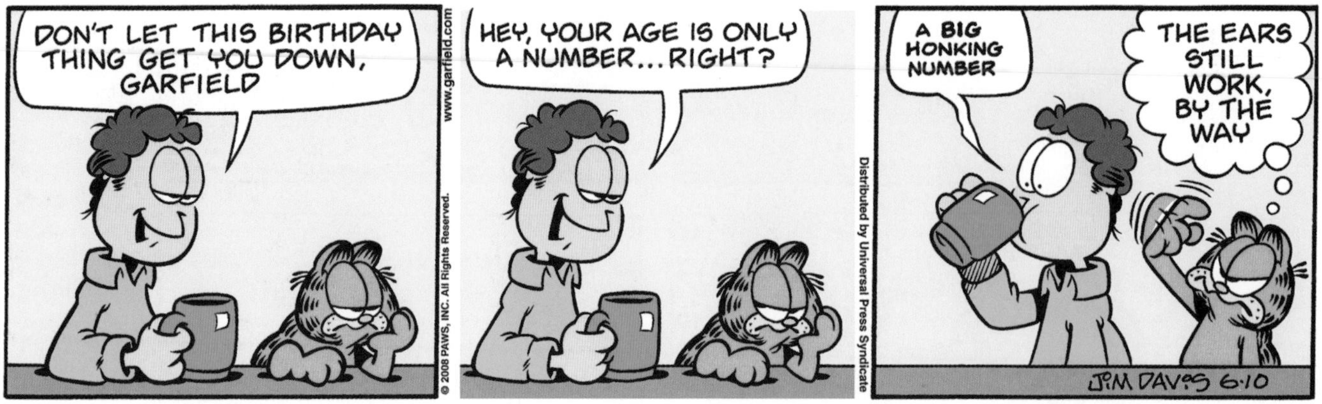
DON'T LET THIS BIRTHDAY THING GET YOU DOWN, GARFIELD
www.garfield.com
© 2008 PAWS, INC. All Rights Reserved.
HEY, YOUR AGE IS ONLY A NUMBER... RIGHT?
Distributed by Universal Press Syndicate
A BIG HONKING NUMBER
THE EARS STILL WORK, BY THE WAY
JIM DAVIS 6-10

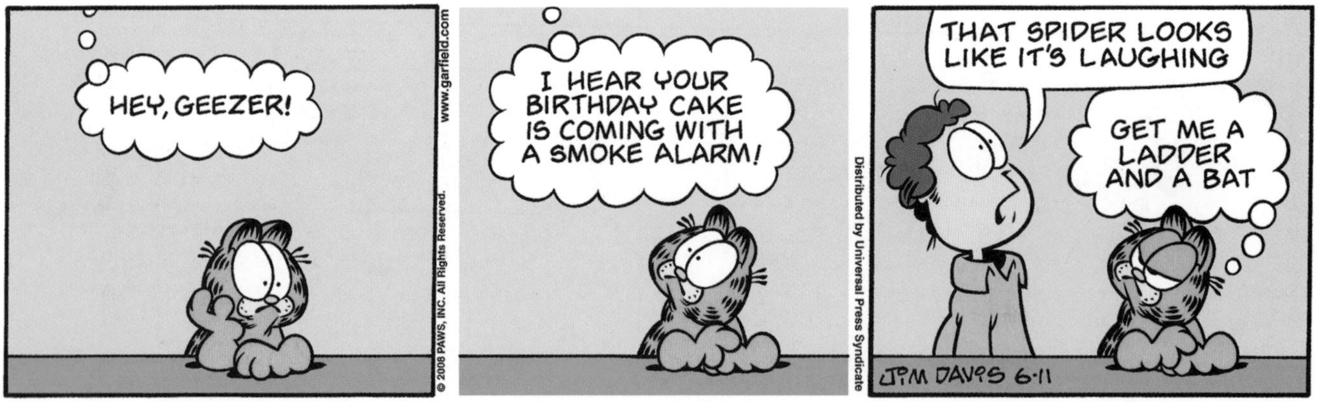
HEY, GEEZER!
www.garfield.com
© 2008 PAWS, INC. All Rights Reserved.
I HEAR YOUR BIRTHDAY CAKE IS COMING WITH A SMOKE ALARM!
Distributed by Universal Press Syndicate
THAT SPIDER LOOKS LIKE IT'S LAUGHING
GET ME A LADDER AND A BAT
JIM DAVIS 6-11

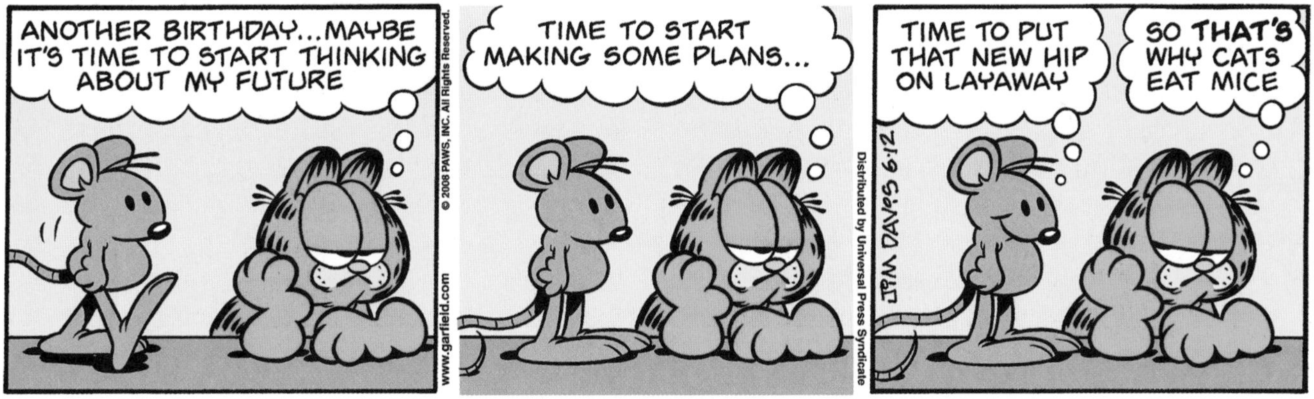
ANOTHER BIRTHDAY...MAYBE IT'S TIME TO START THINKING ABOUT MY FUTURE
© 2008 PAWS, INC. All Rights Reserved.
www.garfield.com
TIME TO START MAKING SOME PLANS...
Distributed by Universal Press Syndicate
TIME TO PUT THAT NEW HIP ON LAYAWAY
SO THAT'S WHY CATS EAT MICE
JIM DAVIS 6·12

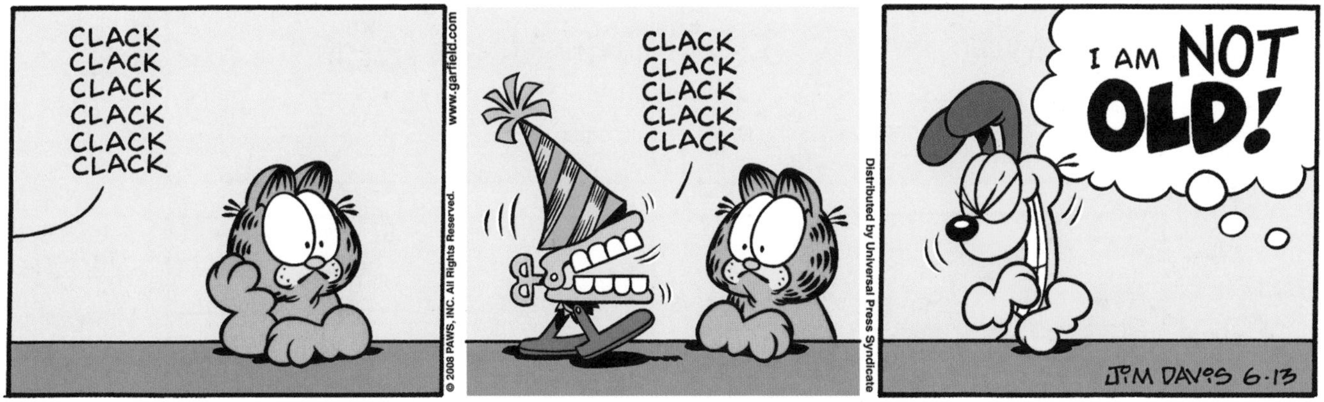
CLACK CLACK CLACK CLACK CLACK CLACK
www.garfield.com
© 2008 PAWS, INC. All Rights Reserved.
CLACK CLACK CLACK CLACK CLACK
Distributed by Universal Press Syndicate
I AM NOT OLD!
JIM DAVIS 6·13

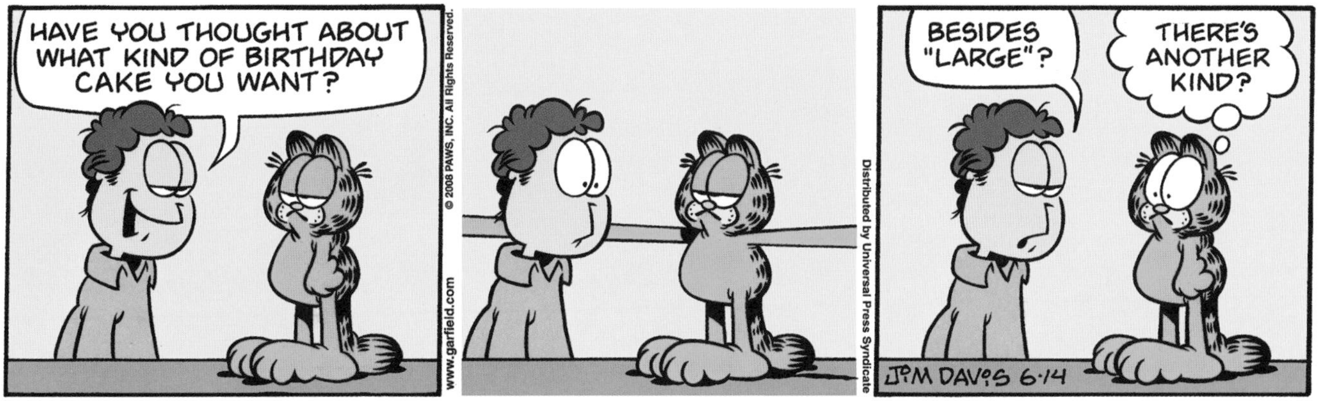
HAVE YOU THOUGHT ABOUT WHAT KIND OF BIRTHDAY CAKE YOU WANT?
© 2008 PAWS, INC. All Rights Reserved.
www.garfield.com
Distributed by Universal Press Syndicate
BESIDES "LARGE"?
THERE'S ANOTHER KIND?
JIM DAVIS 6·14

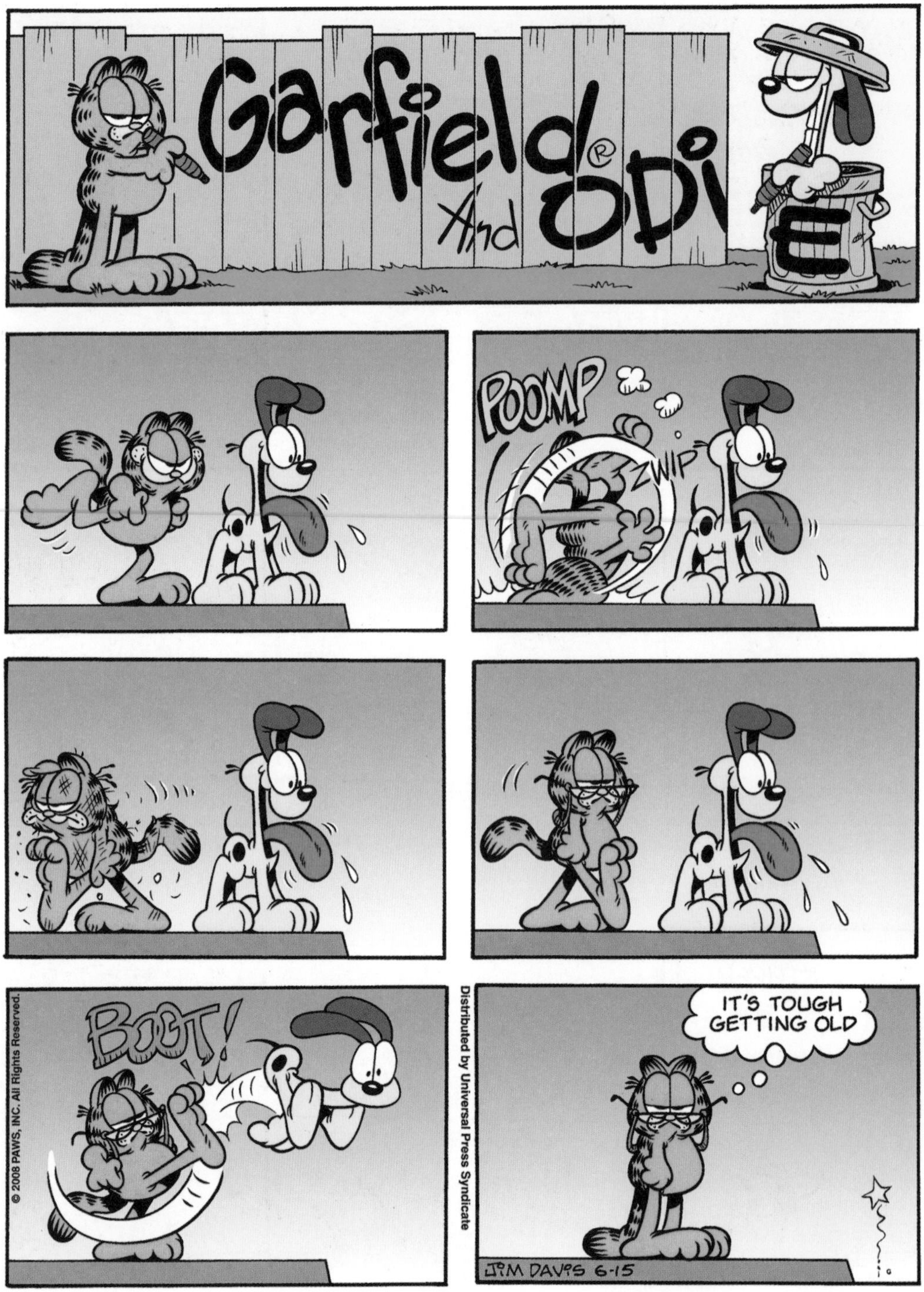
Garfield® And ODIE
POOMP
ZWIP
BOOT!
IT'S TOUGH GETTING OLD
JIM DAVIS 6-15
© 2008 PAWS, INC. All Rights Reserved.
Distributed by Universal Press Syndicate

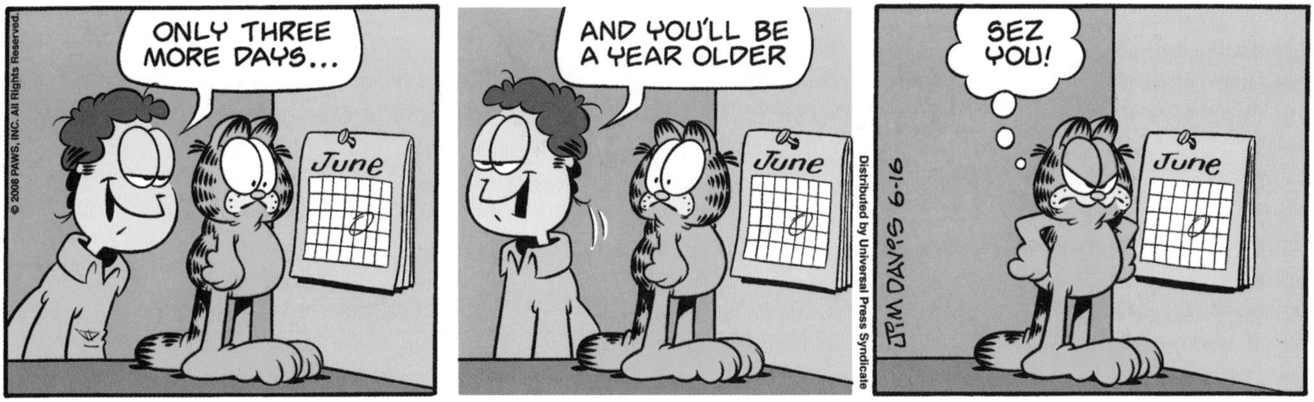
© 2008 PAWS, INC. All Rights Reserved.
ONLY THREE MORE DAYS...
AND YOU'LL BE A YEAR OLDER
Distributed by Universal Press Syndicate
JIM DAVIS 6-16
SEZ YOU!
June

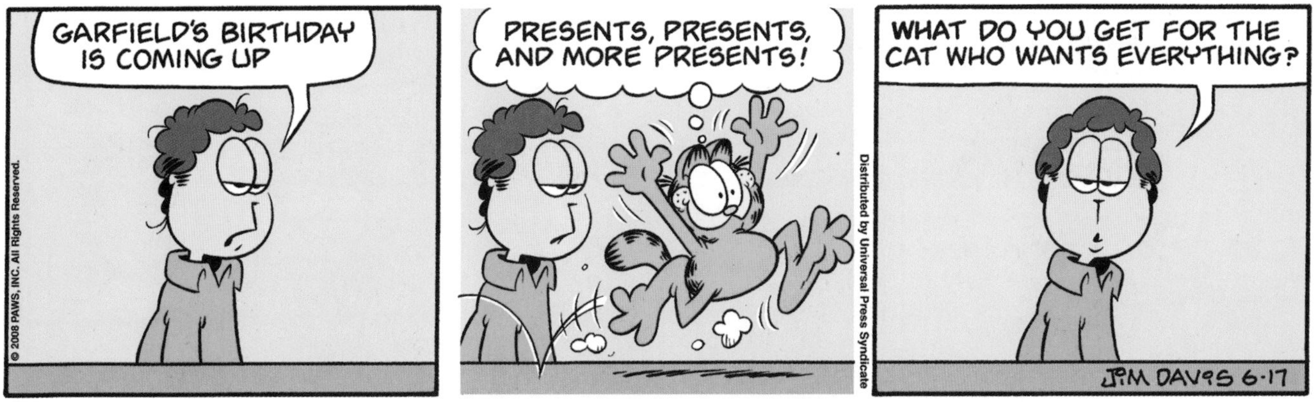
© 2008 PAWS, INC. All Rights Reserved.
GARFIELD'S BIRTHDAY IS COMING UP
PRESENTS, PRESENTS, AND MORE PRESENTS!
Distributed by Universal Press Syndicate
WHAT DO YOU GET FOR THE CAT WHO WANTS EVERYTHING?
JIM DAVIS 6-17

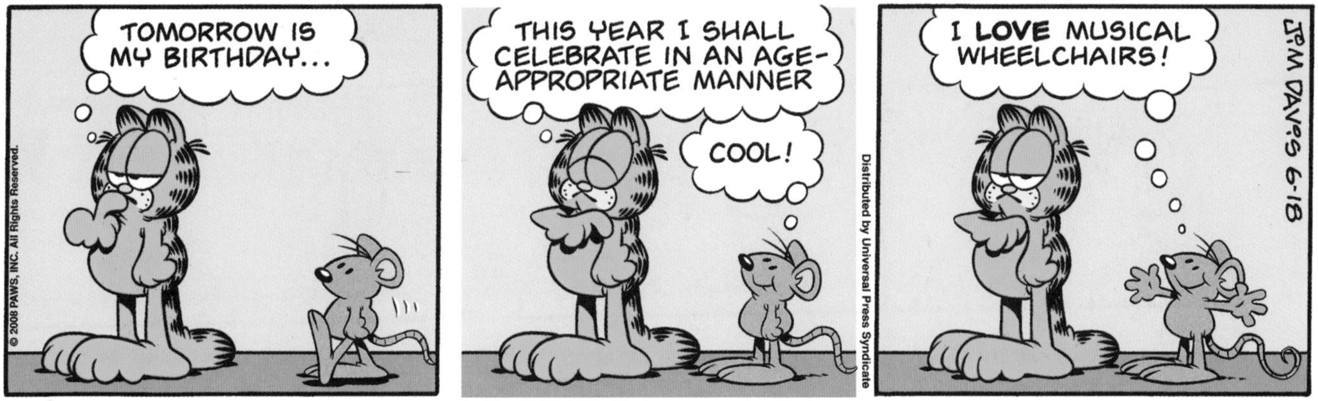
© 2008 PAWS, INC. All Rights Reserved.
TOMORROW IS MY BIRTHDAY...
THIS YEAR I SHALL CELEBRATE IN AN AGE-APPROPRIATE MANNER
COOL!
Distributed by Universal Press Syndicate
I **LOVE** MUSICAL WHEELCHAIRS!
JIM DAVIS 6-18

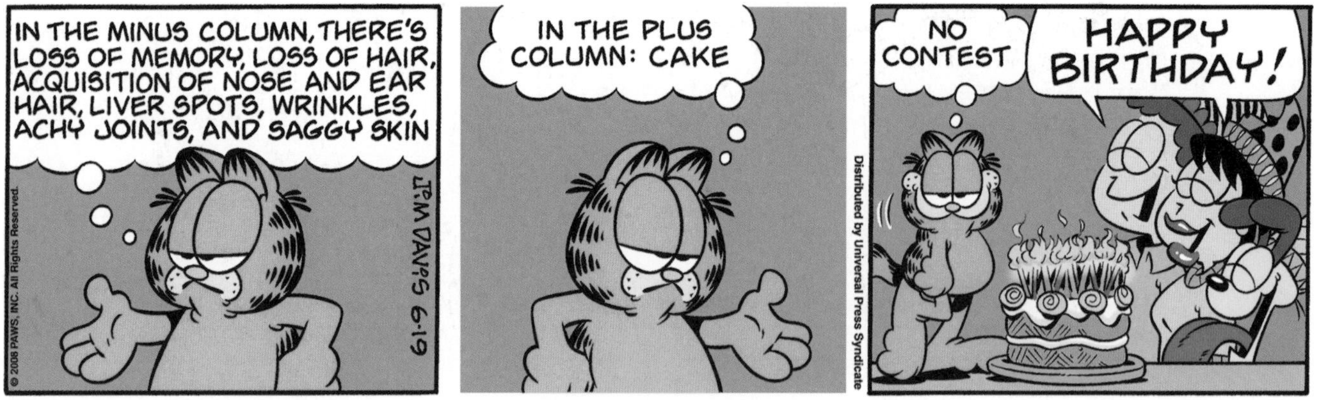
IN THE MINUS COLUMN, THERE'S LOSS OF MEMORY, LOSS OF HAIR, ACQUISITION OF NOSE AND EAR HAIR, LIVER SPOTS, WRINKLES, ACHY JOINTS, AND SAGGY SKIN
© 2008 PAWS, INC. All Rights Reserved.
JIM DAVIS 6·19
IN THE PLUS COLUMN: CAKE
Distributed by Universal Press Syndicate
NO CONTEST
HAPPY BIRTHDAY!

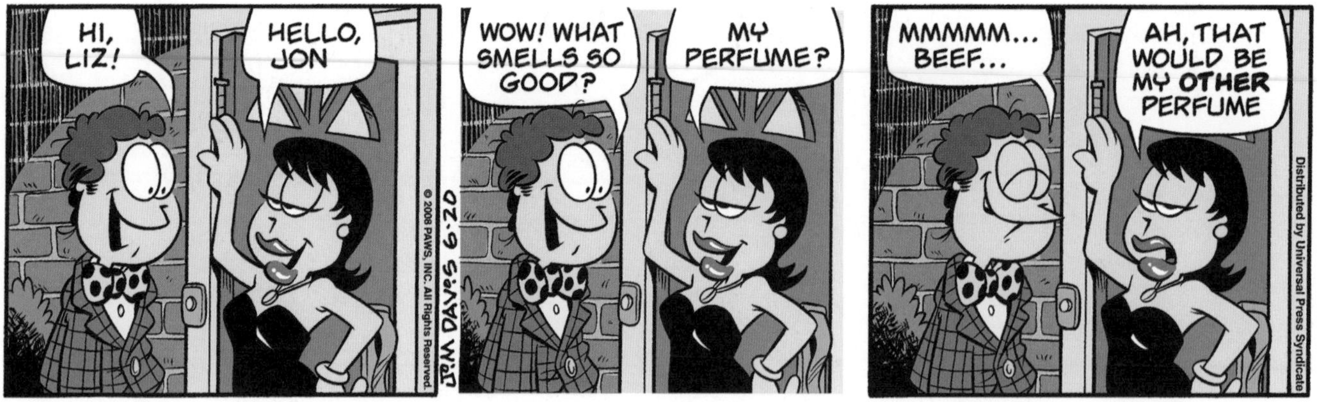
HI, LIZ!
HELLO, JON
© 2008 PAWS, INC. All Rights Reserved.
JIM DAVIS 6·20
WOW! WHAT SMELLS SO GOOD?
MY PERFUME?
MMMMM... BEEF...
AH, THAT WOULD BE MY **OTHER** PERFUME
Distributed by Universal Press Syndicate

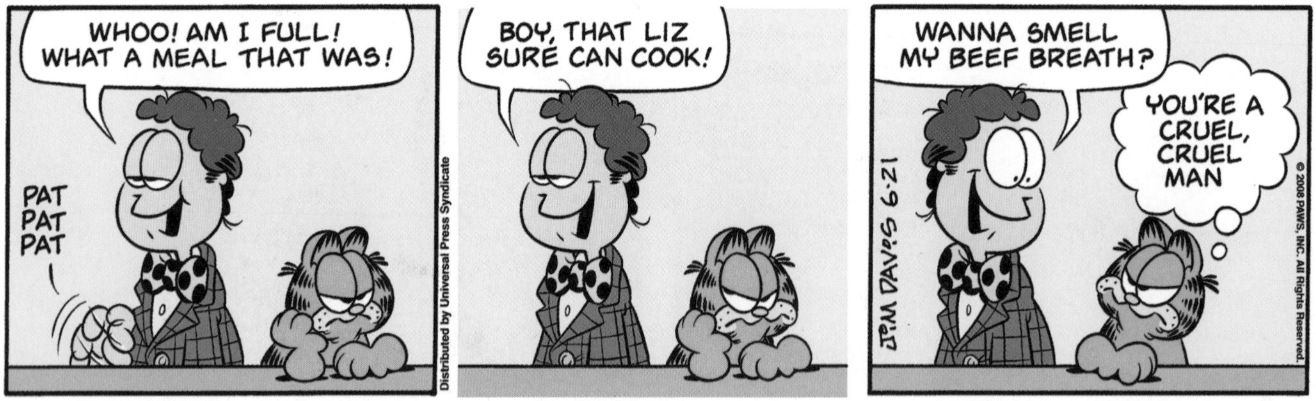
WHOO! AM I FULL! WHAT A MEAL THAT WAS!
PAT PAT PAT
Distributed by Universal Press Syndicate
BOY, THAT LIZ SURE CAN COOK!
JIM DAVIS 6·21
WANNA SMELL MY BEEF BREATH?
YOU'RE A CRUEL, CRUEL MAN
© 2008 PAWS, INC. All Rights Reserved.

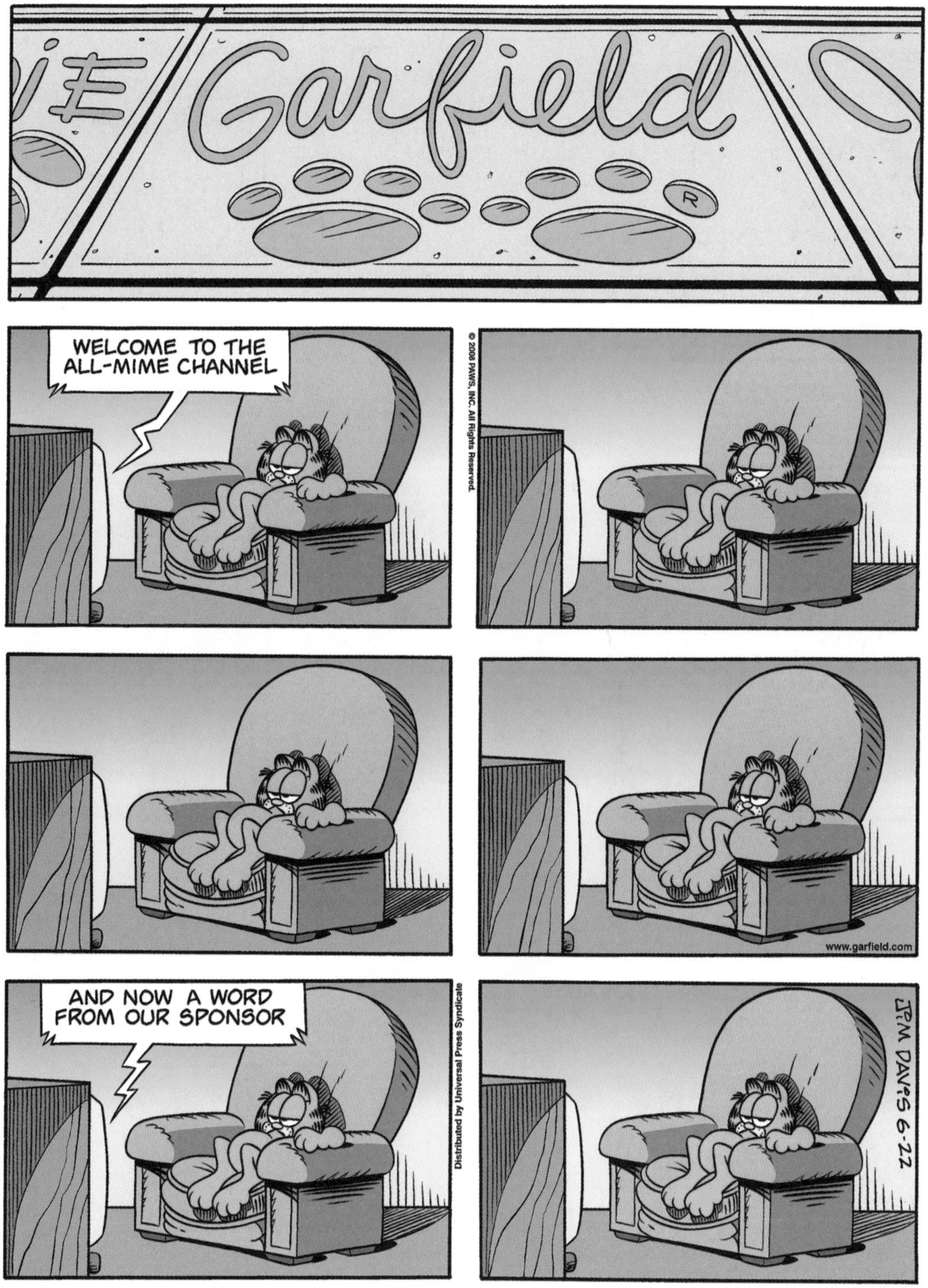
Garfield
WELCOME TO THE ALL-MIME CHANNEL
© 2008 PAWS, INC. All Rights Reserved.
www.garfield.com
AND NOW A WORD FROM OUR SPONSOR
Distributed by Universal Press Syndicate
JPM DAVIS 6-22

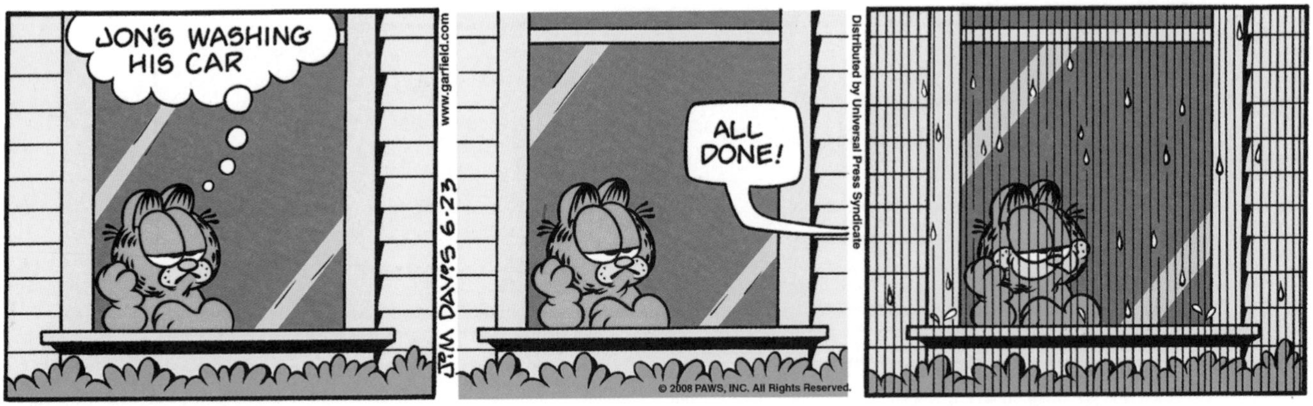
JON'S WASHING HIS CAR
ALL DONE!
JIM DAVIS 6-23
www.garfield.com
© 2008 PAWS, INC. All Rights Reserved.
Distributed by Universal Press Syndicate

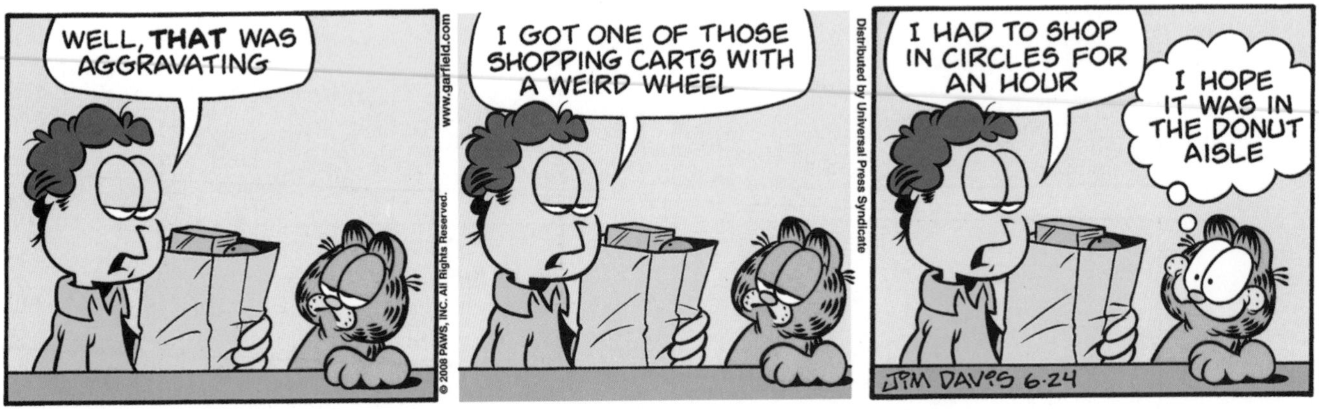
WELL, THAT WAS AGGRAVATING
I GOT ONE OF THOSE SHOPPING CARTS WITH A WEIRD WHEEL
I HAD TO SHOP IN CIRCLES FOR AN HOUR
I HOPE IT WAS IN THE DONUT AISLE
JIM DAVIS 6-24
www.garfield.com
© 2008 PAWS, INC. All Rights Reserved.
Distributed by Universal Press Syndicate

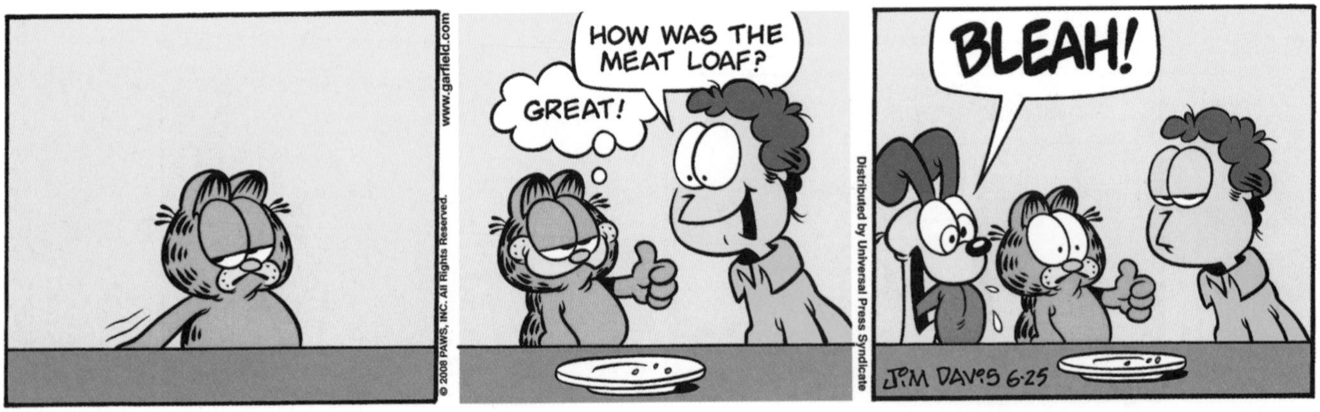
HOW WAS THE MEAT LOAF?
GREAT!
BLEAH!
JIM DAVIS 6-25
www.garfield.com
© 2008 PAWS, INC. All Rights Reserved.
Distributed by Universal Press Syndicate

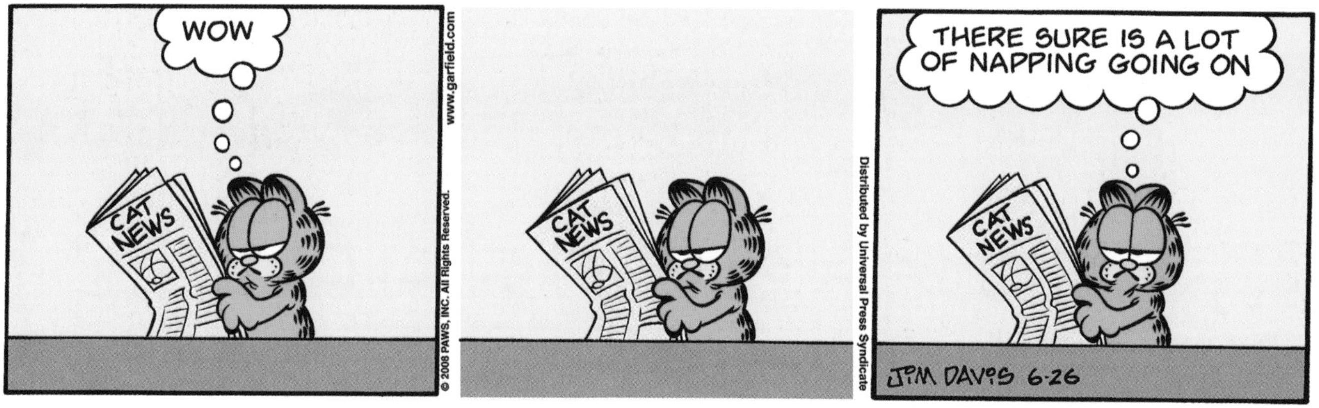
WOW
THERE SURE IS A LOT OF NAPPING GOING ON
CAT NEWS
JIM DAVIS 6-26
© 2008 PAWS, INC. All Rights Reserved.
www.garfield.com
Distributed by Universal Press Syndicate

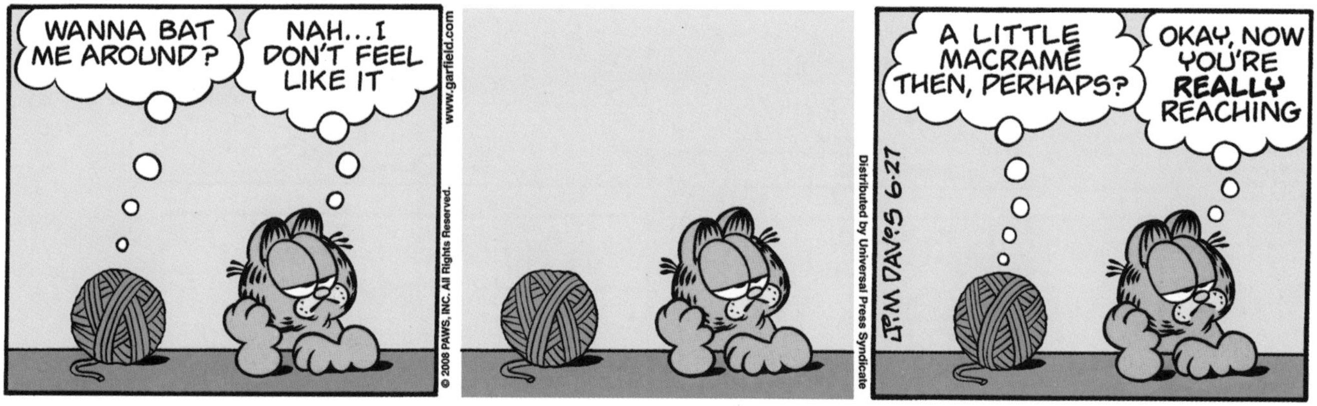
WANNA BAT ME AROUND?
NAH... I DON'T FEEL LIKE IT
A LITTLE MACRAMÉ THEN, PERHAPS?
OKAY, NOW YOU'RE **REALLY** REACHING
JIM DAVIS 6-27
© 2008 PAWS, INC. All Rights Reserved.
www.garfield.com
Distributed by Universal Press Syndicate

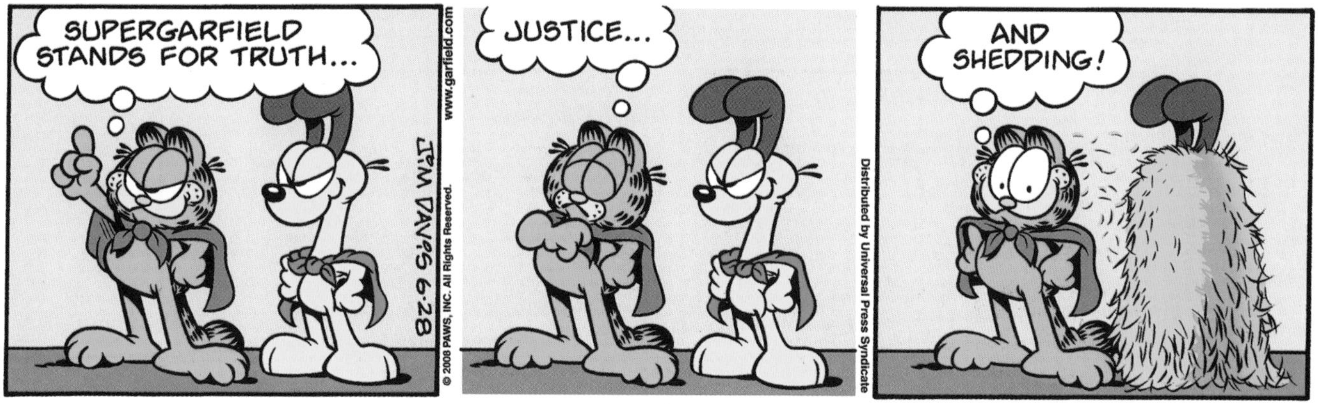
SUPERGARFIELD STANDS FOR TRUTH...
JUSTICE...
AND SHEDDING!
JIM DAVIS 6-28
© 2008 PAWS, INC. All Rights Reserved.
www.garfield.com
Distributed by Universal Press Syndicate

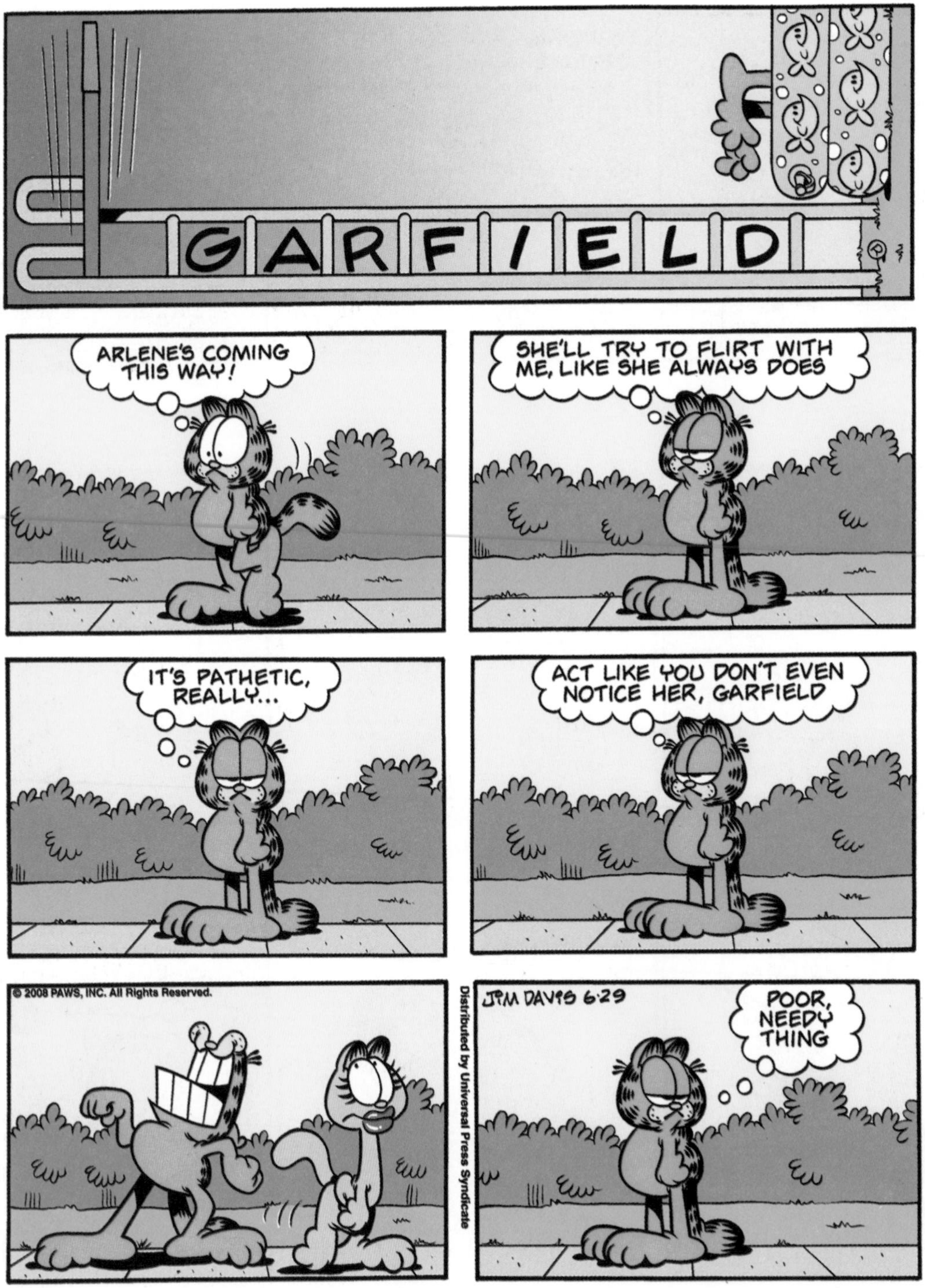
GARFIELD
ARLENE'S COMING THIS WAY!
SHE'LL TRY TO FLIRT WITH ME, LIKE SHE ALWAYS DOES
IT'S PATHETIC, REALLY...
ACT LIKE YOU DON'T EVEN NOTICE HER, GARFIELD
© 2008 PAWS, INC. All Rights Reserved.
Distributed by Universal Press Syndicate
JIM DAVIS 6·29
POOR, NEEDY THING

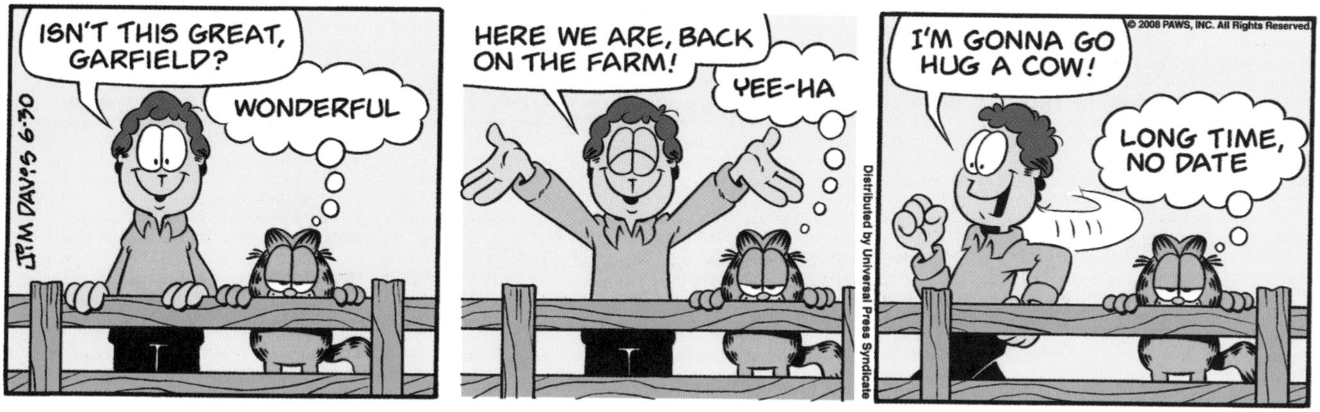
ISN'T THIS GREAT, GARFIELD?
WONDERFUL
JIM DAVIS 6-30
HERE WE ARE, BACK ON THE FARM!
YEE-HA
Distributed by Universal Press Syndicate
I'M GONNA GO HUG A COW!
© 2008 PAWS, INC. All Rights Reserved.
LONG TIME, NO DATE

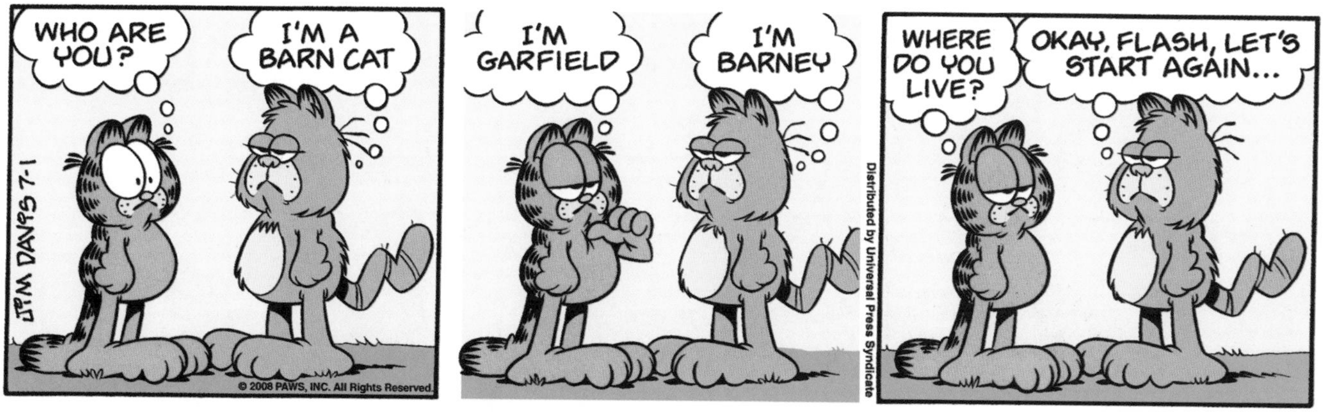
WHO ARE YOU?
I'M A BARN CAT
JIM DAVIS 7-1
© 2008 PAWS, INC. All Rights Reserved.
I'M GARFIELD
I'M BARNEY
Distributed by Universal Press Syndicate
WHERE DO YOU LIVE?
OKAY, FLASH, LET'S START AGAIN...

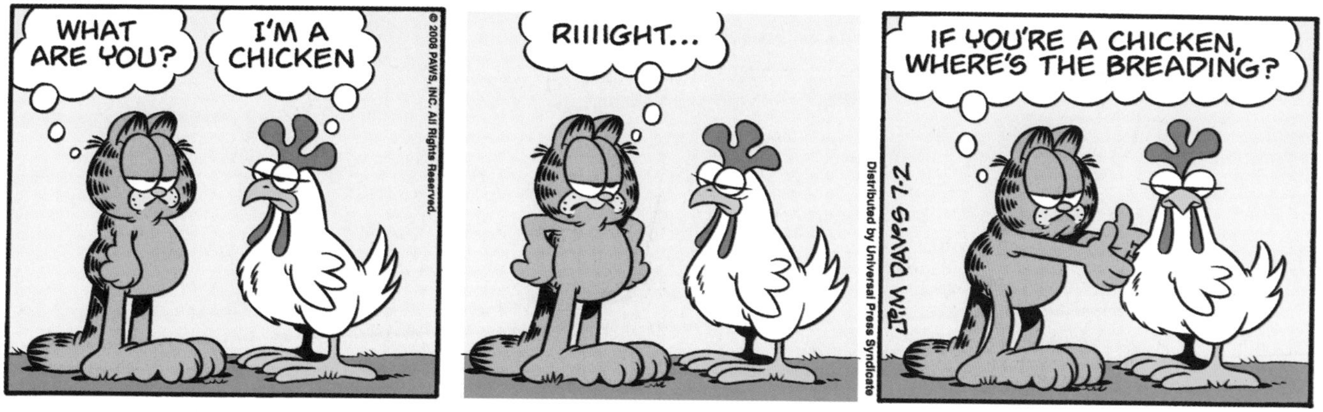
WHAT ARE YOU?
I'M A CHICKEN
© 2008 PAWS, INC. All Rights Reserved.
RIIIIGHT...
Distributed by Universal Press Syndicate
JIM DAVIS 7-2
IF YOU'RE A CHICKEN, WHERE'S THE BREADING?

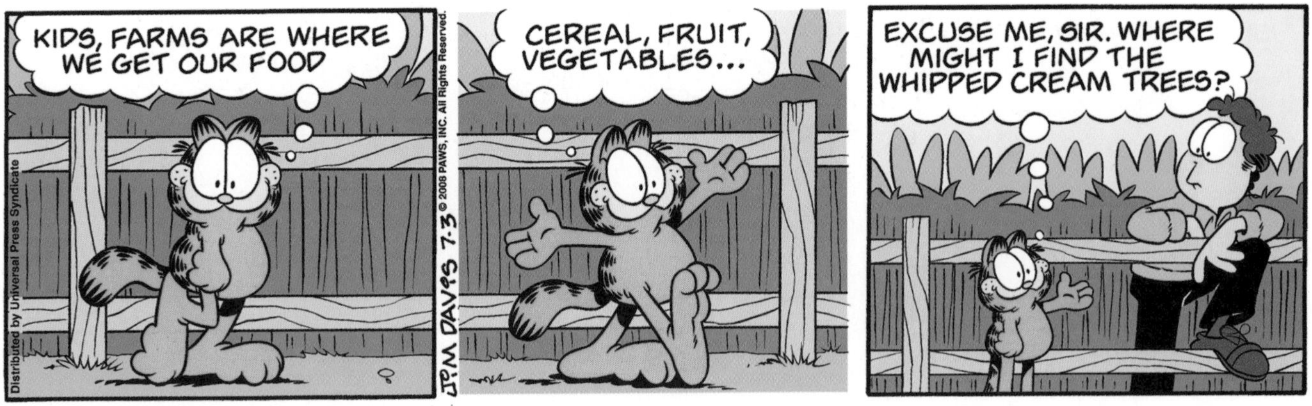
KIDS, FARMS ARE WHERE WE GET OUR FOOD
CEREAL, FRUIT, VEGETABLES...
EXCUSE ME, SIR. WHERE MIGHT I FIND THE WHIPPED CREAM TREES?
JPM DAVPS 7-3
© 2008 PAWS, INC. All Rights Reserved.
Distributed by Universal Press Syndicate

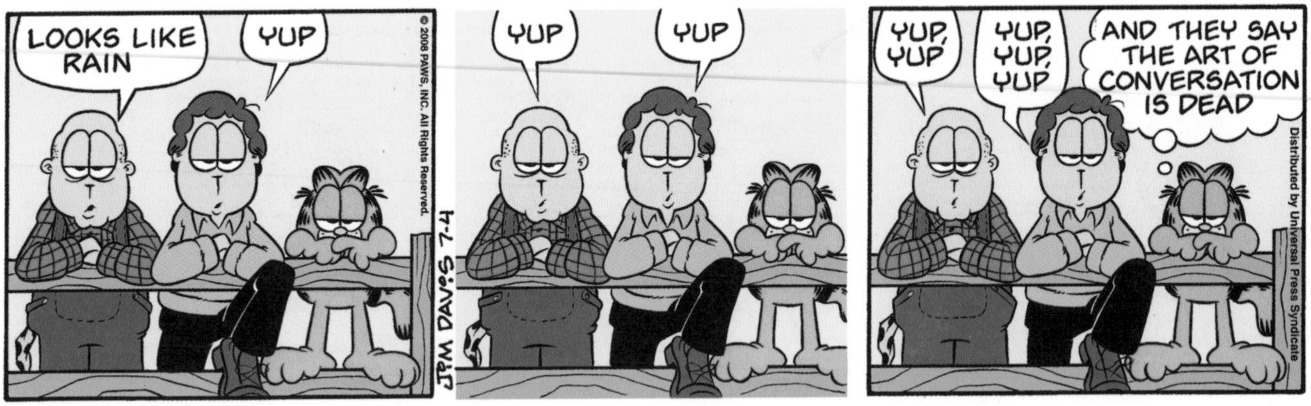
LOOKS LIKE RAIN
YUP
YUP
YUP
YUP, YUP
YUP, YUP, YUP
AND THEY SAY THE ART OF CONVERSATION IS DEAD
JPM DAVPS 7-4
© 2008 PAWS, INC. All Rights Reserved.
Distributed by Universal Press Syndicate

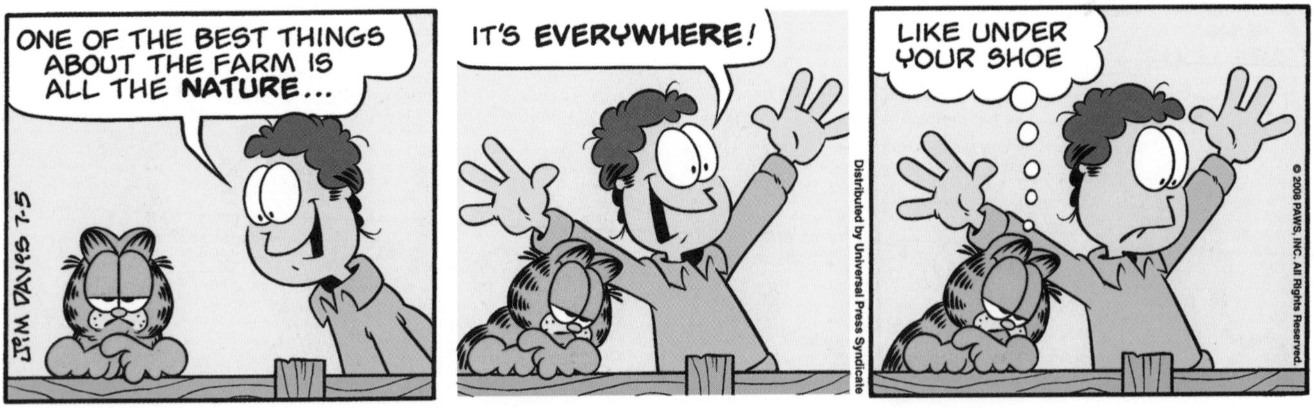
ONE OF THE BEST THINGS ABOUT THE FARM IS ALL THE **NATURE**...
IT'S **EVERYWHERE**!
LIKE UNDER YOUR SHOE
JPM DAVPS 7-5
Distributed by Universal Press Syndicate
© 2008 PAWS, INC. All Rights Reserved.

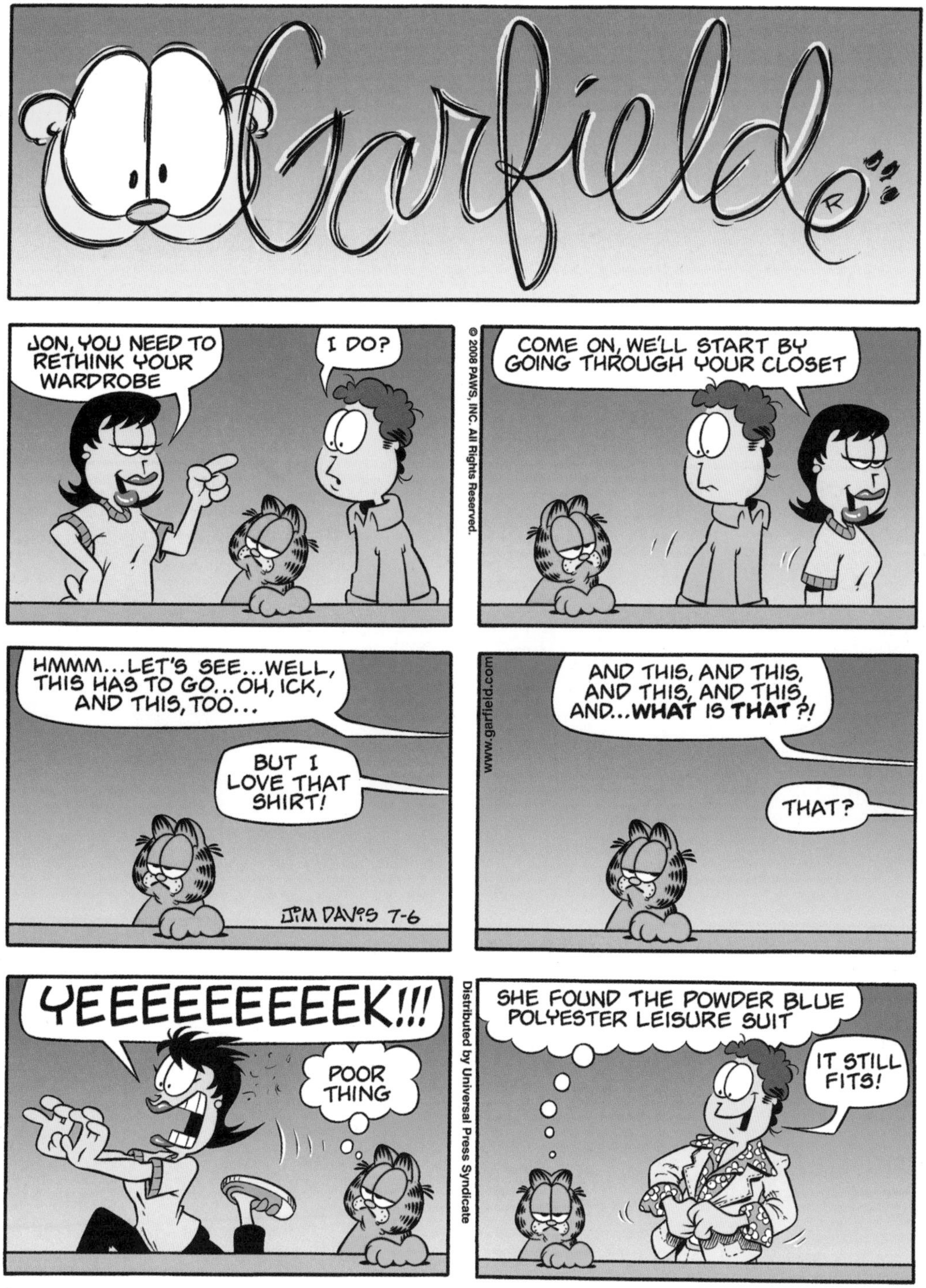
Garfield
JON, YOU NEED TO RETHINK YOUR WARDROBE
I DO?
COME ON, WE'LL START BY GOING THROUGH YOUR CLOSET
HMMM...LET'S SEE...WELL, THIS HAS TO GO...OH, ICK, AND THIS, TOO...
BUT I LOVE THAT SHIRT!
JIM DAVIS 7-6
AND THIS, AND THIS, AND THIS, AND THIS, AND...**WHAT** IS **THAT**?!
THAT?
YEEEEEEEEEK!!!
POOR THING
SHE FOUND THE POWDER BLUE POLYESTER LEISURE SUIT
IT STILL FITS!
© 2008 PAWS, INC. All Rights Reserved.
www.garfield.com
Distributed by Universal Press Syndicate

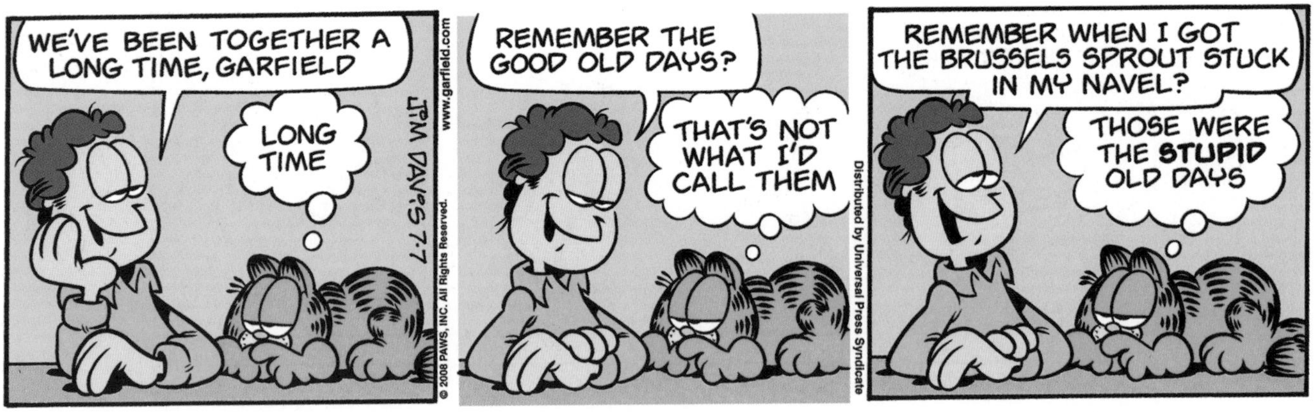
WE'VE BEEN TOGETHER A LONG TIME, GARFIELD
LONG TIME
JIM DAVIS 7-7
© 2008 PAWS, INC. All Rights Reserved.
www.garfield.com
REMEMBER THE GOOD OLD DAYS?
THAT'S NOT WHAT I'D CALL THEM
Distributed by Universal Press Syndicate
REMEMBER WHEN I GOT THE BRUSSELS SPROUT STUCK IN MY NAVEL?
THOSE WERE THE **STUPID** OLD DAYS

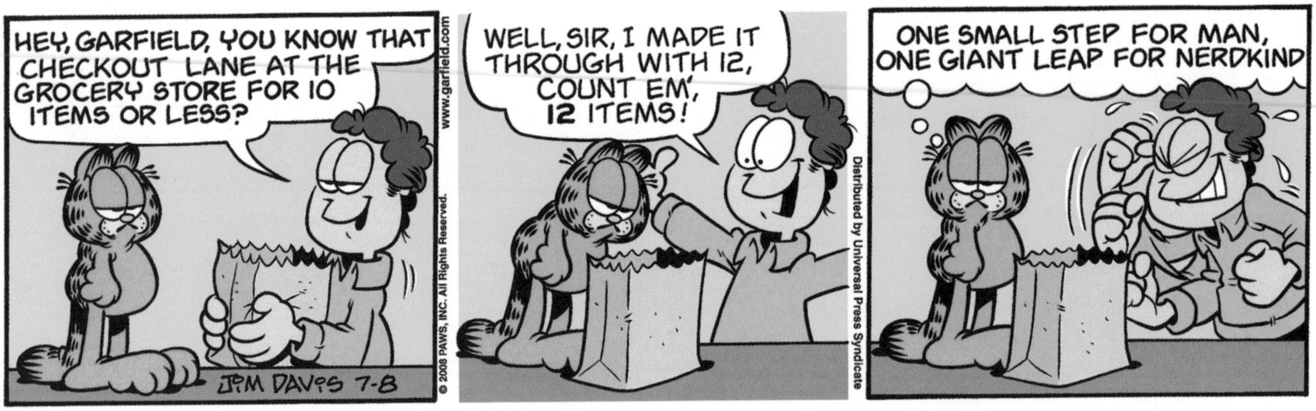
HEY, GARFIELD, YOU KNOW THAT CHECKOUT LANE AT THE GROCERY STORE FOR 10 ITEMS OR LESS?
JIM DAVIS 7-8
© 2008 PAWS, INC. All Rights Reserved.
www.garfield.com
WELL, SIR, I MADE IT THROUGH WITH 12, COUNT EM', **12** ITEMS!
Distributed by Universal Press Syndicate
ONE SMALL STEP FOR MAN, ONE GIANT LEAP FOR NERDKIND

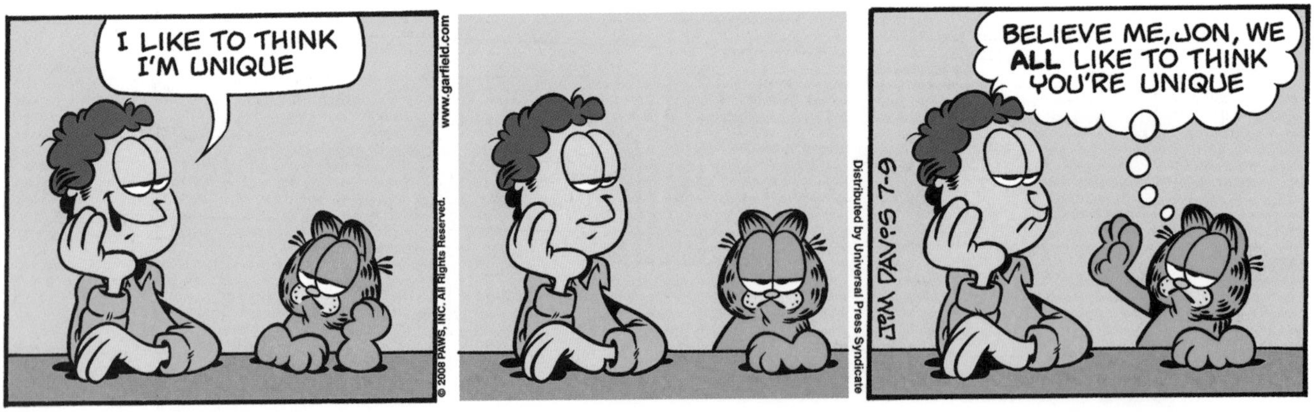
I LIKE TO THINK I'M UNIQUE
© 2008 PAWS, INC. All Rights Reserved.
www.garfield.com
Distributed by Universal Press Syndicate
JIM DAVIS 7-9
BELIEVE ME, JON, WE **ALL** LIKE TO THINK YOU'RE UNIQUE

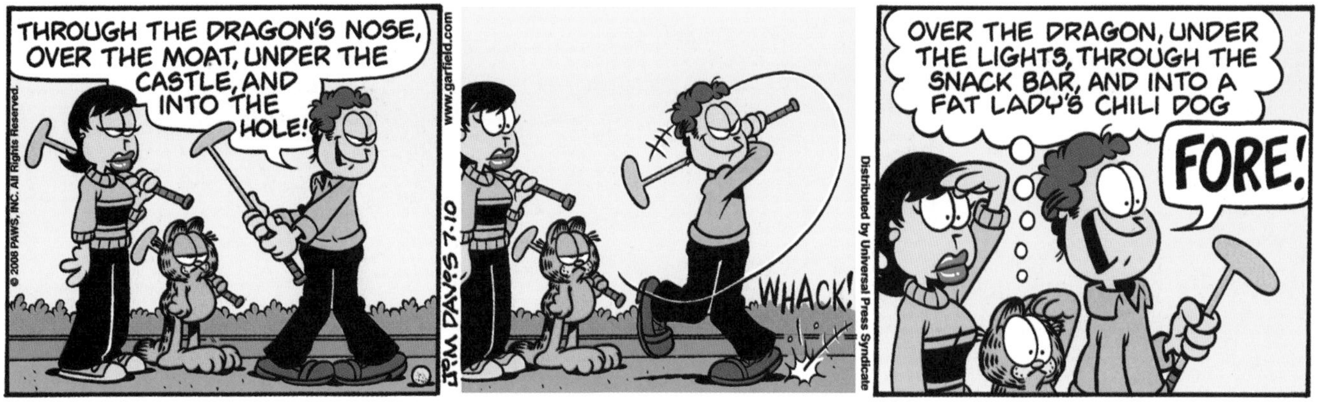
THROUGH THE DRAGON'S NOSE, OVER THE MOAT, UNDER THE CASTLE, AND INTO THE HOLE!
© 2008 PAWS, INC. All Rights Reserved.
www.garfield.com
JIM DAVIS 7-10
WHACK!
Distributed by Universal Press Syndicate
OVER THE DRAGON, UNDER THE LIGHTS, THROUGH THE SNACK BAR, AND INTO A FAT LADY'S CHILI DOG
FORE!

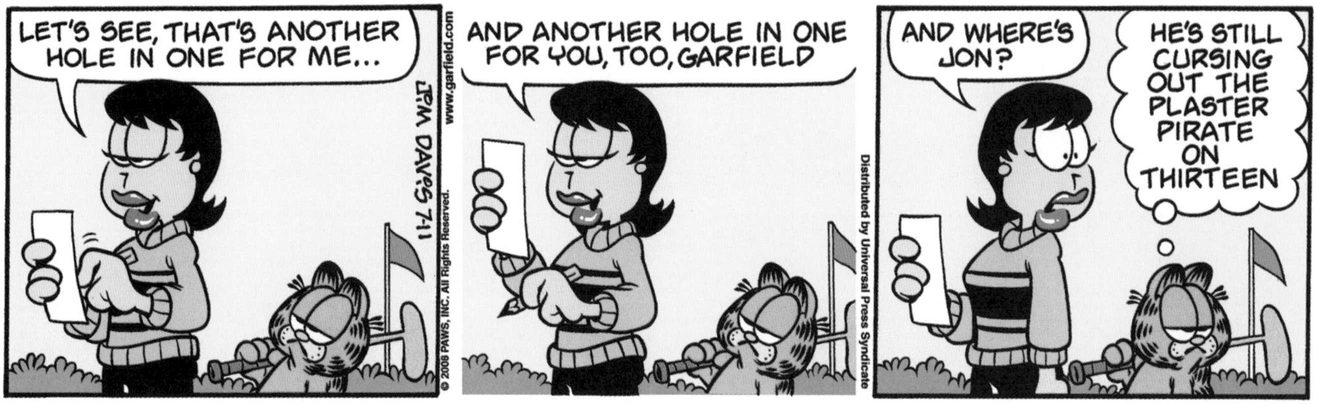
LET'S SEE, THAT'S ANOTHER HOLE IN ONE FOR ME...
JIM DAVIS 7-11
www.garfield.com
© 2008 PAWS, INC. All Rights Reserved.
AND ANOTHER HOLE IN ONE FOR YOU, TOO, GARFIELD
Distributed by Universal Press Syndicate
AND WHERE'S JON?
HE'S STILL CURSING OUT THE PLASTER PIRATE ON THIRTEEN

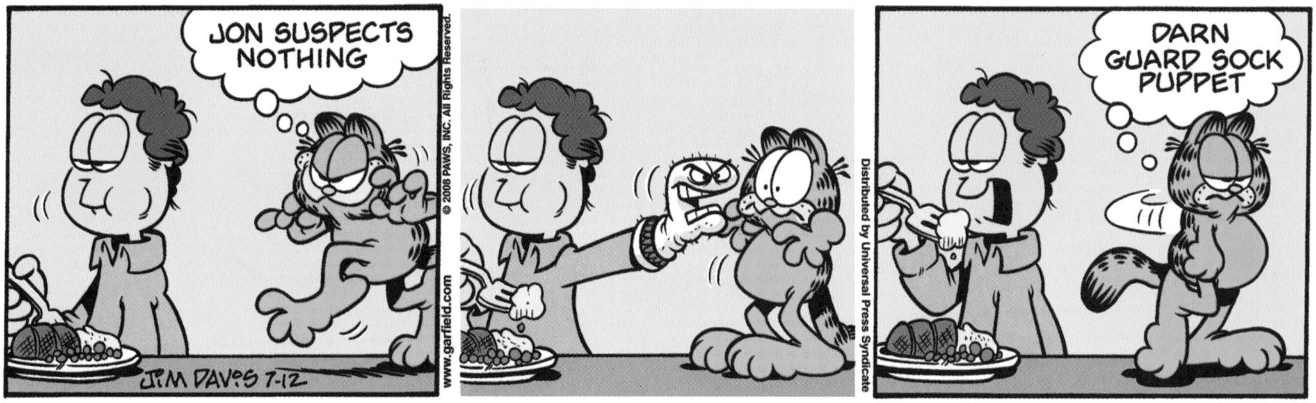
JON SUSPECTS NOTHING
JIM DAVIS 7-12
© 2008 PAWS, INC. All Rights Reserved.
www.garfield.com
Distributed by Universal Press Syndicate
DARN GUARD SOCK PUPPET

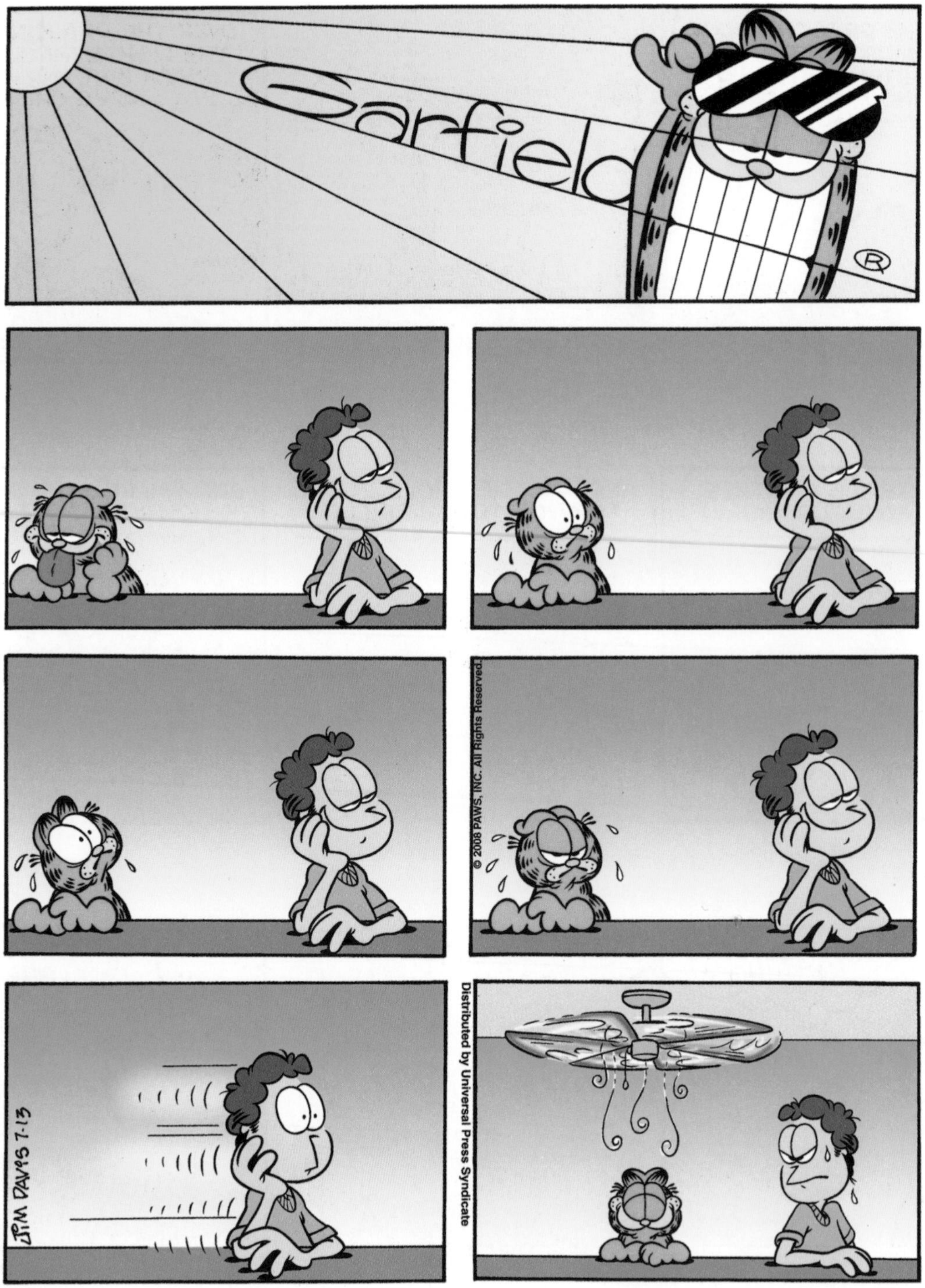
Garfield
®
© 2008 PAWS, INC. All Rights Reserved.
Distributed by Universal Press Syndicate
JIM DAVIS 7-13

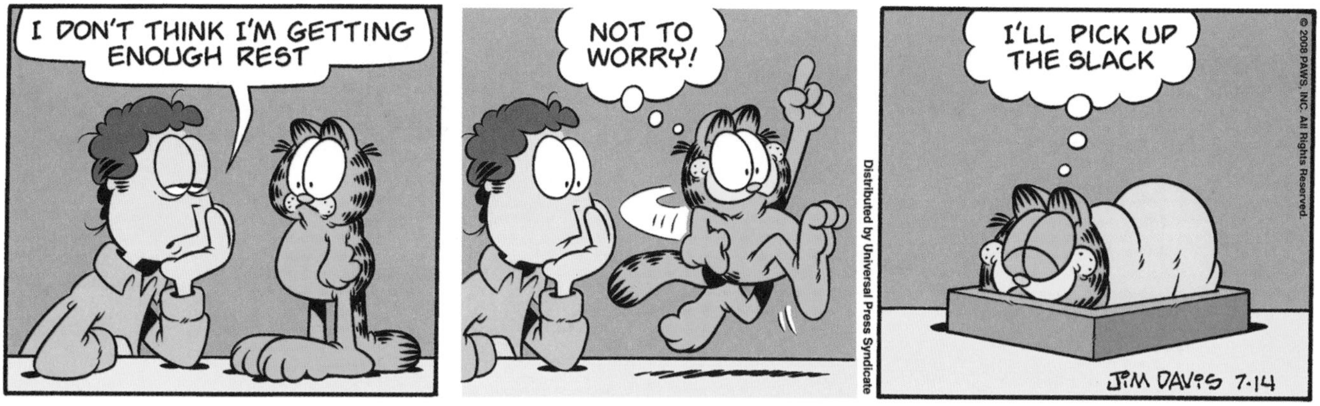
I DON'T THINK I'M GETTING ENOUGH REST
NOT TO WORRY!
I'LL PICK UP THE SLACK
JIM DAVIS 7-14
Distributed by Universal Press Syndicate
© 2008 PAWS, INC. All Rights Reserved.

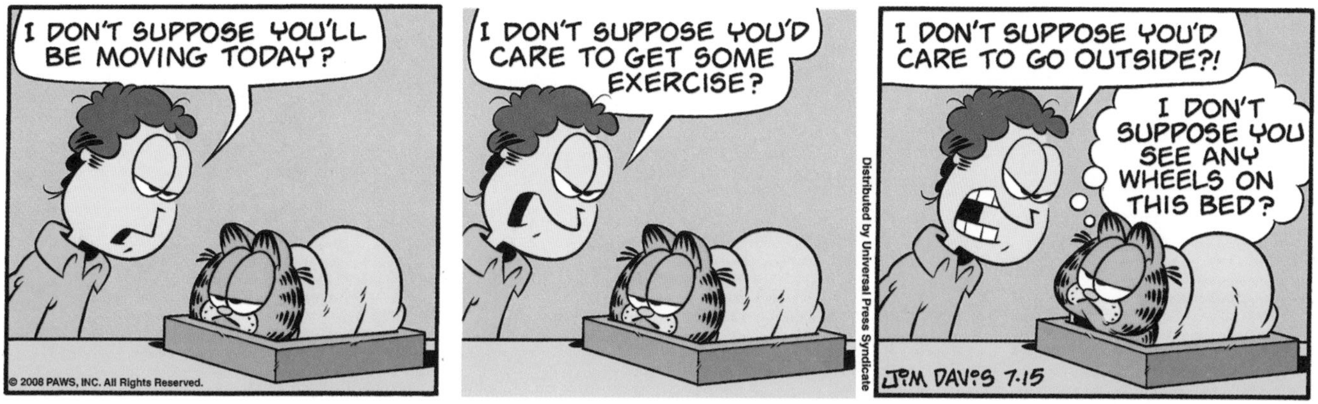
I DON'T SUPPOSE YOU'LL BE MOVING TODAY?
I DON'T SUPPOSE YOU'D CARE TO GET SOME EXERCISE?
I DON'T SUPPOSE YOU'D CARE TO GO OUTSIDE?!
I DON'T SUPPOSE YOU SEE ANY WHEELS ON THIS BED?
JIM DAVIS 7-15
© 2008 PAWS, INC. All Rights Reserved.
Distributed by Universal Press Syndicate

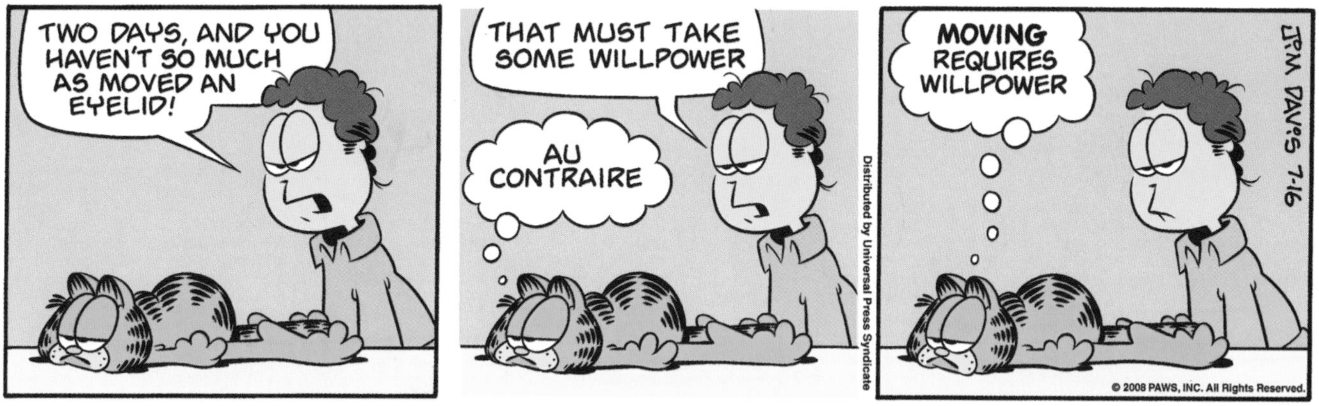
TWO DAYS, AND YOU HAVEN'T SO MUCH AS MOVED AN EYELID!
THAT MUST TAKE SOME WILLPOWER
AU CONTRAIRE
MOVING REQUIRES WILLPOWER
JIM DAVIS 7-16
Distributed by Universal Press Syndicate
© 2008 PAWS, INC. All Rights Reserved.

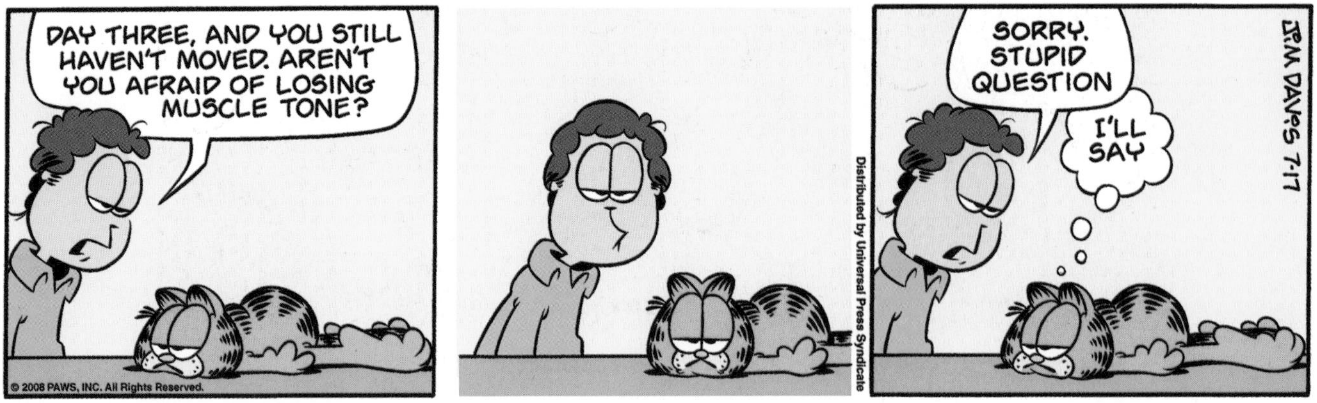
DAY THREE, AND YOU STILL HAVEN'T MOVED. AREN'T YOU AFRAID OF LOSING MUSCLE TONE?
SORRY. STUPID QUESTION
I'LL SAY
JIM DAVIS 7-17
© 2008 PAWS, INC. All Rights Reserved.
Distributed by Universal Press Syndicate

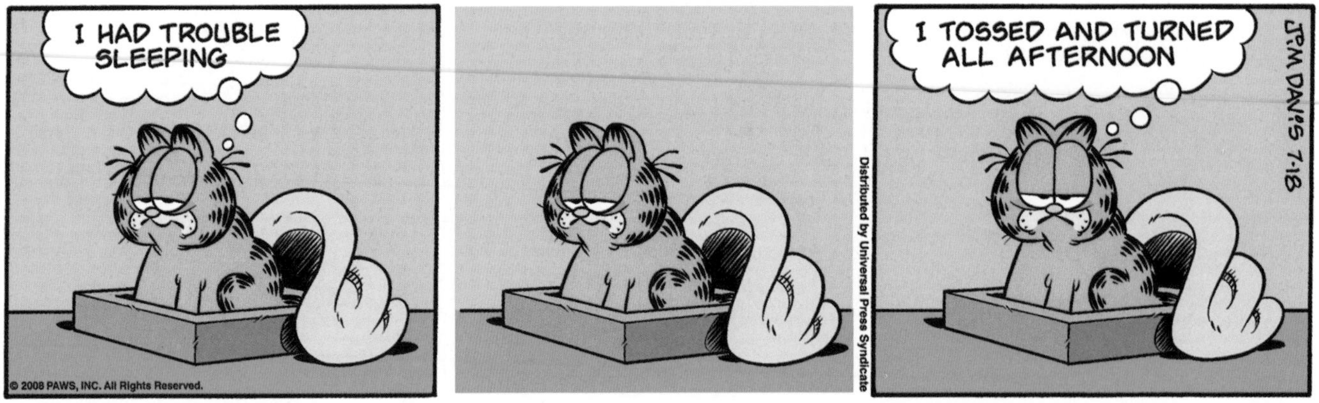
I HAD TROUBLE SLEEPING
I TOSSED AND TURNED ALL AFTERNOON
JIM DAVIS 7-18
© 2008 PAWS, INC. All Rights Reserved.
Distributed by Universal Press Syndicate

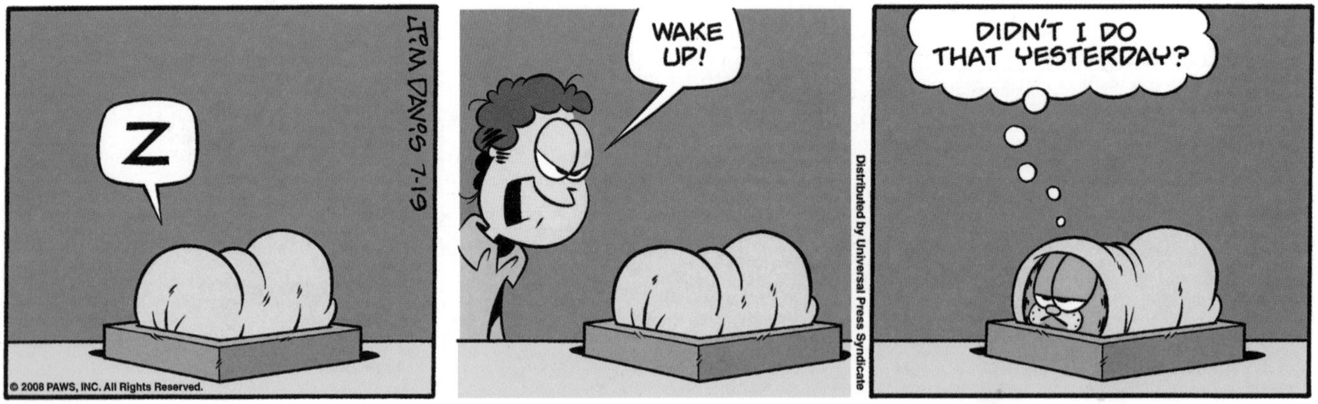
Z
WAKE UP!
DIDN'T I DO THAT YESTERDAY?
JIM DAVIS 7-19
© 2008 PAWS, INC. All Rights Reserved.
Distributed by Universal Press Syndicate

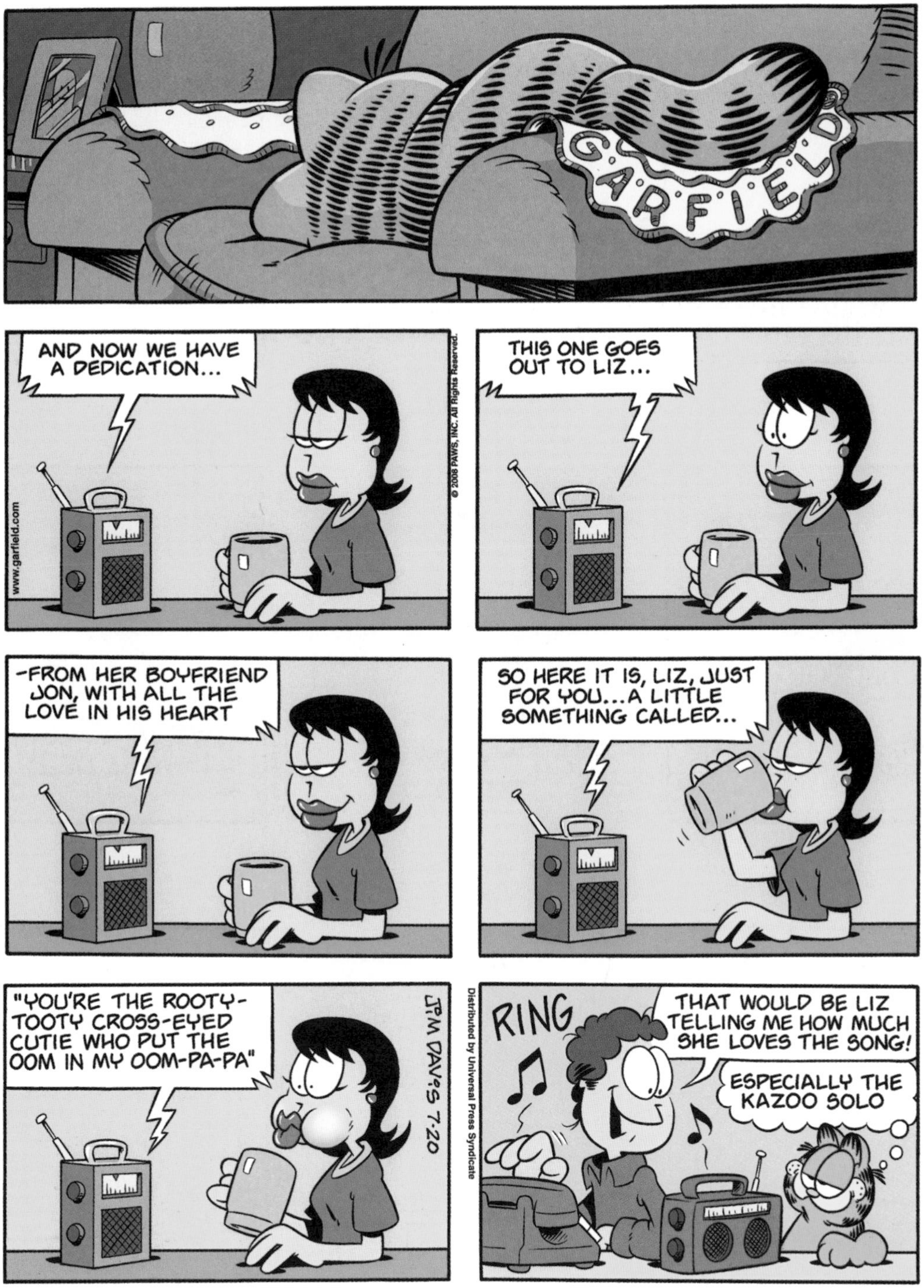
GARFIELD
AND NOW WE HAVE A DEDICATION...
www.garfield.com
© 2008 PAWS, INC. All Rights Reserved.
THIS ONE GOES OUT TO LIZ...
-FROM HER BOYFRIEND JON, WITH ALL THE LOVE IN HIS HEART
SO HERE IT IS, LIZ, JUST FOR YOU...A LITTLE SOMETHING CALLED...
"YOU'RE THE ROOTY-TOOTY CROSS-EYED CUTIE WHO PUT THE OOM IN MY OOM-PA-PA"
JPM DAVIS 7-20
Distributed by Universal Press Syndicate
RING
THAT WOULD BE LIZ TELLING ME HOW MUCH SHE LOVES THE SONG!
ESPECIALLY THE KAZOO SOLO

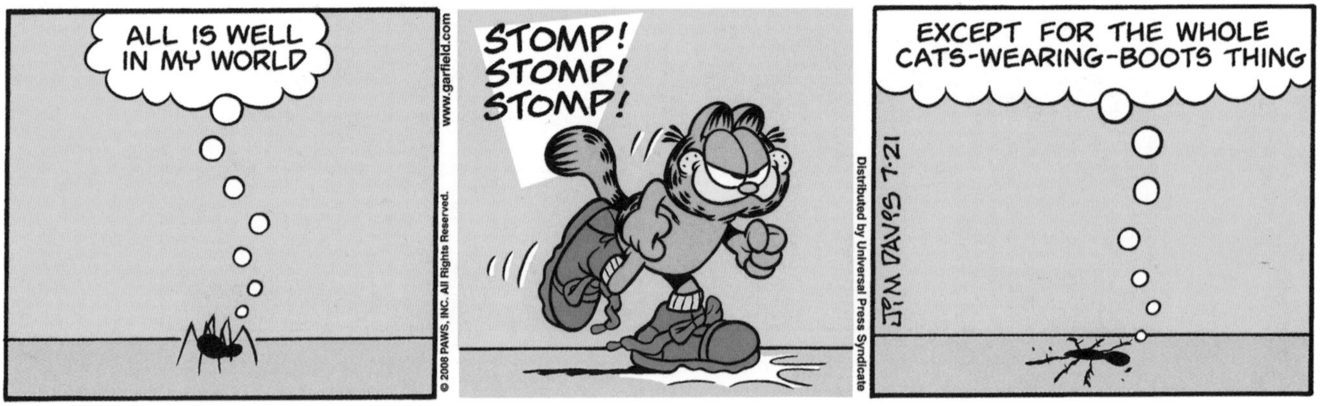
ALL IS WELL IN MY WORLD
www.garfield.com
© 2008 PAWS, INC. All Rights Reserved.
STOMP! STOMP! STOMP!
Distributed by Universal Press Syndicate
EXCEPT FOR THE WHOLE CATS-WEARING-BOOTS THING
JIM DAVIS 7-21

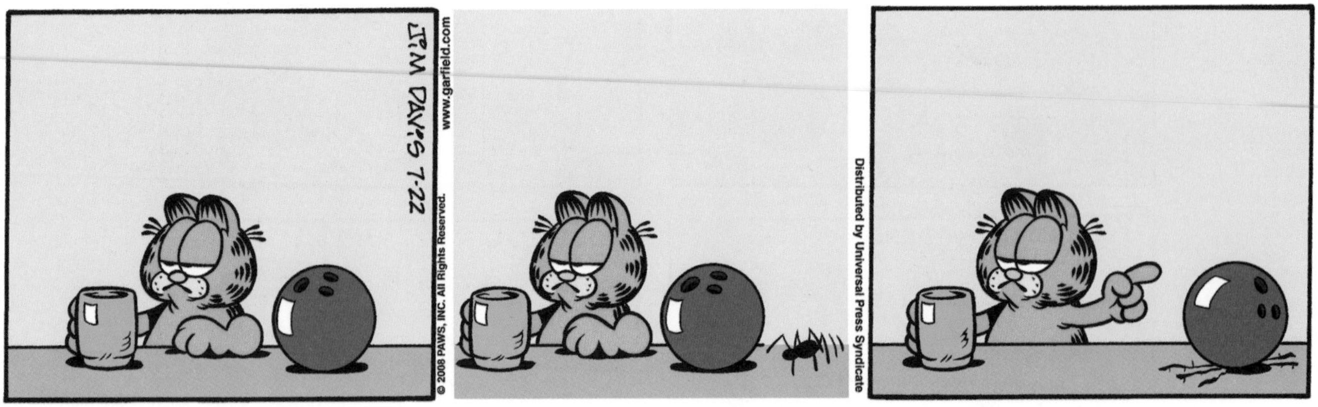
JIM DAVIS 7-22
www.garfield.com
© 2008 PAWS, INC. All Rights Reserved.
Distributed by Universal Press Syndicate

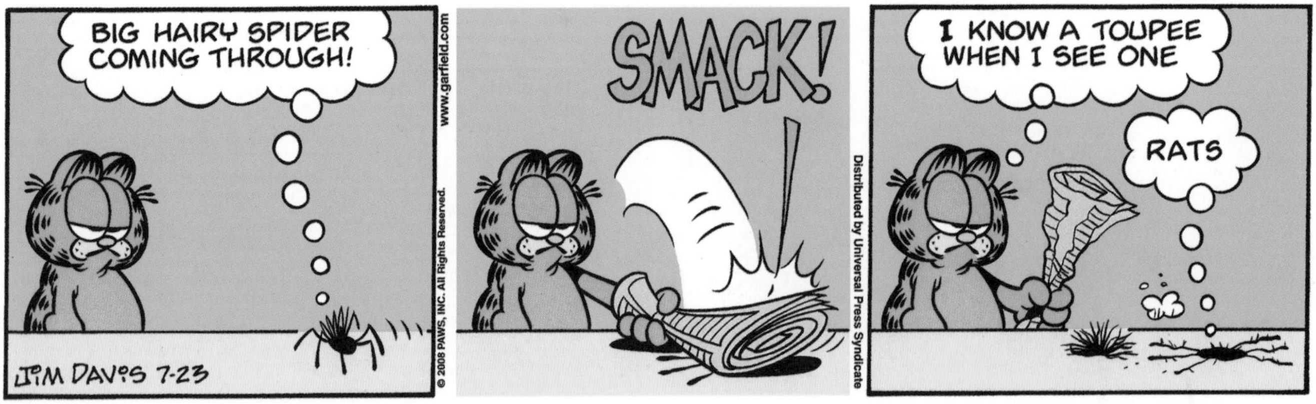
BIG HAIRY SPIDER COMING THROUGH!
JIM DAVIS 7-23
www.garfield.com
© 2008 PAWS, INC. All Rights Reserved.
SMACK!
Distributed by Universal Press Syndicate
I KNOW A TOUPEE WHEN I SEE ONE
RATS

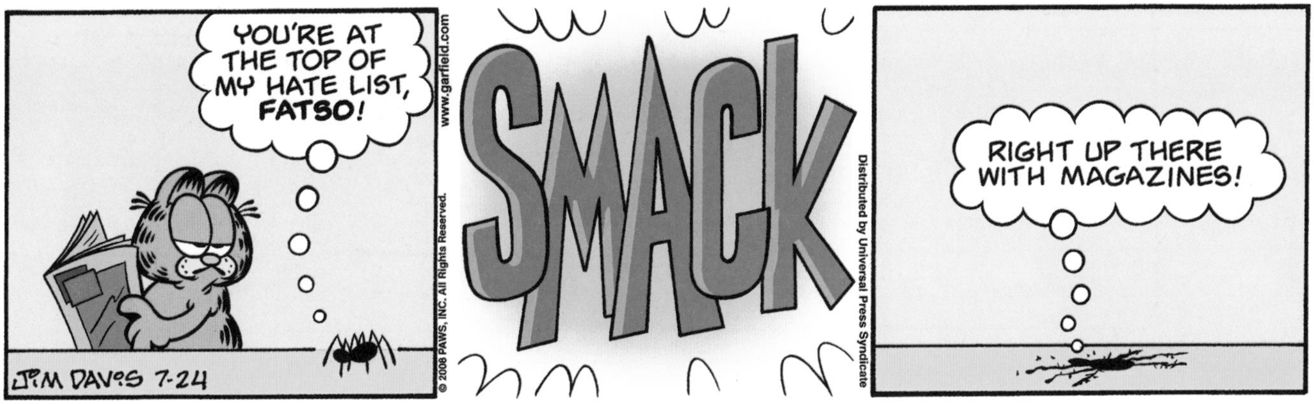
YOU'RE AT THE TOP OF MY HATE LIST, **FATSO!**
SMACK
RIGHT UP THERE WITH MAGAZINES!
JIM DAVIS 7-24
© 2008 PAWS, INC. All Rights Reserved.
www.garfield.com
Distributed by Universal Press Syndicate

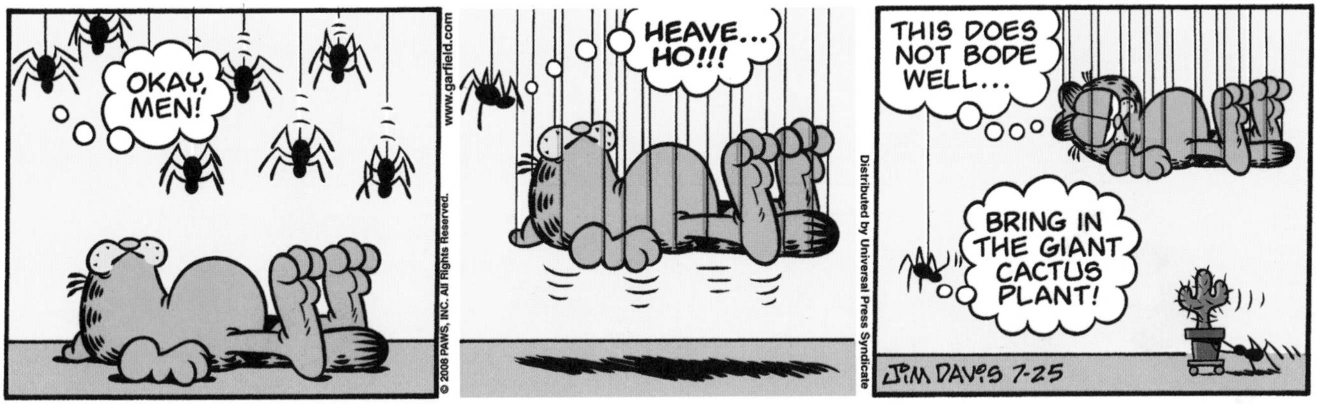
OKAY, MEN!
HEAVE... HO!!!
THIS DOES NOT BODE WELL...
BRING IN THE GIANT CACTUS PLANT!
JIM DAVIS 7-25
© 2008 PAWS, INC. All Rights Reserved.
www.garfield.com
Distributed by Universal Press Syndicate

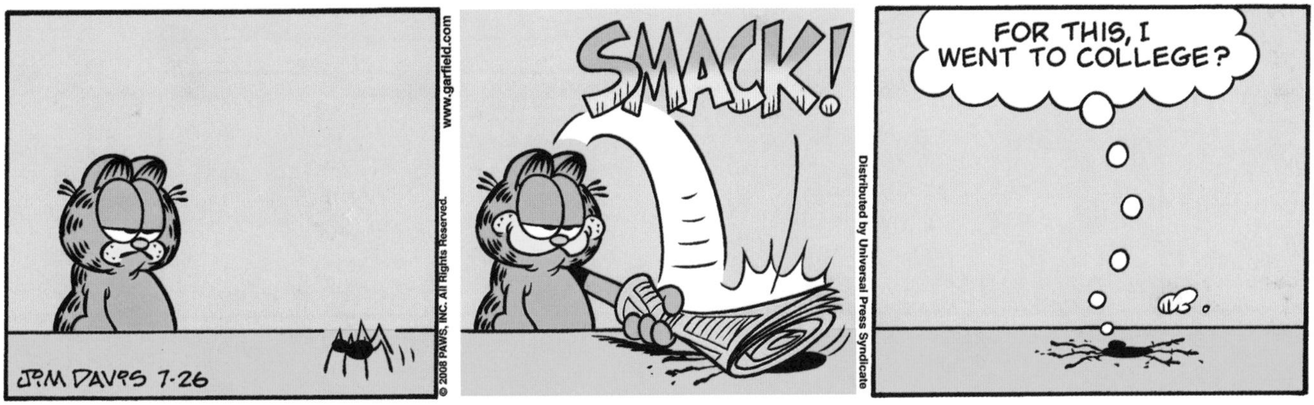
JIM DAVIS 7-26
SMACK!
FOR THIS, I WENT TO COLLEGE?
© 2008 PAWS, INC. All Rights Reserved.
www.garfield.com
Distributed by Universal Press Syndicate

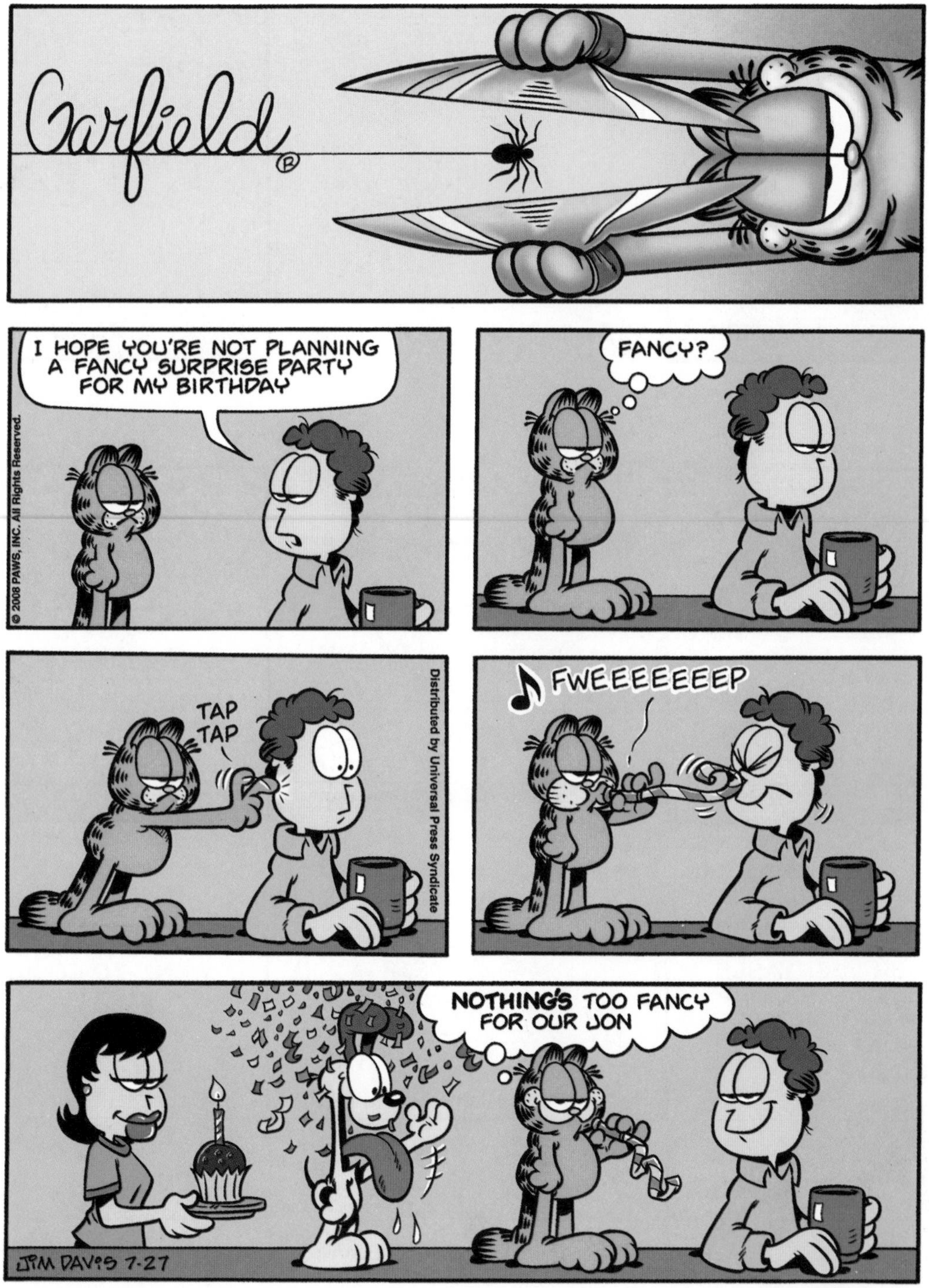
Garfield®
I HOPE YOU'RE NOT PLANNING A FANCY SURPRISE PARTY FOR MY BIRTHDAY
© 2008 PAWS, INC. All Rights Reserved.
FANCY?
TAP TAP
Distributed by Universal Press Syndicate
FWEEEEEEEP
NOTHING'S TOO FANCY FOR OUR JON
JIM DAVIS 7-27

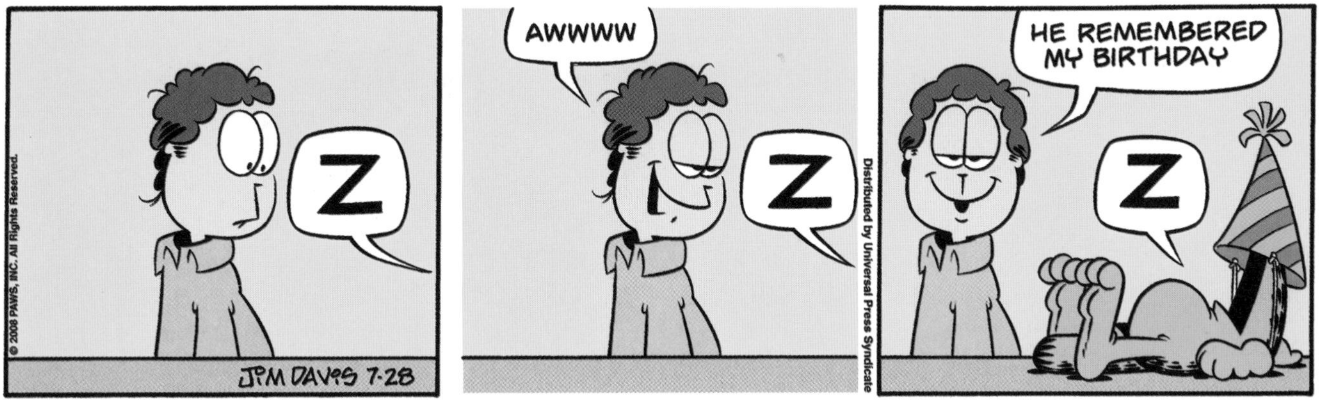
© 2008 PAWS, INC. All Rights Reserved.
Z
JIM DAVIS 7-28
AWWWW
Z
Distributed by Universal Press Syndicate
HE REMEMBERED MY BIRTHDAY
Z

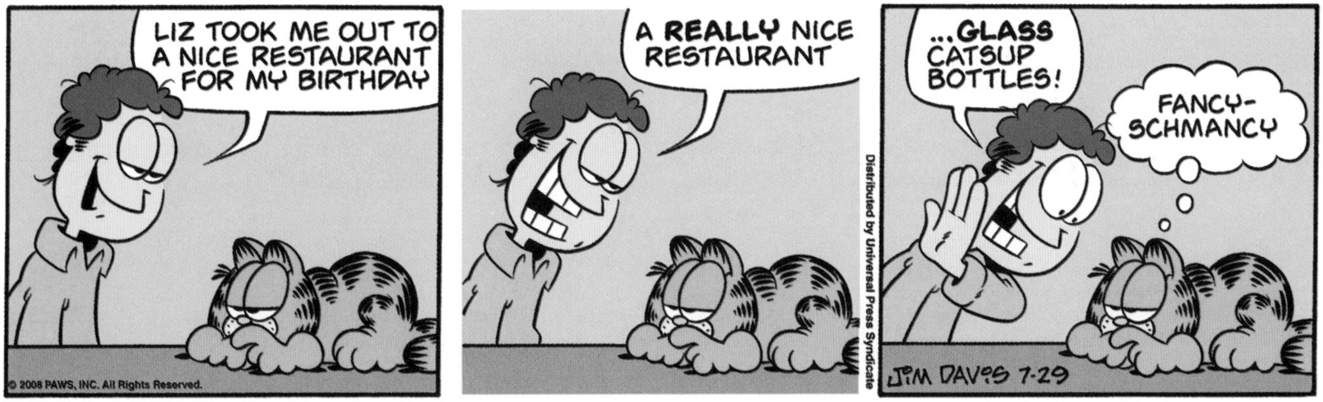
LIZ TOOK ME OUT TO A NICE RESTAURANT FOR MY BIRTHDAY
© 2008 PAWS, INC. All Rights Reserved.
A **REALLY** NICE RESTAURANT
Distributed by Universal Press Syndicate
...**GLASS** CATSUP BOTTLES!
FANCY-SCHMANCY
JIM DAVIS 7-29

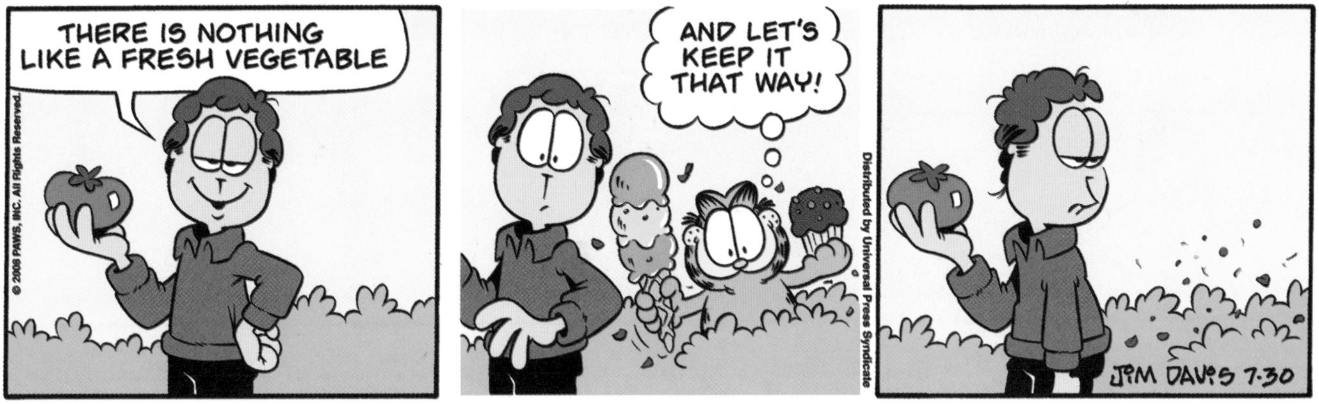
THERE IS NOTHING LIKE A FRESH VEGETABLE
© 2008 PAWS, INC. All Rights Reserved.
AND LET'S KEEP IT THAT WAY!
Distributed by Universal Press Syndicate
JIM DAVIS 7-30

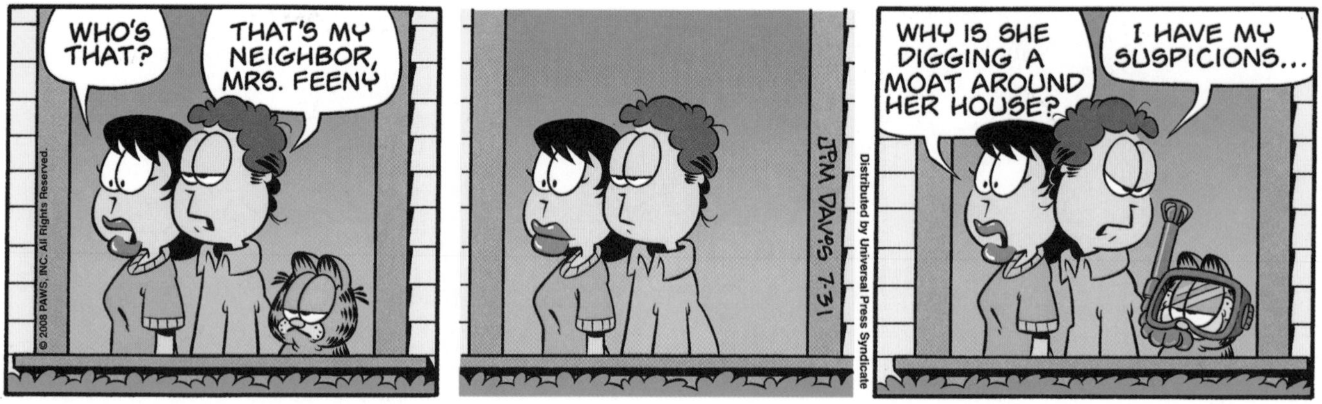
WHO'S THAT?
THAT'S MY NEIGHBOR, MRS. FEENY
WHY IS SHE DIGGING A MOAT AROUND HER HOUSE?
I HAVE MY SUSPICIONS...
JIM DAVIS 7-31
© 2008 PAWS, INC. All Rights Reserved.
Distributed by Universal Press Syndicate

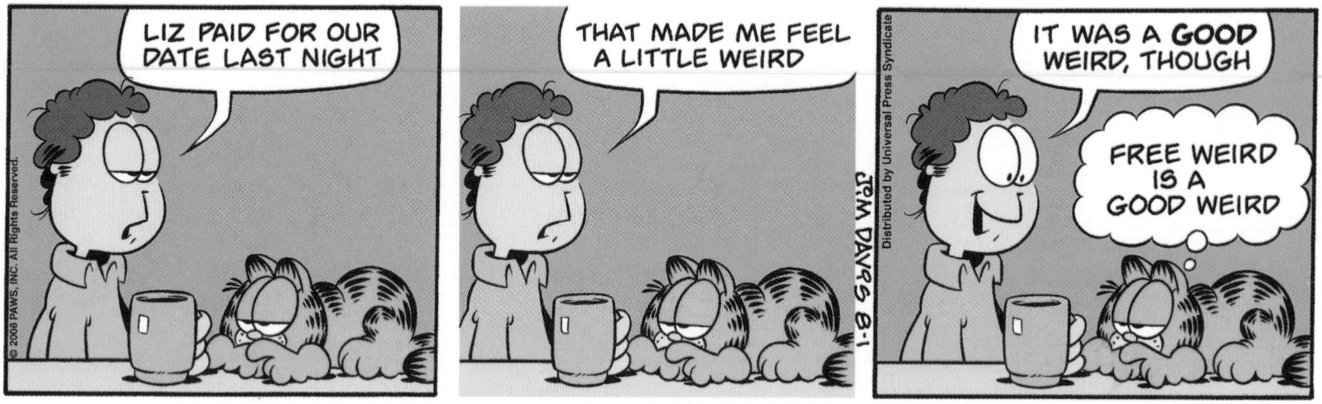
LIZ PAID FOR OUR DATE LAST NIGHT
THAT MADE ME FEEL A LITTLE WEIRD
IT WAS A **GOOD** WEIRD, THOUGH
FREE WEIRD IS A GOOD WEIRD
JIM DAVIS 8-1
© 2008 PAWS, INC. All Rights Reserved.
Distributed by Universal Press Syndicate

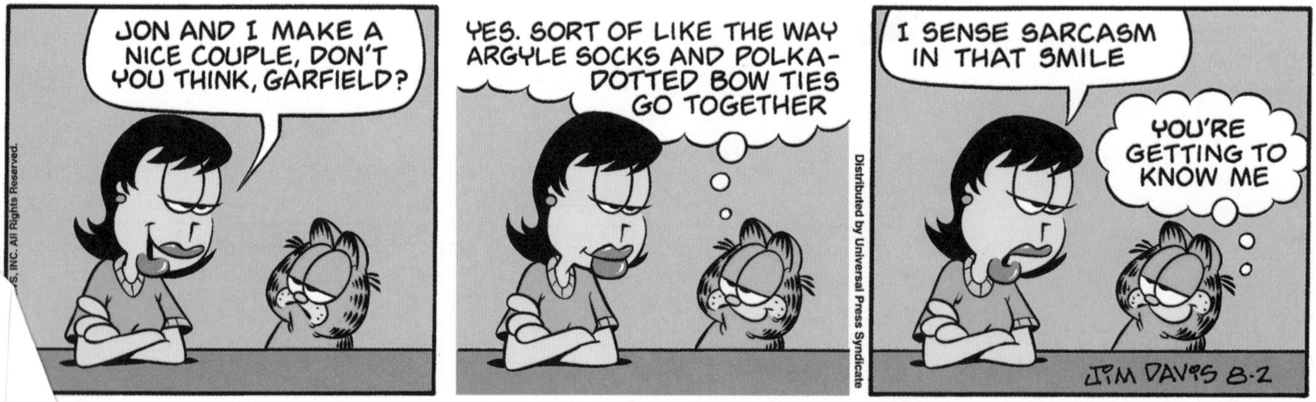
JON AND I MAKE A NICE COUPLE, DON'T YOU THINK, GARFIELD?
YES. SORT OF LIKE THE WAY ARGYLE SOCKS AND POLKA-DOTTED BOW TIES GO TOGETHER
I SENSE SARCASM IN THAT SMILE
YOU'RE GETTING TO KNOW ME
JIM DAVIS 8-2
S, INC. All Rights Reserved.
Distributed by Universal Press Syndicate

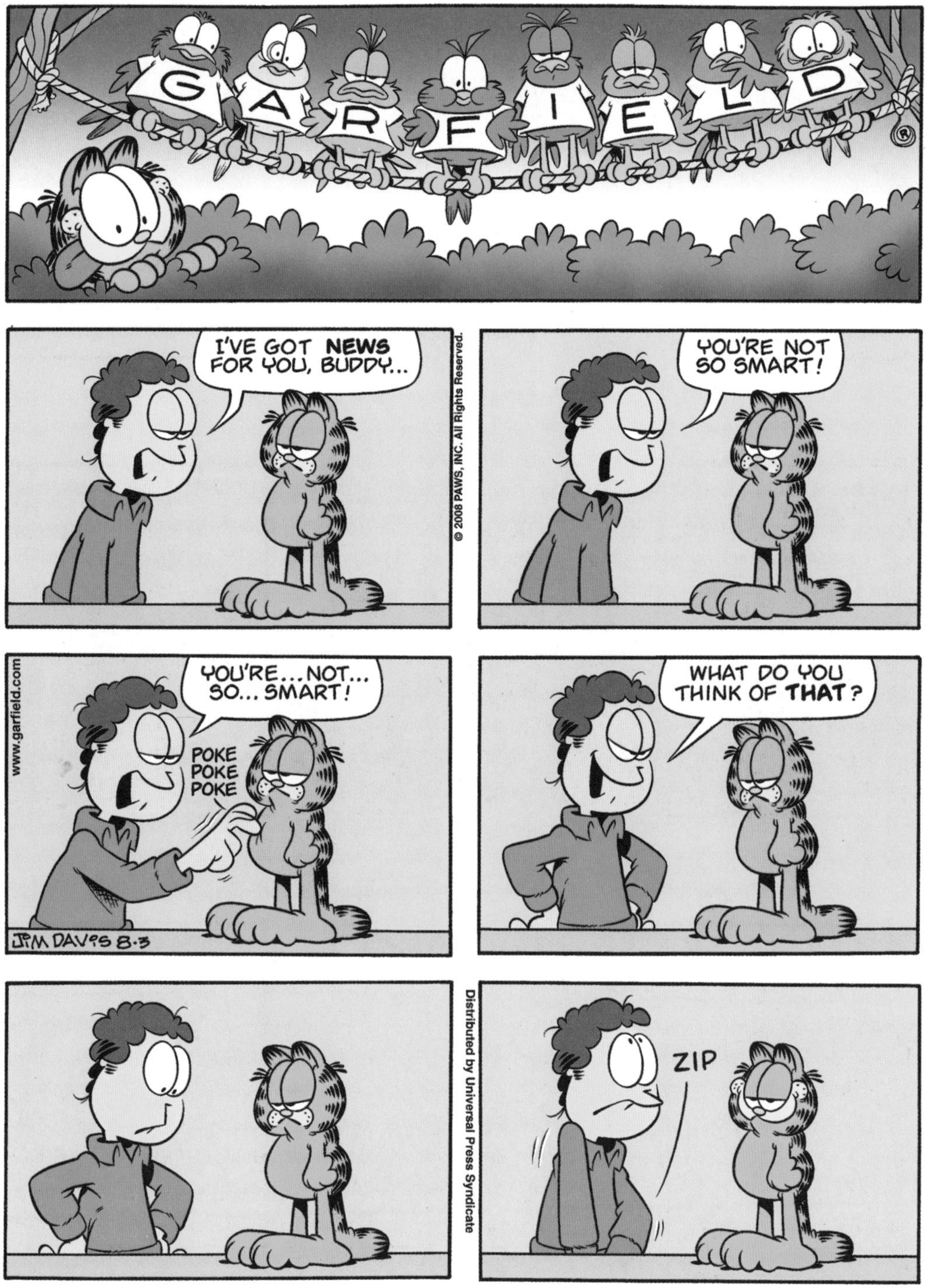
G A R F I E L D
I'VE GOT NEWS FOR YOU, BUDDY...
© 2008 PAWS, INC. All Rights Reserved.
YOU'RE NOT SO SMART!
www.garfield.com
YOU'RE...NOT... SO...SMART!
POKE POKE POKE
JIM DAVIS 8·3
WHAT DO YOU THINK OF THAT?
Distributed by Universal Press Syndicate
ZIP

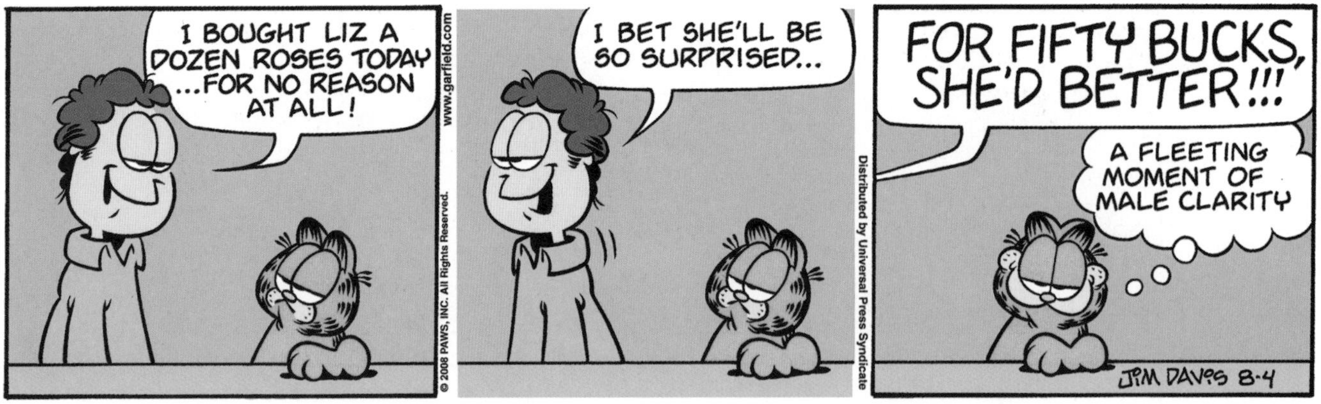
I BOUGHT LIZ A DOZEN ROSES TODAY ...FOR NO REASON AT ALL!
www.garfield.com
© 2008 PAWS, INC. All Rights Reserved.
I BET SHE'LL BE SO SURPRISED...
Distributed by Universal Press Syndicate
FOR FIFTY BUCKS, SHE'D BETTER!!!
A FLEETING MOMENT OF MALE CLARITY
JIM DAVIS 8-4

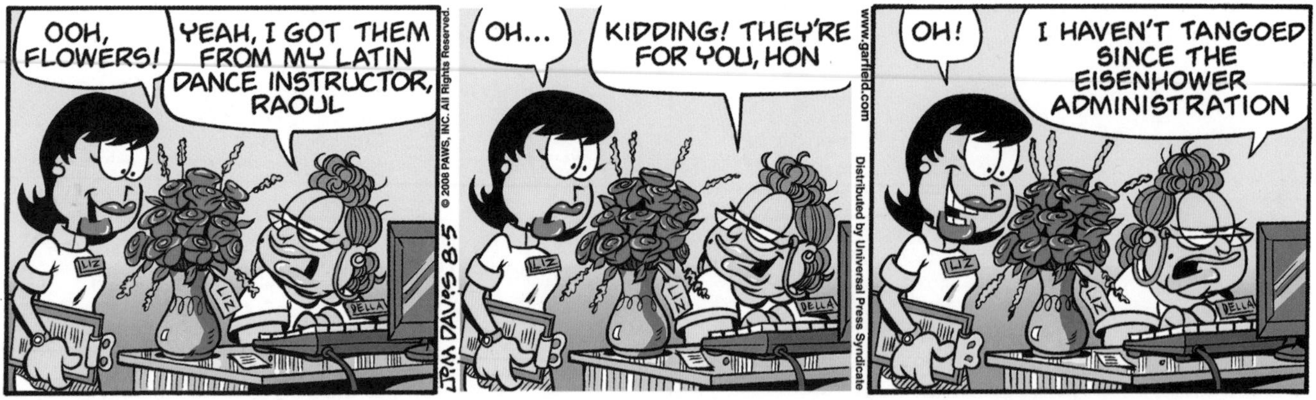
OOH, FLOWERS!
YEAH, I GOT THEM FROM MY LATIN DANCE INSTRUCTOR, RAOUL
LIZ
LIZ
DELLA
© 2008 PAWS, INC. All Rights Reserved.
JIM DAVIS 8-5
OH...
KIDDING! THEY'RE FOR YOU, HON
www.garfield.com
Distributed by Universal Press Syndicate
OH!
I HAVEN'T TANGOED SINCE THE EISENHOWER ADMINISTRATION

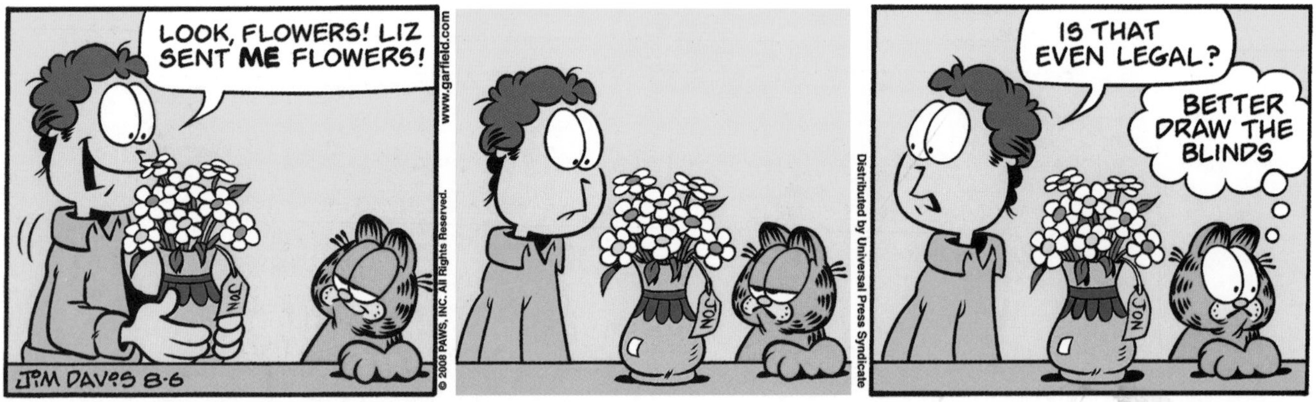
LOOK, FLOWERS! LIZ SENT **ME** FLOWERS!
JON
JIM DAVIS 8-6
www.garfield.com
© 2008 PAWS, INC. All Rights Reserved.
Distributed by Universal Press Syndicate
IS THAT EVEN LEGAL?
BETTER DRAW THE BLINDS

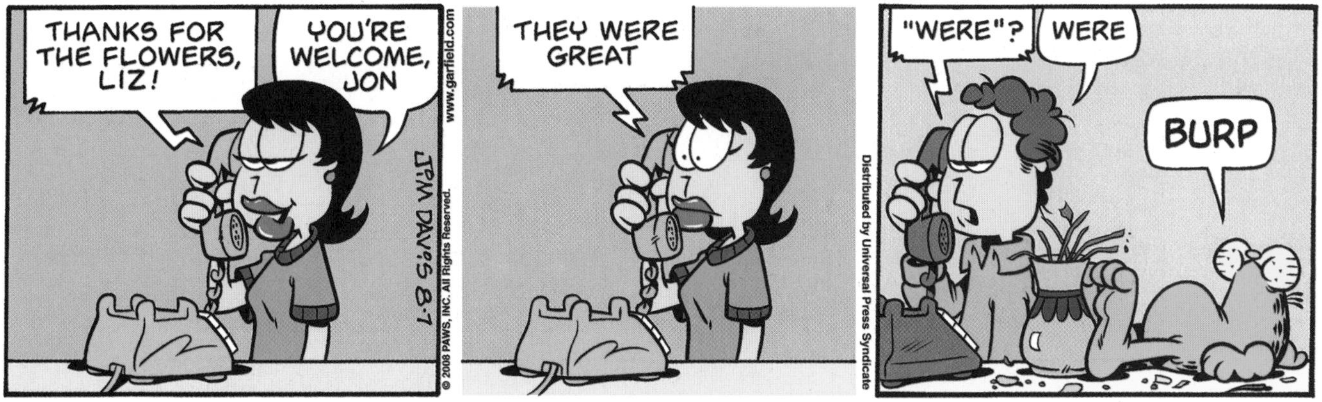
THANKS FOR THE FLOWERS, LIZ!
YOU'RE WELCOME, JON
JIM DAVIS 8-7
© 2008 PAWS, INC. All Rights Reserved.
www.garfield.com
THEY WERE GREAT
Distributed by Universal Press Syndicate
"WERE"?
WERE
BURP

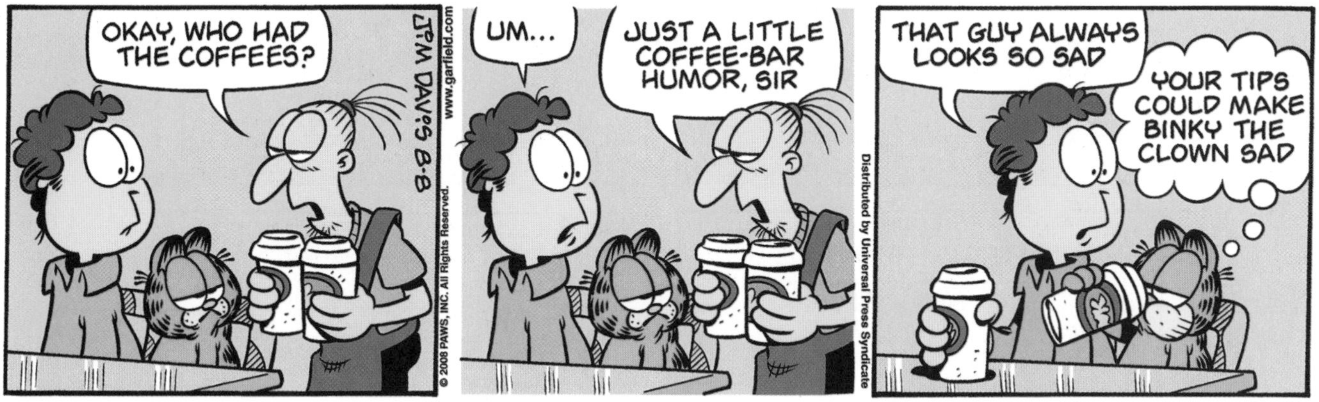
OKAY, WHO HAD THE COFFEES?
JIM DAVIS 8-8
© 2008 PAWS, INC. All Rights Reserved.
www.garfield.com
UM...
JUST A LITTLE COFFEE-BAR HUMOR, SIR
Distributed by Universal Press Syndicate
THAT GUY ALWAYS LOOKS SO SAD
YOUR TIPS COULD MAKE BINKY THE CLOWN SAD

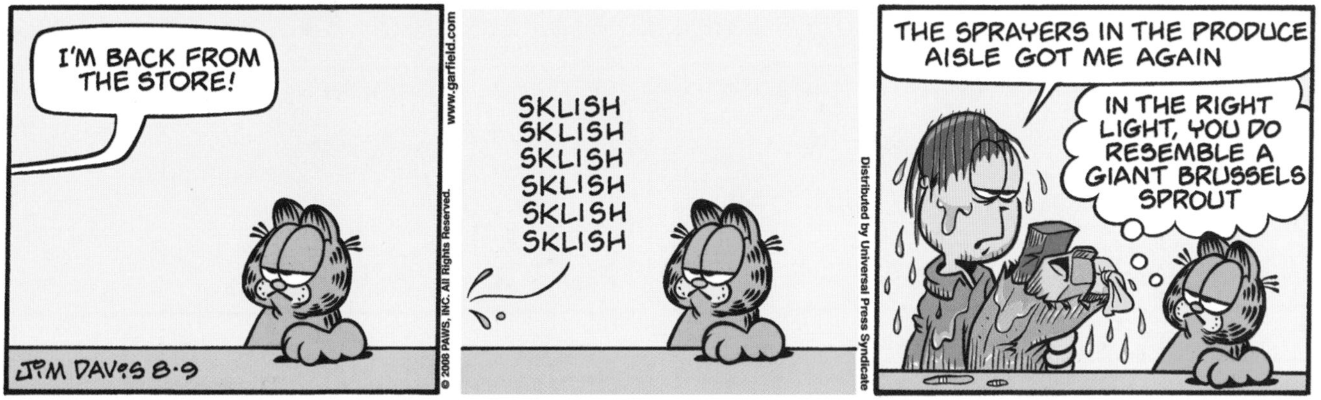
I'M BACK FROM THE STORE!
JIM DAVIS 8-9
© 2008 PAWS, INC. All Rights Reserved.
www.garfield.com
SKLISH
SKLISH
SKLISH
SKLISH
SKLISH
SKLISH
Distributed by Universal Press Syndicate
THE SPRAYERS IN THE PRODUCE AISLE GOT ME AGAIN
IN THE RIGHT LIGHT, YOU DO RESEMBLE A GIANT BRUSSELS SPROUT

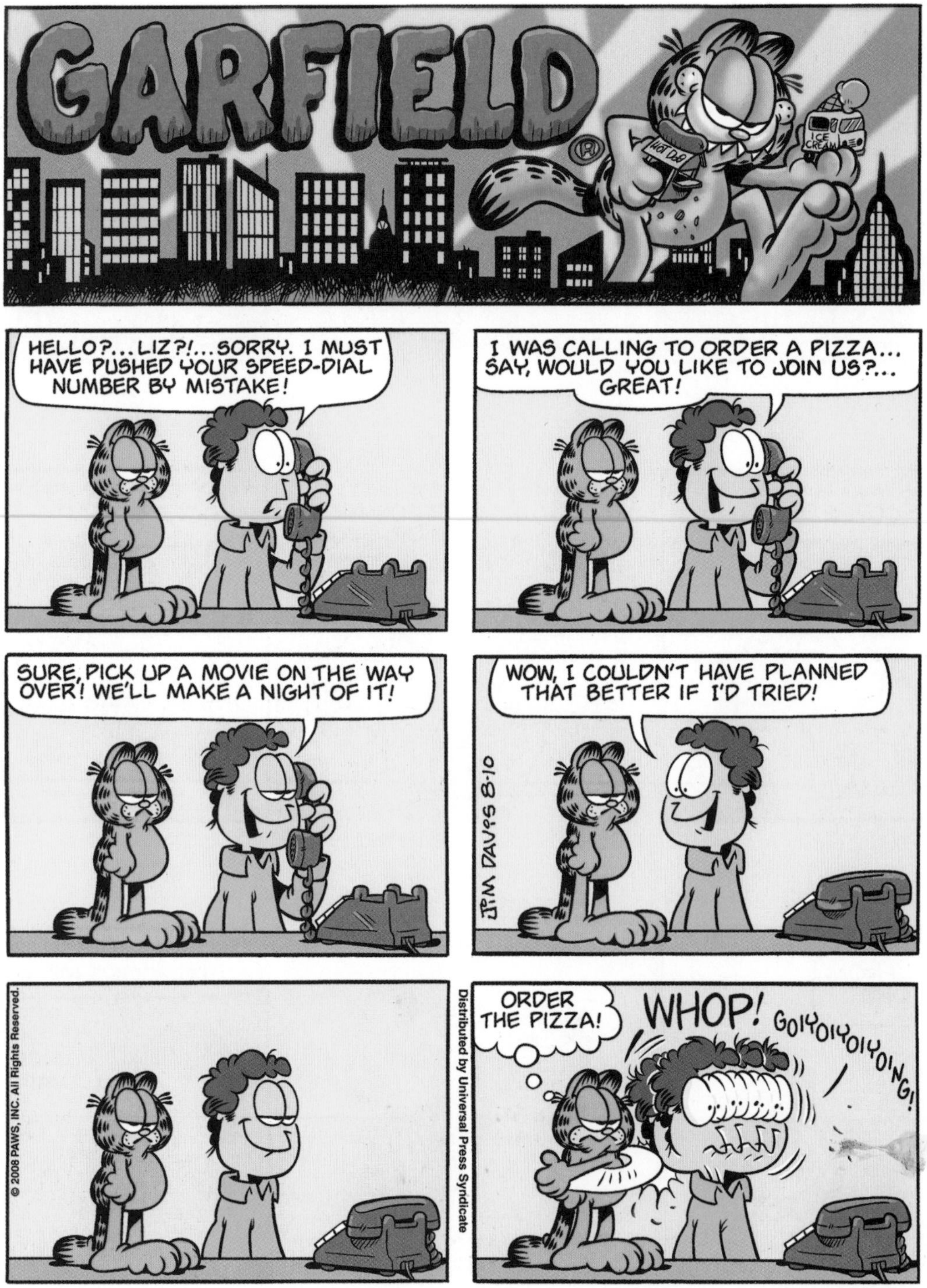
GARFIELD
HOT DOG
ICE CREAM
HELLO?...LIZ?!...SORRY. I MUST HAVE PUSHED YOUR SPEED-DIAL NUMBER BY MISTAKE!
I WAS CALLING TO ORDER A PIZZA... SAY, WOULD YOU LIKE TO JOIN US?... GREAT!
SURE, PICK UP A MOVIE ON THE WAY OVER! WE'LL MAKE A NIGHT OF IT!
WOW, I COULDN'T HAVE PLANNED THAT BETTER IF I'D TRIED!
JIM DAVIS 8-10
ORDER THE PIZZA!
WHOP!
GOIYOIYOIYOIYOING!

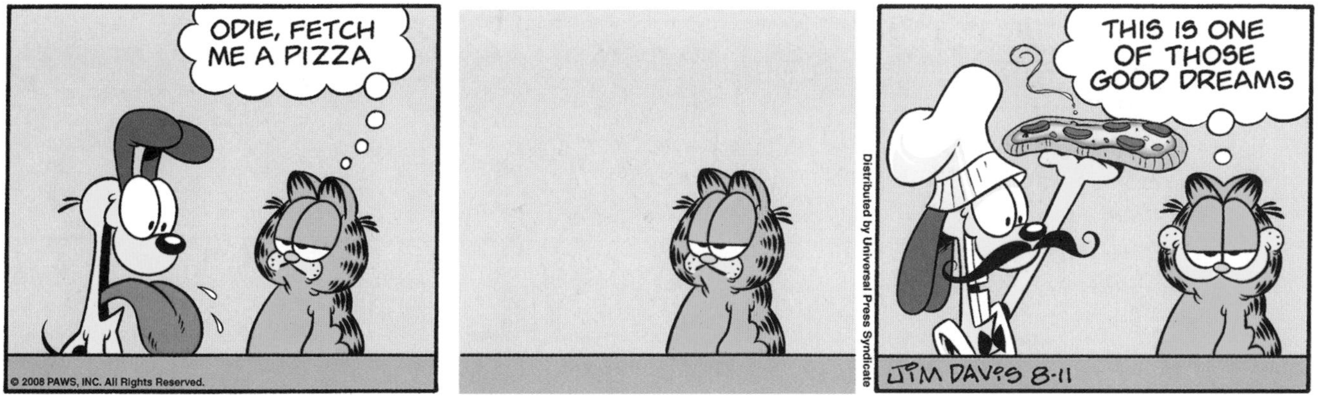
ODIE, FETCH ME A PIZZA
THIS IS ONE OF THOSE GOOD DREAMS
© 2008 PAWS, INC. All Rights Reserved.
Distributed by Universal Press Syndicate
JIM DAVIS 8-11

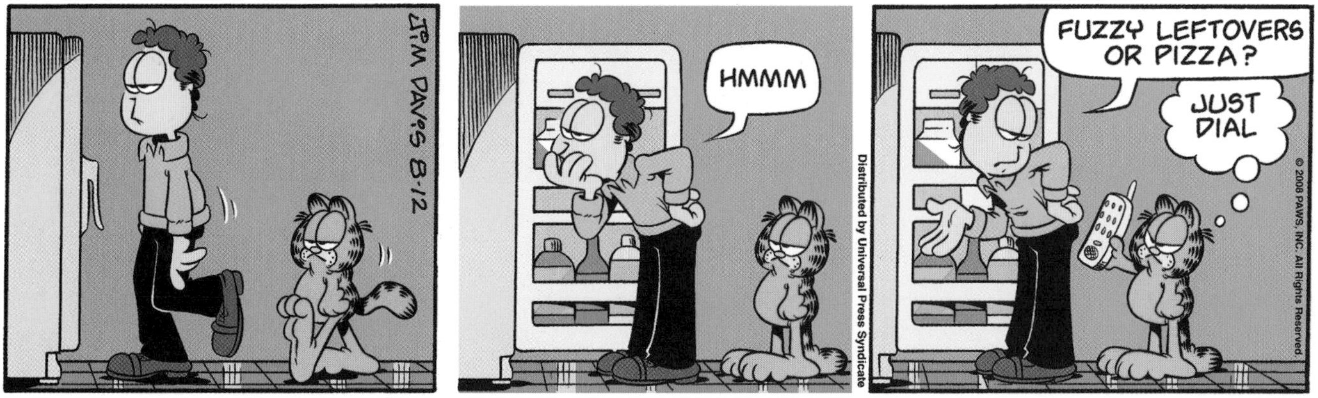
JIM DAVIS 8-12
HMMM
FUZZY LEFTOVERS OR PIZZA?
JUST DIAL
Distributed by Universal Press Syndicate
© 2008 PAWS, INC. All Rights Reserved.

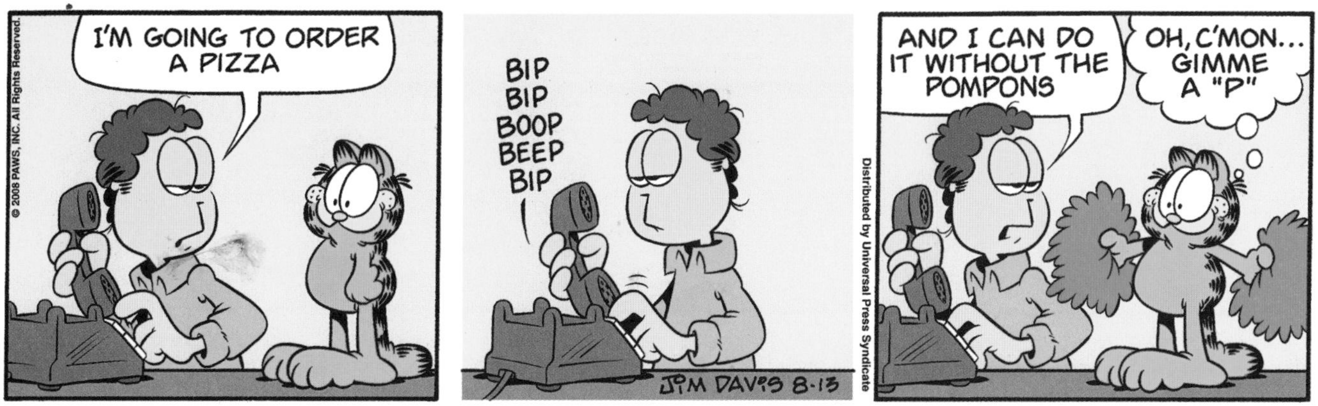
© 2008 PAWS, INC. All Rights Reserved.
I'M GOING TO ORDER A PIZZA
BIP BIP BOOP BEEP BIP
AND I CAN DO IT WITHOUT THE POMPONS
OH, C'MON... GIMME A "P"
Distributed by Universal Press Syndicate
JIM DAVIS 8-13

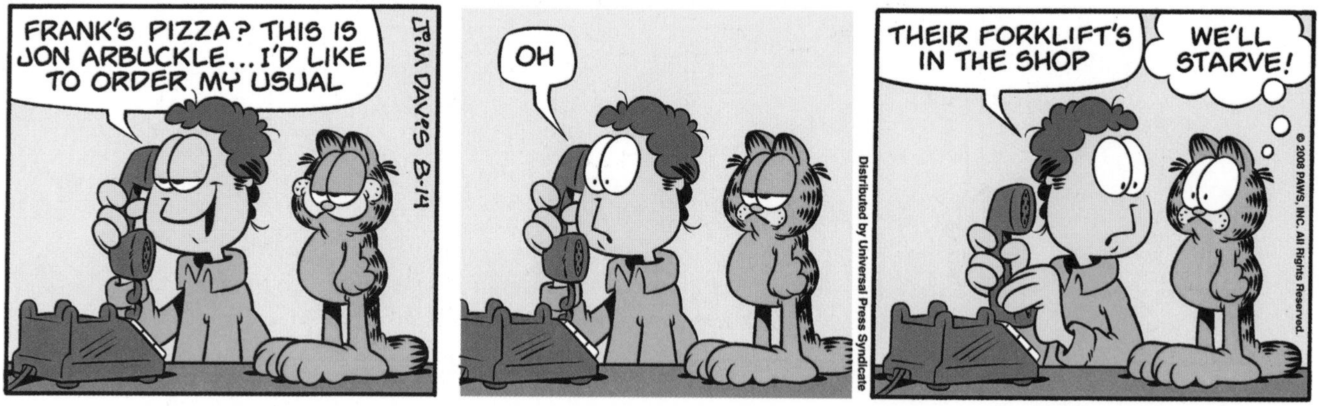
FRANK'S PIZZA? THIS IS JON ARBUCKLE... I'D LIKE TO ORDER MY USUAL
JIM DAVIS 8-14
OH
Distributed by Universal Press Syndicate
THEIR FORKLIFT'S IN THE SHOP
WE'LL STARVE!
© 2008 PAWS, INC. All Rights Reserved.

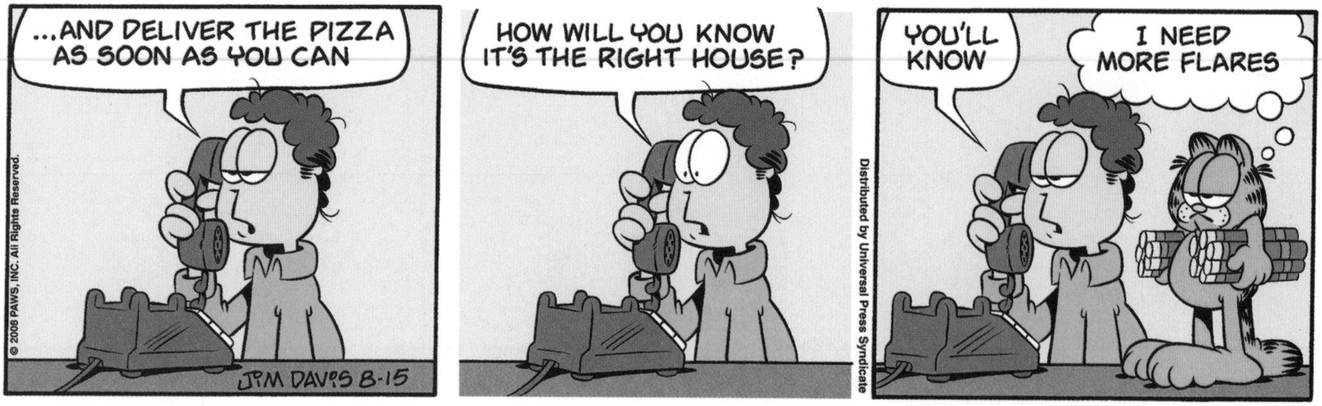
...AND DELIVER THE PIZZA AS SOON AS YOU CAN
© 2008 PAWS, INC. All Rights Reserved.
JIM DAVIS 8-15
HOW WILL YOU KNOW IT'S THE RIGHT HOUSE?
Distributed by Universal Press Syndicate
YOU'LL KNOW
I NEED MORE FLARES

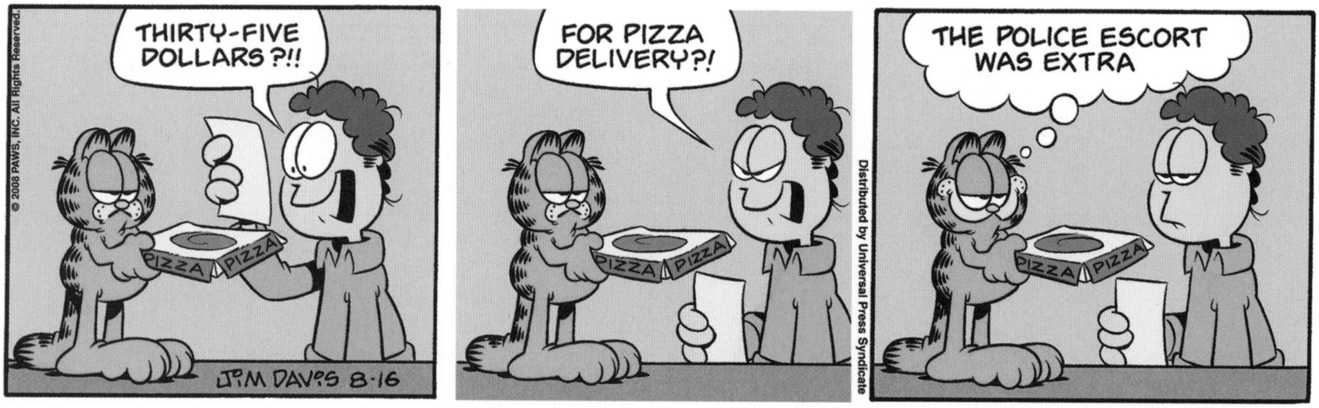
THIRTY-FIVE DOLLARS?!!
© 2008 PAWS, INC. All Rights Reserved.
PIZZA
PIZZA
JIM DAVIS 8-16
FOR PIZZA DELIVERY?!
PIZZA
PIZZA
Distributed by Universal Press Syndicate
THE POLICE ESCORT WAS EXTRA
PIZZA
PIZZA

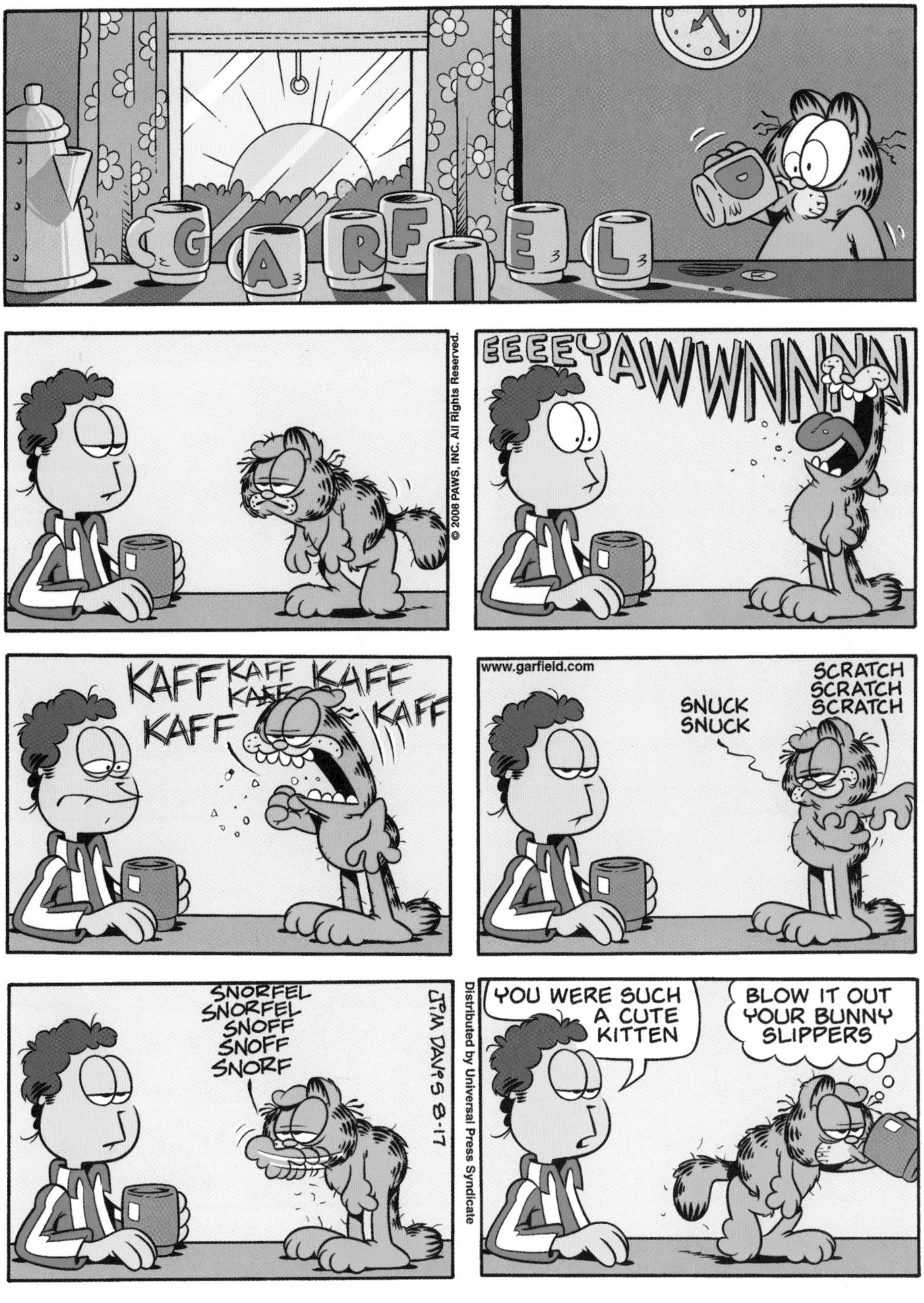

© 2008 PAWS, INC. All Rights Reserved.
EEEEYAWWNNNN
KAFF KAFF KAFF KAFF KAFF KAFF KAFF
www.garfield.com
SNUCK SNUCK
SCRATCH SCRATCH SCRATCH
SNORFEL SNORFEL SNOFF SNOFF SNORF
JPM DAVIS 8-17
Distributed by Universal Press Syndicate
YOU WERE SUCH A CUTE KITTEN
BLOW IT OUT YOUR BUNNY SLIPPERS

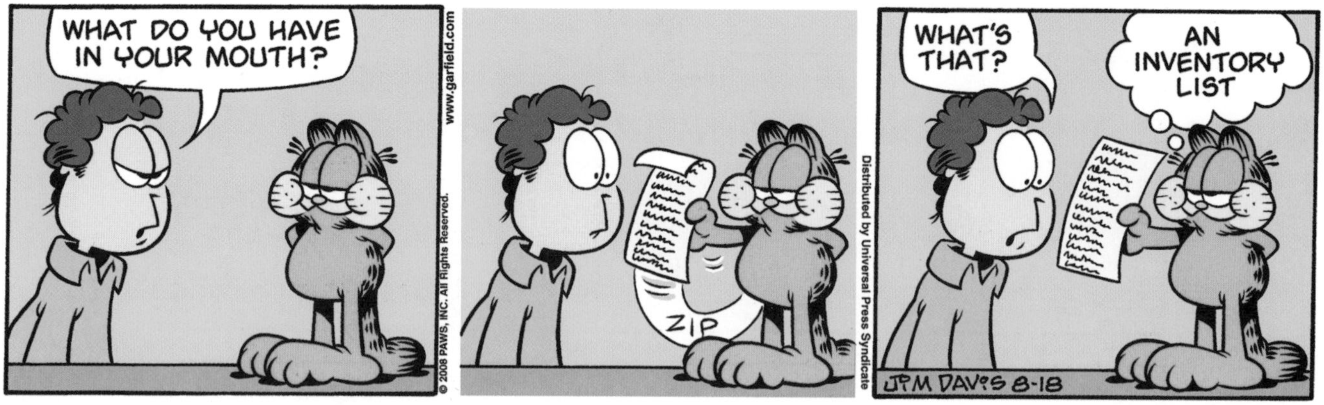
WHAT DO YOU HAVE IN YOUR MOUTH?
ZIP
WHAT'S THAT?
AN INVENTORY LIST
JIM DAVIS 8-18
© 2008 PAWS, INC. All Rights Reserved.
www.garfield.com
Distributed by Universal Press Syndicate

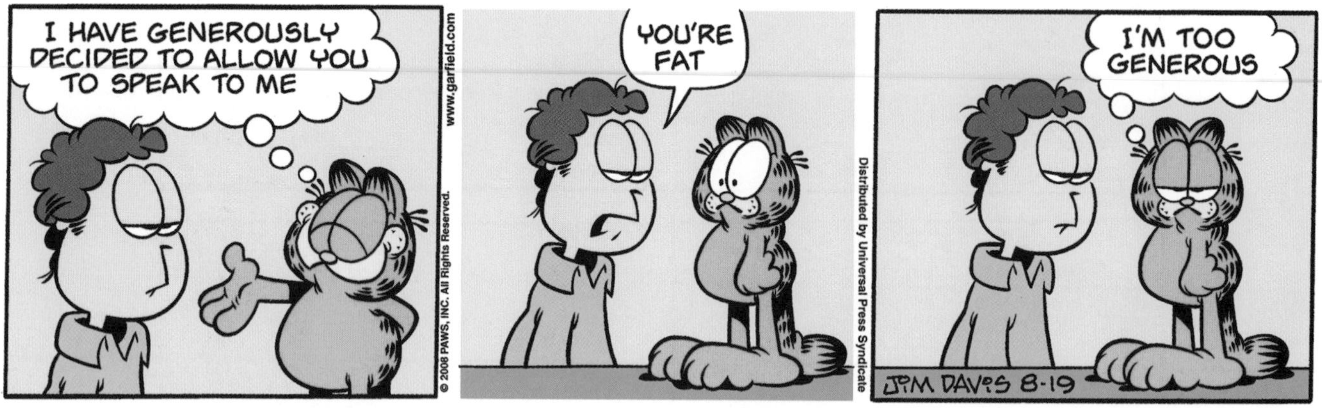
I HAVE GENEROUSLY DECIDED TO ALLOW YOU TO SPEAK TO ME
YOU'RE FAT
I'M TOO GENEROUS
JIM DAVIS 8-19
© 2008 PAWS, INC. All Rights Reserved.
www.garfield.com
Distributed by Universal Press Syndicate

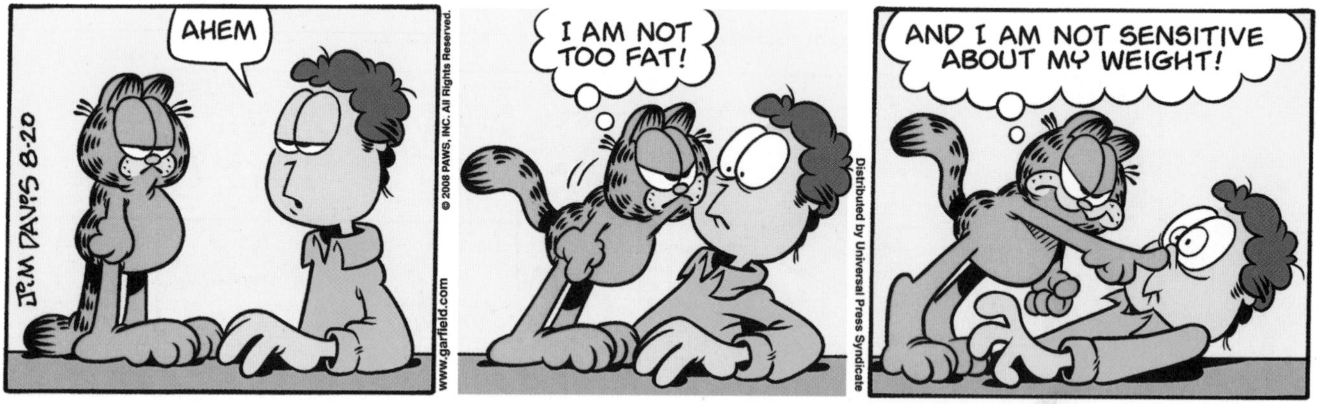
JIM DAVIS 8-20
AHEM
I AM NOT TOO FAT!
AND I AM NOT SENSITIVE ABOUT MY WEIGHT!
© 2008 PAWS, INC. All Rights Reserved.
www.garfield.com
Distributed by Universal Press Syndicate

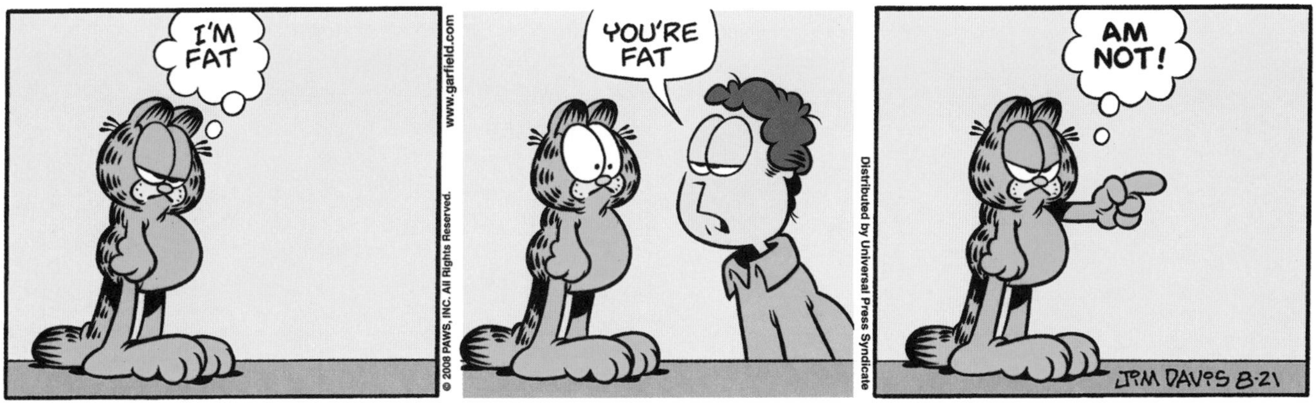
I'M FAT
YOU'RE FAT
AM NOT!
JIM DAVIS 8·21
© 2008 PAWS, INC. All Rights Reserved.
www.garfield.com
Distributed by Universal Press Syndicate

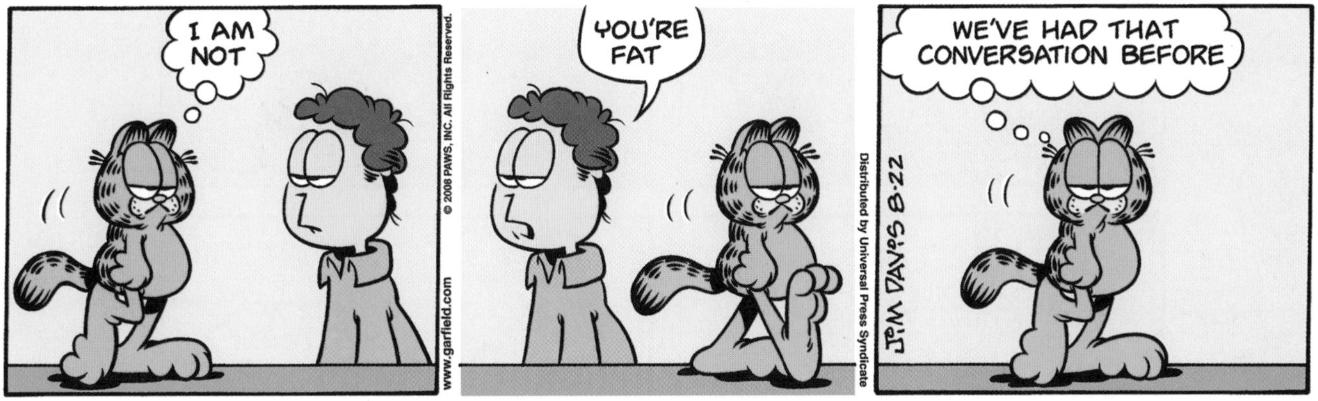
I AM NOT
YOU'RE FAT
WE'VE HAD THAT CONVERSATION BEFORE
JIM DAVIS 8·22
© 2008 PAWS, INC. All Rights Reserved.
www.garfield.com
Distributed by Universal Press Syndicate

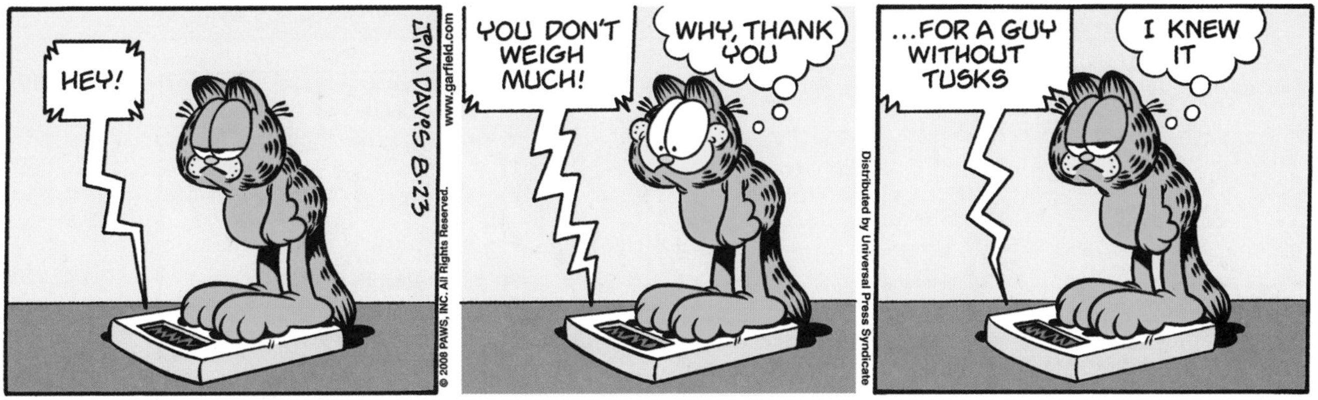
HEY!
YOU DON'T WEIGH MUCH!
WHY, THANK YOU
...FOR A GUY WITHOUT TUSKS
I KNEW IT
JIM DAVIS 8·23
© 2008 PAWS, INC. All Rights Reserved.
www.garfield.com
Distributed by Universal Press Syndicate

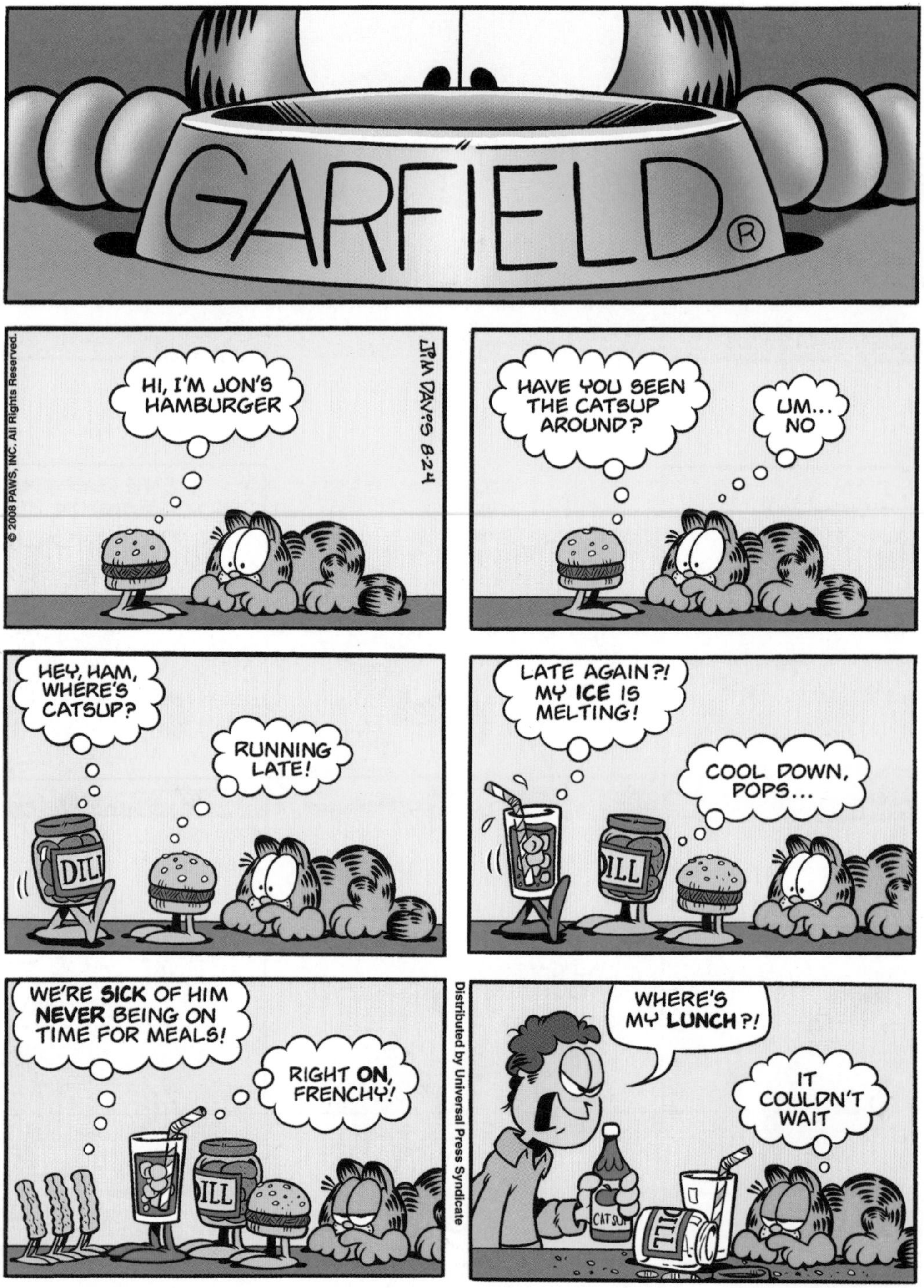
GARFIELD®
© 2008 PAWS, INC. All Rights Reserved.
JPM DAVPS 8-24
HI, I'M JON'S HAMBURGER
HAVE YOU SEEN THE CATSUP AROUND?
UM... NO
HEY, HAM, WHERE'S CATSUP?
RUNNING LATE!
DILL
LATE AGAIN?! MY ICE IS MELTING!
COOL DOWN, POPS...
DILL
WE'RE SICK OF HIM NEVER BEING ON TIME FOR MEALS!
RIGHT ON, FRENCHY!
DILL
Distributed by Universal Press Syndicate
WHERE'S MY LUNCH?!
IT COULDN'T WAIT
CATSUP

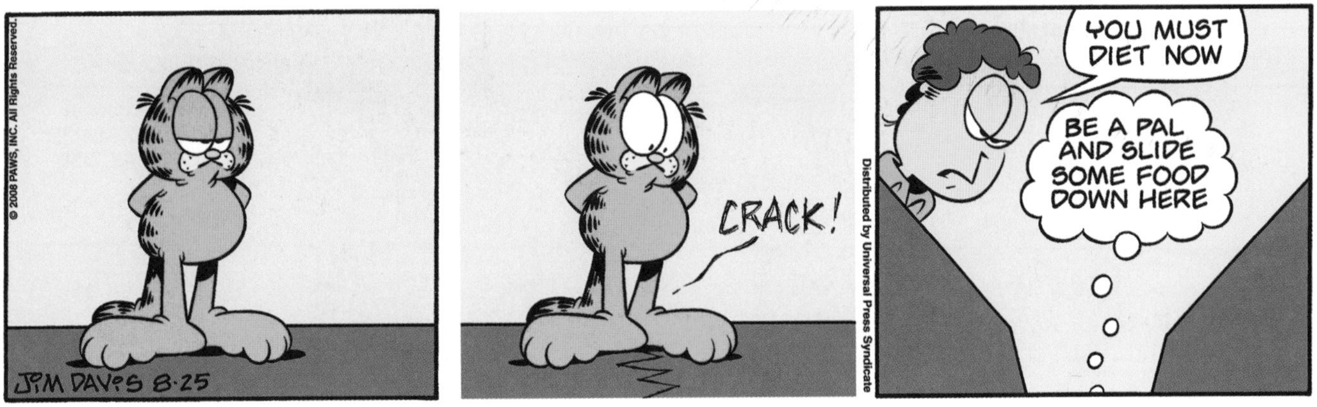
© 2008 PAWS, INC. All Rights Reserved.
JIM DAVIS 8·25
CRACK!
Distributed by Universal Press Syndicate
YOU MUST DIET NOW
BE A PAL AND SLIDE SOME FOOD DOWN HERE

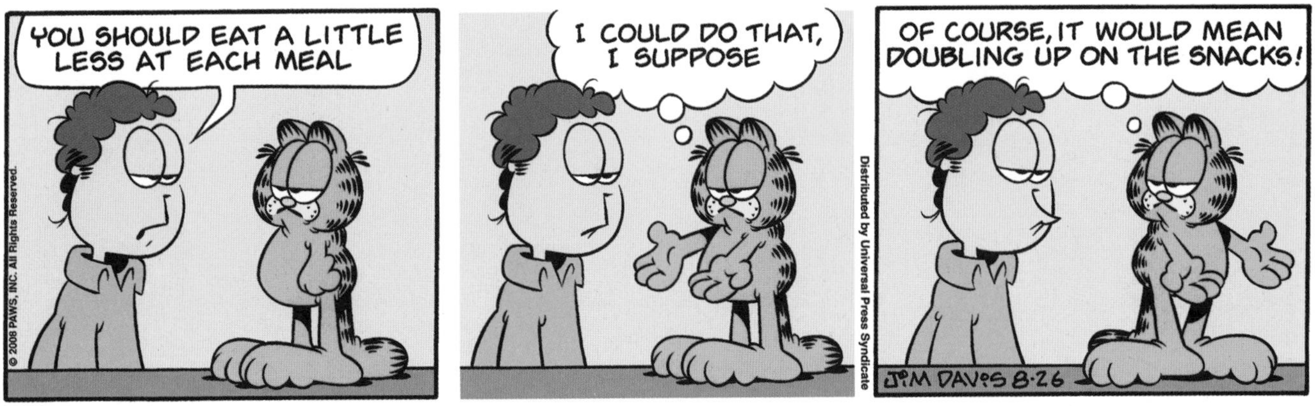
© 2008 PAWS, INC. All Rights Reserved.
YOU SHOULD EAT A LITTLE LESS AT EACH MEAL
I COULD DO THAT, I SUPPOSE
Distributed by Universal Press Syndicate
OF COURSE, IT WOULD MEAN DOUBLING UP ON THE SNACKS!
JIM DAVIS 8·26

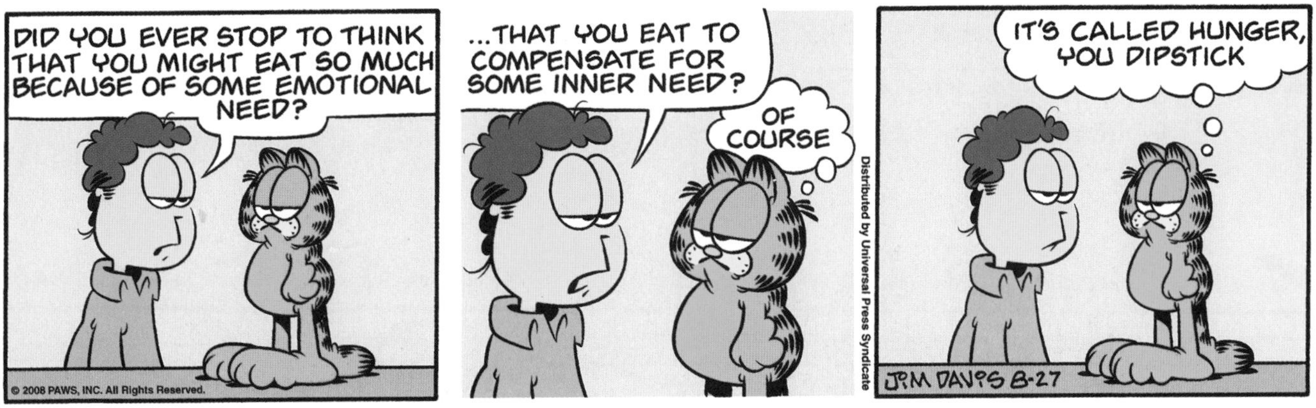
DID YOU EVER STOP TO THINK THAT YOU MIGHT EAT SO MUCH BECAUSE OF SOME EMOTIONAL NEED?
© 2008 PAWS, INC. All Rights Reserved.
...THAT YOU EAT TO COMPENSATE FOR SOME INNER NEED?
OF COURSE
Distributed by Universal Press Syndicate
IT'S CALLED HUNGER, YOU DIPSTICK
JIM DAVIS 8·27

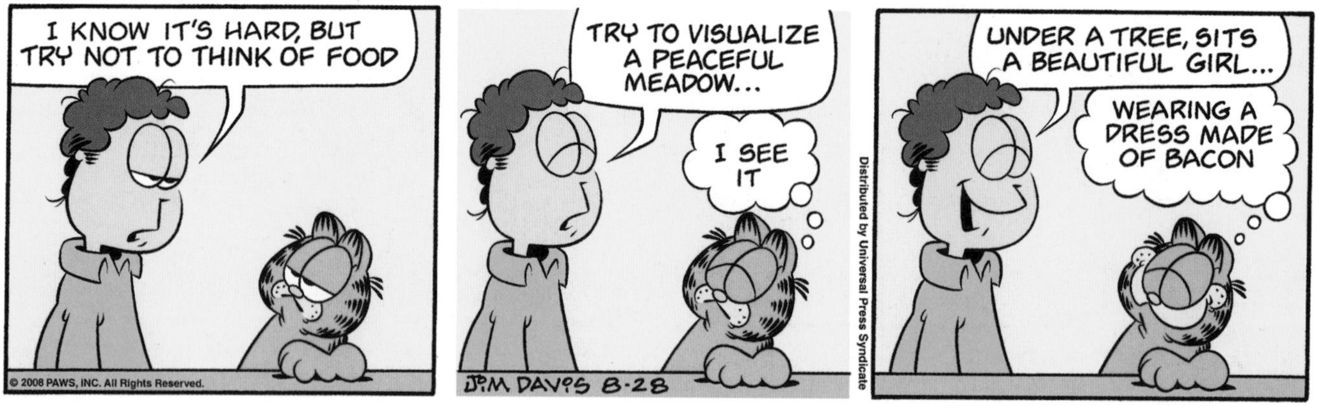
I KNOW IT'S HARD, BUT TRY NOT TO THINK OF FOOD
TRY TO VISUALIZE A PEACEFUL MEADOW...
I SEE IT
UNDER A TREE, SITS A BEAUTIFUL GIRL...
WEARING A DRESS MADE OF BACON
© 2008 PAWS, INC. All Rights Reserved.
JIM DAVIS 8-28
Distributed by Universal Press Syndicate

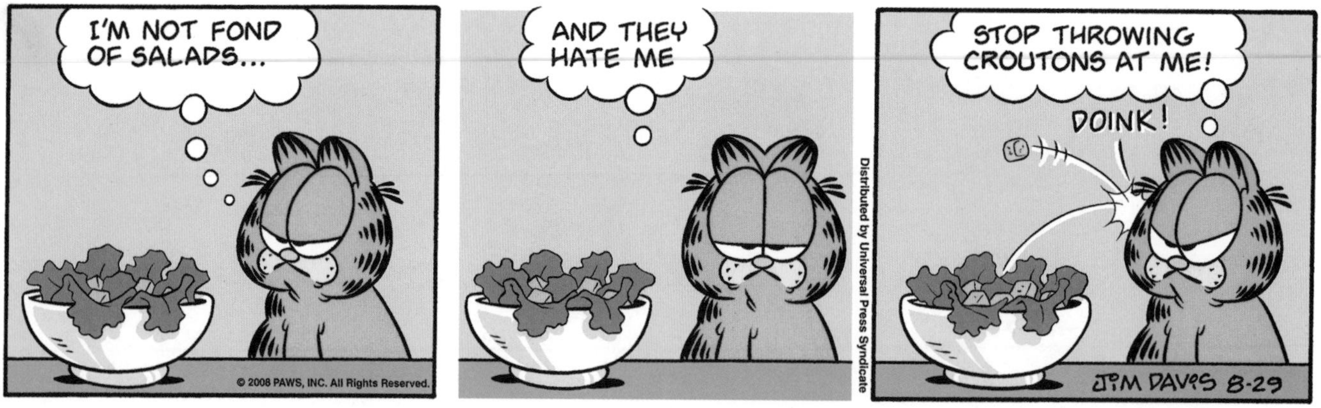
I'M NOT FOND OF SALADS...
AND THEY HATE ME
STOP THROWING CROUTONS AT ME!
DOINK!
© 2008 PAWS, INC. All Rights Reserved.
JIM DAVIS 8-29
Distributed by Universal Press Syndicate

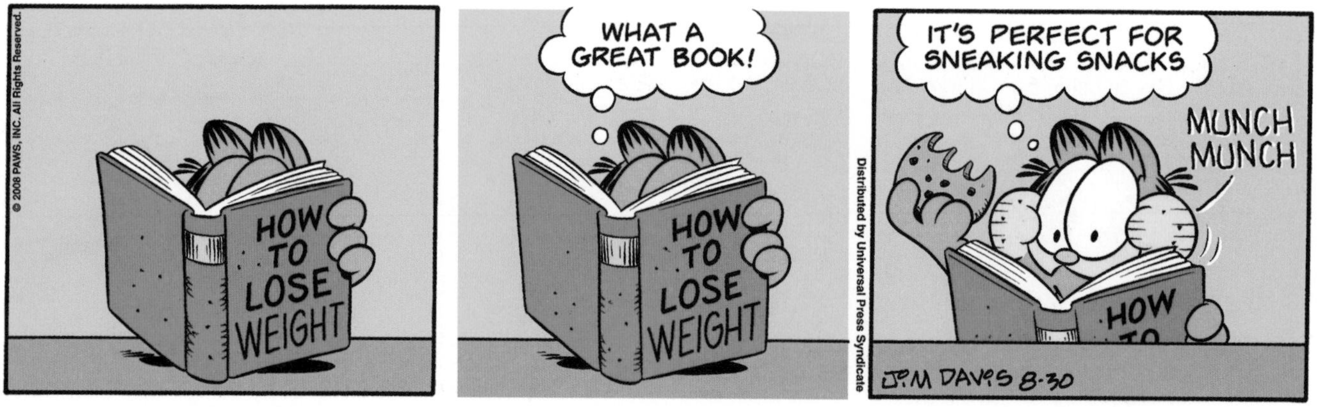
© 2008 PAWS, INC. All Rights Reserved.
HOW TO LOSE WEIGHT
WHAT A GREAT BOOK!
HOW TO LOSE WEIGHT
IT'S PERFECT FOR SNEAKING SNACKS
MUNCH MUNCH
HOW
JIM DAVIS 8-30
Distributed by Universal Press Syndicate

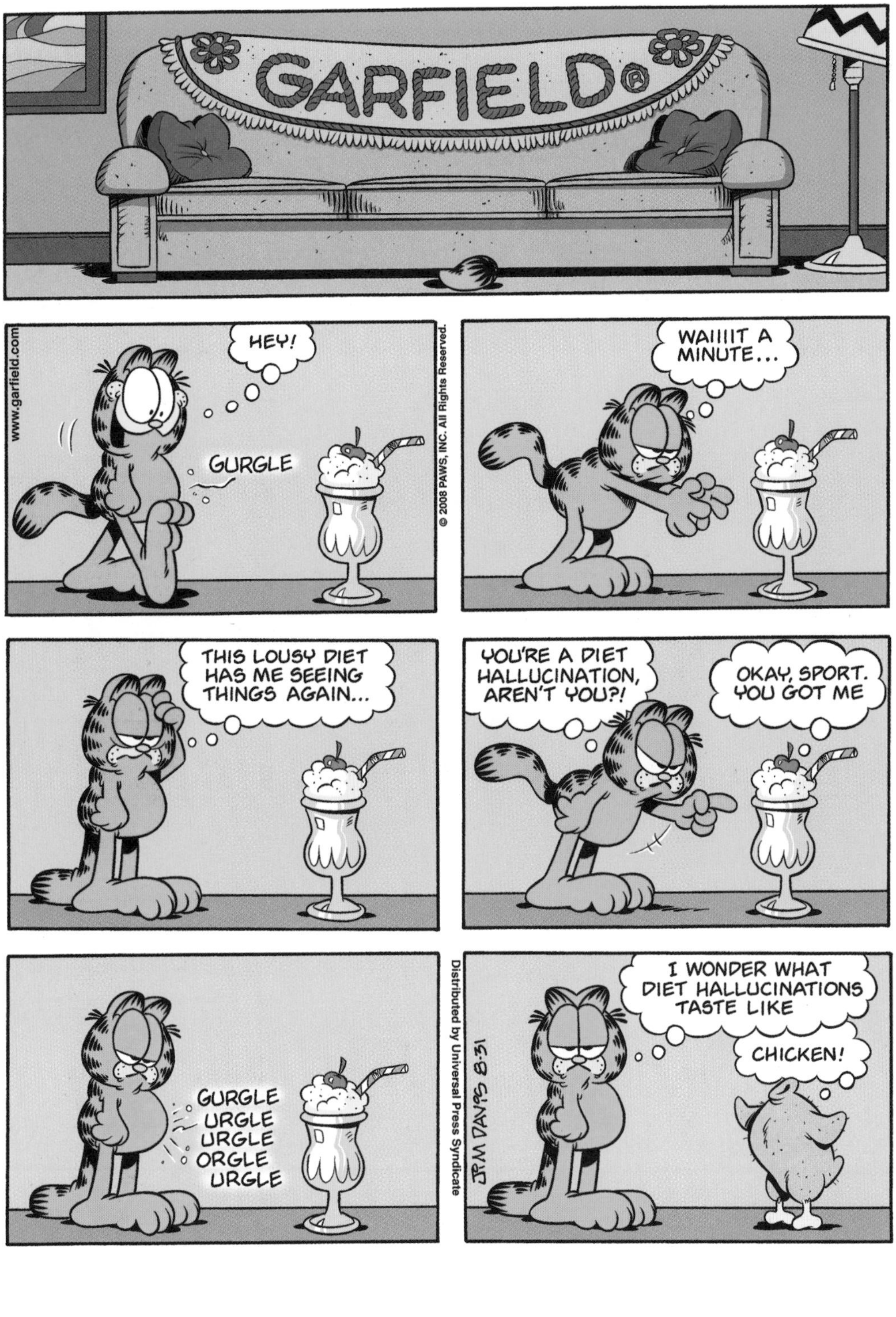
GARFIELD®
www.garfield.com
HEY!
GURGLE
WAIIIIT A MINUTE...
THIS LOUSY DIET HAS ME SEEING THINGS AGAIN...
YOU'RE A DIET HALLUCINATION, AREN'T YOU?!
OKAY, SPORT. YOU GOT ME
GURGLE
URGLE
URGLE
ORGLE
URGLE
I WONDER WHAT DIET HALLUCINATIONS TASTE LIKE
CHICKEN!
JPM DAVPS 8-31
Distributed by Universal Press Syndicate

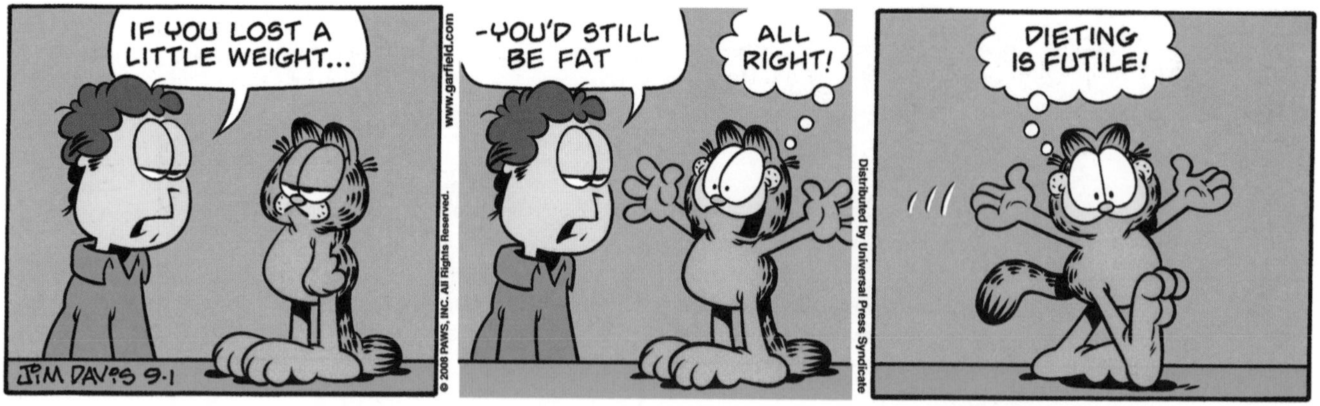
IF YOU LOST A LITTLE WEIGHT...
JIM DAVIS 9-1
www.garfield.com
© 2008 PAWS, INC. All Rights Reserved.
-YOU'D STILL BE FAT
ALL RIGHT!
Distributed by Universal Press Syndicate
DIETING IS FUTILE!

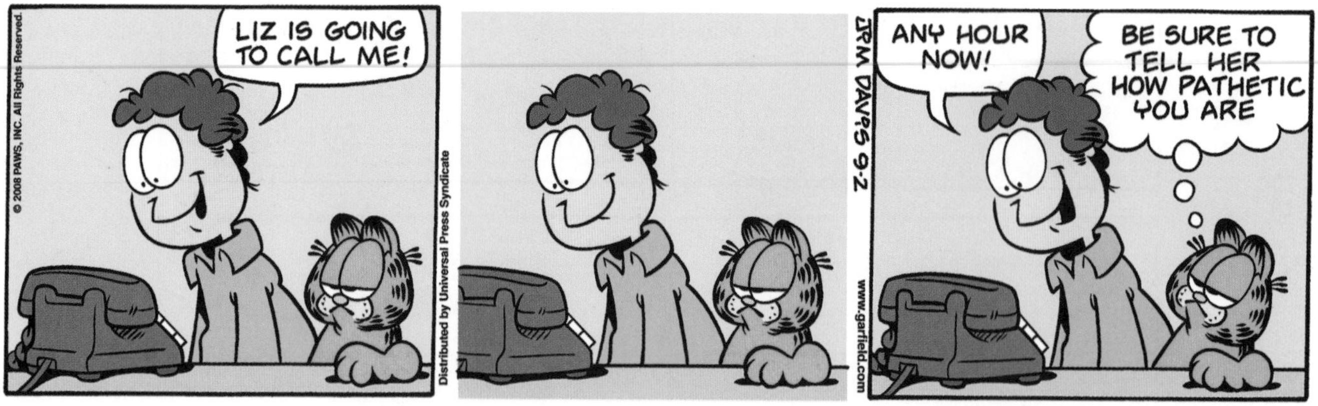
© 2008 PAWS, INC. All Rights Reserved.
LIZ IS GOING TO CALL ME!
Distributed by Universal Press Syndicate
JIM DAVIS 9-2
www.garfield.com
ANY HOUR NOW!
BE SURE TO TELL HER HOW PATHETIC YOU ARE

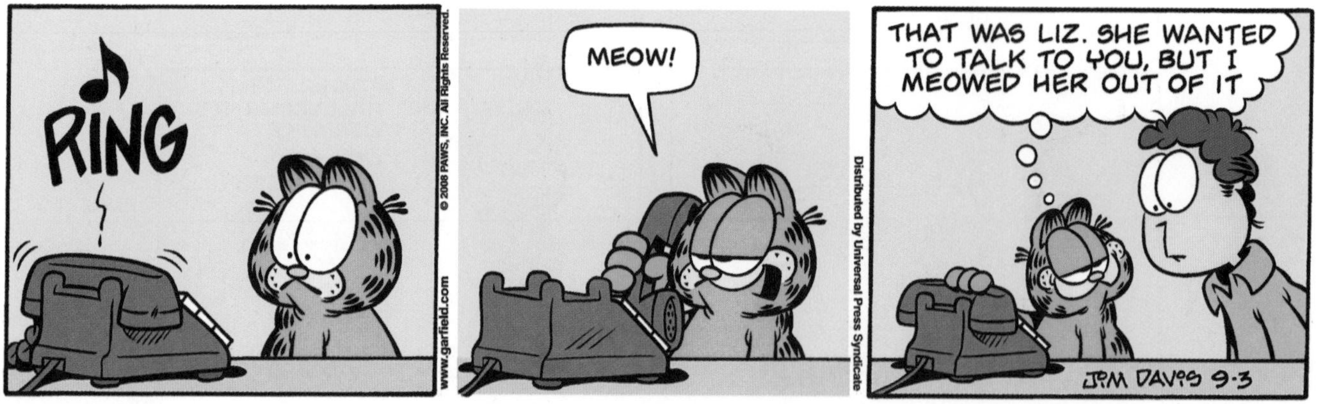
RING
www.garfield.com
© 2008 PAWS, INC. All Rights Reserved.
MEOW!
Distributed by Universal Press Syndicate
THAT WAS LIZ. SHE WANTED TO TALK TO YOU, BUT I MEOWED HER OUT OF IT
JIM DAVIS 9-3

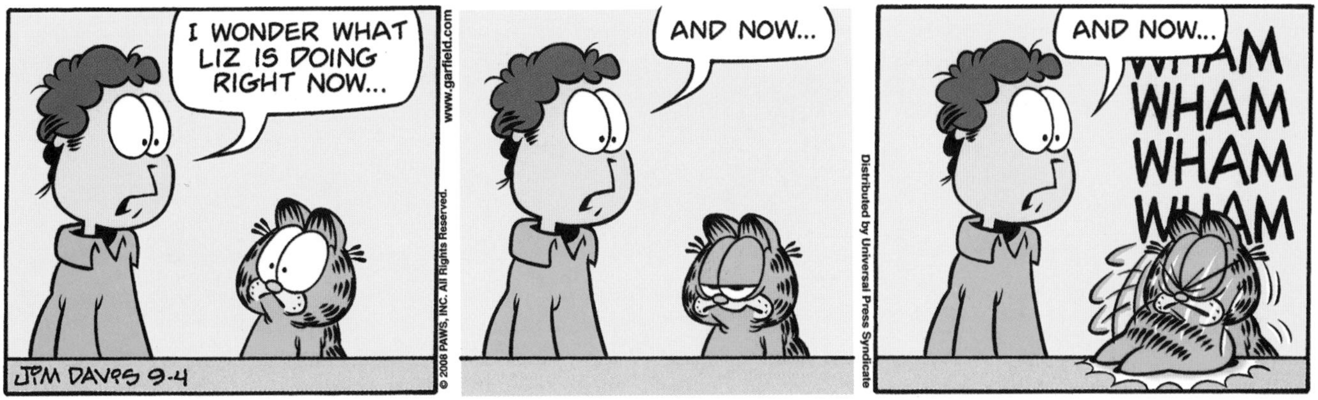
I WONDER WHAT LIZ IS DOING RIGHT NOW...
JIM DAVIS 9-4
www.garfield.com
© 2008 PAWS, INC. All Rights Reserved.
AND NOW...
Distributed by Universal Press Syndicate
AND NOW...
WHAM
WHAM

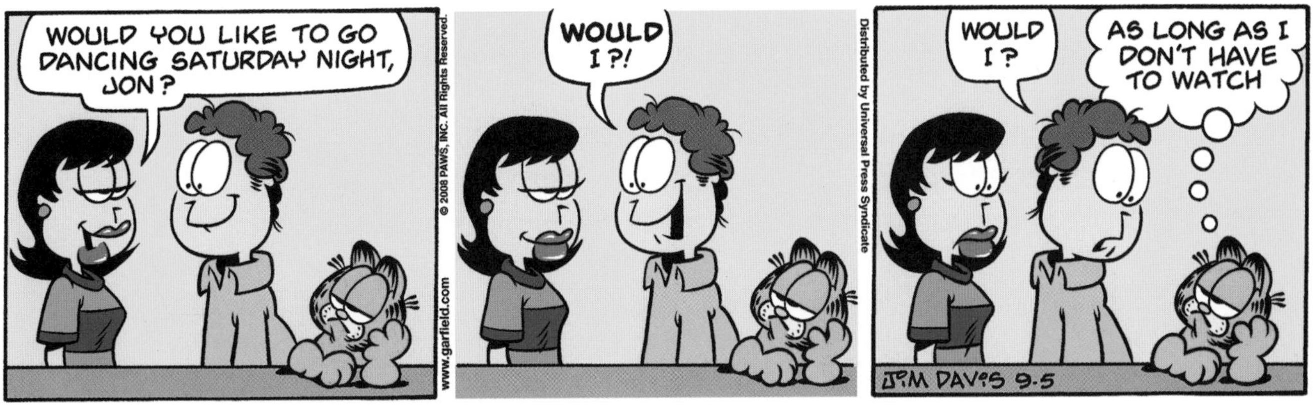
WOULD YOU LIKE TO GO DANCING SATURDAY NIGHT, JON?
© 2008 PAWS, INC. All Rights Reserved.
www.garfield.com
WOULD I?!
Distributed by Universal Press Syndicate
WOULD I?
AS LONG AS I DON'T HAVE TO WATCH
JIM DAVIS 9-5

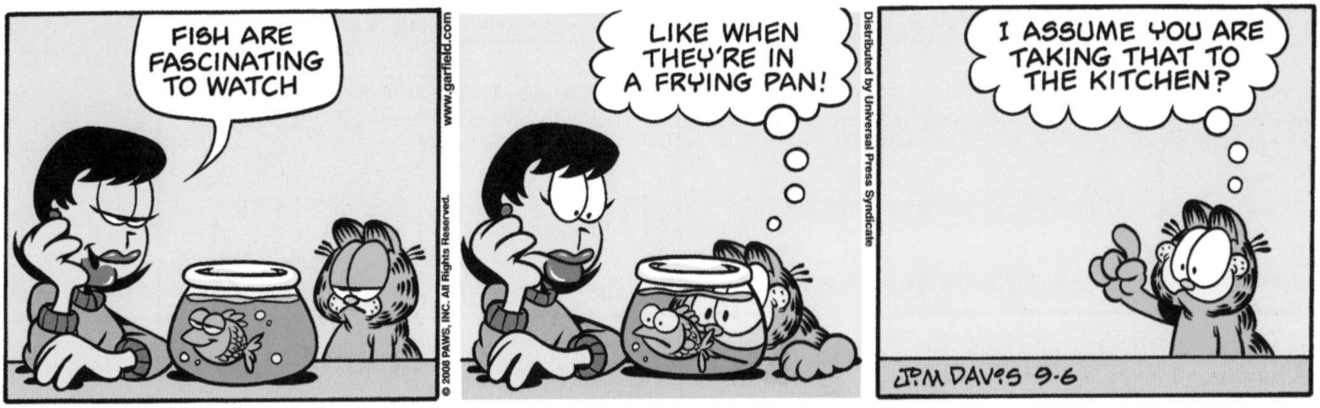
FISH ARE FASCINATING TO WATCH
www.garfield.com
© 2008 PAWS, INC. All Rights Reserved.
LIKE WHEN THEY'RE IN A FRYING PAN!
Distributed by Universal Press Syndicate
I ASSUME YOU ARE TAKING THAT TO THE KITCHEN?
JIM DAVIS 9-6

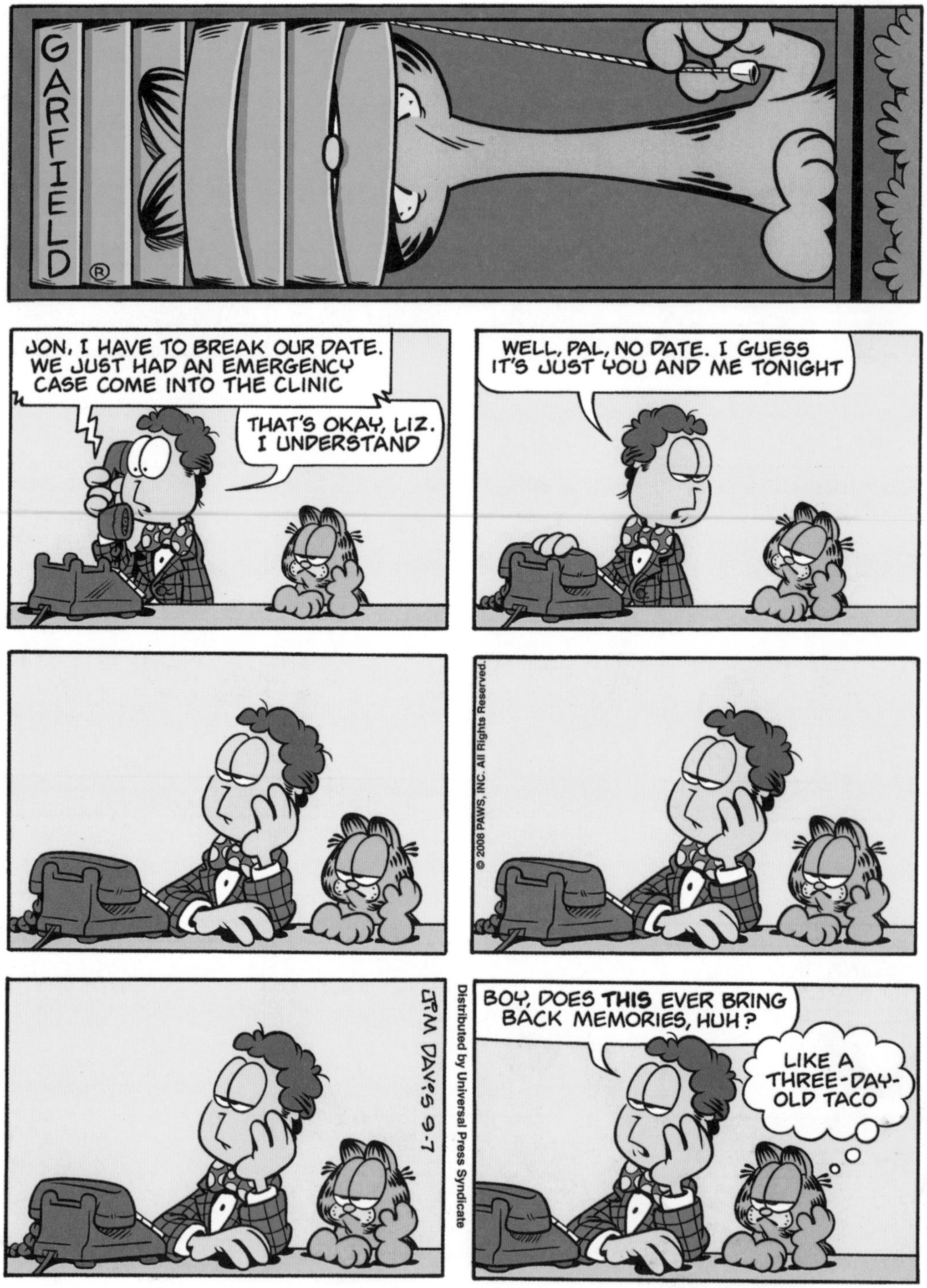
GARFIELD ®
JON, I HAVE TO BREAK OUR DATE. WE JUST HAD AN EMERGENCY CASE COME INTO THE CLINIC
THAT'S OKAY, LIZ. I UNDERSTAND
WELL, PAL, NO DATE. I GUESS IT'S JUST YOU AND ME TONIGHT
© 2008 PAWS, INC. All Rights Reserved.
JPM DAVIS 9-7
Distributed by Universal Press Syndicate
BOY, DOES THIS EVER BRING BACK MEMORIES, HUH?
LIKE A THREE-DAY-OLD TACO

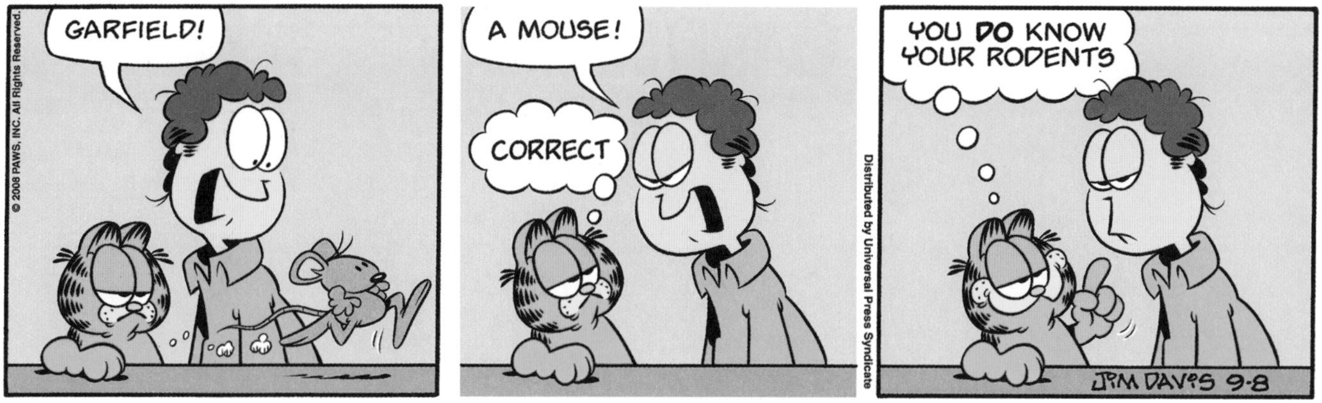
© 2008 PAWS, INC. All Rights Reserved.
GARFIELD!
A MOUSE!
CORRECT
YOU DO KNOW YOUR RODENTS
Distributed by Universal Press Syndicate
JIM DAVIS 9-8

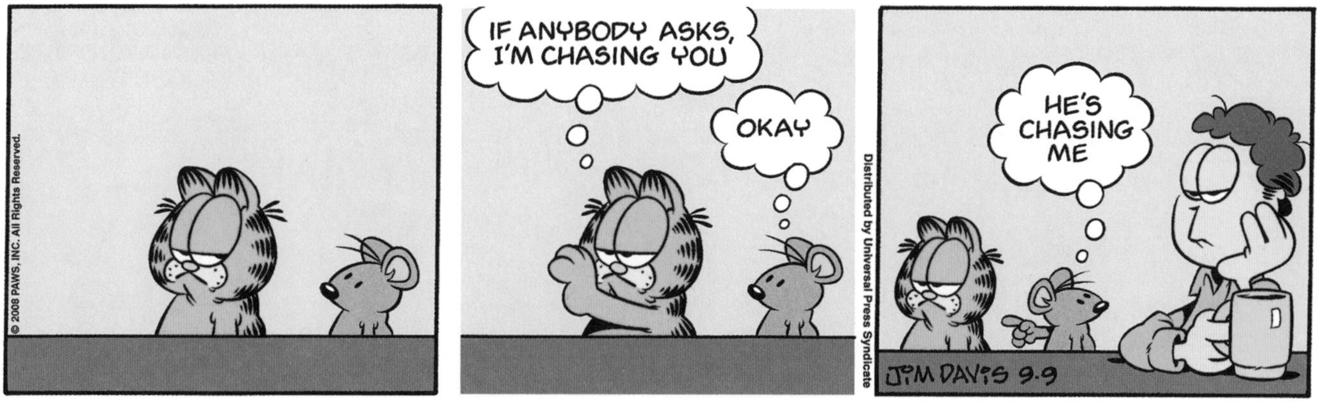
© 2008 PAWS, INC. All Rights Reserved.
IF ANYBODY ASKS, I'M CHASING YOU
OKAY
Distributed by Universal Press Syndicate
HE'S CHASING ME
JIM DAVIS 9-9

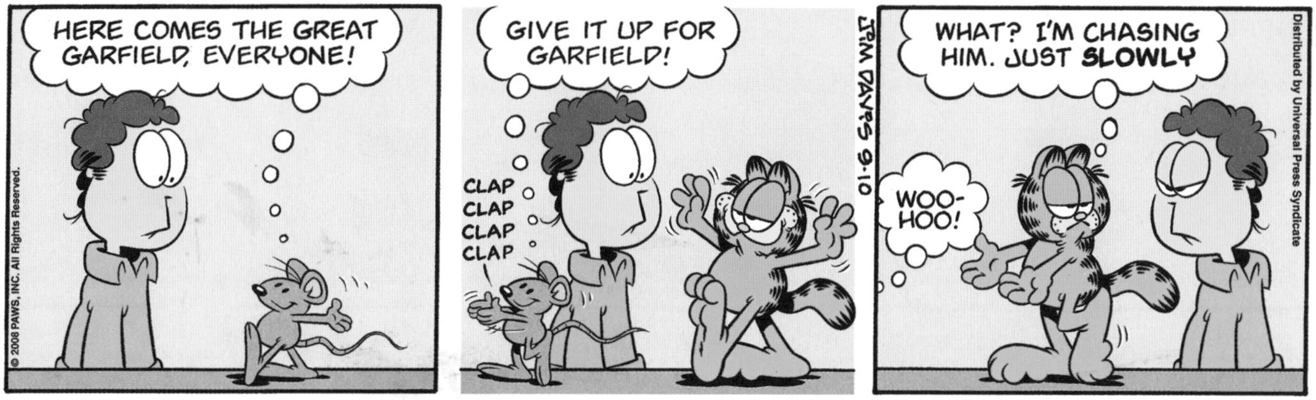
© 2008 PAWS, INC. All Rights Reserved.
HERE COMES THE GREAT GARFIELD, EVERYONE!
GIVE IT UP FOR GARFIELD!
CLAP CLAP CLAP CLAP
JIM DAVIS 9-10
WHAT? I'M CHASING HIM. JUST SLOWLY
WOO-HOO!
Distributed by Universal Press Syndicate

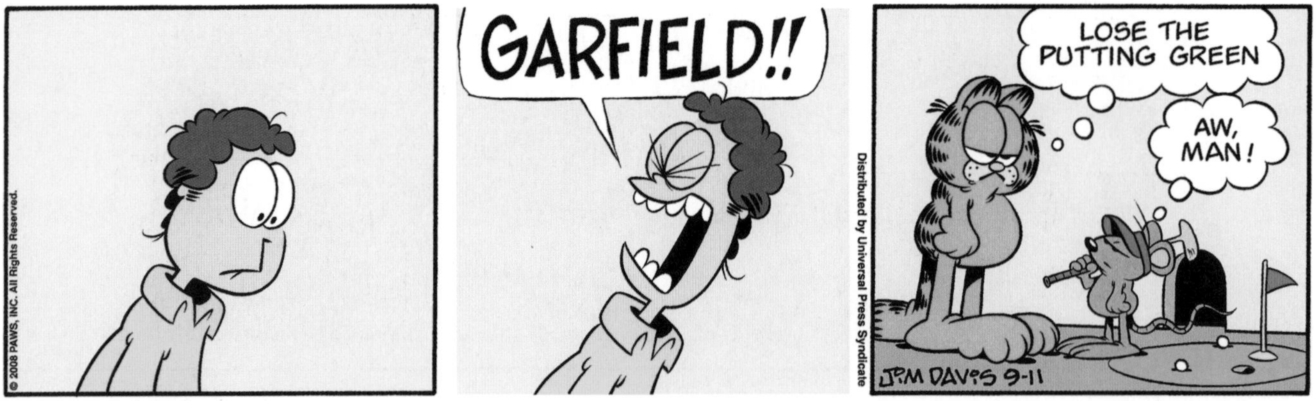
GARFIELD!!
LOSE THE PUTTING GREEN
AW, MAN!
© 2008 PAWS, INC. All Rights Reserved.
Distributed by Universal Press Syndicate
JIM DAVIS 9-11

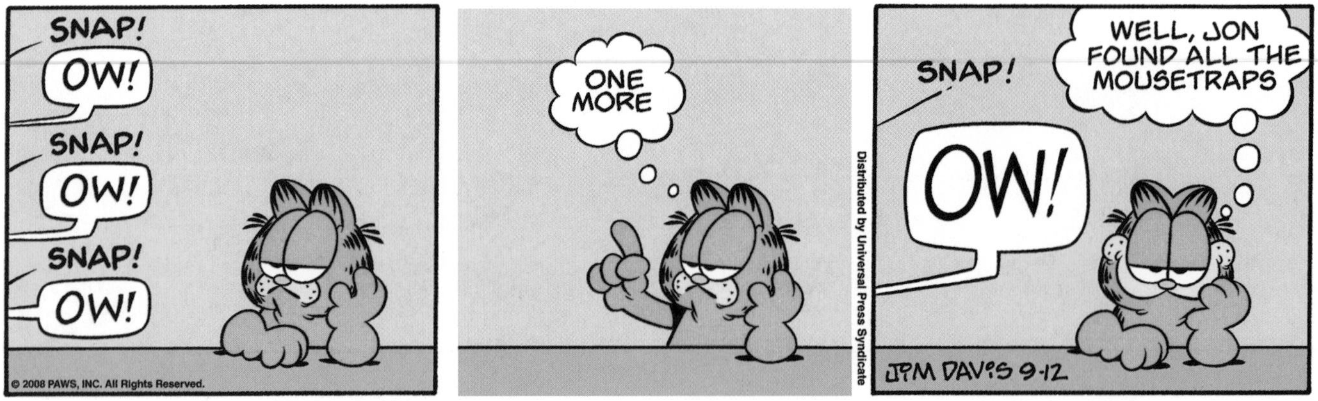
SNAP!
OW!
SNAP!
OW!
SNAP!
OW!
ONE MORE
SNAP!
OW!
WELL, JON FOUND ALL THE MOUSETRAPS
© 2008 PAWS, INC. All Rights Reserved.
Distributed by Universal Press Syndicate
JIM DAVIS 9-12

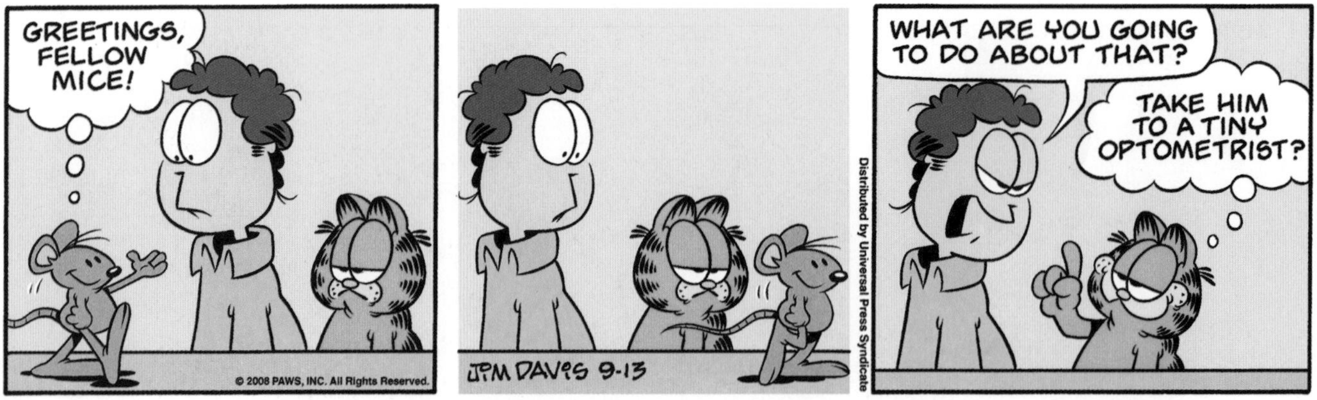
GREETINGS, FELLOW MICE!
WHAT ARE YOU GOING TO DO ABOUT THAT?
TAKE HIM TO A TINY OPTOMETRIST?
© 2008 PAWS, INC. All Rights Reserved.
Distributed by Universal Press Syndicate
JIM DAVIS 9-13

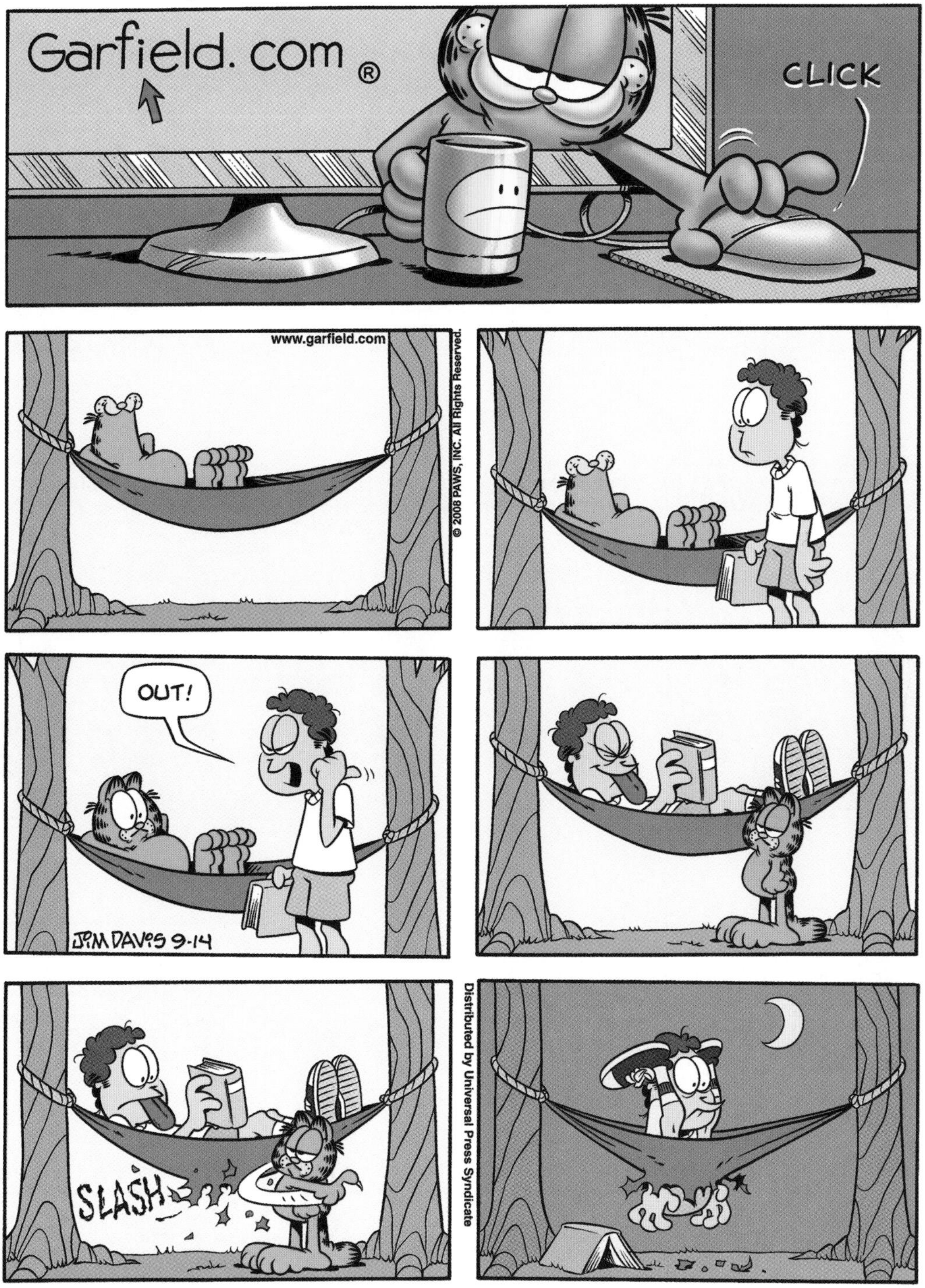
Garfield.com ®
CLICK
www.garfield.com
© 2008 PAWS, INC. All Rights Reserved.
OUT!
JIM DAVIS 9-14
Distributed by Universal Press Syndicate
SLASH

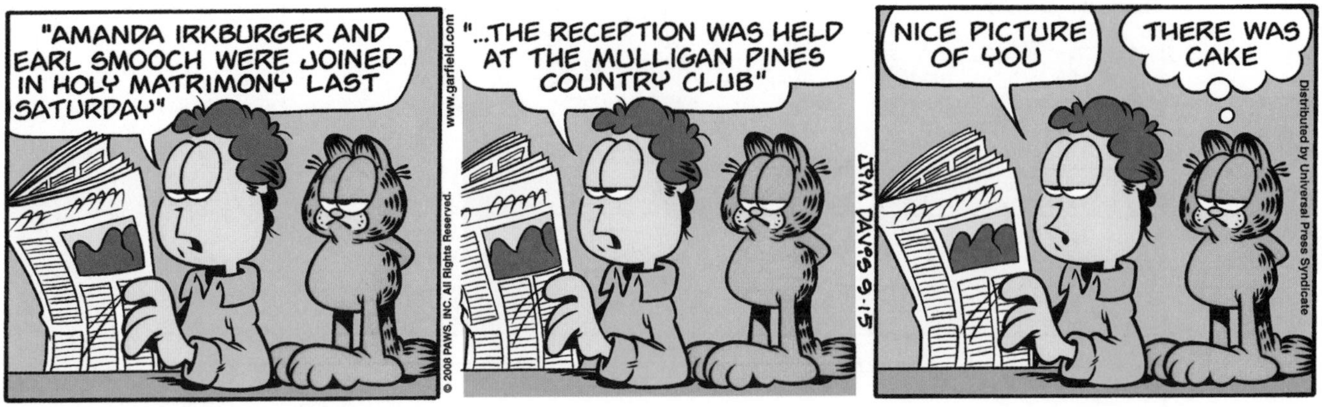
"AMANDA IRKBURGER AND EARL SMOOCH WERE JOINED IN HOLY MATRIMONY LAST SATURDAY"
"...THE RECEPTION WAS HELD AT THE MULLIGAN PINES COUNTRY CLUB"
NICE PICTURE OF YOU
THERE WAS CAKE
JIM DAVIS 9-15

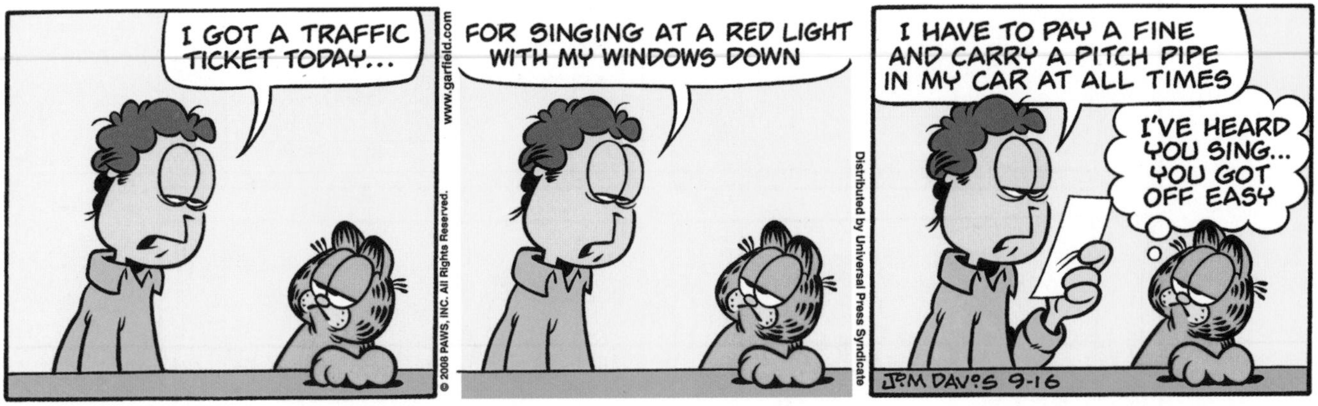
I GOT A TRAFFIC TICKET TODAY...
FOR SINGING AT A RED LIGHT WITH MY WINDOWS DOWN
I HAVE TO PAY A FINE AND CARRY A PITCH PIPE IN MY CAR AT ALL TIMES
I'VE HEARD YOU SING... YOU GOT OFF EASY
JIM DAVIS 9-16

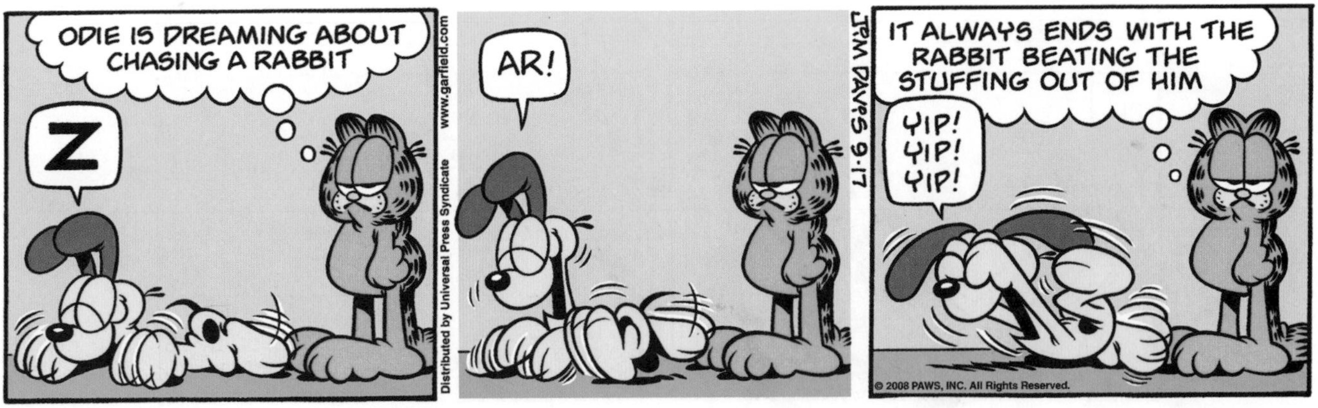
Z
ODIE IS DREAMING ABOUT CHASING A RABBIT
AR!
JIM DAVIS 9-17
IT ALWAYS ENDS WITH THE RABBIT BEATING THE STUFFING OUT OF HIM
YIP! YIP! YIP!

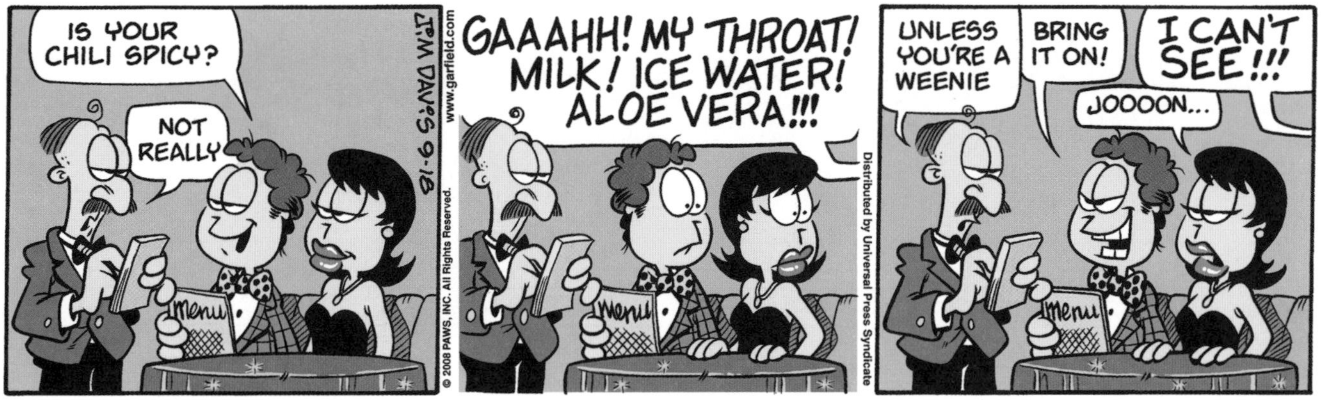
IS YOUR CHILI SPICY?
NOT REALLY
JIM DAVIS 9-18
© 2008 PAWS, INC. All Rights Reserved.
www.garfield.com
GAAAHH! MY THROAT! MILK! ICE WATER! ALOE VERA!!!
Distributed by Universal Press Syndicate
UNLESS YOU'RE A WEENIE
BRING IT ON!
JOOOON...
I CAN'T SEE!!!

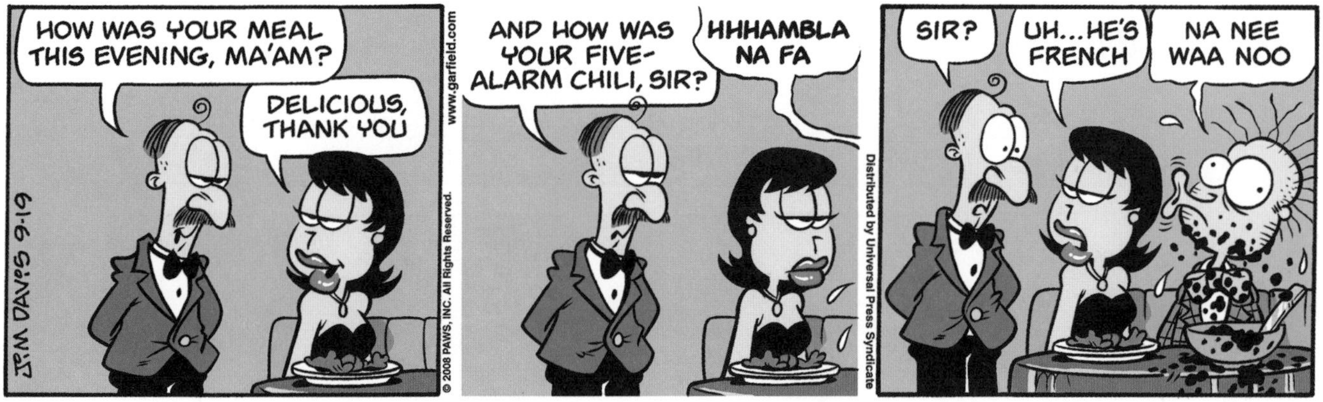
HOW WAS YOUR MEAL THIS EVENING, MA'AM?
DELICIOUS, THANK YOU
JIM DAVIS 9-19
© 2008 PAWS, INC. All Rights Reserved.
www.garfield.com
AND HOW WAS YOUR FIVE-ALARM CHILI, SIR?
HHHAMBLA NA FA
Distributed by Universal Press Syndicate
SIR?
UH...HE'S FRENCH
NA NEE WAA NOO

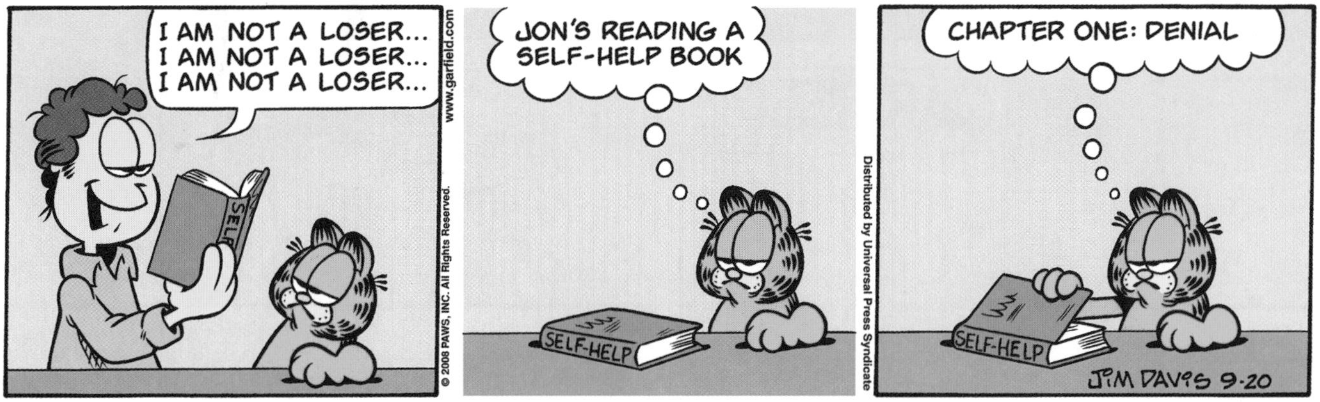
I AM NOT A LOSER...
I AM NOT A LOSER...
I AM NOT A LOSER...
SELF
© 2008 PAWS, INC. All Rights Reserved.
www.garfield.com
JON'S READING A SELF-HELP BOOK
SELF-HELP
Distributed by Universal Press Syndicate
CHAPTER ONE: DENIAL
SELF-HELP
JIM DAVIS 9-20

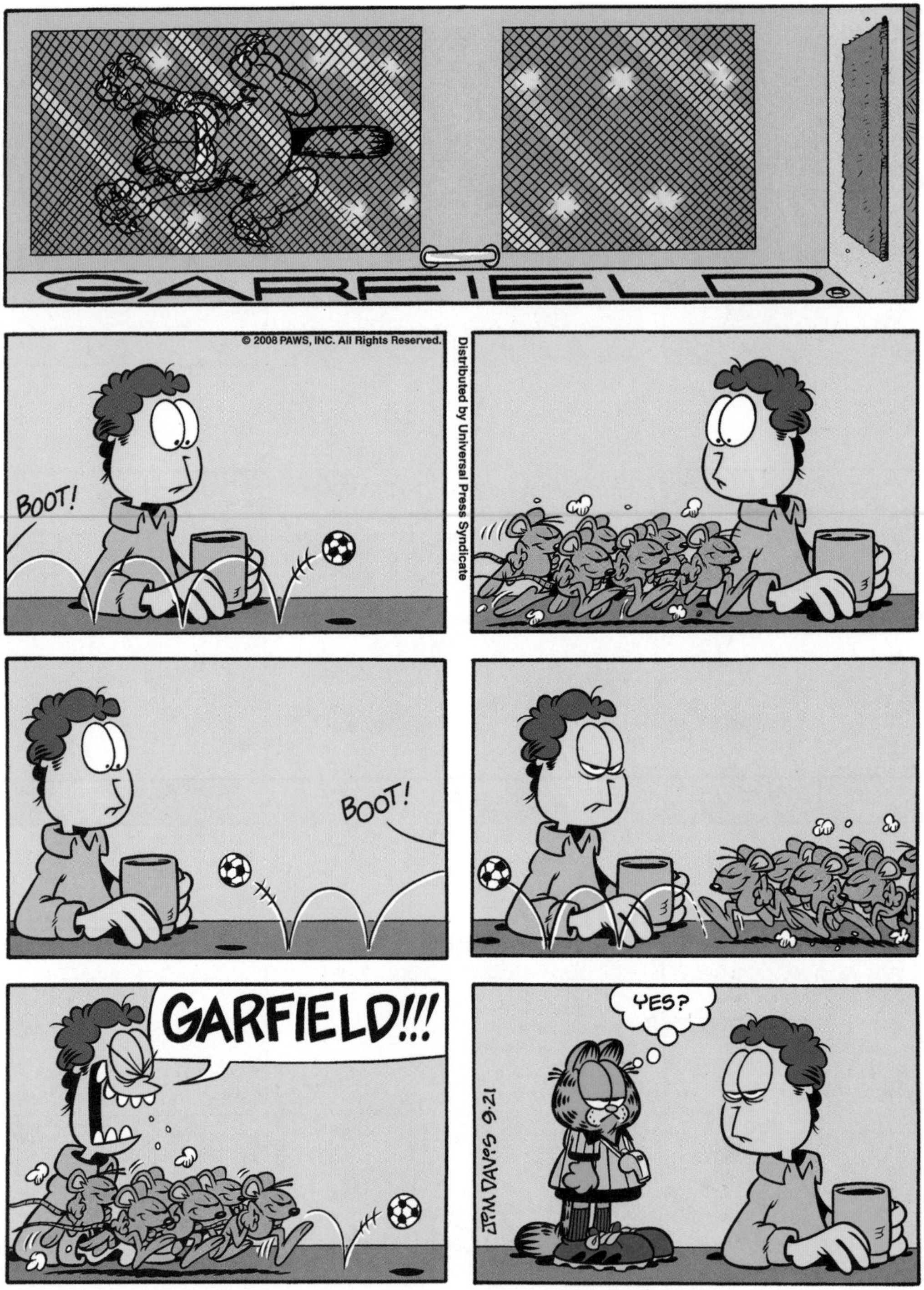
GARFIELD
© 2008 PAWS, INC. All Rights Reserved.
Distributed by Universal Press Syndicate
BOOT!
BOOT!
GARFIELD!!!
YES?
JPM DAVPS 9·21

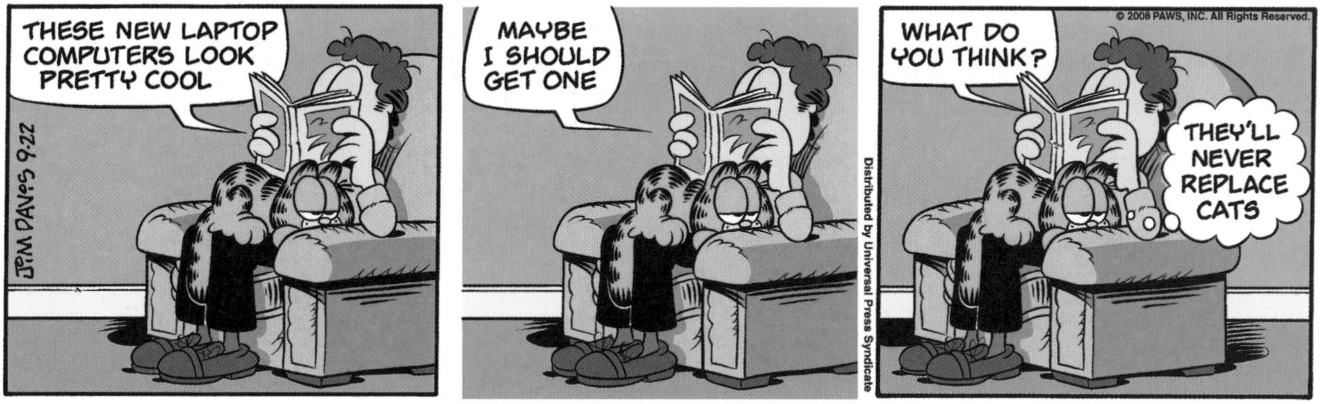
THESE NEW LAPTOP COMPUTERS LOOK PRETTY COOL
JIM DAVIS 9.22
MAYBE I SHOULD GET ONE
Distributed by Universal Press Syndicate
© 2008 PAWS, INC. All Rights Reserved.
WHAT DO YOU THINK?
THEY'LL NEVER REPLACE CATS

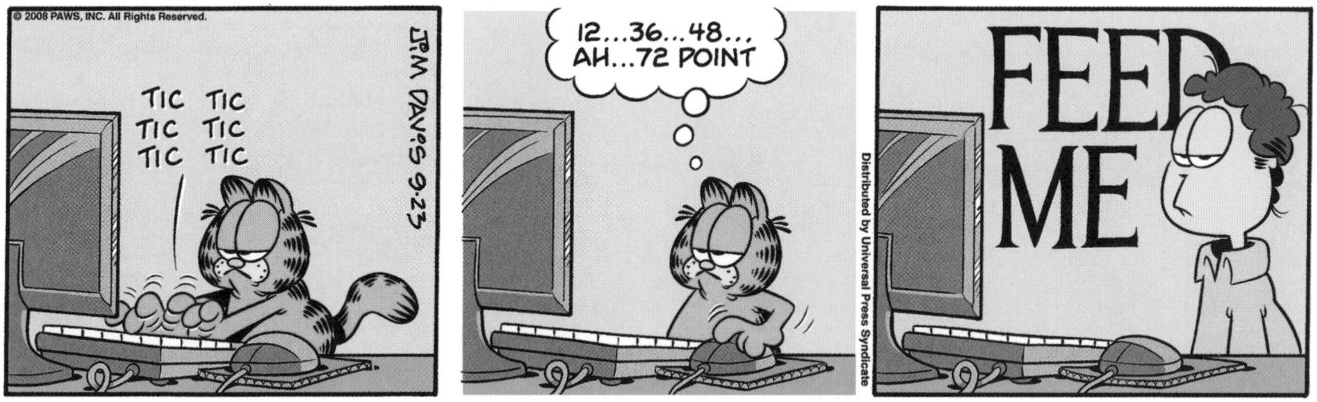
© 2008 PAWS, INC. All Rights Reserved.
JIM DAVIS 9.23
TIC TIC
TIC TIC
TIC TIC
12...36...48... AH...72 POINT
Distributed by Universal Press Syndicate
FEED ME

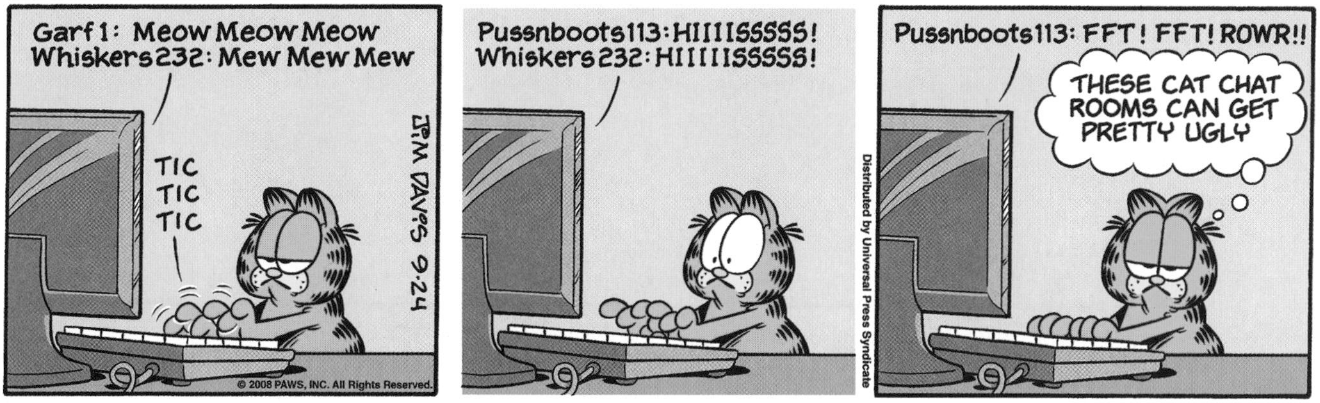
Garf1: Meow Meow Meow
Whiskers232: Mew Mew Mew
TIC
TIC
TIC
JIM DAVIS 9.24
© 2008 PAWS, INC. All Rights Reserved.
Pussnboots113: HIIIIISSSSS!
Whiskers232: HIIIIISSSSS!
Distributed by Universal Press Syndicate
Pussnboots113: FFT! FFT! ROWR!!
THESE CAT CHAT ROOMS CAN GET PRETTY UGLY

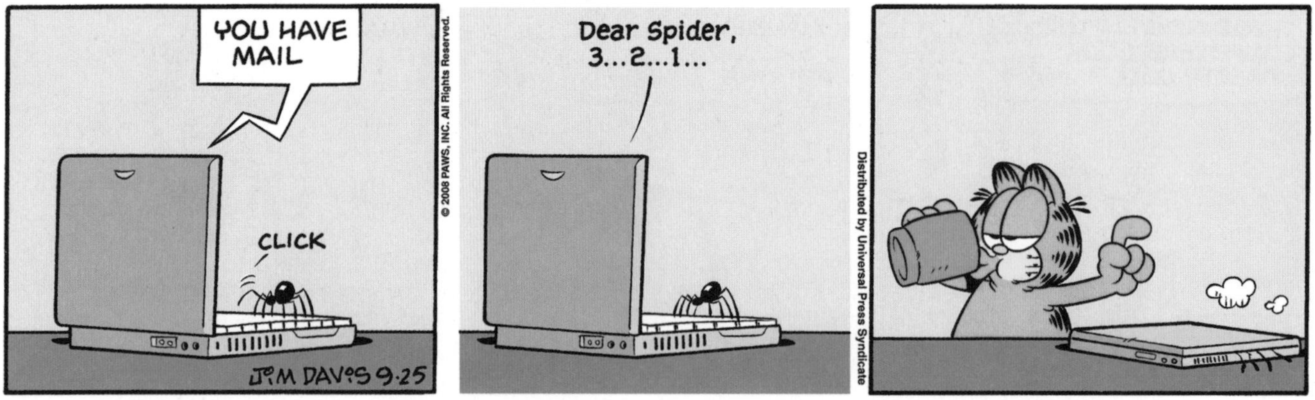
YOU HAVE MAIL
CLICK
JIM DAVIS 9·25
© 2008 PAWS, INC. All Rights Reserved.
Dear Spider, 3...2...1...
Distributed by Universal Press Syndicate

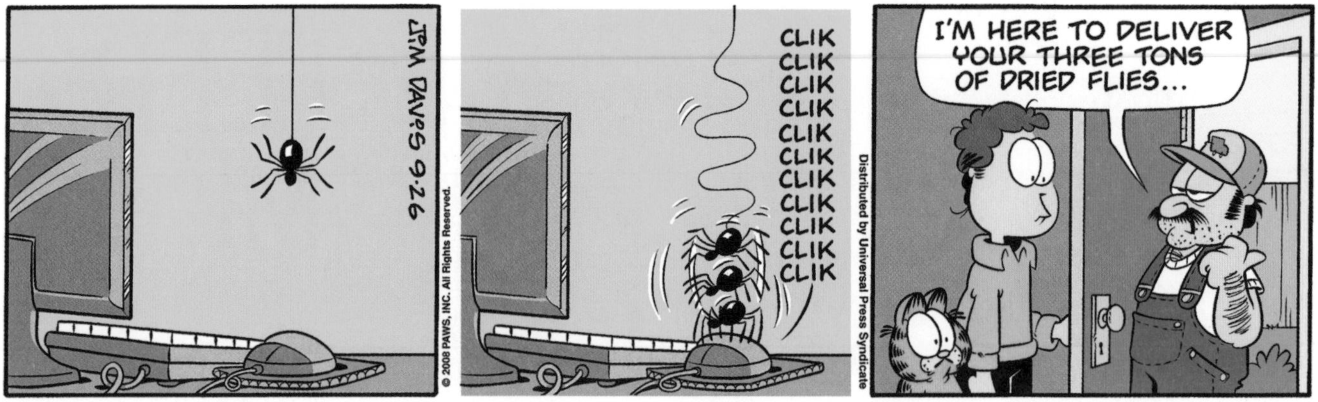
JIM DAVIS 9·26
© 2008 PAWS, INC. All Rights Reserved.
CLIK CLIK CLIK CLIK CLIK CLIK CLIK CLIK CLIK CLIK CLIK
Distributed by Universal Press Syndicate
I'M HERE TO DELIVER YOUR THREE TONS OF DRIED FLIES...

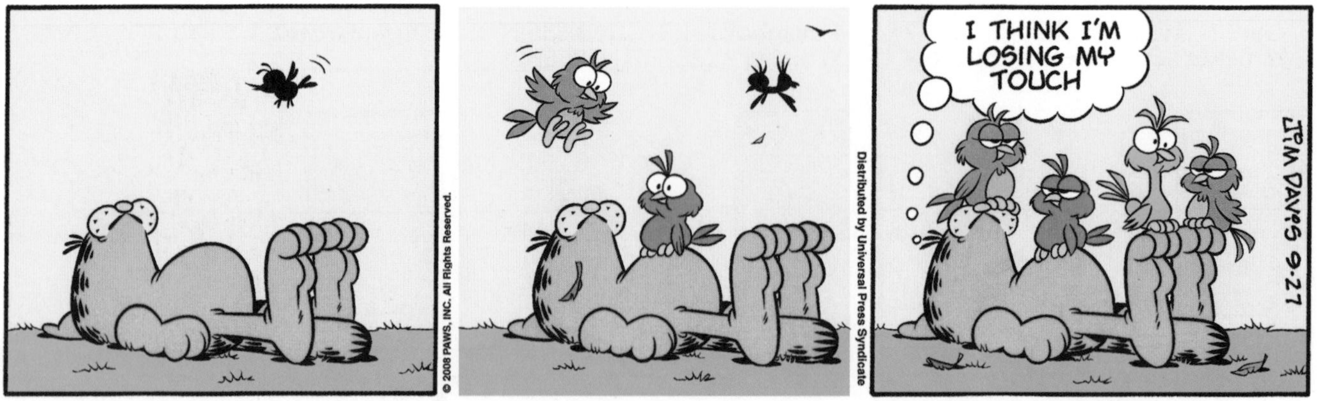
© 2008 PAWS, INC. All Rights Reserved.
Distributed by Universal Press Syndicate
I THINK I'M LOSING MY TOUCH
JIM DAVIS 9·27

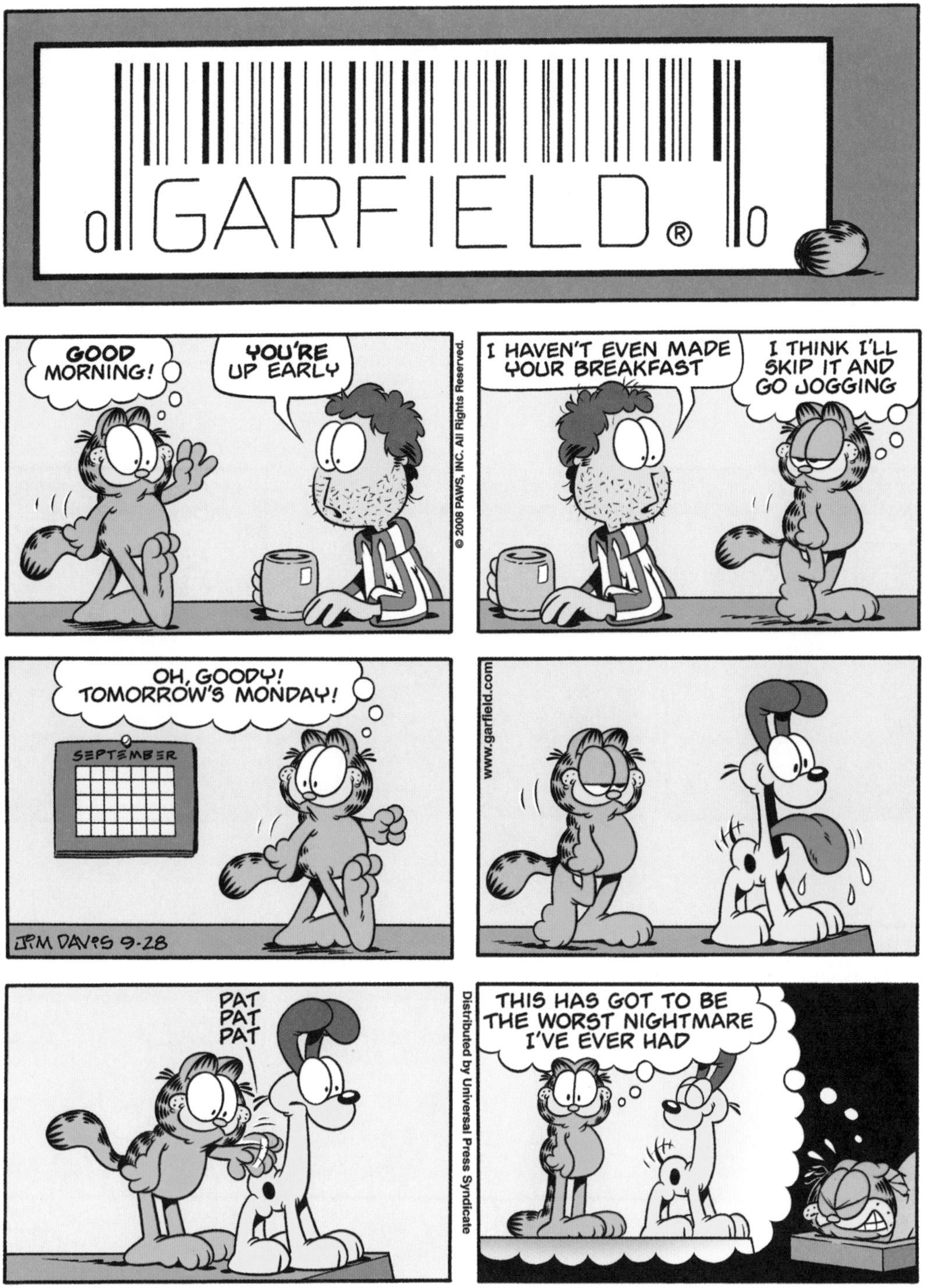
GARFIELD®
GOOD MORNING!
YOU'RE UP EARLY
© 2008 PAWS, INC. All Rights Reserved.
I HAVEN'T EVEN MADE YOUR BREAKFAST
I THINK I'LL SKIP IT AND GO JOGGING
OH, GOODY! TOMORROW'S MONDAY!
SEPTEMBER
JIM DAVIS 9-28
www.garfield.com
PAT PAT PAT
Distributed by Universal Press Syndicate
THIS HAS GOT TO BE THE WORST NIGHTMARE I'VE EVER HAD

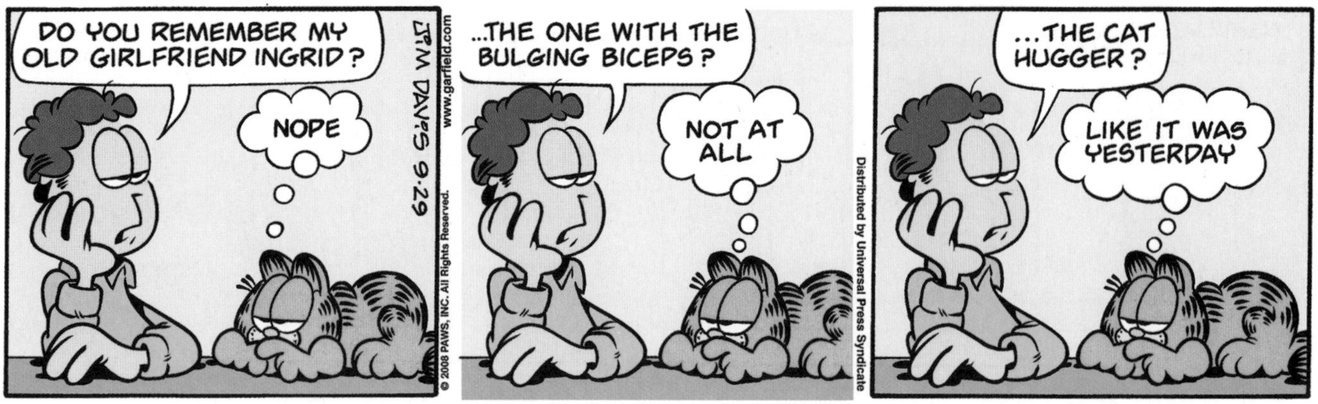
DO YOU REMEMBER MY OLD GIRLFRIEND INGRID?
NOPE
JIM DAVIS 9-29
© 2008 PAWS, INC. All Rights Reserved. www.garfield.com
...THE ONE WITH THE BULGING BICEPS?
NOT AT ALL
Distributed by Universal Press Syndicate
...THE CAT HUGGER?
LIKE IT WAS YESTERDAY

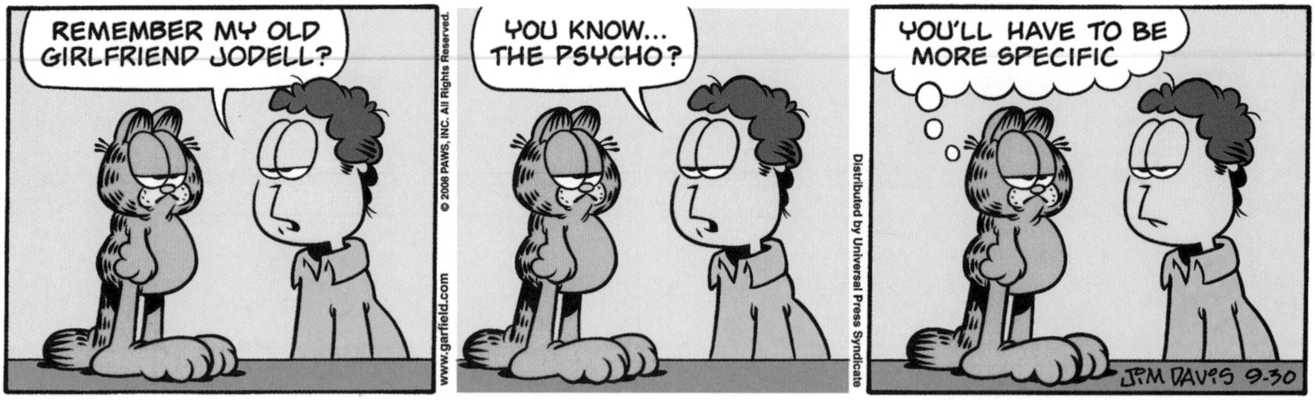
REMEMBER MY OLD GIRLFRIEND JODELL?
© 2008 PAWS, INC. All Rights Reserved. www.garfield.com
YOU KNOW... THE PSYCHO?
Distributed by Universal Press Syndicate
YOU'LL HAVE TO BE MORE SPECIFIC
JIM DAVIS 9-30

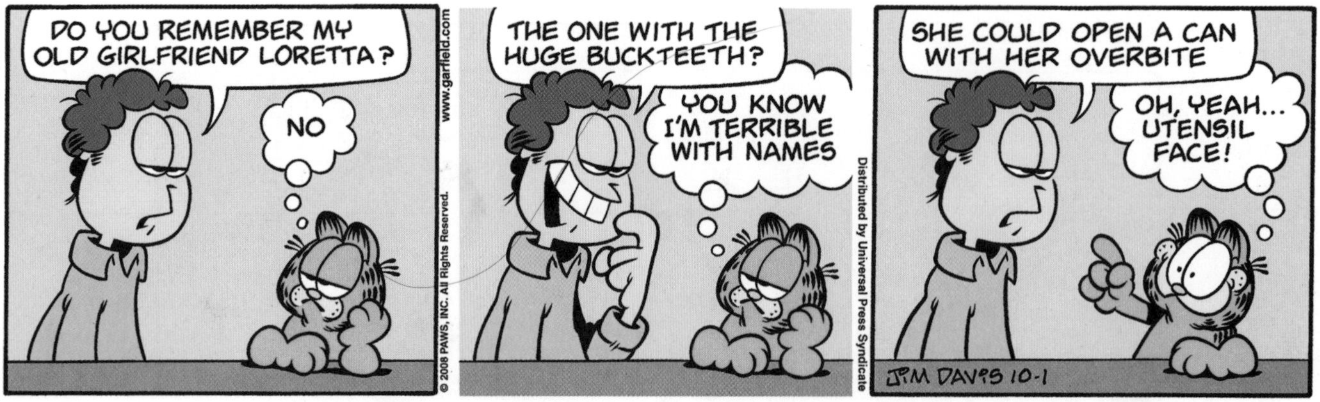
DO YOU REMEMBER MY OLD GIRLFRIEND LORETTA?
NO
© 2008 PAWS, INC. All Rights Reserved. www.garfield.com
THE ONE WITH THE HUGE BUCKTEETH?
YOU KNOW I'M TERRIBLE WITH NAMES
Distributed by Universal Press Syndicate
SHE COULD OPEN A CAN WITH HER OVERBITE
OH, YEAH... UTENSIL FACE!
JIM DAVIS 10-1

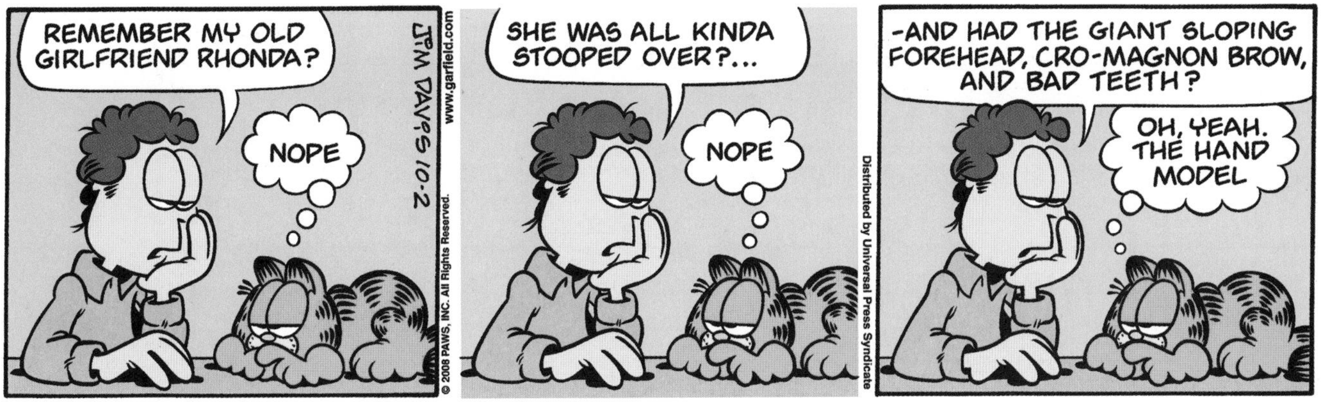
REMEMBER MY OLD GIRLFRIEND RHONDA?
NOPE
SHE WAS ALL KINDA STOOPED OVER?...
NOPE
-AND HAD THE GIANT SLOPING FOREHEAD, CRO-MAGNON BROW, AND BAD TEETH?
OH, YEAH. THE HAND MODEL
JIM DAVIS 10-2

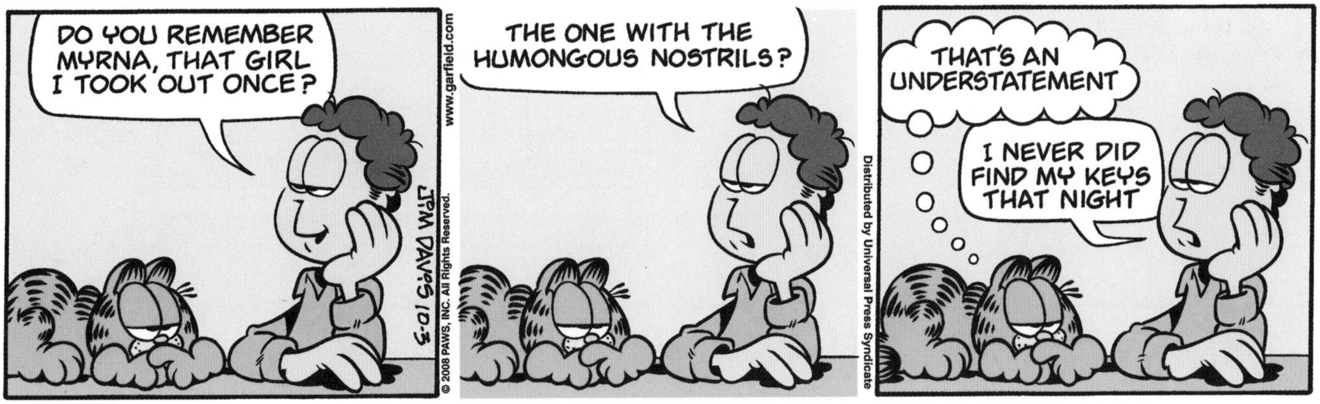
DO YOU REMEMBER MYRNA, THAT GIRL I TOOK OUT ONCE?
THE ONE WITH THE HUMONGOUS NOSTRILS?
THAT'S AN UNDERSTATEMENT
I NEVER DID FIND MY KEYS THAT NIGHT
JIM DAVIS 10-3

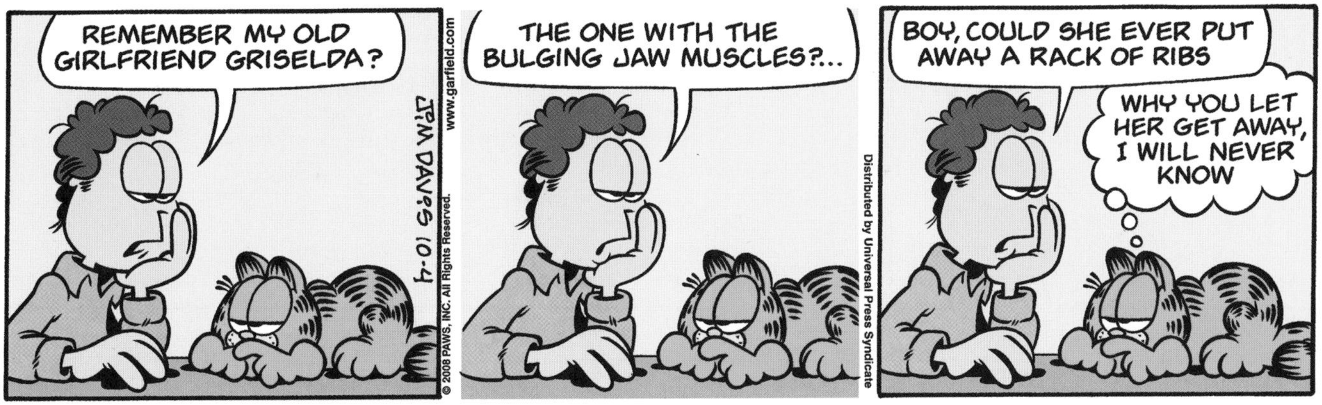
REMEMBER MY OLD GIRLFRIEND GRISELDA?
THE ONE WITH THE BULGING JAW MUSCLES?...
BOY, COULD SHE EVER PUT AWAY A RACK OF RIBS
WHY YOU LET HER GET AWAY, I WILL NEVER KNOW
JIM DAVIS 10-4

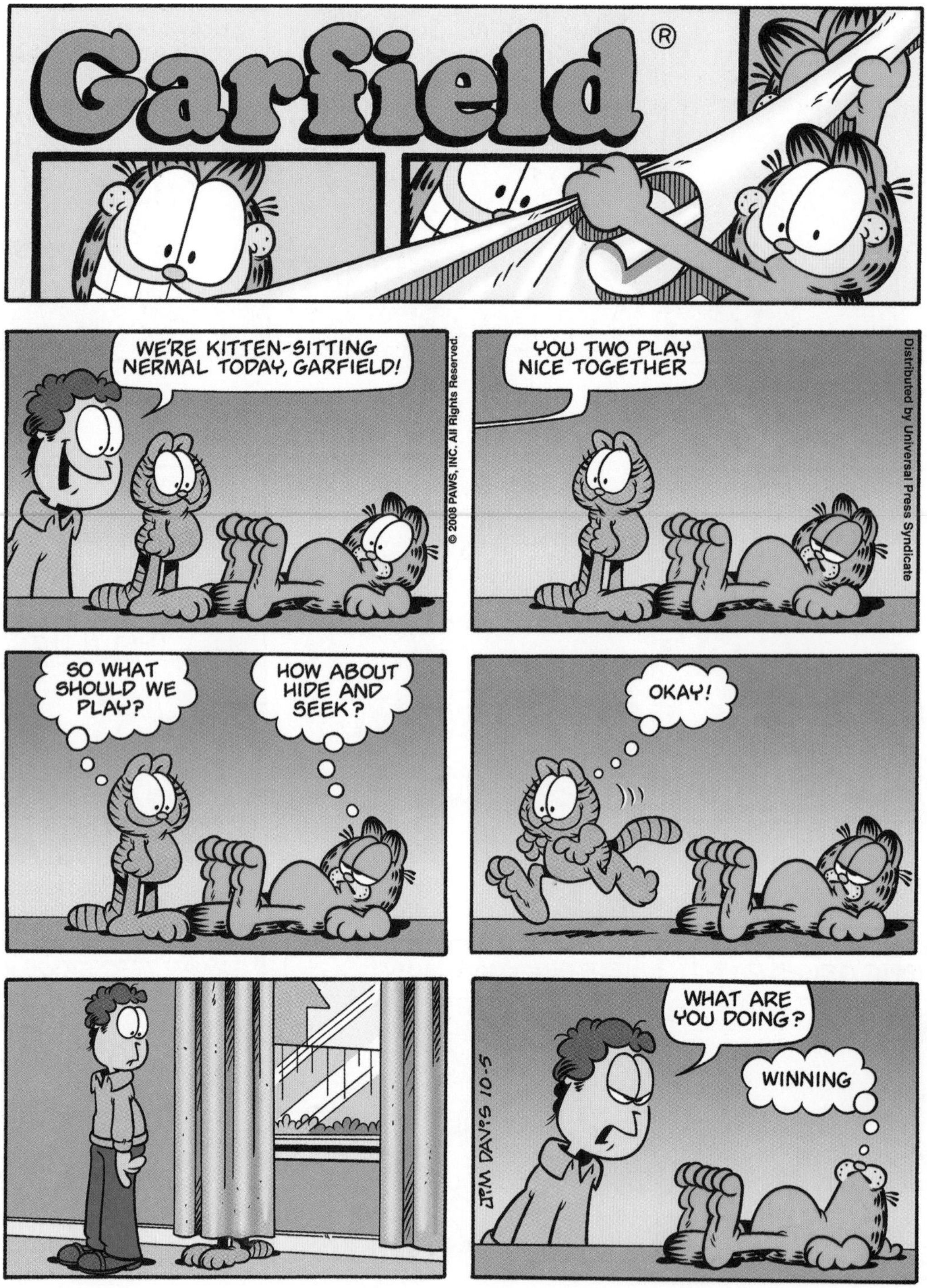
Garfield®
© 2008 PAWS, INC. All Rights Reserved.
Distributed by Universal Press Syndicate
WE'RE KITTEN-SITTING NERMAL TODAY, GARFIELD!
YOU TWO PLAY NICE TOGETHER
SO WHAT SHOULD WE PLAY?
HOW ABOUT HIDE AND SEEK?
OKAY!
JPM DAVIS 10-5
WHAT ARE YOU DOING?
WINNING

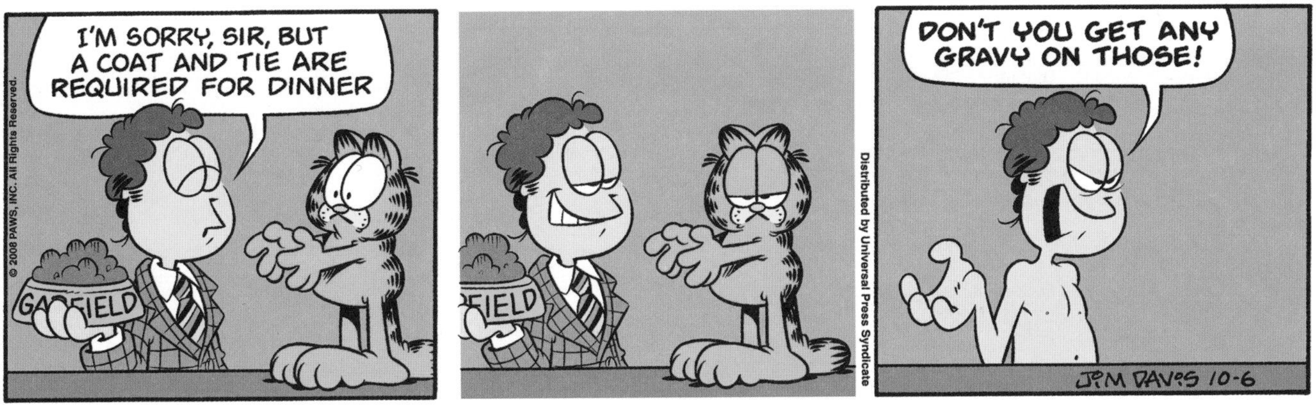
I'M SORRY, SIR, BUT A COAT AND TIE ARE REQUIRED FOR DINNER
GARFIELD
DON'T YOU GET ANY GRAVY ON THOSE!
JIM DAVIS 10-6
© 2008 PAWS, INC. All Rights Reserved.
Distributed by Universal Press Syndicate

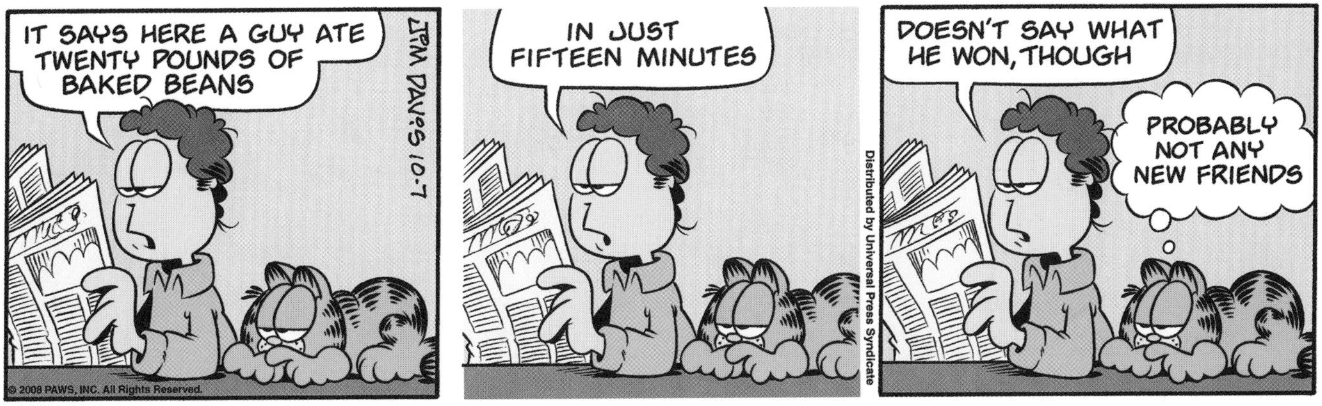
IT SAYS HERE A GUY ATE TWENTY POUNDS OF BAKED BEANS
JIM DAVIS 10-7
IN JUST FIFTEEN MINUTES
DOESN'T SAY WHAT HE WON, THOUGH
PROBABLY NOT ANY NEW FRIENDS
© 2008 PAWS, INC. All Rights Reserved.
Distributed by Universal Press Syndicate

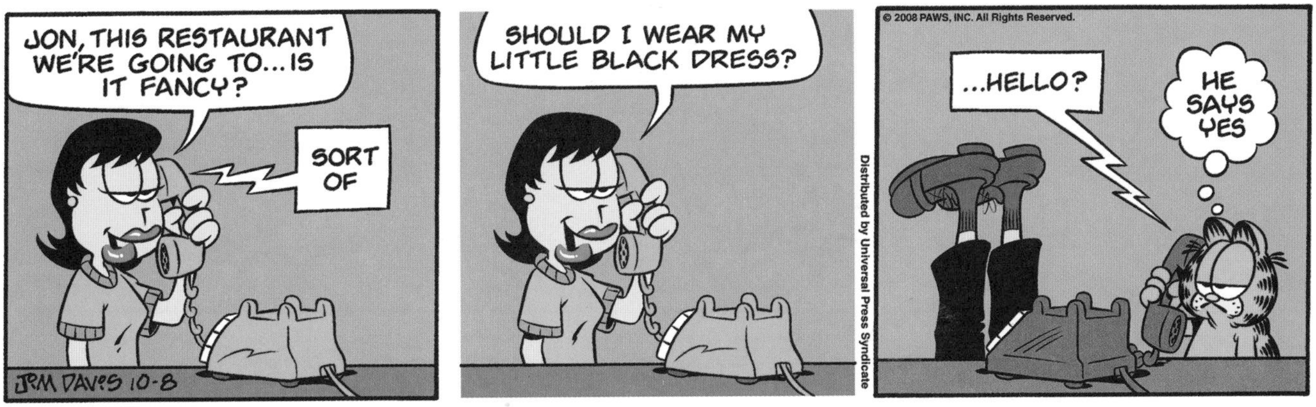
JON, THIS RESTAURANT WE'RE GOING TO... IS IT FANCY?
SORT OF
JIM DAVIS 10-8
SHOULD I WEAR MY LITTLE BLACK DRESS?
...HELLO?
HE SAYS YES
© 2008 PAWS, INC. All Rights Reserved.
Distributed by Universal Press Syndicate

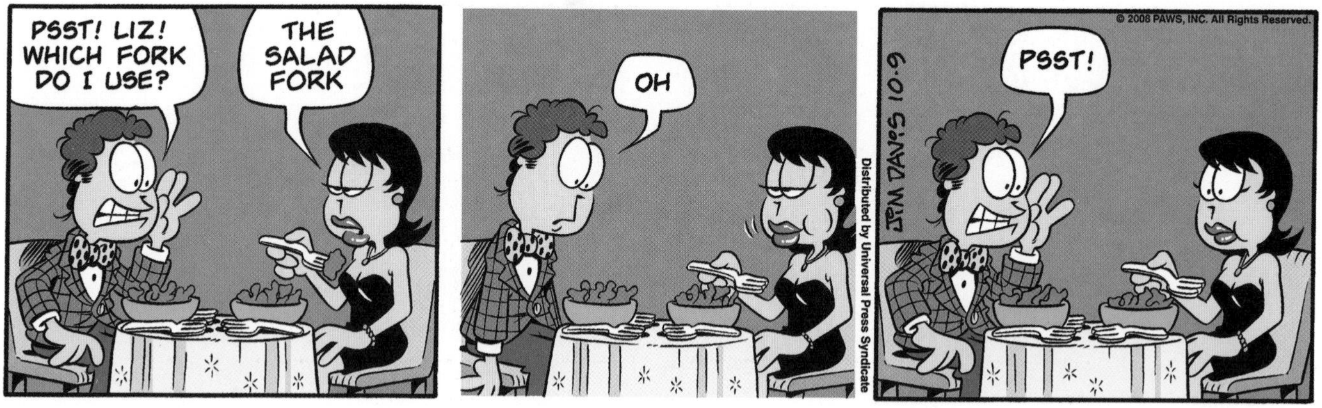
PSST! LIZ! WHICH FORK DO I USE?
THE SALAD FORK
OH
PSST!
JIM DAVIS 10-9
© 2008 PAWS, INC. All Rights Reserved.
Distributed by Universal Press Syndicate

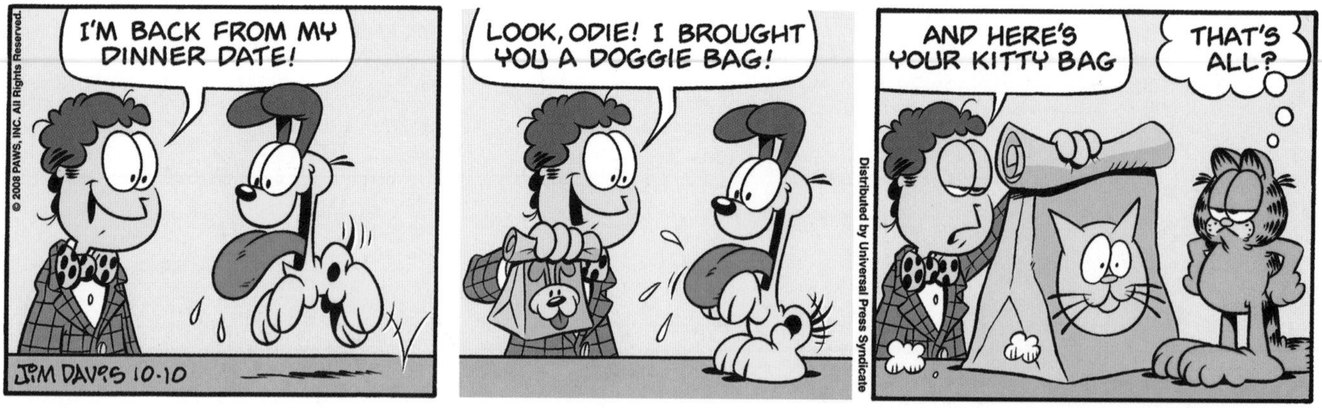
I'M BACK FROM MY DINNER DATE!
LOOK, ODIE! I BROUGHT YOU A DOGGIE BAG!
AND HERE'S YOUR KITTY BAG
THAT'S ALL?
JIM DAVIS 10-10
© 2008 PAWS, INC. All Rights Reserved.
Distributed by Universal Press Syndicate

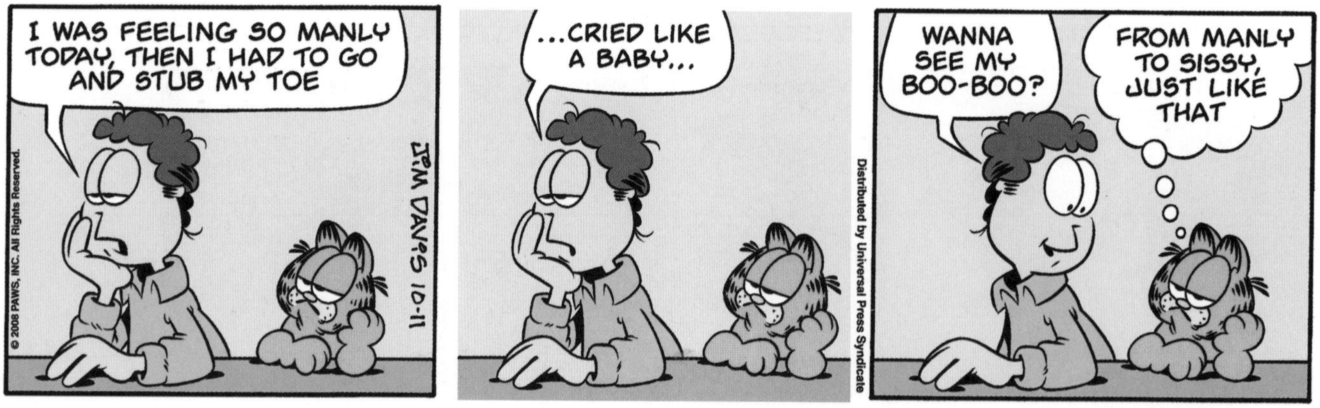
I WAS FEELING SO MANLY TODAY, THEN I HAD TO GO AND STUB MY TOE
...CRIED LIKE A BABY...
WANNA SEE MY BOO-BOO?
FROM MANLY TO SISSY, JUST LIKE THAT
JIM DAVIS 10-11
© 2008 PAWS, INC. All Rights Reserved.
Distributed by Universal Press Syndicate

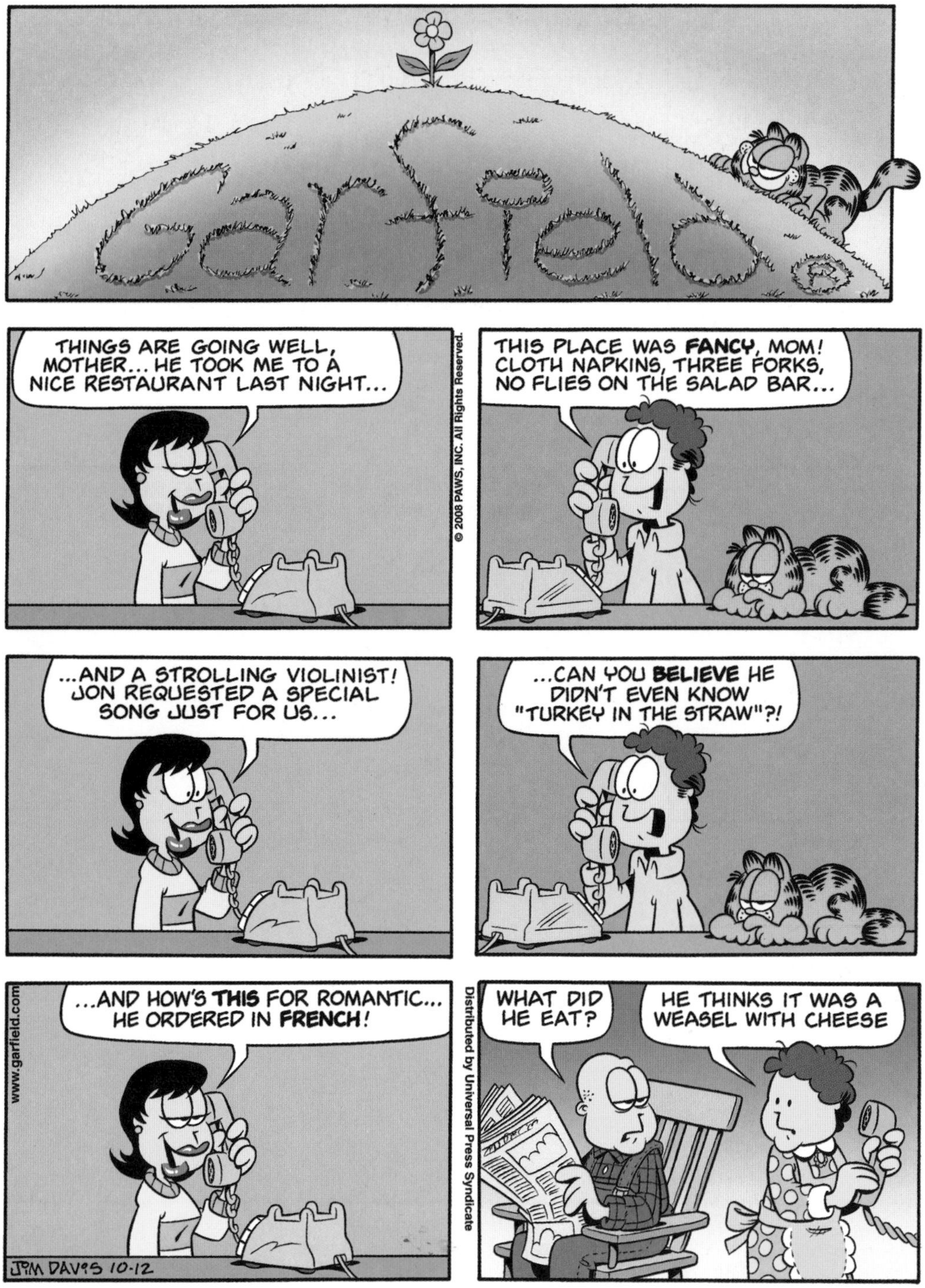

garfield
THINGS ARE GOING WELL, MOTHER... HE TOOK ME TO A NICE RESTAURANT LAST NIGHT...
© 2008 PAWS, INC. All Rights Reserved.
THIS PLACE WAS FANCY, MOM! CLOTH NAPKINS, THREE FORKS, NO FLIES ON THE SALAD BAR...
...AND A STROLLING VIOLINIST! JON REQUESTED A SPECIAL SONG JUST FOR US...
...CAN YOU BELIEVE HE DIDN'T EVEN KNOW "TURKEY IN THE STRAW"?!
www.garfield.com
...AND HOW'S THIS FOR ROMANTIC... HE ORDERED IN FRENCH!
JIM DAVIS 10-12
Distributed by Universal Press Syndicate
WHAT DID HE EAT?
HE THINKS IT WAS A WEASEL WITH CHEESE

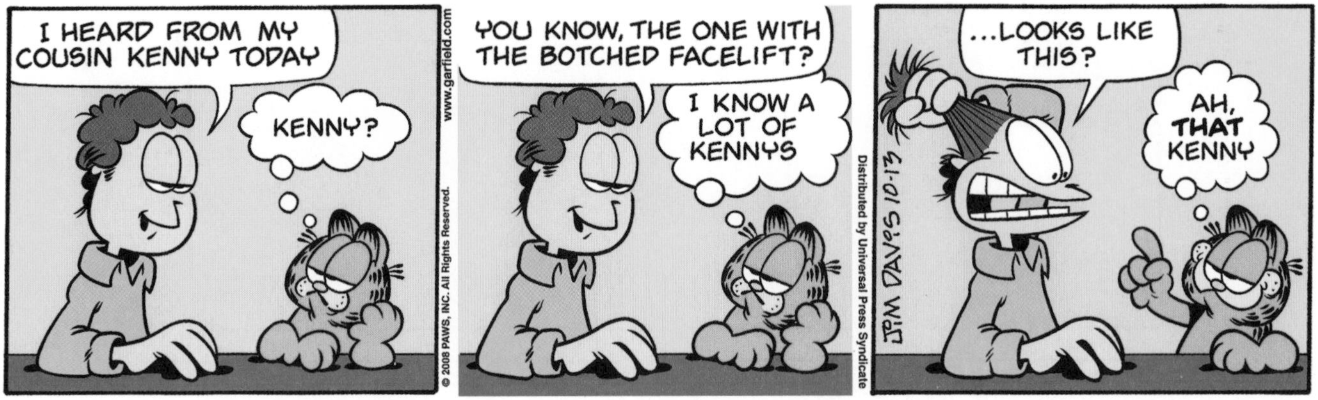
I HEARD FROM MY COUSIN KENNY TODAY
KENNY?
© 2008 PAWS, INC. All Rights Reserved. www.garfield.com
YOU KNOW, THE ONE WITH THE BOTCHED FACELIFT?
I KNOW A LOT OF KENNYS
Distributed by Universal Press Syndicate
JIM DAVIS 10-13
...LOOKS LIKE THIS?
AH, **THAT** KENNY

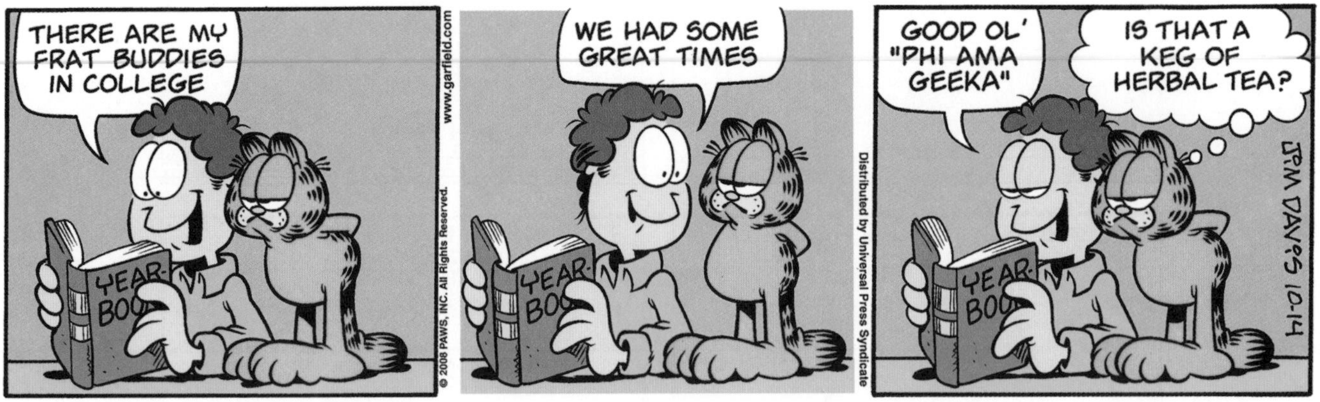
THERE ARE MY FRAT BUDDIES IN COLLEGE
YEAR-BOO
© 2008 PAWS, INC. All Rights Reserved. www.garfield.com
WE HAD SOME GREAT TIMES
Distributed by Universal Press Syndicate
GOOD OL' "PHI AMA GEEKA"
IS THAT A KEG OF HERBAL TEA?
JIM DAVIS 10-14

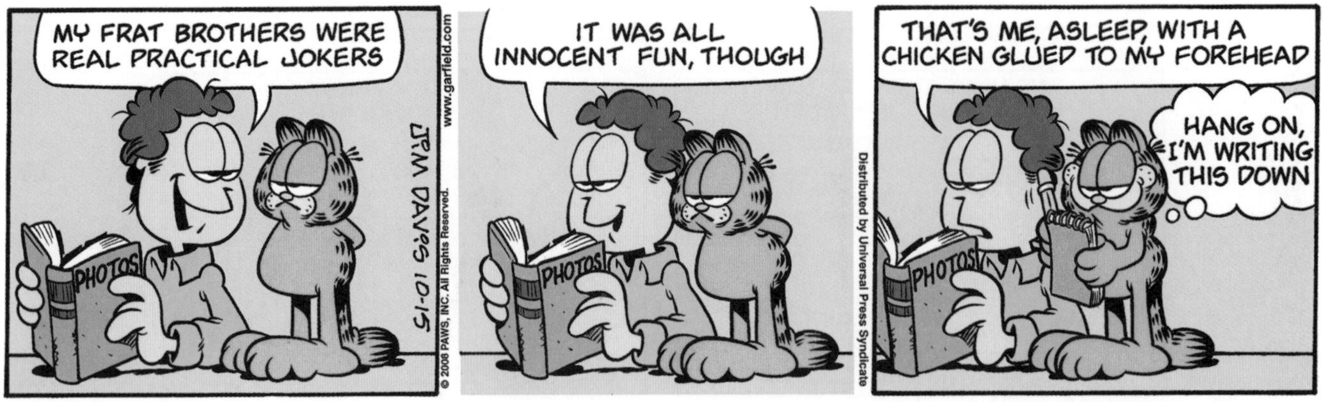
MY FRAT BROTHERS WERE REAL PRACTICAL JOKERS
PHOTOS
JIM DAVIS 10-15
© 2008 PAWS, INC. All Rights Reserved. www.garfield.com
IT WAS ALL INNOCENT FUN, THOUGH
Distributed by Universal Press Syndicate
THAT'S ME, ASLEEP, WITH A CHICKEN GLUED TO MY FOREHEAD
HANG ON, I'M WRITING THIS DOWN

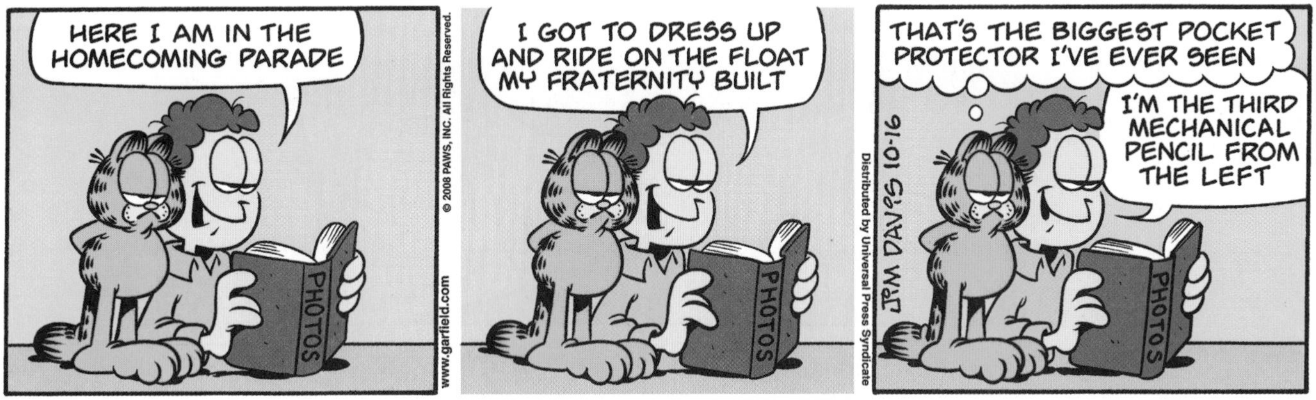
HERE I AM IN THE HOMECOMING PARADE
I GOT TO DRESS UP AND RIDE ON THE FLOAT MY FRATERNITY BUILT
THAT'S THE BIGGEST POCKET PROTECTOR I'VE EVER SEEN
I'M THE THIRD MECHANICAL PENCIL FROM THE LEFT
PHOTOS
JIM DAVIS 10-16

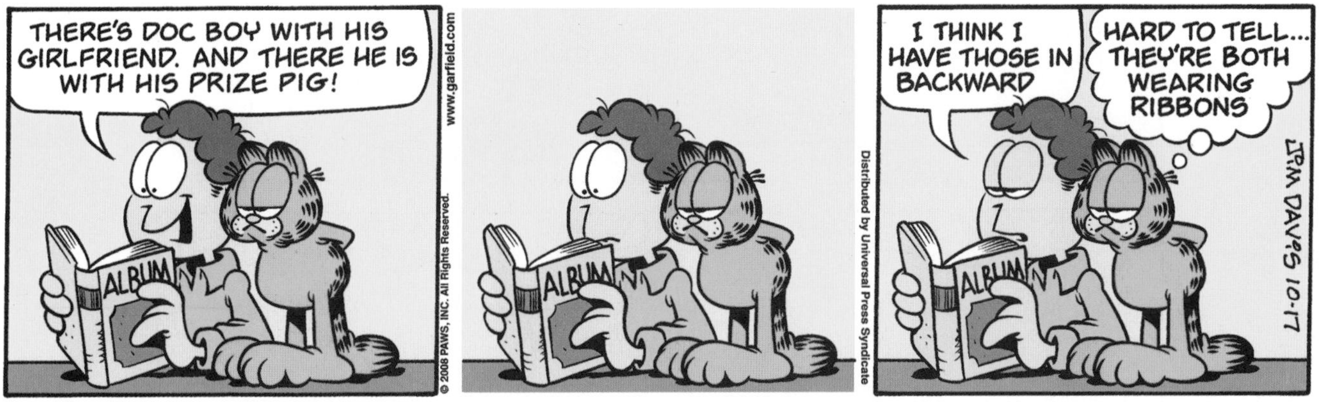
THERE'S DOC BOY WITH HIS GIRLFRIEND. AND THERE HE IS WITH HIS PRIZE PIG!
ALBUM
I THINK I HAVE THOSE IN BACKWARD
HARD TO TELL... THEY'RE BOTH WEARING RIBBONS
JIM DAVIS 10-17

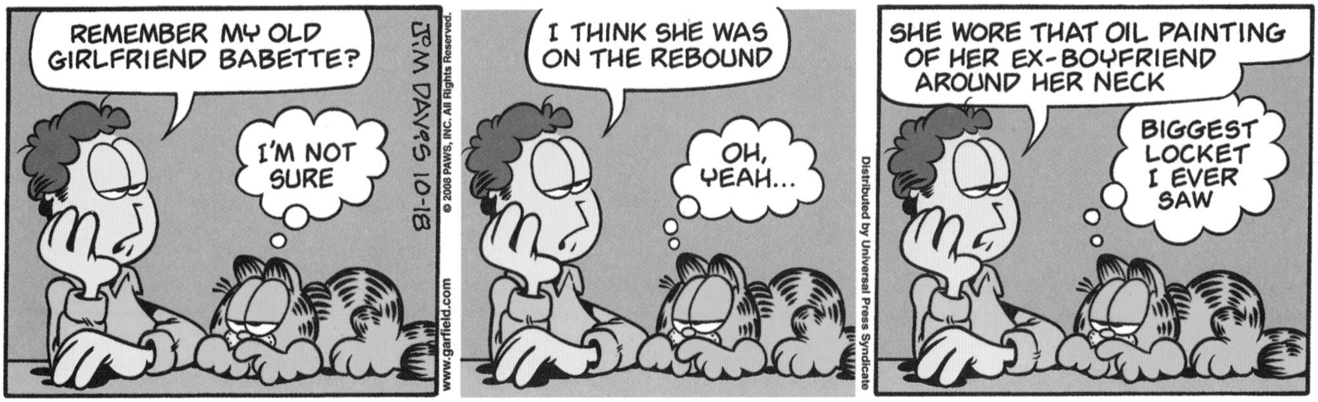
REMEMBER MY OLD GIRLFRIEND BABETTE?
I'M NOT SURE
JIM DAVIS 10-18
I THINK SHE WAS ON THE REBOUND
OH, YEAH...
SHE WORE THAT OIL PAINTING OF HER EX-BOYFRIEND AROUND HER NECK
BIGGEST LOCKET I EVER SAW

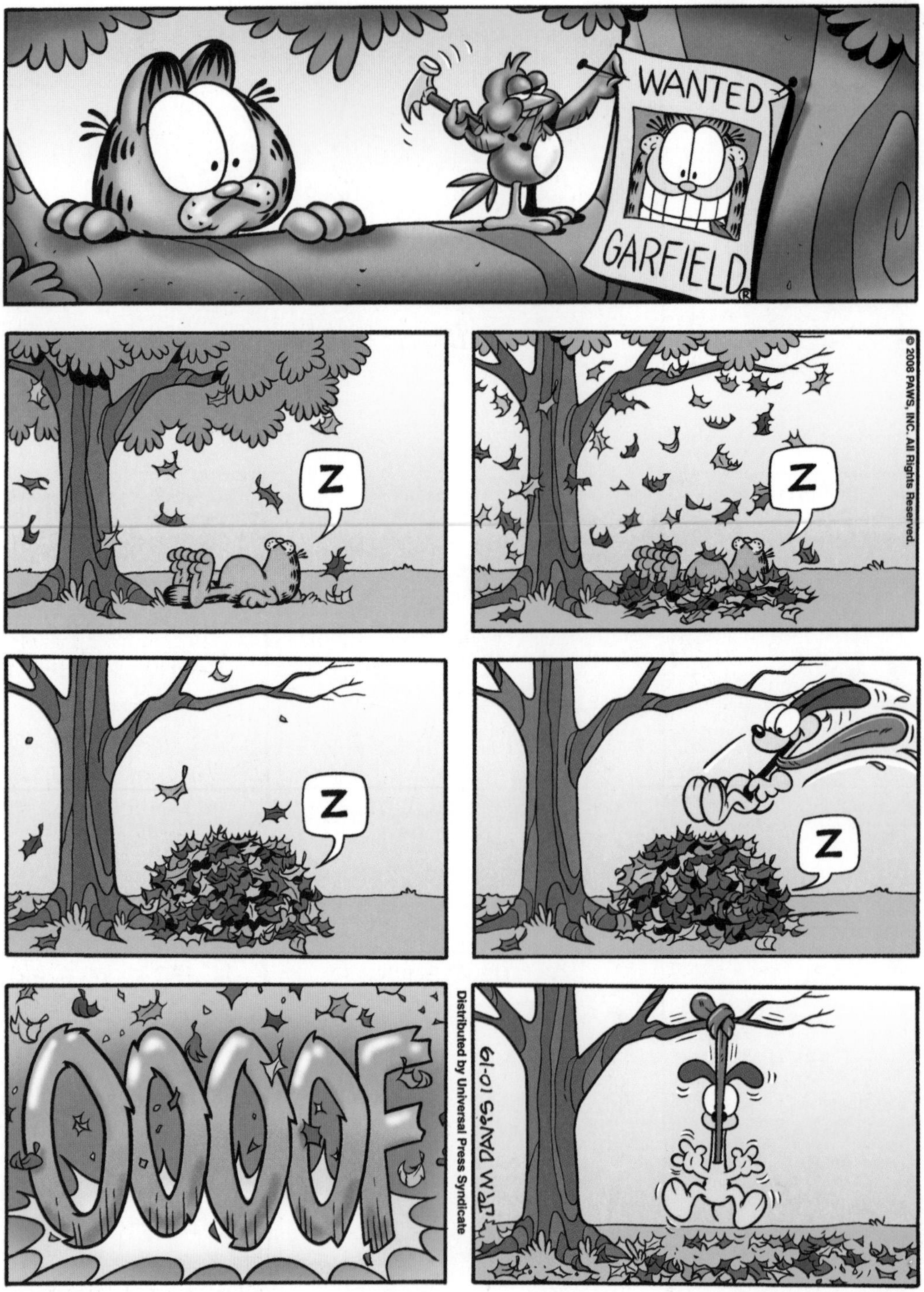
WANTED
GARFIELD®
Z
Z
Z
Z
OOOOF
© 2008 PAWS, INC. All Rights Reserved.
JIM DAVIS 10-19
Distributed by Universal Press Syndicate

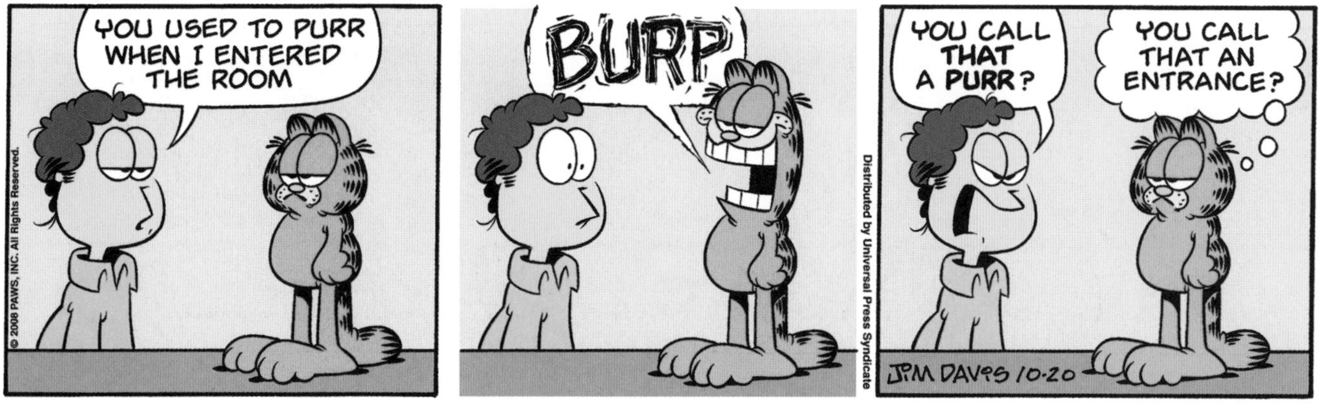
YOU USED TO PURR WHEN I ENTERED THE ROOM
BURP
YOU CALL **THAT** A **PURR**?
YOU CALL THAT AN ENTRANCE?
JIM DAVIS 10-20

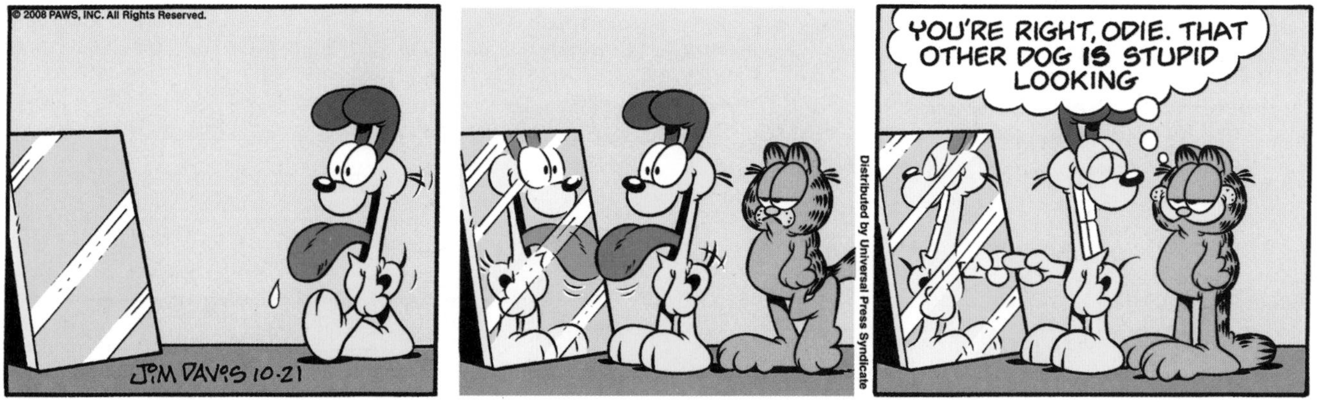
JIM DAVIS 10-21
YOU'RE RIGHT, ODIE. THAT OTHER DOG **IS** STUPID LOOKING

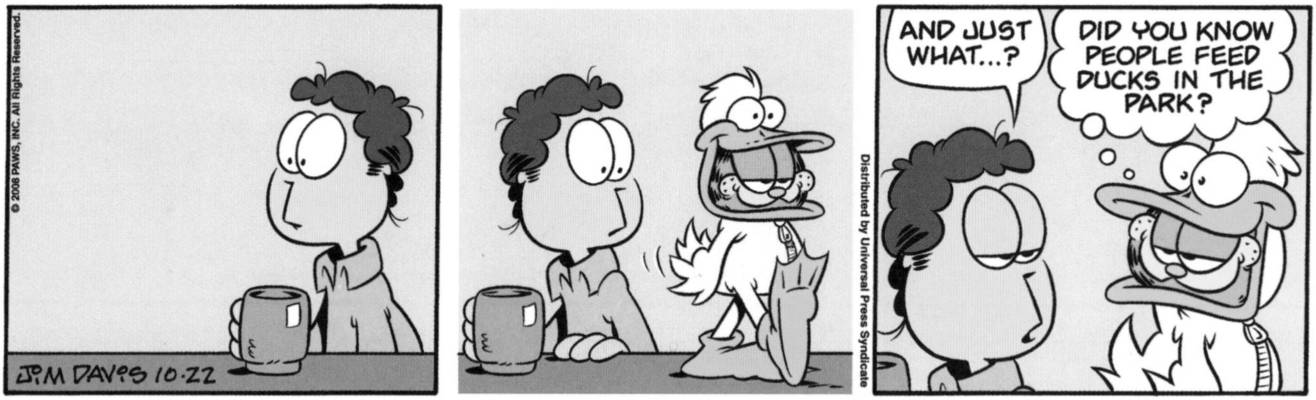
JIM DAVIS 10-22
AND JUST WHAT...?
DID YOU KNOW PEOPLE FEED DUCKS IN THE PARK?

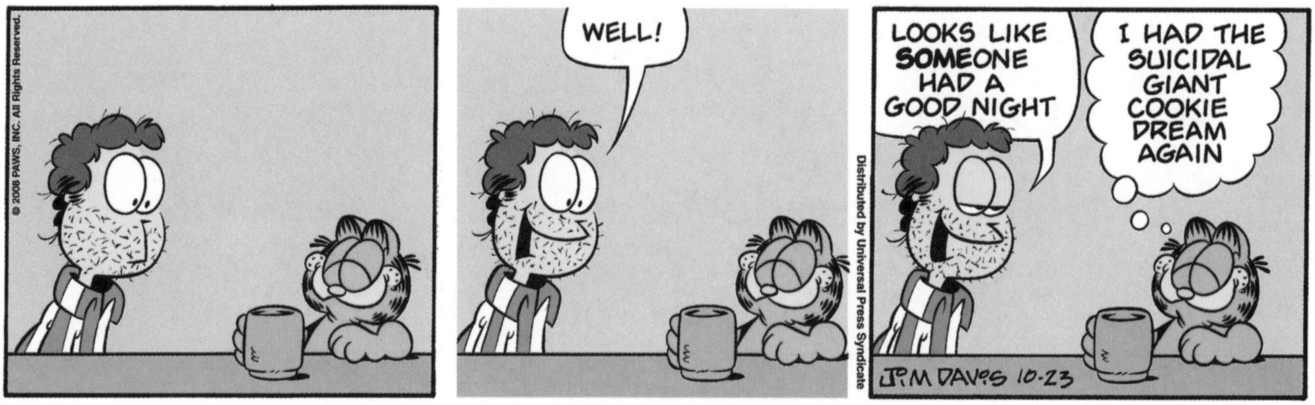
© 2008 PAWS, INC. All Rights Reserved.
WELL!
LOOKS LIKE **SOME**ONE HAD A GOOD NIGHT
I HAD THE SUICIDAL GIANT COOKIE DREAM AGAIN
Distributed by Universal Press Syndicate
JIM DAVIS 10-23

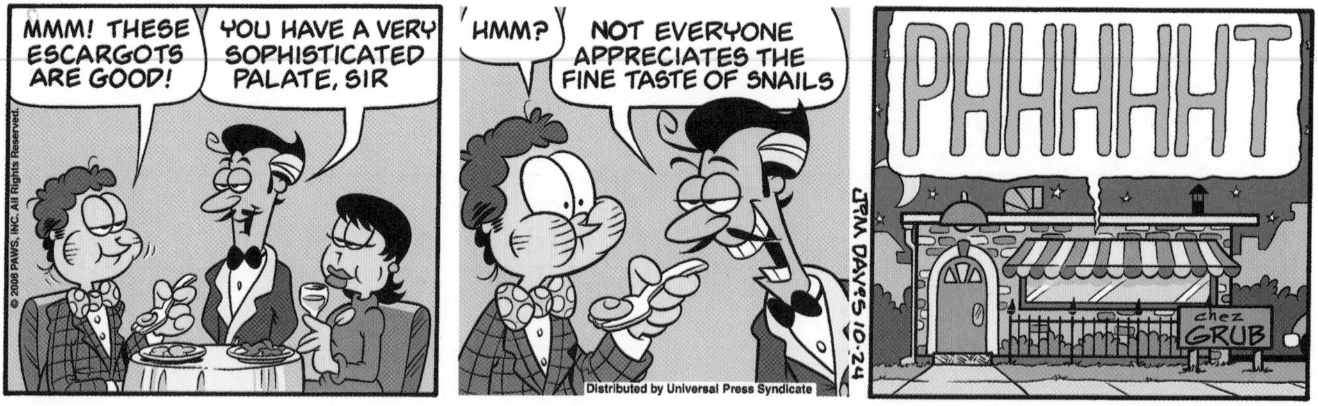
© 2008 PAWS, INC. All Rights Reserved.
MMM! THESE ESCARGOTS ARE GOOD!
YOU HAVE A VERY SOPHISTICATED PALATE, SIR
HMM?
NOT EVERYONE APPRECIATES THE FINE TASTE OF SNAILS
JIM DAVIS 10-24
Distributed by Universal Press Syndicate
PHHHHHT
chez GRUB

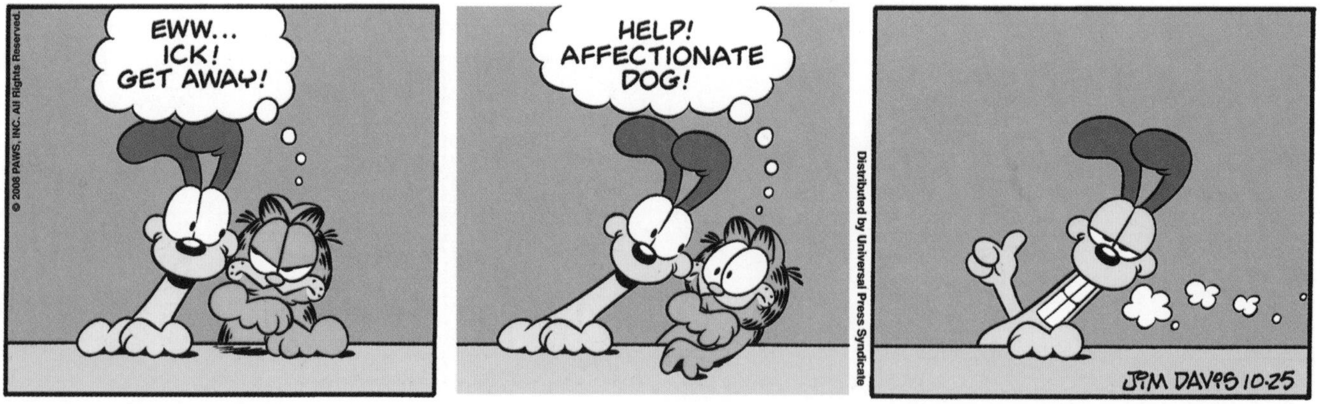
© 2008 PAWS, INC. All Rights Reserved.
EWW... ICK! GET AWAY!
HELP! AFFECTIONATE DOG!
Distributed by Universal Press Syndicate
JIM DAVIS 10-25

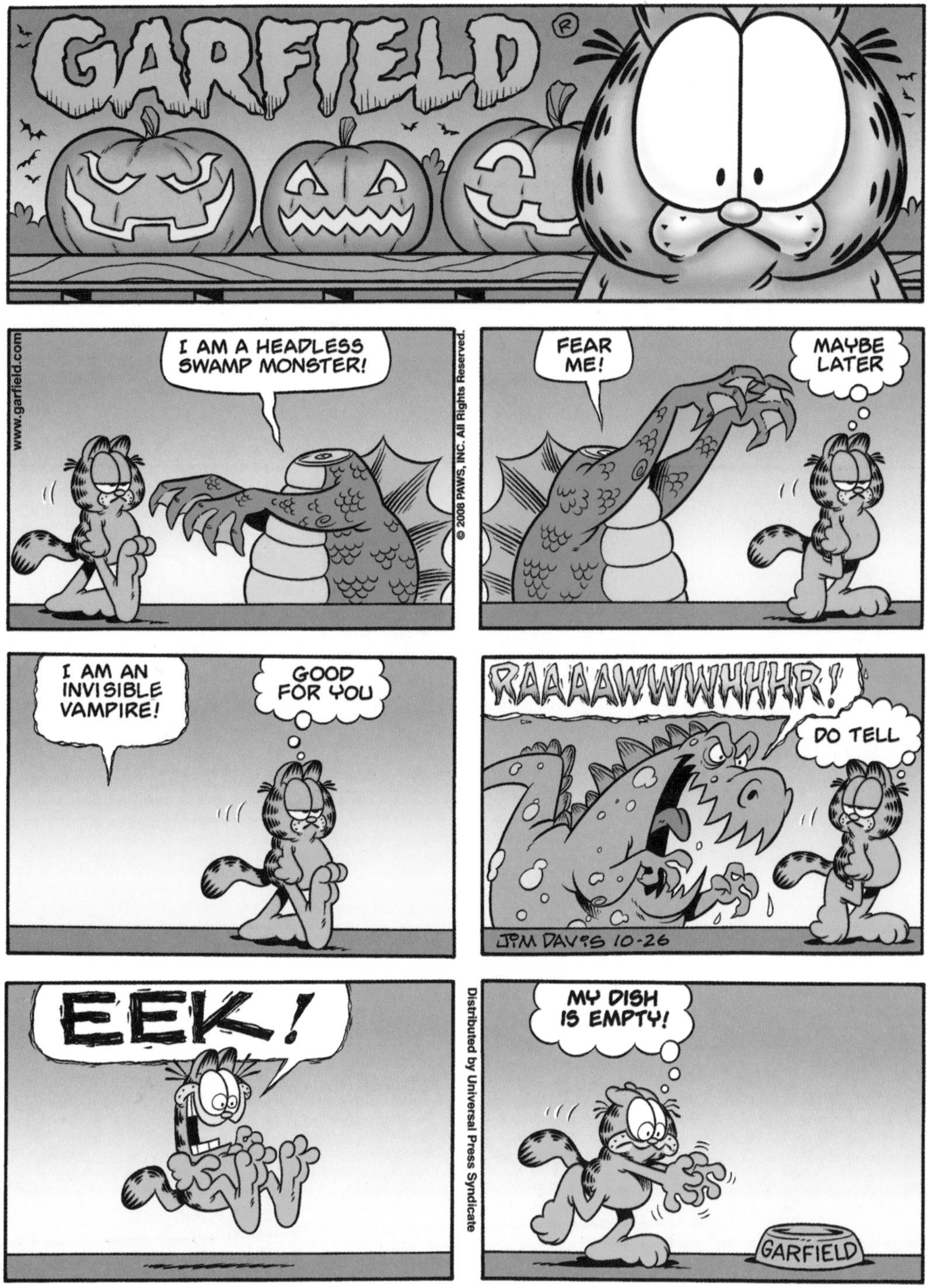
GARFIELD®
www.garfield.com
I AM A HEADLESS SWAMP MONSTER!
© 2008 PAWS, INC. All Rights Reserved.
FEAR ME!
MAYBE LATER
I AM AN INVISIBLE VAMPIRE!
GOOD FOR YOU
RAAAAWWWHHHR!
DO TELL
JIM DAVIS 10-26
EEK!
Distributed by Universal Press Syndicate
MY DISH IS EMPTY!
GARFIELD

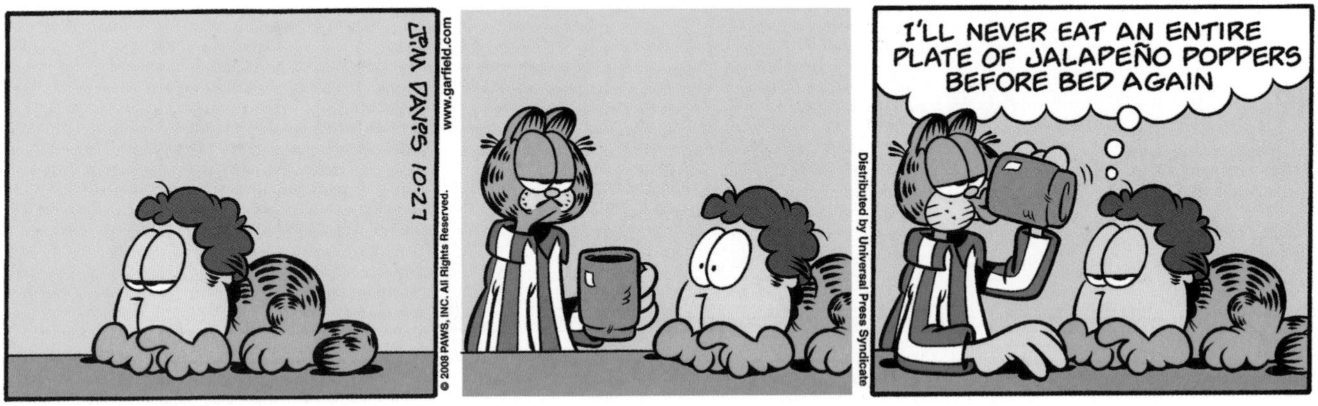
JIM DAVIS 10-27
© 2008 PAWS, INC. All Rights Reserved. www.garfield.com
I'LL NEVER EAT AN ENTIRE PLATE OF JALAPEÑO POPPERS BEFORE BED AGAIN
Distributed by Universal Press Syndicate

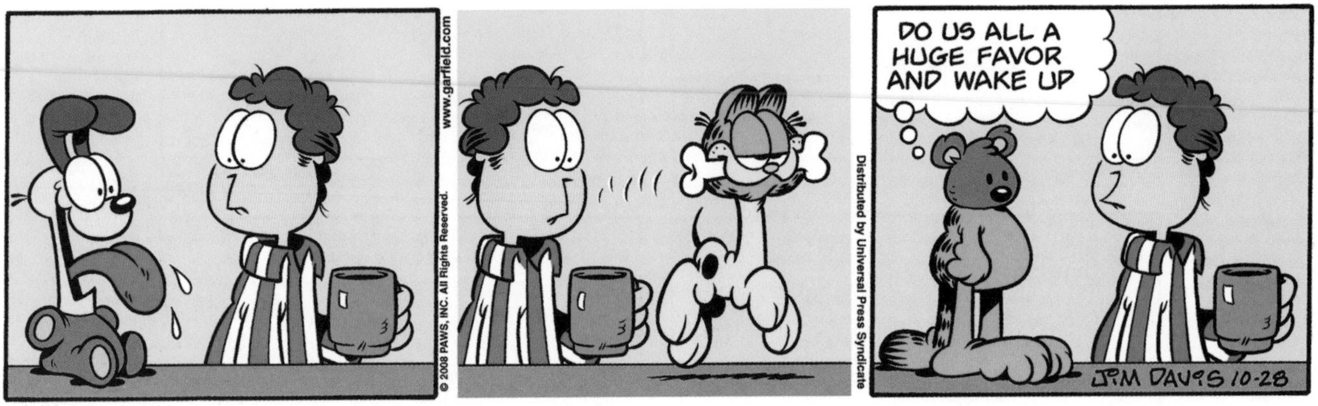
© 2008 PAWS, INC. All Rights Reserved. www.garfield.com
Distributed by Universal Press Syndicate
DO US ALL A HUGE FAVOR AND WAKE UP
JIM DAVIS 10-28

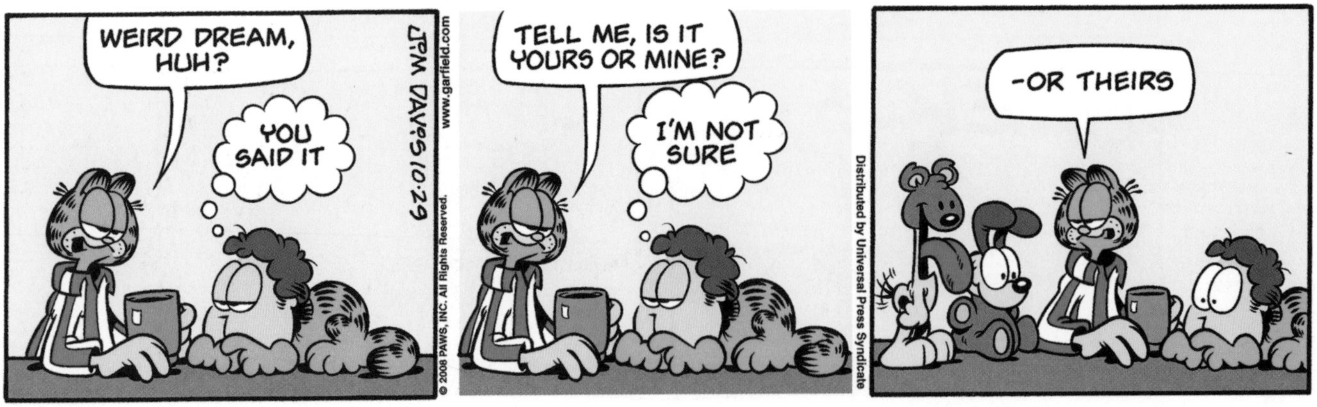
WEIRD DREAM, HUH?
YOU SAID IT
JIM DAVIS 10-29
© 2008 PAWS, INC. All Rights Reserved. www.garfield.com
TELL ME, IS IT YOURS OR MINE?
I'M NOT SURE
Distributed by Universal Press Syndicate
-OR THEIRS

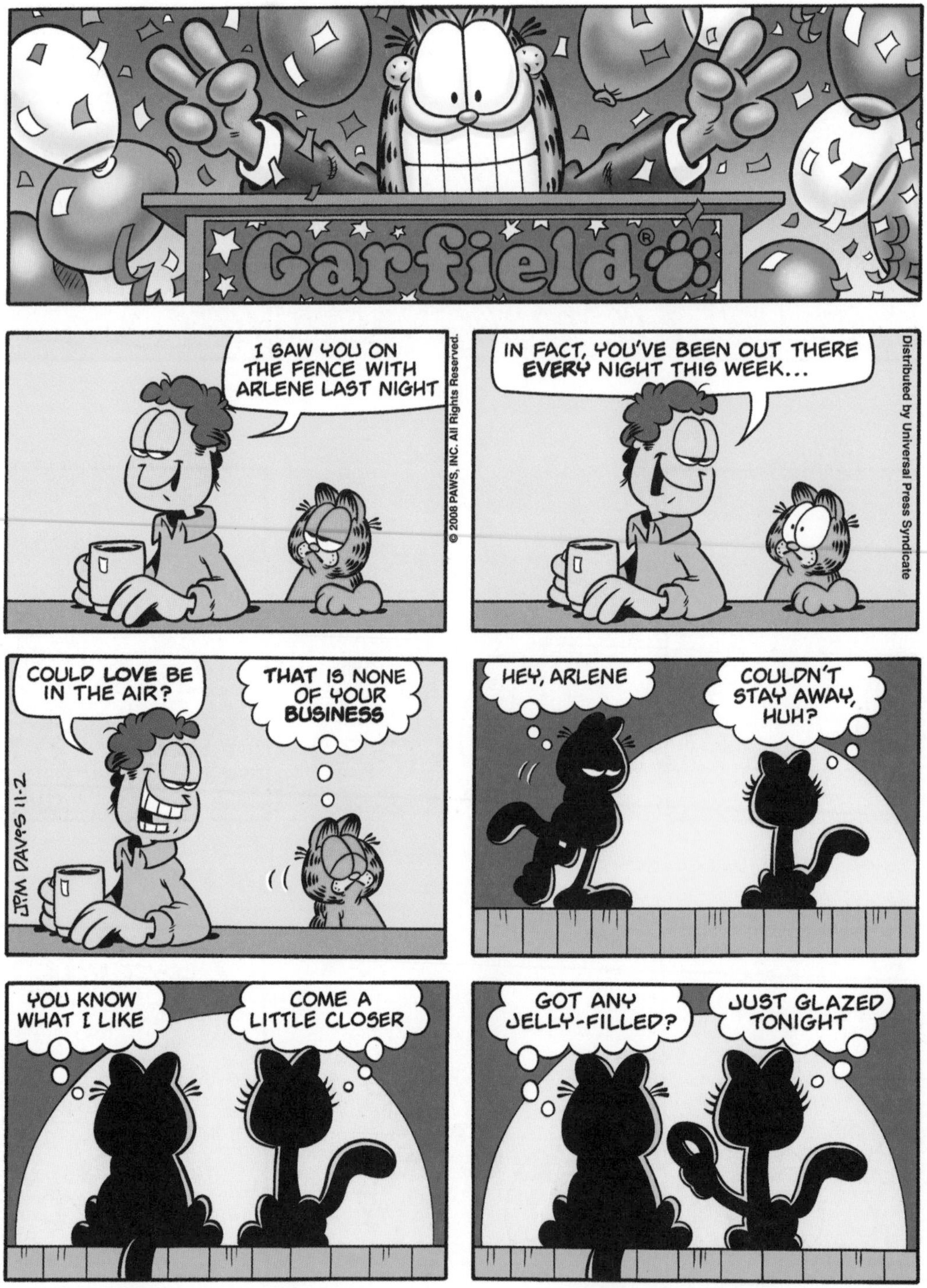

Garfield®
I SAW YOU ON THE FENCE WITH ARLENE LAST NIGHT
© 2008 PAWS, INC. All Rights Reserved.
IN FACT, YOU'VE BEEN OUT THERE EVERY NIGHT THIS WEEK...
Distributed by Universal Press Syndicate
COULD LOVE BE IN THE AIR?
THAT IS NONE OF YOUR BUSINESS
JIM DAVIS 11-2
HEY, ARLENE
COULDN'T STAY AWAY, HUH?
YOU KNOW WHAT I LIKE
COME A LITTLE CLOSER
GOT ANY JELLY-FILLED?
JUST GLAZED TONIGHT

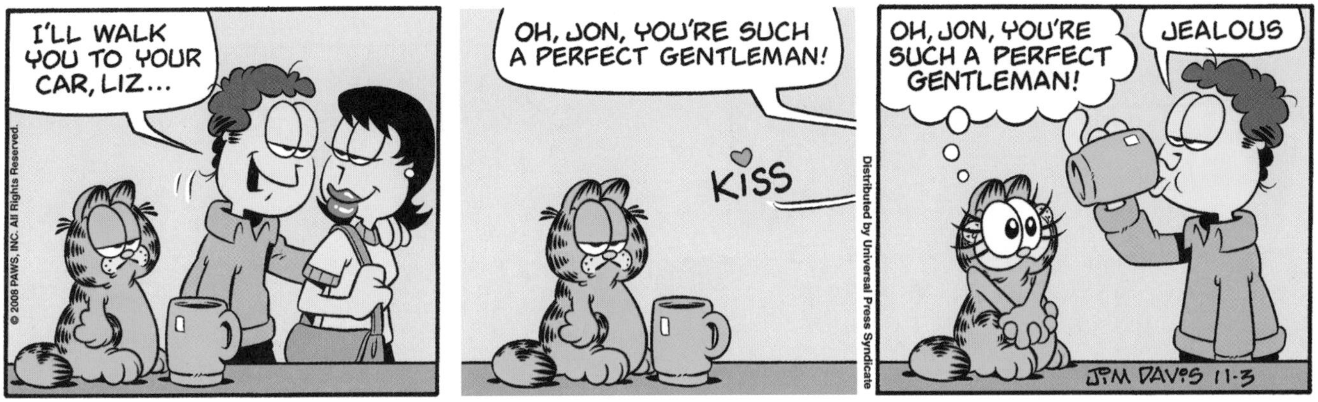
I'LL WALK YOU TO YOUR CAR, LIZ...
OH, JON, YOU'RE SUCH A PERFECT GENTLEMAN!
KISS
OH, JON, YOU'RE SUCH A PERFECT GENTLEMAN!
JEALOUS
JIM DAVIS 11-3
© 2008 PAWS, INC. All Rights Reserved.
Distributed by Universal Press Syndicate

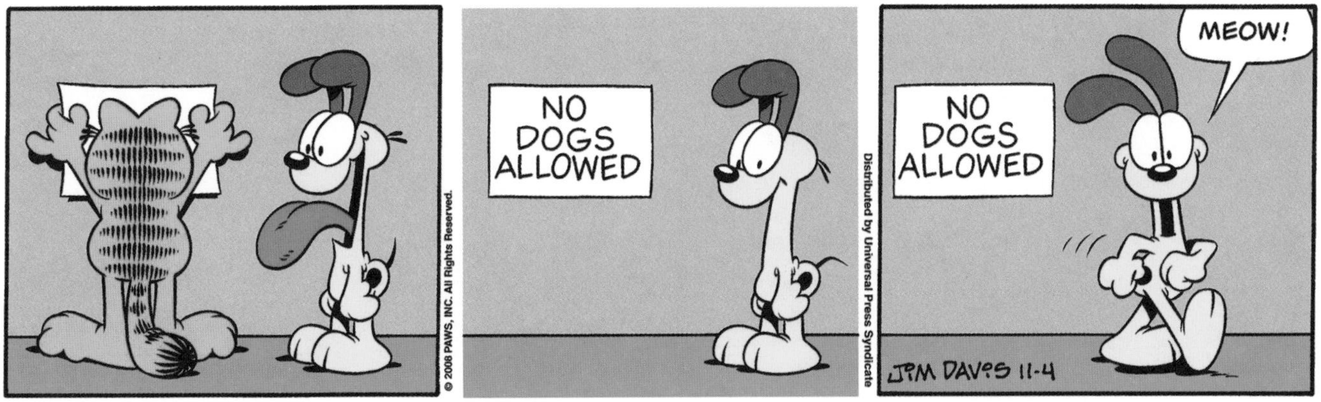
NO DOGS ALLOWED
NO DOGS ALLOWED
MEOW!
JIM DAVIS 11-4
© 2008 PAWS, INC. All Rights Reserved.
Distributed by Universal Press Syndicate

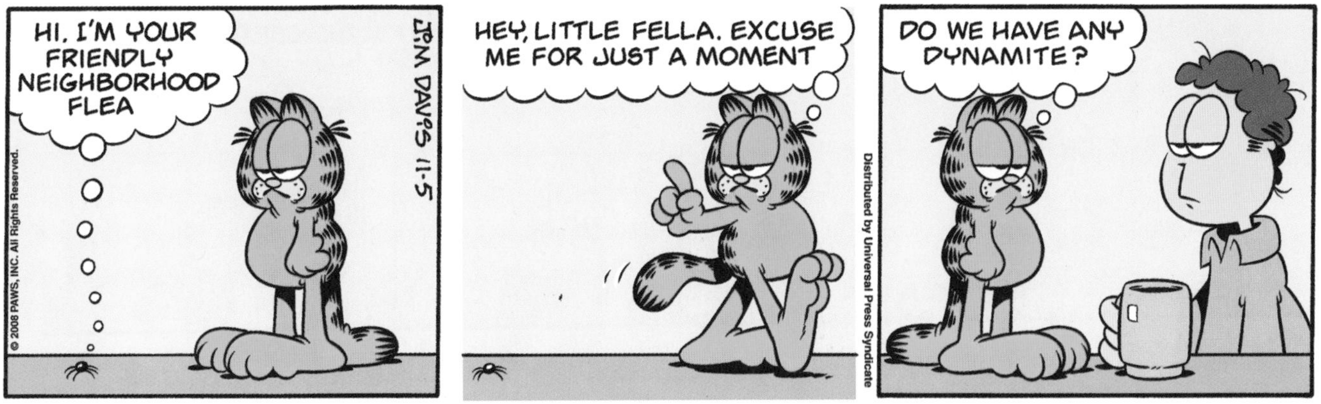
HI. I'M YOUR FRIENDLY NEIGHBORHOOD FLEA
JIM DAVIS 11-5
HEY, LITTLE FELLA. EXCUSE ME FOR JUST A MOMENT
DO WE HAVE ANY DYNAMITE?
© 2008 PAWS, INC. All Rights Reserved.
Distributed by Universal Press Syndicate

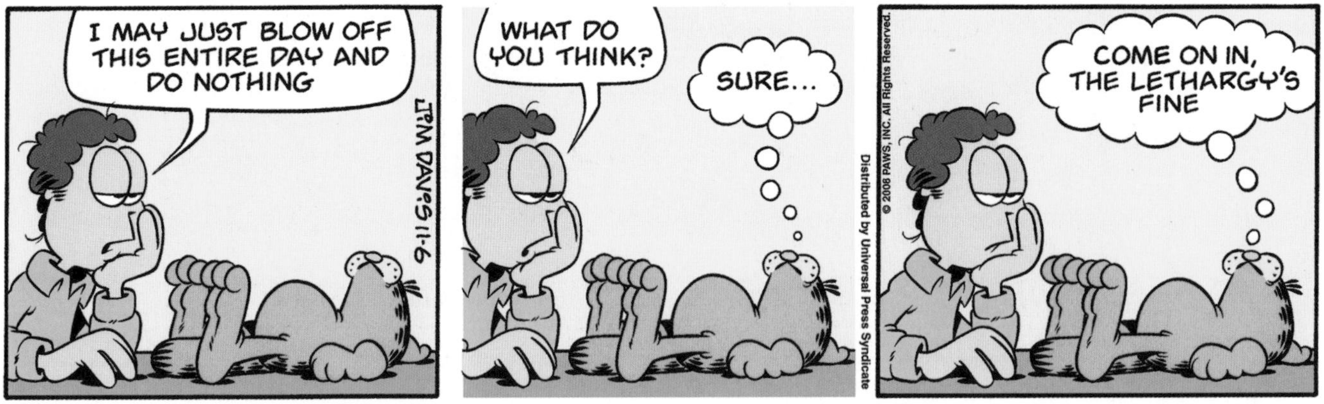
I MAY JUST BLOW OFF THIS ENTIRE DAY AND DO NOTHING
JIM DAVIS 11-6
WHAT DO YOU THINK?
SURE...
© 2008 PAWS, INC. All Rights Reserved.
Distributed by Universal Press Syndicate
COME ON IN, THE LETHARGY'S FINE

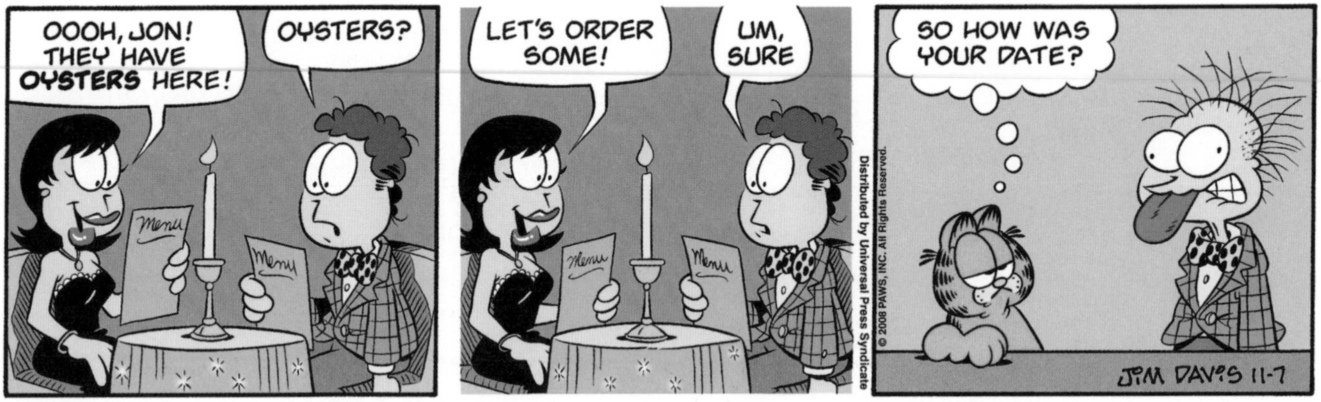
OOOH, JON! THEY HAVE **OYSTERS** HERE!
OYSTERS?
Menu
Menu
LET'S ORDER SOME!
UM, SURE
Menu
Menu
© 2008 PAWS, INC. All Rights Reserved.
Distributed by Universal Press Syndicate
SO HOW WAS YOUR DATE?
JIM DAVIS 11-7

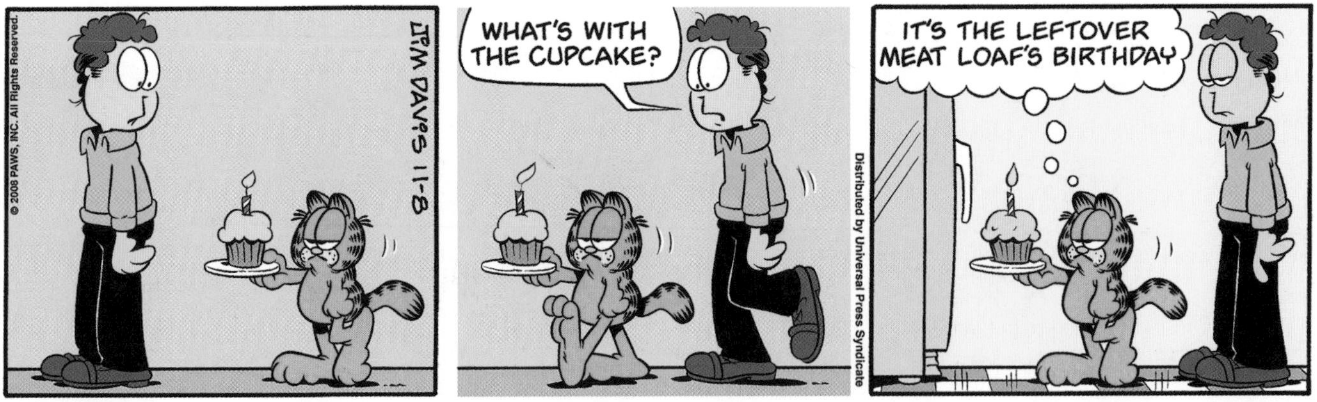
© 2008 PAWS, INC. All Rights Reserved.
JIM DAVIS 11-8
WHAT'S WITH THE CUPCAKE?
Distributed by Universal Press Syndicate
IT'S THE LEFTOVER MEAT LOAF'S BIRTHDAY

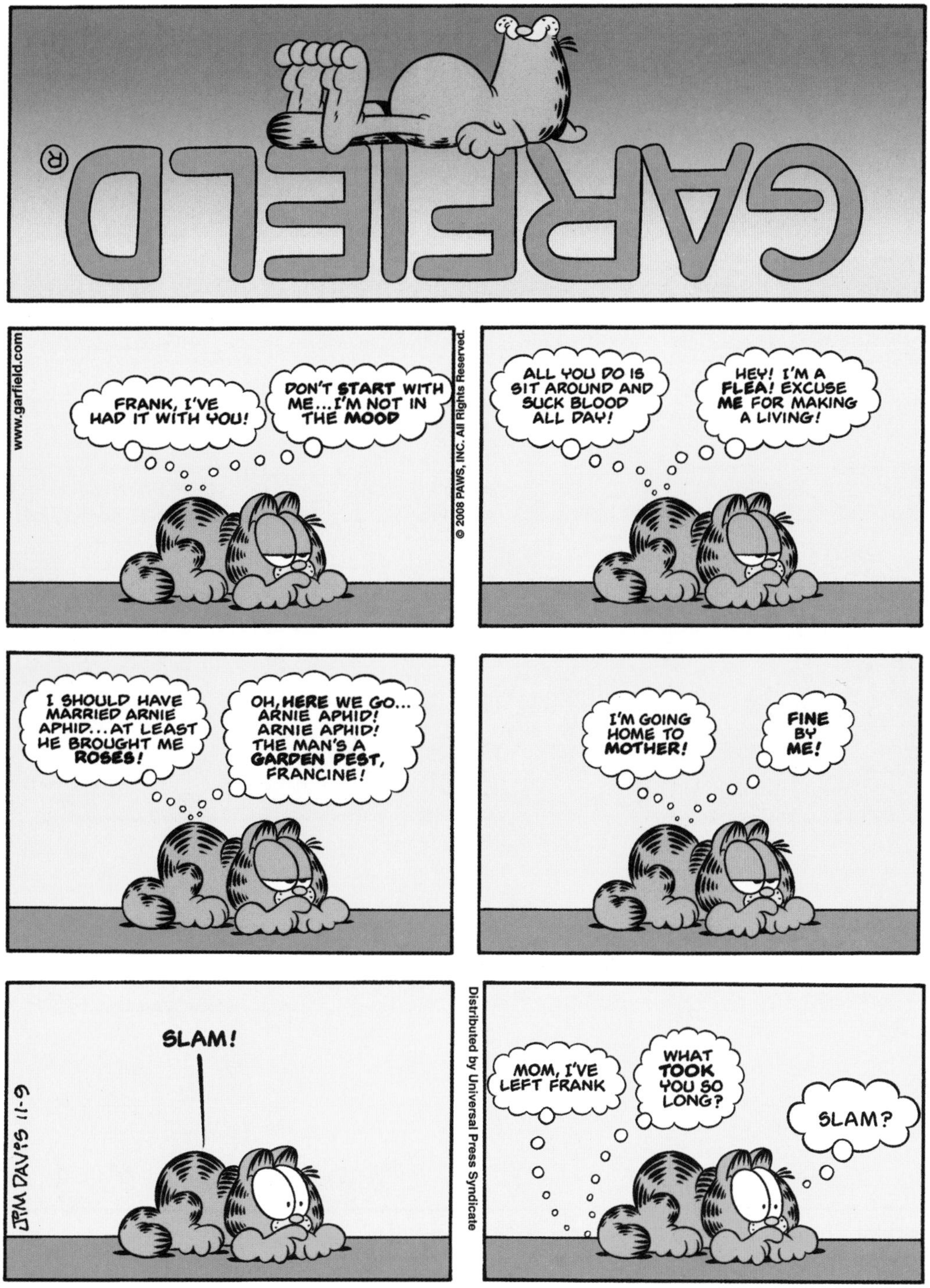
GARFIELD®
www.garfield.com
© 2008 PAWS, INC. All Rights Reserved.
FRANK, I'VE HAD IT WITH YOU!
DON'T START WITH ME... I'M NOT IN THE MOOD
ALL YOU DO IS SIT AROUND AND SUCK BLOOD ALL DAY!
HEY! I'M A FLEA! EXCUSE ME FOR MAKING A LIVING!
I SHOULD HAVE MARRIED ARNIE APHID... AT LEAST HE BROUGHT ME ROSES!
OH, HERE WE GO... ARNIE APHID! ARNIE APHID! THE MAN'S A GARDEN PEST, FRANCINE!
I'M GOING HOME TO MOTHER!
FINE BY ME!
SLAM!
JPM DAVIS 11-9
Distributed by Universal Press Syndicate
MOM, I'VE LEFT FRANK
WHAT TOOK YOU SO LONG?
SLAM?

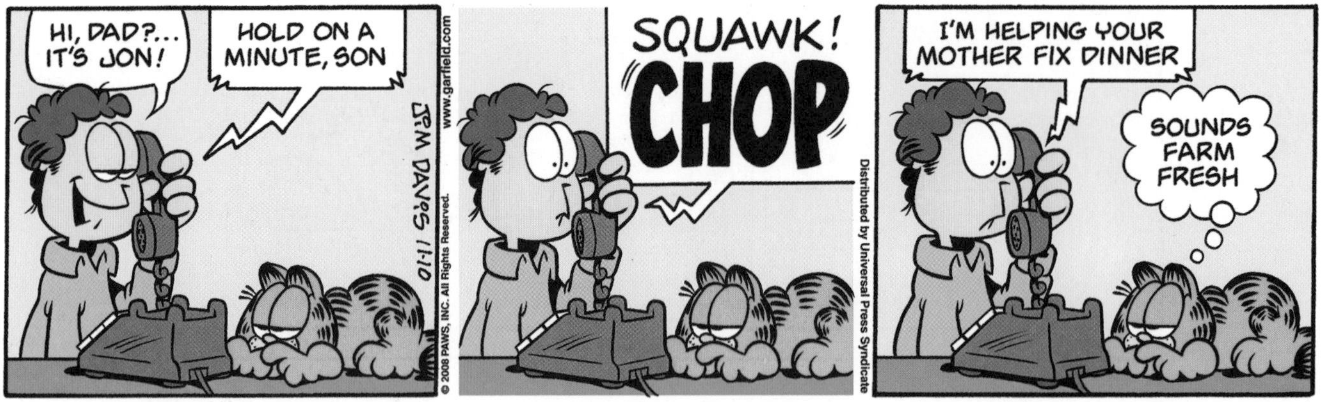
HI, DAD?... IT'S JON!
HOLD ON A MINUTE, SON
JIM DAVIS 11-10
www.garfield.com
© 2008 PAWS, INC. All Rights Reserved.
SQUAWK!
CHOP
Distributed by Universal Press Syndicate
I'M HELPING YOUR MOTHER FIX DINNER
SOUNDS FARM FRESH

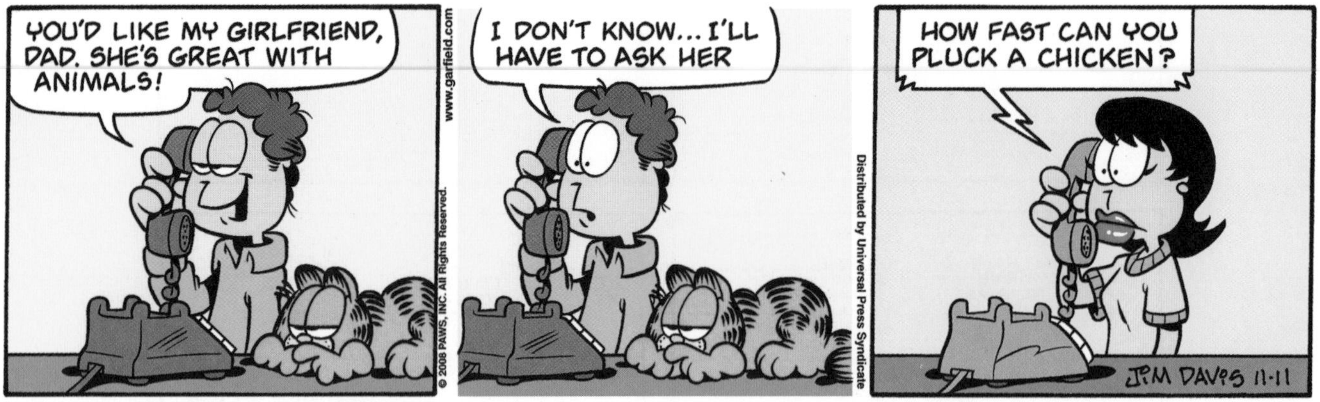
YOU'D LIKE MY GIRLFRIEND, DAD. SHE'S GREAT WITH ANIMALS!
www.garfield.com
© 2008 PAWS, INC. All Rights Reserved.
I DON'T KNOW... I'LL HAVE TO ASK HER
Distributed by Universal Press Syndicate
HOW FAST CAN YOU PLUCK A CHICKEN?
JIM DAVIS 11-11

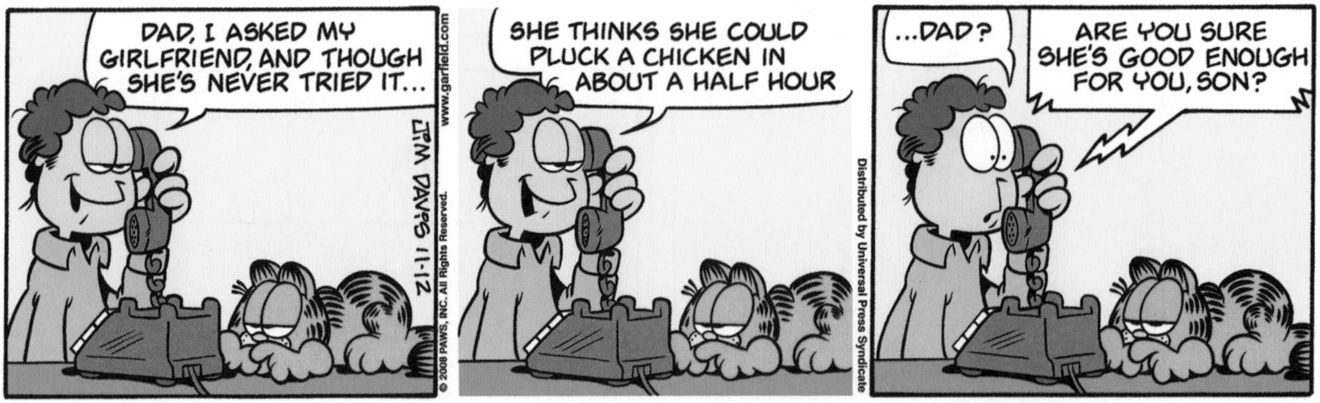
DAD, I ASKED MY GIRLFRIEND, AND THOUGH SHE'S NEVER TRIED IT...
JIM DAVIS 11-12
www.garfield.com
© 2008 PAWS, INC. All Rights Reserved.
SHE THINKS SHE COULD PLUCK A CHICKEN IN ABOUT A HALF HOUR
Distributed by Universal Press Syndicate
...DAD?
ARE YOU SURE SHE'S GOOD ENOUGH FOR YOU, SON?

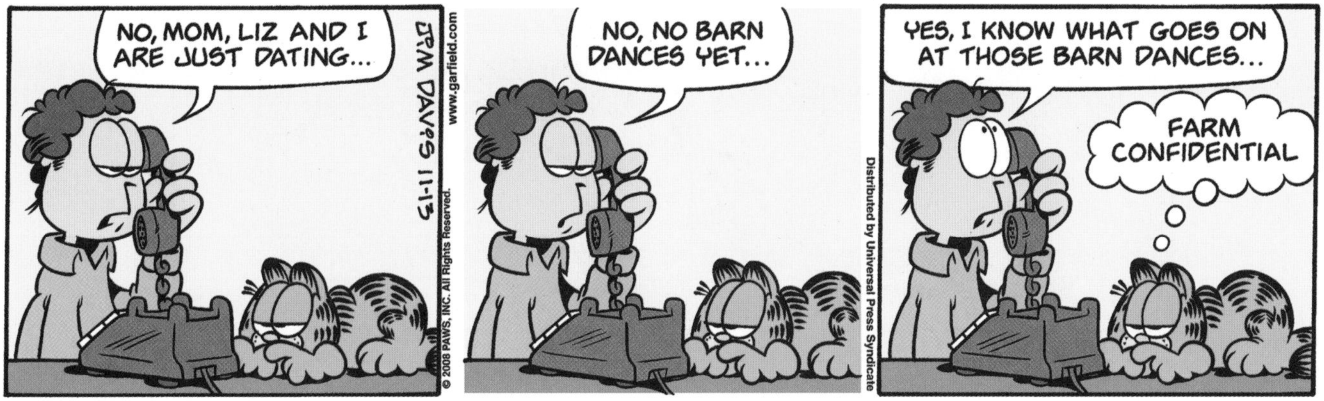

NO, MOM, LIZ AND I ARE JUST DATING...
JIM DAVIS 11-13
www.garfield.com
© 2008 PAWS, INC. All Rights Reserved.
NO, NO BARN DANCES YET...
Distributed by Universal Press Syndicate
YES, I KNOW WHAT GOES ON AT THOSE BARN DANCES...
FARM CONFIDENTIAL

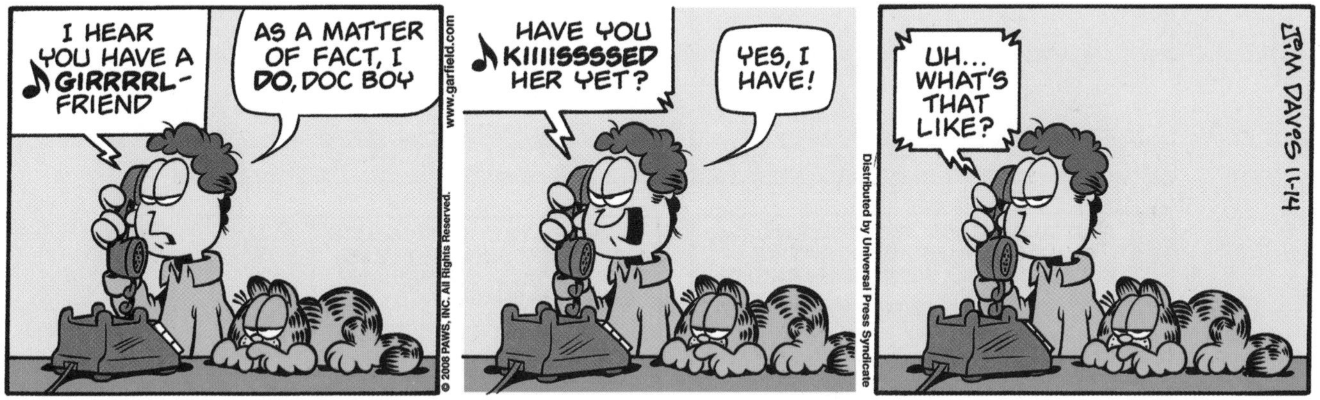

I HEAR YOU HAVE A ♪GIRRRRL-FRIEND
AS A MATTER OF FACT, I DO, DOC BOY
www.garfield.com
© 2008 PAWS, INC. All Rights Reserved.
♪HAVE YOU KIIIISSSSED HER YET?
YES, I HAVE!
Distributed by Universal Press Syndicate
UH... WHAT'S THAT LIKE?
JIM DAVIS 11-14

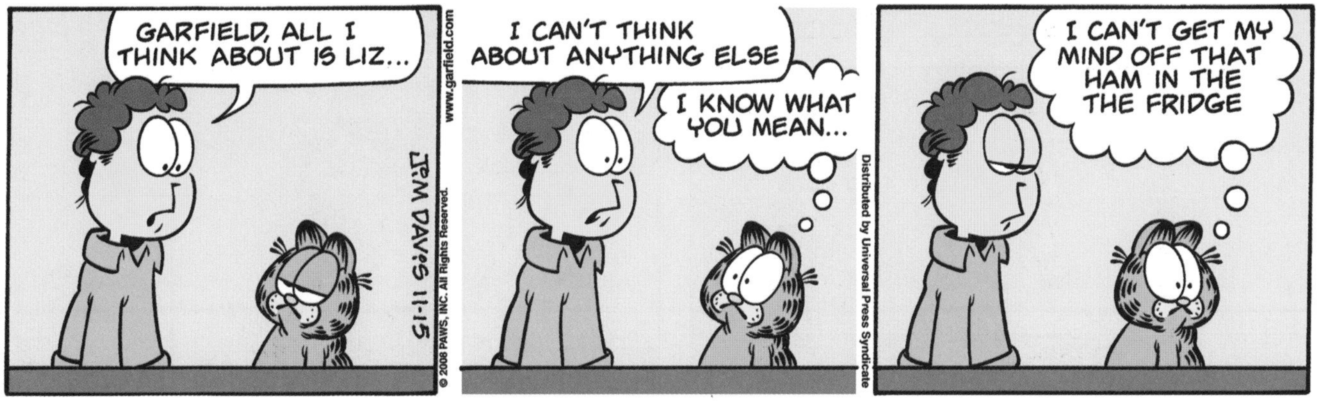

GARFIELD, ALL I THINK ABOUT IS LIZ...
www.garfield.com
JIM DAVIS 11-15
© 2008 PAWS, INC. All Rights Reserved.
I CAN'T THINK ABOUT ANYTHING ELSE
I KNOW WHAT YOU MEAN...
Distributed by Universal Press Syndicate
I CAN'T GET MY MIND OFF THAT HAM IN THE THE FRIDGE

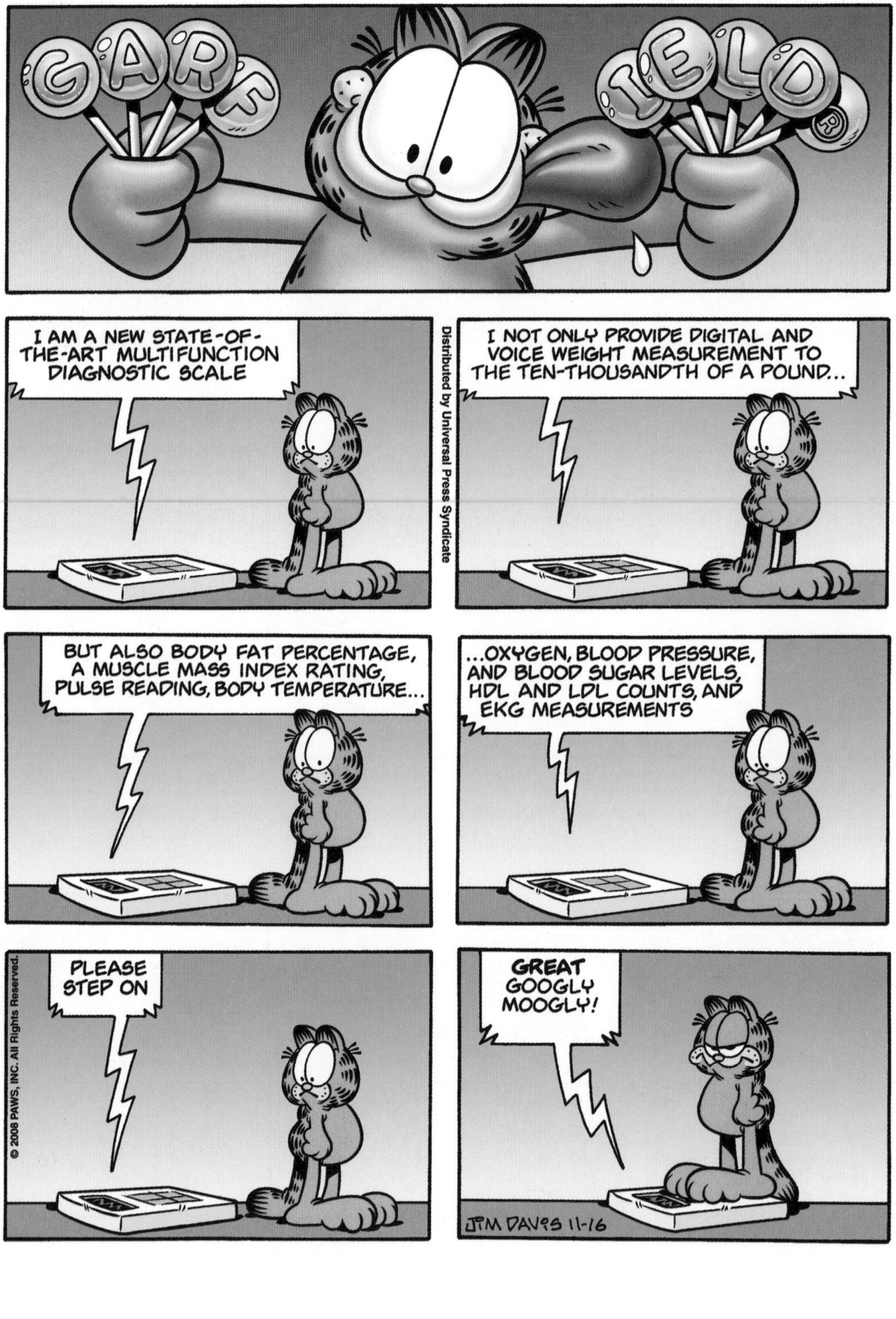

GARFIELD®
I AM A NEW STATE-OF-THE-ART MULTIFUNCTION DIAGNOSTIC SCALE
I NOT ONLY PROVIDE DIGITAL AND VOICE WEIGHT MEASUREMENT TO THE TEN-THOUSANDTH OF A POUND...
BUT ALSO BODY FAT PERCENTAGE, A MUSCLE MASS INDEX RATING, PULSE READING, BODY TEMPERATURE...
...OXYGEN, BLOOD PRESSURE, AND BLOOD SUGAR LEVELS, HDL AND LDL COUNTS, AND EKG MEASUREMENTS
PLEASE STEP ON
GREAT GOOGLY MOOGLY!
JIM DAVIS 11-16
Distributed by Universal Press Syndicate
© 2008 PAWS, INC. All Rights Reserved.

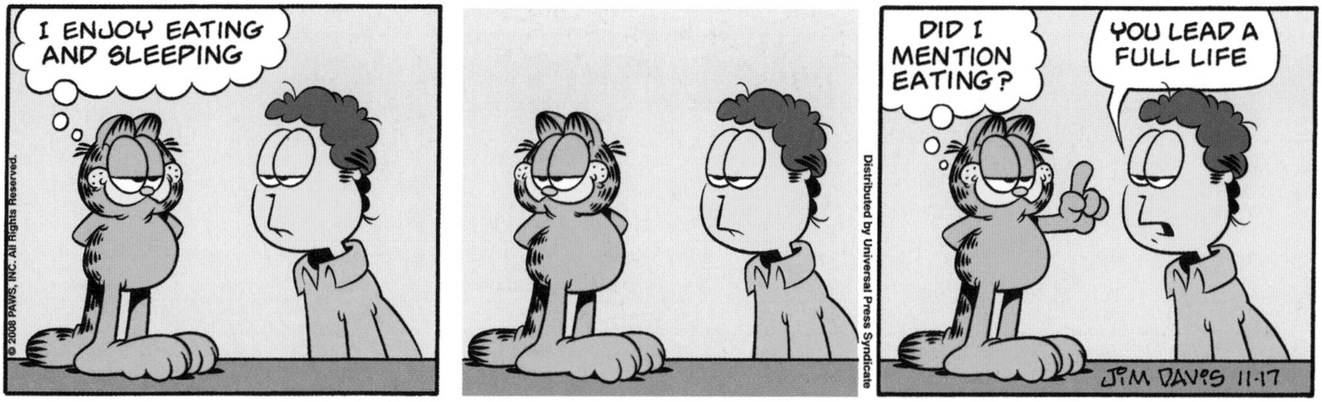
I ENJOY EATING AND SLEEPING
DID I MENTION EATING?
YOU LEAD A FULL LIFE
JIM DAVIS 11-17
© 2008 PAWS, INC. All Rights Reserved.
Distributed by Universal Press Syndicate

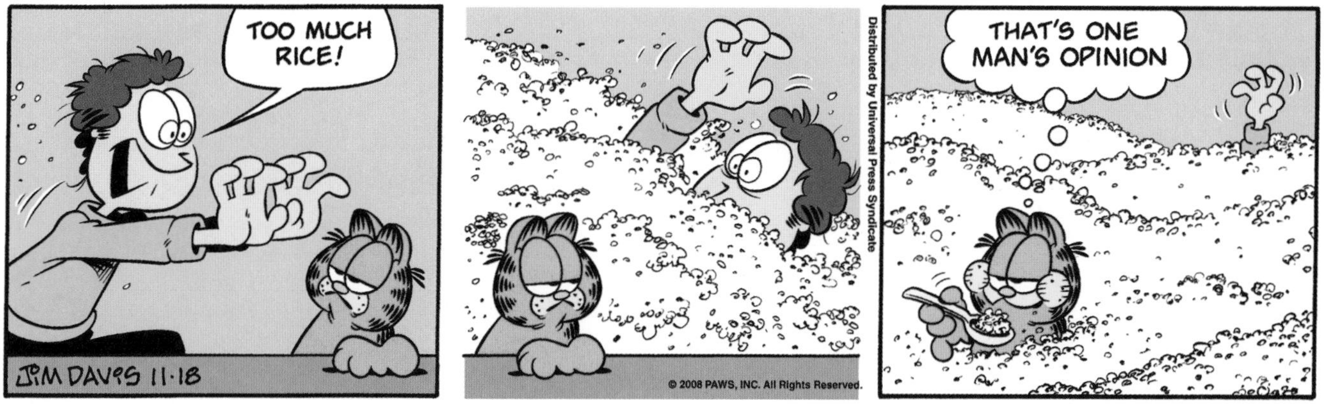
TOO MUCH RICE!
THAT'S ONE MAN'S OPINION
JIM DAVIS 11-18
© 2008 PAWS, INC. All Rights Reserved.
Distributed by Universal Press Syndicate

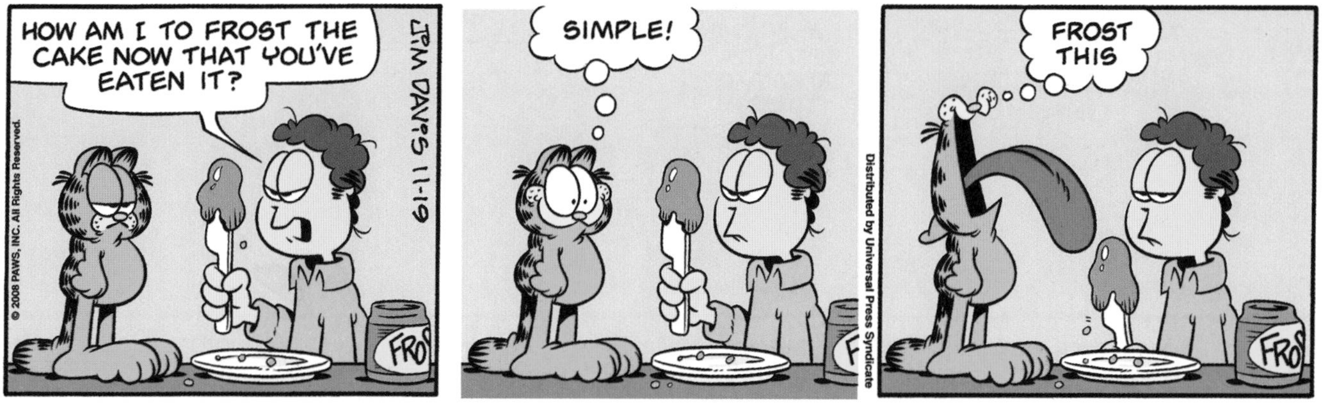
HOW AM I TO FROST THE CAKE NOW THAT YOU'VE EATEN IT?
SIMPLE!
FROST THIS
JIM DAVIS 11-19
© 2008 PAWS, INC. All Rights Reserved.
Distributed by Universal Press Syndicate

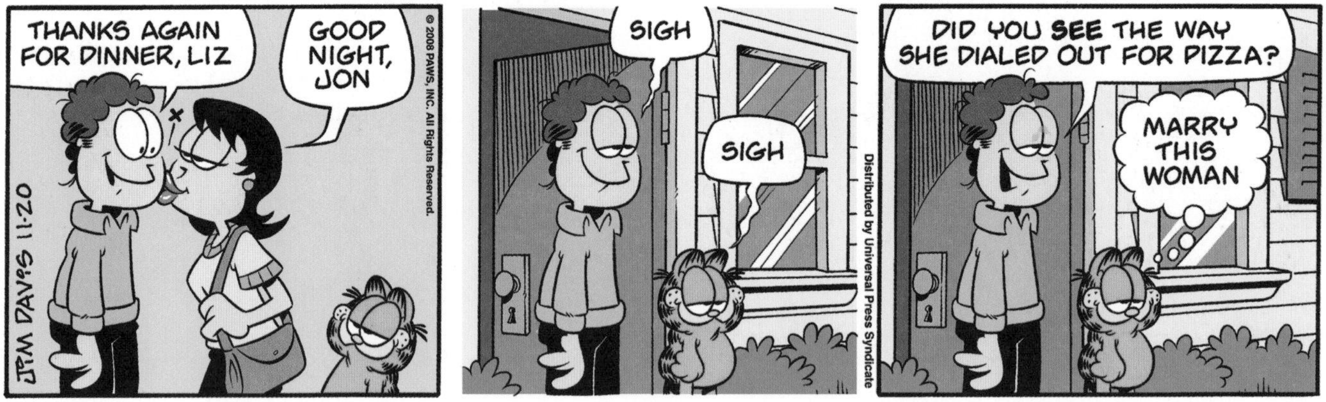
THANKS AGAIN FOR DINNER, LIZ
GOOD NIGHT, JON
© 2008 PAWS, INC. All Rights Reserved.
JIM DAVIS 11-20
SIGH
SIGH
Distributed by Universal Press Syndicate
DID YOU SEE THE WAY SHE DIALED OUT FOR PIZZA?
MARRY THIS WOMAN

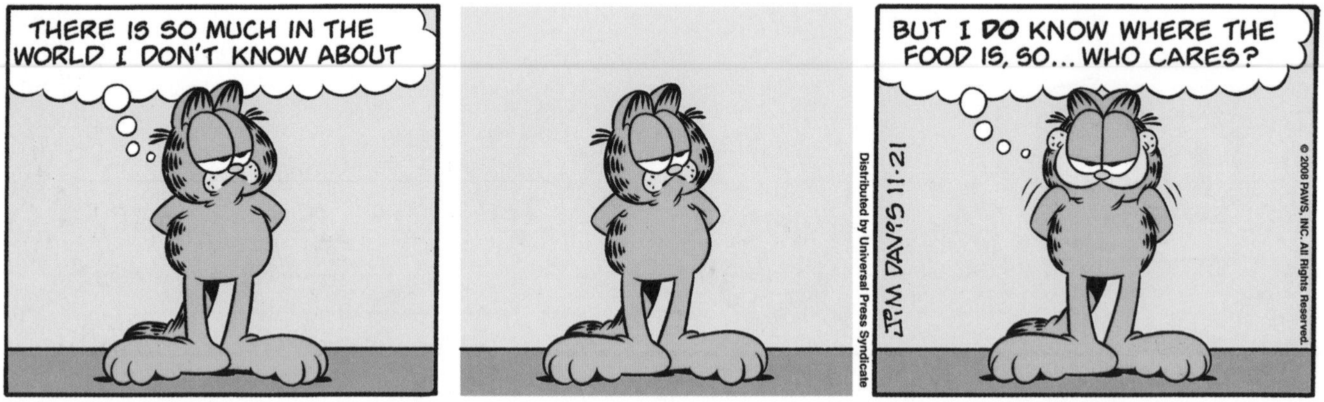
THERE IS SO MUCH IN THE WORLD I DON'T KNOW ABOUT
Distributed by Universal Press Syndicate
JIM DAVIS 11-21
BUT I DO KNOW WHERE THE FOOD IS, SO... WHO CARES?
© 2008 PAWS, INC. All Rights Reserved.

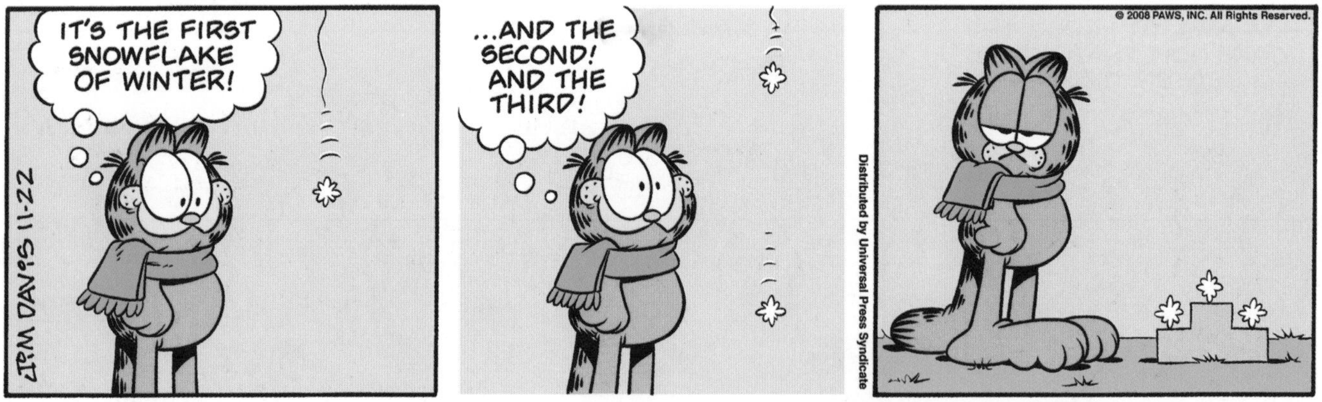
IT'S THE FIRST SNOWFLAKE OF WINTER!
JIM DAVIS 11-22
...AND THE SECOND! AND THE THIRD!
Distributed by Universal Press Syndicate
© 2008 PAWS, INC. All Rights Reserved.

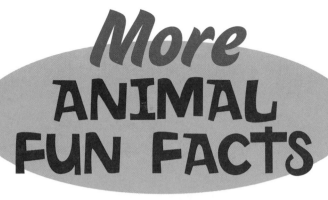

More ANIMAL FUN FACTS

THE SKIN OF A HIPPOPOTAMUS PRODUCES A PINK FLUID THAT PROTECTS IT AGAINST SUNBURN AND INFECTIONS.

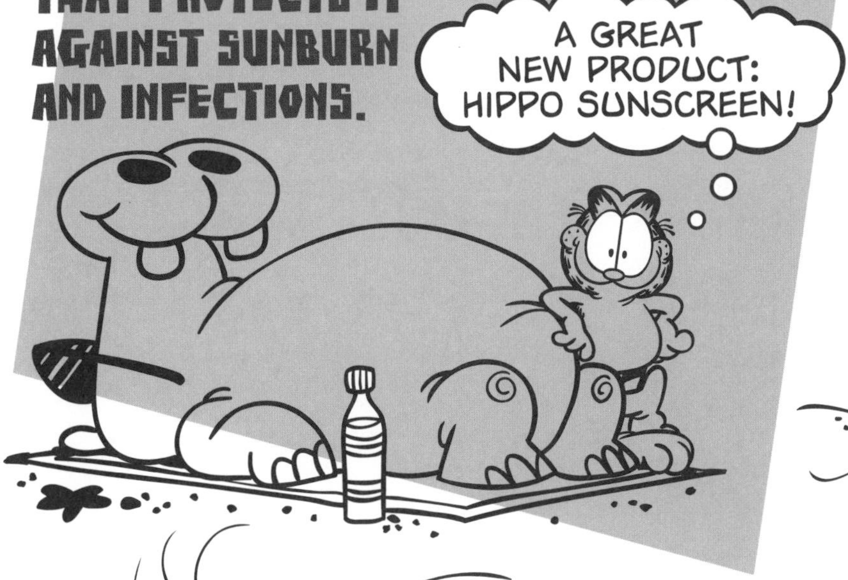
A GREAT NEW PRODUCT: HIPPO SUNSCREEN!

A DROMEDARY HAS ONE HUMP; A CAMEL HAS TWO HUMPS.

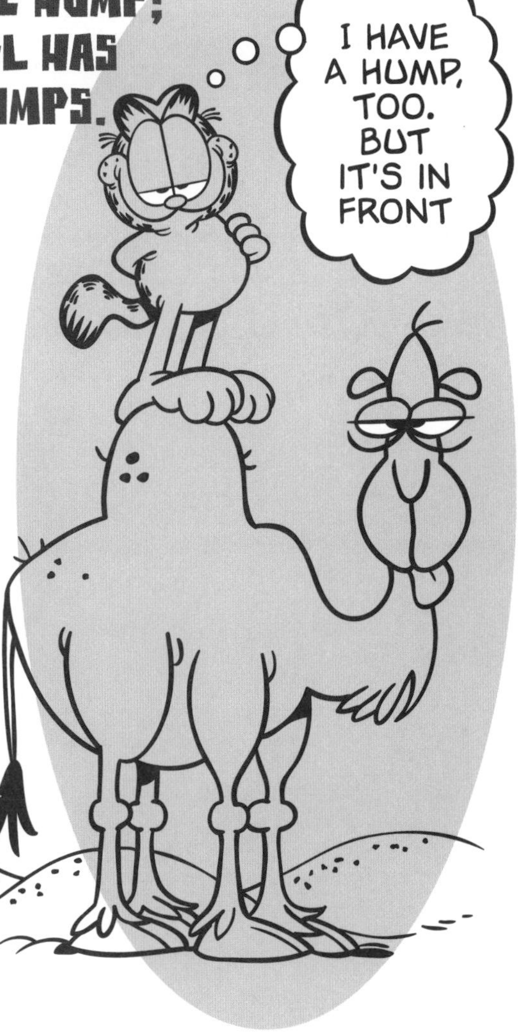
I HAVE A HUMP, TOO. BUT IT'S IN FRONT

A CHEETAH CAN RUN 75 MPH.

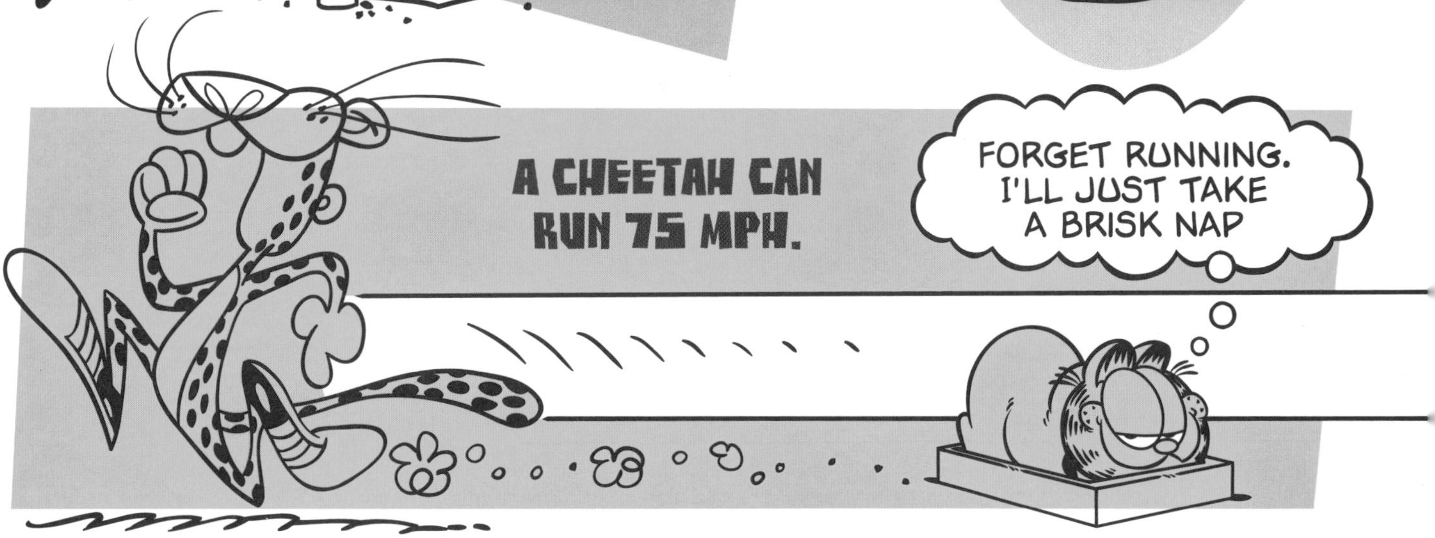
FORGET RUNNING. I'LL JUST TAKE A BRISK NAP

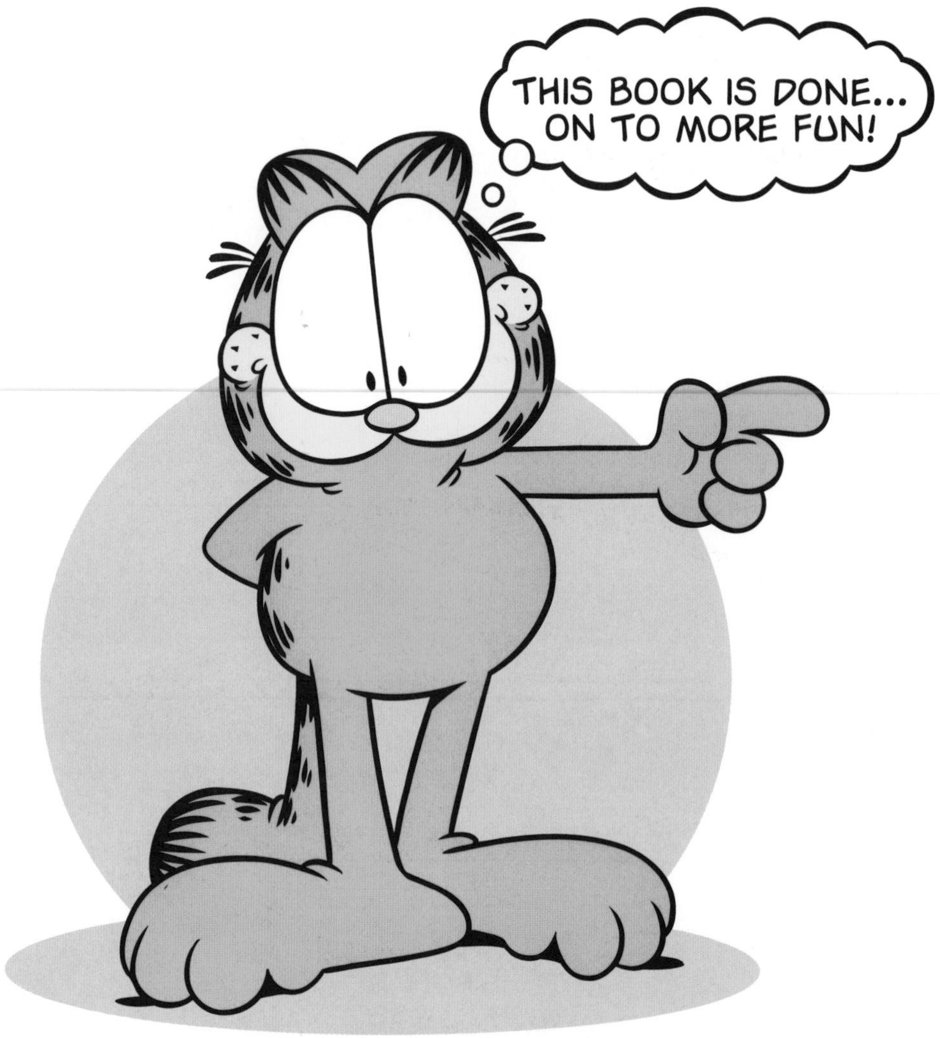
THIS BOOK IS DONE... ON TO MORE FUN!

Garfield
Brings Home the Bacon

BY JIM DAVIS

Ballantine Books ● **New York**

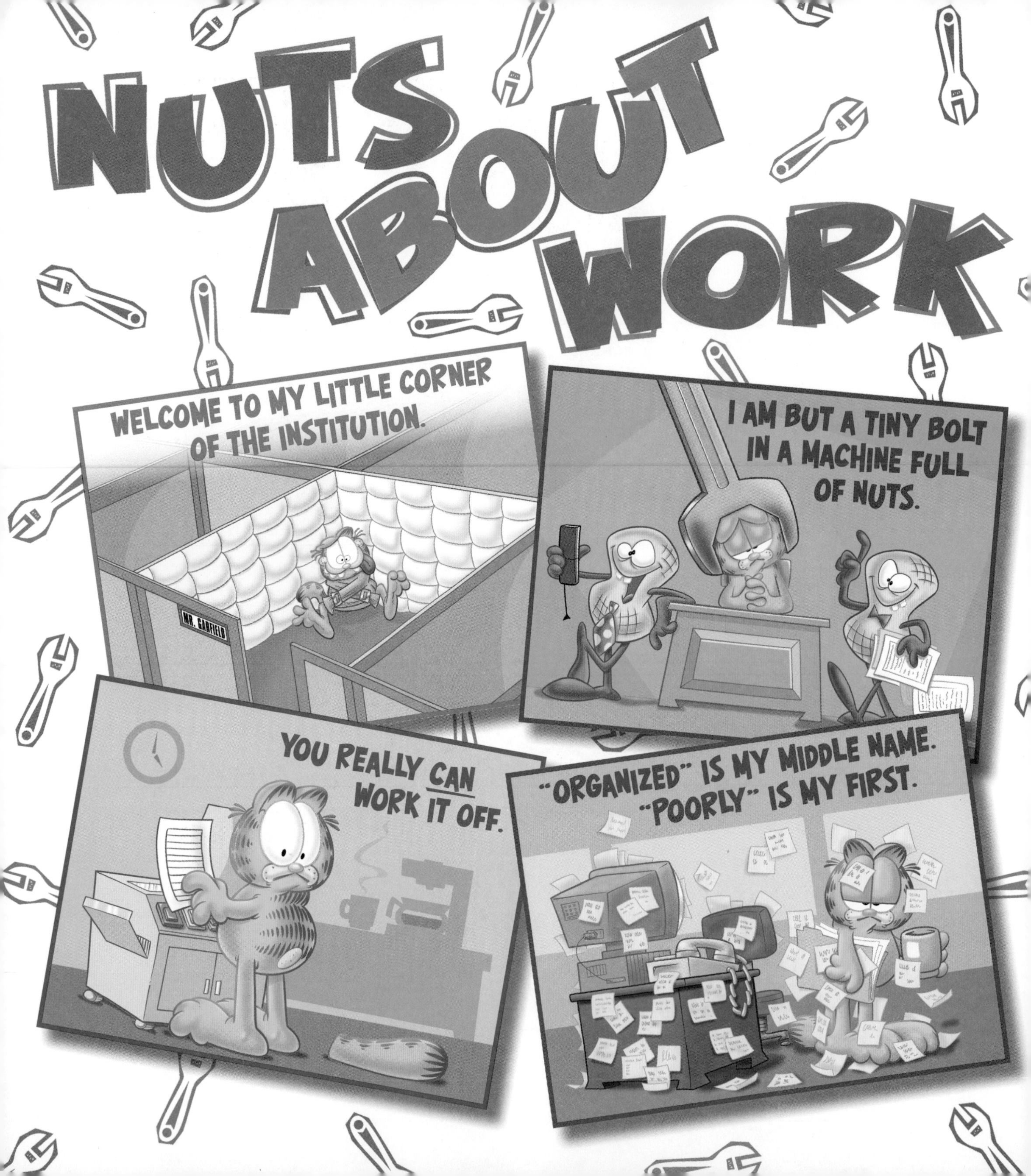

NUTS ABOUT WORK
WELCOME TO MY LITTLE CORNER OF THE INSTITUTION.
MR. GARFIELD
I AM BUT A TINY BOLT IN A MACHINE FULL OF NUTS.
YOU REALLY CAN WORK IT OFF.
"ORGANIZED" IS MY MIDDLE NAME. "POORLY" IS MY FIRST.

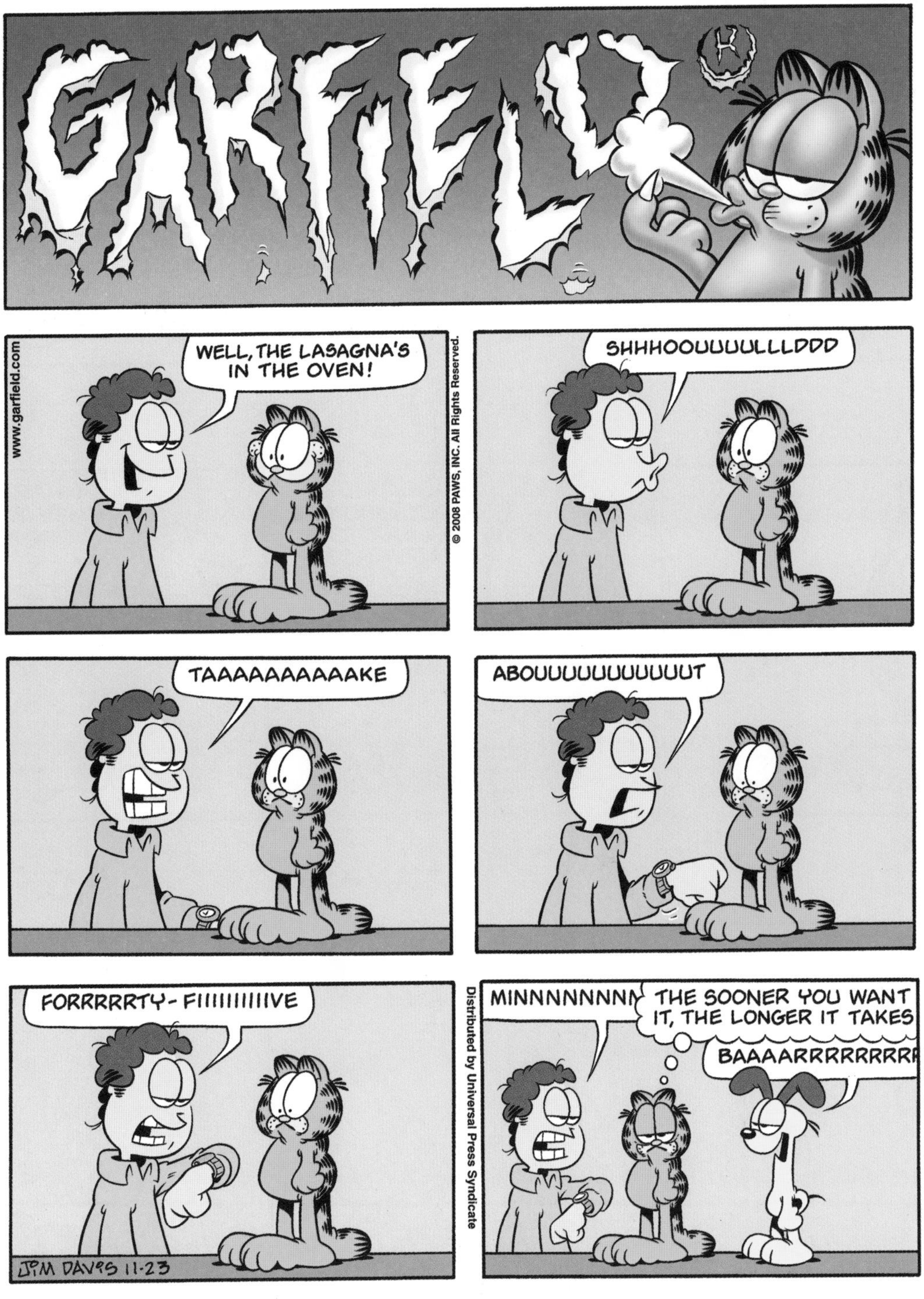
GARFIELD
www.garfield.com
WELL, THE LASAGNA'S IN THE OVEN!
© 2008 PAWS, INC. All Rights Reserved.
SHHHOOUUUUULLLDDD
TAAAAAAAAAAKE
ABOUUUUUUUUUUUT
FORRRRRTY- FIIIIIIIIIIVE
JIM DAVIS 11-23
Distributed by Universal Press Syndicate
MINNNNNNNN
THE SOONER YOU WANT IT, THE LONGER IT TAKES
BAAAARRRRRRRRR

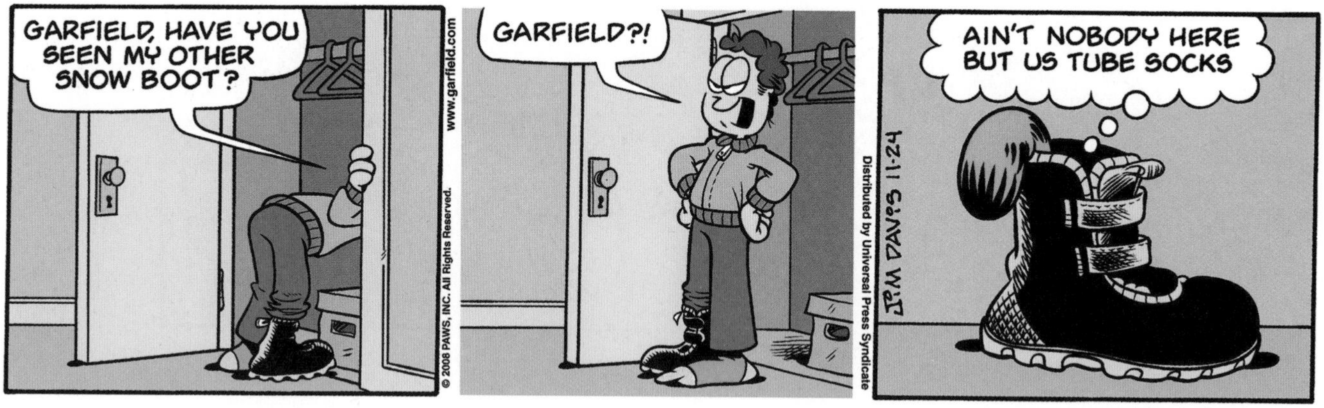
GARFIELD, HAVE YOU SEEN MY OTHER SNOW BOOT?
© 2008 PAWS, INC. All Rights Reserved. www.garfield.com
GARFIELD?!
Distributed by Universal Press Syndicate
AIN'T NOBODY HERE BUT US TUBE SOCKS
JIM DAVIS 11-24

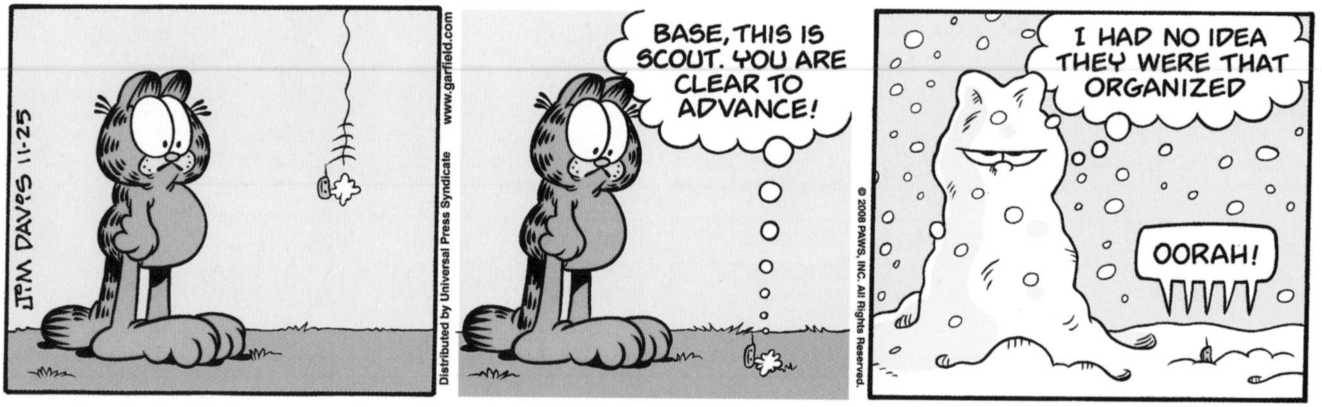
JIM DAVIS 11-25
Distributed by Universal Press Syndicate www.garfield.com
BASE, THIS IS SCOUT. YOU ARE CLEAR TO ADVANCE!
© 2008 PAWS, INC. All Rights Reserved.
I HAD NO IDEA THEY WERE THAT ORGANIZED
OORAH!

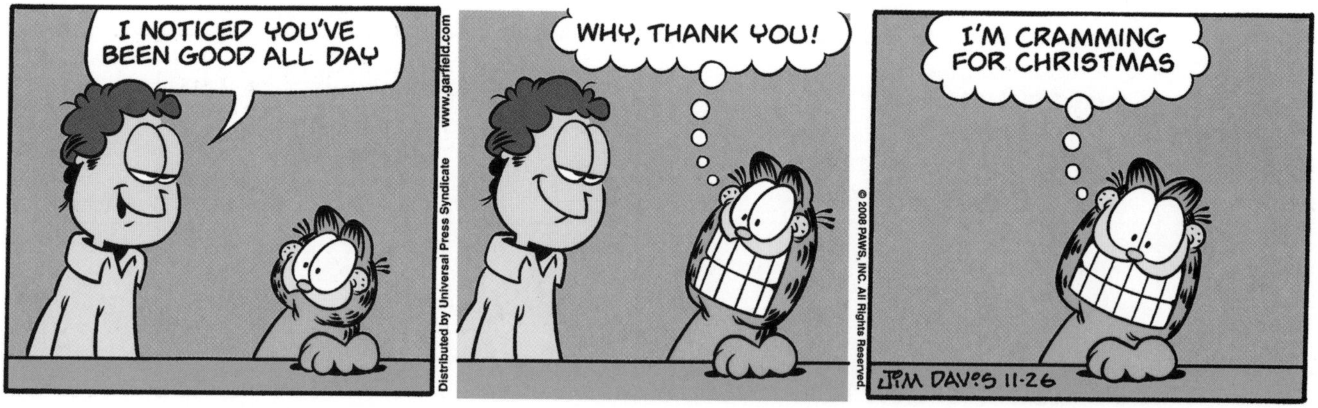
I NOTICED YOU'VE BEEN GOOD ALL DAY
Distributed by Universal Press Syndicate www.garfield.com
WHY, THANK YOU!
© 2008 PAWS, INC. All Rights Reserved.
I'M CRAMMING FOR CHRISTMAS
JIM DAVIS 11-26

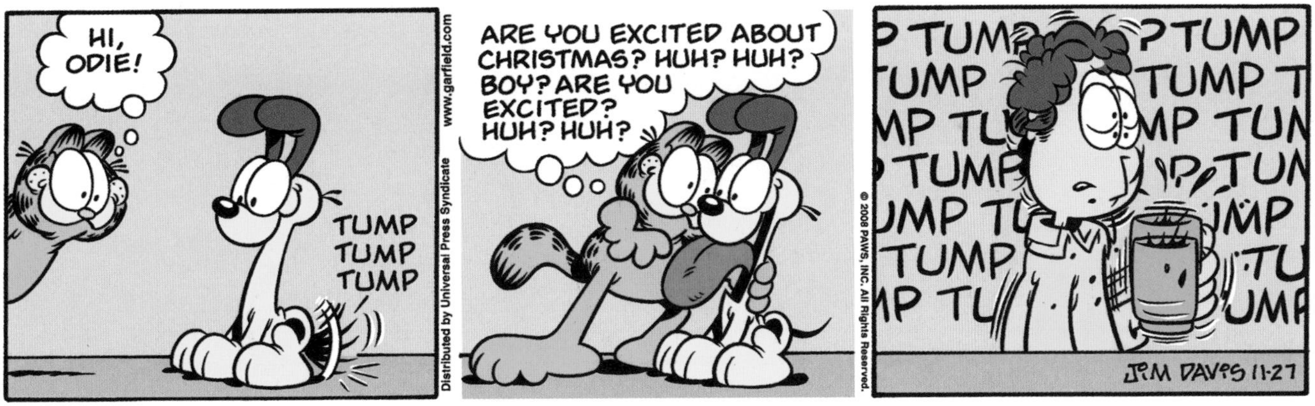
HI, ODIE!
TUMP TUMP TUMP
Distributed by Universal Press Syndicate www.garfield.com
ARE YOU EXCITED ABOUT CHRISTMAS? HUH? HUH? BOY? ARE YOU EXCITED? HUH? HUH?
© 2008 PAWS, INC. All Rights Reserved.
TUMP TUMP TUMP TUMP TUMP
JIM DAVIS 11-27

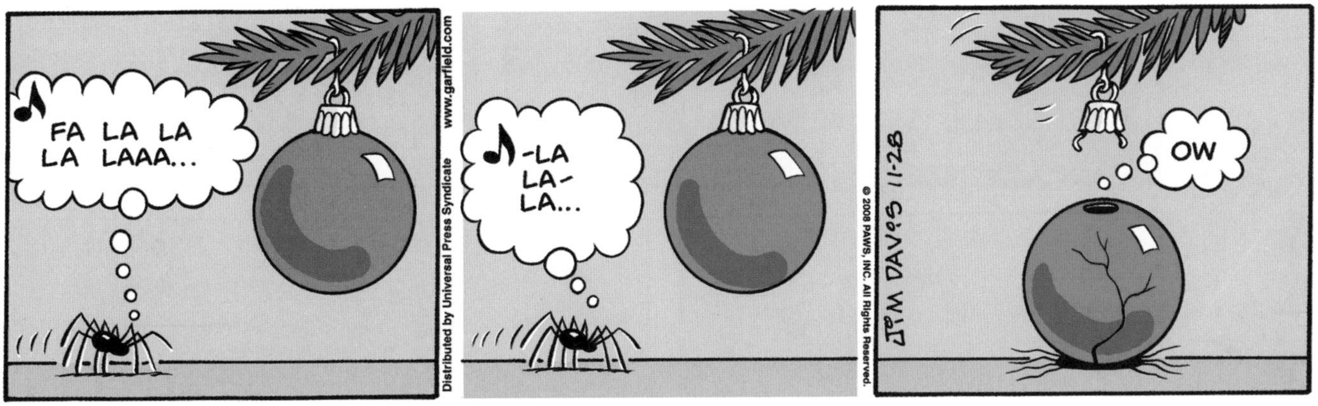
FA LA LA LA LAAA...
Distributed by Universal Press Syndicate www.garfield.com
-LA LA-LA...
© 2008 PAWS, INC. All Rights Reserved.
JIM DAVIS 11-28
OW

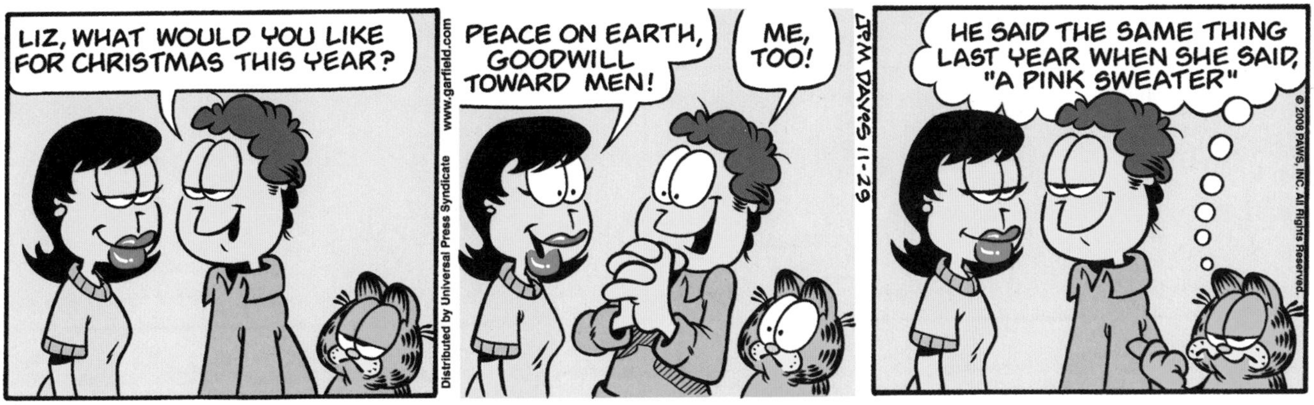
LIZ, WHAT WOULD YOU LIKE FOR CHRISTMAS THIS YEAR?
Distributed by Universal Press Syndicate www.garfield.com
PEACE ON EARTH, GOODWILL TOWARD MEN!
ME, TOO!
JIM DAVIS 11-29
HE SAID THE SAME THING LAST YEAR WHEN SHE SAID, "A PINK SWEATER"
© 2008 PAWS, INC. All Rights Reserved.

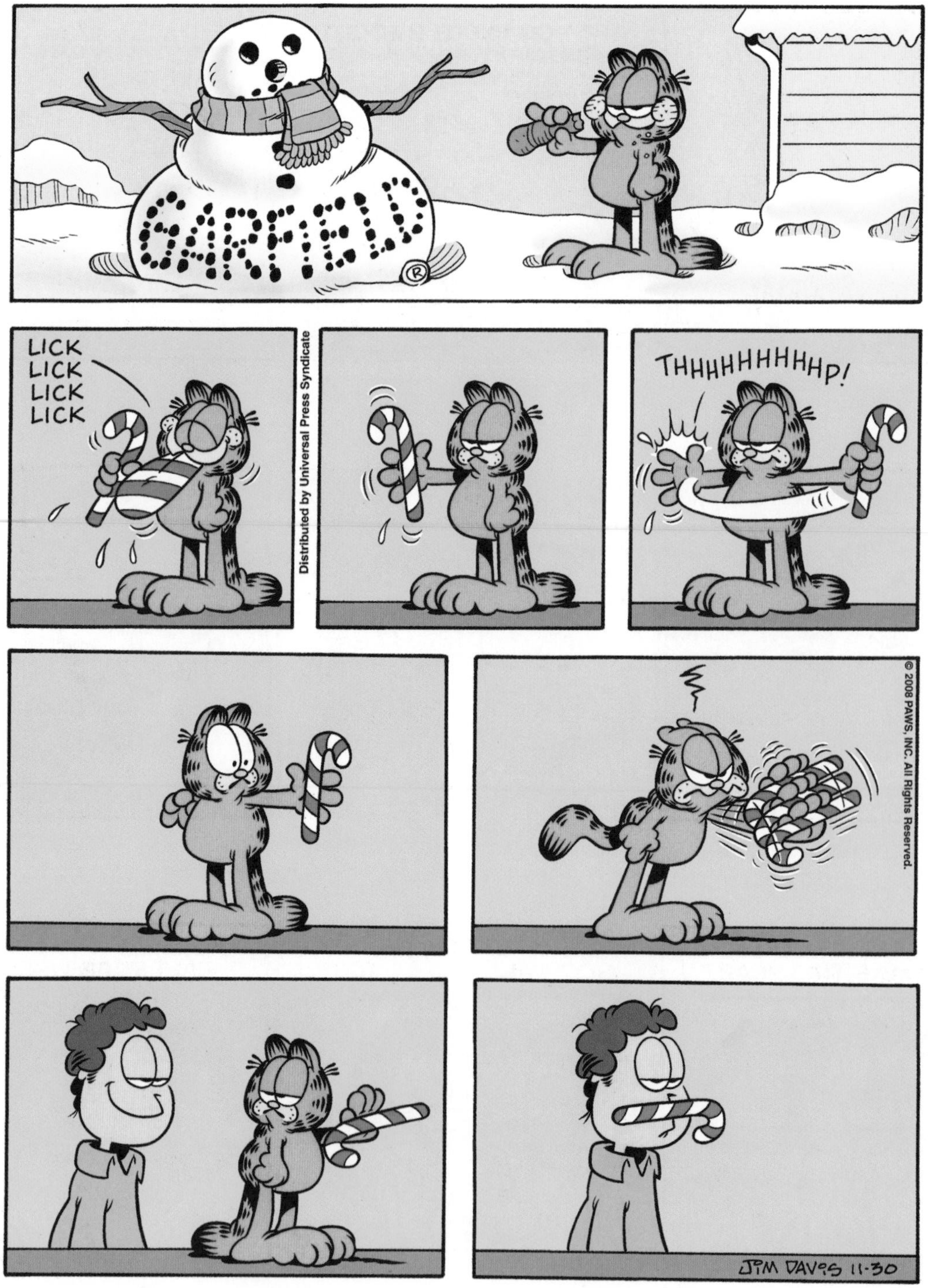
GARFIELD®
Distributed by Universal Press Syndicate
LICK
LICK
LICK
LICK
THHHHHHHHHP!
© 2008 PAWS, INC. All Rights Reserved.
JIM DAVIS 11-30

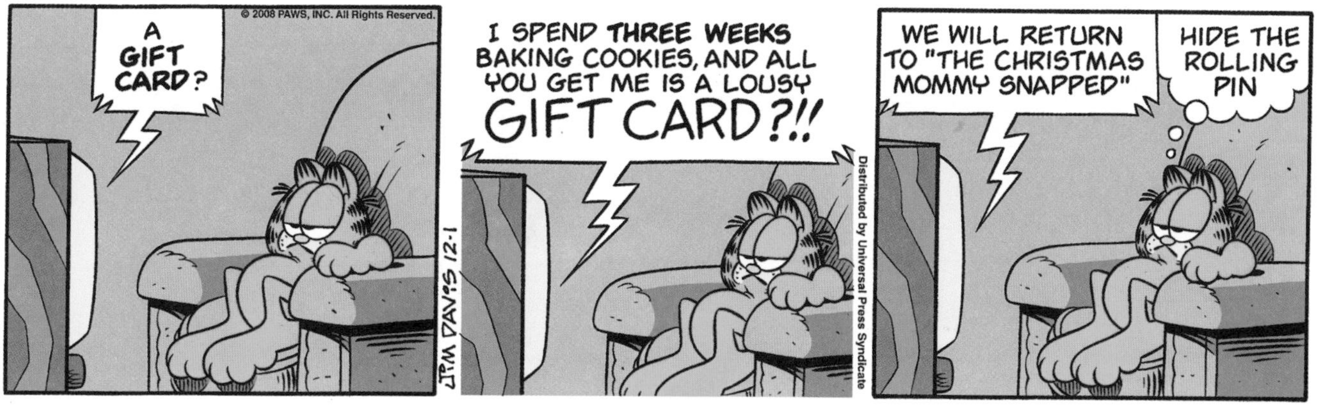
© 2008 PAWS, INC. All Rights Reserved.
A GIFT CARD?
JIM DAVIS 12-1
I SPEND THREE WEEKS BAKING COOKIES, AND ALL YOU GET ME IS A LOUSY GIFT CARD?!!
Distributed by Universal Press Syndicate
WE WILL RETURN TO "THE CHRISTMAS MOMMY SNAPPED"
HIDE THE ROLLING PIN

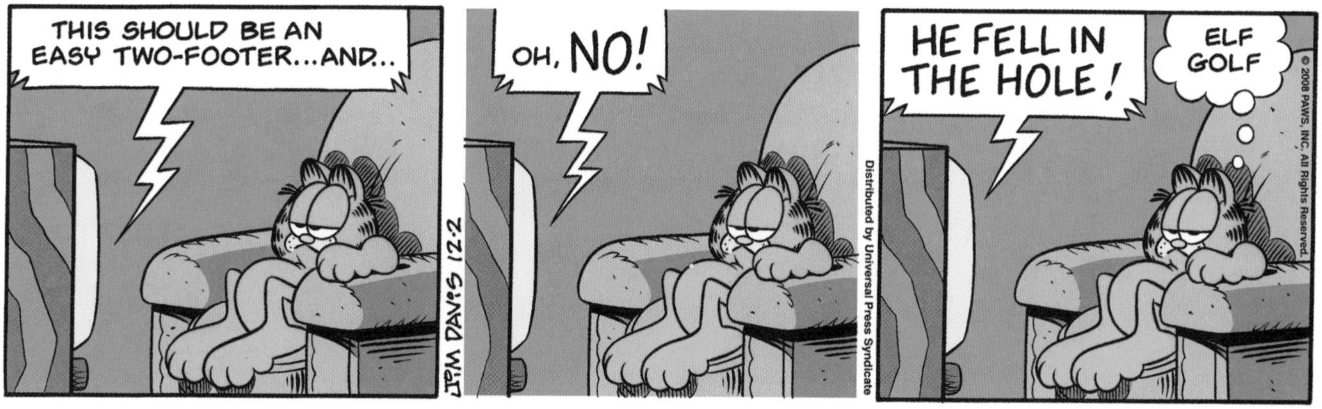
THIS SHOULD BE AN EASY TWO-FOOTER...AND...
JIM DAVIS 12-2
OH, NO!
Distributed by Universal Press Syndicate
HE FELL IN THE HOLE!
ELF GOLF
© 2008 PAWS, INC. All Rights Reserved.

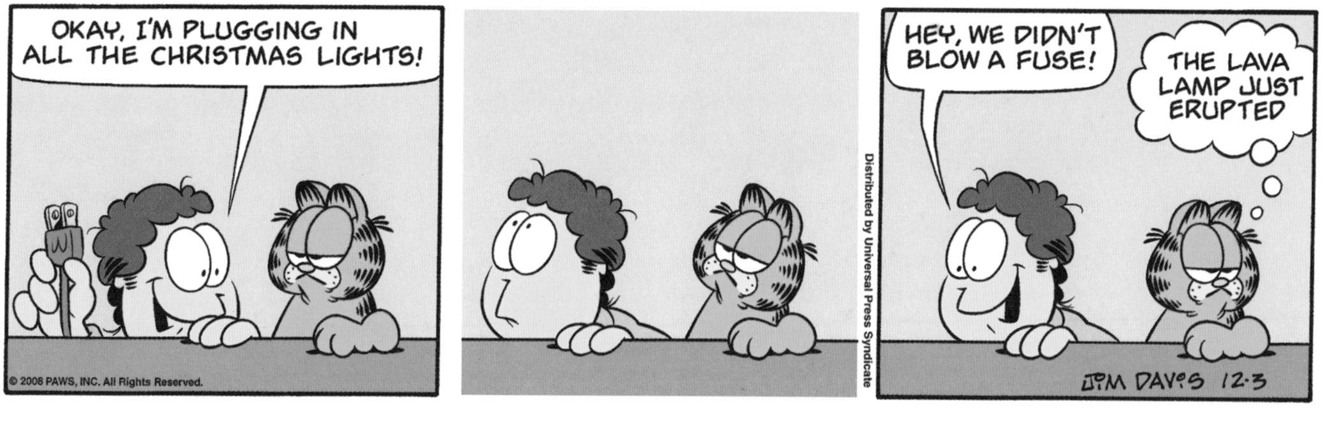
OKAY, I'M PLUGGING IN ALL THE CHRISTMAS LIGHTS!
© 2008 PAWS, INC. All Rights Reserved.
Distributed by Universal Press Syndicate
HEY, WE DIDN'T BLOW A FUSE!
THE LAVA LAMP JUST ERUPTED
JIM DAVIS 12-3

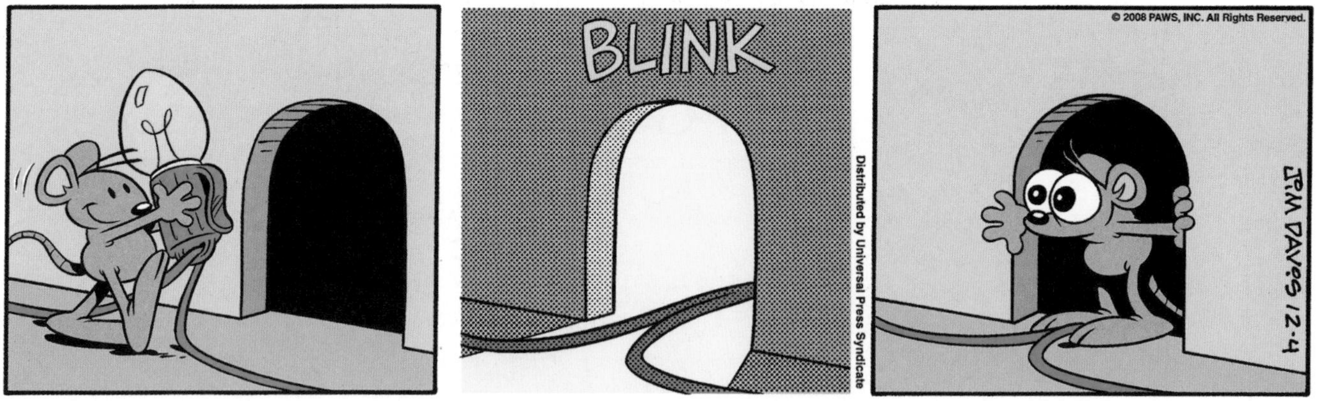
BLINK
Distributed by Universal Press Syndicate
© 2008 PAWS, INC. All Rights Reserved.
JIM DAVIS 12·4

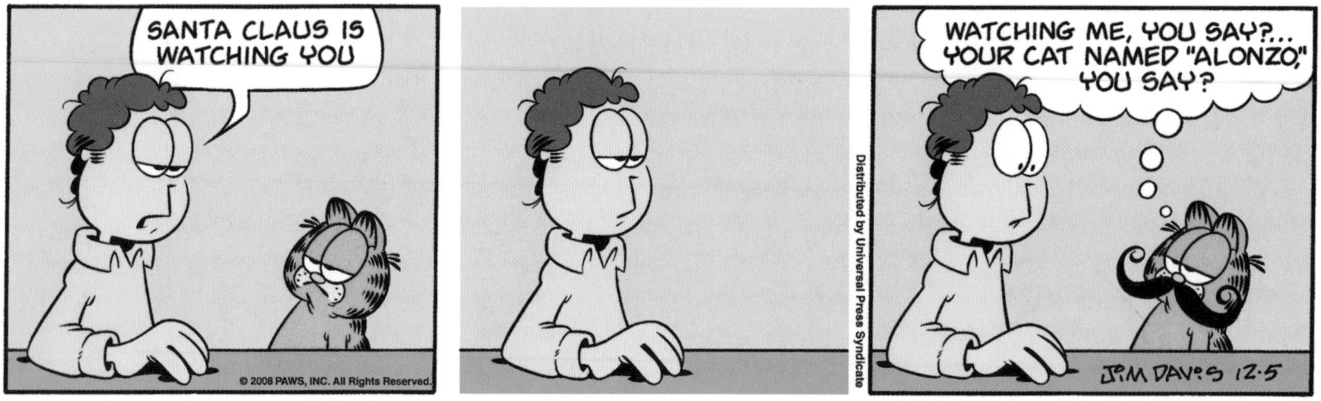
SANTA CLAUS IS WATCHING YOU
© 2008 PAWS, INC. All Rights Reserved.
Distributed by Universal Press Syndicate
WATCHING ME, YOU SAY?... YOUR CAT NAMED "ALONZO," YOU SAY?
JIM DAVIS 12·5

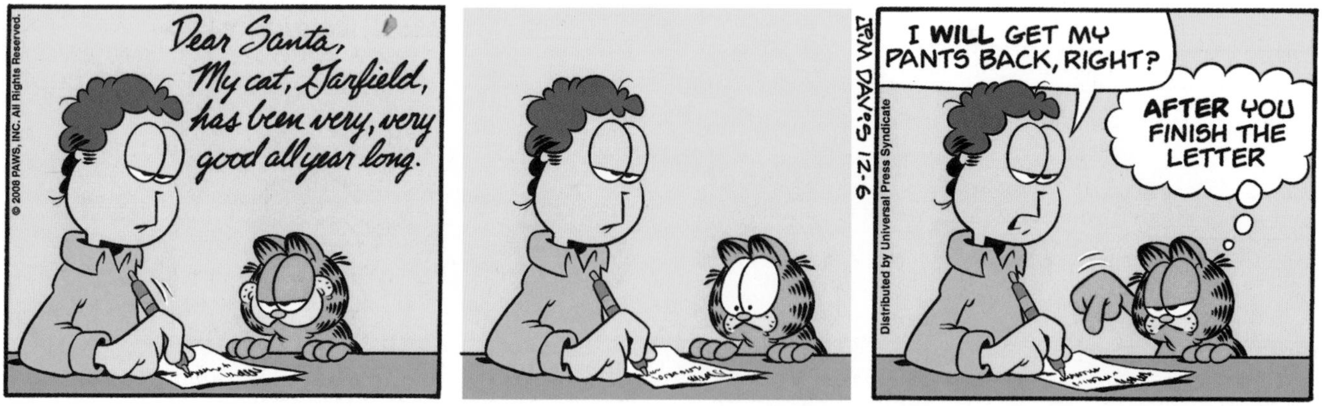
© 2008 PAWS, INC. All Rights Reserved.
Dear Santa,
My cat, Garfield, has been very, very good all year long.
JIM DAVIS 12·6
Distributed by Universal Press Syndicate
I WILL GET MY PANTS BACK, RIGHT?
AFTER YOU FINISH THE LETTER

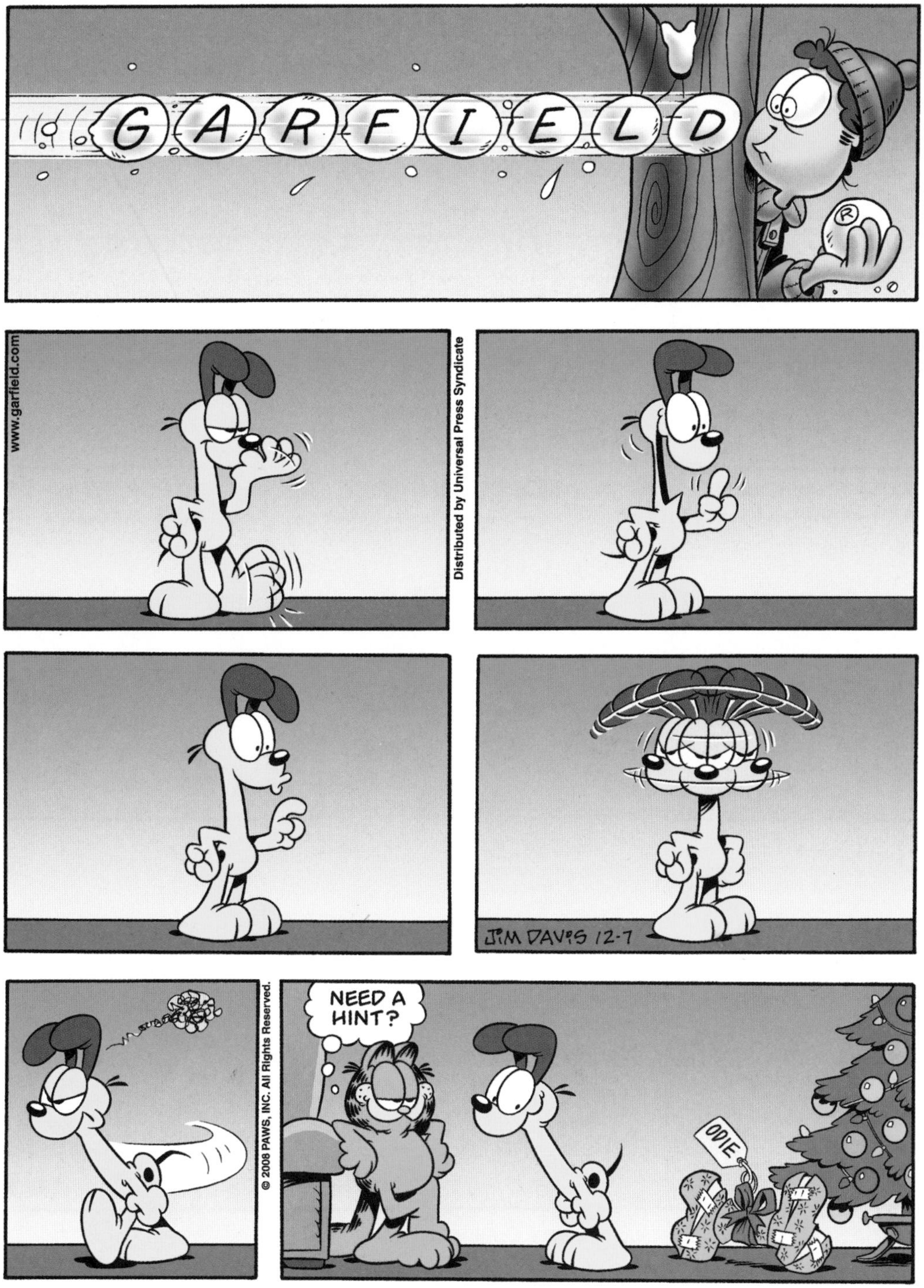
GARFIELD
www.garfield.com
Distributed by Universal Press Syndicate
JIM DAVIS 12-7
© 2008 PAWS, INC. All Rights Reserved.
NEED A HINT?
ODIE

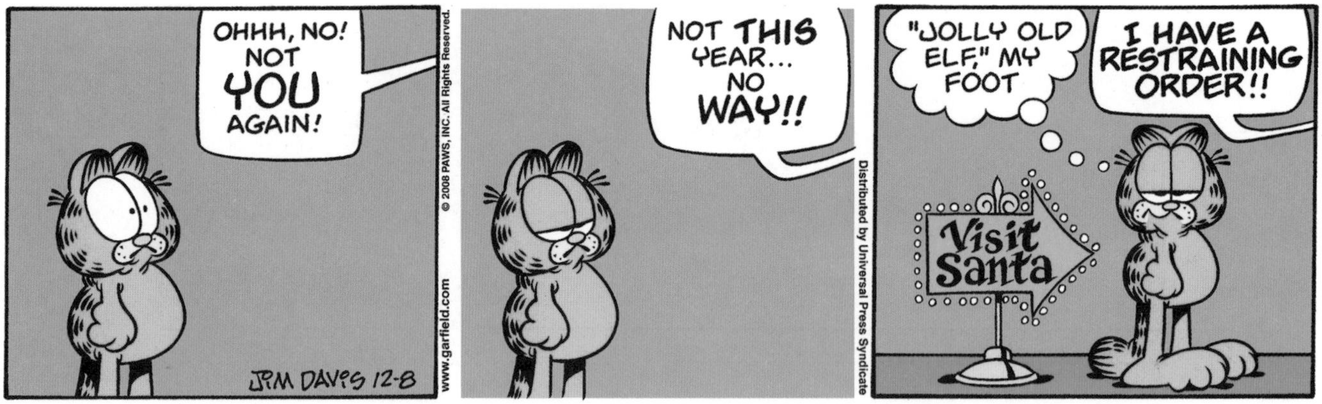
OHHH, NO! NOT YOU AGAIN!
JIM DAVIS 12-8
© 2008 PAWS, INC. All Rights Reserved.
www.garfield.com
NOT THIS YEAR... NO WAY!!
Distributed by Universal Press Syndicate
"JOLLY OLD ELF," MY FOOT
I HAVE A RESTRAINING ORDER!!
Visit Santa

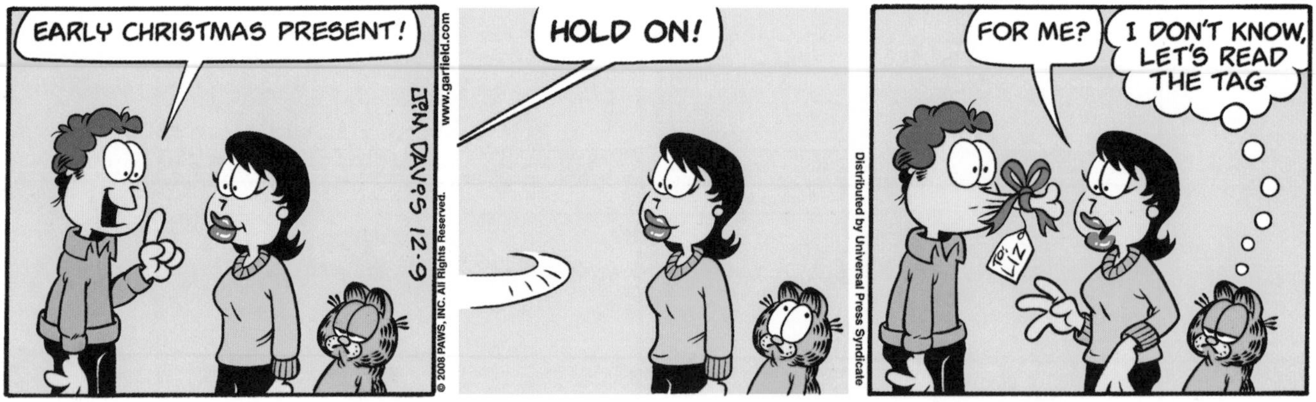
EARLY CHRISTMAS PRESENT!
JIM DAVIS 12-9
www.garfield.com
© 2008 PAWS, INC. All Rights Reserved.
HOLD ON!
Distributed by Universal Press Syndicate
FOR ME?
I DON'T KNOW, LET'S READ THE TAG
TO: LIZ

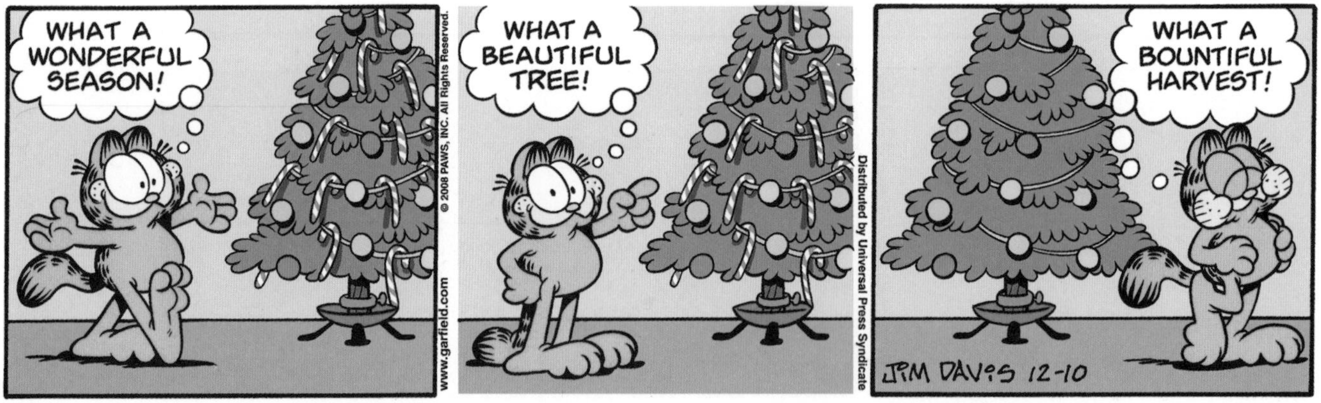
WHAT A WONDERFUL SEASON!
© 2008 PAWS, INC. All Rights Reserved.
www.garfield.com
WHAT A BEAUTIFUL TREE!
Distributed by Universal Press Syndicate
WHAT A BOUNTIFUL HARVEST!
JIM DAVIS 12-10

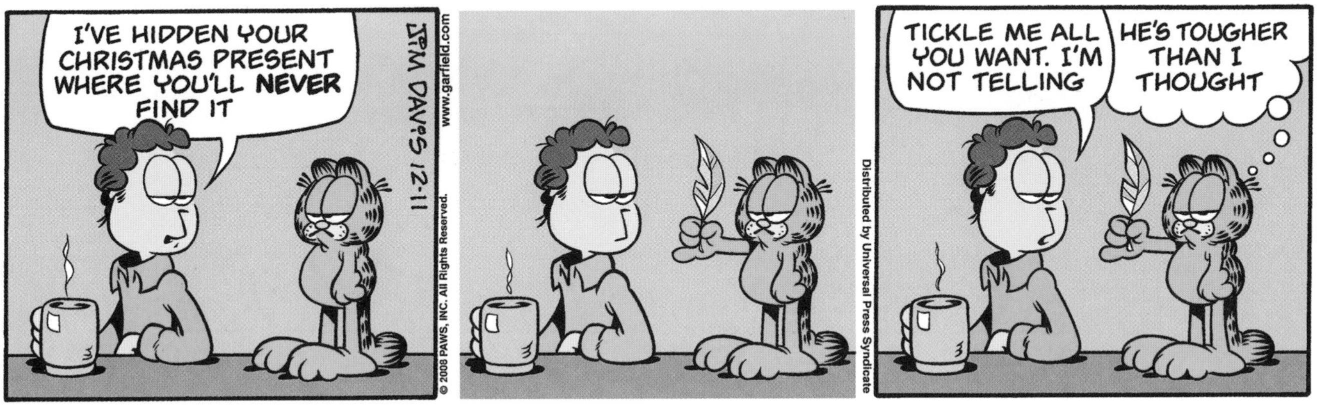
I'VE HIDDEN YOUR CHRISTMAS PRESENT WHERE YOU'LL **NEVER** FIND IT
JIM DAVIS 12-11
www.garfield.com
© 2008 PAWS, INC. All Rights Reserved.
TICKLE ME ALL YOU WANT. I'M NOT TELLING
HE'S TOUGHER THAN I THOUGHT
Distributed by Universal Press Syndicate

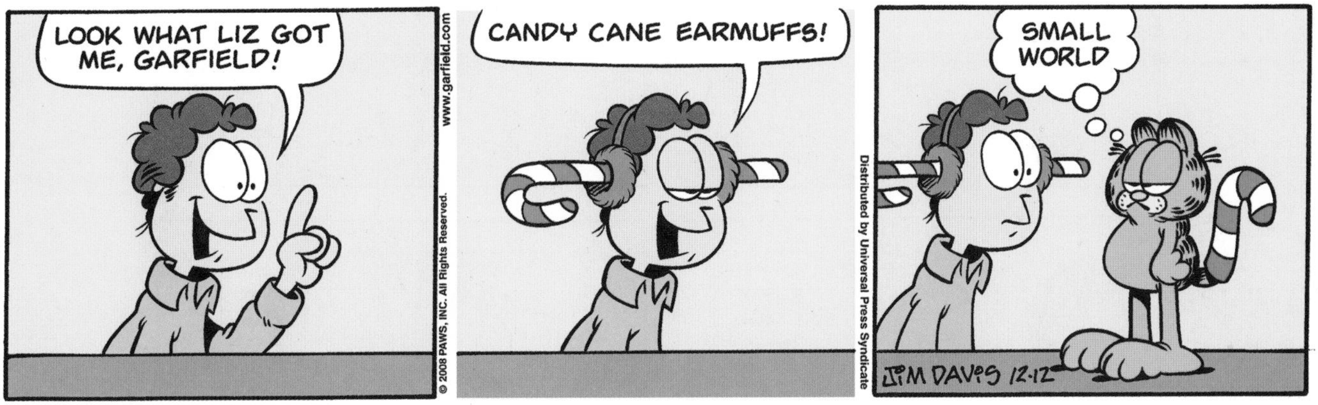
LOOK WHAT LIZ GOT ME, GARFIELD!
www.garfield.com
© 2008 PAWS, INC. All Rights Reserved.
CANDY CANE EARMUFFS!
Distributed by Universal Press Syndicate
SMALL WORLD
JIM DAVIS 12-12

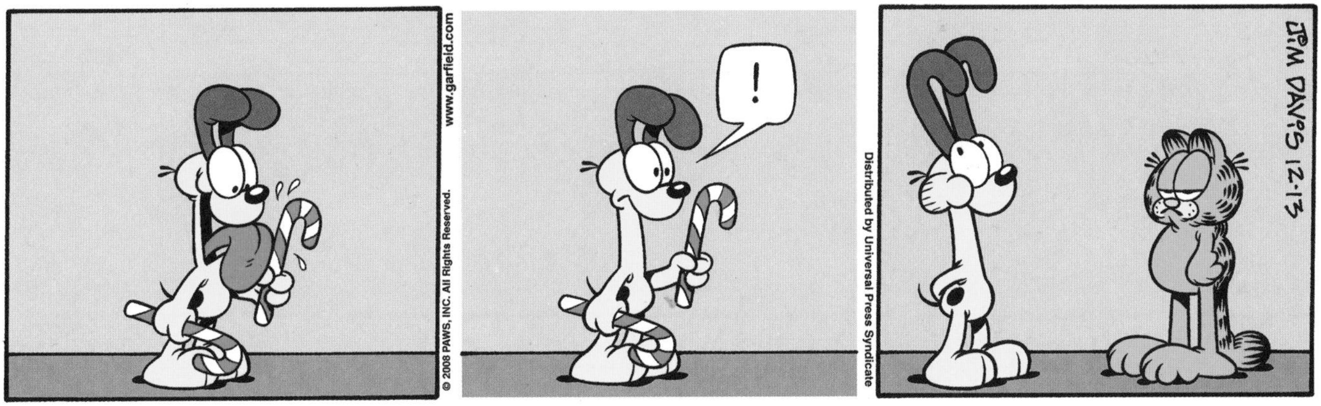
www.garfield.com
© 2008 PAWS, INC. All Rights Reserved.
!
Distributed by Universal Press Syndicate
JIM DAVIS 12-13

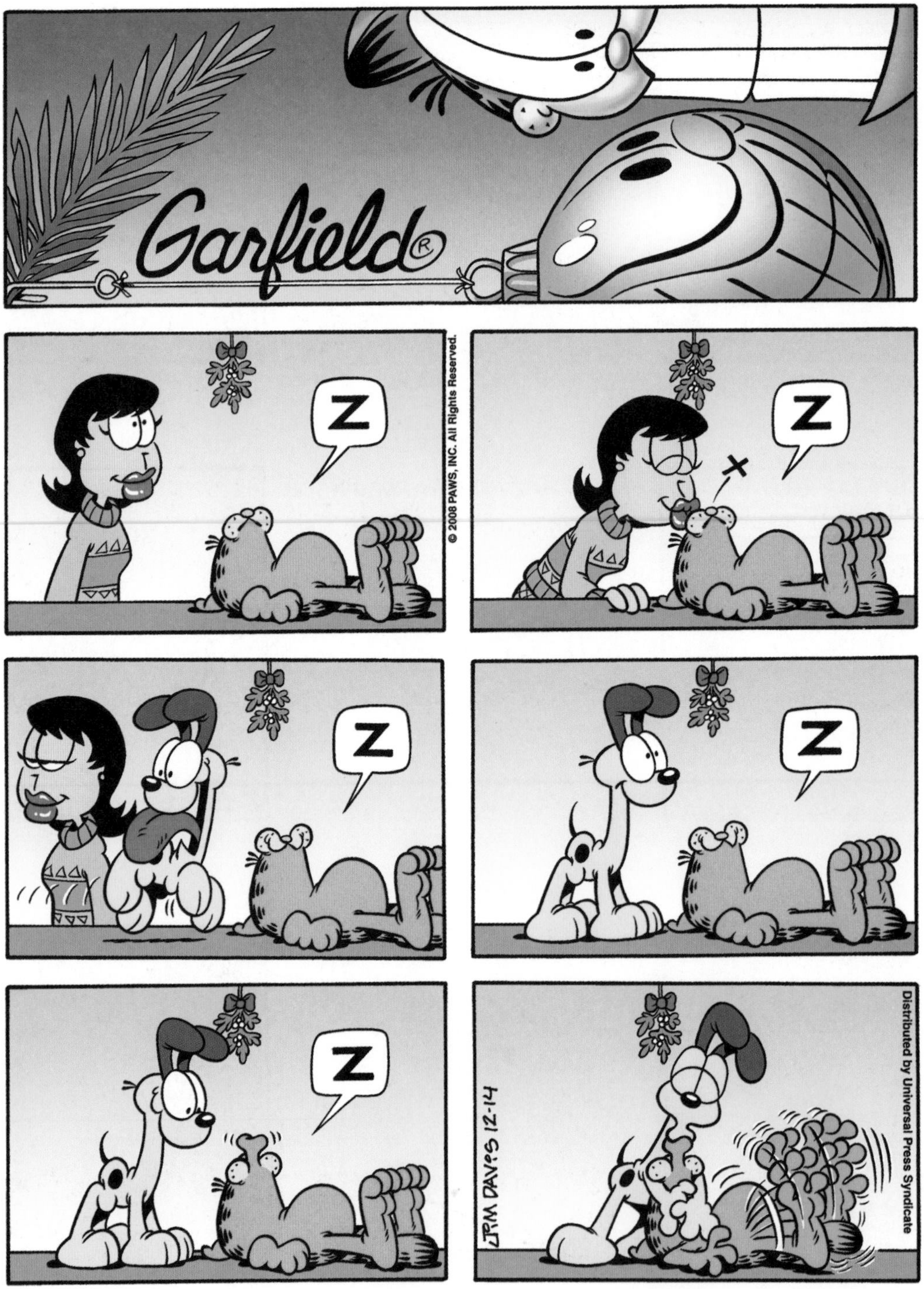
Garfield®
Z
Z
Z
Z
Z
© 2008 PAWS, INC. All Rights Reserved.
JIM DAVIS 12-14
Distributed by Universal Press Syndicate

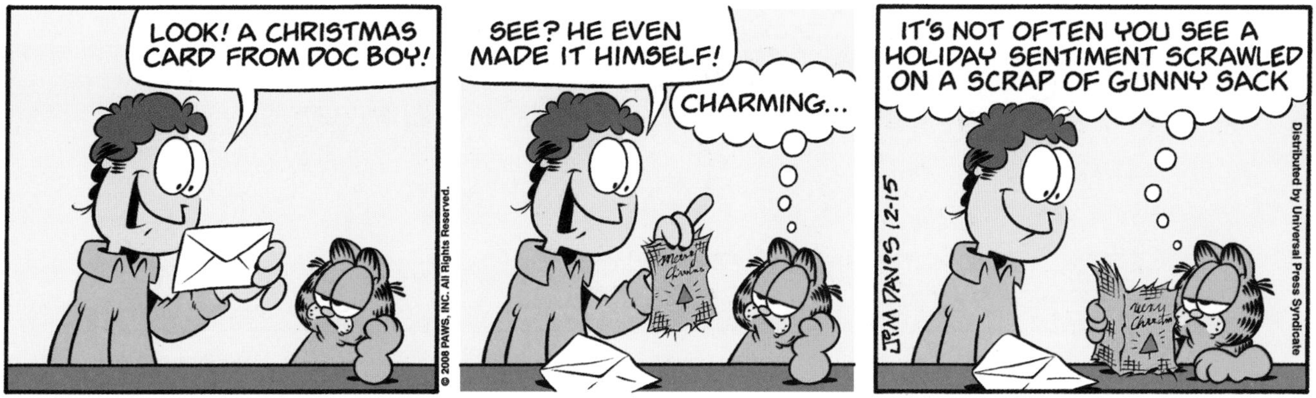
LOOK! A CHRISTMAS CARD FROM DOC BOY!
© 2008 PAWS, INC. All Rights Reserved.
SEE? HE EVEN MADE IT HIMSELF!
CHARMING...
IT'S NOT OFTEN YOU SEE A HOLIDAY SENTIMENT SCRAWLED ON A SCRAP OF GUNNY SACK
JIM DAVIS 12-15
Distributed by Universal Press Syndicate

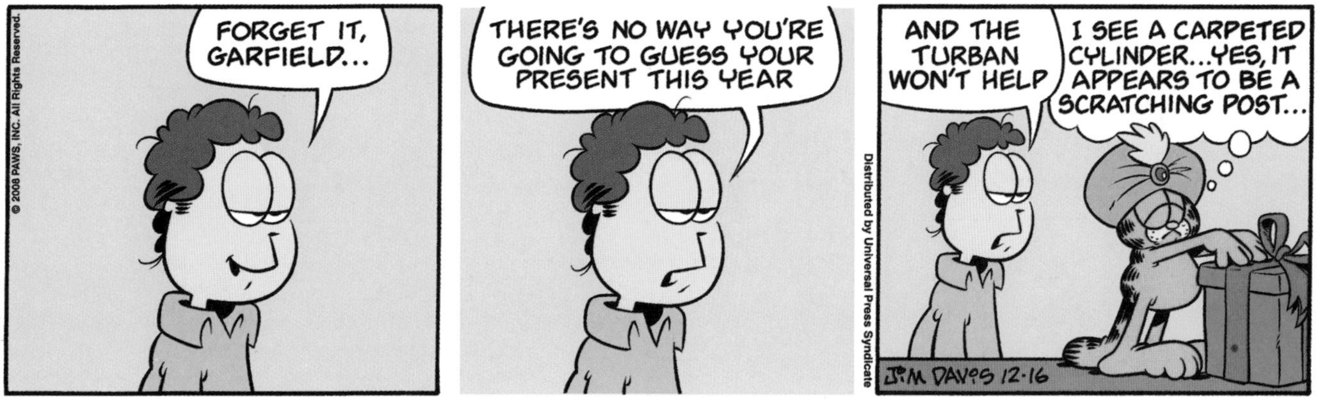
© 2008 PAWS, INC. All Rights Reserved.
FORGET IT, GARFIELD...
THERE'S NO WAY YOU'RE GOING TO GUESS YOUR PRESENT THIS YEAR
Distributed by Universal Press Syndicate
AND THE TURBAN WON'T HELP
I SEE A CARPETED CYLINDER...YES, IT APPEARS TO BE A SCRATCHING POST...
JIM DAVIS 12-16

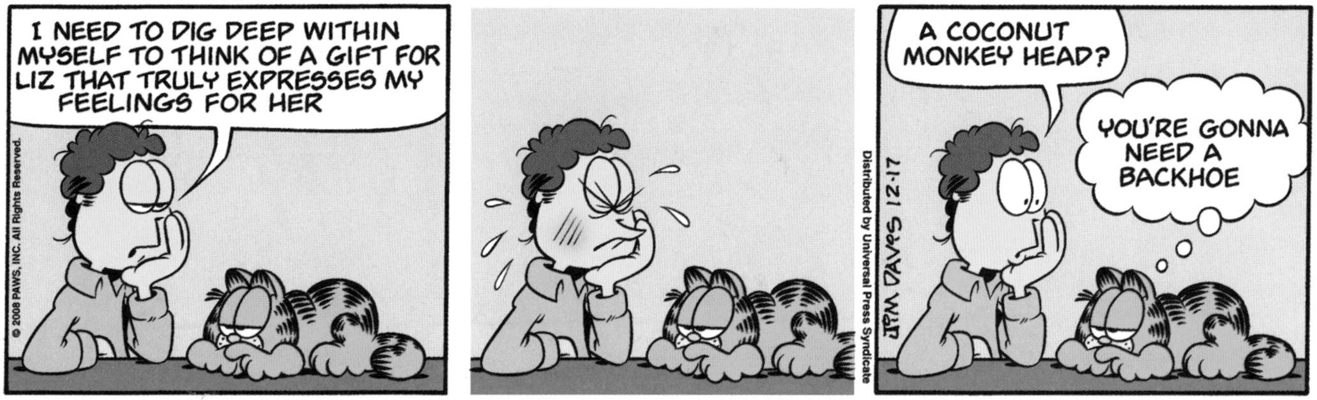
I NEED TO DIG DEEP WITHIN MYSELF TO THINK OF A GIFT FOR LIZ THAT TRULY EXPRESSES MY FEELINGS FOR HER
© 2008 PAWS, INC. All Rights Reserved.
Distributed by Universal Press Syndicate
JIM DAVIS 12-17
A COCONUT MONKEY HEAD?
YOU'RE GONNA NEED A BACKHOE

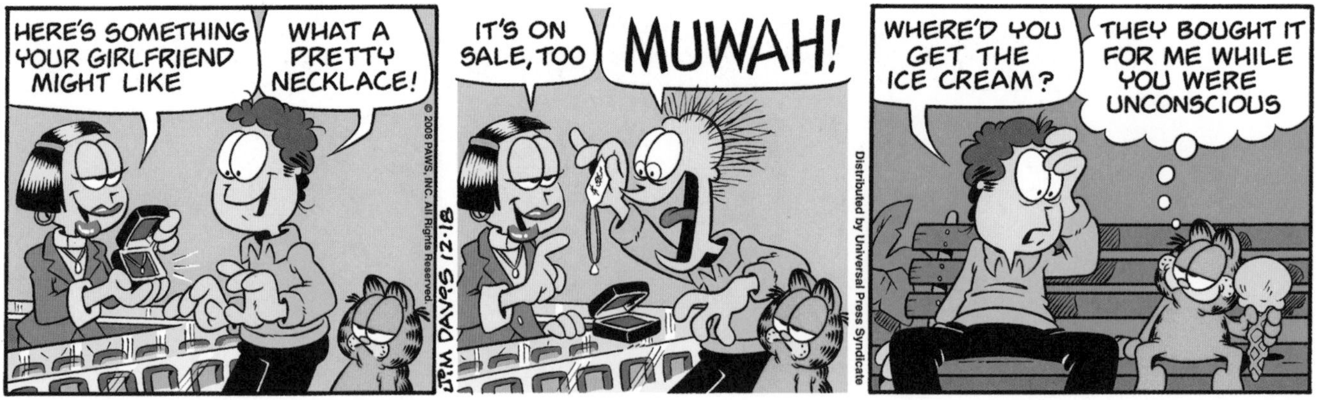
HERE'S SOMETHING YOUR GIRLFRIEND MIGHT LIKE
WHAT A PRETTY NECKLACE!
© 2008 PAWS, INC. All Rights Reserved.
JIM DAVIS 12·18
IT'S ON SALE, TOO
MUWAH!
Distributed by Universal Press Syndicate
WHERE'D YOU GET THE ICE CREAM?
THEY BOUGHT IT FOR ME WHILE YOU WERE UNCONSCIOUS

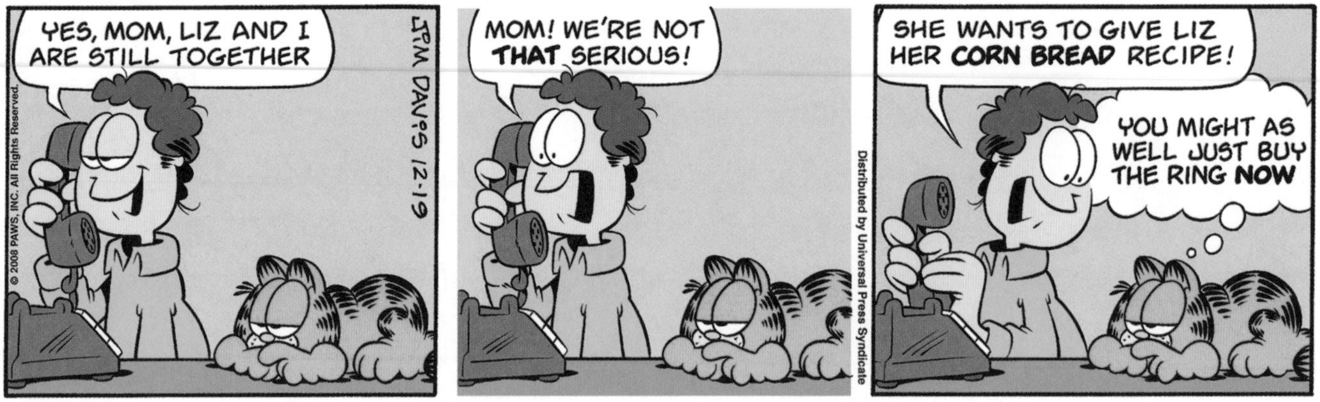
YES, MOM, LIZ AND I ARE STILL TOGETHER
© 2008 PAWS, INC. All Rights Reserved.
JIM DAVIS 12·19
MOM! WE'RE NOT **THAT** SERIOUS!
Distributed by Universal Press Syndicate
SHE WANTS TO GIVE LIZ HER **CORN BREAD** RECIPE!
YOU MIGHT AS WELL JUST BUY THE RING **NOW**

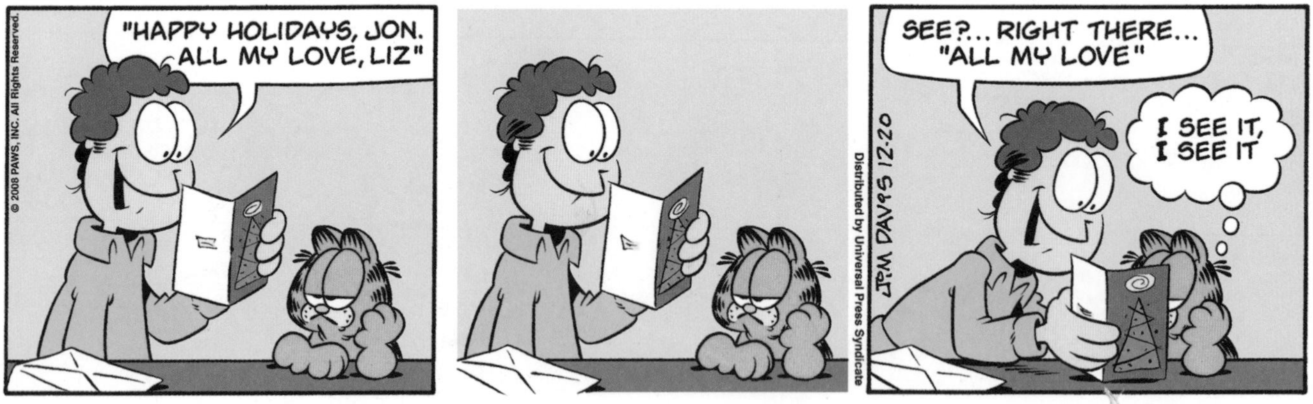
© 2008 PAWS, INC. All Rights Reserved.
"HAPPY HOLIDAYS, JON. ALL MY LOVE, LIZ"
Distributed by Universal Press Syndicate
JIM DAVIS 12·20
SEE?... RIGHT THERE... "ALL MY LOVE"
I SEE IT, **I** SEE IT

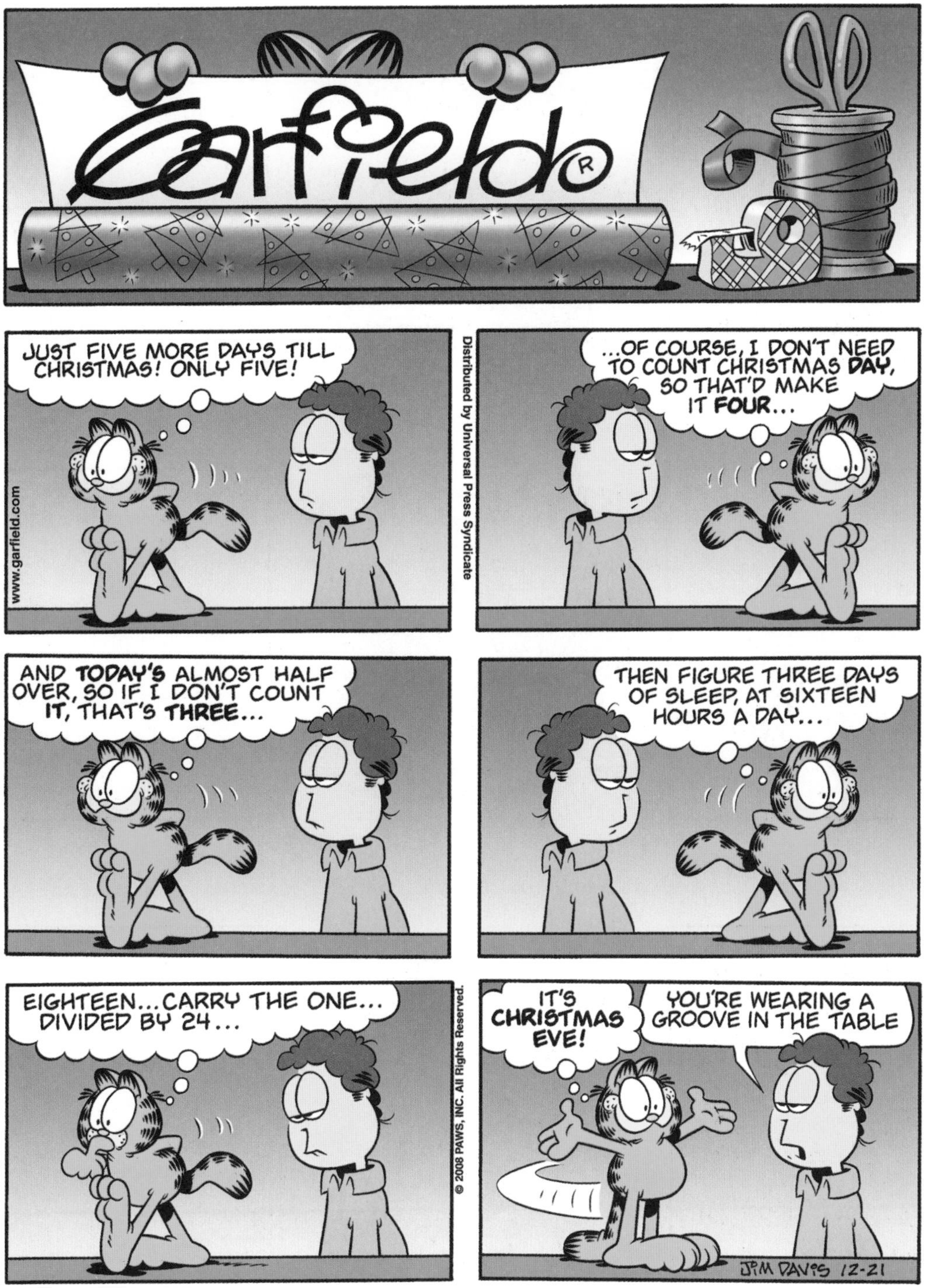
Garfield®
JUST FIVE MORE DAYS TILL CHRISTMAS! ONLY FIVE!
www.garfield.com
Distributed by Universal Press Syndicate
...OF COURSE, I DON'T NEED TO COUNT CHRISTMAS DAY, SO THAT'D MAKE IT FOUR...
AND TODAY'S ALMOST HALF OVER, SO IF I DON'T COUNT IT, THAT'S THREE...
THEN FIGURE THREE DAYS OF SLEEP, AT SIXTEEN HOURS A DAY...
EIGHTEEN...CARRY THE ONE... DIVIDED BY 24...
© 2008 PAWS, INC. All Rights Reserved.
IT'S CHRISTMAS EVE!
YOU'RE WEARING A GROOVE IN THE TABLE
JIM DAVIS 12-21

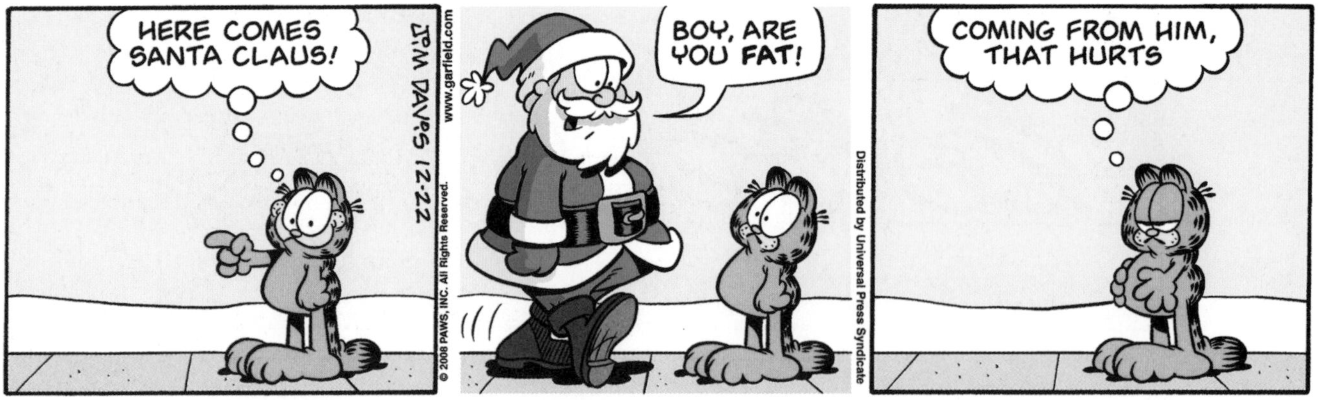
HERE COMES SANTA CLAUS!
JIM DAVIS 12-22
www.garfield.com
© 2008 PAWS, INC. All Rights Reserved.
BOY, ARE YOU FAT!
Distributed by Universal Press Syndicate
COMING FROM HIM, THAT HURTS

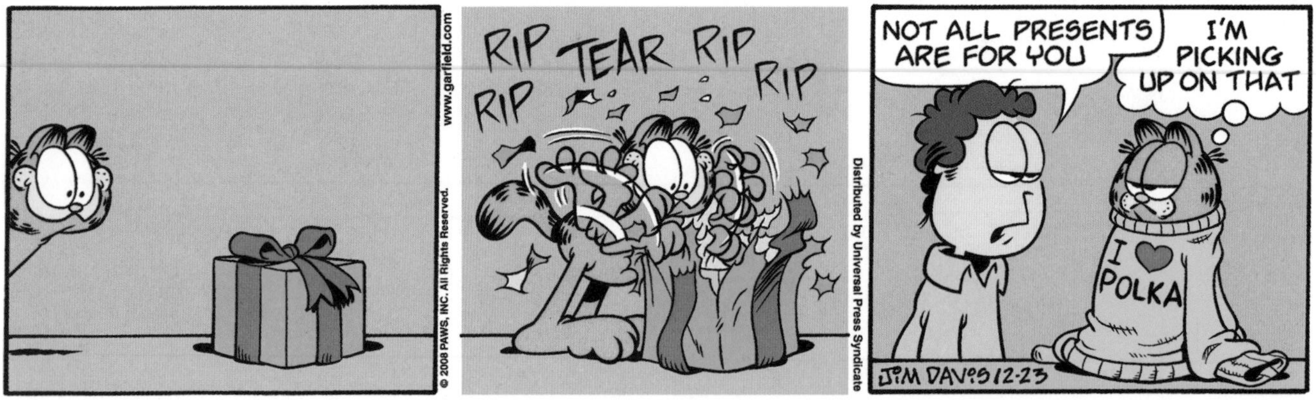
www.garfield.com
© 2008 PAWS, INC. All Rights Reserved.
RIP TEAR RIP
RIP RIP
Distributed by Universal Press Syndicate
NOT ALL PRESENTS ARE FOR YOU
I'M PICKING UP ON THAT
I ♥ POLKA
JIM DAVIS 12-23

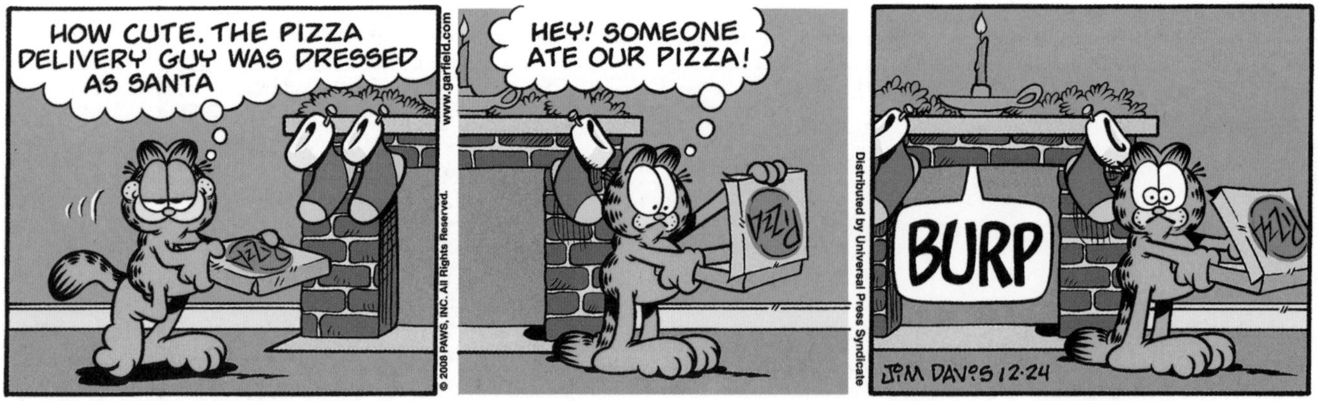
HOW CUTE. THE PIZZA DELIVERY GUY WAS DRESSED AS SANTA
www.garfield.com
© 2008 PAWS, INC. All Rights Reserved.
HEY! SOMEONE ATE OUR PIZZA!
Distributed by Universal Press Syndicate
BURP
JIM DAVIS 12-24

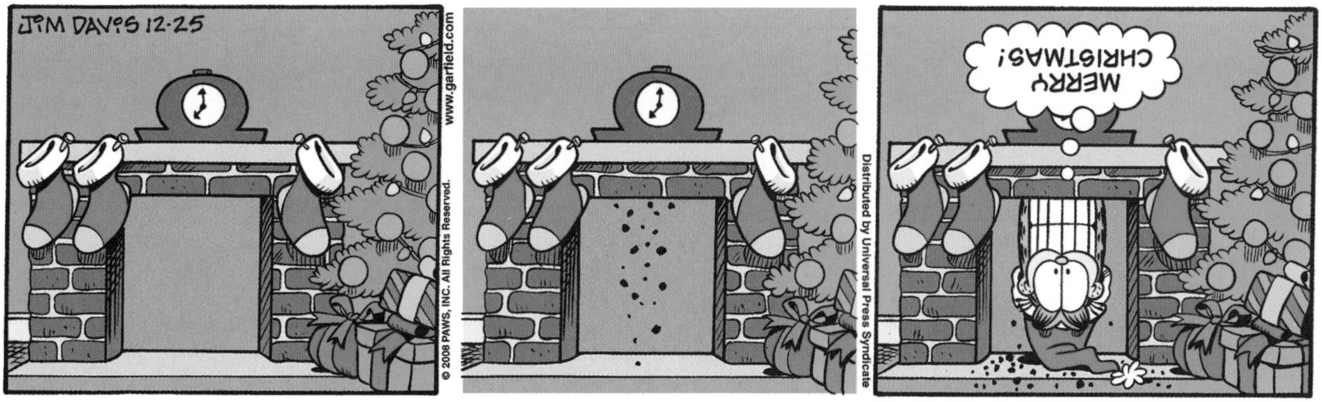
JIM DAVIS 12-25
www.garfield.com
© 2008 PAWS, INC. All Rights Reserved.
Distributed by Universal Press Syndicate
MERRY CHRISTMAS!

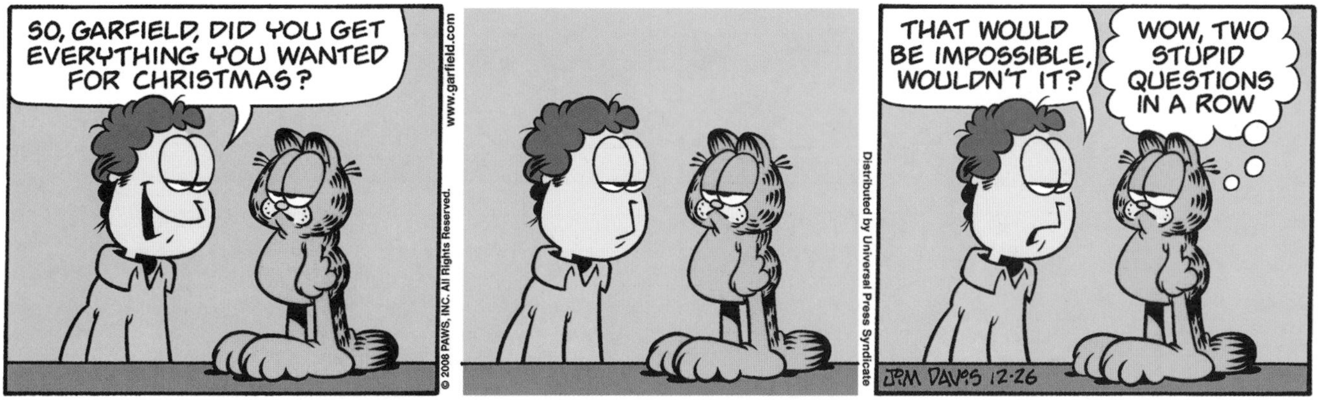
SO, GARFIELD, DID YOU GET EVERYTHING YOU WANTED FOR CHRISTMAS?
www.garfield.com
© 2008 PAWS, INC. All Rights Reserved.
Distributed by Universal Press Syndicate
THAT WOULD BE IMPOSSIBLE, WOULDN'T IT?
WOW, TWO STUPID QUESTIONS IN A ROW
JIM DAVIS 12-26

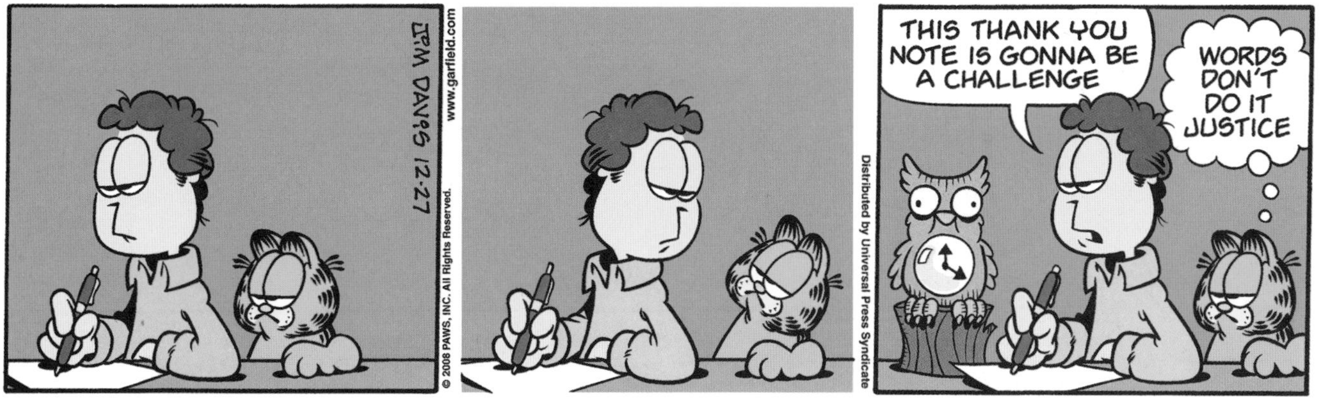
JIM DAVIS 12-27
www.garfield.com
© 2008 PAWS, INC. All Rights Reserved.
Distributed by Universal Press Syndicate
THIS THANK YOU NOTE IS GONNA BE A CHALLENGE
WORDS DON'T DO IT JUSTICE

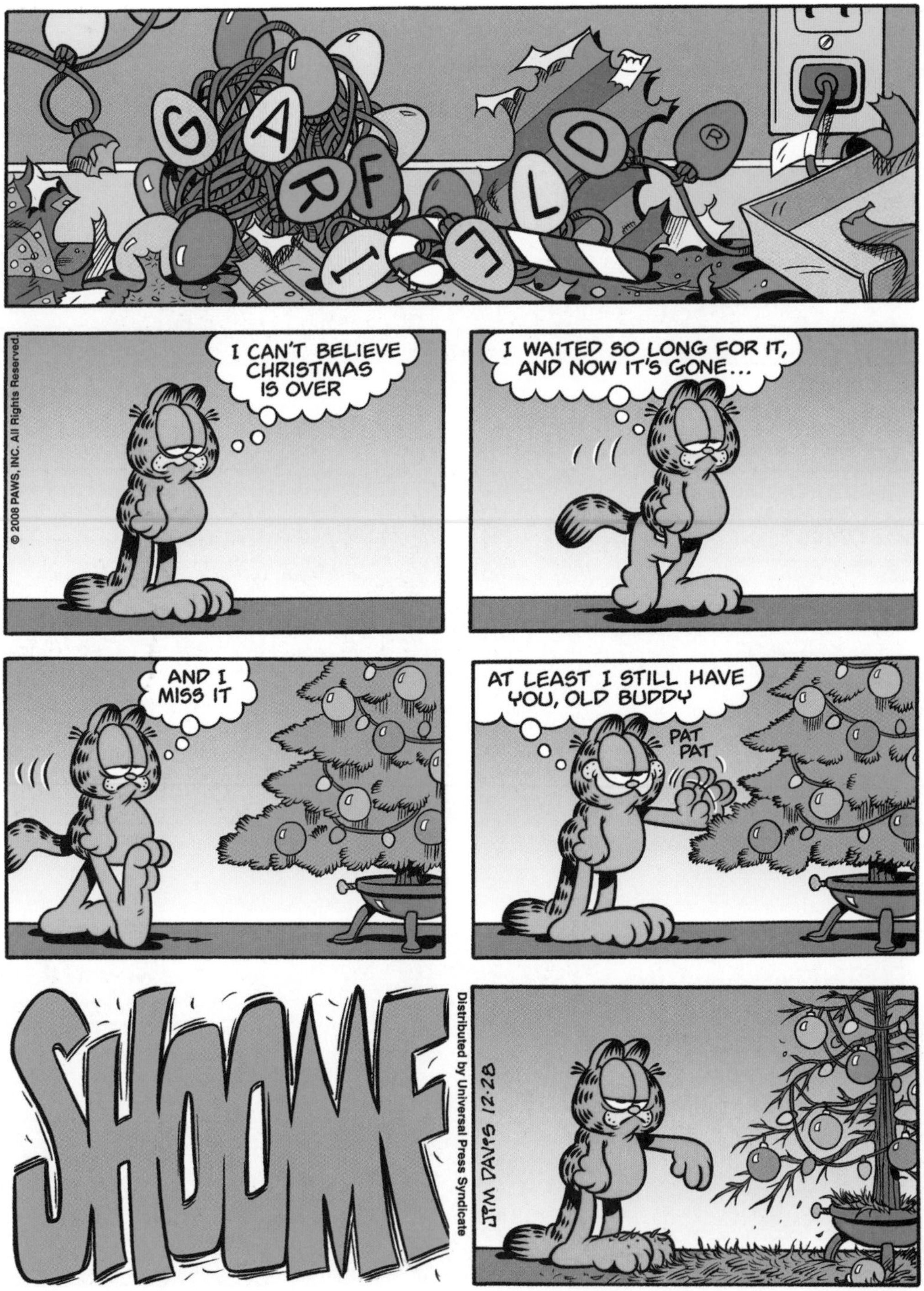
GARFIELD®
I CAN'T BELIEVE CHRISTMAS IS OVER
I WAITED SO LONG FOR IT, AND NOW IT'S GONE...
AND I MISS IT
AT LEAST I STILL HAVE YOU, OLD BUDDY
PAT PAT
SHOOMF
JPM DAVPS 12·28

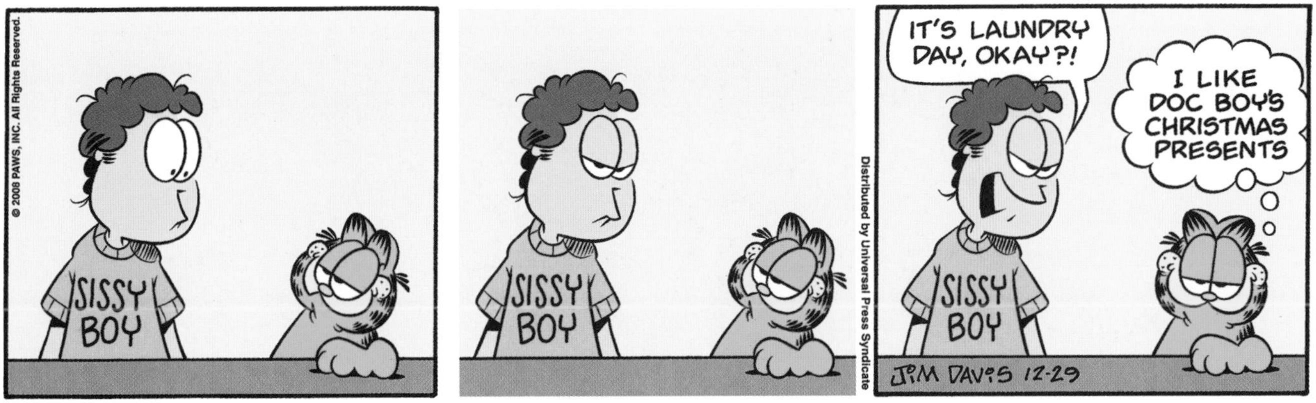
© 2008 PAWS, INC. All Rights Reserved.
SISSY BOY
IT'S LAUNDRY DAY, OKAY?!
I LIKE DOC BOY'S CHRISTMAS PRESENTS
JIM DAVIS 12-29
Distributed by Universal Press Syndicate

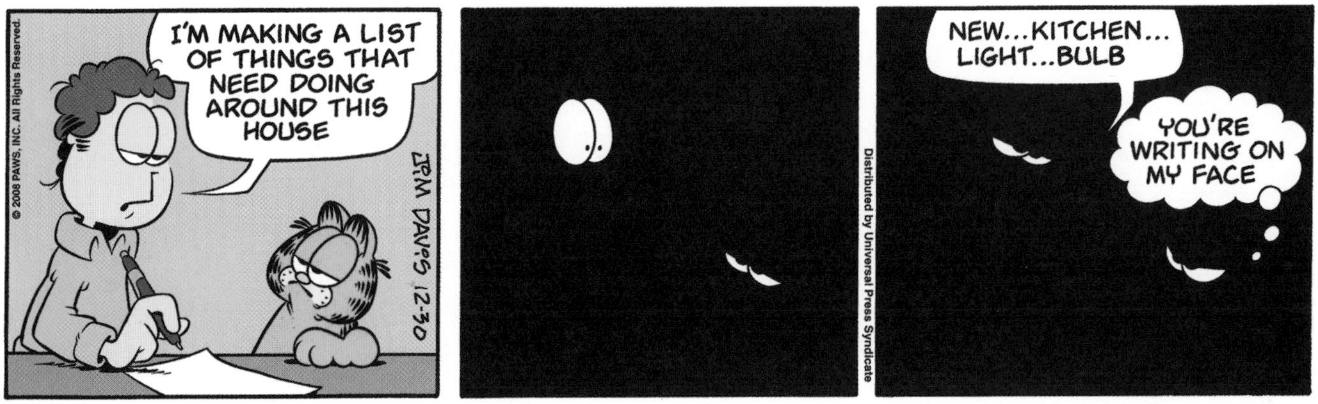
© 2008 PAWS, INC. All Rights Reserved.
I'M MAKING A LIST OF THINGS THAT NEED DOING AROUND THIS HOUSE
JIM DAVIS 12-30
NEW... KITCHEN... LIGHT... BULB
YOU'RE WRITING ON MY FACE
Distributed by Universal Press Syndicate

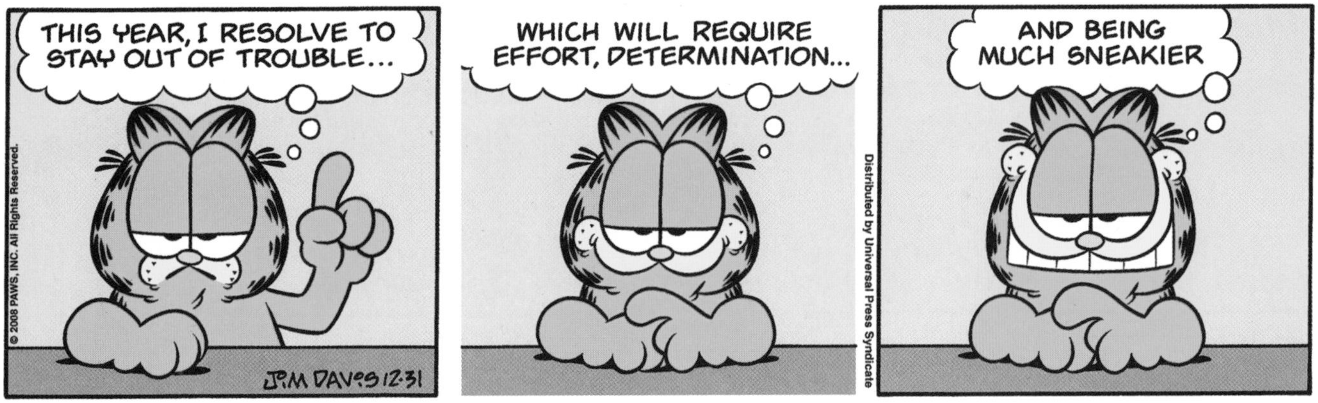
© 2008 PAWS, INC. All Rights Reserved.
THIS YEAR, I RESOLVE TO STAY OUT OF TROUBLE...
JIM DAVIS 12-31
WHICH WILL REQUIRE EFFORT, DETERMINATION...
AND BEING MUCH SNEAKIER
Distributed by Universal Press Syndicate

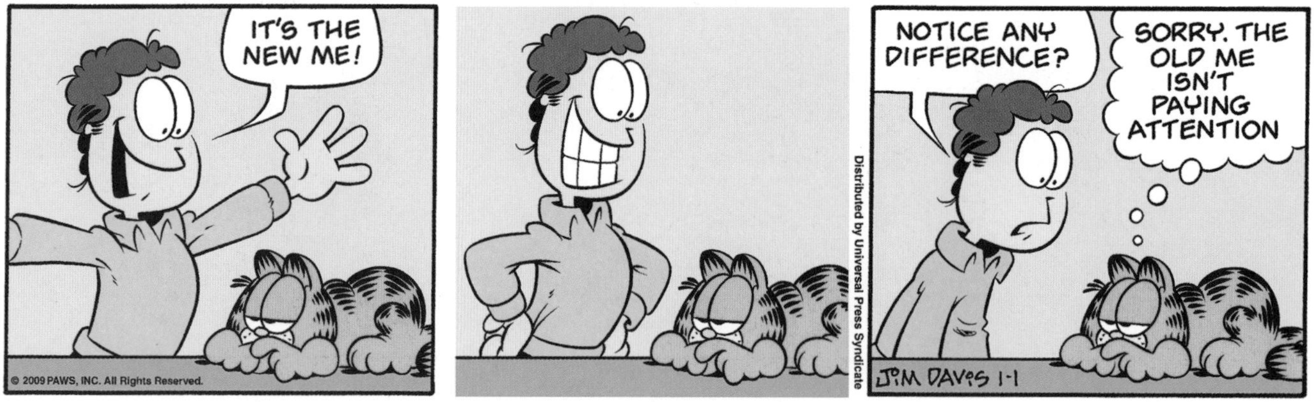
IT'S THE NEW ME!
NOTICE ANY DIFFERENCE?
SORRY. THE OLD ME ISN'T PAYING ATTENTION
© 2009 PAWS, INC. All Rights Reserved.
Distributed by Universal Press Syndicate
JIM DAVIS 1-1

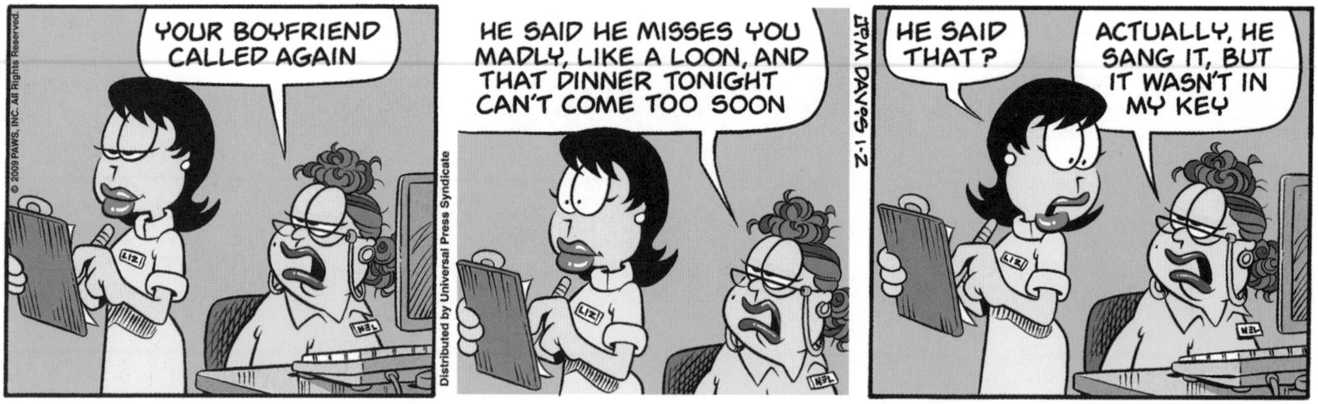
YOUR BOYFRIEND CALLED AGAIN
HE SAID HE MISSES YOU MADLY, LIKE A LOON, AND THAT DINNER TONIGHT CAN'T COME TOO SOON
HE SAID THAT?
ACTUALLY, HE SANG IT, BUT IT WASN'T IN MY KEY
© 2009 PAWS, INC. All Rights Reserved.
Distributed by Universal Press Syndicate
JIM DAVIS 1-2

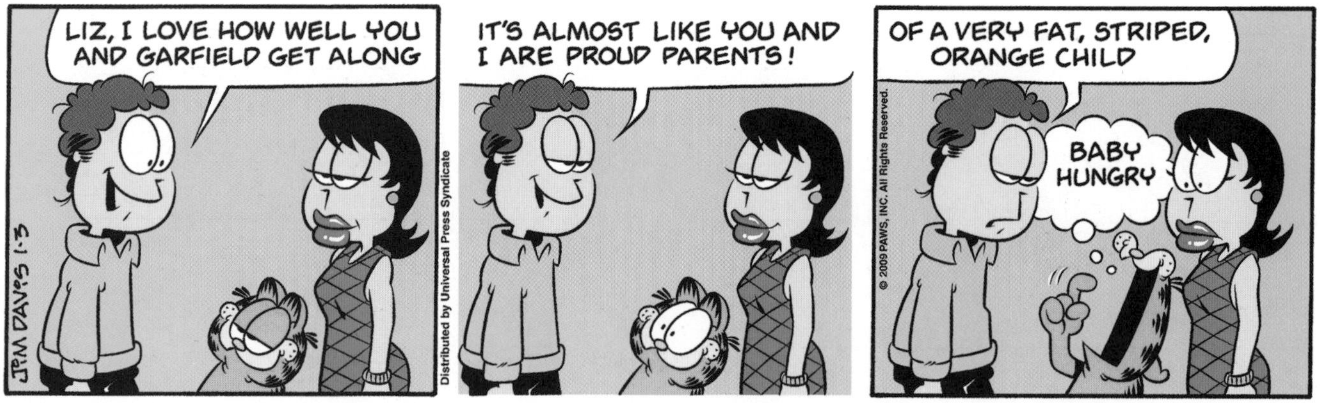
LIZ, I LOVE HOW WELL YOU AND GARFIELD GET ALONG
IT'S ALMOST LIKE YOU AND I ARE PROUD PARENTS!
OF A VERY FAT, STRIPED, ORANGE CHILD
BABY HUNGRY
JIM DAVIS 1-3
Distributed by Universal Press Syndicate
© 2009 PAWS, INC. All Rights Reserved.

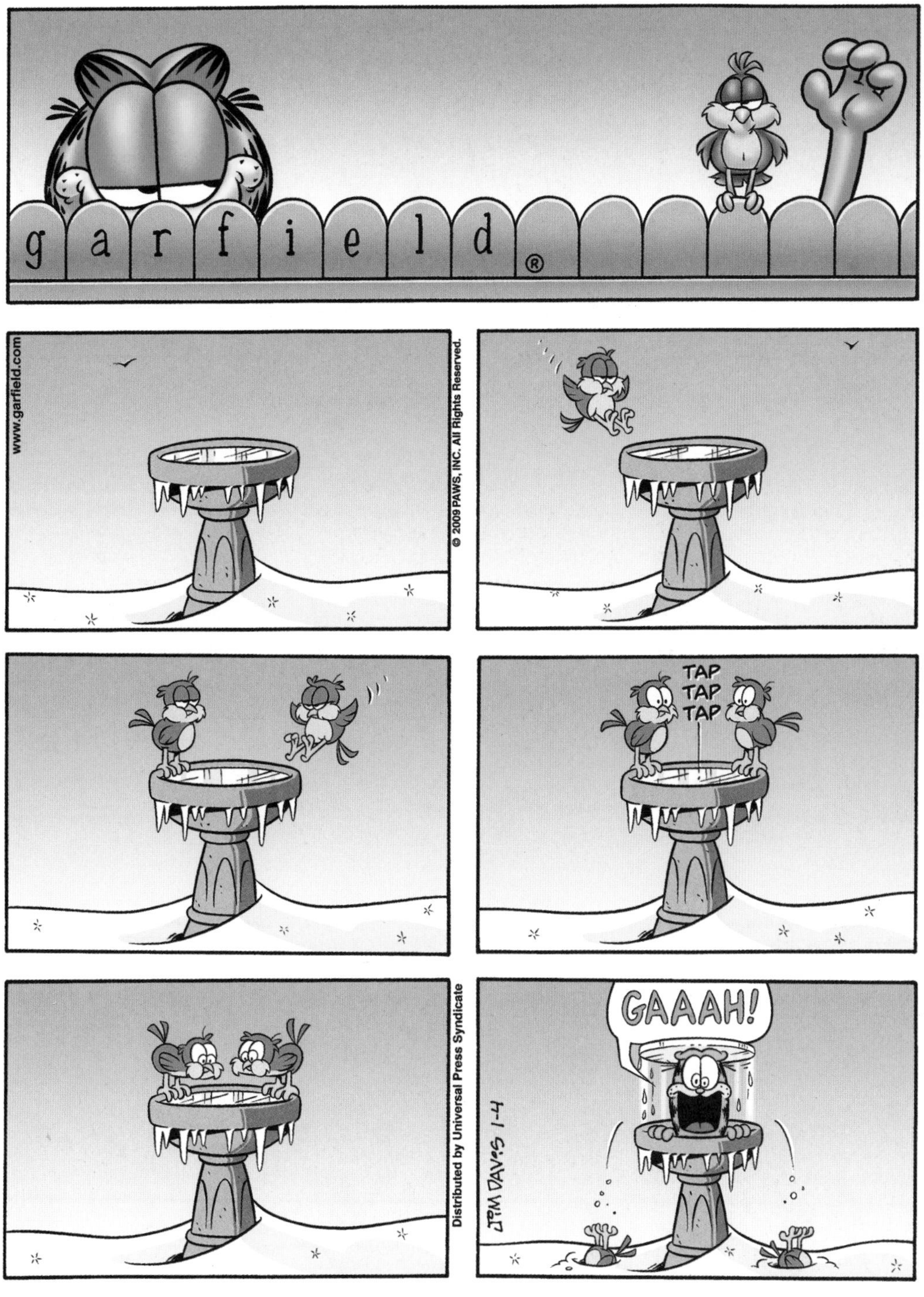
garfield®
www.garfield.com
© 2009 PAWS, INC. All Rights Reserved.
TAP TAP TAP
Distributed by Universal Press Syndicate
JIM DAVIS 1-4
GAAAH!

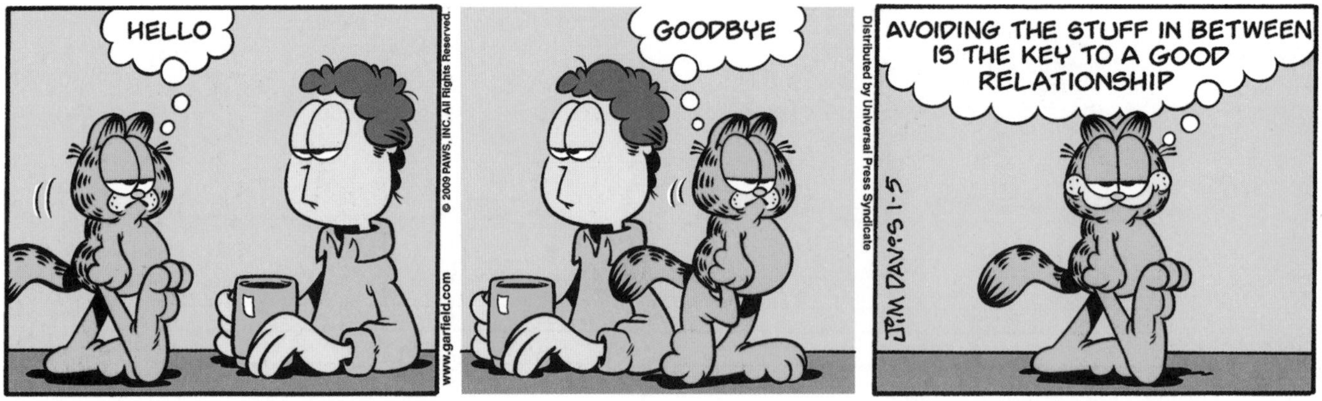
HELLO
© 2009 PAWS, INC. All Rights Reserved.
www.garfield.com
GOODBYE
Distributed by Universal Press Syndicate
AVOIDING THE STUFF IN BETWEEN IS THE KEY TO A GOOD RELATIONSHIP
JPM DAVIS 1-5

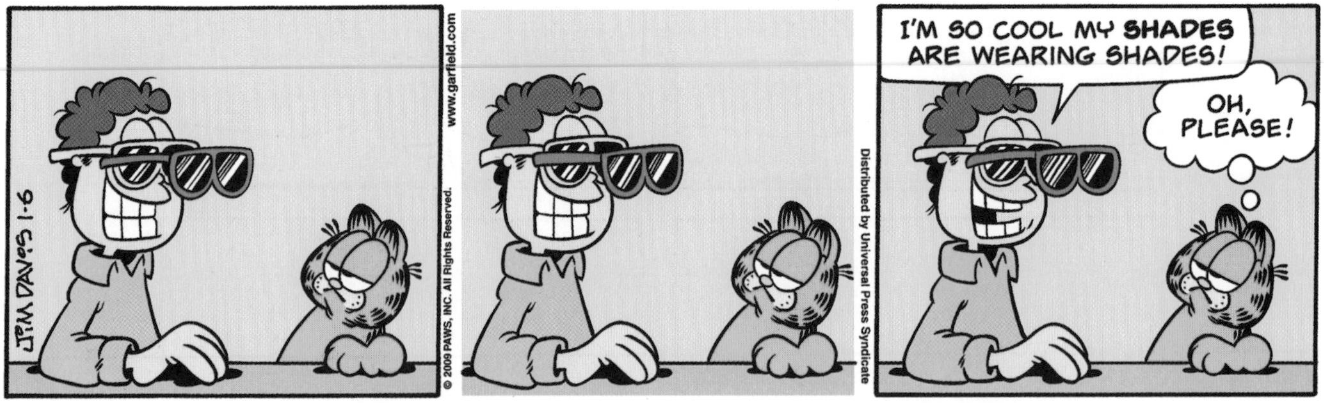
JPM DAVIS 1-6
www.garfield.com
© 2009 PAWS, INC. All Rights Reserved.
Distributed by Universal Press Syndicate
I'M SO COOL MY **SHADES** ARE WEARING SHADES!
OH, PLEASE!

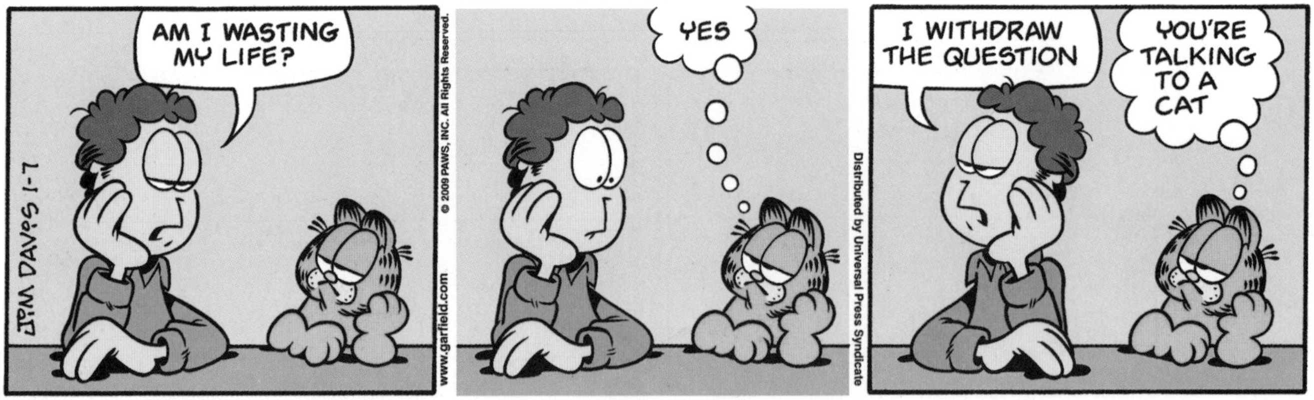
JPM DAVIS 1-7
AM I WASTING MY LIFE?
© 2009 PAWS, INC. All Rights Reserved.
www.garfield.com
YES
Distributed by Universal Press Syndicate
I WITHDRAW THE QUESTION
YOU'RE TALKING TO A CAT

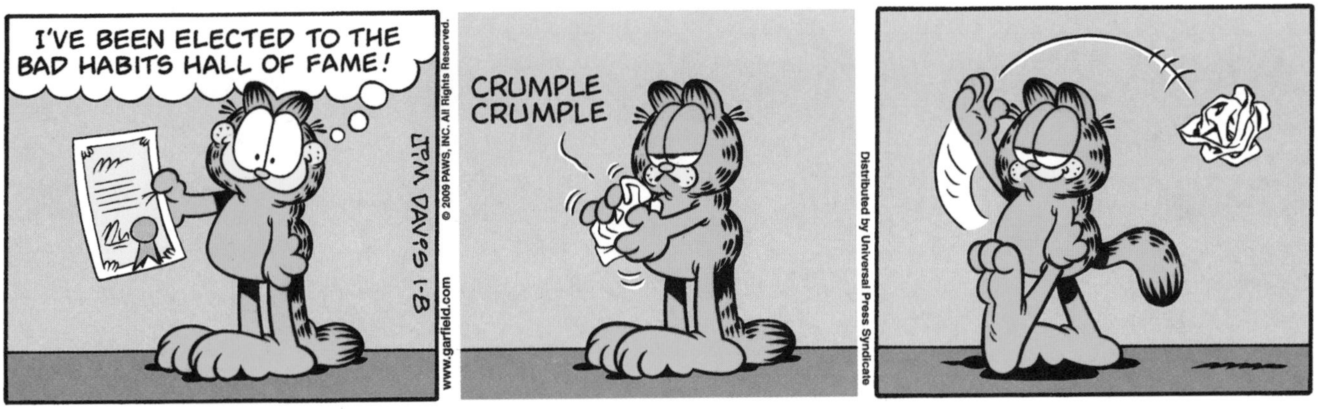
I'VE BEEN ELECTED TO THE BAD HABITS HALL OF FAME!
JPM DAVPS 1-8
© 2009 PAWS, INC. All Rights Reserved.
www.garfield.com
CRUMPLE CRUMPLE
Distributed by Universal Press Syndicate

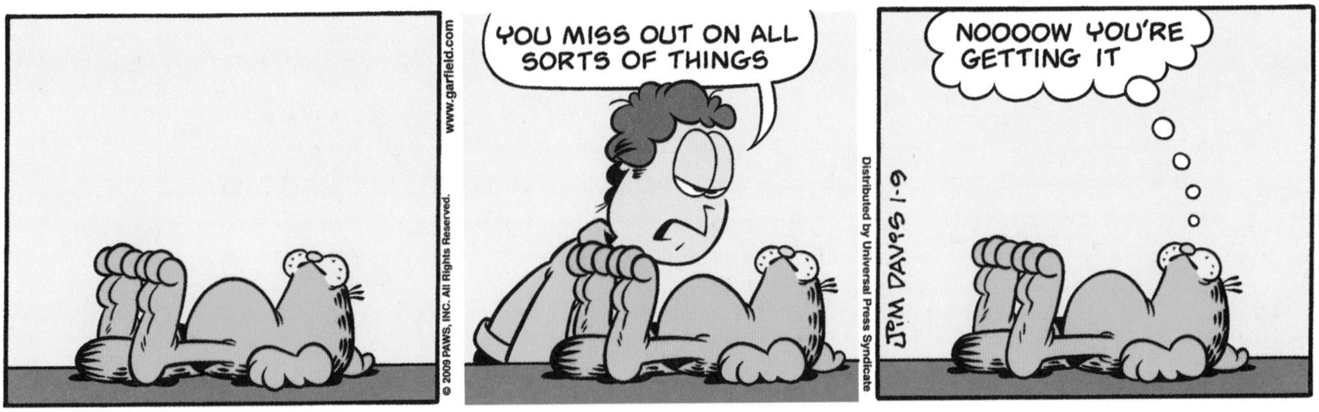
© 2009 PAWS, INC. All Rights Reserved.
www.garfield.com
YOU MISS OUT ON ALL SORTS OF THINGS
Distributed by Universal Press Syndicate
JPM DAVPS 1-9
NOOOOW YOU'RE GETTING IT

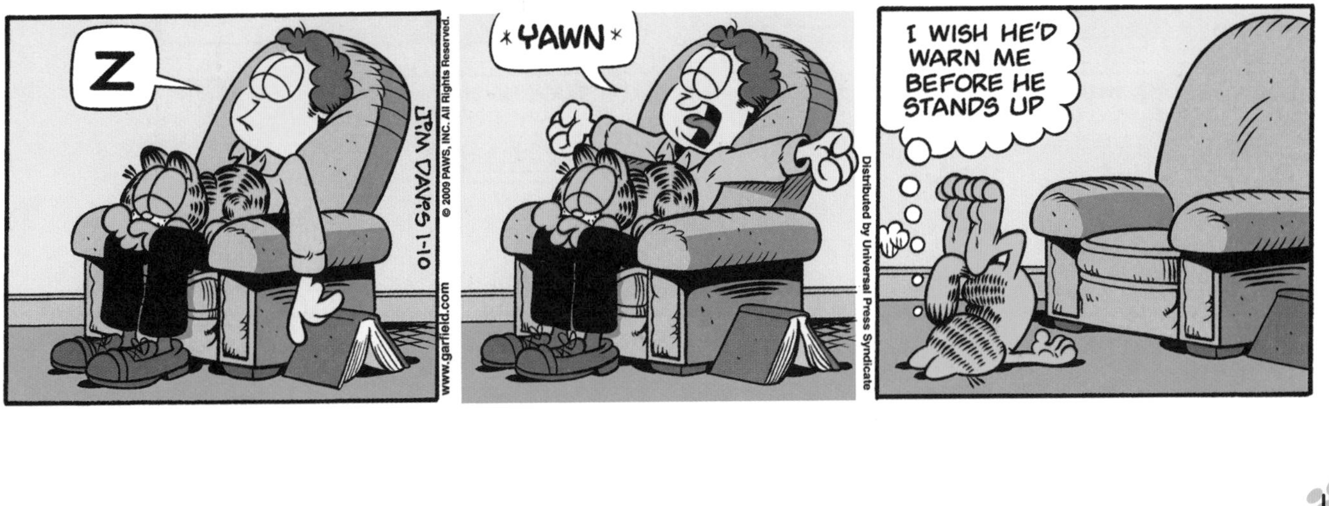
Z
JPM DAVPS 1-10
© 2009 PAWS, INC. All Rights Reserved.
www.garfield.com
YAWN
Distributed by Universal Press Syndicate
I WISH HE'D WARN ME BEFORE HE STANDS UP

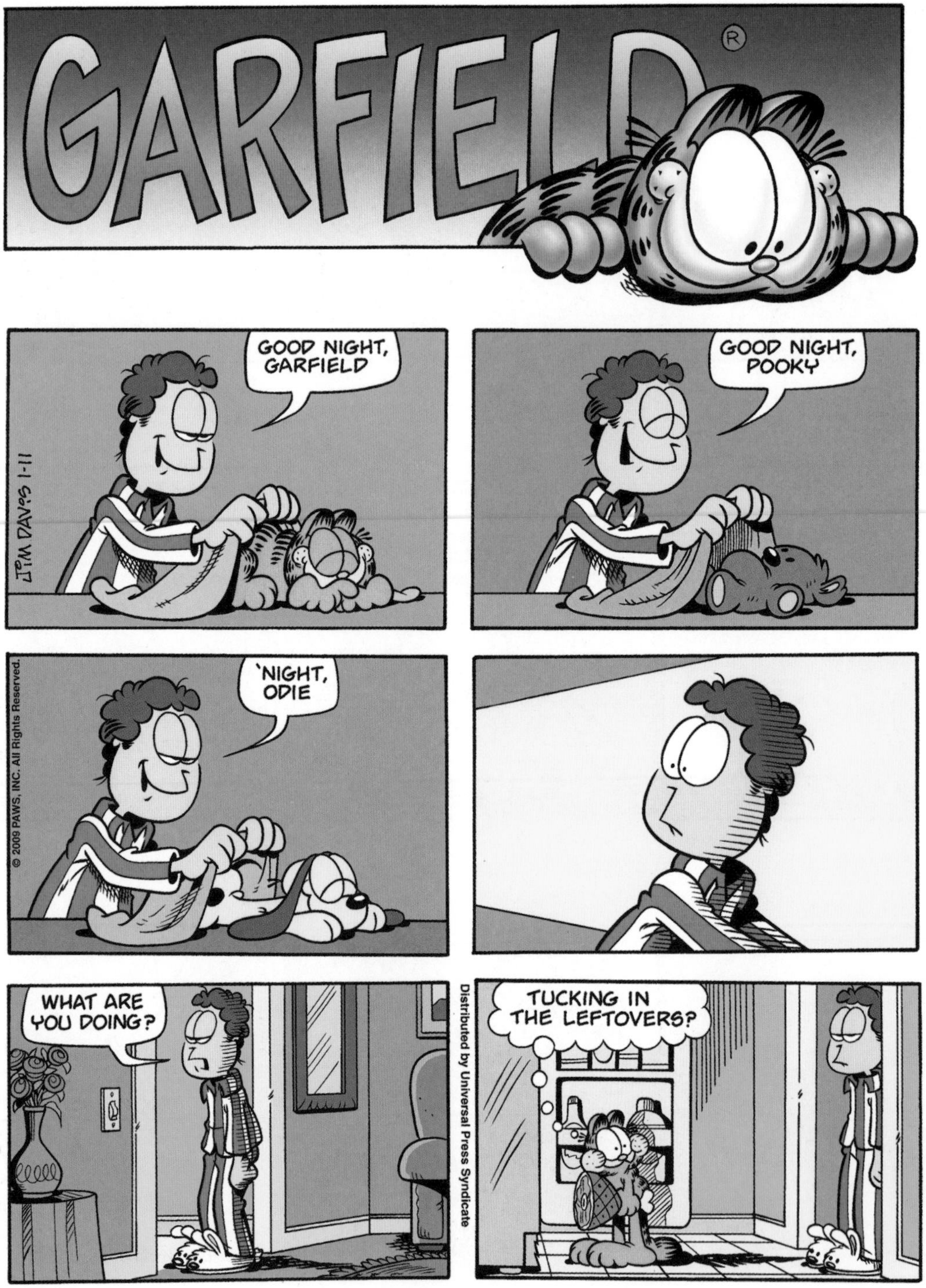
GARFIELD
JPM DAVPS 1-11
GOOD NIGHT, GARFIELD
GOOD NIGHT, POOKY
'NIGHT, ODIE
© 2009 PAWS, INC. All Rights Reserved.
WHAT ARE YOU DOING?
Distributed by Universal Press Syndicate
TUCKING IN THE LEFTOVERS?

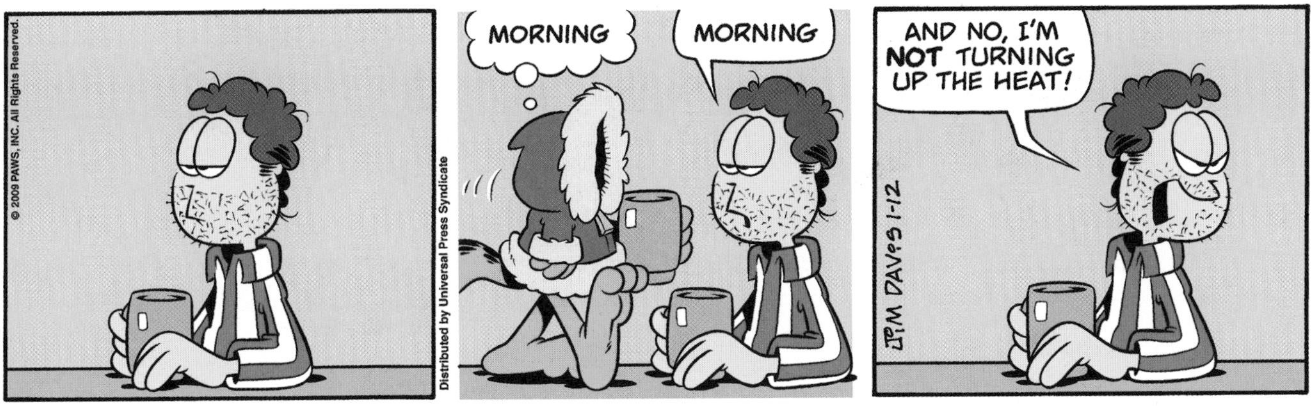
© 2009 PAWS, INC. All Rights Reserved.
Distributed by Universal Press Syndicate
MORNING
MORNING
AND NO, I'M **NOT** TURNING UP THE HEAT!
JIM DAVIS 1-12

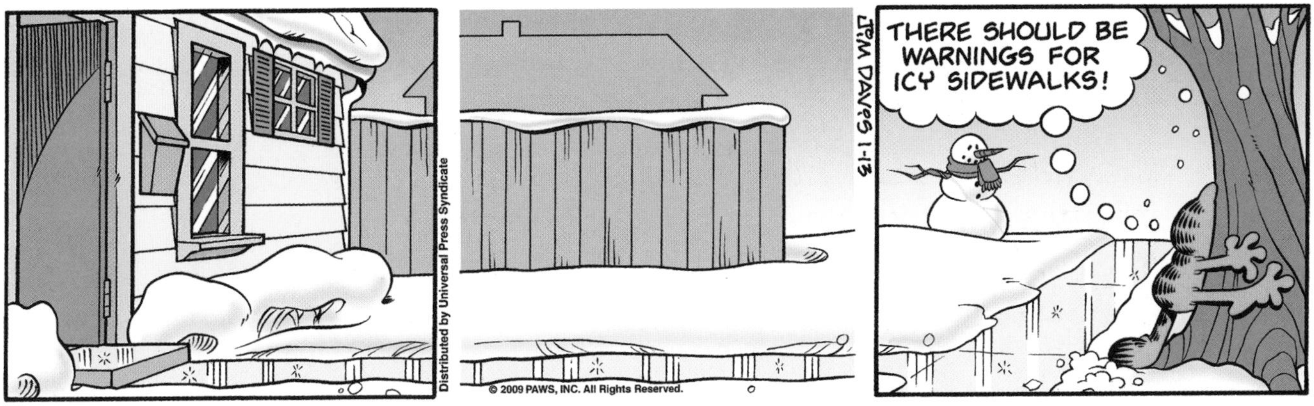
Distributed by Universal Press Syndicate
© 2009 PAWS, INC. All Rights Reserved.
JIM DAVIS 1-13
THERE SHOULD BE WARNINGS FOR ICY SIDEWALKS!

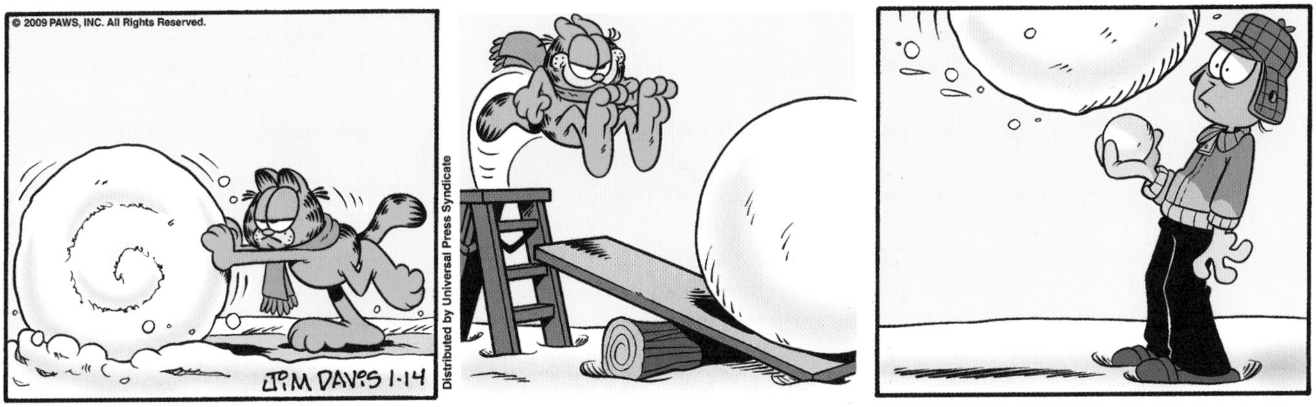
© 2009 PAWS, INC. All Rights Reserved.
JIM DAVIS 1-14
Distributed by Universal Press Syndicate

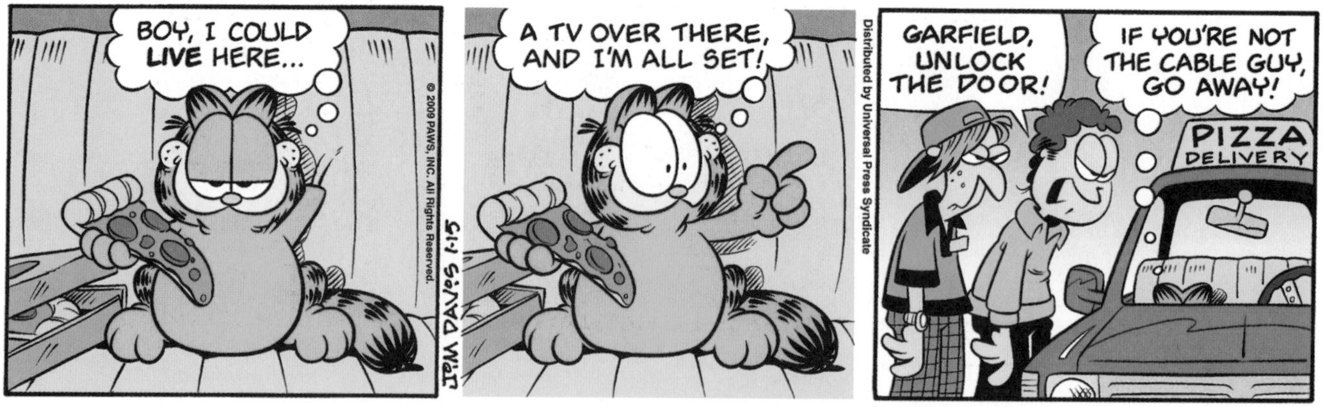
BOY, I COULD **LIVE** HERE...
A TV OVER THERE, AND I'M ALL SET!
GARFIELD, UNLOCK THE DOOR!
IF YOU'RE NOT THE CABLE GUY, GO AWAY!
PIZZA DELIVERY
JPM DAVIS 1-15
© 2009 PAWS, INC. All Rights Reserved.
Distributed by Universal Press Syndicate

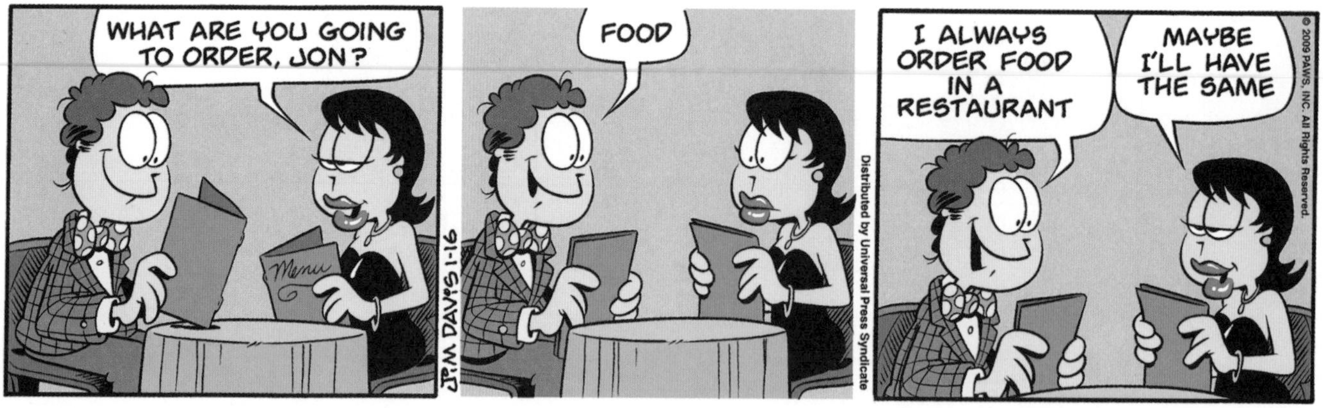
WHAT ARE YOU GOING TO ORDER, JON?
Menu
FOOD
I ALWAYS ORDER FOOD IN A RESTAURANT
MAYBE I'LL HAVE THE SAME
JPM DAVIS 1-16
© 2009 PAWS, INC. All Rights Reserved.
Distributed by Universal Press Syndicate

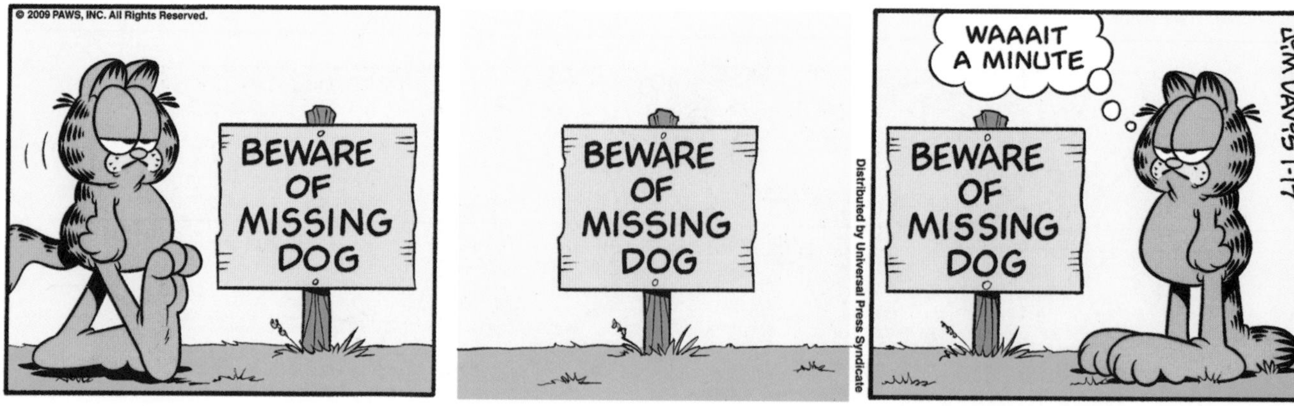
© 2009 PAWS, INC. All Rights Reserved.
BEWARE OF MISSING DOG
BEWARE OF MISSING DOG
WAAAIT A MINUTE
BEWARE OF MISSING DOG
JPM DAVIS 1-17
Distributed by Universal Press Syndicate

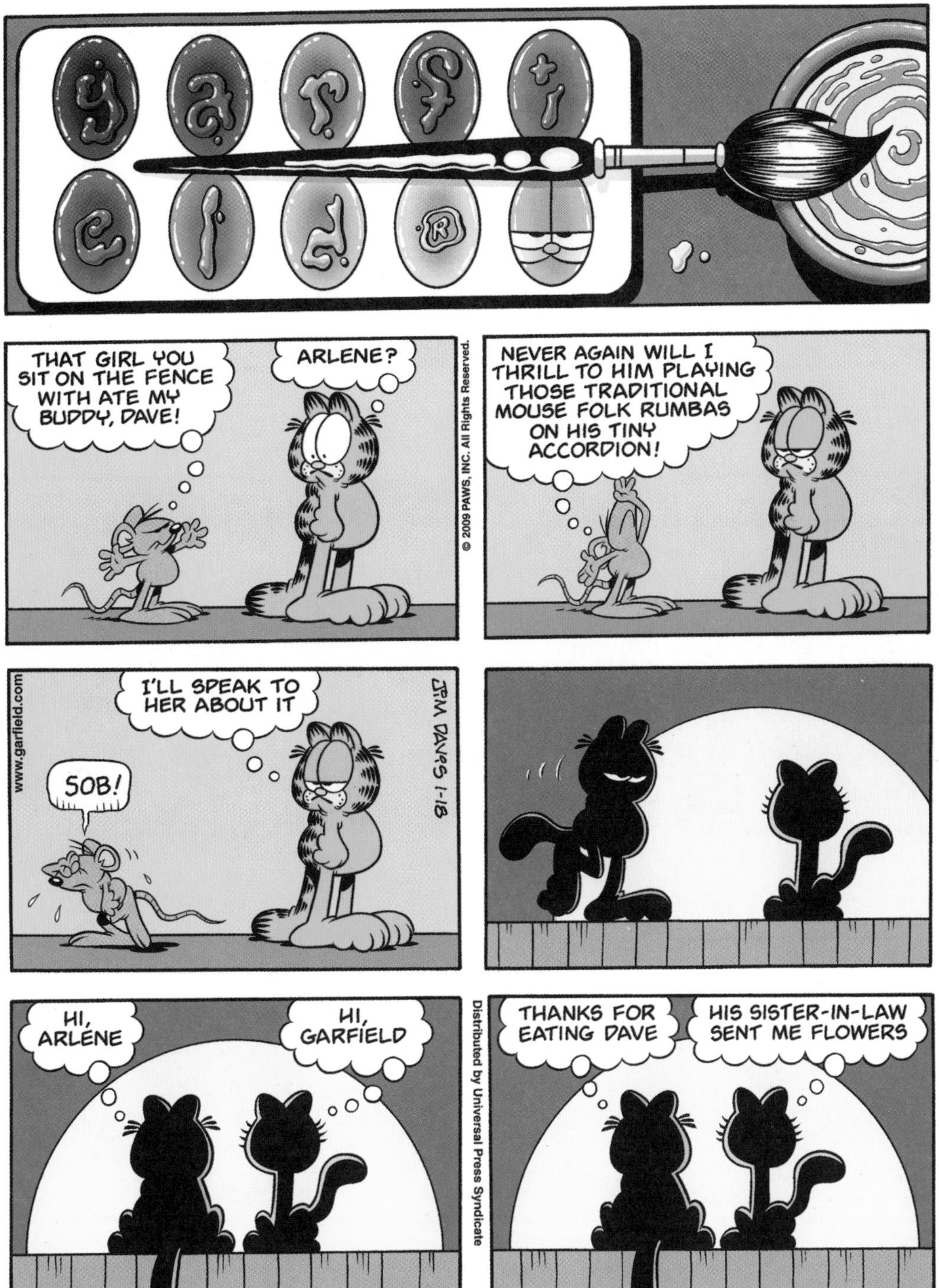
garfield
THAT GIRL YOU SIT ON THE FENCE WITH ATE MY BUDDY, DAVE!
ARLENE?
NEVER AGAIN WILL I THRILL TO HIM PLAYING THOSE TRADITIONAL MOUSE FOLK RUMBAS ON HIS TINY ACCORDION!
© 2009 PAWS, INC. All Rights Reserved.
www.garfield.com
SOB!
I'LL SPEAK TO HER ABOUT IT
JIM DAVIS 1-18
HI, ARLENE
HI, GARFIELD
Distributed by Universal Press Syndicate
THANKS FOR EATING DAVE
HIS SISTER-IN-LAW SENT ME FLOWERS

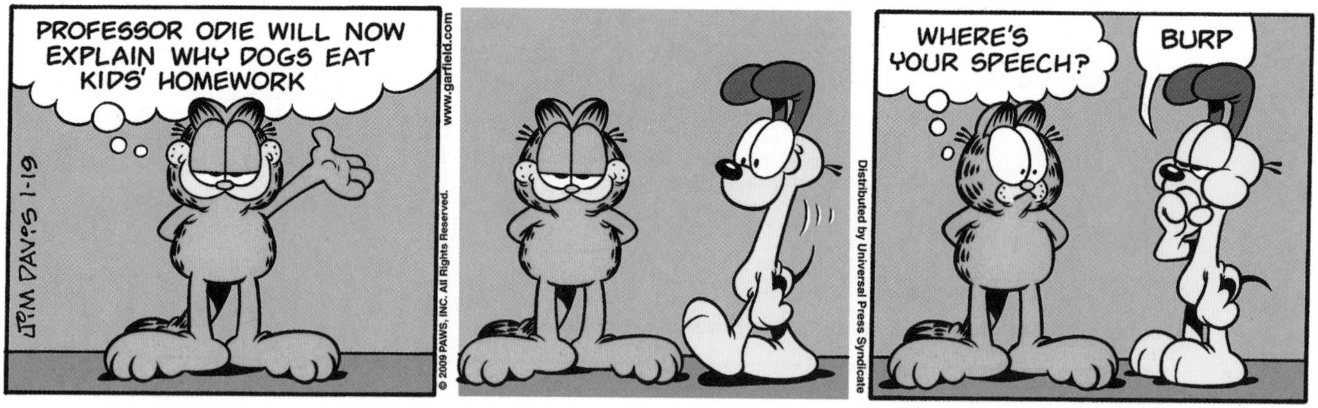
PROFESSOR ODIE WILL NOW EXPLAIN WHY DOGS EAT KIDS' HOMEWORK
JIM DAVIS 1-19
© 2009 PAWS, INC. All Rights Reserved. www.garfield.com
WHERE'S YOUR SPEECH?
BURP
Distributed by Universal Press Syndicate

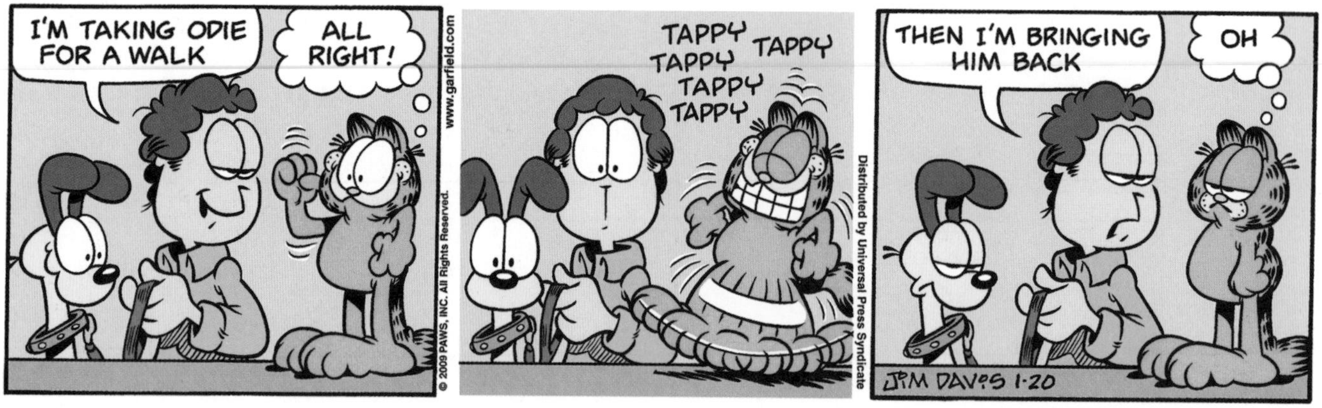
I'M TAKING ODIE FOR A WALK
ALL RIGHT!
© 2009 PAWS, INC. All Rights Reserved. www.garfield.com
TAPPY TAPPY TAPPY TAPPY TAPPY
Distributed by Universal Press Syndicate
THEN I'M BRINGING HIM BACK
OH
JIM DAVIS 1-20

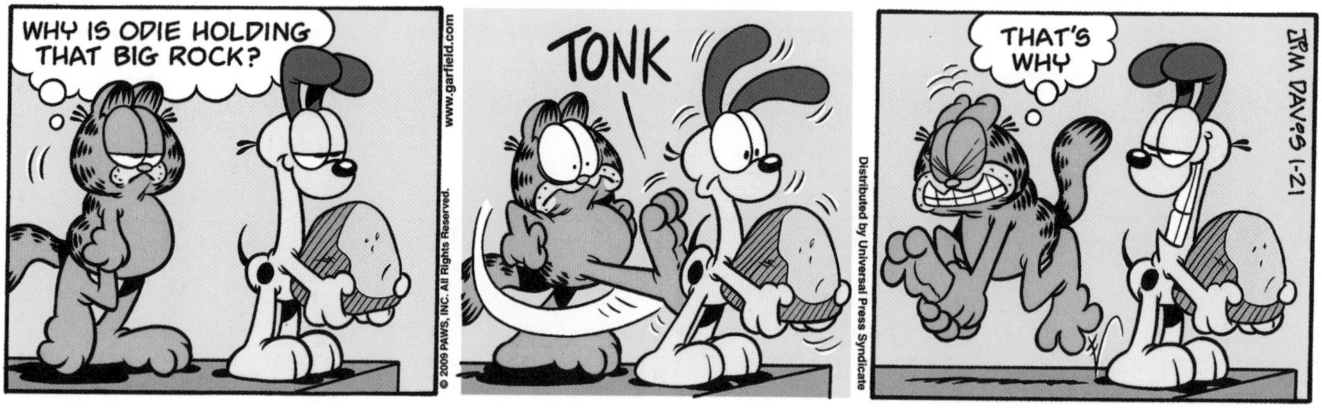
WHY IS ODIE HOLDING THAT BIG ROCK?
© 2009 PAWS, INC. All Rights Reserved. www.garfield.com
TONK
Distributed by Universal Press Syndicate
THAT'S WHY
JIM DAVIS 1-21

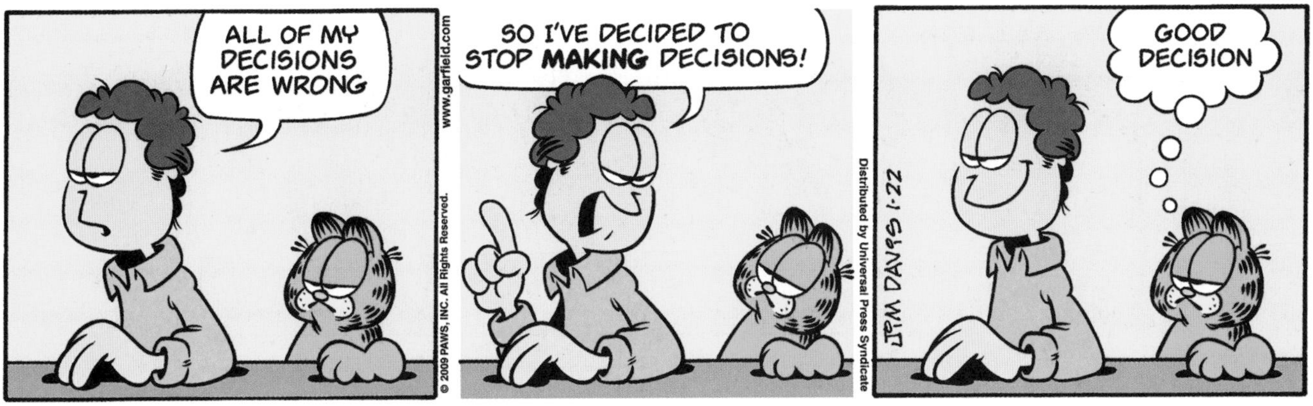
ALL OF MY DECISIONS ARE WRONG
© 2009 PAWS, INC. All Rights Reserved. www.garfield.com
SO I'VE DECIDED TO STOP **MAKING** DECISIONS!
Distributed by Universal Press Syndicate
JIM DAVIS 1-22
GOOD DECISION

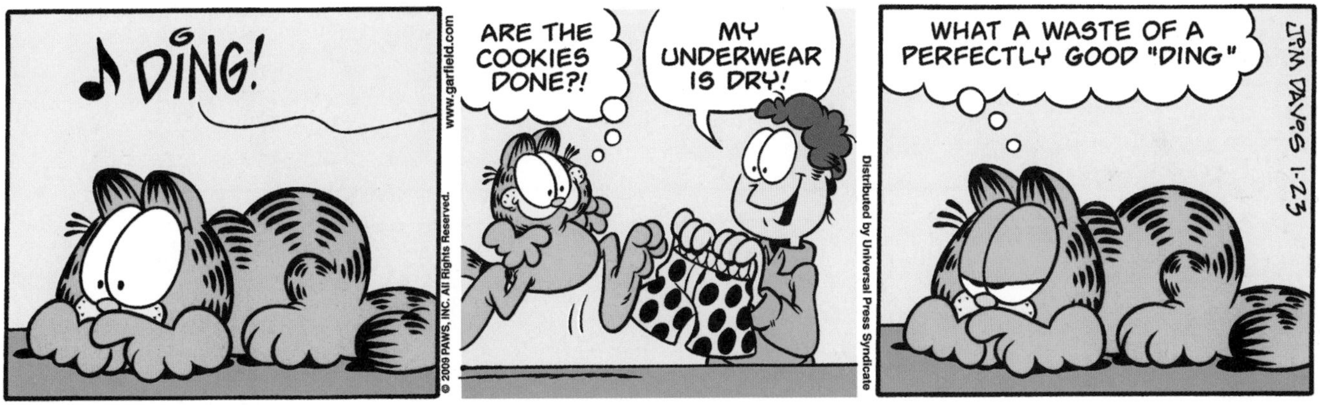
DING!
© 2009 PAWS, INC. All Rights Reserved. www.garfield.com
ARE THE COOKIES DONE?!
MY UNDERWEAR IS DRY!
Distributed by Universal Press Syndicate
WHAT A WASTE OF A PERFECTLY GOOD "DING"
JIM DAVIS 1-23

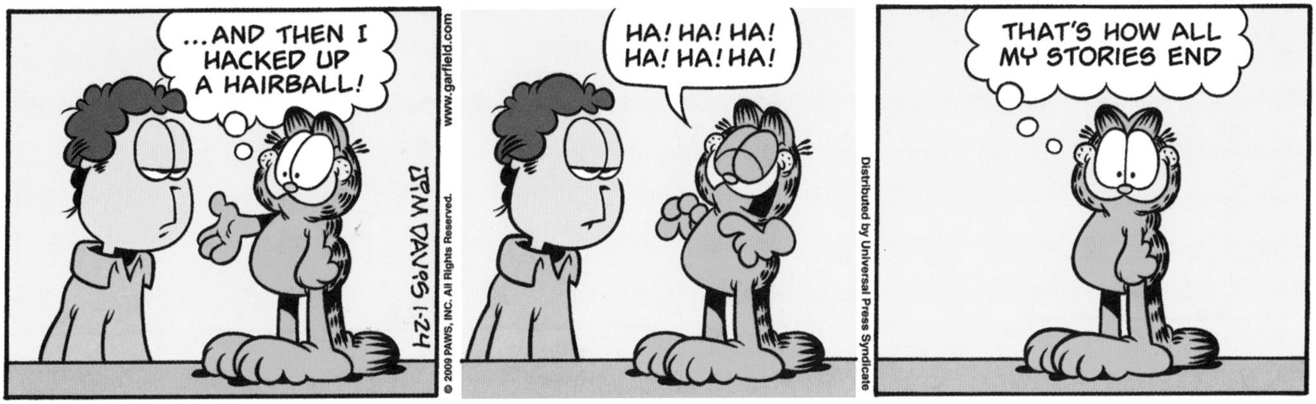
...AND THEN I HACKED UP A HAIRBALL!
JIM DAVIS 1-24
© 2009 PAWS, INC. All Rights Reserved. www.garfield.com
HA! HA! HA! HA! HA! HA!
Distributed by Universal Press Syndicate
THAT'S HOW ALL MY STORIES END

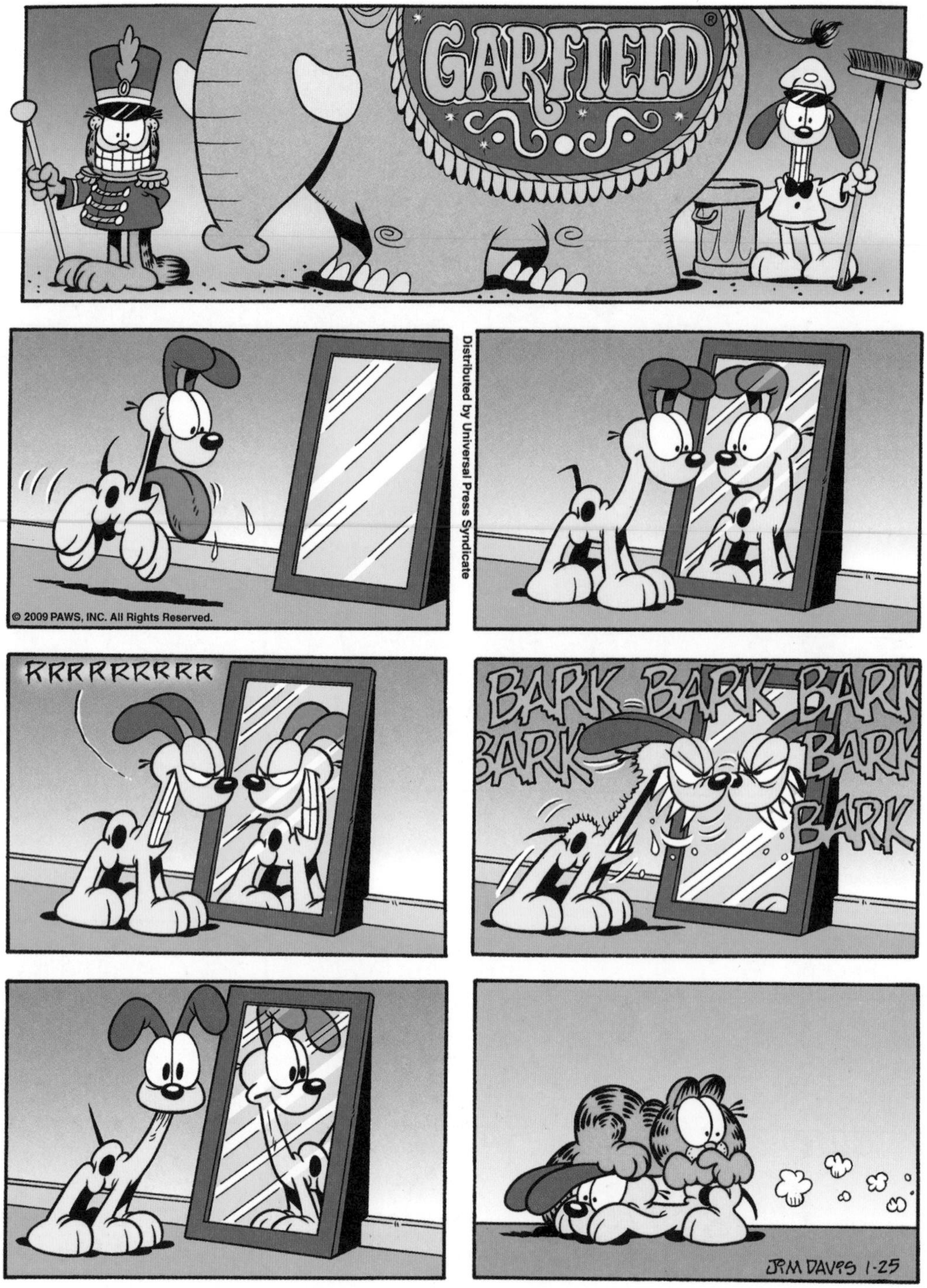
GARFIELD®
Distributed by Universal Press Syndicate
© 2009 PAWS, INC. All Rights Reserved.
RRRRRRRRRR
BARK BARK BARK
BARK BARK
BARK
JIM DAVIS 1-25

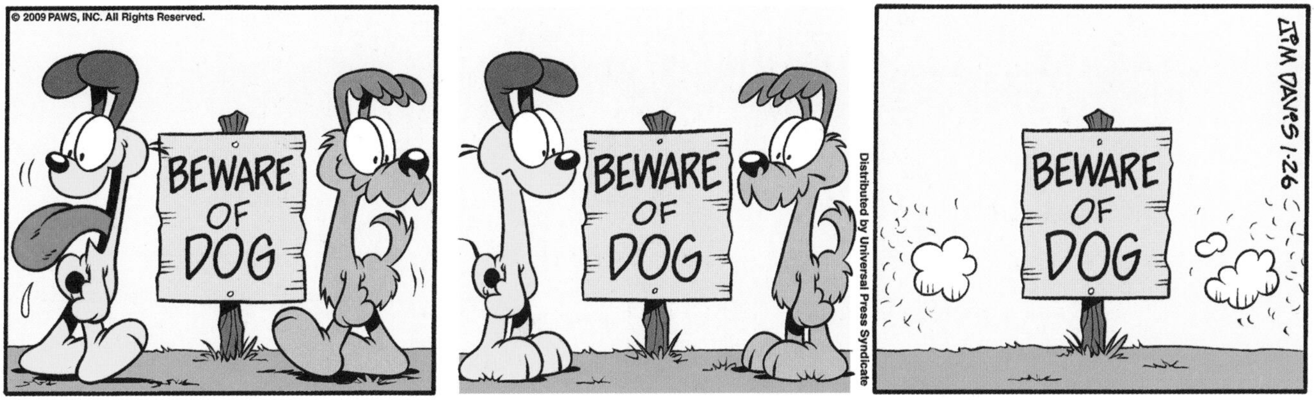
© 2009 PAWS, INC. All Rights Reserved.
BEWARE OF DOG
BEWARE OF DOG
Distributed by Universal Press Syndicate
BEWARE OF DOG
JIM DAVIS 1-26

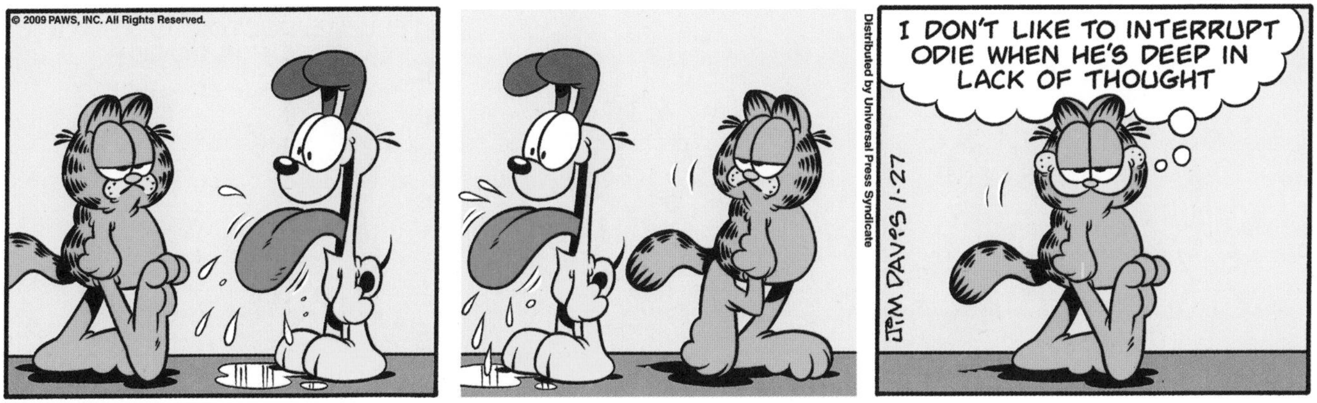
© 2009 PAWS, INC. All Rights Reserved.
Distributed by Universal Press Syndicate
JIM DAVIS 1-27
I DON'T LIKE TO INTERRUPT ODIE WHEN HE'S DEEP IN LACK OF THOUGHT

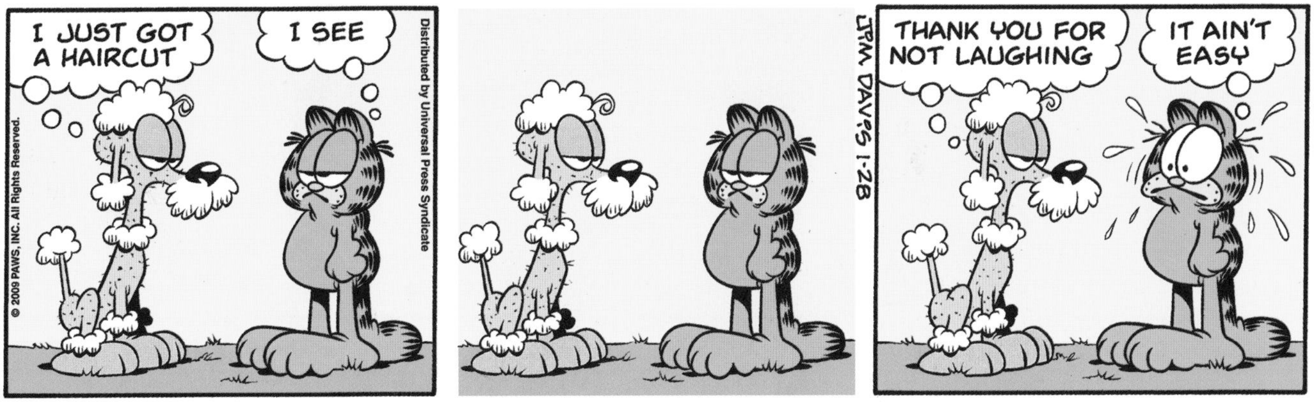
© 2009 PAWS, INC. All Rights Reserved.
I JUST GOT A HAIRCUT
I SEE
Distributed by Universal Press Syndicate
JIM DAVIS 1-28
THANK YOU FOR NOT LAUGHING
IT AIN'T EASY

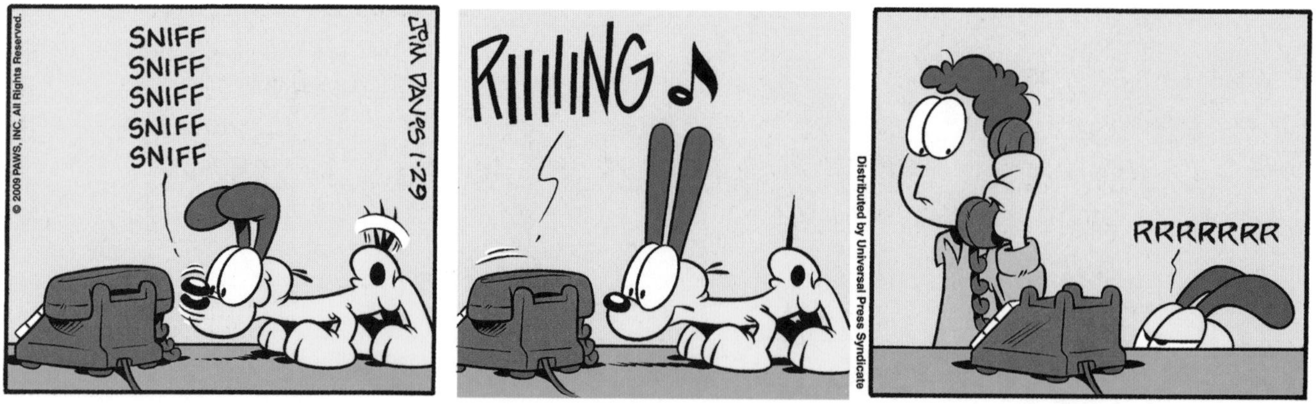
© 2009 PAWS, INC. All Rights Reserved.
SNIFF SNIFF SNIFF SNIFF SNIFF
JIM DAVIS 1-29
RIIIIING
Distributed by Universal Press Syndicate
RRRRRRR

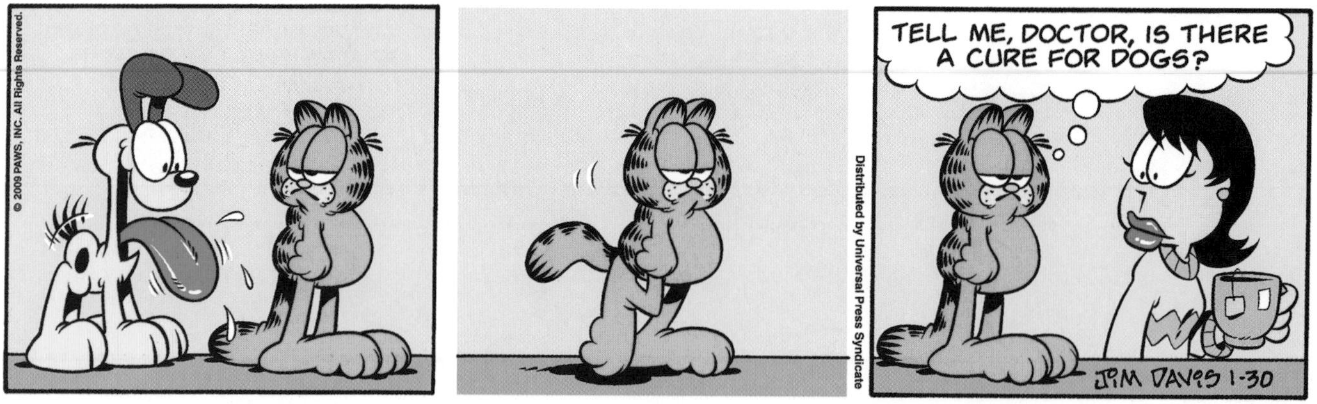
© 2009 PAWS, INC. All Rights Reserved.
Distributed by Universal Press Syndicate
TELL ME, DOCTOR, IS THERE A CURE FOR DOGS?
JIM DAVIS 1-30

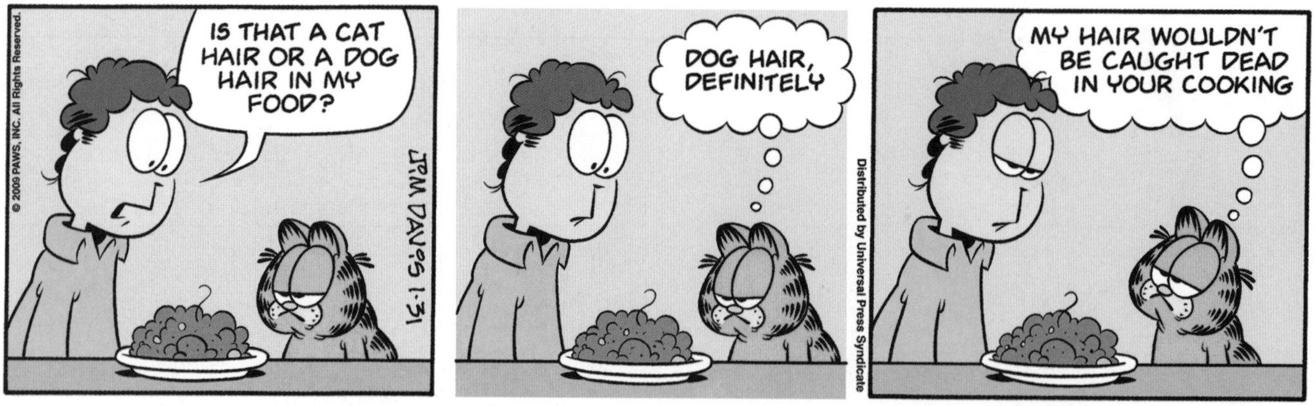
© 2009 PAWS, INC. All Rights Reserved.
IS THAT A CAT HAIR OR A DOG HAIR IN MY FOOD?
JIM DAVIS 1-31
DOG HAIR, DEFINITELY
Distributed by Universal Press Syndicate
MY HAIR WOULDN'T BE CAUGHT DEAD IN YOUR COOKING

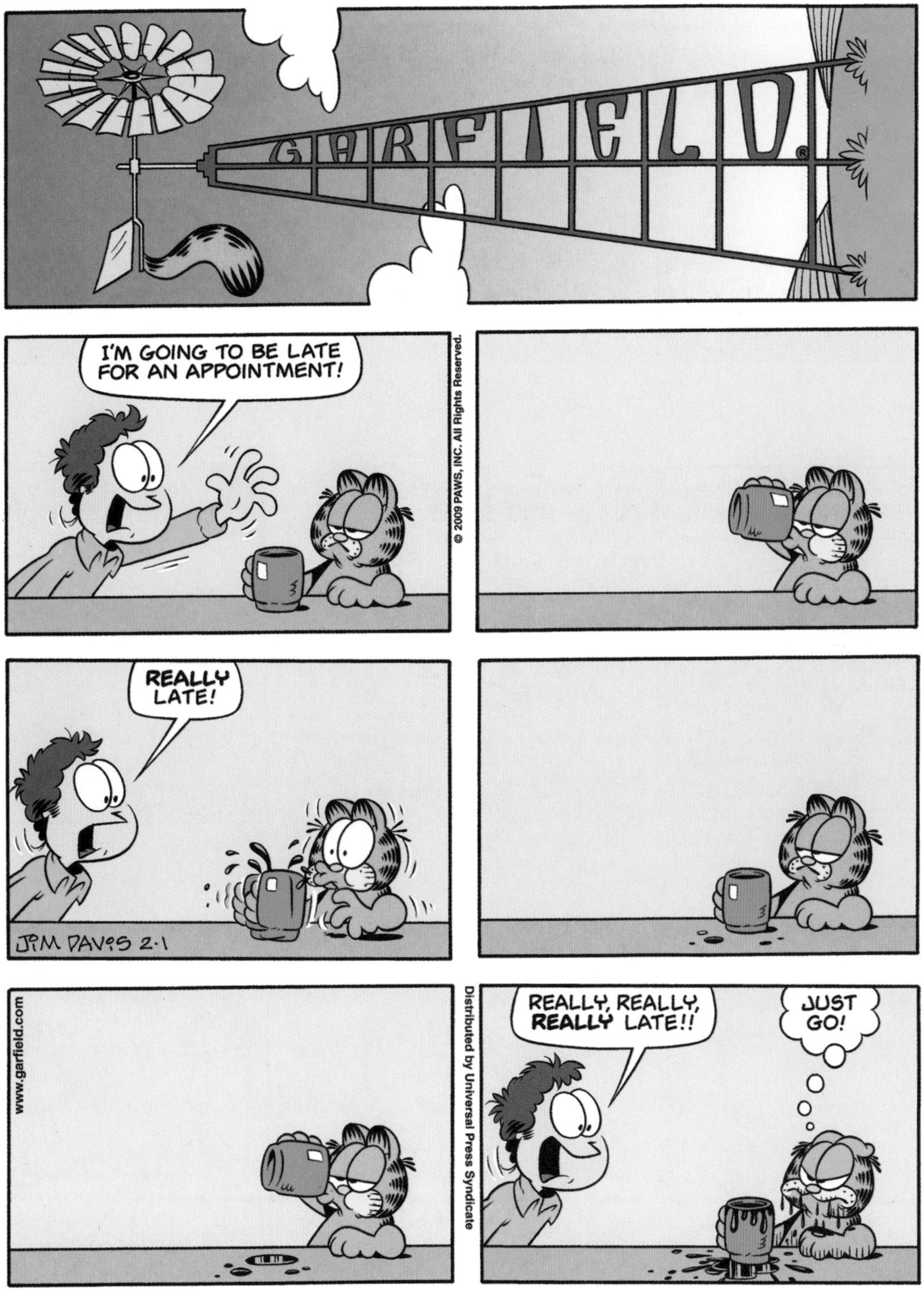
GARFIELD®
I'M GOING TO BE LATE FOR AN APPOINTMENT!
© 2009 PAWS, INC. All Rights Reserved.
REALLY LATE!
JIM DAVIS 2-1
www.garfield.com
Distributed by Universal Press Syndicate
REALLY, REALLY, **REALLY** LATE!!
JUST GO!

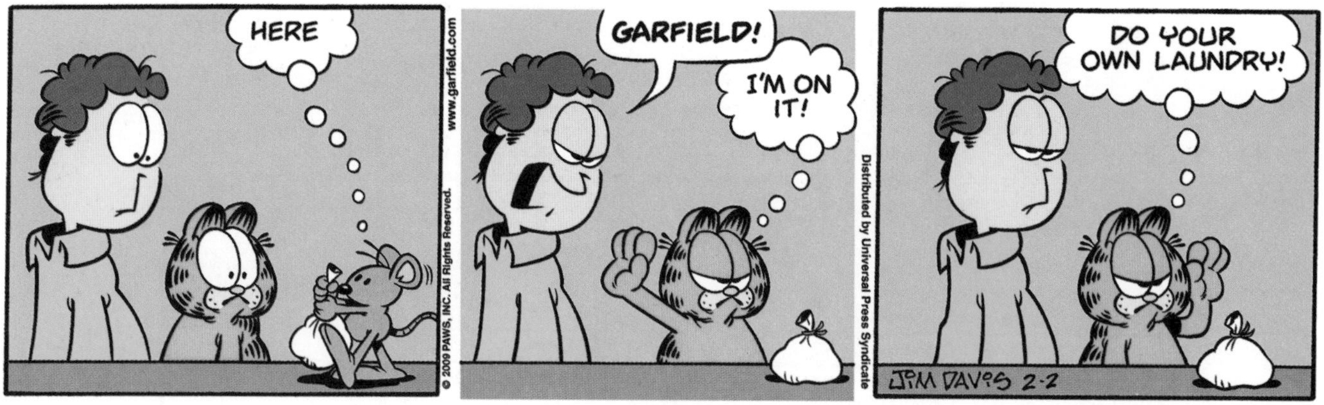
HERE
www.garfield.com
© 2009 PAWS, INC. All Rights Reserved.
GARFIELD!
I'M ON IT!
Distributed by Universal Press Syndicate
DO YOUR OWN LAUNDRY!
JIM DAVIS 2-2

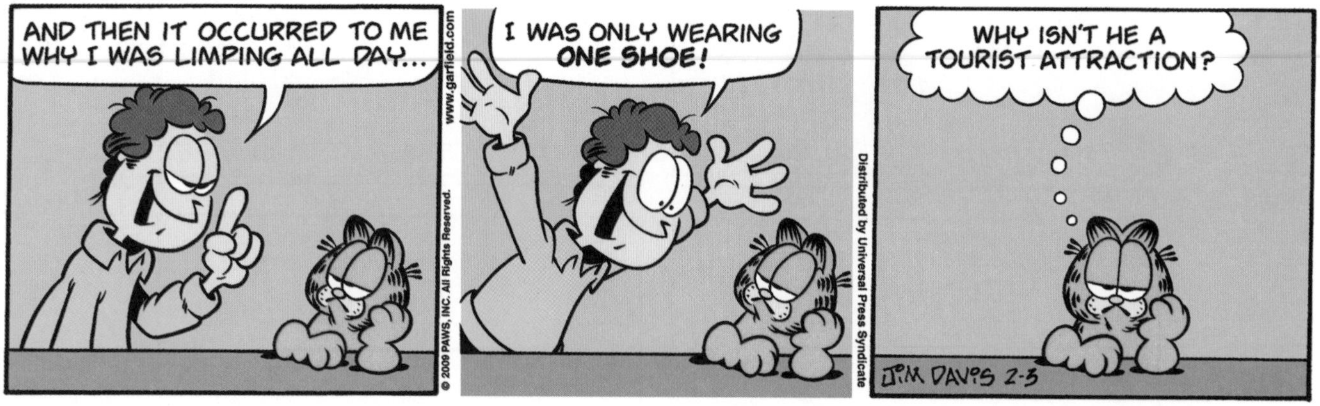
AND THEN IT OCCURRED TO ME WHY I WAS LIMPING ALL DAY...
www.garfield.com
© 2009 PAWS, INC. All Rights Reserved.
I WAS ONLY WEARING **ONE SHOE**!
Distributed by Universal Press Syndicate
WHY ISN'T HE A TOURIST ATTRACTION?
JIM DAVIS 2-3

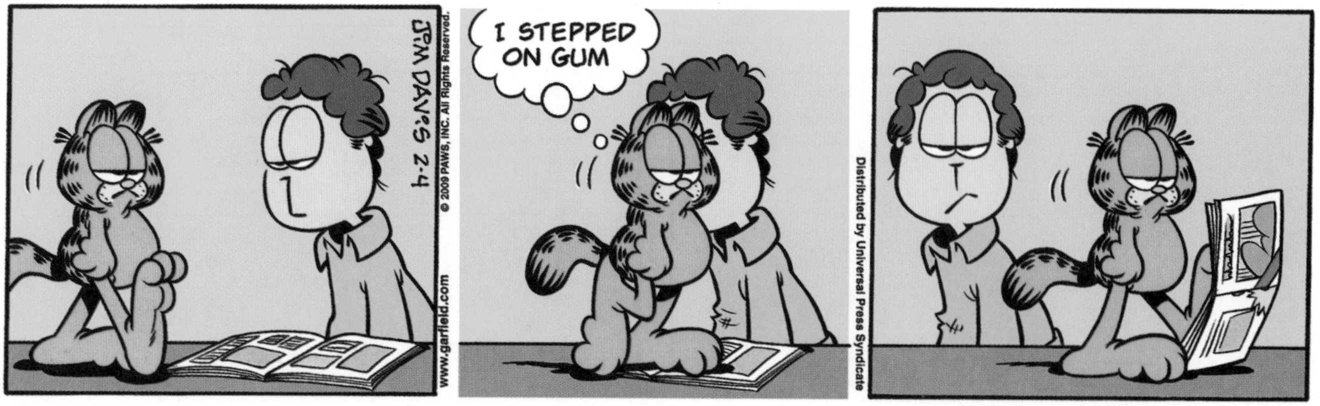
JIM DAVIS 2-4
© 2009 PAWS, INC. All Rights Reserved.
www.garfield.com
I STEPPED ON GUM
Distributed by Universal Press Syndicate

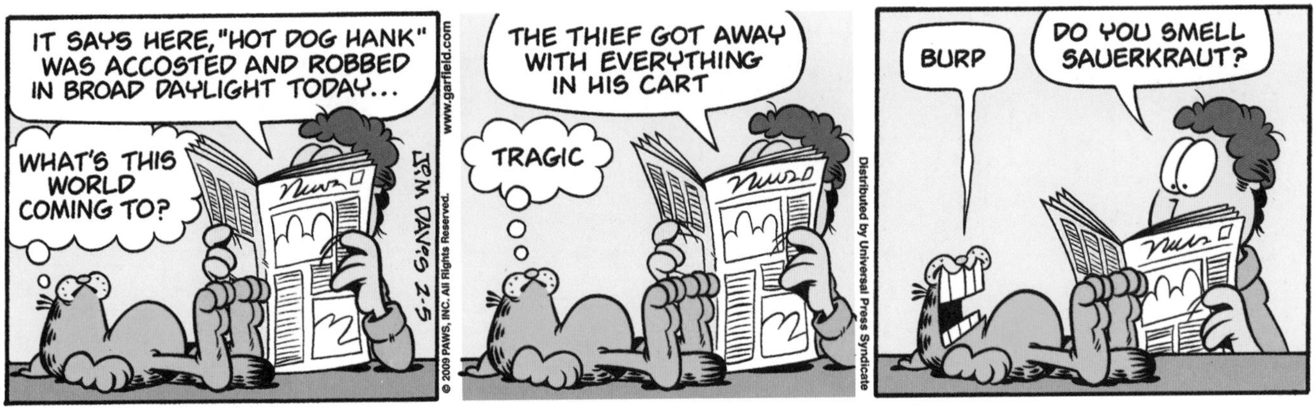
IT SAYS HERE, "HOT DOG HANK" WAS ACCOSTED AND ROBBED IN BROAD DAYLIGHT TODAY...
WHAT'S THIS WORLD COMING TO?
JIM DAVIS 2-5
THE THIEF GOT AWAY WITH EVERYTHING IN HIS CART
TRAGIC
BURP
DO YOU SMELL SAUERKRAUT?
© 2009 PAWS, INC. All Rights Reserved.
www.garfield.com
Distributed by Universal Press Syndicate

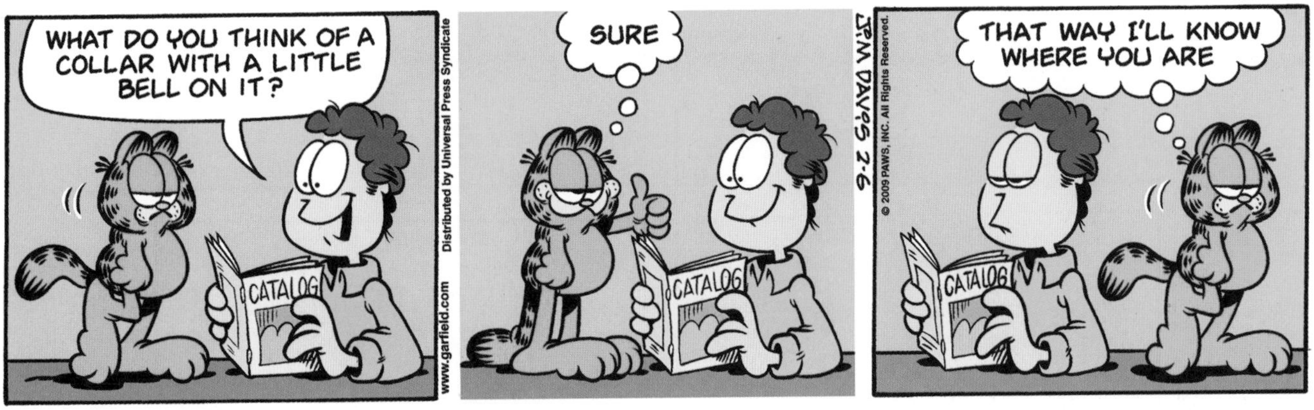
WHAT DO YOU THINK OF A COLLAR WITH A LITTLE BELL ON IT?
CATALOG
SURE
THAT WAY I'LL KNOW WHERE YOU ARE
JIM DAVIS 2-6
© 2009 PAWS, INC. All Rights Reserved.
www.garfield.com
Distributed by Universal Press Syndicate

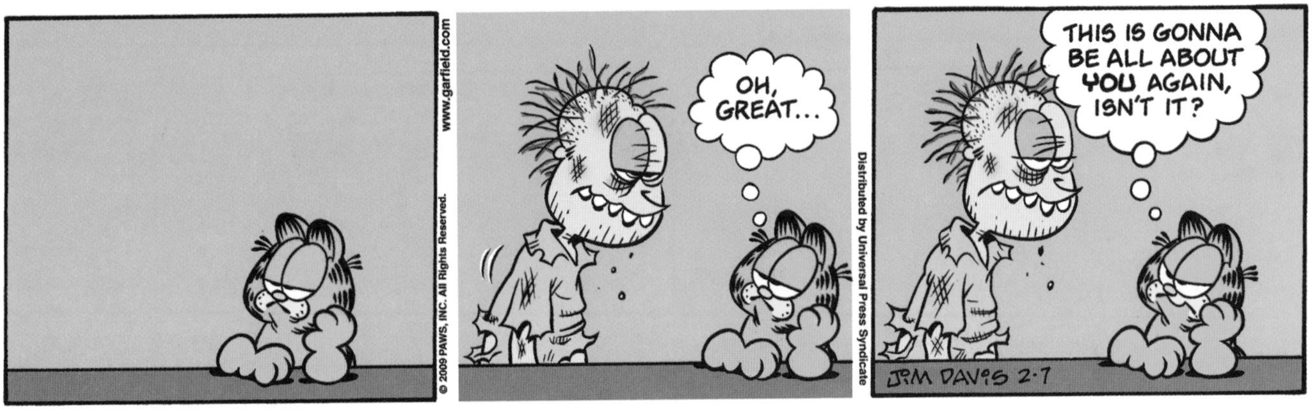
OH, GREAT...
THIS IS GONNA BE ALL ABOUT **YOU** AGAIN, ISN'T IT?
JIM DAVIS 2-7
© 2009 PAWS, INC. All Rights Reserved.
www.garfield.com
Distributed by Universal Press Syndicate

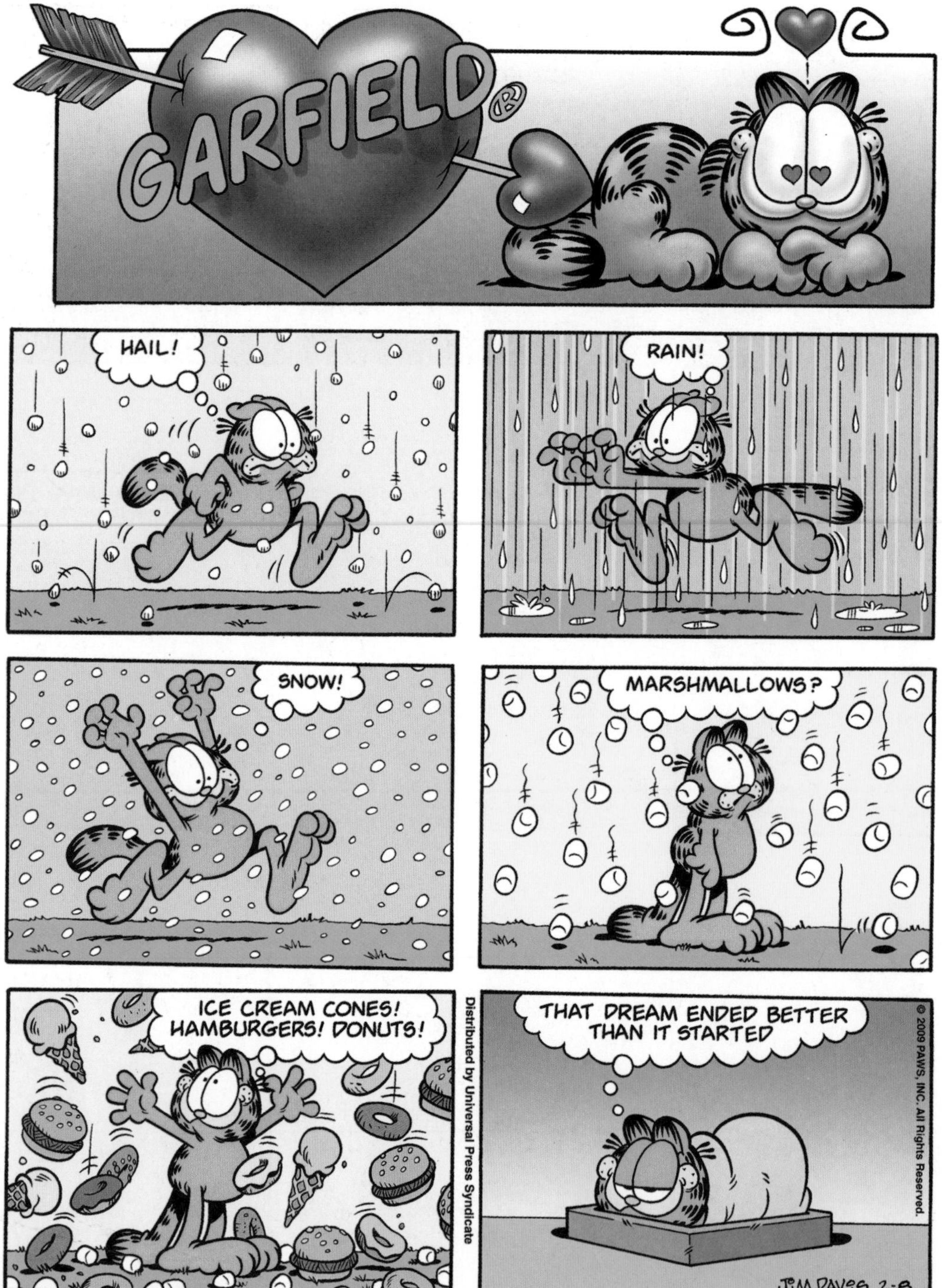
GARFIELD®
HAIL!
RAIN!
SNOW!
MARSHMALLOWS?
ICE CREAM CONES! HAMBURGERS! DONUTS!
THAT DREAM ENDED BETTER THAN IT STARTED
Distributed by Universal Press Syndicate
© 2009 PAWS, INC. All Rights Reserved.
JIM DAVIS 2-8

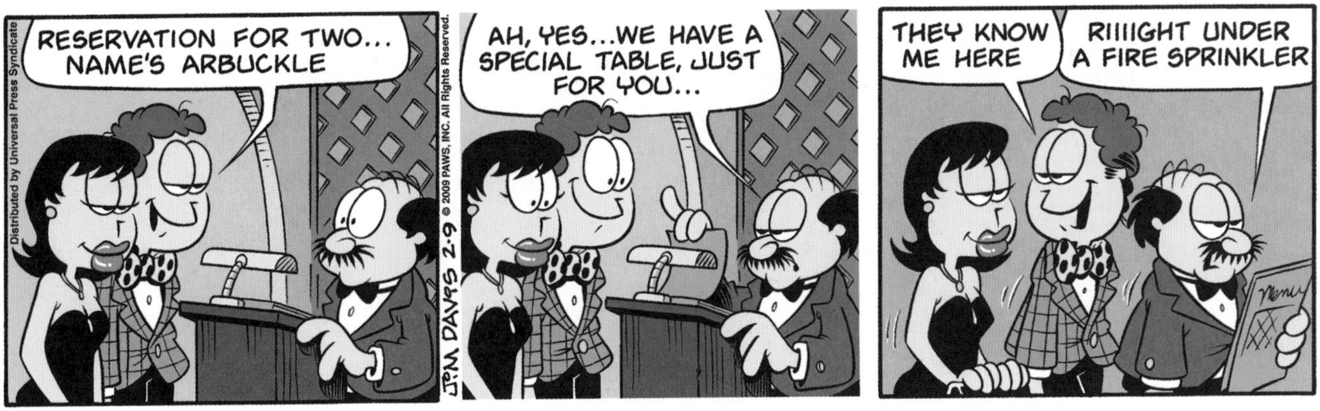
Distributed by Universal Press Syndicate
RESERVATION FOR TWO... NAME'S ARBUCKLE
JPM DAVPS 2-9
© 2009 PAWS, INC. All Rights Reserved.
AH, YES...WE HAVE A SPECIAL TABLE, JUST FOR YOU...
THEY KNOW ME HERE
RIIIIGHT UNDER A FIRE SPRINKLER
Menu

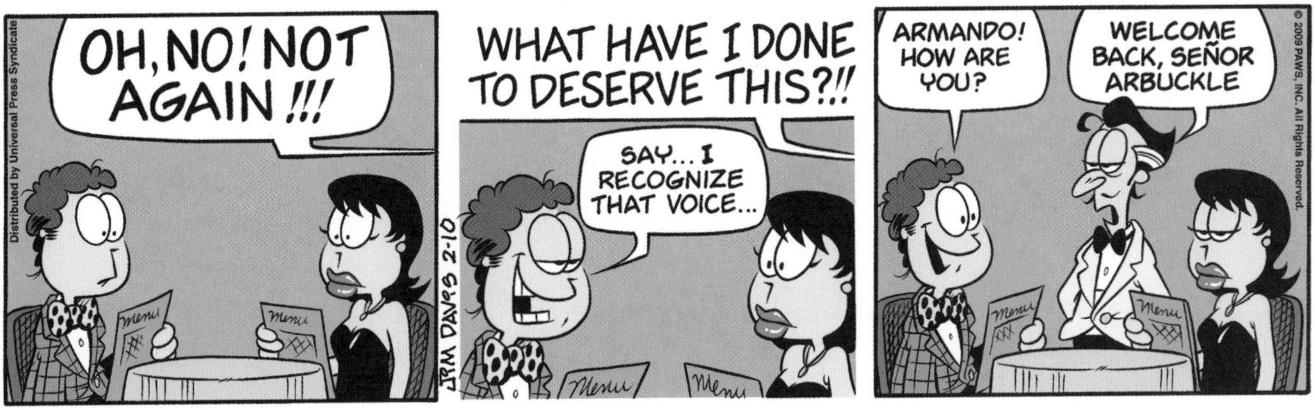
Distributed by Universal Press Syndicate
OH, NO! NOT AGAIN!!!
Menu
Menu
JPM DAVPS 2-10
WHAT HAVE I DONE TO DESERVE THIS?!!
SAY... I RECOGNIZE THAT VOICE...
Menu
Menu
ARMANDO! HOW ARE YOU?
WELCOME BACK, SEÑOR ARBUCKLE
Menu
Menu
© 2009 PAWS, INC. All Rights Reserved.

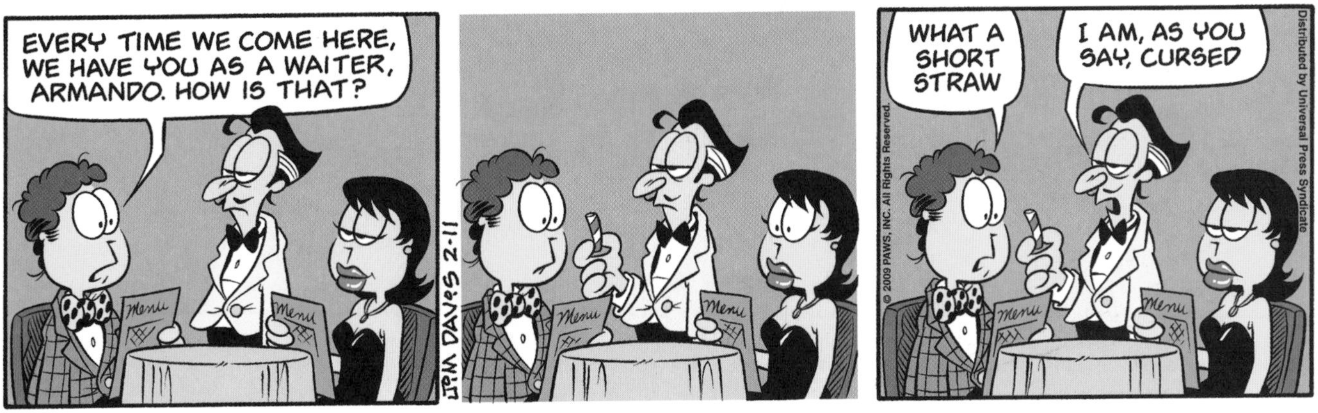
EVERY TIME WE COME HERE, WE HAVE YOU AS A WAITER, ARMANDO. HOW IS THAT?
Menu
Menu
JPM DAVPS 2-11
Menu
Menu
© 2009 PAWS, INC. All Rights Reserved.
WHAT A SHORT STRAW
I AM, AS YOU SAY, CURSED
Menu
Menu
Distributed by Universal Press Syndicate

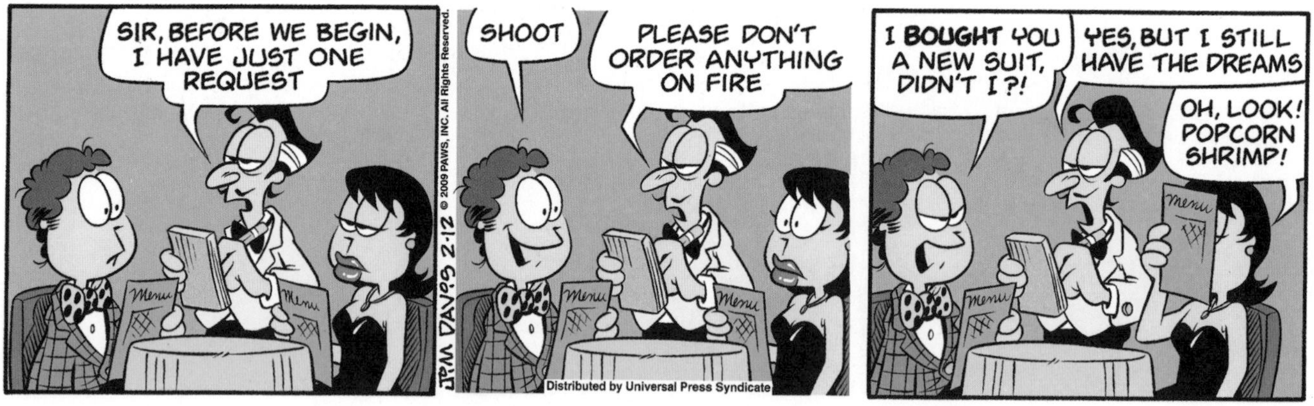
SIR, BEFORE WE BEGIN, I HAVE JUST ONE REQUEST
JPM DAVIS 2-12
© 2009 PAWS, INC. All Rights Reserved.
SHOOT
PLEASE DON'T ORDER ANYTHING ON FIRE
Menu
Distributed by Universal Press Syndicate
I **BOUGHT** YOU A NEW SUIT, DIDN'T I?!
YES, BUT I STILL HAVE THE DREAMS
OH, LOOK! POPCORN SHRIMP!

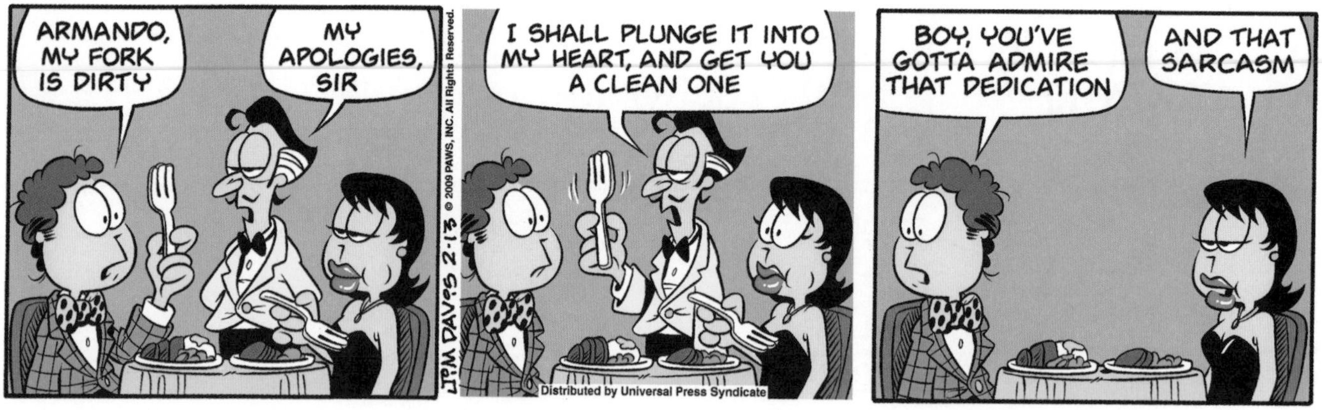
ARMANDO, MY FORK IS DIRTY
MY APOLOGIES, SIR
JPM DAVIS 2-13
© 2009 PAWS, INC. All Rights Reserved.
I SHALL PLUNGE IT INTO MY HEART, AND GET YOU A CLEAN ONE
Distributed by Universal Press Syndicate
BOY, YOU'VE GOTTA ADMIRE THAT DEDICATION
AND THAT SARCASM

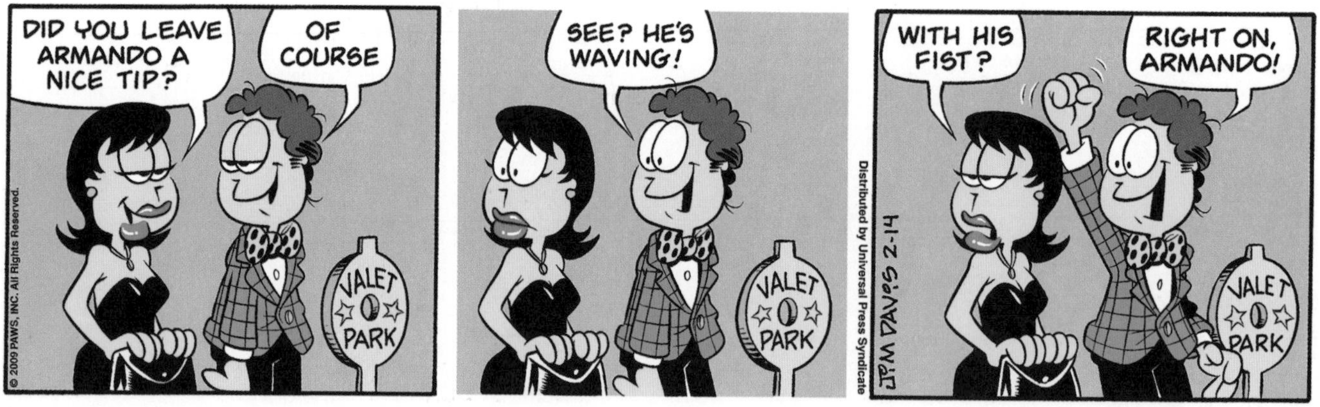
DID YOU LEAVE ARMANDO A NICE TIP?
OF COURSE
© 2009 PAWS, INC. All Rights Reserved.
VALET PARK
SEE? HE'S WAVING!
JPM DAVIS 2-14
Distributed by Universal Press Syndicate
WITH HIS FIST?
RIGHT ON, ARMANDO!

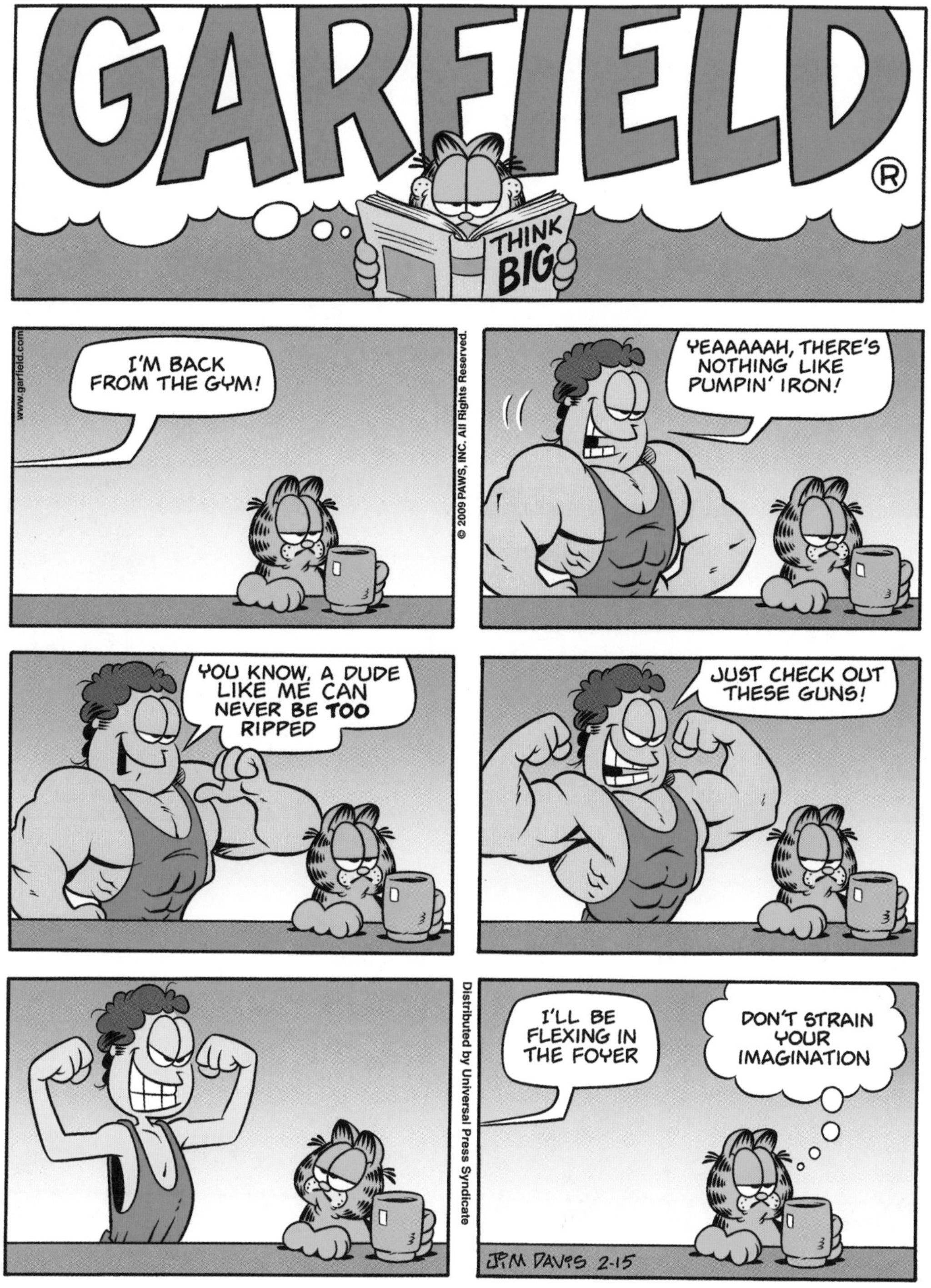
GARFIELD®
THINK BIG
www.garfield.com
I'M BACK FROM THE GYM!
© 2009 PAWS, INC. All Rights Reserved.
YEAAAAAH, THERE'S NOTHING LIKE PUMPIN' IRON!
YOU KNOW, A DUDE LIKE ME CAN NEVER BE **TOO** RIPPED
JUST CHECK OUT THESE GUNS!
Distributed by Universal Press Syndicate
I'LL BE FLEXING IN THE FOYER
DON'T STRAIN YOUR IMAGINATION
JIM DAVIS 2-15

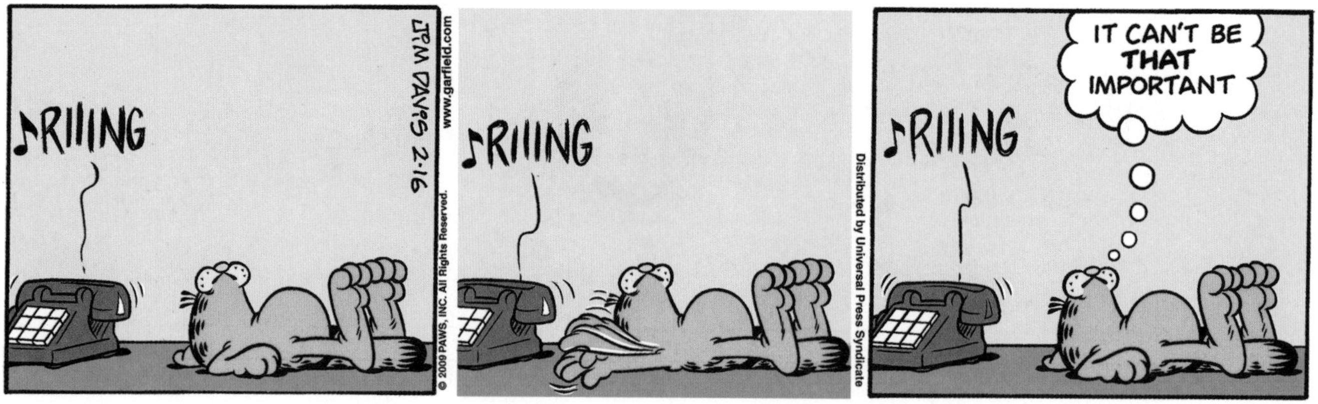
♪RIIING
JIM DAVIS 2-16
www.garfield.com
© 2009 PAWS, INC. All Rights Reserved.
♪RIIING
Distributed by Universal Press Syndicate
♪RIIING
IT CAN'T BE **THAT** IMPORTANT

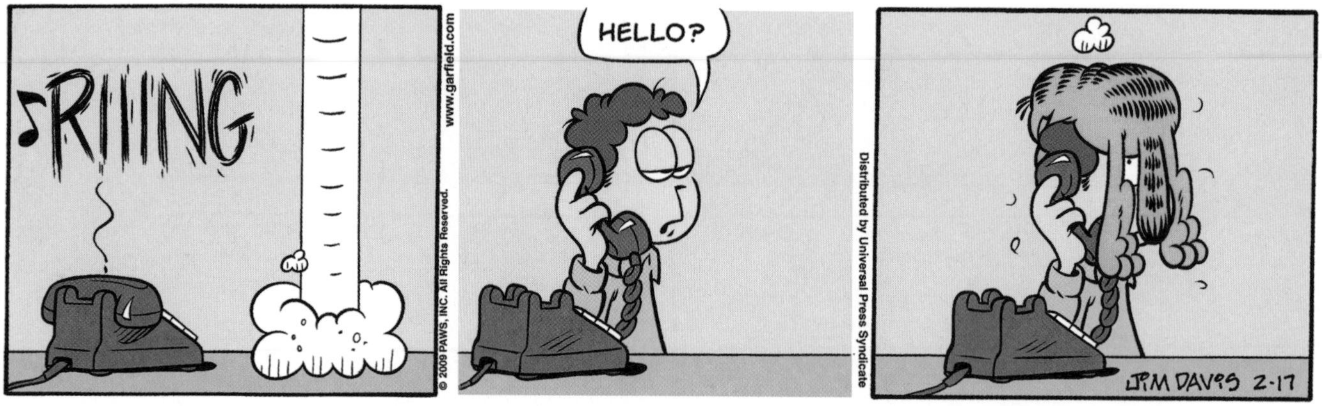
♪RIIING
www.garfield.com
© 2009 PAWS, INC. All Rights Reserved.
HELLO?
Distributed by Universal Press Syndicate
JIM DAVIS 2-17

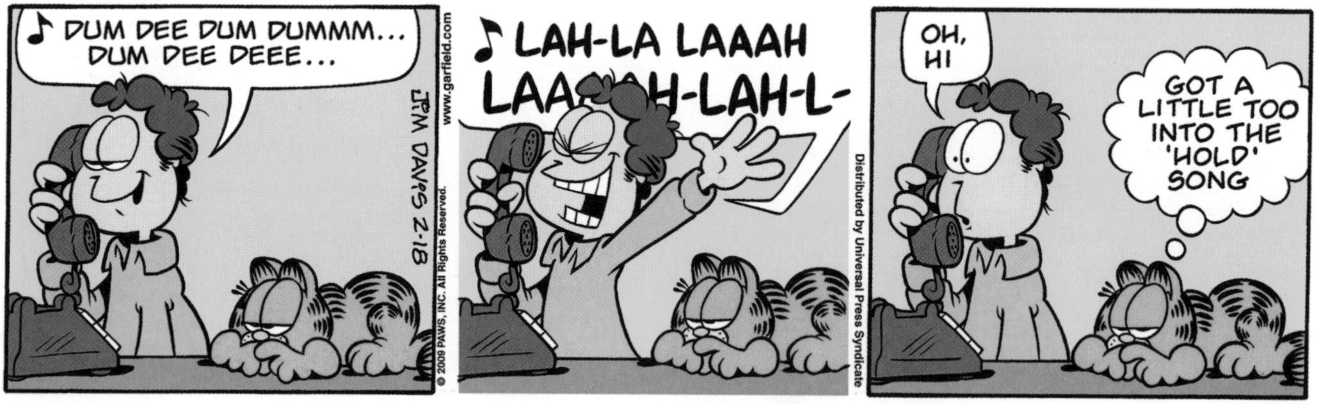
♪ DUM DEE DUM DUMMM... DUM DEE DEEE...
JIM DAVIS 2-18
www.garfield.com
© 2009 PAWS, INC. All Rights Reserved.
♪ LAH-LA LAAAH
LAA H-LAH-L-
Distributed by Universal Press Syndicate
OH, HI
GOT A LITTLE TOO INTO THE 'HOLD' SONG

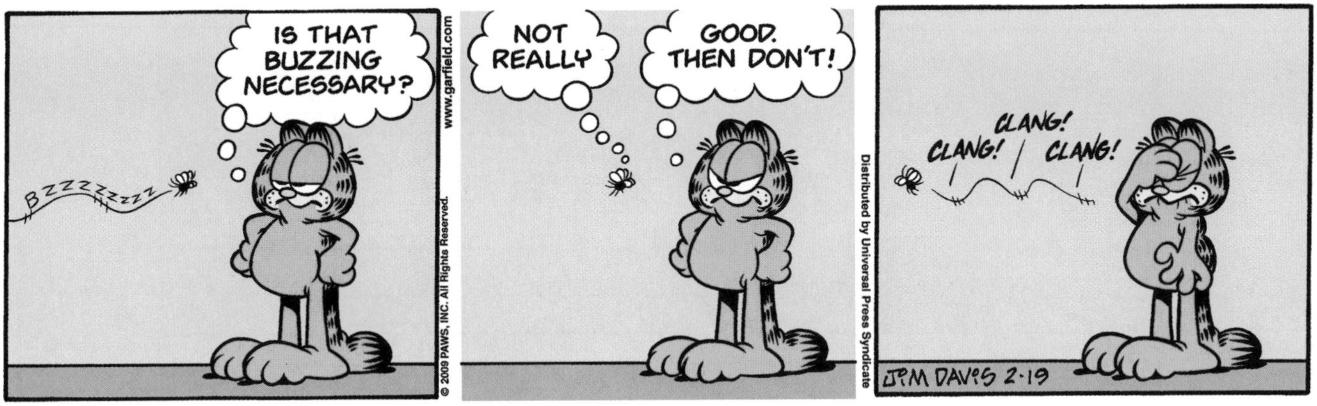
IS THAT BUZZING NECESSARY?
BZZZZZZZZZ
© 2009 PAWS, INC. All Rights Reserved.
www.garfield.com
NOT REALLY
GOOD. THEN DON'T!
Distributed by Universal Press Syndicate
CLANG! CLANG! CLANG!
JIM DAVIS 2-19

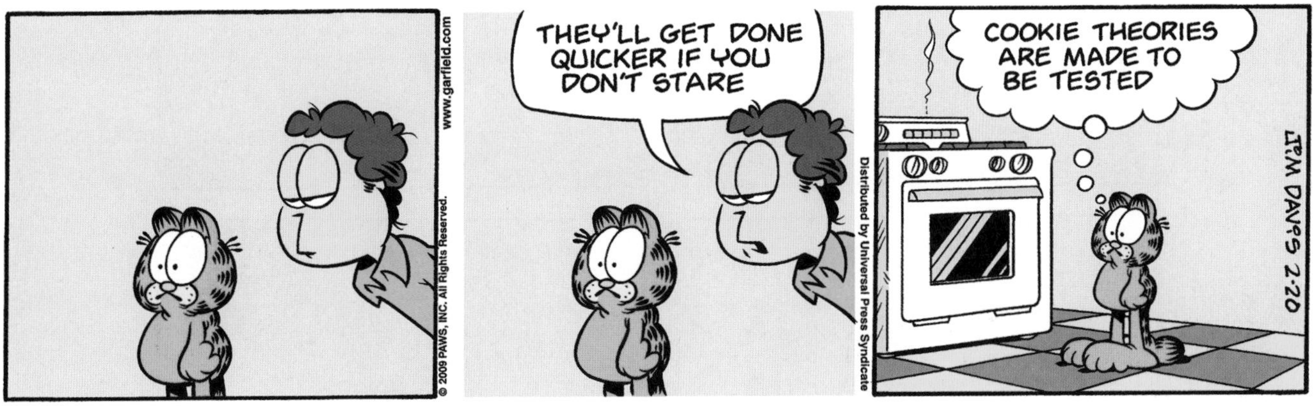
© 2009 PAWS, INC. All Rights Reserved.
www.garfield.com
THEY'LL GET DONE QUICKER IF YOU DON'T STARE
Distributed by Universal Press Syndicate
COOKIE THEORIES ARE MADE TO BE TESTED
JIM DAVIS 2-20

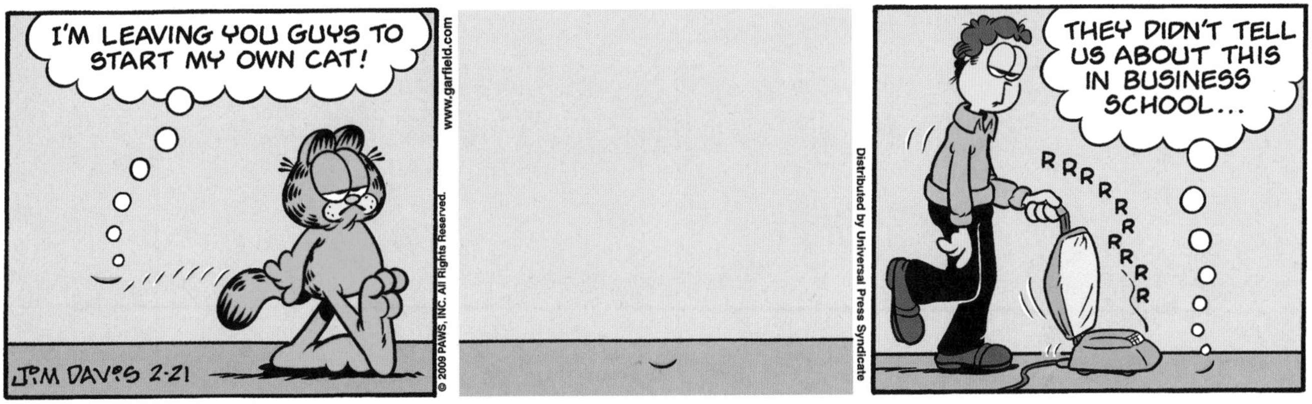
I'M LEAVING YOU GUYS TO START MY OWN CAT!
JIM DAVIS 2-21
© 2009 PAWS, INC. All Rights Reserved.
www.garfield.com
Distributed by Universal Press Syndicate
RRRRRRRRRR
THEY DIDN'T TELL US ABOUT THIS IN BUSINESS SCHOOL...

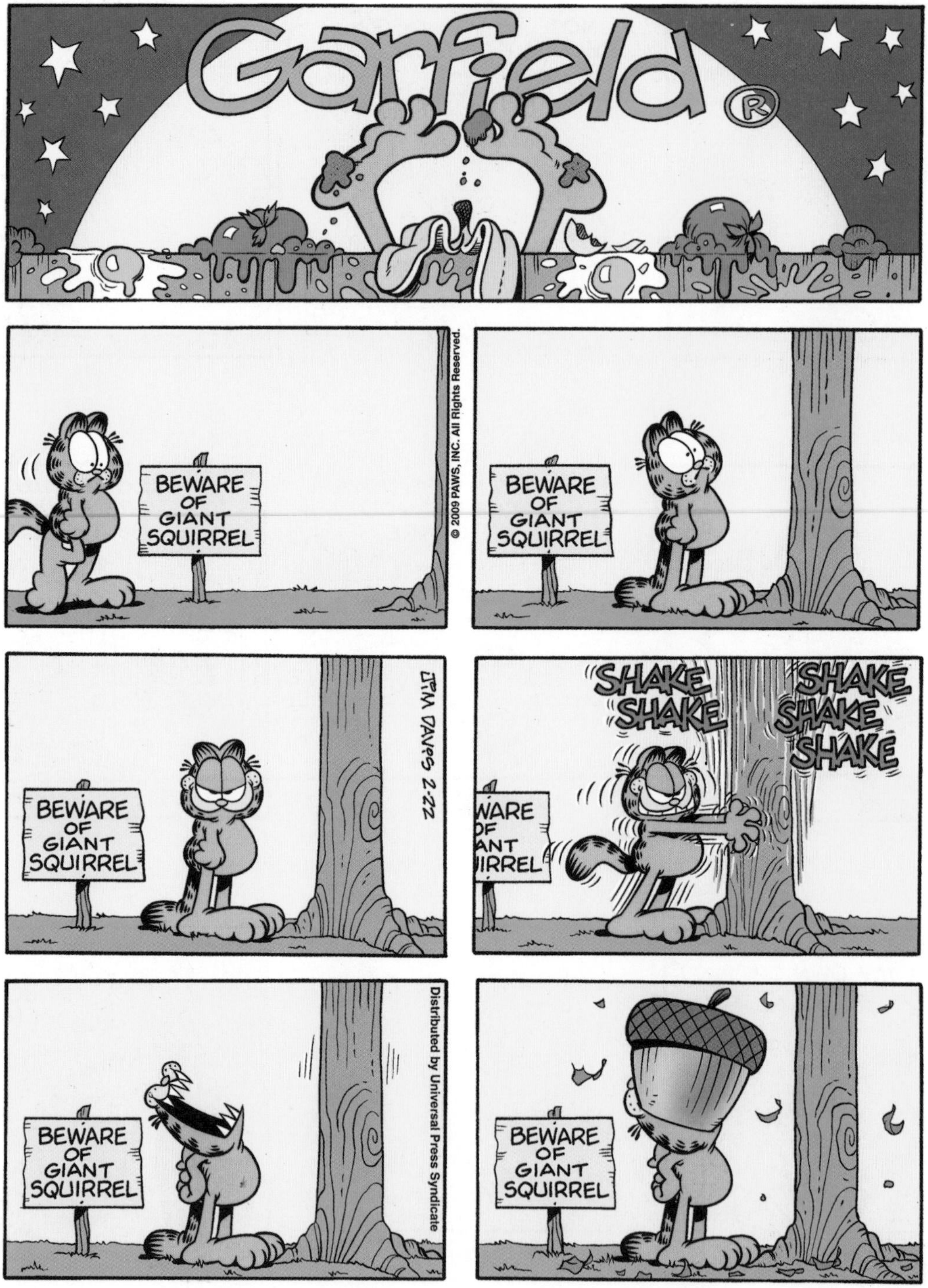
Garfield®
BEWARE OF GIANT SQUIRREL
© 2009 PAWS, INC. All Rights Reserved.
BEWARE OF GIANT SQUIRREL
BEWARE OF GIANT SQUIRREL
JIM DAVIS 2-22
SHAKE SHAKE
SHAKE SHAKE SHAKE
WARE OF ANT IRREL
BEWARE OF GIANT SQUIRREL
Distributed by Universal Press Syndicate
BEWARE OF GIANT SQUIRREL

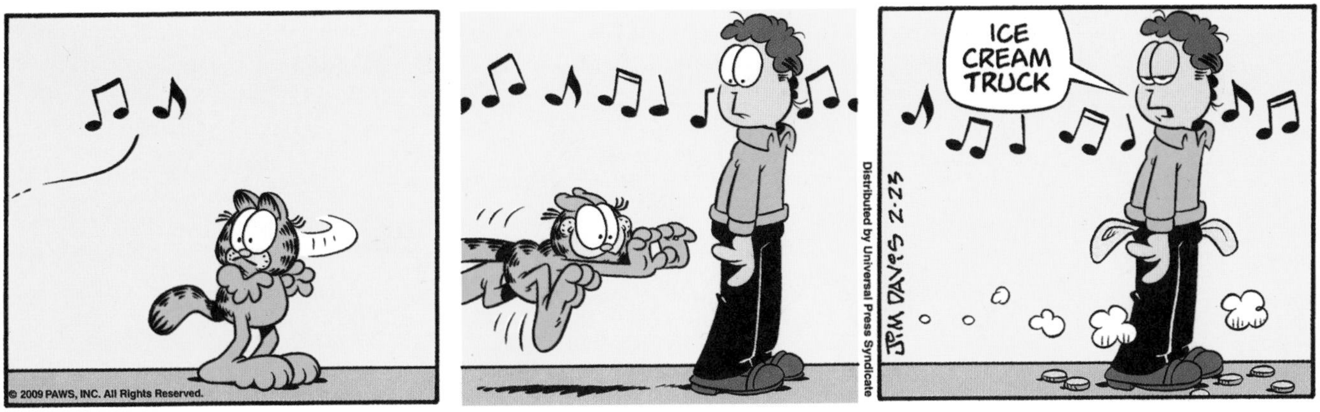
© 2009 PAWS, INC. All Rights Reserved.
Distributed by Universal Press Syndicate
JIM DAVIS 2-23
ICE CREAM TRUCK

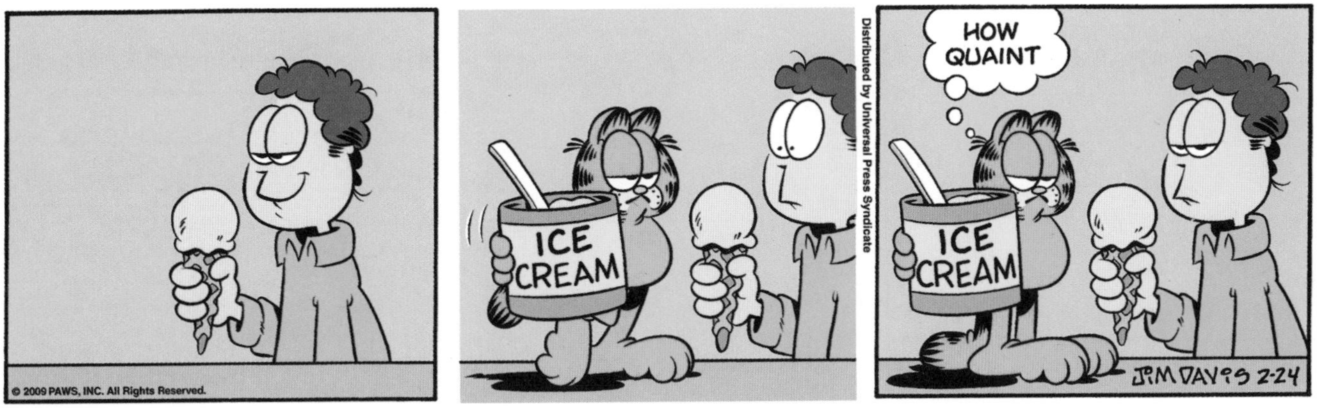
© 2009 PAWS, INC. All Rights Reserved.
Distributed by Universal Press Syndicate
ICE CREAM
HOW QUAINT
ICE CREAM
JIM DAVIS 2-24

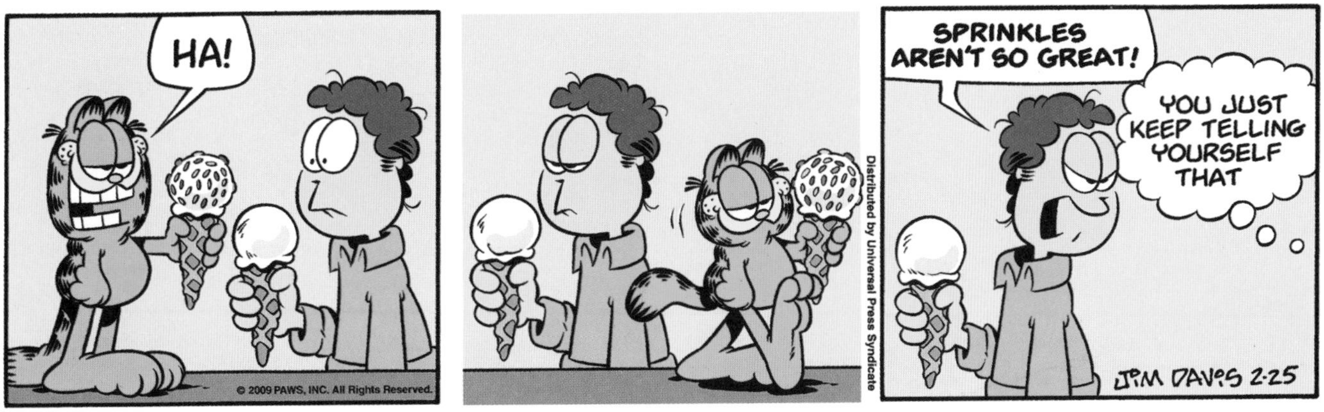
HA!
© 2009 PAWS, INC. All Rights Reserved.
Distributed by Universal Press Syndicate
SPRINKLES AREN'T SO GREAT!
YOU JUST KEEP TELLING YOURSELF THAT
JIM DAVIS 2-25

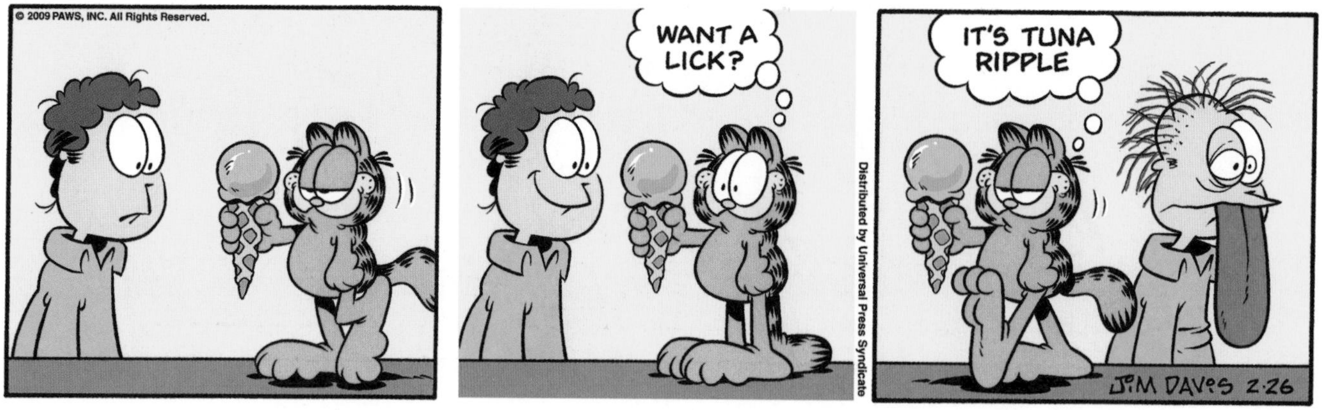
© 2009 PAWS, INC. All Rights Reserved.
WANT A LICK?
Distributed by Universal Press Syndicate
IT'S TUNA RIPPLE
JIM DAVIS 2·26

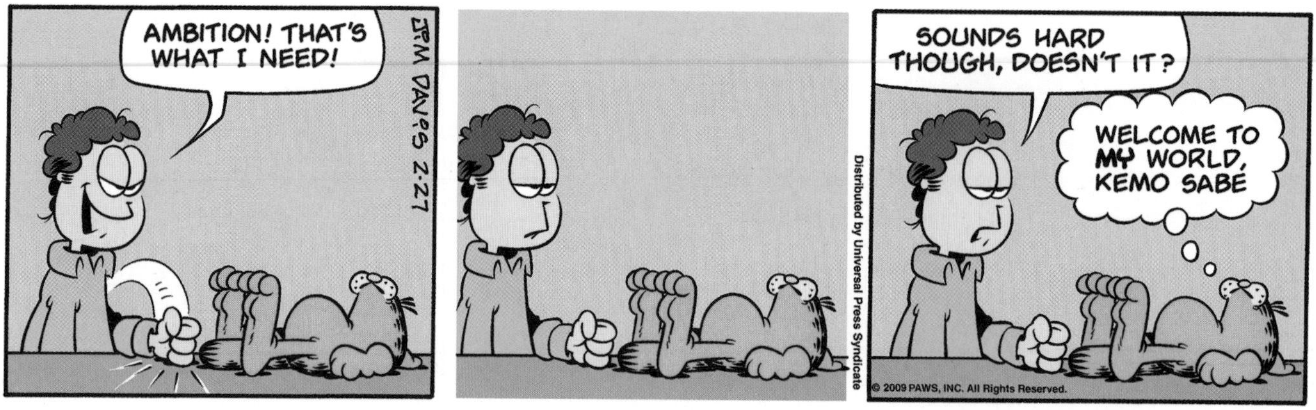
AMBITION! THAT'S WHAT I NEED!
JIM DAVIS 2·27
Distributed by Universal Press Syndicate
SOUNDS HARD THOUGH, DOESN'T IT?
WELCOME TO MY WORLD, KEMO SABE
© 2009 PAWS, INC. All Rights Reserved.

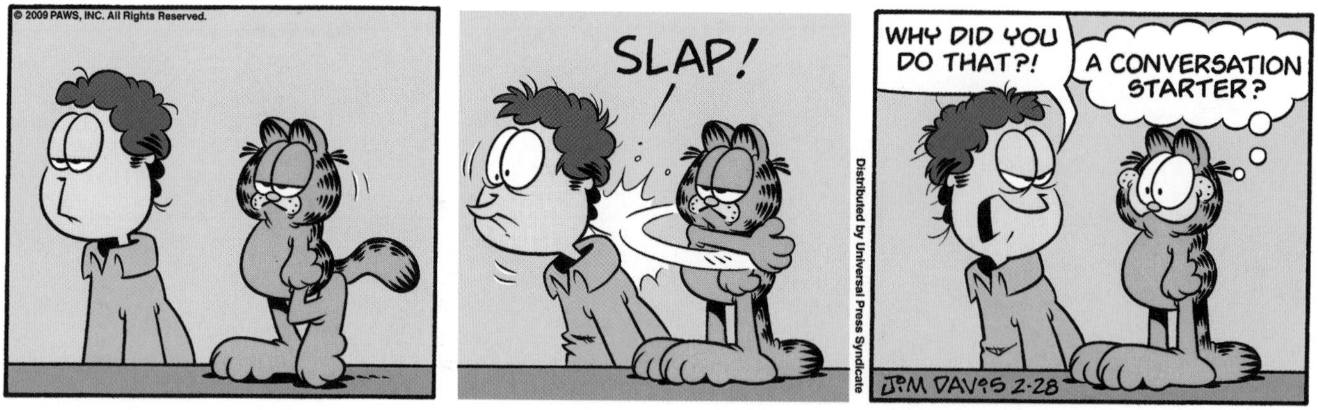
© 2009 PAWS, INC. All Rights Reserved.
SLAP!
Distributed by Universal Press Syndicate
WHY DID YOU DO THAT?!
A CONVERSATION STARTER?
JIM DAVIS 2·28

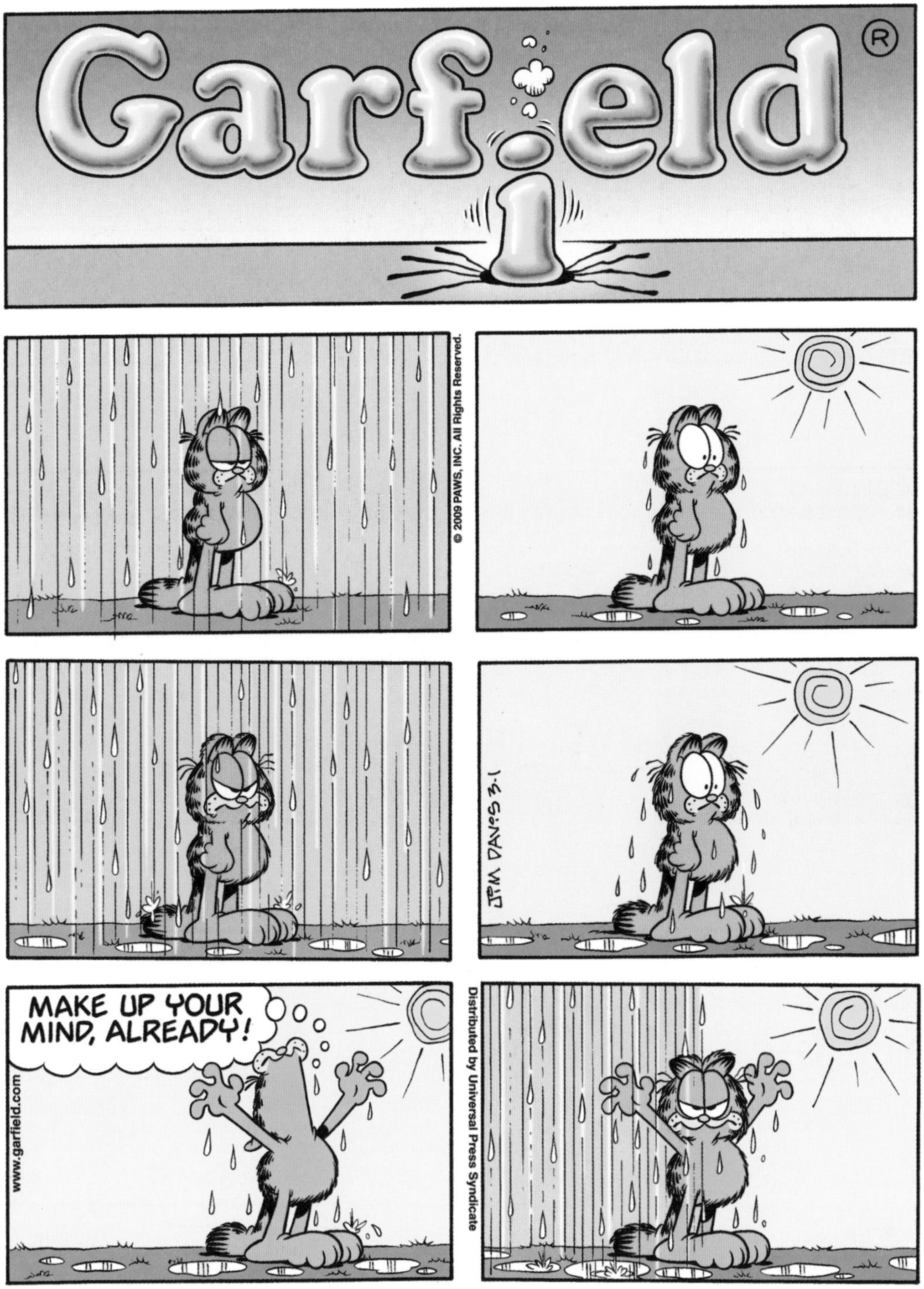
Garfield®
© 2009 PAWS, INC. All Rights Reserved.
JIM DAVIS 3-1
MAKE UP YOUR MIND, ALREADY!
www.garfield.com
Distributed by Universal Press Syndicate

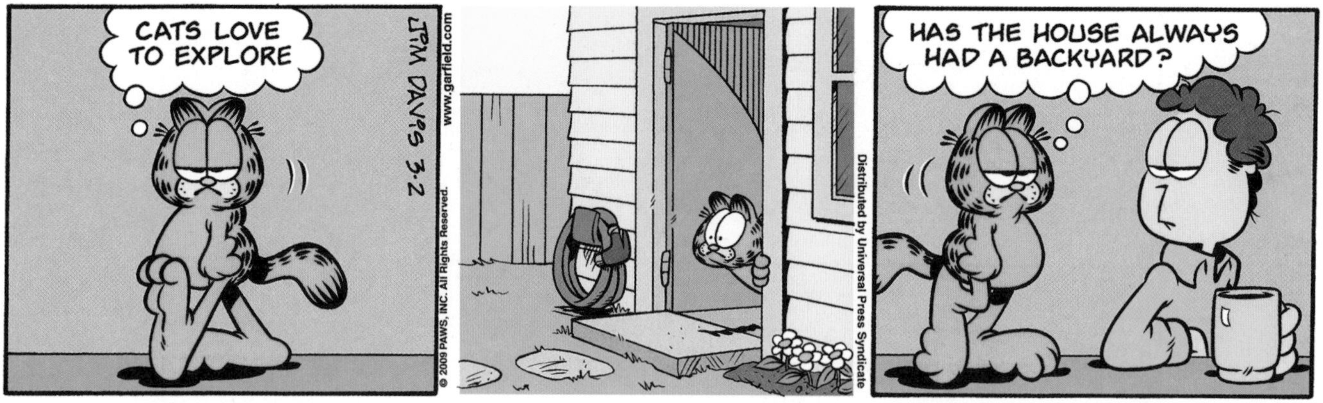
CATS LOVE TO EXPLORE
JIM DAVIS 3-2
www.garfield.com
© 2009 PAWS, INC. All Rights Reserved.
Distributed by Universal Press Syndicate
HAS THE HOUSE ALWAYS HAD A BACKYARD?

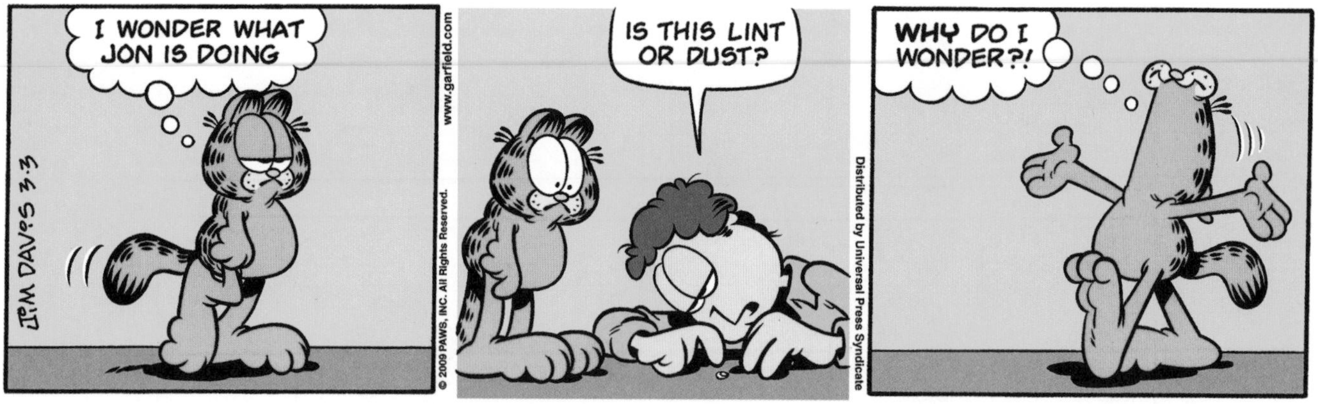
I WONDER WHAT JON IS DOING
JIM DAVIS 3-3
www.garfield.com
© 2009 PAWS, INC. All Rights Reserved.
IS THIS LINT OR DUST?
Distributed by Universal Press Syndicate
WHY DO I WONDER?!

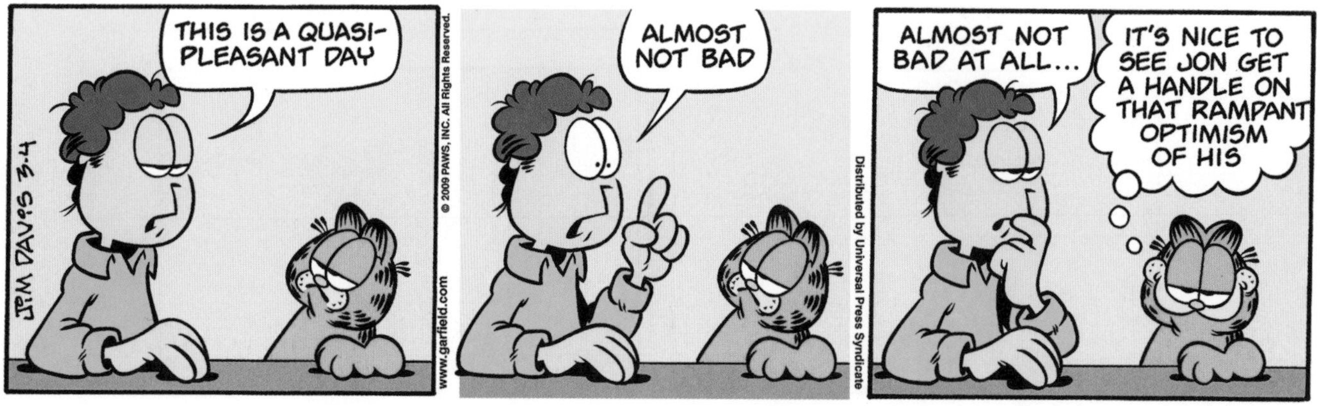
THIS IS A QUASI-PLEASANT DAY
JIM DAVIS 3-4
© 2009 PAWS, INC. All Rights Reserved.
www.garfield.com
ALMOST NOT BAD
Distributed by Universal Press Syndicate
ALMOST NOT BAD AT ALL...
IT'S NICE TO SEE JON GET A HANDLE ON THAT RAMPANT OPTIMISM OF HIS

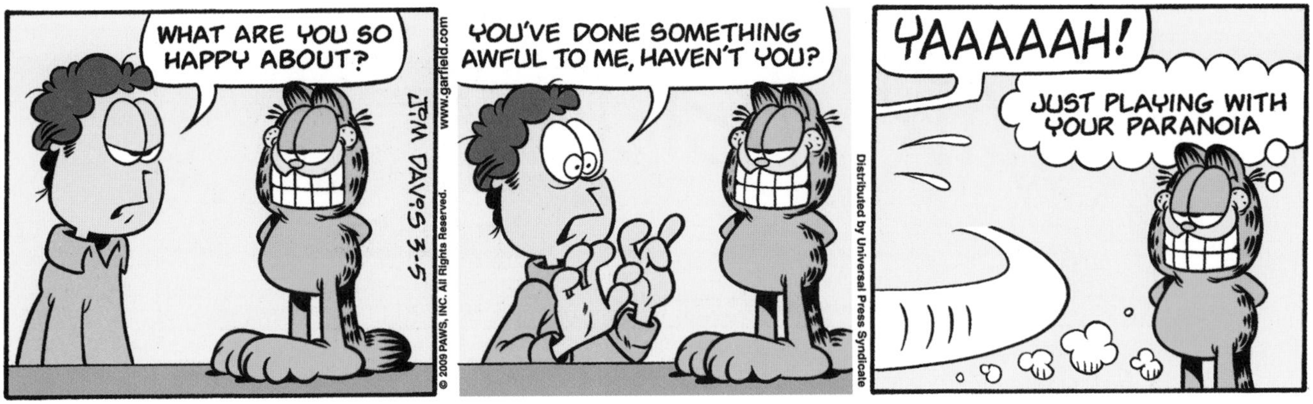
WHAT ARE YOU SO HAPPY ABOUT?
JIM DAVIS 3-5
© 2009 PAWS, INC. All Rights Reserved. www.garfield.com
YOU'VE DONE SOMETHING AWFUL TO ME, HAVEN'T YOU?
Distributed by Universal Press Syndicate
YAAAAAH!
JUST PLAYING WITH YOUR PARANOIA

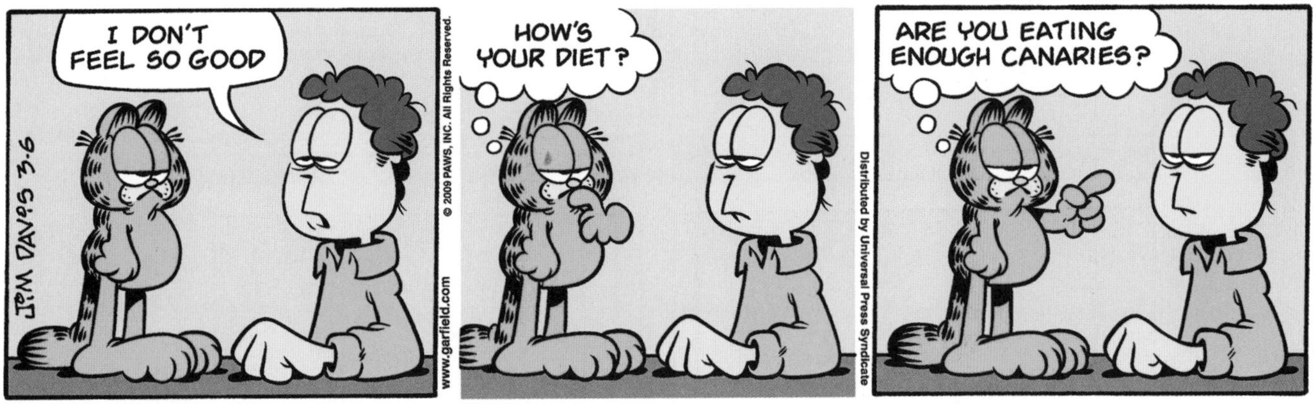
I DON'T FEEL SO GOOD
JIM DAVIS 3-6
© 2009 PAWS, INC. All Rights Reserved. www.garfield.com
HOW'S YOUR DIET?
Distributed by Universal Press Syndicate
ARE YOU EATING ENOUGH CANARIES?

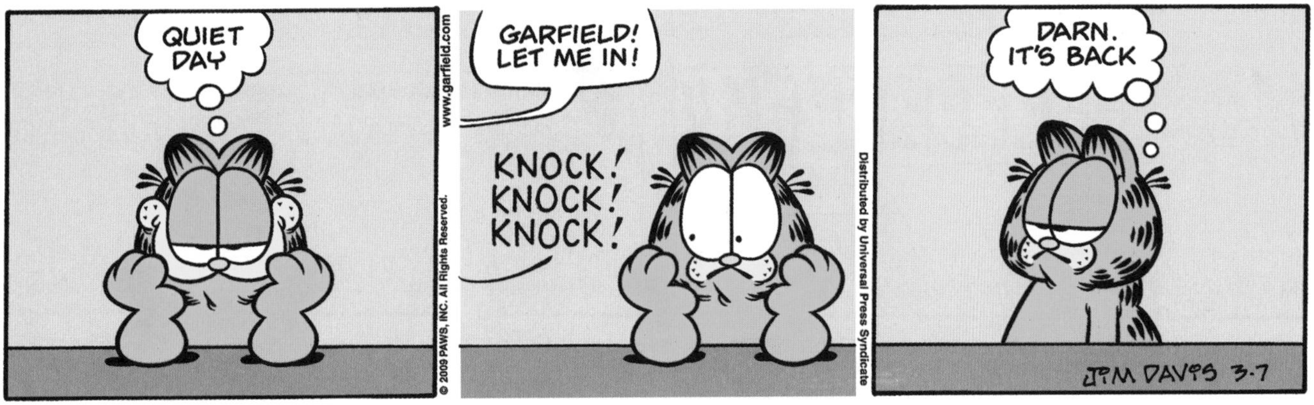
QUIET DAY
© 2009 PAWS, INC. All Rights Reserved. www.garfield.com
GARFIELD! LET ME IN!
KNOCK! KNOCK! KNOCK!
Distributed by Universal Press Syndicate
DARN. IT'S BACK
JIM DAVIS 3-7

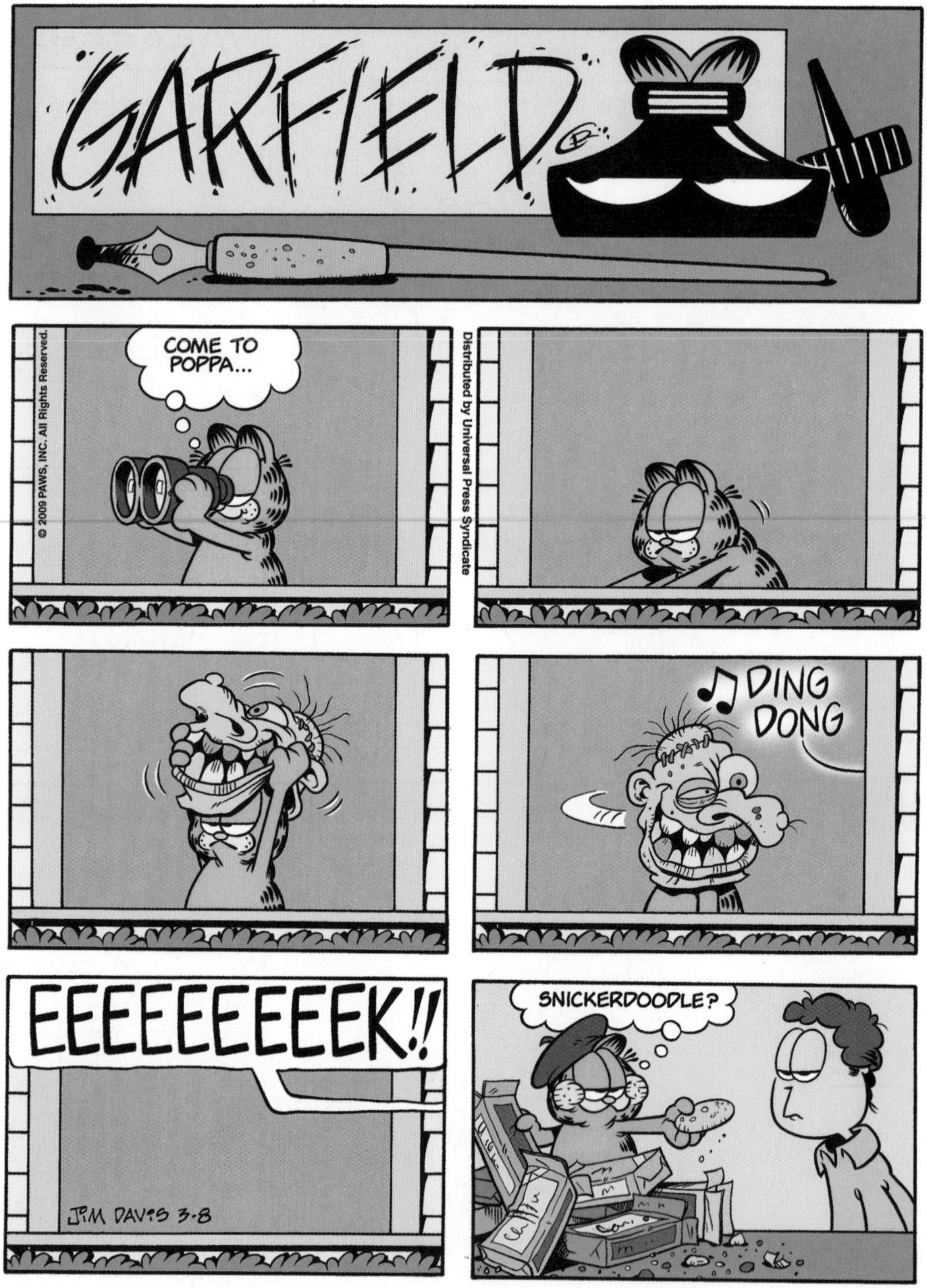
GARFIELD
© 2009 PAWS, INC. All Rights Reserved.
Distributed by Universal Press Syndicate
COME TO POPPA...
DING DONG
EEEEEEEEEK!!
JIM DAVIS 3-8
SNICKERDOODLE?

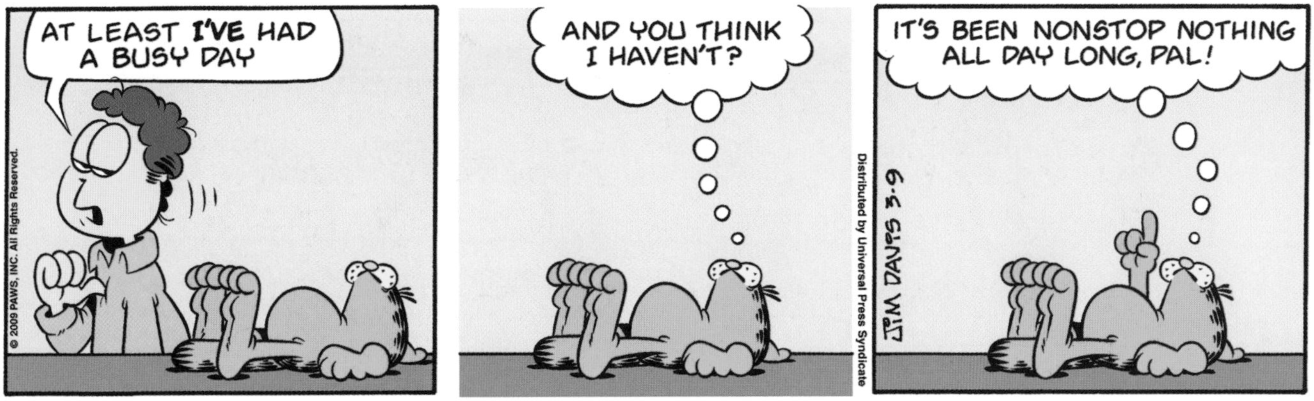
© 2009 PAWS, INC. All Rights Reserved.
AT LEAST I'VE HAD A BUSY DAY
AND YOU THINK I HAVEN'T?
Distributed by Universal Press Syndicate
JIM DAVIS 3-9
IT'S BEEN NONSTOP NOTHING ALL DAY LONG, PAL!

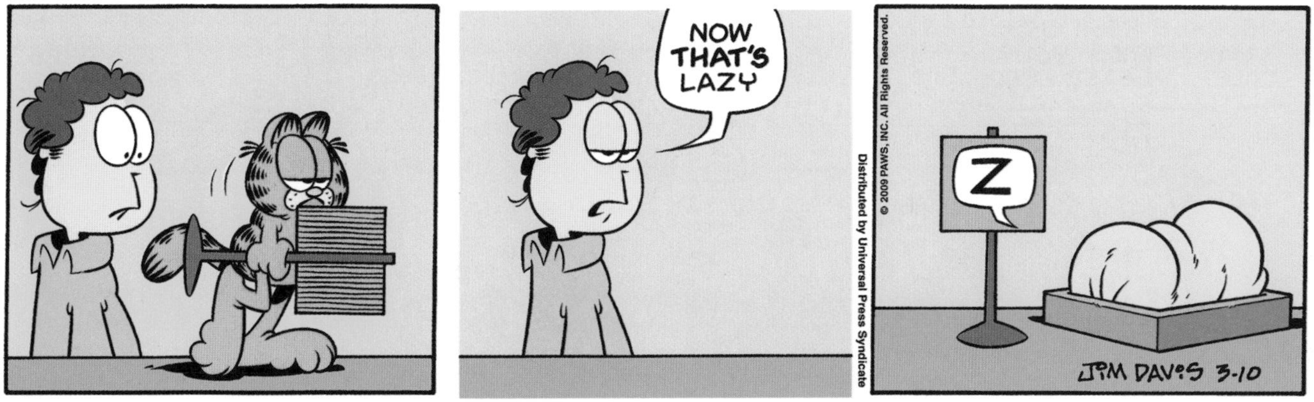
NOW THAT'S LAZY
Distributed by Universal Press Syndicate
© 2009 PAWS, INC. All Rights Reserved.
Z
JIM DAVIS 3-10

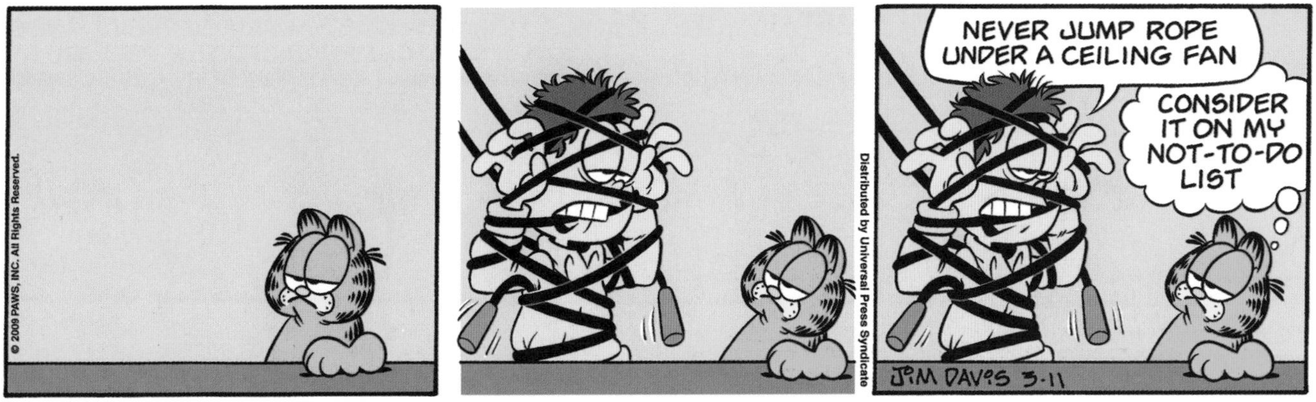
© 2009 PAWS, INC. All Rights Reserved.
Distributed by Universal Press Syndicate
NEVER JUMP ROPE UNDER A CEILING FAN
CONSIDER IT ON MY NOT-TO-DO LIST
JIM DAVIS 3-11

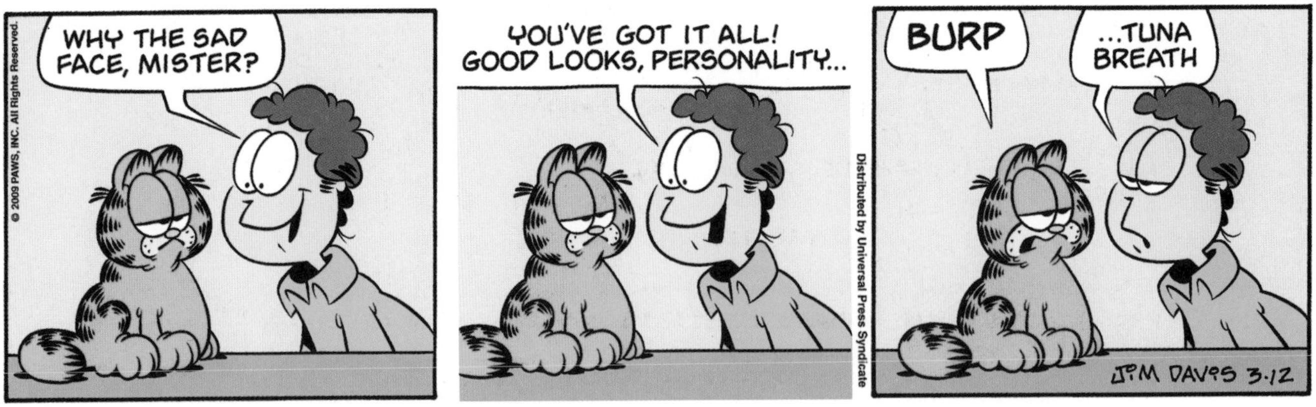
© 2009 PAWS, INC. All Rights Reserved.
WHY THE SAD FACE, MISTER?
YOU'VE GOT IT ALL! GOOD LOOKS, PERSONALITY...
Distributed by Universal Press Syndicate
BURP
...TUNA BREATH
JIM DAVIS 3-12

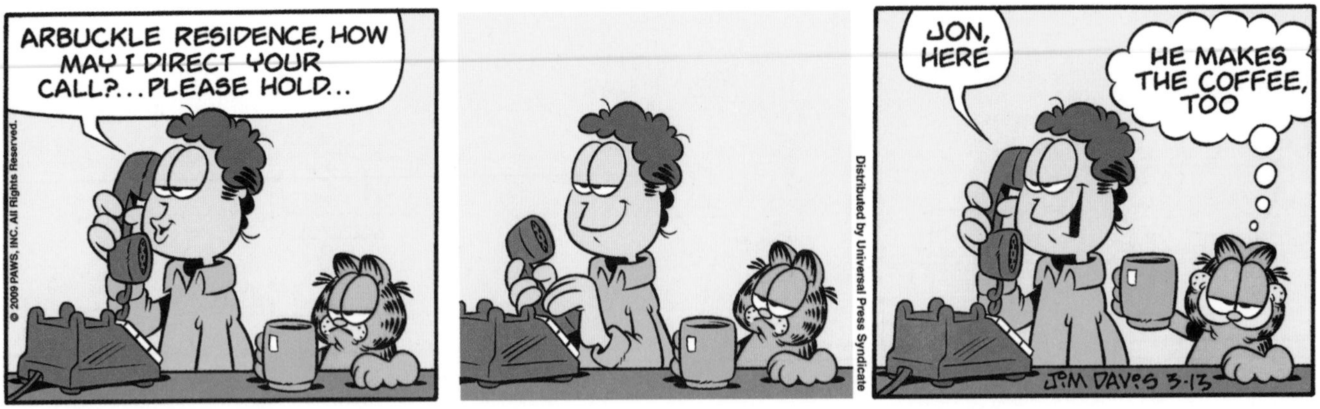
© 2009 PAWS, INC. All Rights Reserved.
ARBUCKLE RESIDENCE, HOW MAY I DIRECT YOUR CALL?... PLEASE HOLD...
Distributed by Universal Press Syndicate
JON, HERE
HE MAKES THE COFFEE, TOO
JIM DAVIS 3-13

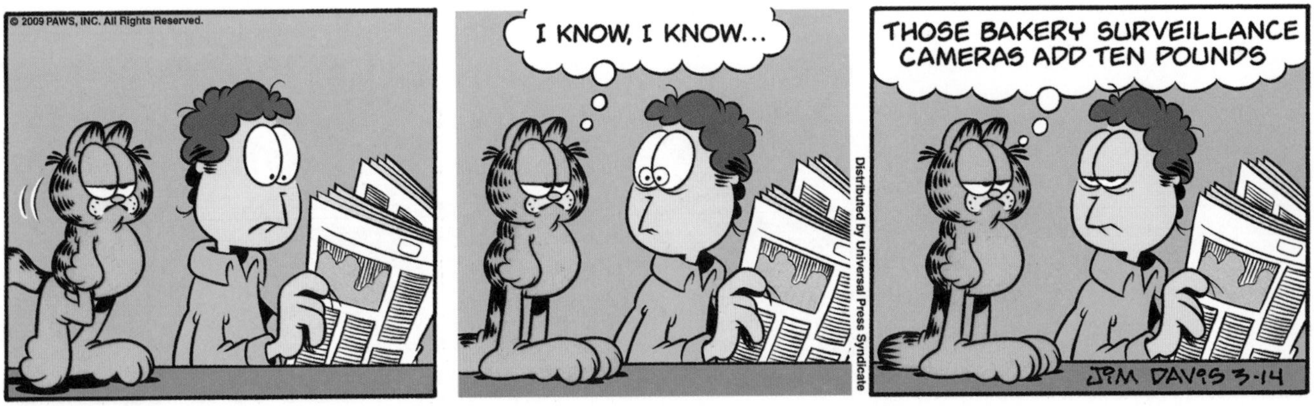
© 2009 PAWS, INC. All Rights Reserved.
I KNOW, I KNOW...
Distributed by Universal Press Syndicate
THOSE BAKERY SURVEILLANCE CAMERAS ADD TEN POUNDS
JIM DAVIS 3-14

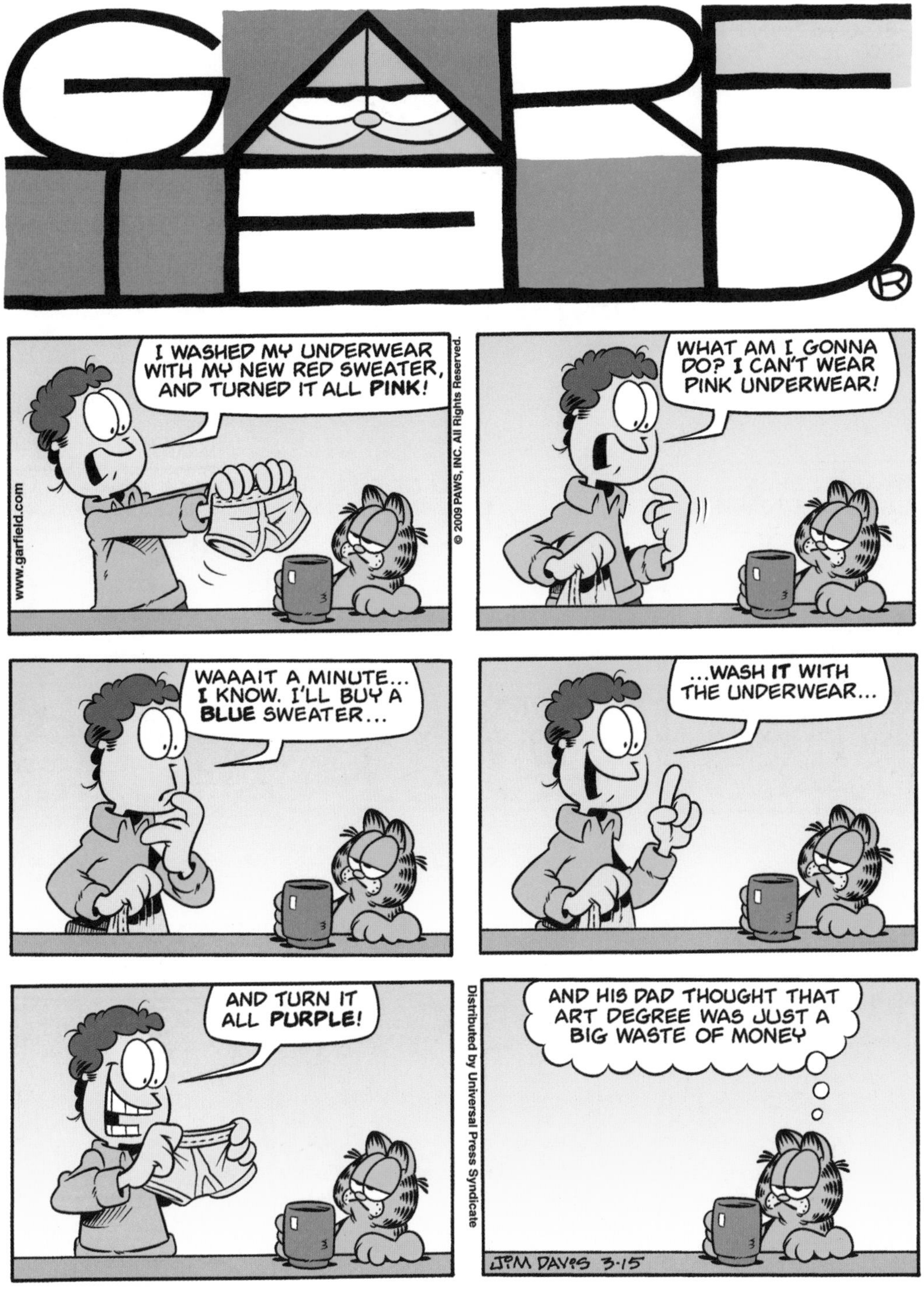
GARFIELD
I WASHED MY UNDERWEAR WITH MY NEW RED SWEATER, AND TURNED IT ALL PINK!
www.garfield.com
© 2009 PAWS, INC. All Rights Reserved.
WHAT AM I GONNA DO? I CAN'T WEAR PINK UNDERWEAR!
WAAAIT A MINUTE... I KNOW. I'LL BUY A BLUE SWEATER...
...WASH IT WITH THE UNDERWEAR...
AND TURN IT ALL PURPLE!
Distributed by Universal Press Syndicate
AND HIS DAD THOUGHT THAT ART DEGREE WAS JUST A BIG WASTE OF MONEY
JIM DAVIS 3-15

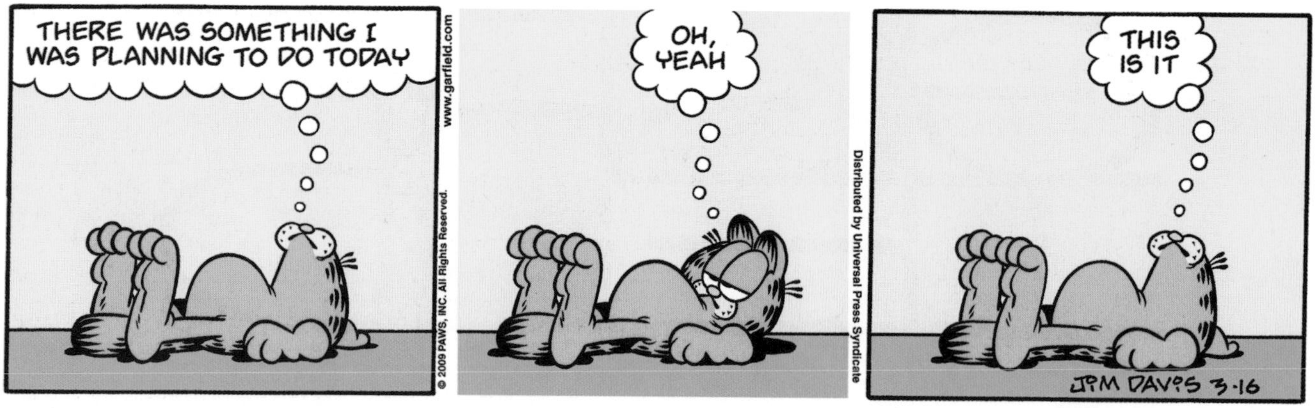
THERE WAS SOMETHING I WAS PLANNING TO DO TODAY
www.garfield.com
© 2009 PAWS, INC. All Rights Reserved.
OH, YEAH
Distributed by Universal Press Syndicate
THIS IS IT
JIM DAVIS 3-16

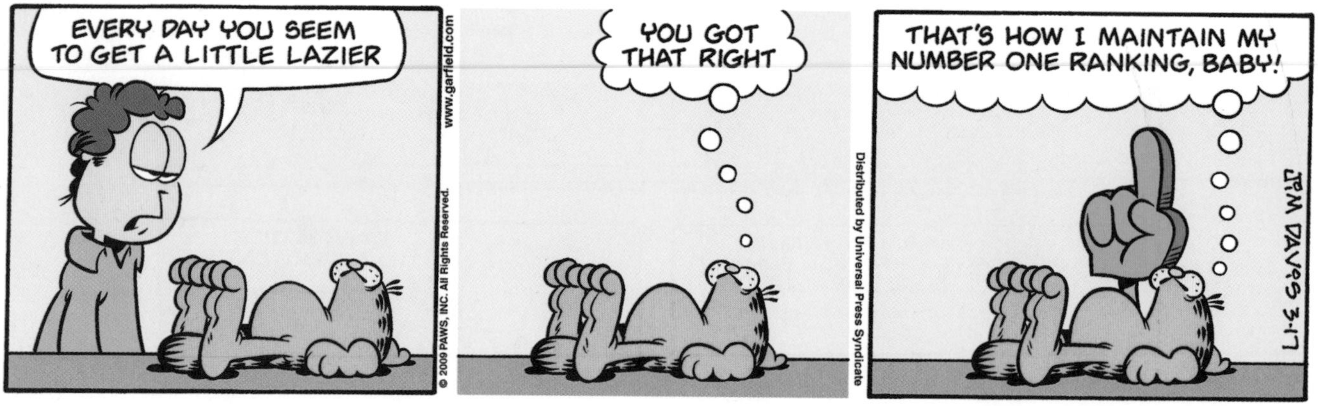
EVERY DAY YOU SEEM TO GET A LITTLE LAZIER
www.garfield.com
© 2009 PAWS, INC. All Rights Reserved.
YOU GOT THAT RIGHT
Distributed by Universal Press Syndicate
THAT'S HOW I MAINTAIN MY NUMBER ONE RANKING, BABY!
JIM DAVIS 3-17

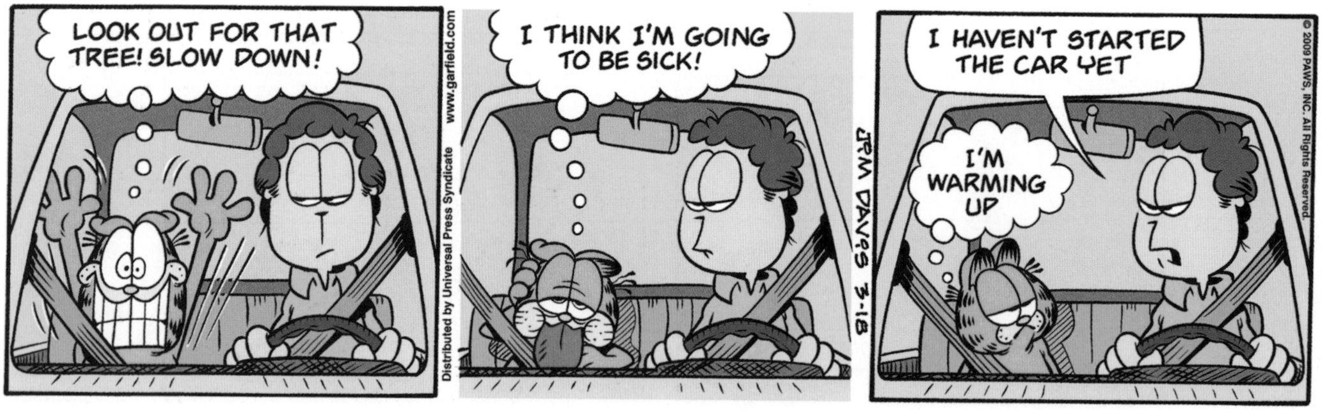
LOOK OUT FOR THAT TREE! SLOW DOWN!
www.garfield.com
Distributed by Universal Press Syndicate
I THINK I'M GOING TO BE SICK!
JIM DAVIS 3-18
I HAVEN'T STARTED THE CAR YET
I'M WARMING UP
© 2009 PAWS, INC. All Rights Reserved.

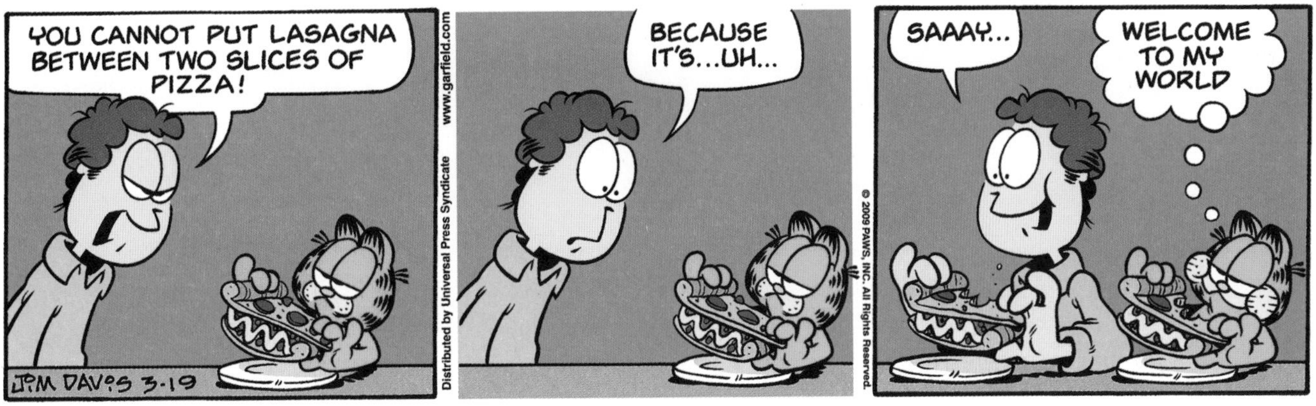
YOU CANNOT PUT LASAGNA BETWEEN TWO SLICES OF PIZZA!
JIM DAVIS 3-19
www.garfield.com
Distributed by Universal Press Syndicate
BECAUSE IT'S...UH...
© 2009 PAWS, INC. All Rights Reserved.
SAAAY...
WELCOME TO MY WORLD

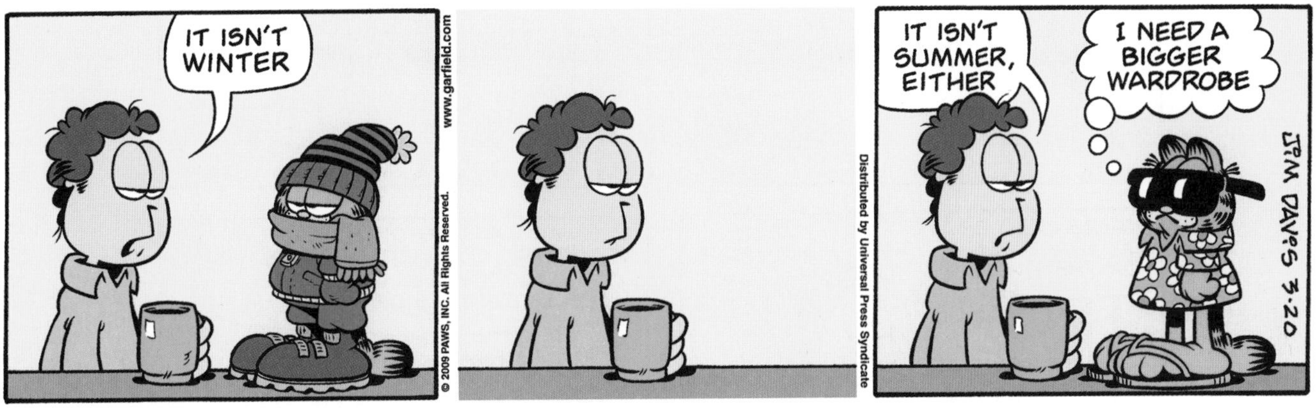
IT ISN'T WINTER
www.garfield.com
© 2009 PAWS, INC. All Rights Reserved.
Distributed by Universal Press Syndicate
IT ISN'T SUMMER, EITHER
I NEED A BIGGER WARDROBE
JIM DAVIS 3-20

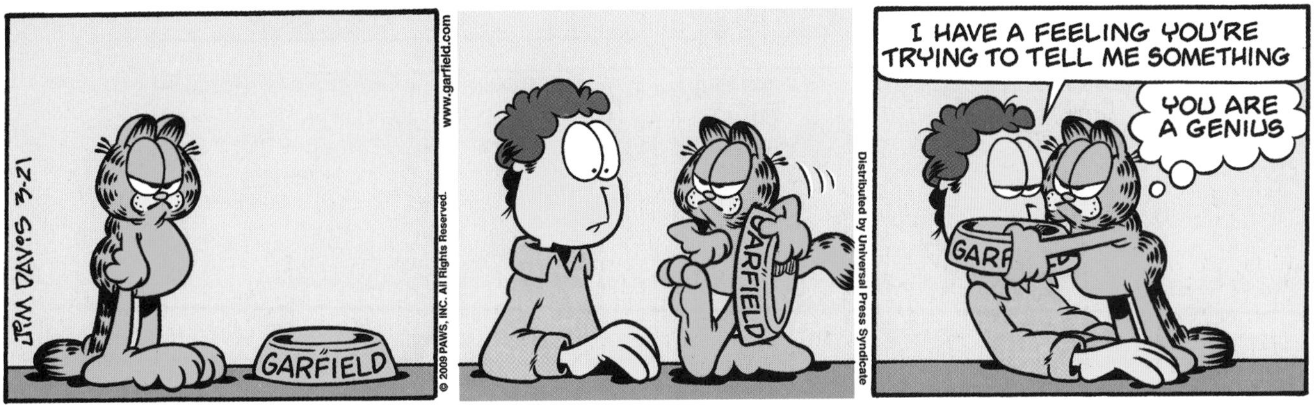
JIM DAVIS 3-21
GARFIELD
www.garfield.com
© 2009 PAWS, INC. All Rights Reserved.
GARFIELD
Distributed by Universal Press Syndicate
I HAVE A FEELING YOU'RE TRYING TO TELL ME SOMETHING
YOU ARE A GENIUS
GARF

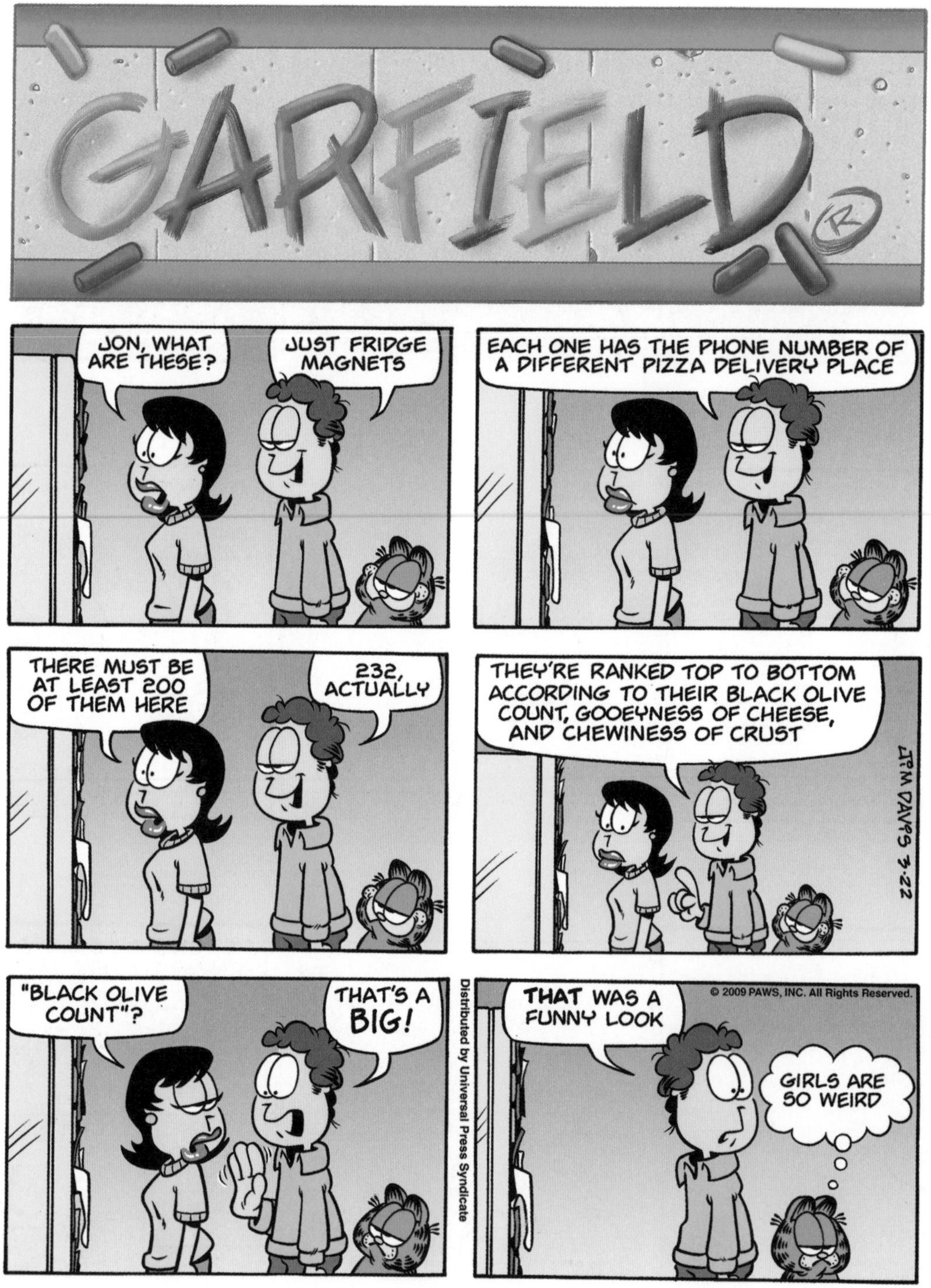
GARFIELD®
JON, WHAT ARE THESE?
JUST FRIDGE MAGNETS
EACH ONE HAS THE PHONE NUMBER OF A DIFFERENT PIZZA DELIVERY PLACE
THERE MUST BE AT LEAST 200 OF THEM HERE
232, ACTUALLY
THEY'RE RANKED TOP TO BOTTOM ACCORDING TO THEIR BLACK OLIVE COUNT, GOOEYNESS OF CHEESE, AND CHEWINESS OF CRUST
JIM DAVIS 3-22
"BLACK OLIVE COUNT"?
THAT'S A BIG!
Distributed by Universal Press Syndicate
© 2009 PAWS, INC. All Rights Reserved.
THAT WAS A FUNNY LOOK
GIRLS ARE SO WEIRD

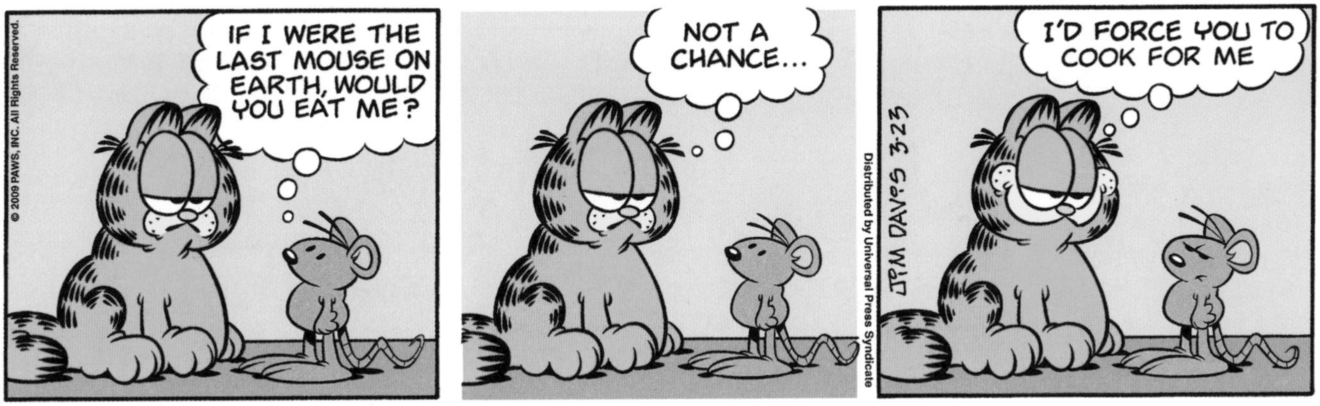
© 2009 PAWS, INC. All Rights Reserved.
IF I WERE THE LAST MOUSE ON EARTH, WOULD YOU EAT ME?
NOT A CHANCE...
Distributed by Universal Press Syndicate
JIM DAVIS 3-23
I'D FORCE YOU TO COOK FOR ME

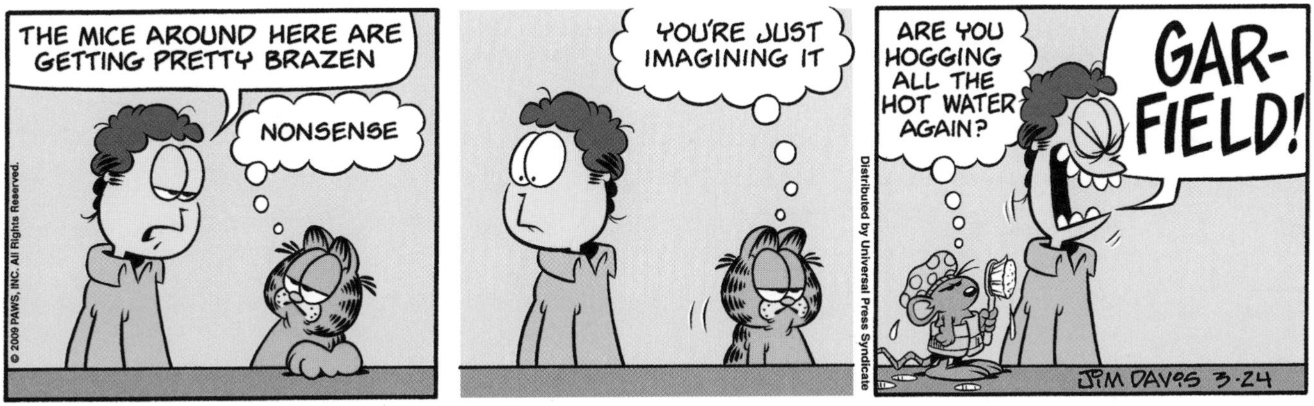
© 2009 PAWS, INC. All Rights Reserved.
THE MICE AROUND HERE ARE GETTING PRETTY BRAZEN
NONSENSE
YOU'RE JUST IMAGINING IT
Distributed by Universal Press Syndicate
ARE YOU HOGGING ALL THE HOT WATER AGAIN?
GAR-FIELD!
JIM DAVIS 3-24

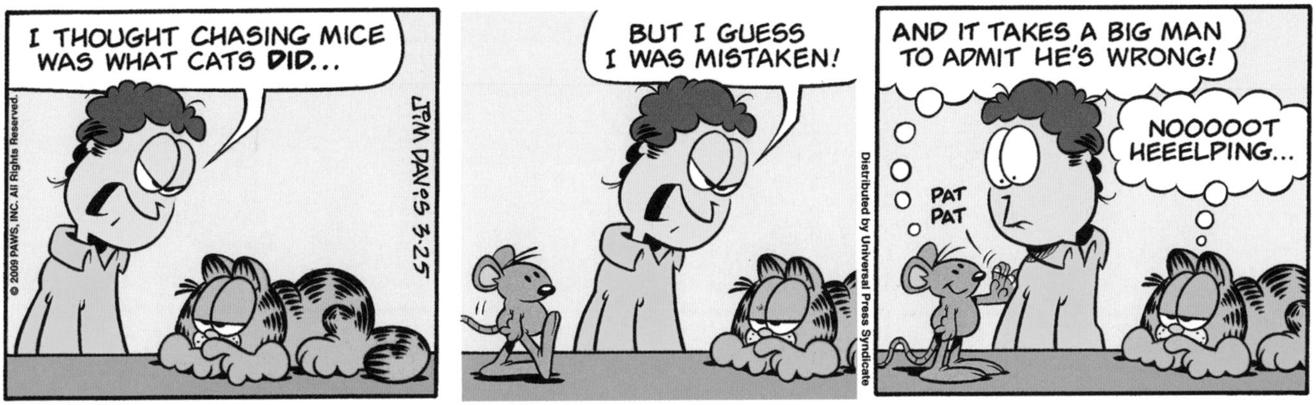
© 2009 PAWS, INC. All Rights Reserved.
I THOUGHT CHASING MICE WAS WHAT CATS DID...
JIM DAVIS 3-25
BUT I GUESS I WAS MISTAKEN!
Distributed by Universal Press Syndicate
AND IT TAKES A BIG MAN TO ADMIT HE'S WRONG!
NOOOOOT HEEELPING...
PAT PAT

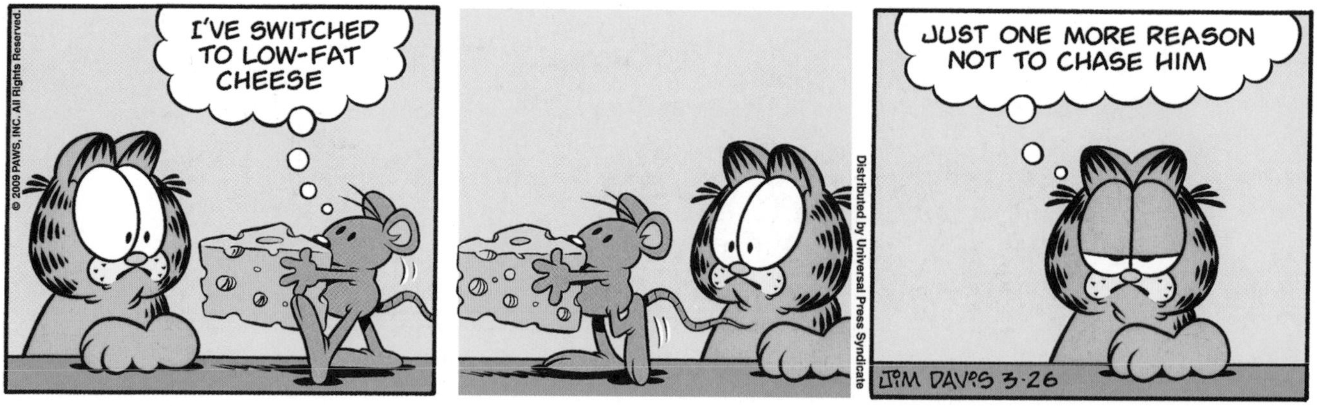
I'VE SWITCHED TO LOW-FAT CHEESE
JUST ONE MORE REASON NOT TO CHASE HIM
© 2009 PAWS, INC. All Rights Reserved.
Distributed by Universal Press Syndicate
JIM DAVIS 3-26

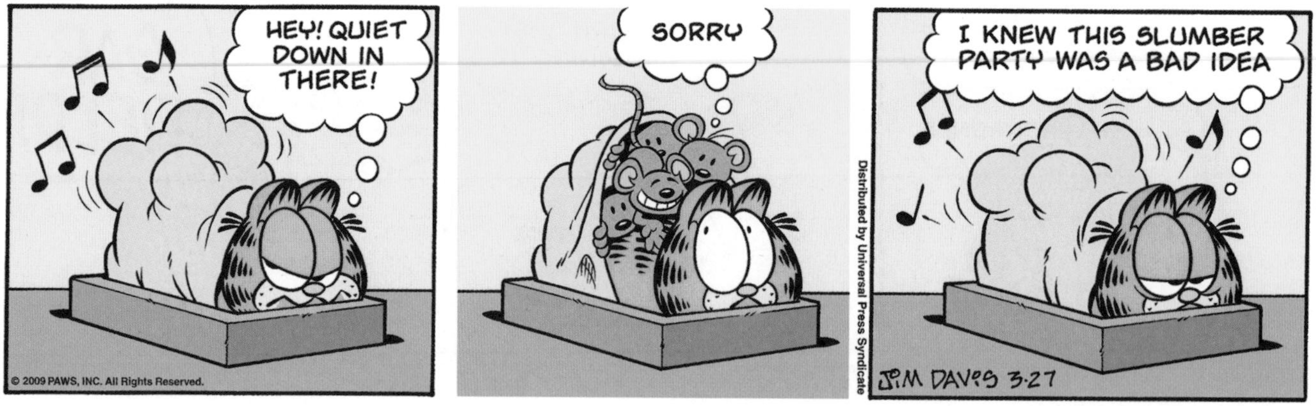
HEY! QUIET DOWN IN THERE!
SORRY
I KNEW THIS SLUMBER PARTY WAS A BAD IDEA
© 2009 PAWS, INC. All Rights Reserved.
Distributed by Universal Press Syndicate
JIM DAVIS 3-27

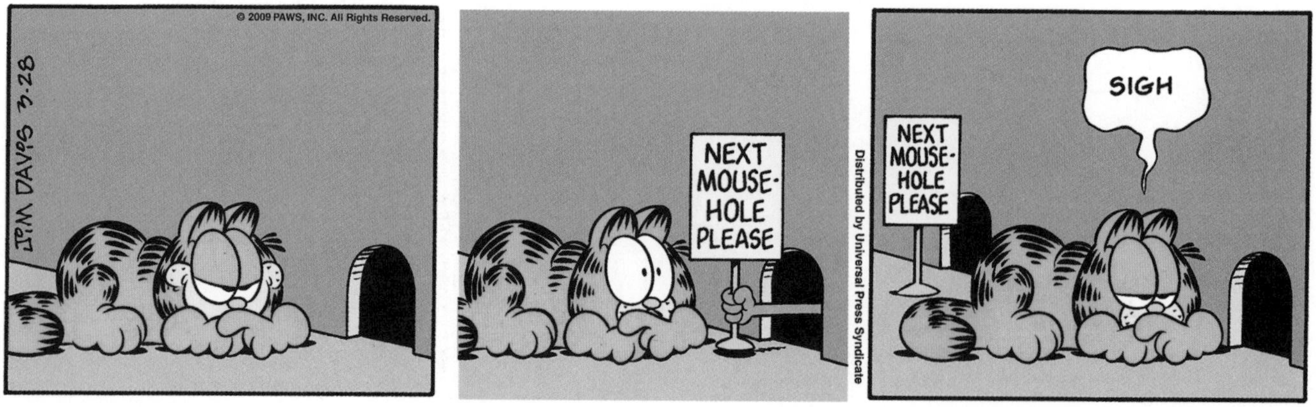
© 2009 PAWS, INC. All Rights Reserved.
JIM DAVIS 3-28
NEXT MOUSE-HOLE PLEASE
NEXT MOUSE-HOLE PLEASE
SIGH
Distributed by Universal Press Syndicate

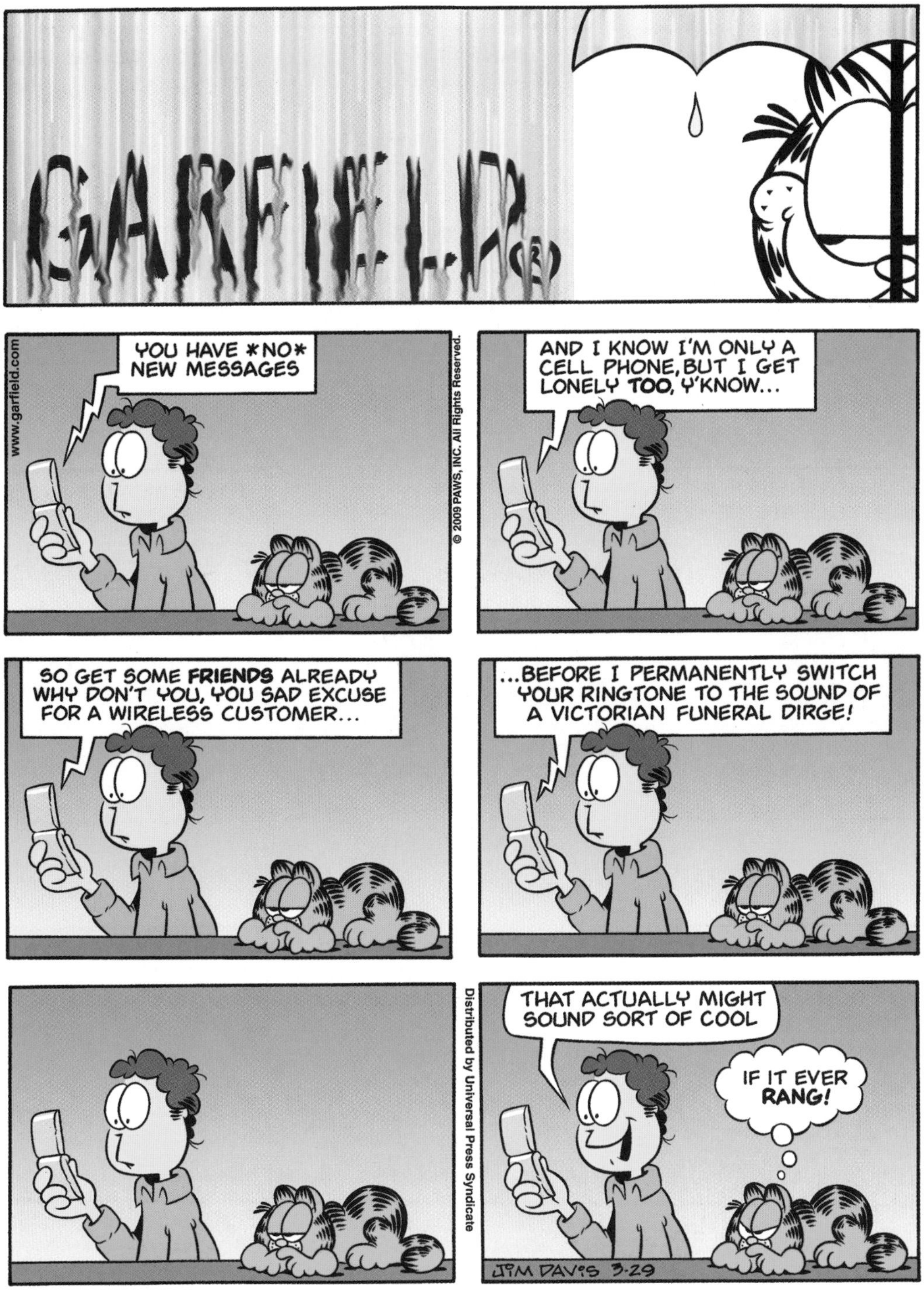
GARFIELD
www.garfield.com
YOU HAVE *NO* NEW MESSAGES
© 2009 PAWS, INC. All Rights Reserved.
AND I KNOW I'M ONLY A CELL PHONE, BUT I GET LONELY TOO, Y'KNOW...
SO GET SOME FRIENDS ALREADY WHY DON'T YOU, YOU SAD EXCUSE FOR A WIRELESS CUSTOMER...
...BEFORE I PERMANENTLY SWITCH YOUR RINGTONE TO THE SOUND OF A VICTORIAN FUNERAL DIRGE!
Distributed by Universal Press Syndicate
THAT ACTUALLY MIGHT SOUND SORT OF COOL
IF IT EVER RANG!
JIM DAVIS 3-29

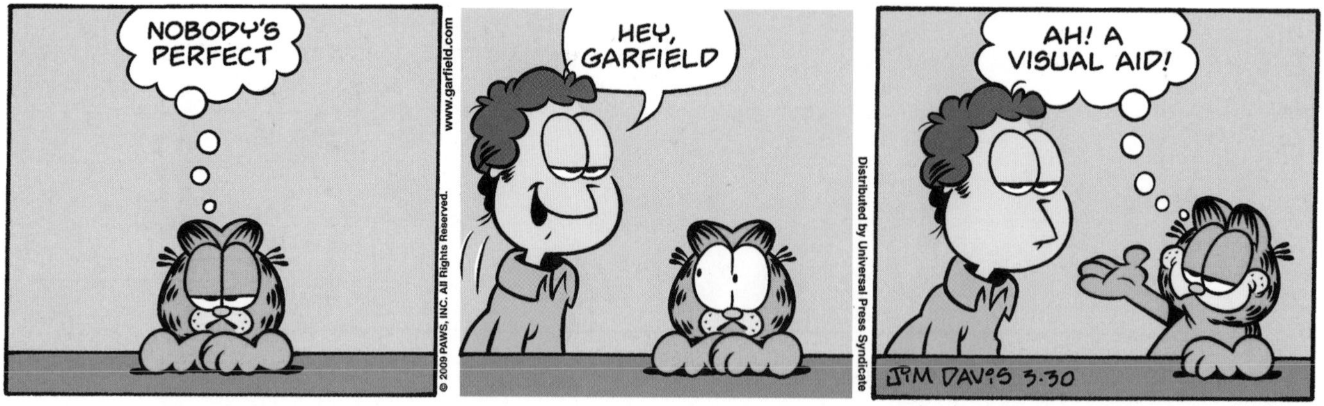
NOBODY'S PERFECT
© 2009 PAWS, INC. All Rights Reserved. www.garfield.com
HEY, GARFIELD
Distributed by Universal Press Syndicate
AH! A VISUAL AID!
JIM DAVIS 3-30

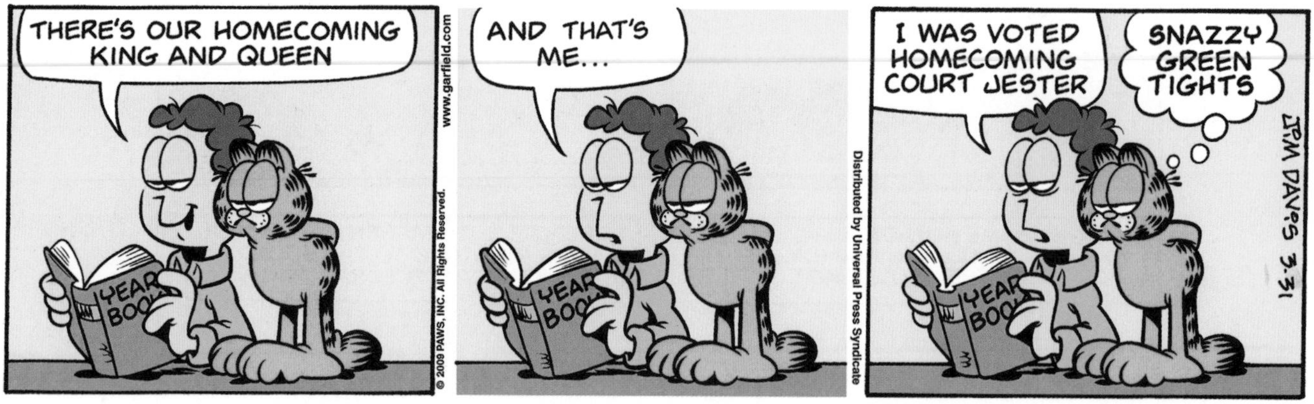
THERE'S OUR HOMECOMING KING AND QUEEN
YEAR BOOK
© 2009 PAWS, INC. All Rights Reserved. www.garfield.com
AND THAT'S ME...
Distributed by Universal Press Syndicate
I WAS VOTED HOMECOMING COURT JESTER
SNAZZY GREEN TIGHTS
JIM DAVIS 3-31

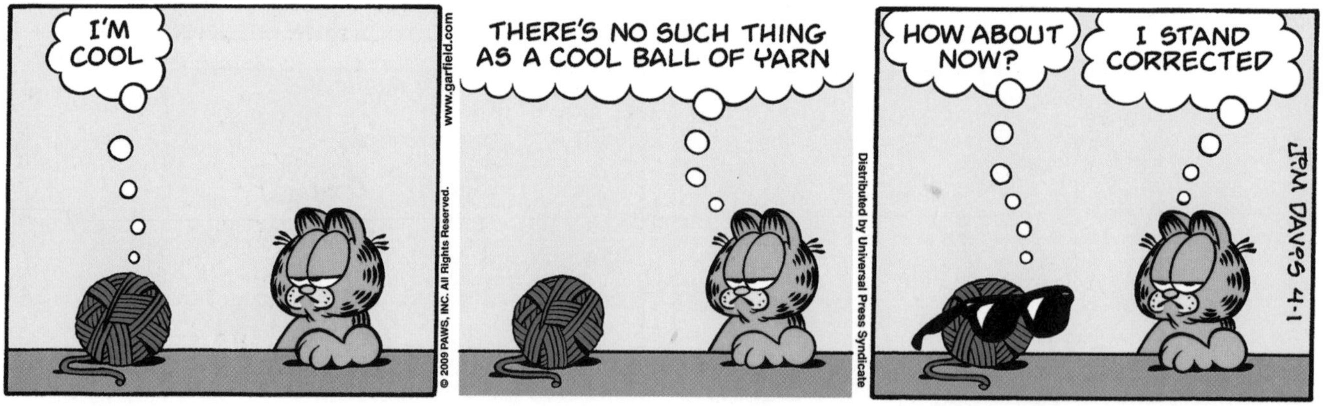
I'M COOL
© 2009 PAWS, INC. All Rights Reserved. www.garfield.com
THERE'S NO SUCH THING AS A COOL BALL OF YARN
Distributed by Universal Press Syndicate
HOW ABOUT NOW?
I STAND CORRECTED
JIM DAVIS 4-1

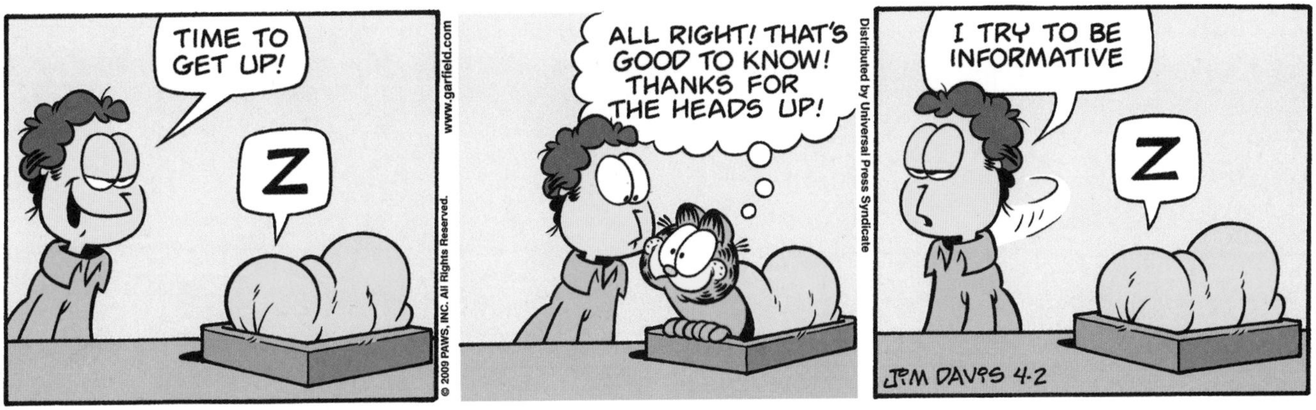
TIME TO GET UP!
Z
© 2009 PAWS, INC. All Rights Reserved.
www.garfield.com
ALL RIGHT! THAT'S GOOD TO KNOW! THANKS FOR THE HEADS UP!
Distributed by Universal Press Syndicate
I TRY TO BE INFORMATIVE
Z
JIM DAVIS 4-2

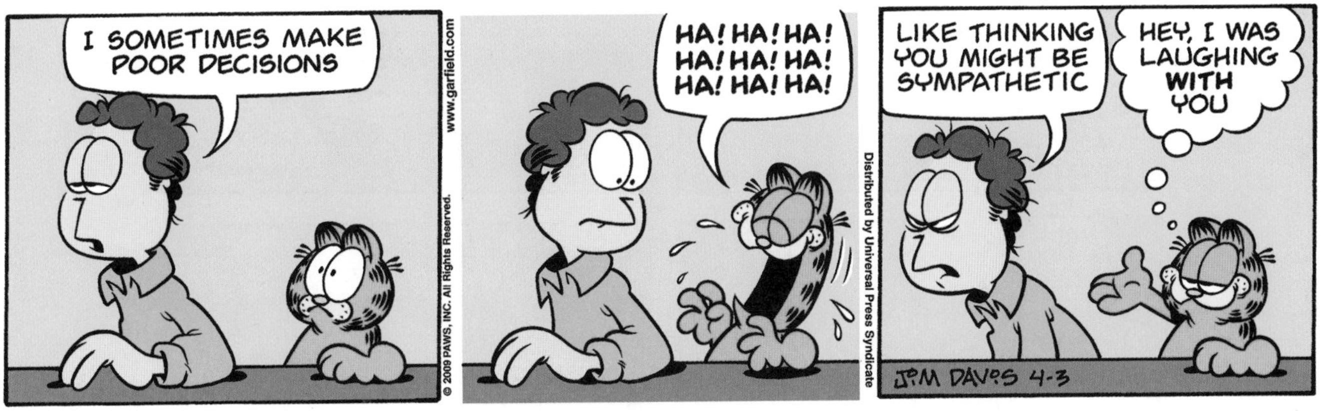
I SOMETIMES MAKE POOR DECISIONS
© 2009 PAWS, INC. All Rights Reserved.
www.garfield.com
HA! HA! HA! HA! HA! HA! HA! HA! HA!
Distributed by Universal Press Syndicate
LIKE THINKING YOU MIGHT BE SYMPATHETIC
HEY, I WAS LAUGHING WITH YOU
JIM DAVIS 4-3

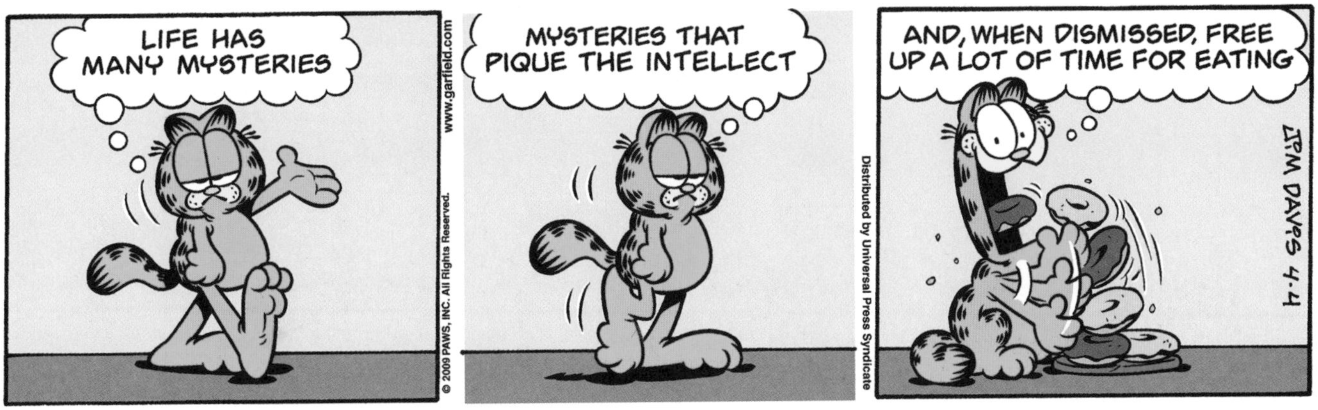
LIFE HAS MANY MYSTERIES
© 2009 PAWS, INC. All Rights Reserved.
www.garfield.com
MYSTERIES THAT PIQUE THE INTELLECT
Distributed by Universal Press Syndicate
AND, WHEN DISMISSED, FREE UP A LOT OF TIME FOR EATING
JIM DAVIS 4-4

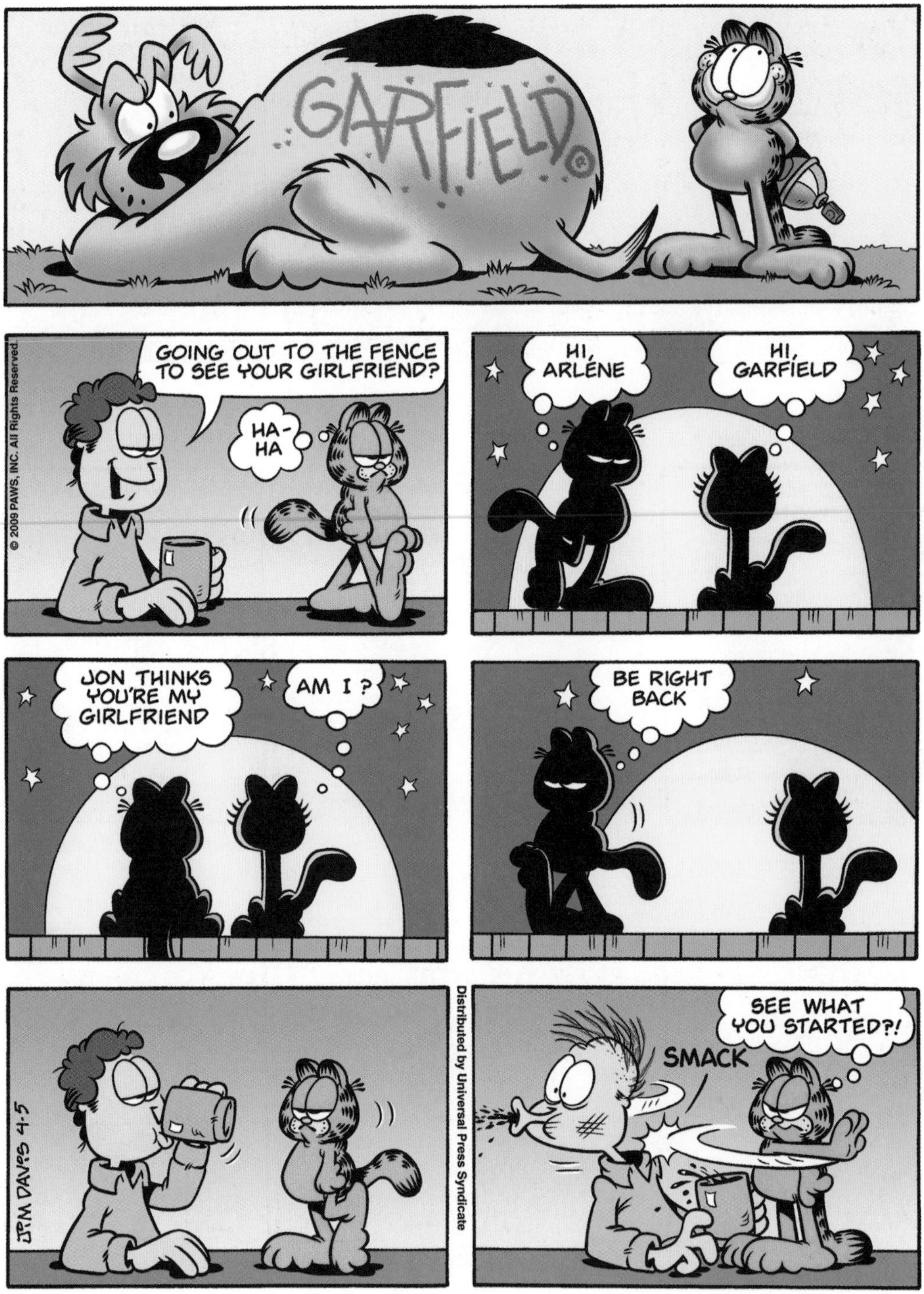
GARFIELD®
© 2009 PAWS, INC. All Rights Reserved.
GOING OUT TO THE FENCE TO SEE YOUR GIRLFRIEND?
HA-HA
HI, ARLENE
HI, GARFIELD
JON THINKS YOU'RE MY GIRLFRIEND
AM I?
BE RIGHT BACK
JIM DAVIS 4-5
Distributed by Universal Press Syndicate
SEE WHAT YOU STARTED?!
SMACK

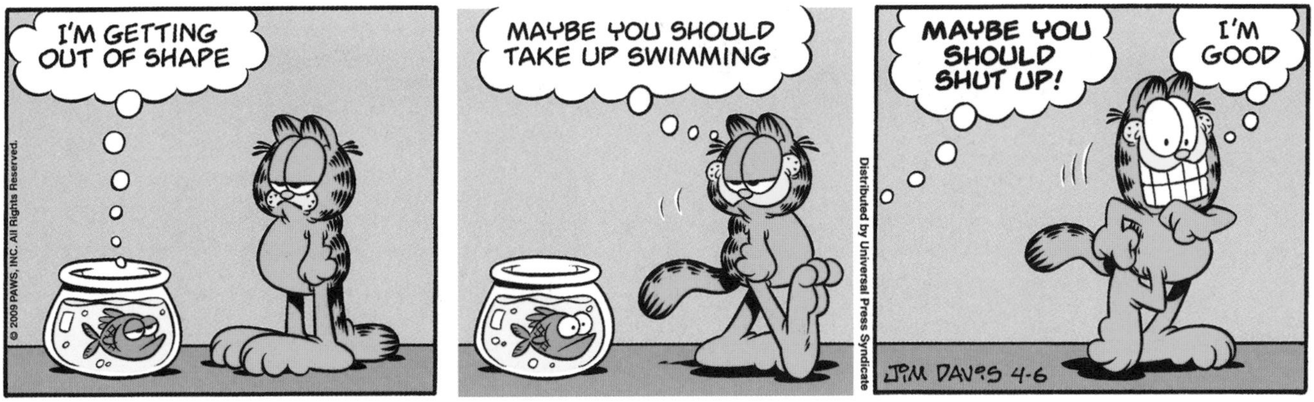
I'M GETTING OUT OF SHAPE
© 2009 PAWS, INC. All Rights Reserved.
MAYBE YOU SHOULD TAKE UP SWIMMING
Distributed by Universal Press Syndicate
MAYBE YOU SHOULD SHUT UP!
I'M GOOD
JIM DAVIS 4-6

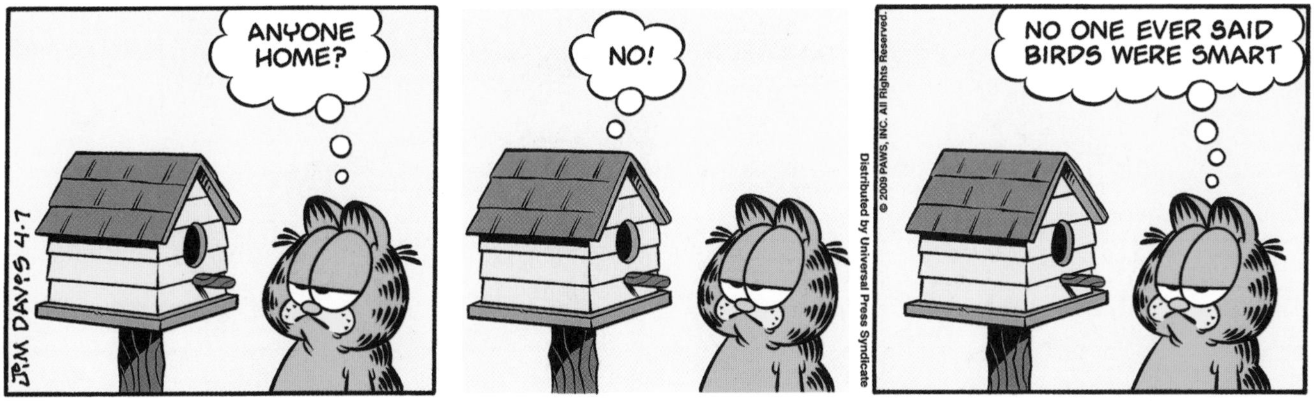
ANYONE HOME?
JIM DAVIS 4-7
NO!
Distributed by Universal Press Syndicate
© 2009 PAWS, INC. All Rights Reserved.
NO ONE EVER SAID BIRDS WERE SMART

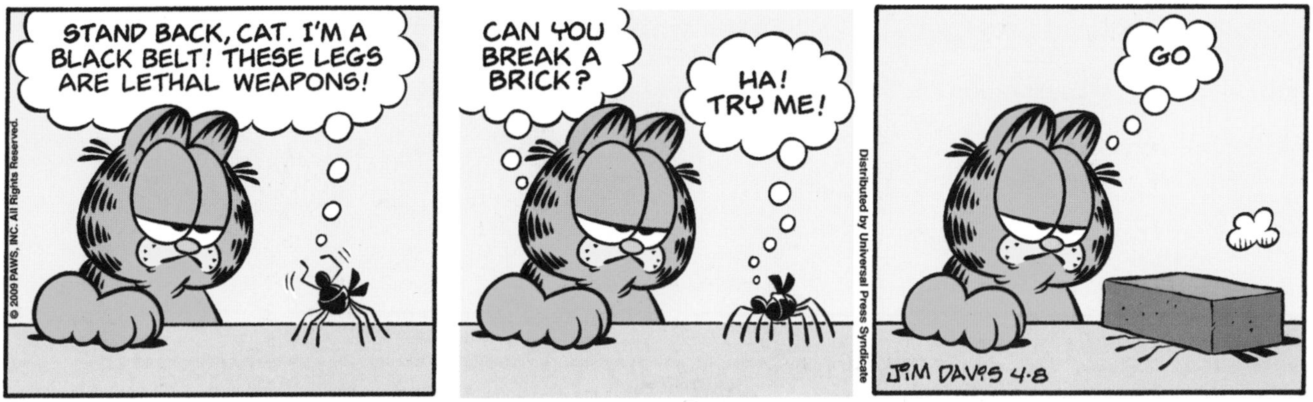
STAND BACK, CAT. I'M A BLACK BELT! THESE LEGS ARE LETHAL WEAPONS!
© 2009 PAWS, INC. All Rights Reserved.
CAN YOU BREAK A BRICK?
HA! TRY ME!
Distributed by Universal Press Syndicate
GO
JIM DAVIS 4-8

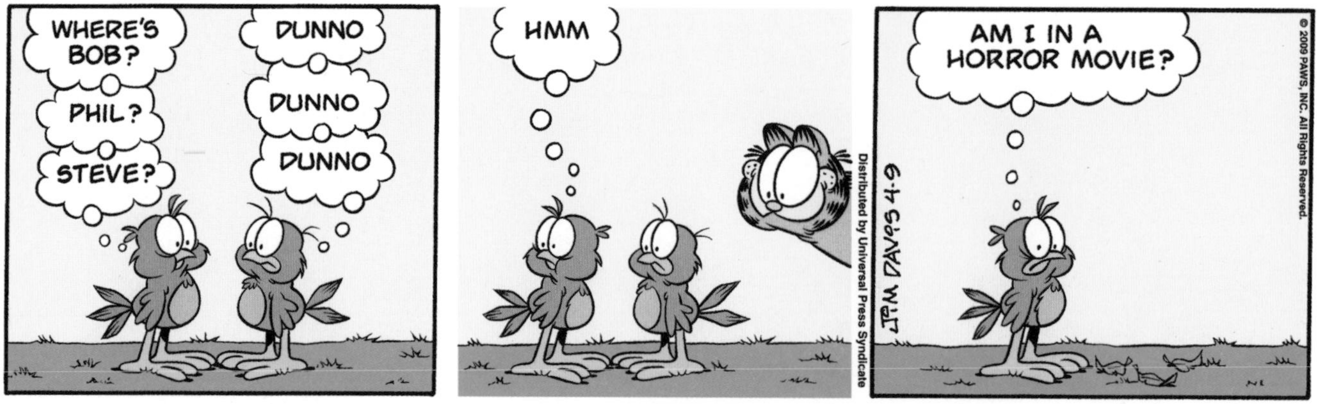
WHERE'S BOB?
PHIL?
STEVE?
DUNNO
DUNNO
DUNNO
HMM
JIM DAVIS 4-9
Distributed by Universal Press Syndicate
AM I IN A HORROR MOVIE?
© 2009 PAWS, INC. All Rights Reserved.

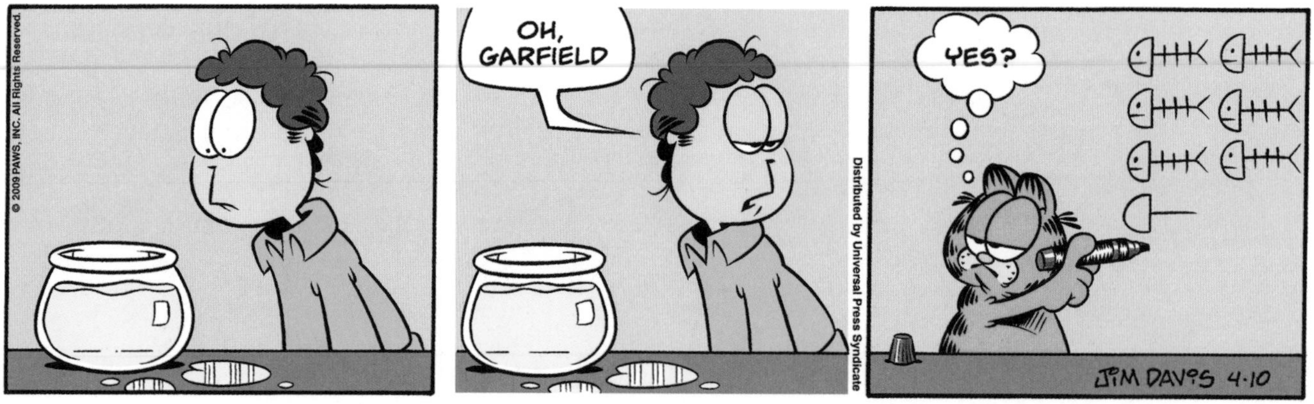
© 2009 PAWS, INC. All Rights Reserved.
OH, GARFIELD
Distributed by Universal Press Syndicate
YES?
JIM DAVIS 4-10

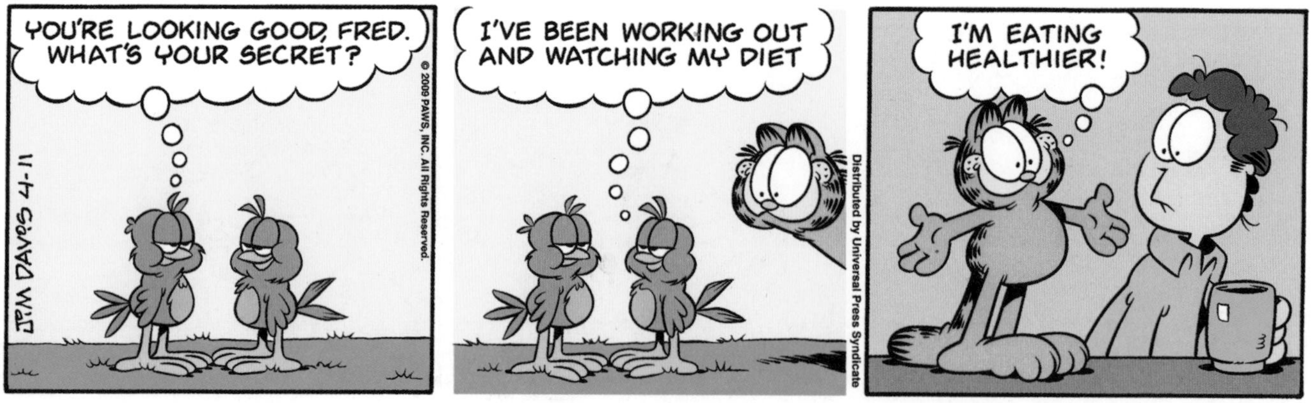
YOU'RE LOOKING GOOD, FRED. WHAT'S YOUR SECRET?
JIM DAVIS 4-11
© 2009 PAWS, INC. All Rights Reserved.
I'VE BEEN WORKING OUT AND WATCHING MY DIET
Distributed by Universal Press Syndicate
I'M EATING HEALTHIER!

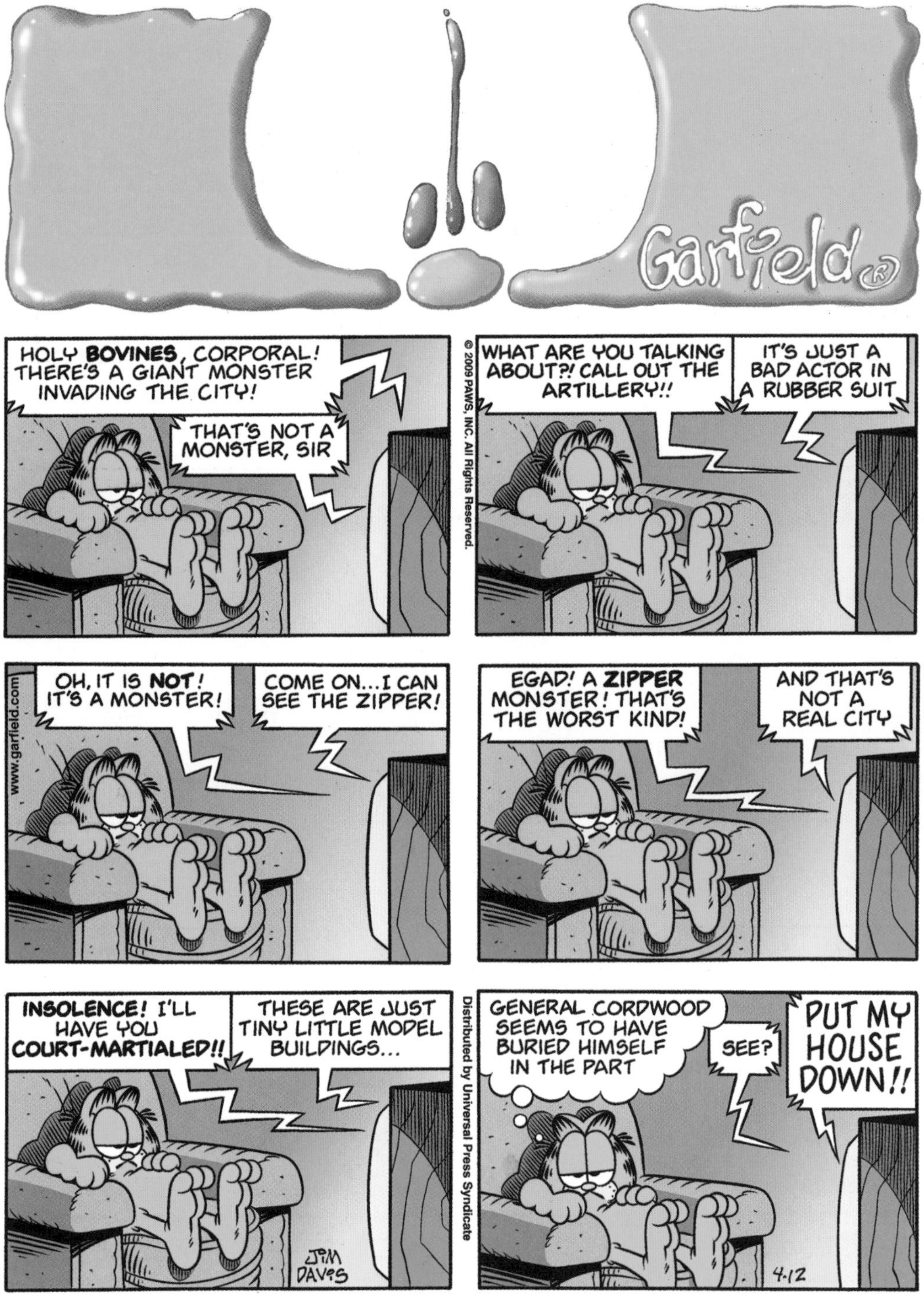
Garfield®
HOLY BOVINES, CORPORAL! THERE'S A GIANT MONSTER INVADING THE CITY!
THAT'S NOT A MONSTER, SIR
WHAT ARE YOU TALKING ABOUT?! CALL OUT THE ARTILLERY!!
IT'S JUST A BAD ACTOR IN A RUBBER SUIT
OH, IT IS NOT! IT'S A MONSTER!
COME ON...I CAN SEE THE ZIPPER!
EGAD! A ZIPPER MONSTER! THAT'S THE WORST KIND!
AND THAT'S NOT A REAL CITY
INSOLENCE! I'LL HAVE YOU COURT-MARTIALED!!
THESE ARE JUST TINY LITTLE MODEL BUILDINGS...
GENERAL CORDWOOD SEEMS TO HAVE BURIED HIMSELF IN THE PART
SEE?
PUT MY HOUSE DOWN!!
JIM DAVIS
4-12
© 2009 PAWS, INC. All Rights Reserved.
www.garfield.com
Distributed by Universal Press Syndicate

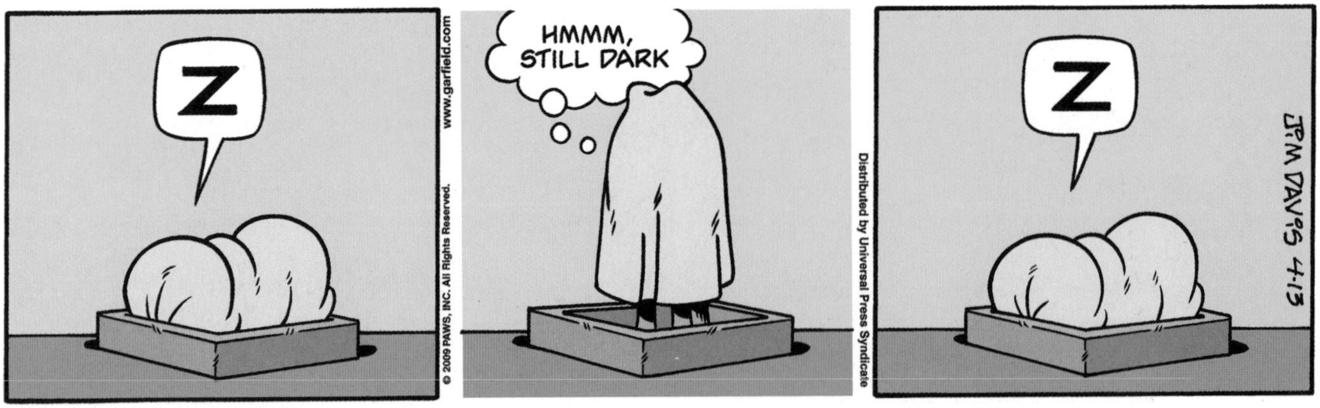
Z
HMMM, STILL DARK
Z
JIM DAVIS 4-13

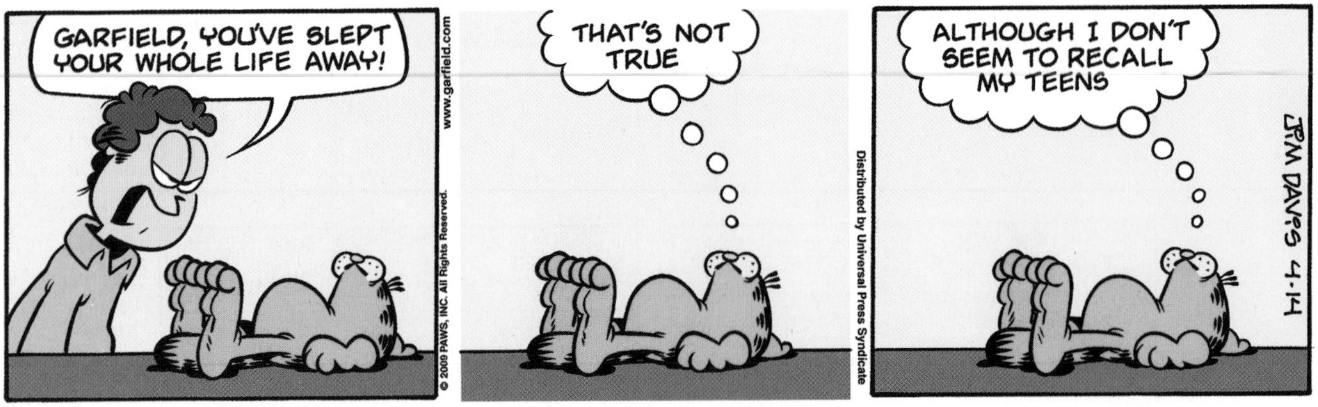
GARFIELD, YOU'VE SLEPT YOUR WHOLE LIFE AWAY!
THAT'S NOT TRUE
ALTHOUGH I DON'T SEEM TO RECALL MY TEENS
JIM DAVIS 4-14

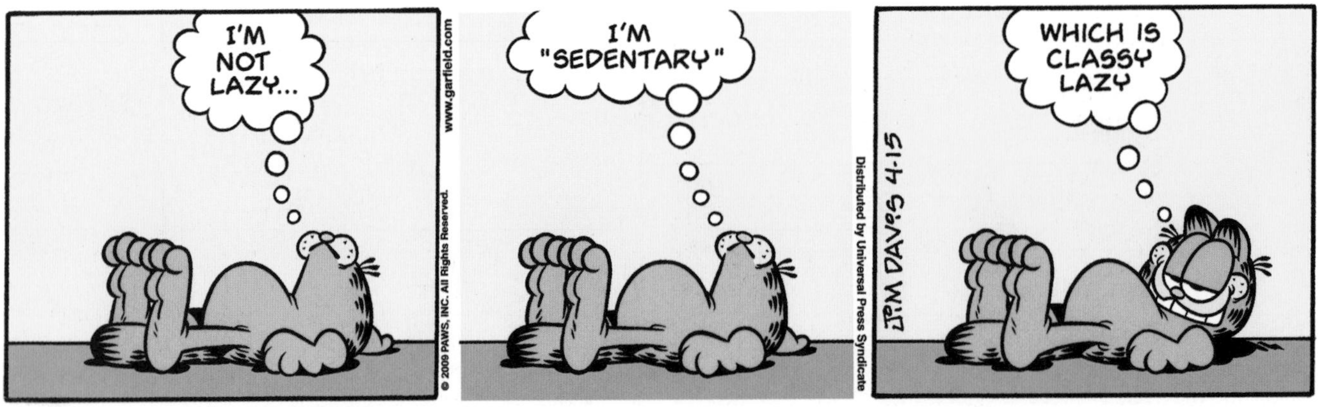
I'M NOT LAZY...
I'M "SEDENTARY"
WHICH IS CLASSY LAZY
JIM DAVIS 4-15

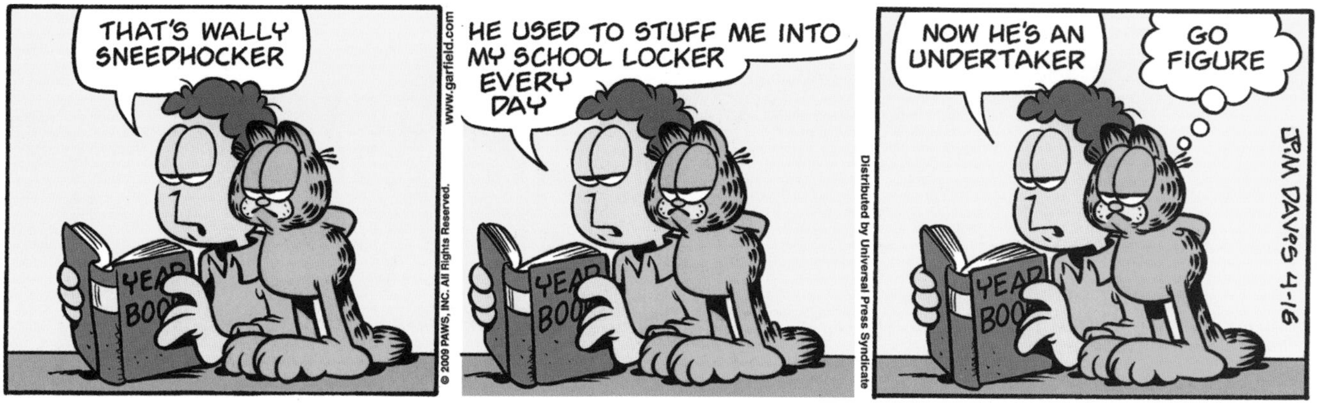
THAT'S WALLY SNEEDHOCKER
HE USED TO STUFF ME INTO MY SCHOOL LOCKER
EVERY DAY
NOW HE'S AN UNDERTAKER
GO FIGURE
JIM DAVIS 4-16
© 2009 PAWS, INC. All Rights Reserved. www.garfield.com
Distributed by Universal Press Syndicate

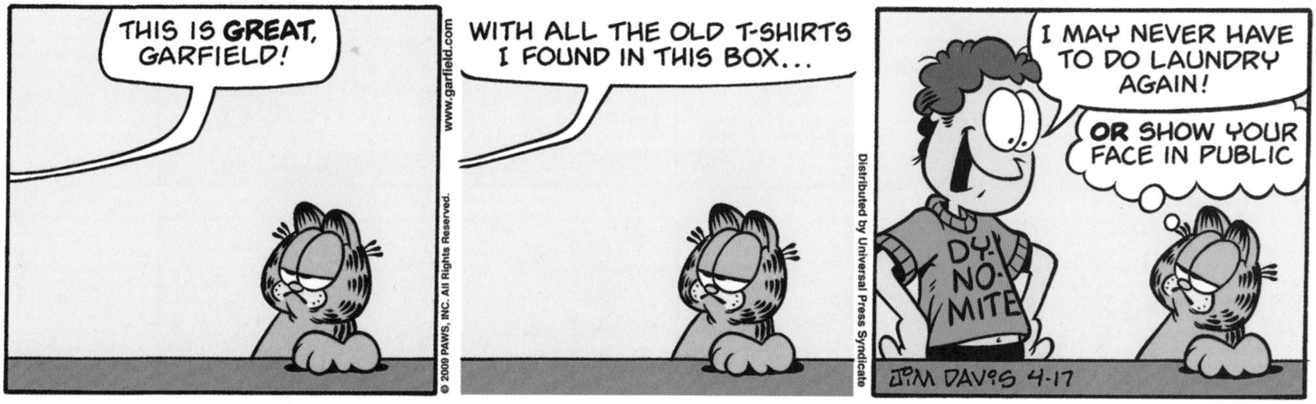
THIS IS **GREAT**, GARFIELD!
WITH ALL THE OLD T-SHIRTS I FOUND IN THIS BOX...
I MAY NEVER HAVE TO DO LAUNDRY AGAIN!
OR SHOW YOUR FACE IN PUBLIC
DY-NO-MITE
JIM DAVIS 4-17
© 2009 PAWS, INC. All Rights Reserved. www.garfield.com
Distributed by Universal Press Syndicate

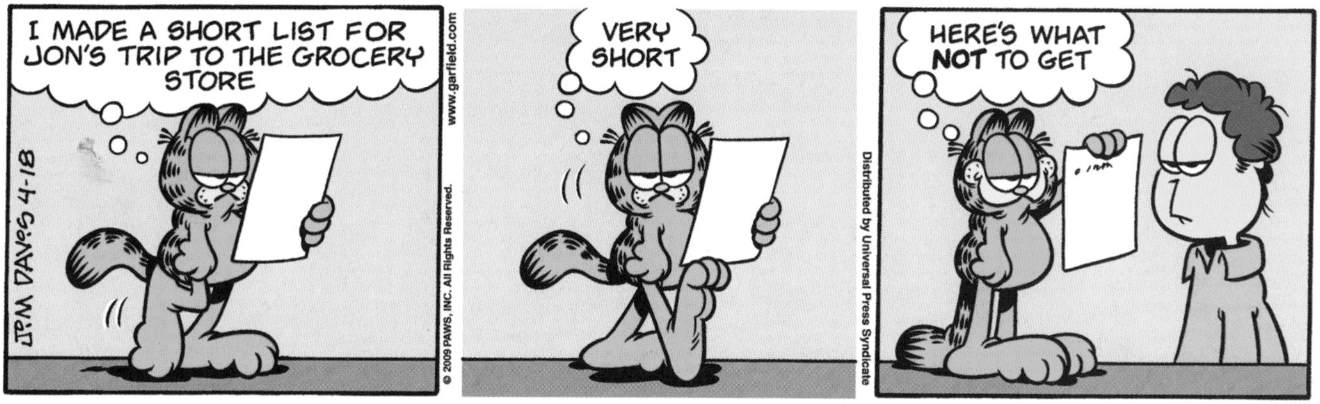
I MADE A SHORT LIST FOR JON'S TRIP TO THE GROCERY STORE
JIM DAVIS 4-18
VERY SHORT
HERE'S WHAT **NOT** TO GET
© 2009 PAWS, INC. All Rights Reserved. www.garfield.com
Distributed by Universal Press Syndicate

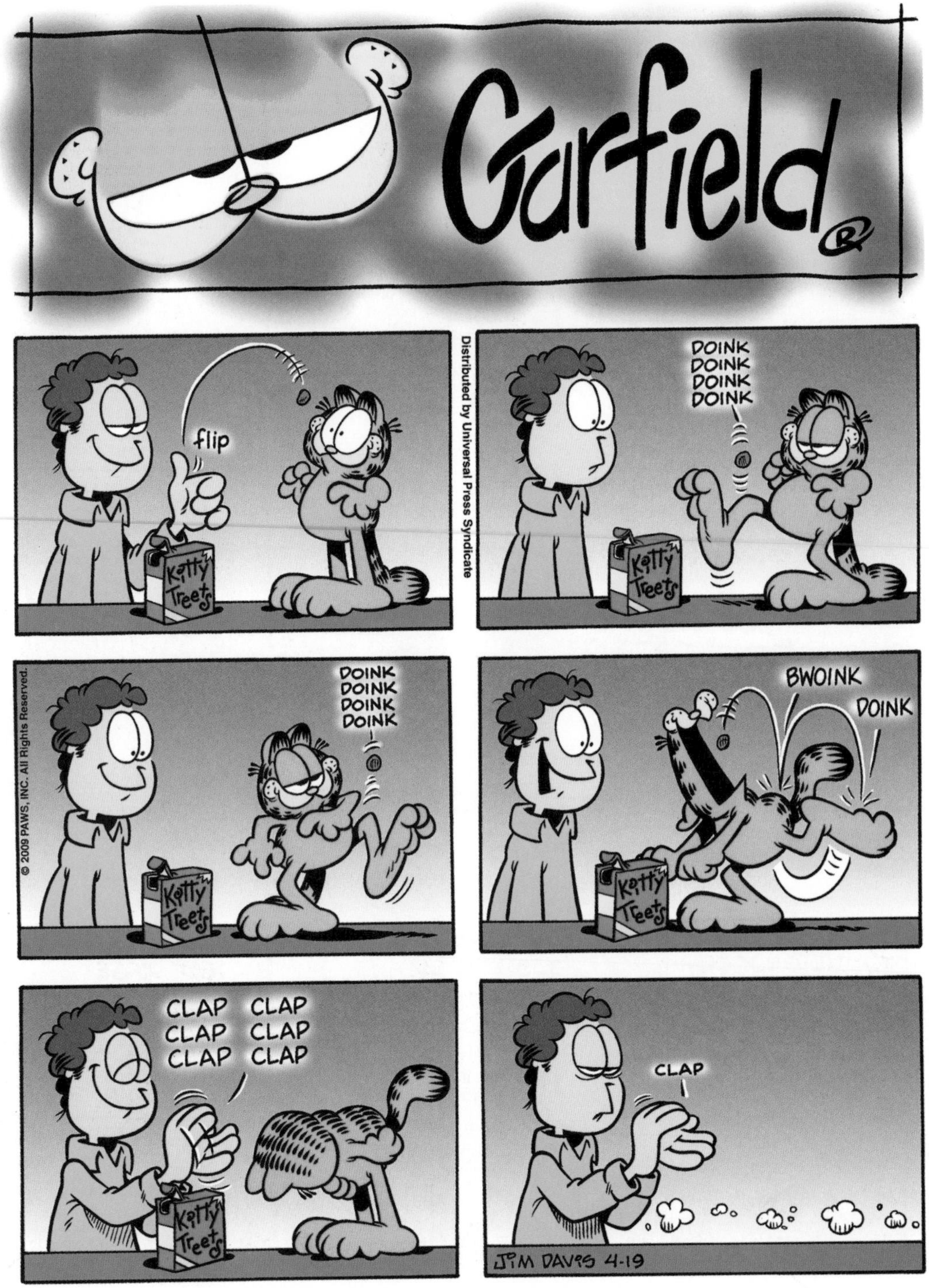
Garfield®
Distributed by Universal Press Syndicate
flip
Katty Treets
DOINK
DOINK
DOINK
DOINK
© 2009 PAWS, INC. All Rights Reserved.
DOINK
DOINK
DOINK
DOINK
BWOINK
DOINK
CLAP CLAP
CLAP CLAP
CLAP CLAP
CLAP
JIM DAVIS 4-19

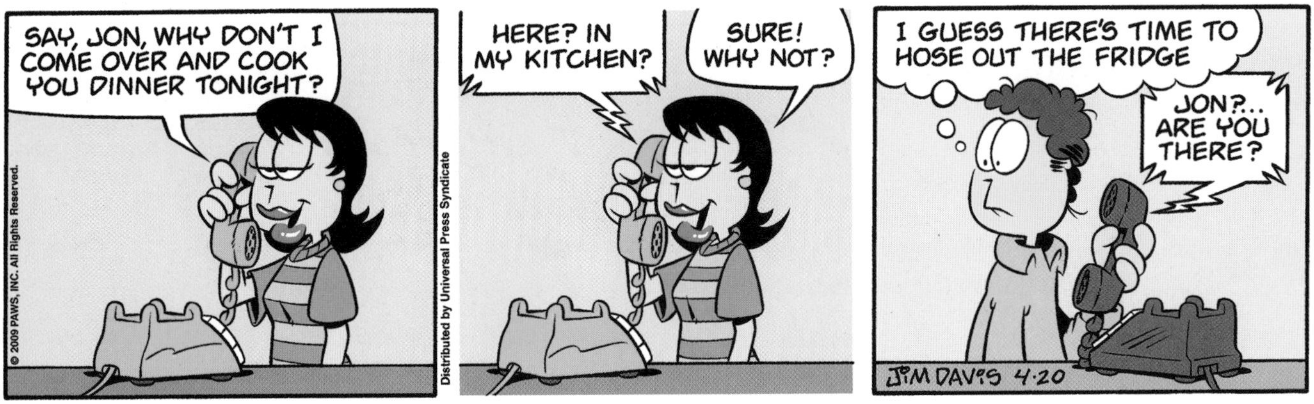
SAY, JON, WHY DON'T I COME OVER AND COOK YOU DINNER TONIGHT?
HERE? IN MY KITCHEN?
SURE! WHY NOT?
I GUESS THERE'S TIME TO HOSE OUT THE FRIDGE
JON?... ARE YOU THERE?
JIM DAVIS 4·20
© 2009 PAWS, INC. All Rights Reserved.
Distributed by Universal Press Syndicate

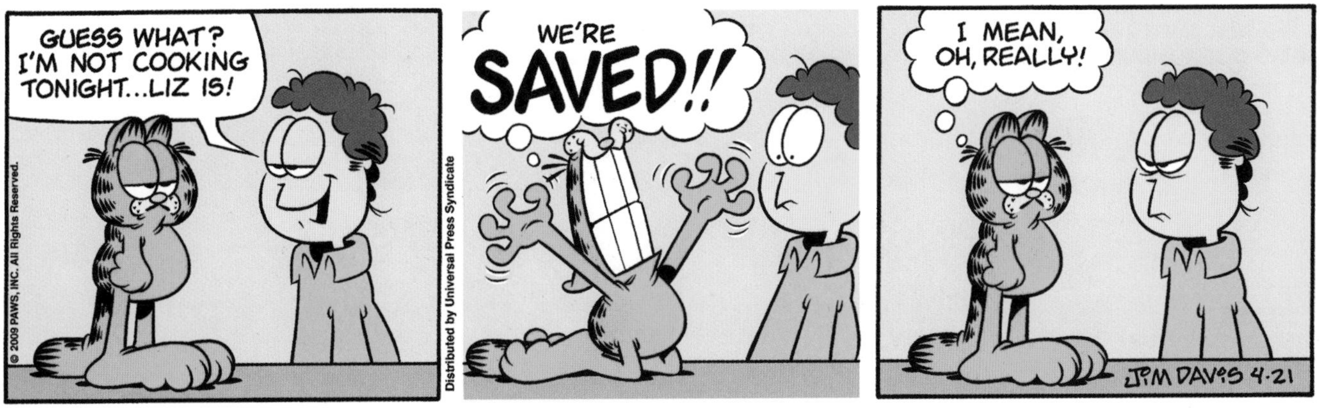
GUESS WHAT? I'M NOT COOKING TONIGHT...LIZ IS!
WE'RE SAVED!!
I MEAN, OH, REALLY!
JIM DAVIS 4·21
© 2009 PAWS, INC. All Rights Reserved.
Distributed by Universal Press Syndicate

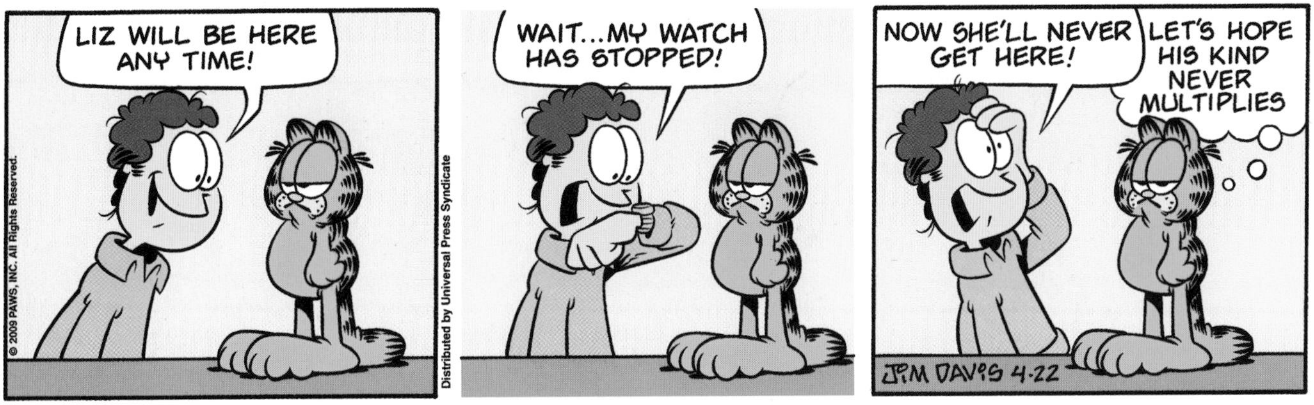
LIZ WILL BE HERE ANY TIME!
WAIT...MY WATCH HAS STOPPED!
NOW SHE'LL NEVER GET HERE!
LET'S HOPE HIS KIND NEVER MULTIPLIES
JIM DAVIS 4·22
© 2009 PAWS, INC. All Rights Reserved.
Distributed by Universal Press Syndicate

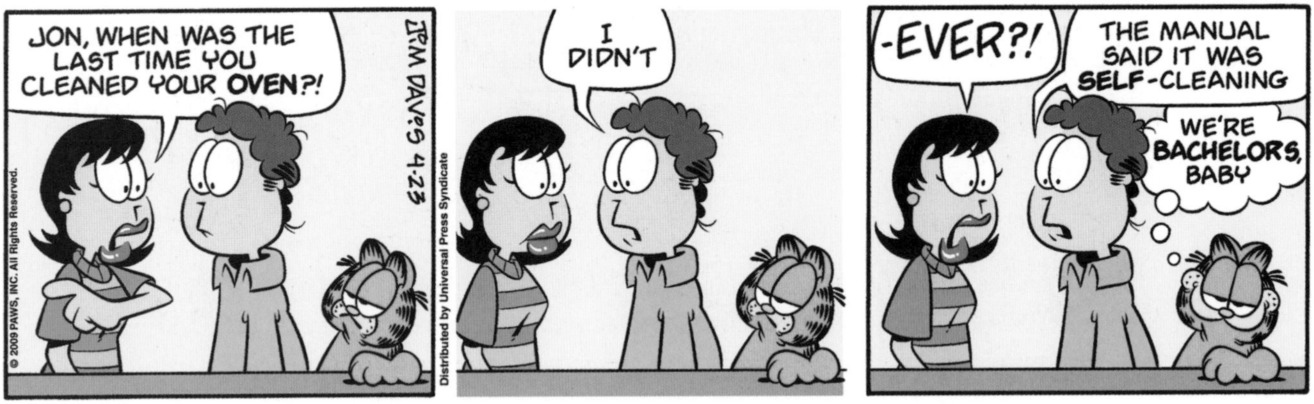
JON, WHEN WAS THE LAST TIME YOU CLEANED YOUR **OVEN**?!
JIM DAVIS 4·23
© 2009 PAWS, INC. All Rights Reserved.
I DIDN'T
Distributed by Universal Press Syndicate
-EVER?!
THE MANUAL SAID IT WAS **SELF**-CLEANING
WE'RE **BACHELORS**, BABY

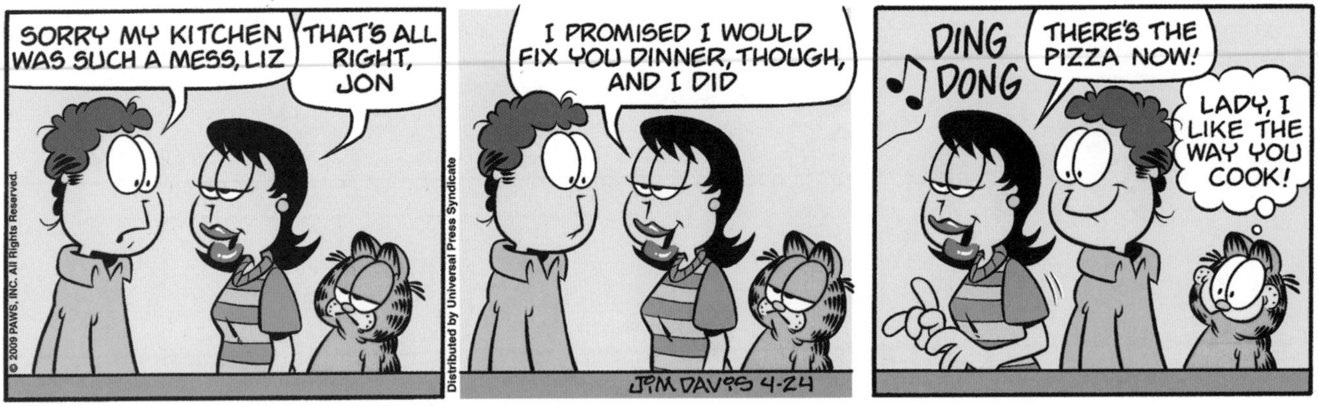
SORRY MY KITCHEN WAS SUCH A MESS, LIZ
THAT'S ALL RIGHT, JON
© 2009 PAWS, INC. All Rights Reserved.
I PROMISED I WOULD FIX YOU DINNER, THOUGH, AND I DID
Distributed by Universal Press Syndicate
JIM DAVIS 4-24
DING DONG
THERE'S THE PIZZA NOW!
LADY, I LIKE THE WAY YOU COOK!

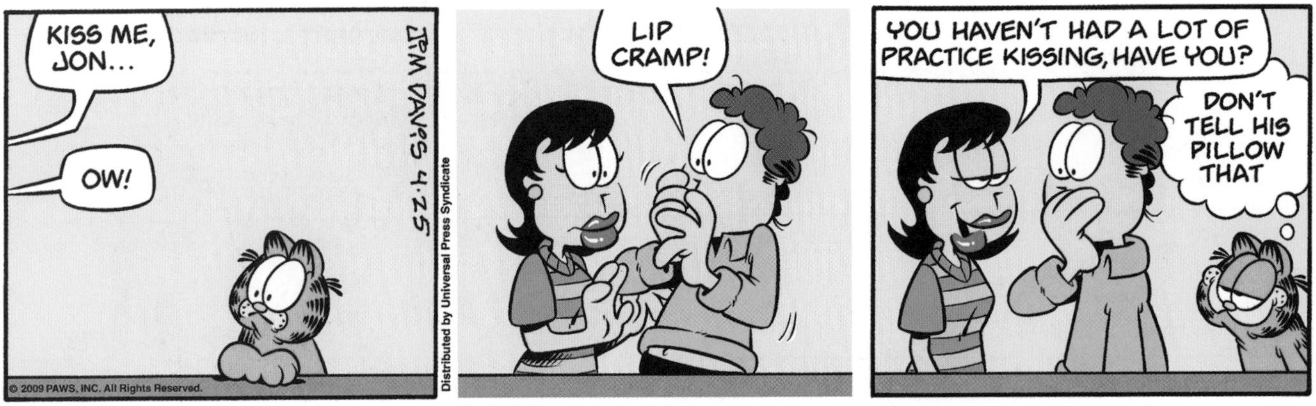
KISS ME, JON...
OW!
JIM DAVIS 4·25
© 2009 PAWS, INC. All Rights Reserved.
LIP CRAMP!
Distributed by Universal Press Syndicate
YOU HAVEN'T HAD A LOT OF PRACTICE KISSING, HAVE YOU?
DON'T TELL HIS PILLOW THAT

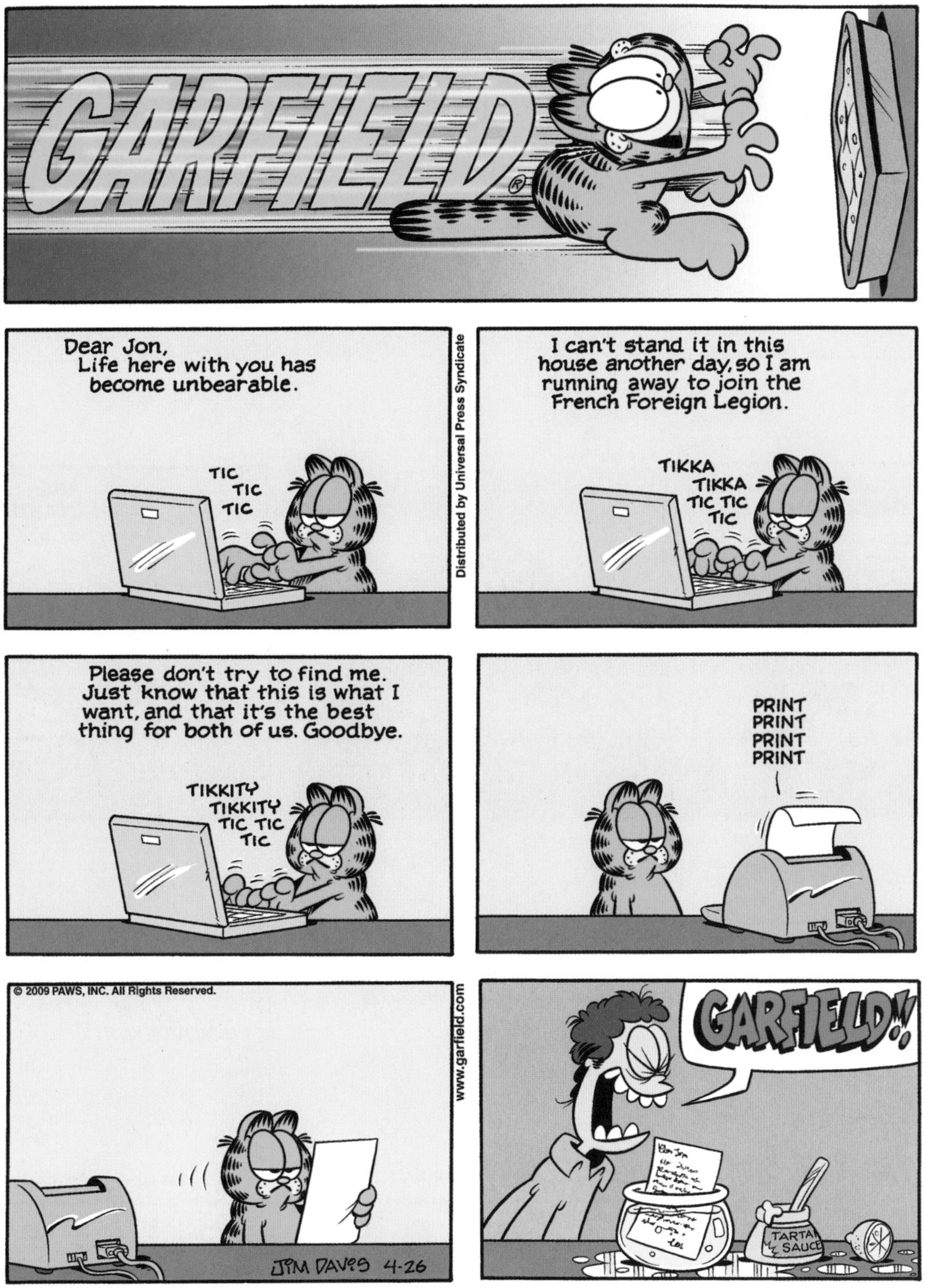
GARFIELD®
Dear Jon, Life here with you has become unbearable.
TIC TIC TIC
Distributed by Universal Press Syndicate
I can't stand it in this house another day, so I am running away to join the French Foreign Legion.
TIKKA TIKKA TIC TIC TIC
Please don't try to find me. Just know that this is what I want, and that it's the best thing for both of us. Goodbye.
TIKKITY TIKKITY TIC TIC TIC
PRINT PRINT PRINT PRINT
© 2009 PAWS, INC. All Rights Reserved.
www.garfield.com
JIM DAVIS 4-26
GARFIELD!!
TARTAR SAUCE

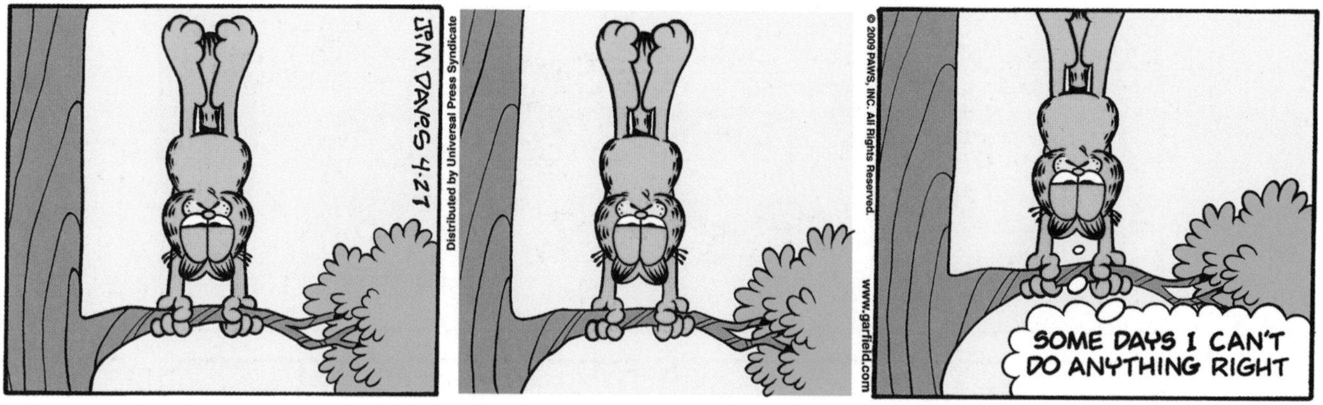
JIM DAVIS 4-27
Distributed by Universal Press Syndicate
© 2009 PAWS, INC. All Rights Reserved.
www.garfield.com
SOME DAYS I CAN'T DO ANYTHING RIGHT

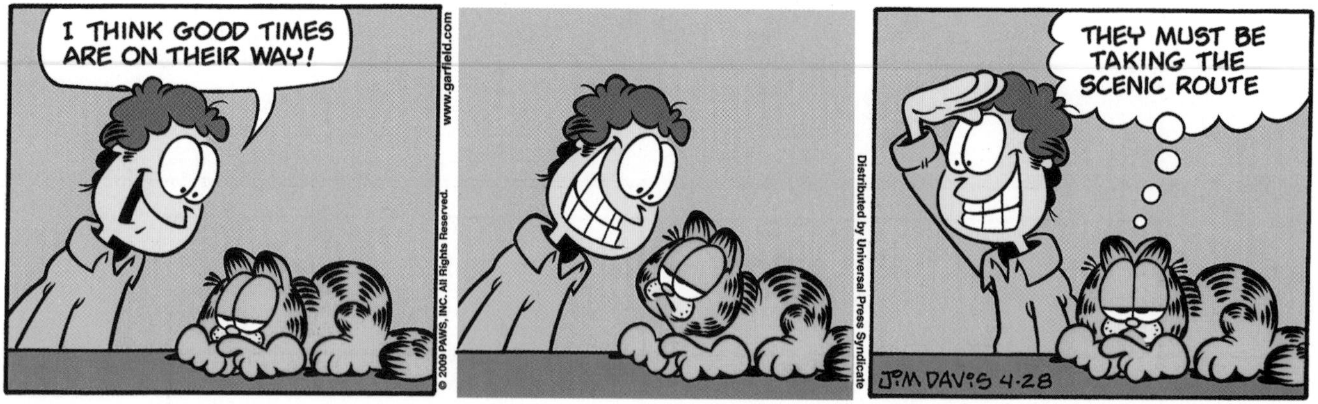
I THINK GOOD TIMES ARE ON THEIR WAY!
www.garfield.com
© 2009 PAWS, INC. All Rights Reserved.
Distributed by Universal Press Syndicate
THEY MUST BE TAKING THE SCENIC ROUTE
JIM DAVIS 4-28

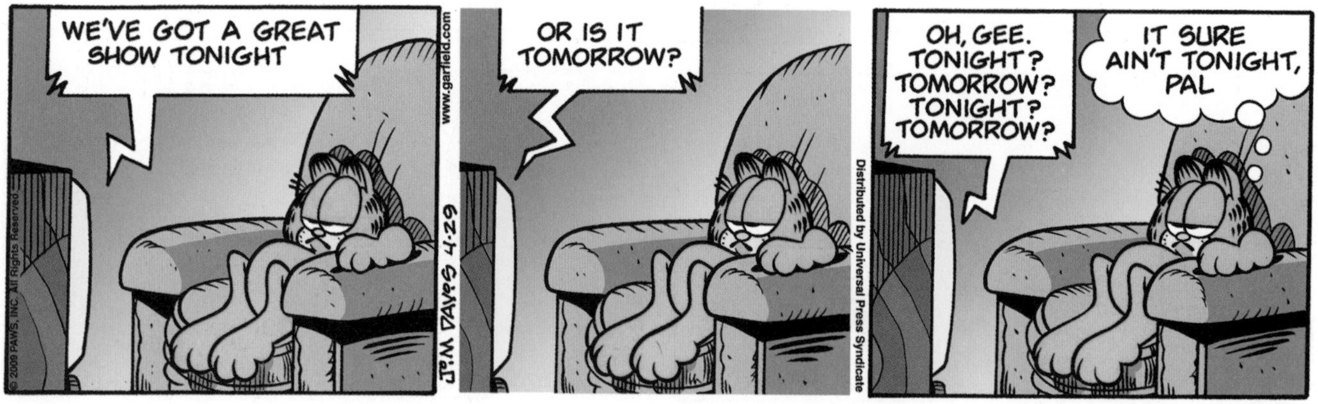
WE'VE GOT A GREAT SHOW TONIGHT
© 2009 PAWS, INC. All Rights Reserved.
www.garfield.com
JIM DAVIS 4-29
OR IS IT TOMORROW?
Distributed by Universal Press Syndicate
OH, GEE. TONIGHT? TOMORROW? TONIGHT? TOMORROW?
IT SURE AIN'T TONIGHT, PAL

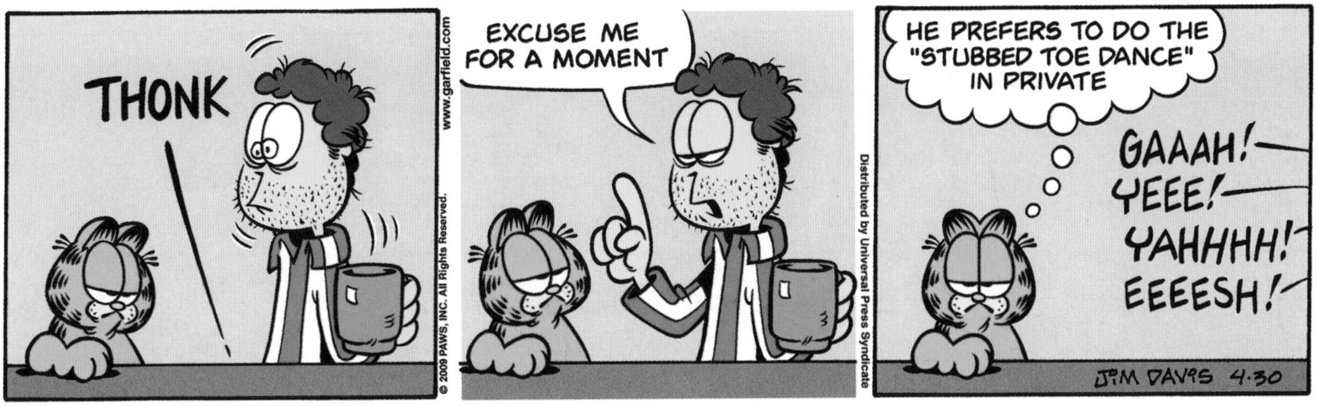
THONK
EXCUSE ME FOR A MOMENT
HE PREFERS TO DO THE "STUBBED TOE DANCE" IN PRIVATE
GAAAH! YEEE! YAHHHH! EEEESH!
JIM DAVIS 4-30

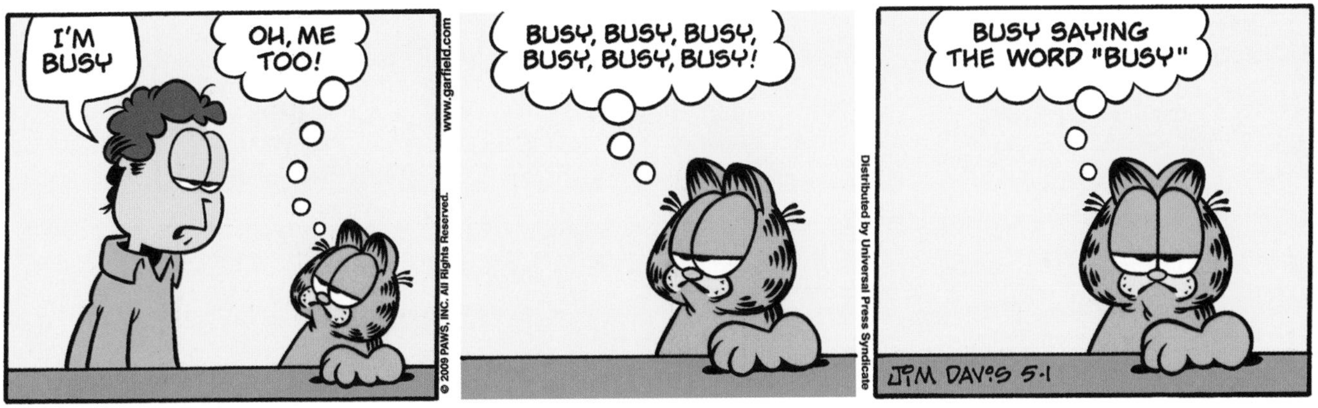
I'M BUSY
OH, ME TOO!
BUSY, BUSY, BUSY, BUSY, BUSY, BUSY!
BUSY SAYING THE WORD "BUSY"
JIM DAVIS 5-1

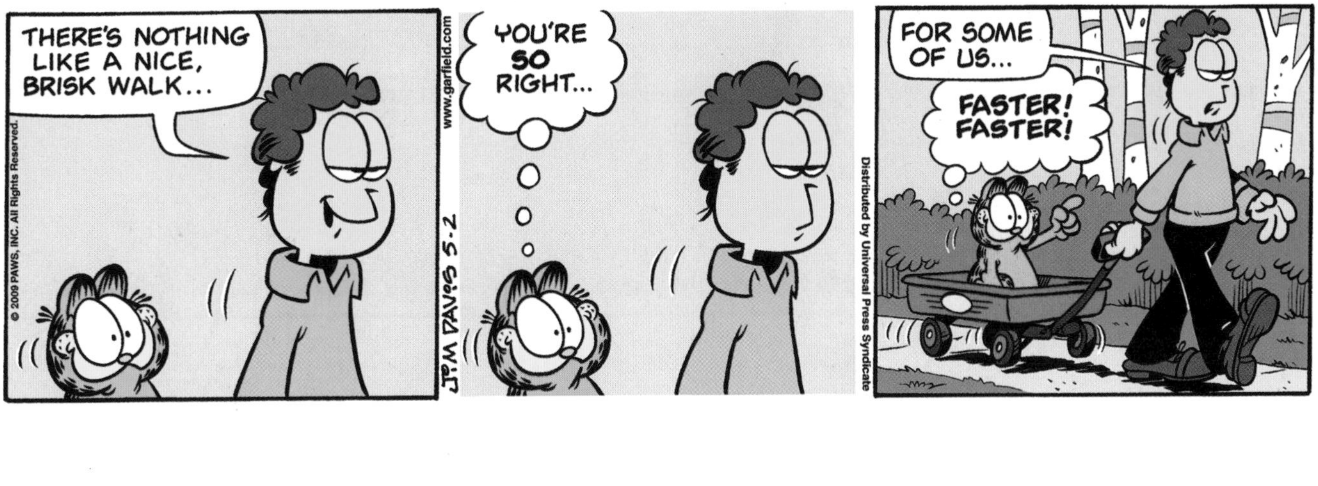
THERE'S NOTHING LIKE A NICE, BRISK WALK...
YOU'RE SO RIGHT...
FOR SOME OF US...
FASTER! FASTER!
JIM DAVIS 5-2

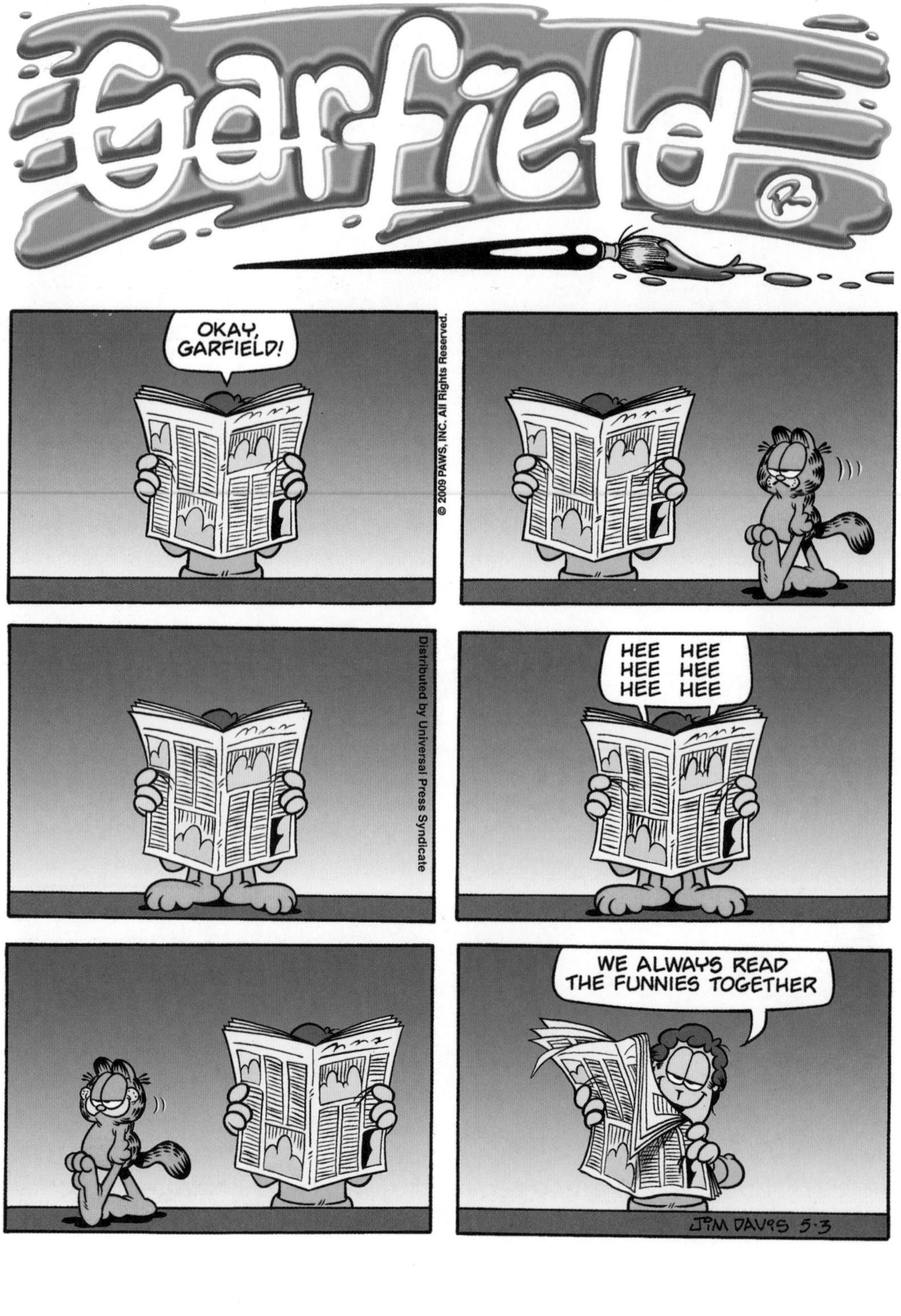
Garfield®
OKAY, GARFIELD!
© 2009 PAWS, INC. All Rights Reserved.
Distributed by Universal Press Syndicate
HEE HEE HEE HEE HEE HEE
WE ALWAYS READ THE FUNNIES TOGETHER
JIM DAVIS 5-3

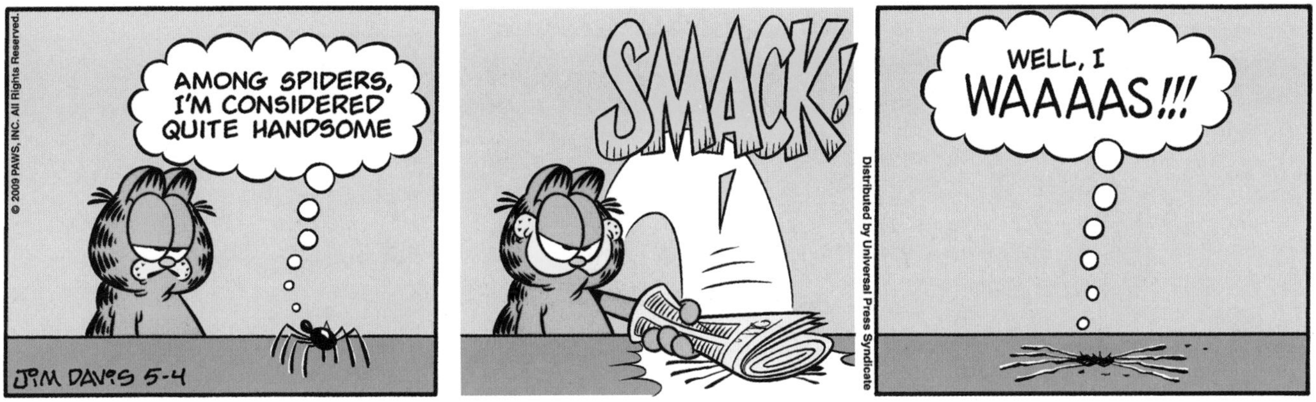
© 2009 PAWS, INC. All Rights Reserved.
AMONG SPIDERS, I'M CONSIDERED QUITE HANDSOME
JIM DAVIS 5-4
SMACK!
Distributed by Universal Press Syndicate
WELL, I WAAAAS!!!

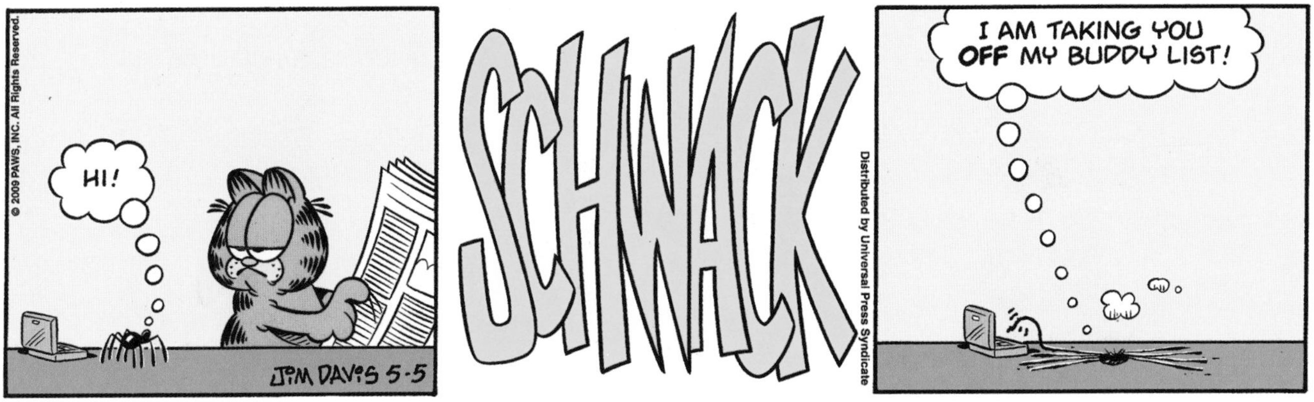
© 2009 PAWS, INC. All Rights Reserved.
HI!
JIM DAVIS 5-5
SCHWACK
Distributed by Universal Press Syndicate
I AM TAKING YOU OFF MY BUDDY LIST!

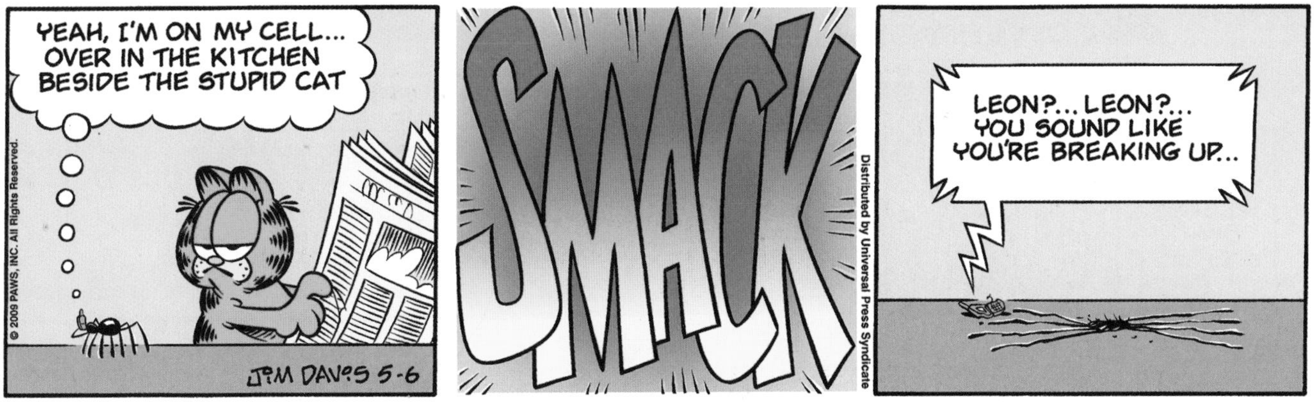
YEAH, I'M ON MY CELL... OVER IN THE KITCHEN BESIDE THE STUPID CAT
© 2009 PAWS, INC. All Rights Reserved.
JIM DAVIS 5-6
SMACK
Distributed by Universal Press Syndicate
LEON?... LEON?... YOU SOUND LIKE YOU'RE BREAKING UP...

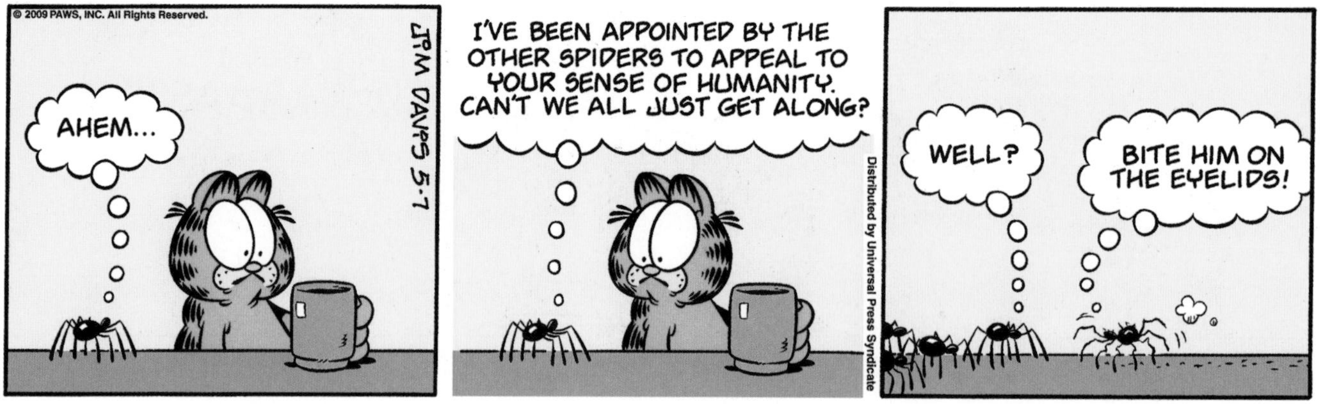
© 2009 PAWS, INC. All Rights Reserved.
JIM DAVIS 5-7
AHEM...
I'VE BEEN APPOINTED BY THE OTHER SPIDERS TO APPEAL TO YOUR SENSE OF HUMANITY. CAN'T WE ALL JUST GET ALONG?
Distributed by Universal Press Syndicate
WELL?
BITE HIM ON THE EYELIDS!

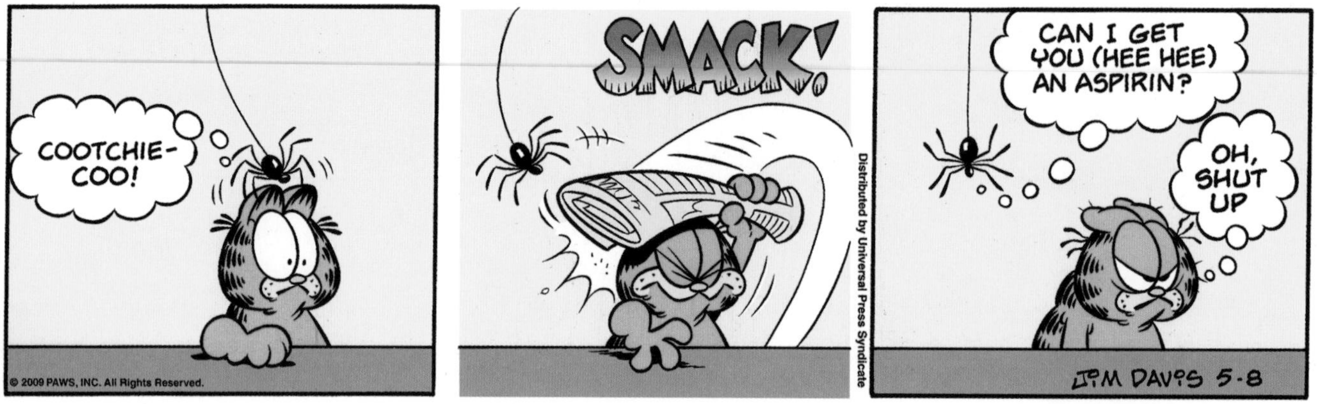
© 2009 PAWS, INC. All Rights Reserved.
COOTCHIE-COO!
SMACK!
Distributed by Universal Press Syndicate
CAN I GET YOU (HEE HEE) AN ASPIRIN?
OH, SHUT UP
JIM DAVIS 5-8

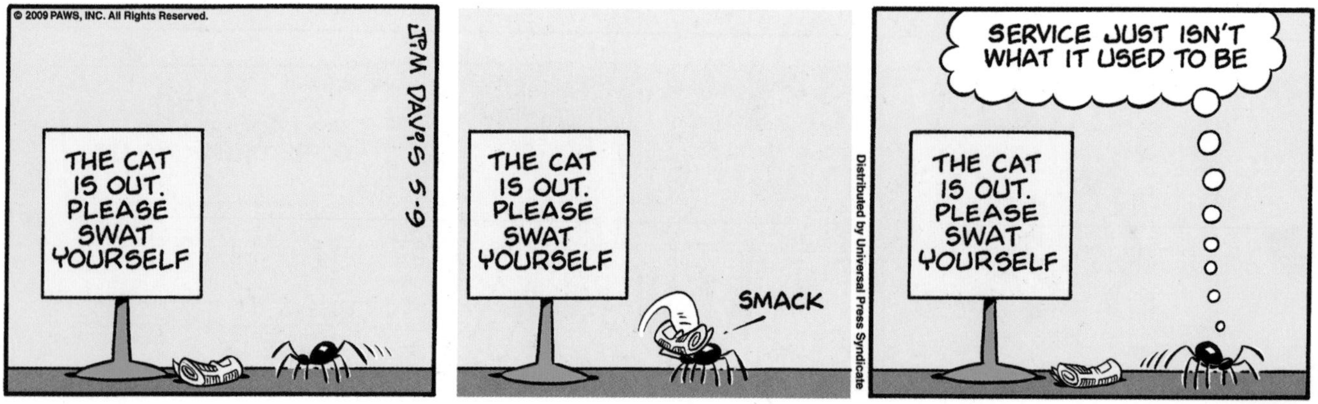
© 2009 PAWS, INC. All Rights Reserved.
JIM DAVIS 5-9
THE CAT IS OUT. PLEASE SWAT YOURSELF
THE CAT IS OUT. PLEASE SWAT YOURSELF
SMACK
Distributed by Universal Press Syndicate
SERVICE JUST ISN'T WHAT IT USED TO BE
THE CAT IS OUT. PLEASE SWAT YOURSELF

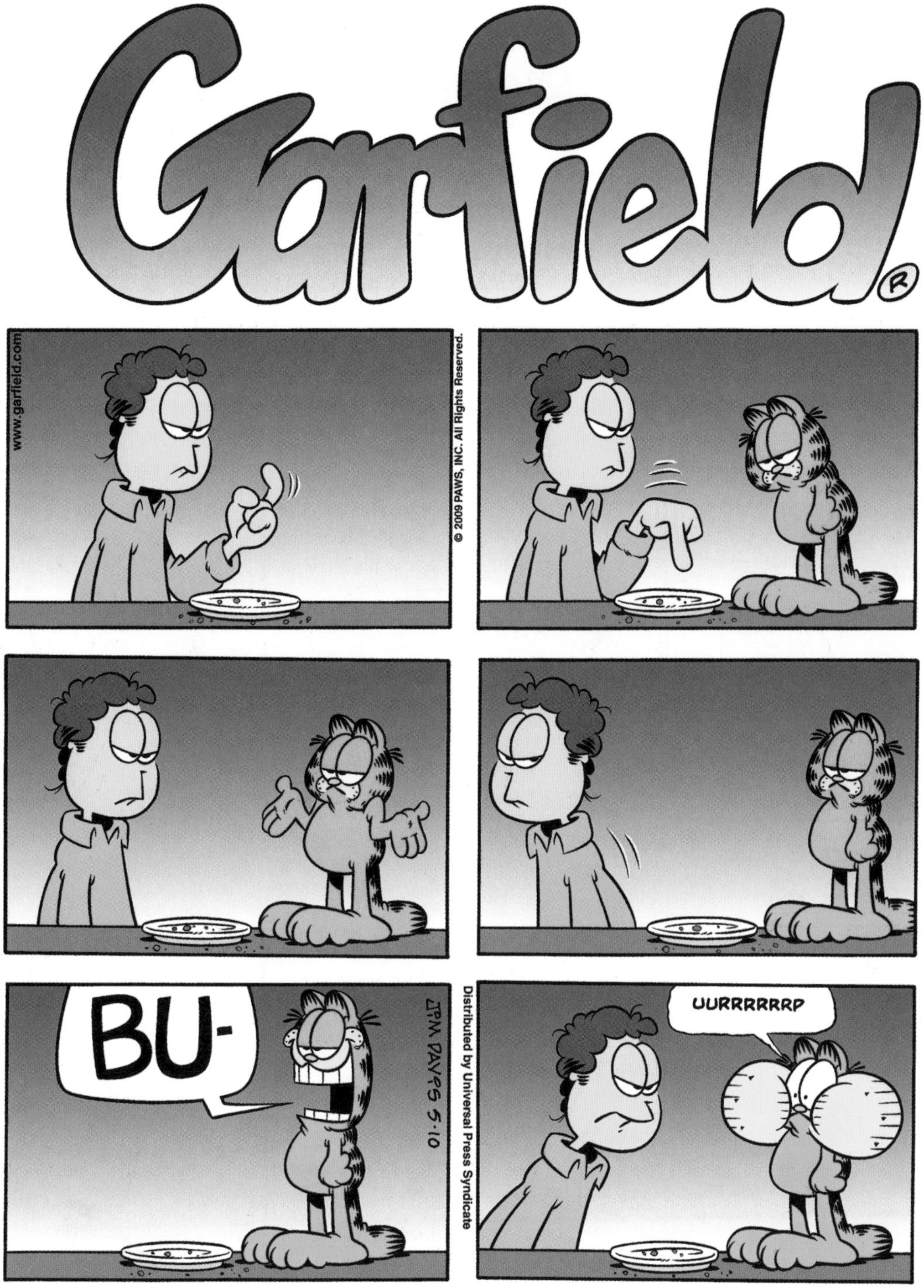
Garfield
www.garfield.com
© 2009 PAWS, INC. All Rights Reserved.
BU-
JPM DAVIS 5-10
Distributed by Universal Press Syndicate
UURRRRRRP

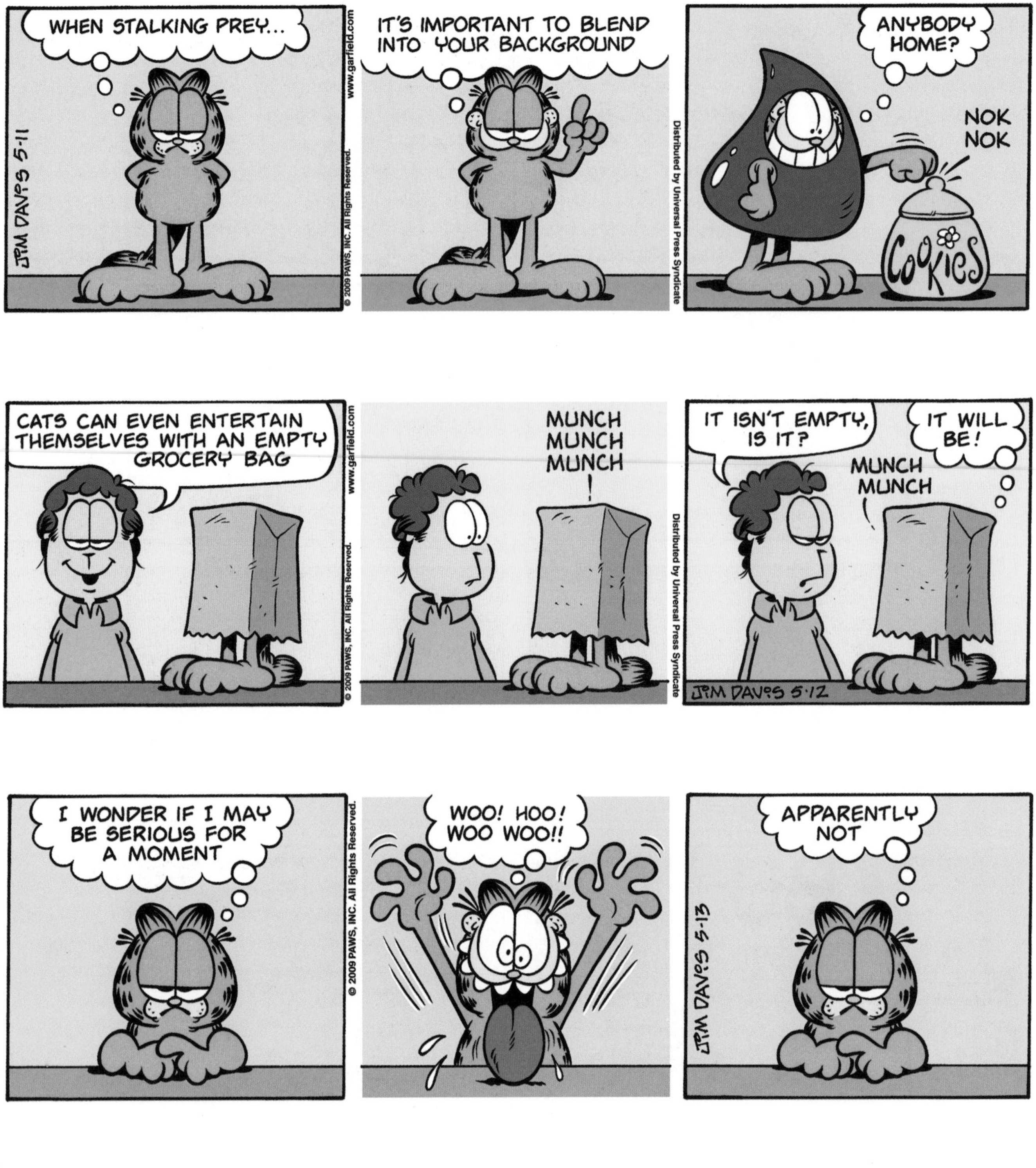
WHEN STALKING PREY...
JPM DAVPS 5-11
IT'S IMPORTANT TO BLEND INTO YOUR BACKGROUND
ANYBODY HOME?
NOK NOK
COOKIES
CATS CAN EVEN ENTERTAIN THEMSELVES WITH AN EMPTY GROCERY BAG
MUNCH MUNCH MUNCH
IT ISN'T EMPTY, IS IT?
MUNCH MUNCH
IT WILL BE!
JPM DAVPS 5-12
I WONDER IF I MAY BE SERIOUS FOR A MOMENT
WOO! HOO! WOO WOO!!
JPM DAVPS 5-13
APPARENTLY NOT

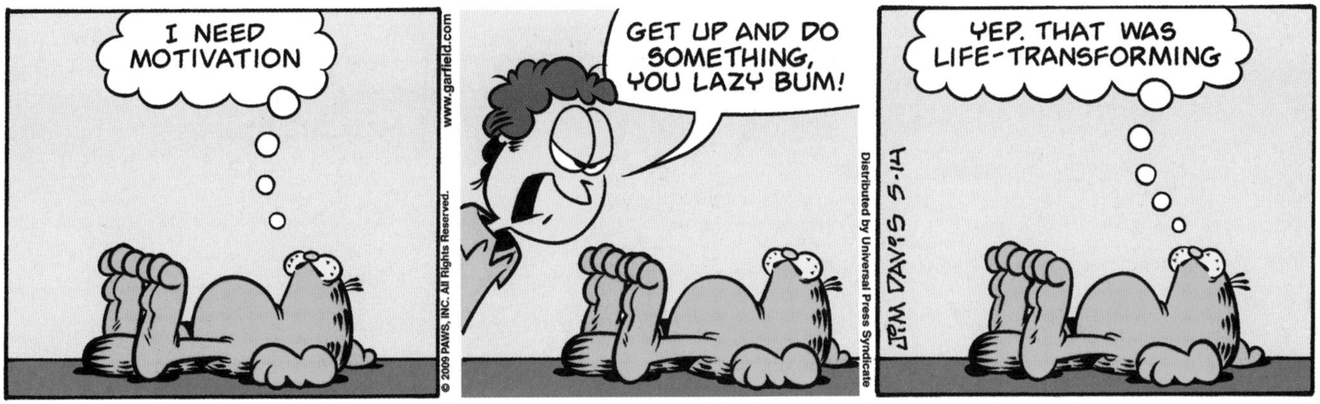
I NEED MOTIVATION
© 2009 PAWS, INC. All Rights Reserved. www.garfield.com
GET UP AND DO SOMETHING, YOU LAZY BUM!
Distributed by Universal Press Syndicate
JIM DAVIS 5-14
YEP. THAT WAS LIFE-TRANSFORMING

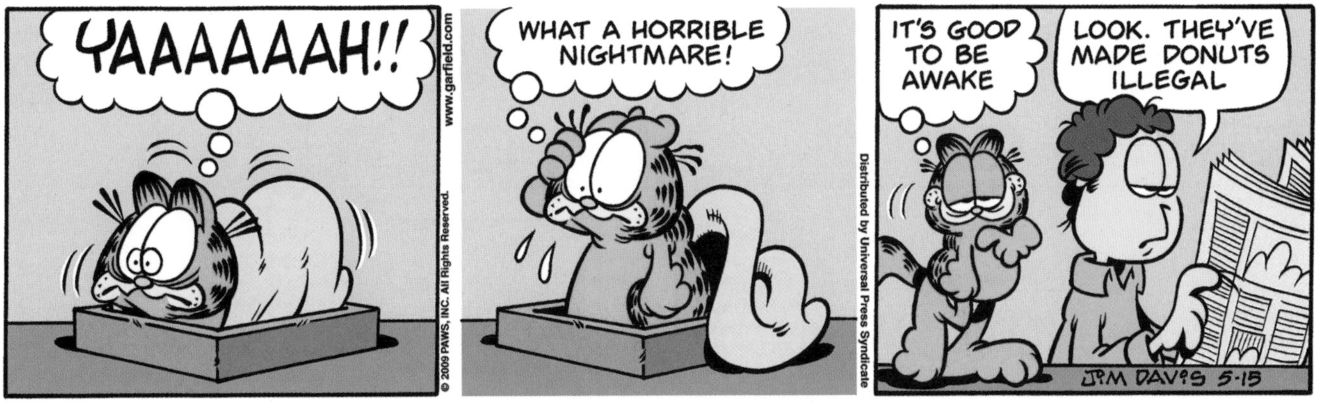
YAAAAAAH!!
© 2009 PAWS, INC. All Rights Reserved. www.garfield.com
WHAT A HORRIBLE NIGHTMARE!
Distributed by Universal Press Syndicate
IT'S GOOD TO BE AWAKE
LOOK. THEY'VE MADE DONUTS ILLEGAL
JIM DAVIS 5-15

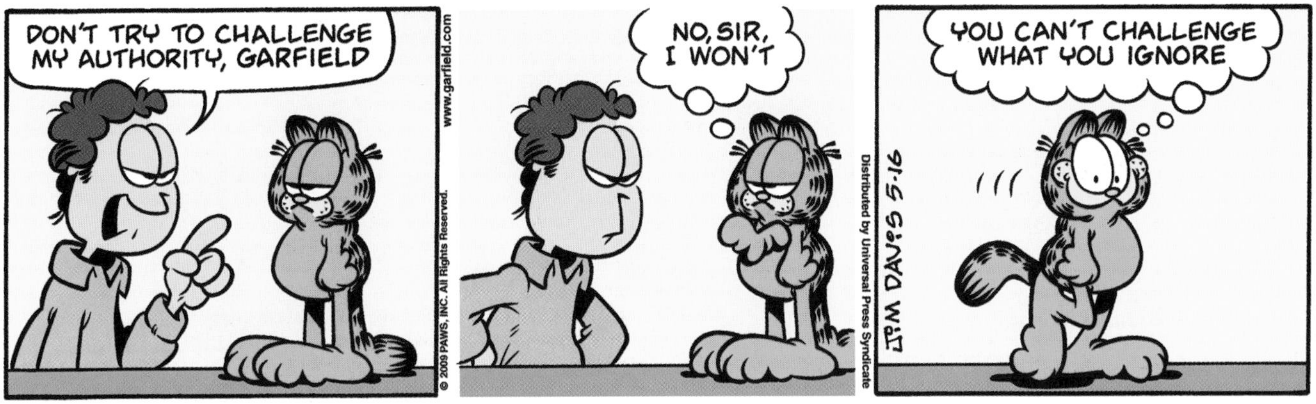
DON'T TRY TO CHALLENGE MY AUTHORITY, GARFIELD
© 2009 PAWS, INC. All Rights Reserved. www.garfield.com
NO, SIR, I WON'T
Distributed by Universal Press Syndicate
JIM DAVIS 5-16
YOU CAN'T CHALLENGE WHAT YOU IGNORE

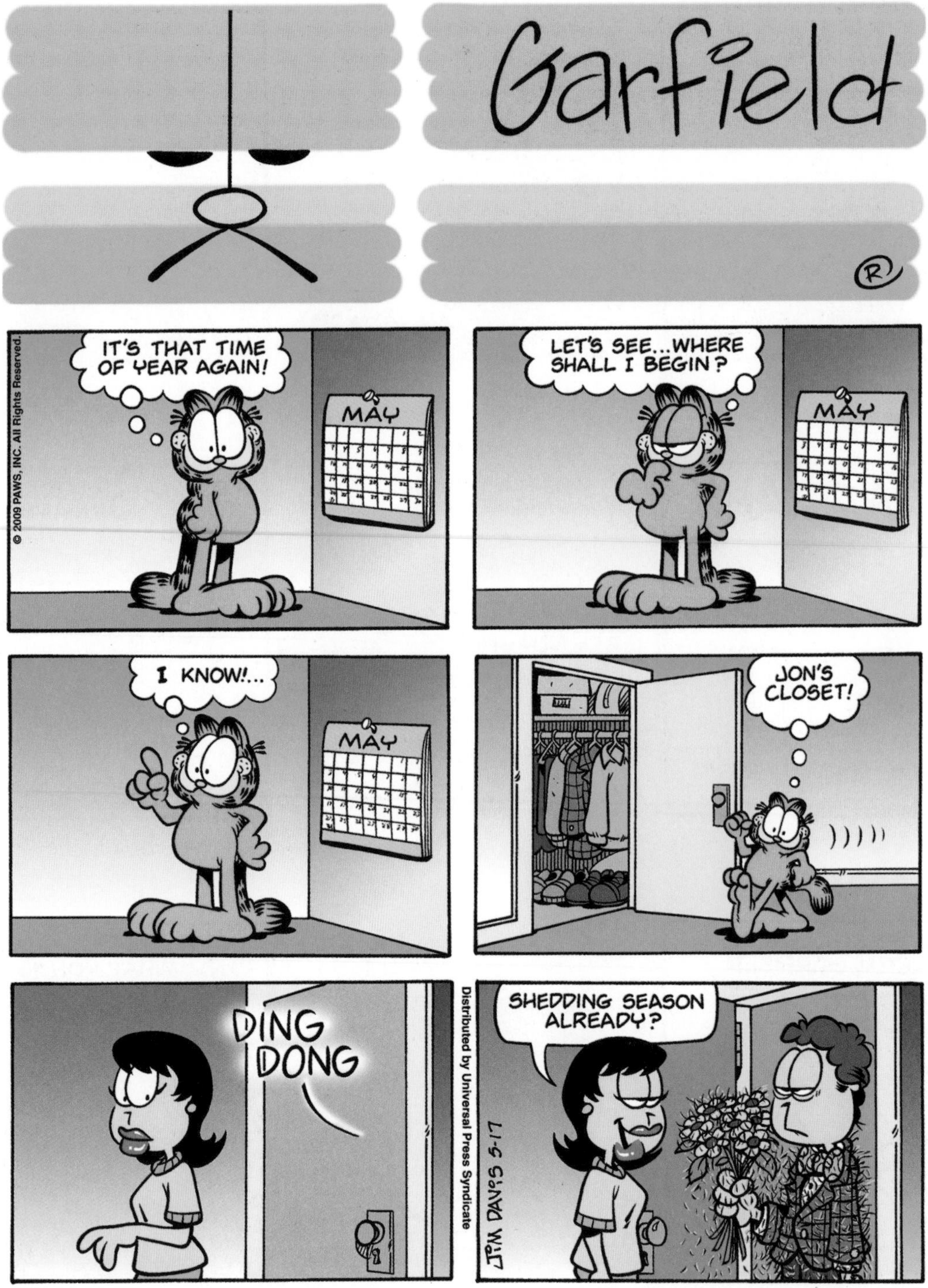
Garfield
IT'S THAT TIME OF YEAR AGAIN!
MAY
LET'S SEE...WHERE SHALL I BEGIN?
I KNOW!...
JON'S CLOSET!
DING DONG
SHEDDING SEASON ALREADY?
JPM DAVIS 5-17

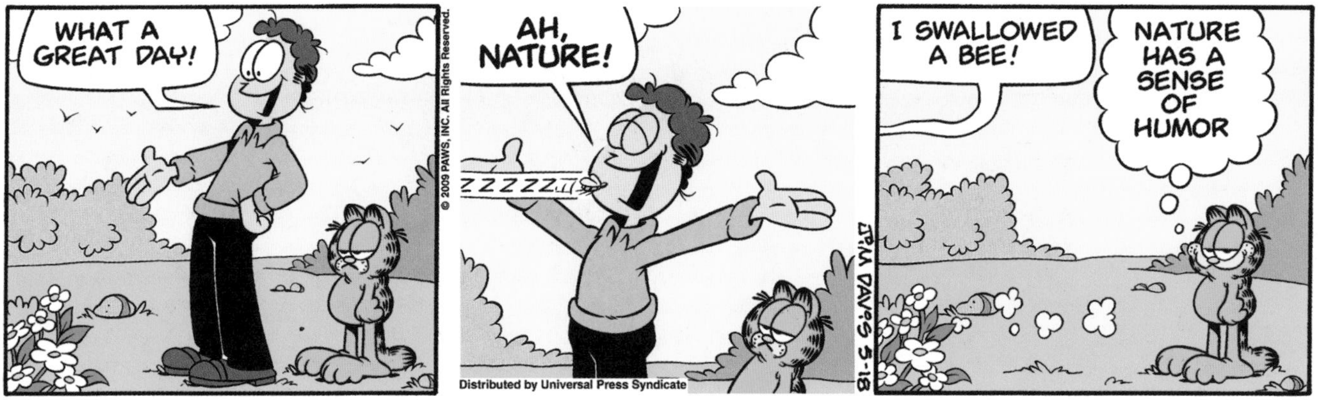
WHAT A GREAT DAY!
© 2009 PAWS, INC. All Rights Reserved.
AH, NATURE!
ZZZZZZ
Distributed by Universal Press Syndicate
JIM DAVIS 5-18
I SWALLOWED A BEE!
NATURE HAS A SENSE OF HUMOR

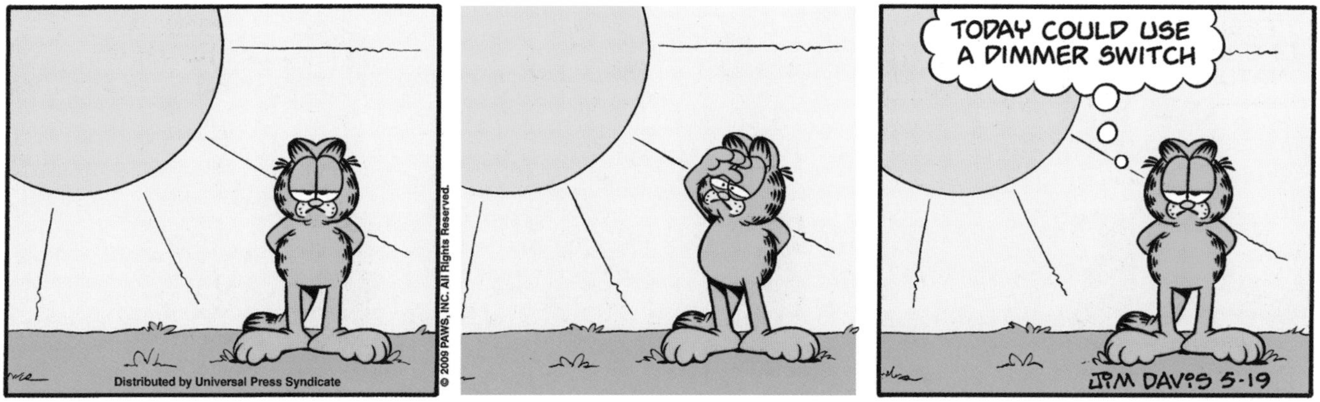
Distributed by Universal Press Syndicate
© 2009 PAWS, INC. All Rights Reserved.
TODAY COULD USE A DIMMER SWITCH
JIM DAVIS 5-19

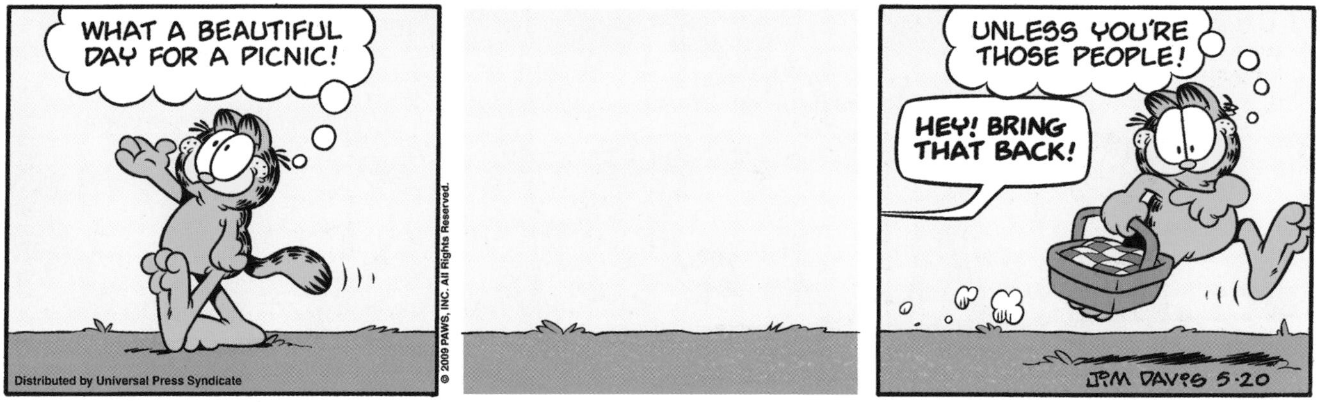
WHAT A BEAUTIFUL DAY FOR A PICNIC!
Distributed by Universal Press Syndicate
© 2009 PAWS, INC. All Rights Reserved.
UNLESS YOU'RE THOSE PEOPLE!
HEY! BRING THAT BACK!
JIM DAVIS 5-20

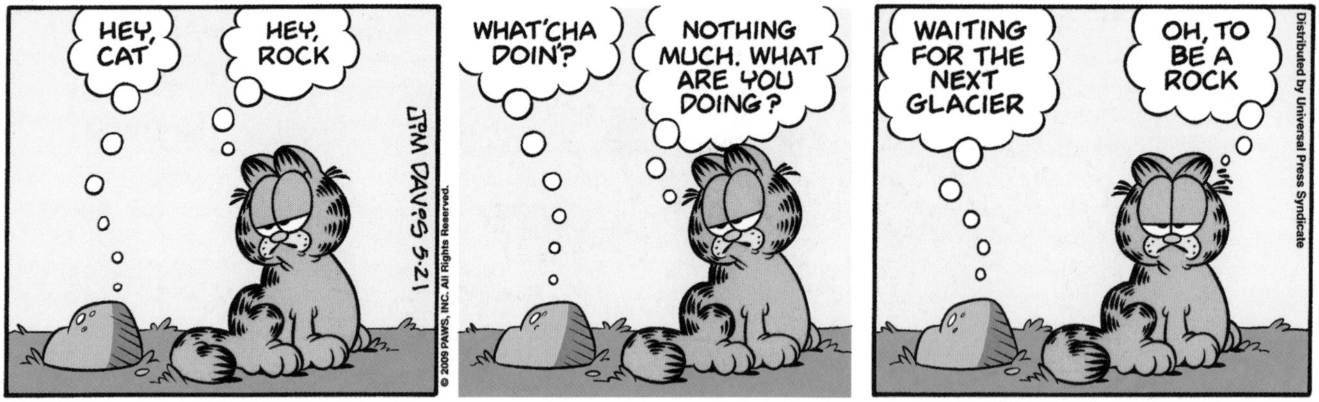
HEY, CAT
HEY, ROCK
JIM DAVIS 5-21
© 2009 PAWS, INC. All Rights Reserved.
WHAT'CHA DOIN'?
NOTHING MUCH. WHAT ARE YOU DOING?
WAITING FOR THE NEXT GLACIER
OH, TO BE A ROCK
Distributed by Universal Press Syndicate

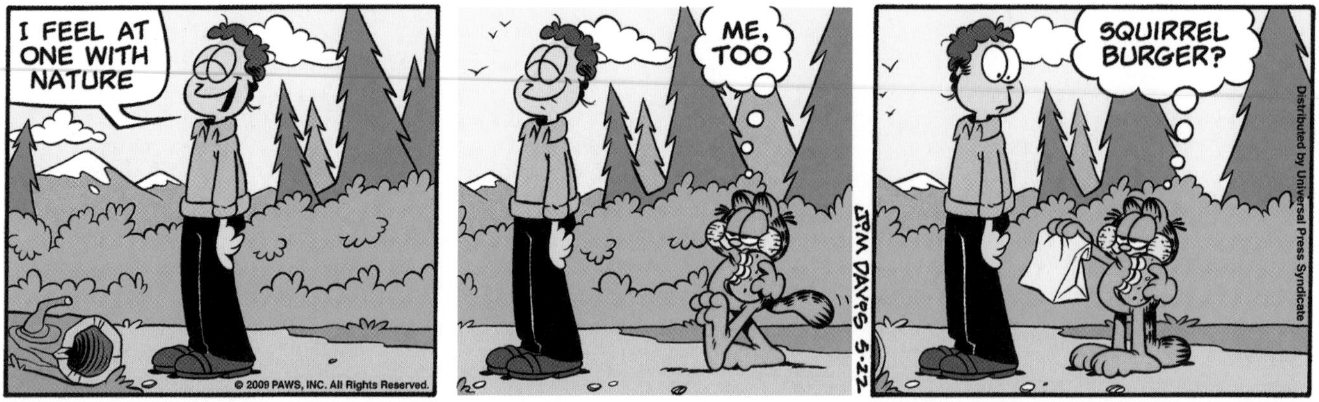
I FEEL AT ONE WITH NATURE
© 2009 PAWS, INC. All Rights Reserved.
ME, TOO
JIM DAVIS 5-22
SQUIRREL BURGER?
Distributed by Universal Press Syndicate

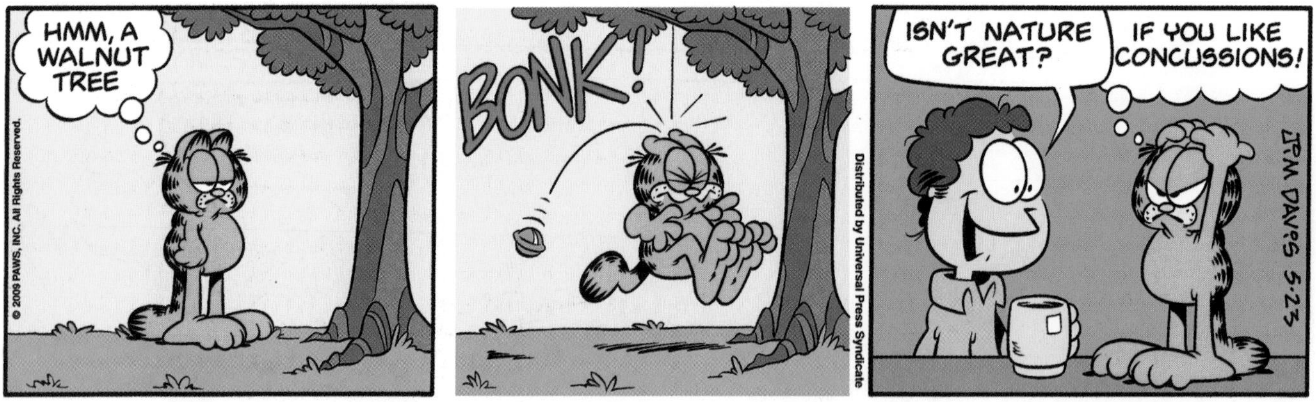
HMM, A WALNUT TREE
© 2009 PAWS, INC. All Rights Reserved.
BONK!
Distributed by Universal Press Syndicate
ISN'T NATURE GREAT?
IF YOU LIKE CONCUSSIONS!
JIM DAVIS 5-23

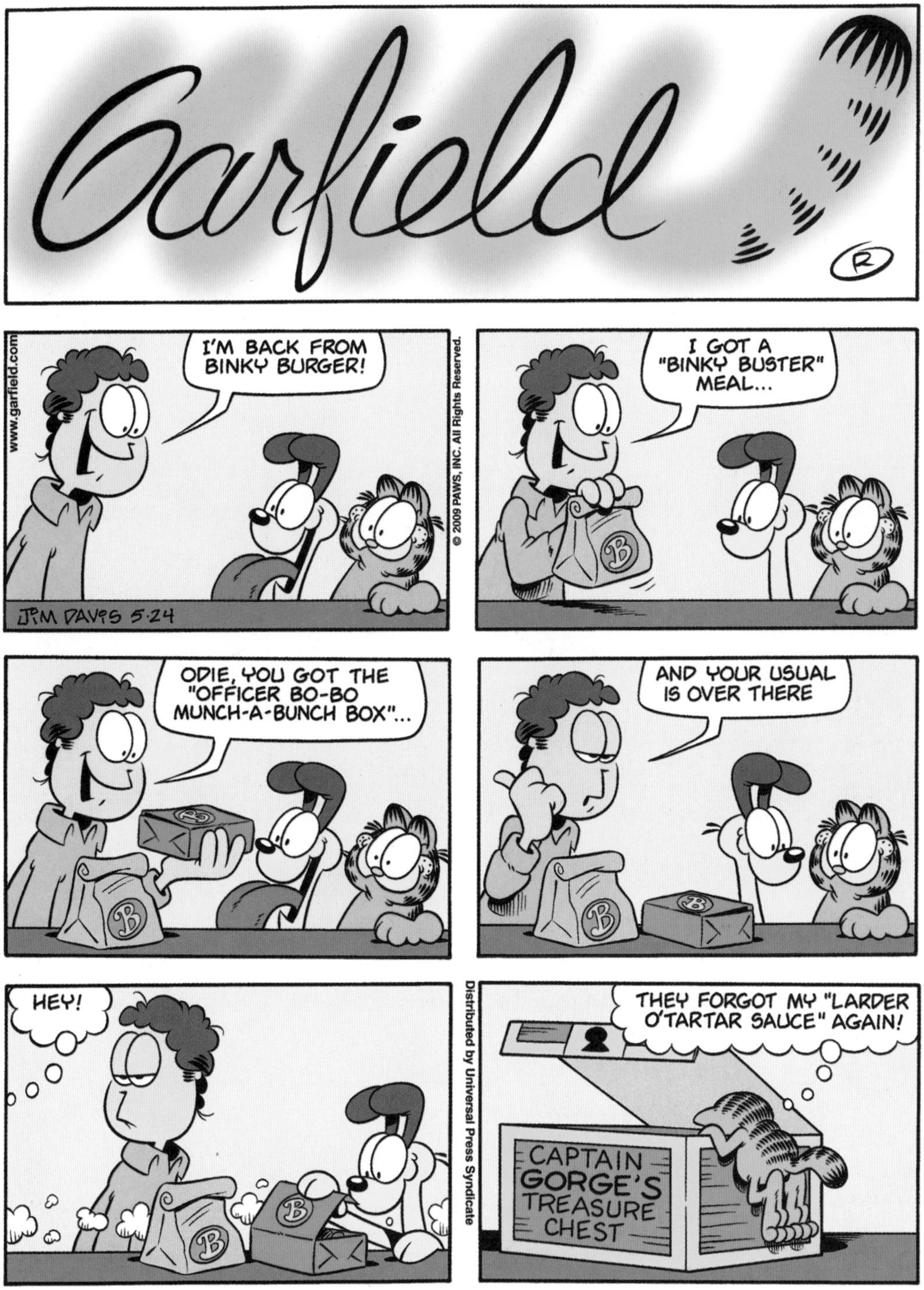
Garfield
I'M BACK FROM BINKY BURGER!
JIM DAVIS 5·24
www.garfield.com
© 2009 PAWS, INC. All Rights Reserved.
I GOT A "BINKY BUSTER" MEAL...
ODIE, YOU GOT THE "OFFICER BO-BO MUNCH-A-BUNCH BOX"...
AND YOUR USUAL IS OVER THERE
HEY!
Distributed by Universal Press Syndicate
THEY FORGOT MY "LARDER O'TARTAR SAUCE" AGAIN!
CAPTAIN GORGE'S TREASURE CHEST

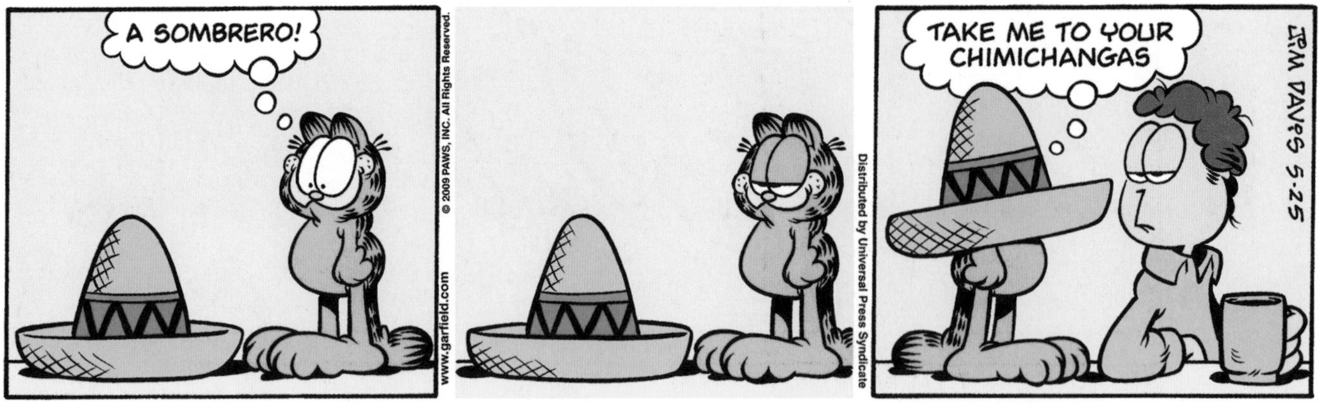
A SOMBRERO!
© 2009 PAWS, INC. All Rights Reserved.
www.garfield.com
Distributed by Universal Press Syndicate
TAKE ME TO YOUR CHIMICHANGAS
JIM DAVIS 5-25

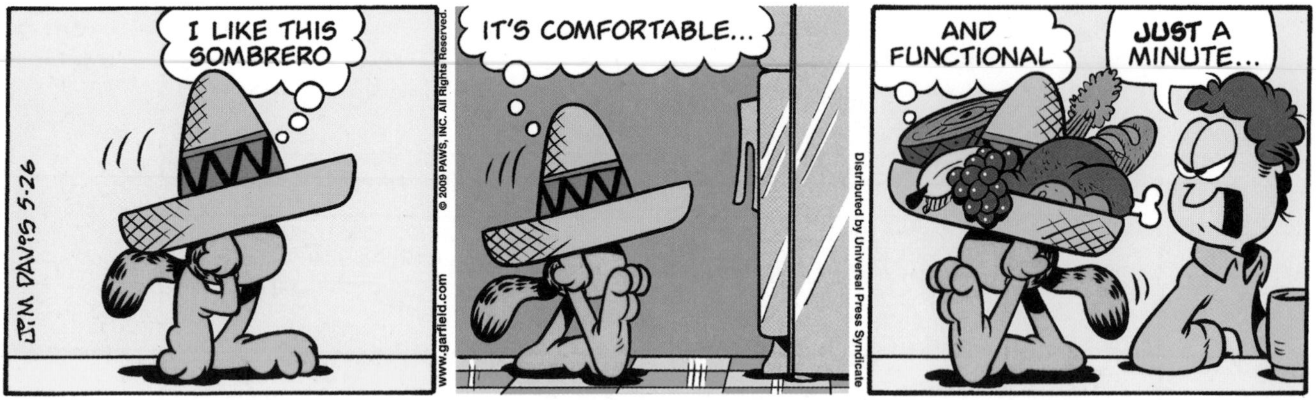
JIM DAVIS 5-26
I LIKE THIS SOMBRERO
© 2009 PAWS, INC. All Rights Reserved.
www.garfield.com
IT'S COMFORTABLE...
Distributed by Universal Press Syndicate
AND FUNCTIONAL
JUST A MINUTE...

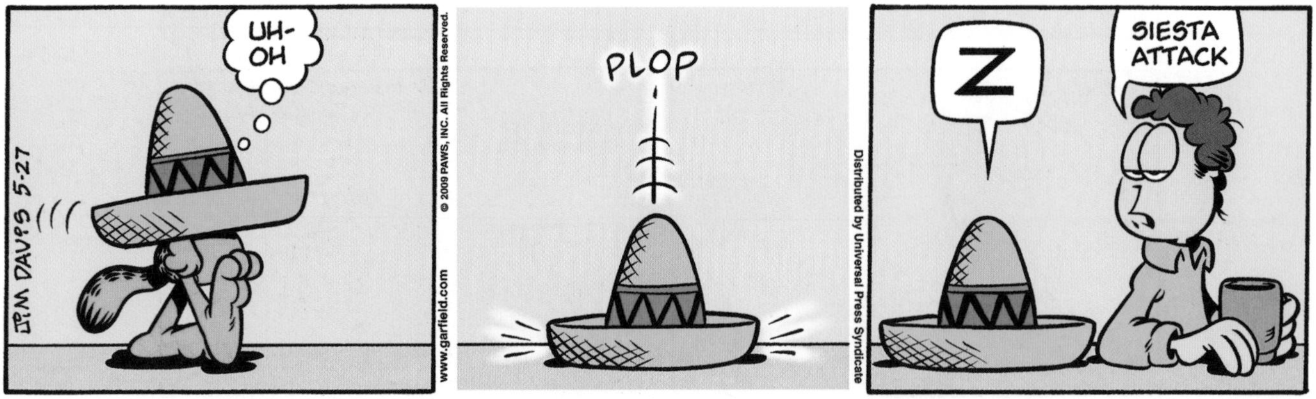
JIM DAVIS 5-27
UH-OH
© 2009 PAWS, INC. All Rights Reserved.
www.garfield.com
PLOP
Distributed by Universal Press Syndicate
Z
SIESTA ATTACK

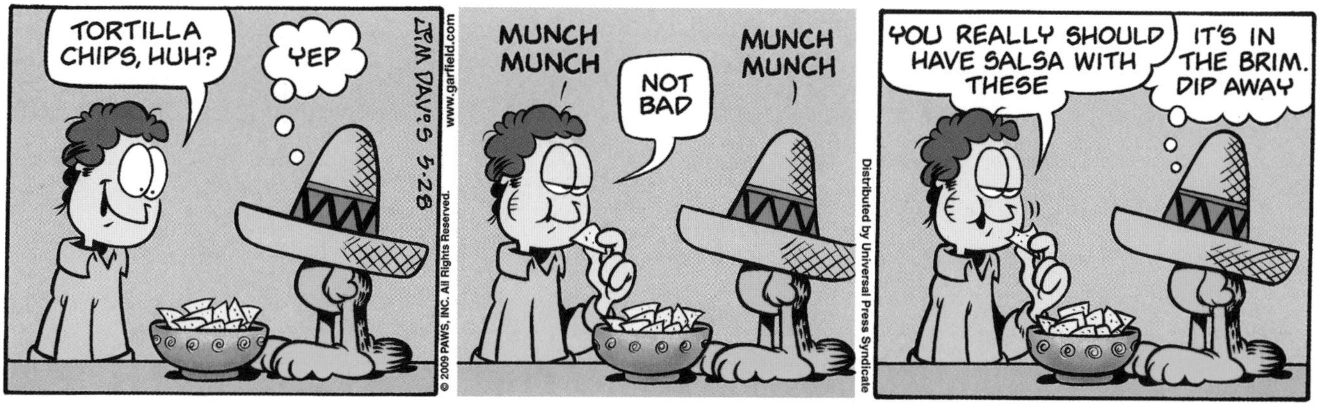
TORTILLA CHIPS, HUH?
YEP
JIM DAVIS 5-28
www.garfield.com
© 2009 PAWS, INC. All Rights Reserved.
MUNCH MUNCH
NOT BAD
MUNCH MUNCH
Distributed by Universal Press Syndicate
YOU REALLY SHOULD HAVE SALSA WITH THESE
IT'S IN THE BRIM. DIP AWAY

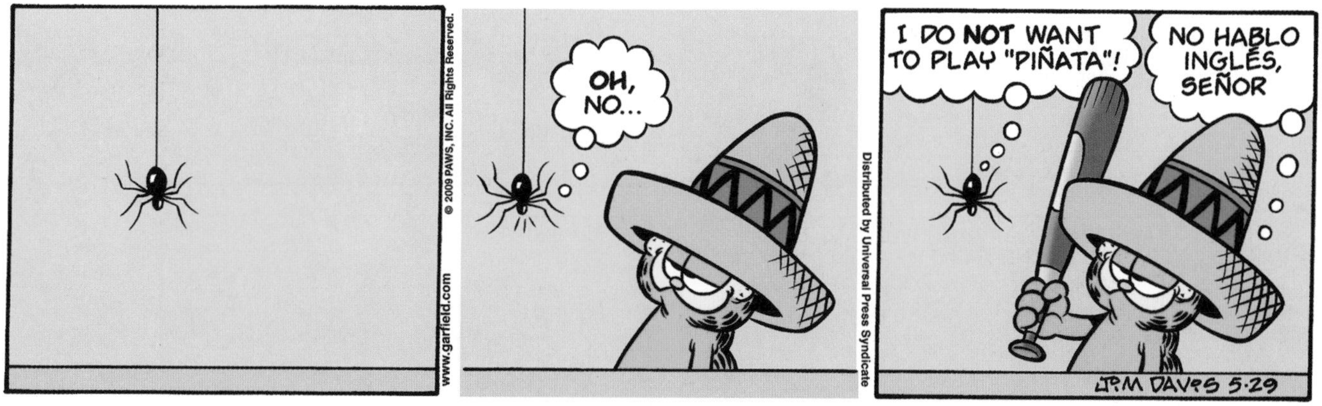
www.garfield.com
© 2009 PAWS, INC. All Rights Reserved.
OH, NO...
Distributed by Universal Press Syndicate
I DO **NOT** WANT TO PLAY "PIÑATA"!
NO HABLO INGLÉS, SEÑOR
JIM DAVIS 5-29

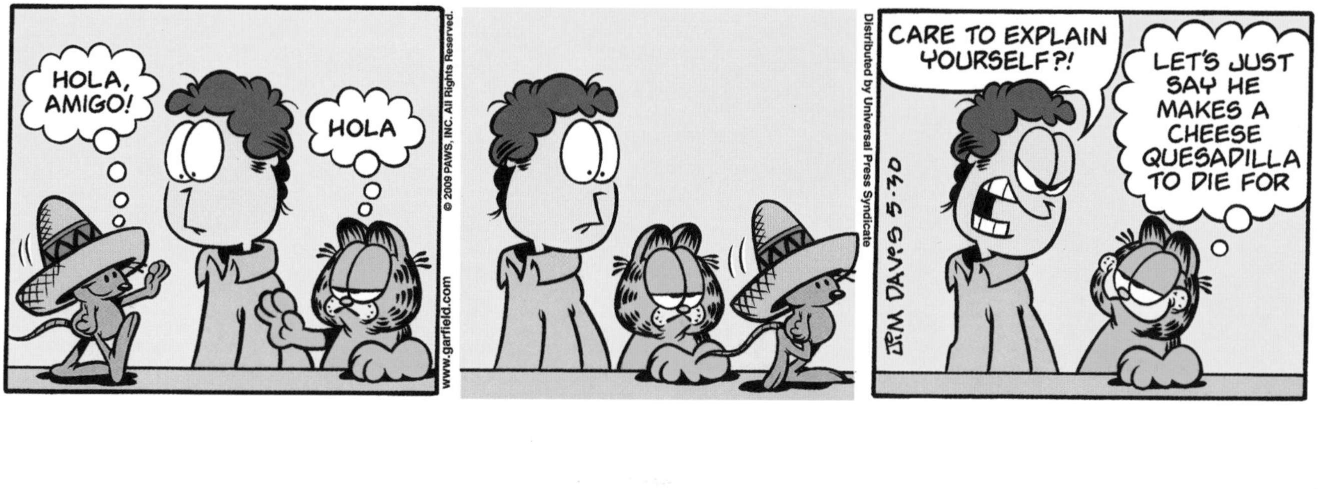
HOLA, AMIGO!
HOLA
www.garfield.com
© 2009 PAWS, INC. All Rights Reserved.
Distributed by Universal Press Syndicate
JIM DAVIS 5-30
CARE TO EXPLAIN YOURSELF?!
LET'S JUST SAY HE MAKES A CHEESE QUESADILLA TO DIE FOR

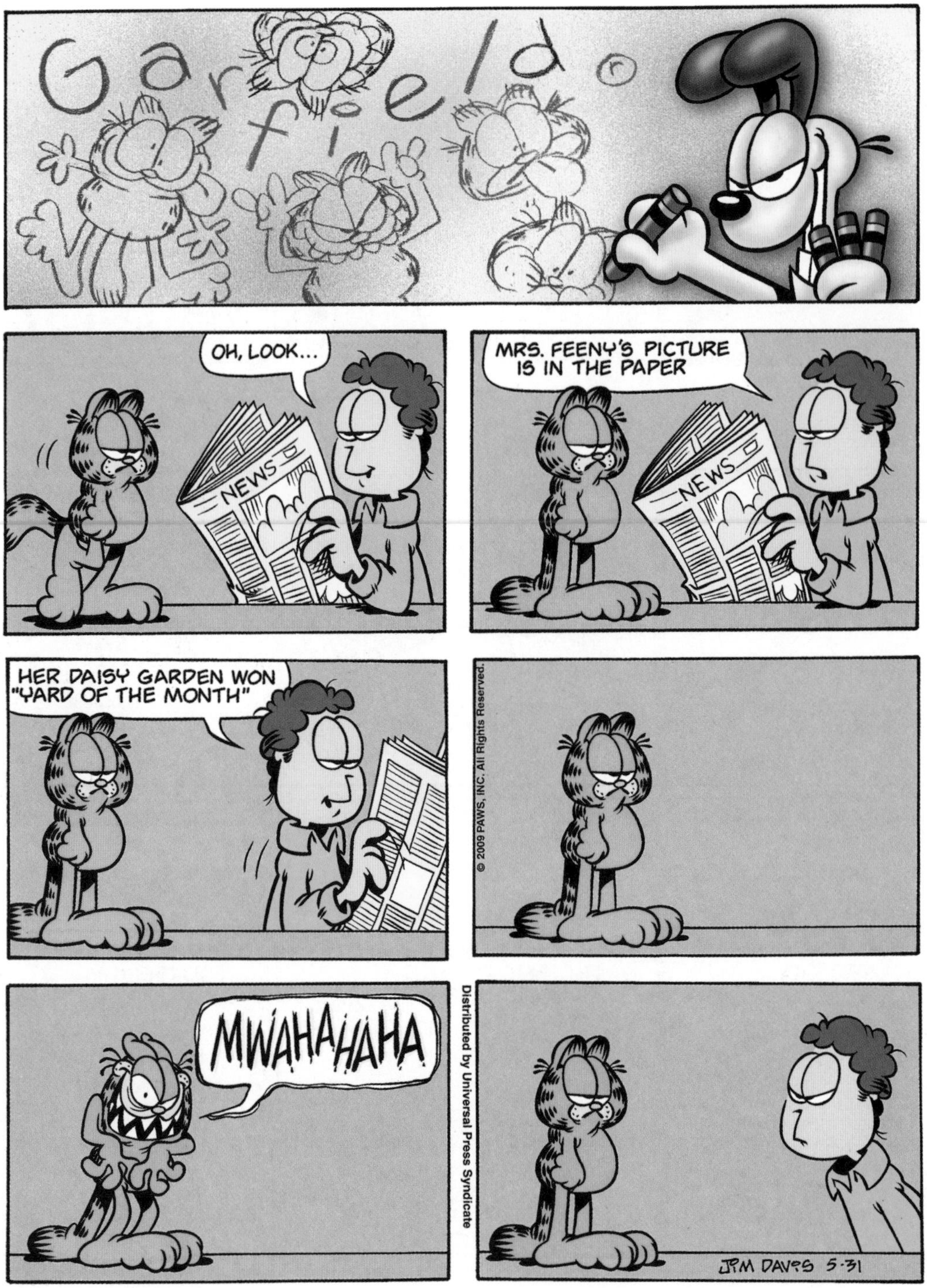
Garfield®
OH, LOOK...
MRS. FEENY'S PICTURE IS IN THE PAPER
NEWS
HER DAISY GARDEN WON "YARD OF THE MONTH"
© 2009 PAWS, INC. All Rights Reserved.
MWAHAHAHA
Distributed by Universal Press Syndicate
JIM DAVIS 5-31

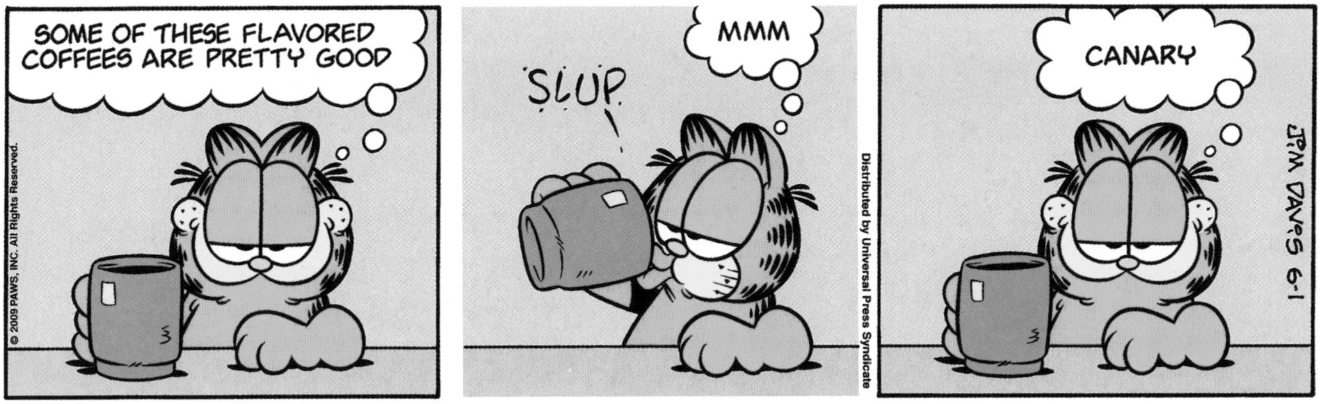
SOME OF THESE FLAVORED COFFEES ARE PRETTY GOOD
SLUP
MMM
CANARY
JIM DAVIS 6-1
© 2009 PAWS, INC. All Rights Reserved.
Distributed by Universal Press Syndicate

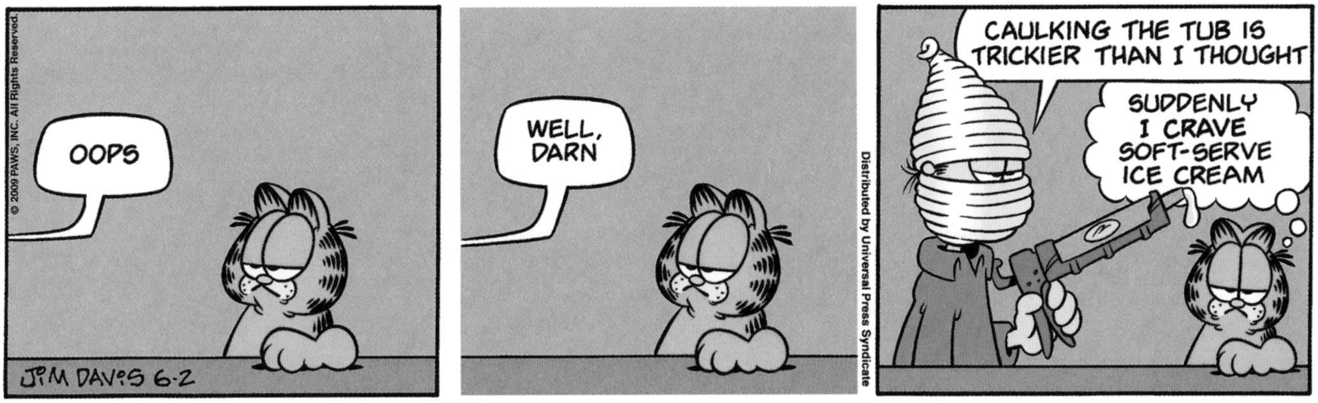
OOPS
WELL, DARN
CAULKING THE TUB IS TRICKIER THAN I THOUGHT
SUDDENLY I CRAVE SOFT-SERVE ICE CREAM
JIM DAVIS 6-2
© 2009 PAWS, INC. All Rights Reserved.
Distributed by Universal Press Syndicate

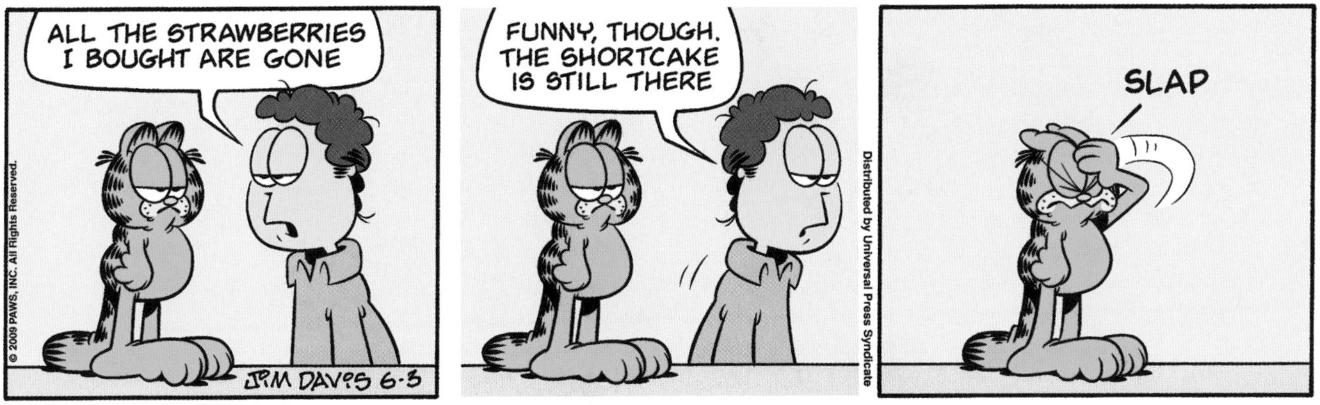
ALL THE STRAWBERRIES I BOUGHT ARE GONE
FUNNY, THOUGH. THE SHORTCAKE IS STILL THERE
SLAP
JIM DAVIS 6-3
© 2009 PAWS, INC. All Rights Reserved.
Distributed by Universal Press Syndicate

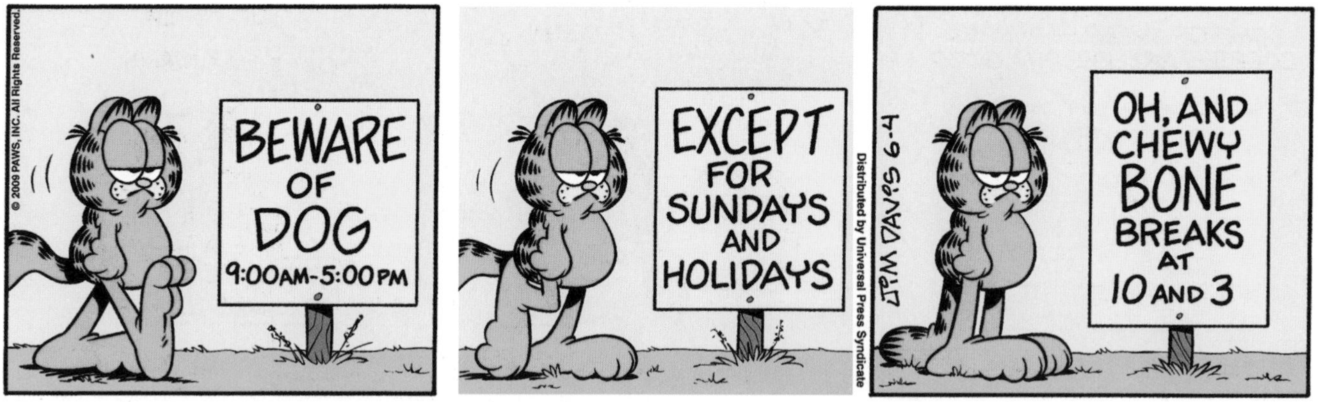
© 2009 PAWS, INC. All Rights Reserved.
BEWARE OF DOG 9:00AM-5:00PM
EXCEPT FOR SUNDAYS AND HOLIDAYS
Distributed by Universal Press Syndicate
JIM DAVIS 6-4
OH, AND CHEWY BONE BREAKS AT 10 AND 3

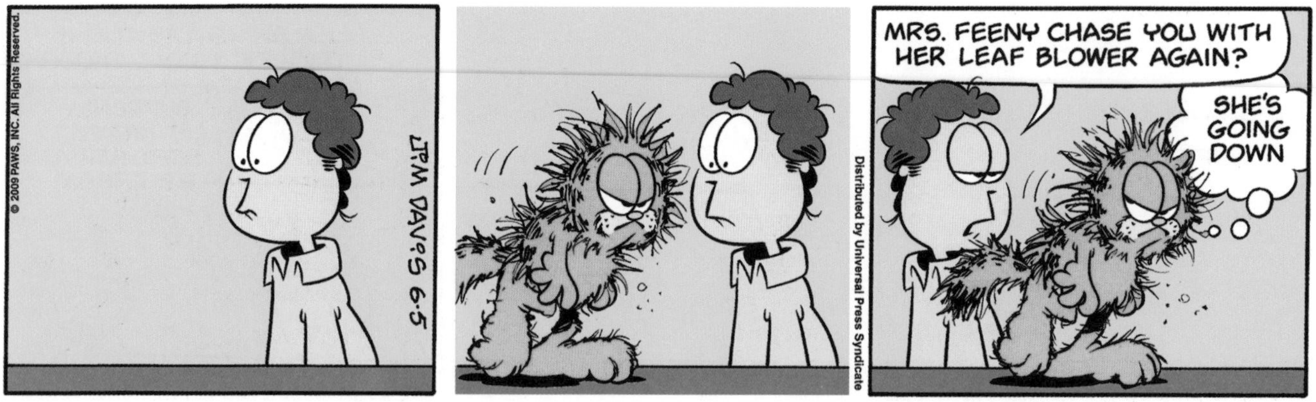
© 2009 PAWS, INC. All Rights Reserved.
JIM DAVIS 6-5
Distributed by Universal Press Syndicate
MRS. FEENY CHASE YOU WITH HER LEAF BLOWER AGAIN?
SHE'S GOING DOWN

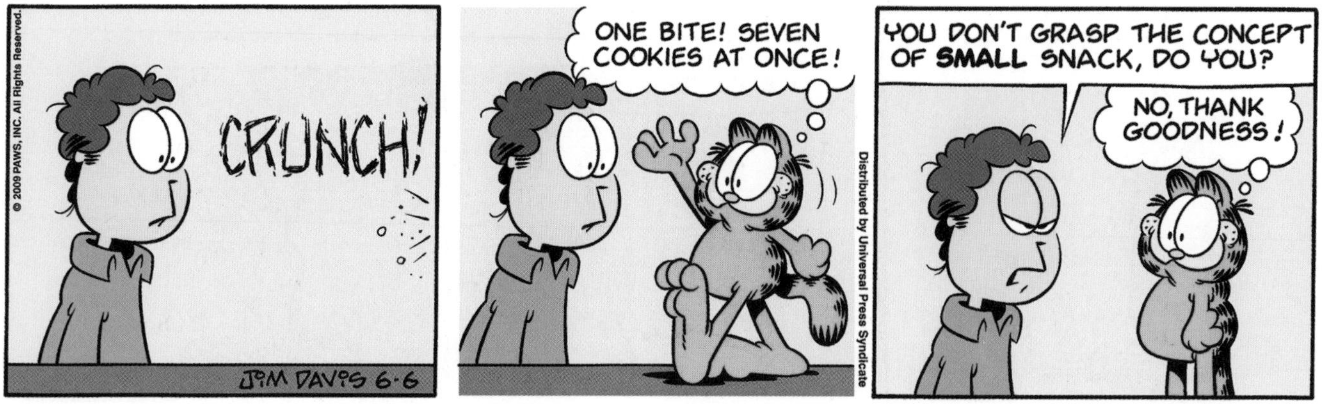
© 2009 PAWS, INC. All Rights Reserved.
CRUNCH!
JIM DAVIS 6-6
ONE BITE! SEVEN COOKIES AT ONCE!
Distributed by Universal Press Syndicate
YOU DON'T GRASP THE CONCEPT OF **SMALL** SNACK, DO YOU?
NO, THANK GOODNESS!

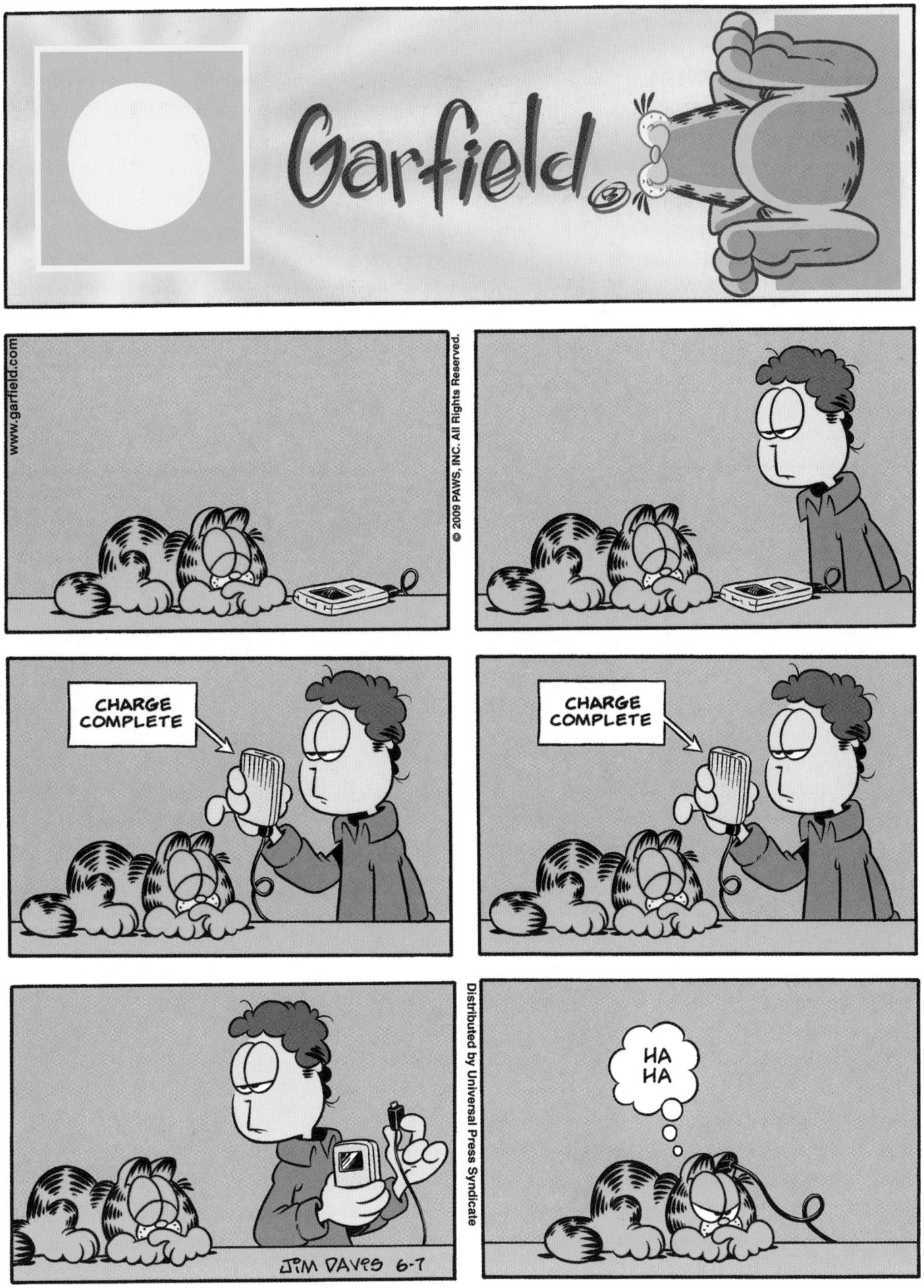
Garfield
www.garfield.com
© 2009 PAWS, INC. All Rights Reserved.
CHARGE COMPLETE
CHARGE COMPLETE
Distributed by Universal Press Syndicate
JIM DAVIS 6-7
HA HA

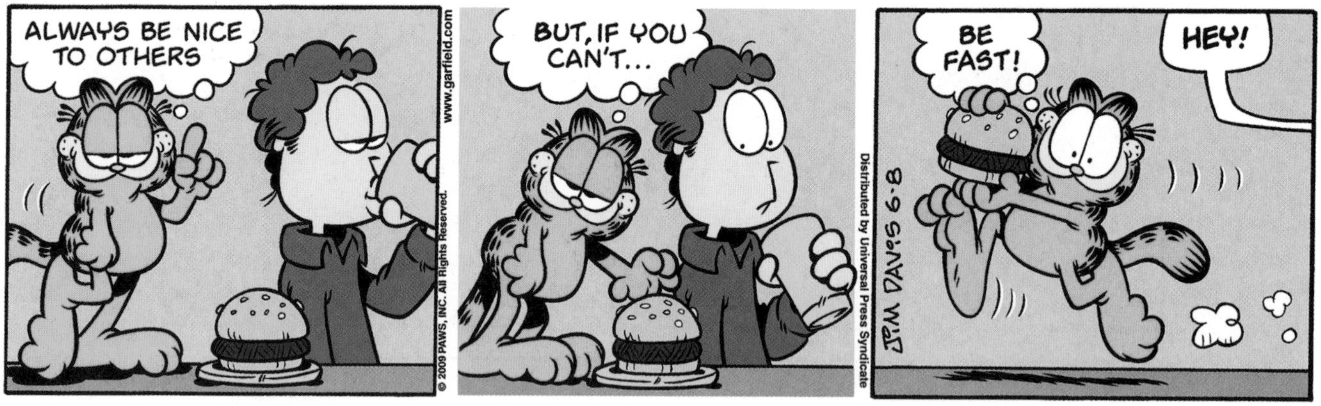
ALWAYS BE NICE TO OTHERS
www.garfield.com
© 2009 PAWS, INC. All Rights Reserved.
BUT, IF YOU CAN'T...
Distributed by Universal Press Syndicate
BE FAST!
HEY!
JIM DAVIS 6-8

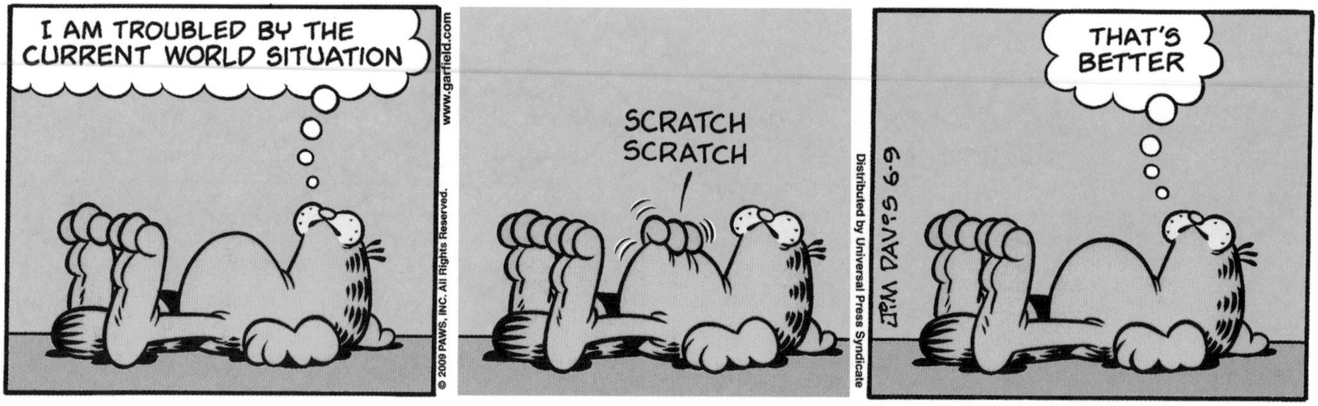
I AM TROUBLED BY THE CURRENT WORLD SITUATION
www.garfield.com
© 2009 PAWS, INC. All Rights Reserved.
SCRATCH SCRATCH
Distributed by Universal Press Syndicate
JIM DAVIS 6-9
THAT'S BETTER

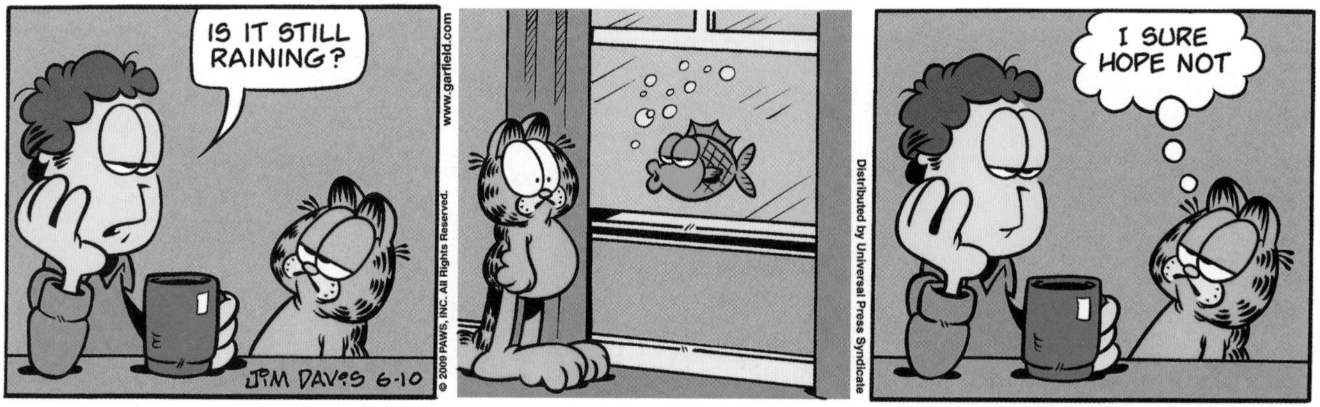
IS IT STILL RAINING?
JIM DAVIS 6-10
www.garfield.com
© 2009 PAWS, INC. All Rights Reserved.
Distributed by Universal Press Syndicate
I SURE HOPE NOT

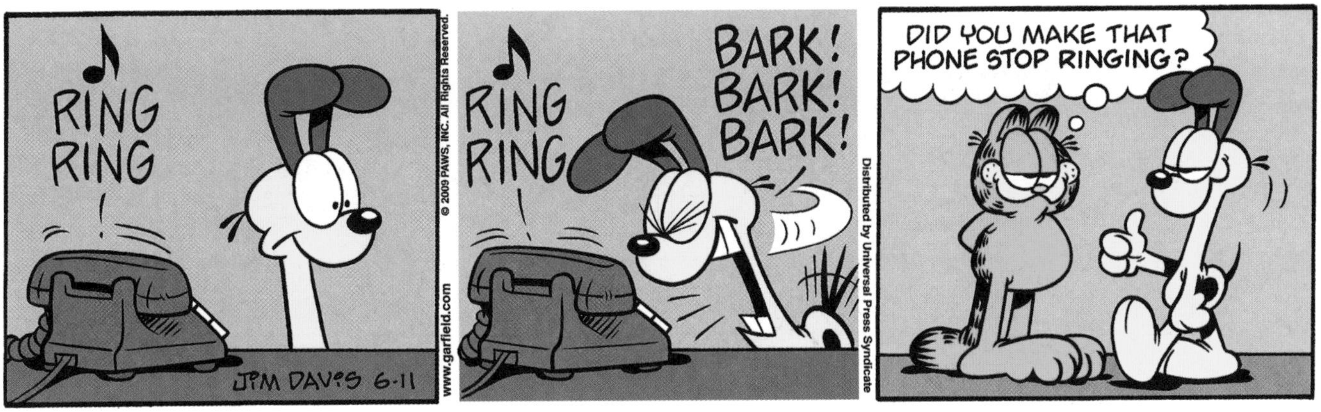
RING RING
JIM DAVIS 6-11
© 2009 PAWS, INC. All Rights Reserved.
www.garfield.com
RING RING
BARK! BARK! BARK!
Distributed by Universal Press Syndicate
DID YOU MAKE THAT PHONE STOP RINGING?

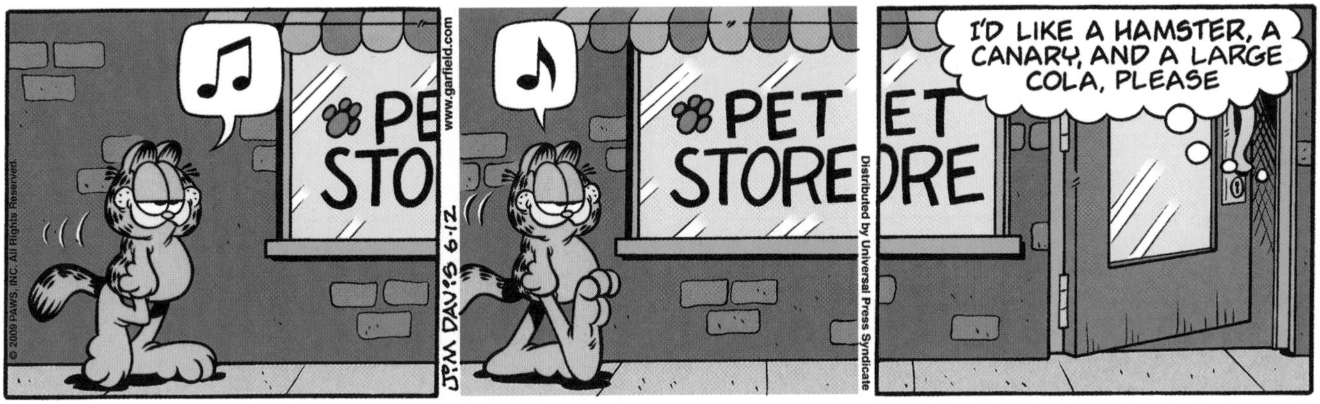
© 2009 PAWS, INC. All Rights Reserved.
PET STORE
www.garfield.com
JIM DAVIS 6-12
PET STORE
Distributed by Universal Press Syndicate
PET STORE
I'D LIKE A HAMSTER, A CANARY, AND A LARGE COLA, PLEASE

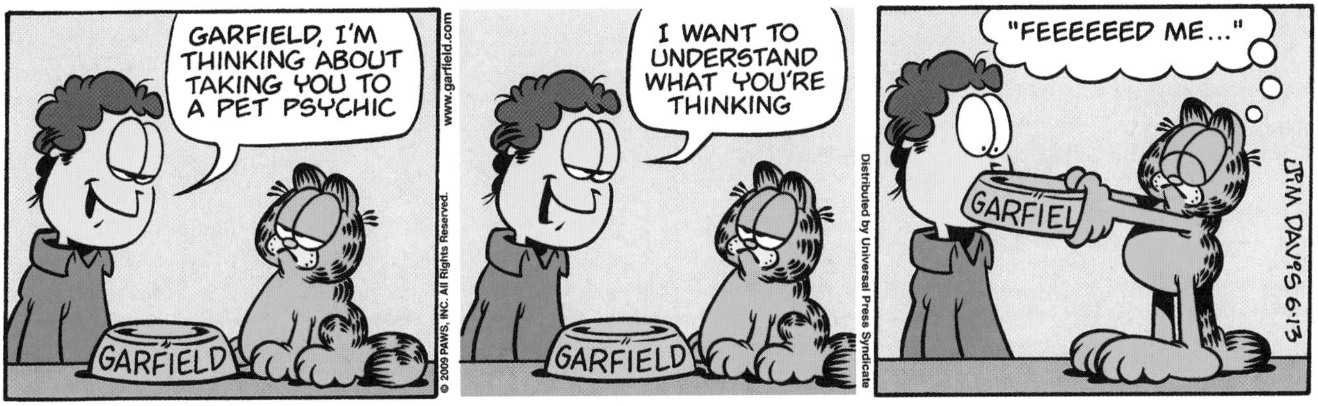
GARFIELD, I'M THINKING ABOUT TAKING YOU TO A PET PSYCHIC
GARFIELD
© 2009 PAWS, INC. All Rights Reserved.
www.garfield.com
I WANT TO UNDERSTAND WHAT YOU'RE THINKING
GARFIELD
Distributed by Universal Press Syndicate
"FEEEEEED ME..."
GARFIEL
JIM DAVIS 6-13

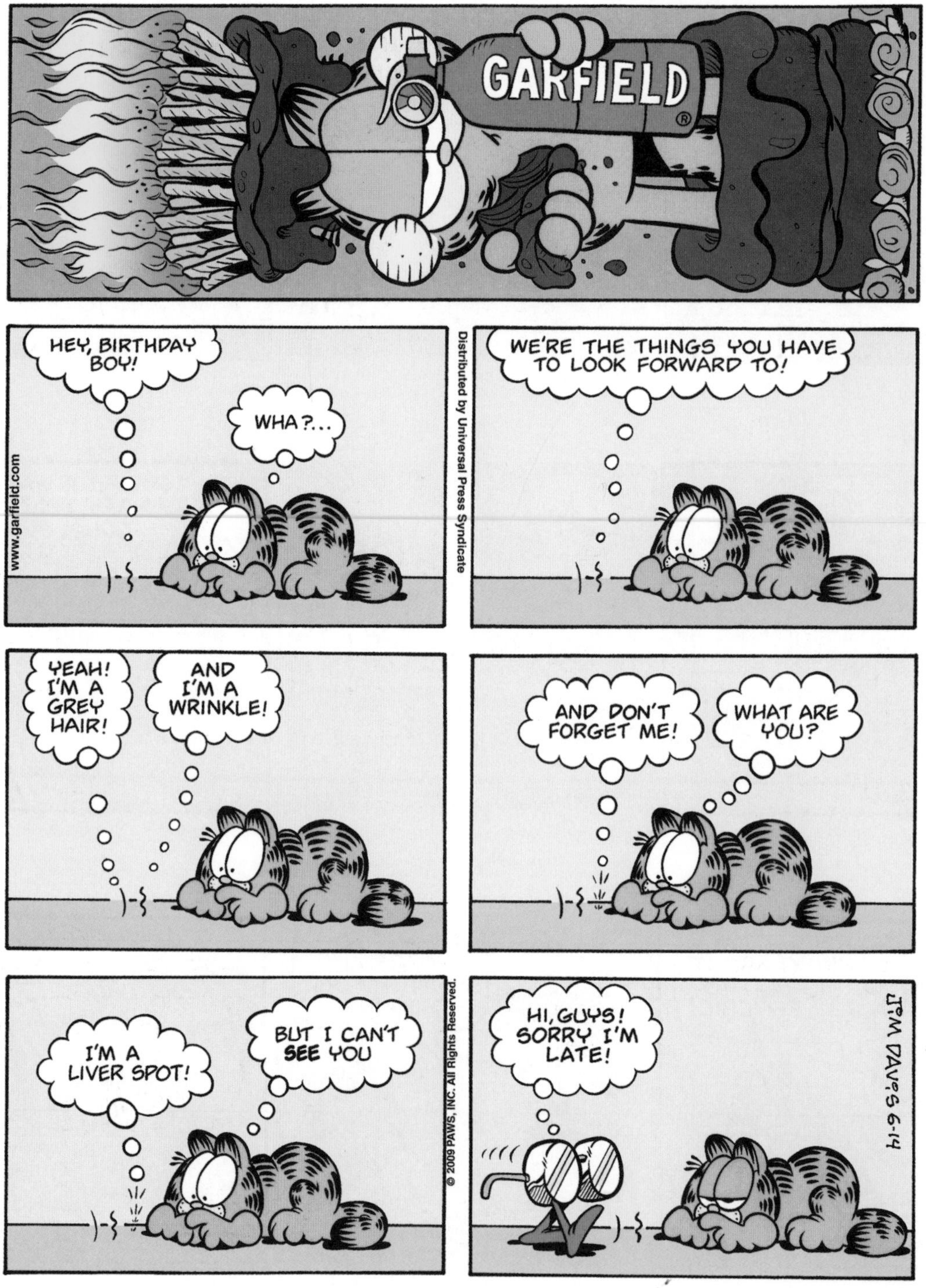
GARFIELD
HEY, BIRTHDAY BOY!
WHA?...
WE'RE THE THINGS YOU HAVE TO LOOK FORWARD TO!
YEAH! I'M A GREY HAIR!
AND I'M A WRINKLE!
AND DON'T FORGET ME!
WHAT ARE YOU?
I'M A LIVER SPOT!
BUT I CAN'T SEE YOU
HI, GUYS! SORRY I'M LATE!
JIM DAVIS 6-14

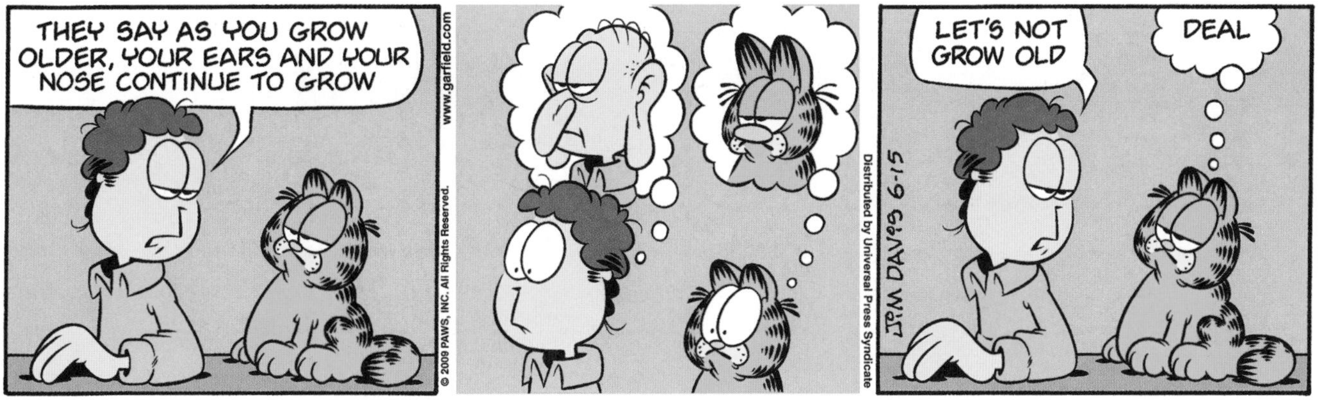
THEY SAY AS YOU GROW OLDER, YOUR EARS AND YOUR NOSE CONTINUE TO GROW
www.garfield.com
© 2009 PAWS, INC. All Rights Reserved.
Distributed by Universal Press Syndicate
JIM DAVIS 6-15
LET'S NOT GROW OLD
DEAL

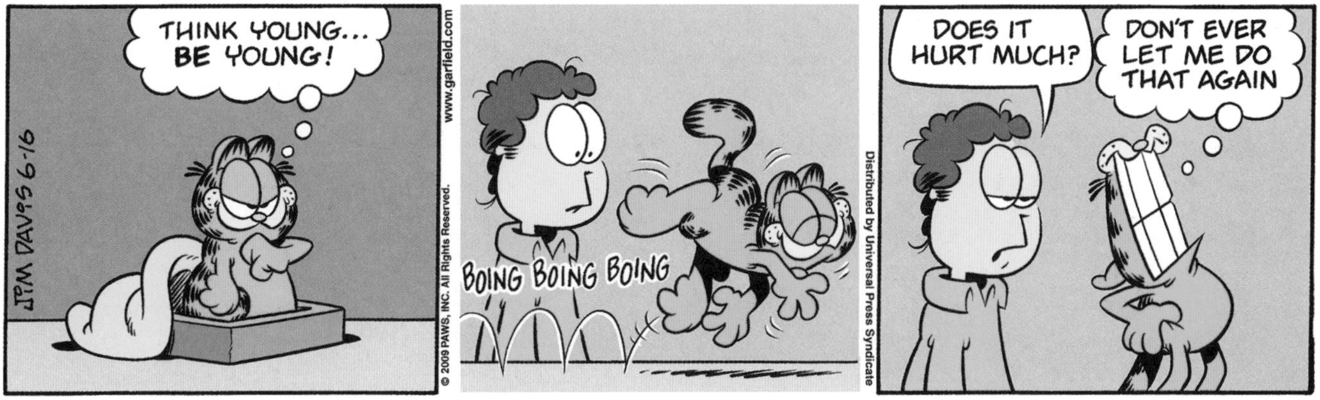
THINK YOUNG... BE YOUNG!
JIM DAVIS 6-16
www.garfield.com
© 2009 PAWS, INC. All Rights Reserved.
BOING BOING BOING
Distributed by Universal Press Syndicate
DOES IT HURT MUCH?
DON'T EVER LET ME DO THAT AGAIN

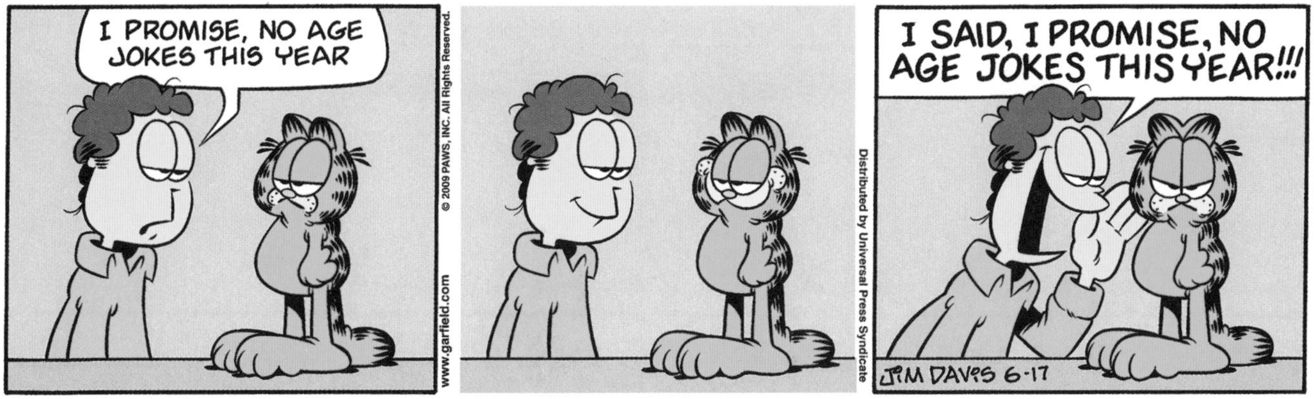
I PROMISE, NO AGE JOKES THIS YEAR
© 2009 PAWS, INC. All Rights Reserved.
www.garfield.com
Distributed by Universal Press Syndicate
I SAID, I PROMISE, NO AGE JOKES THIS YEAR!!!
JIM DAVIS 6-17

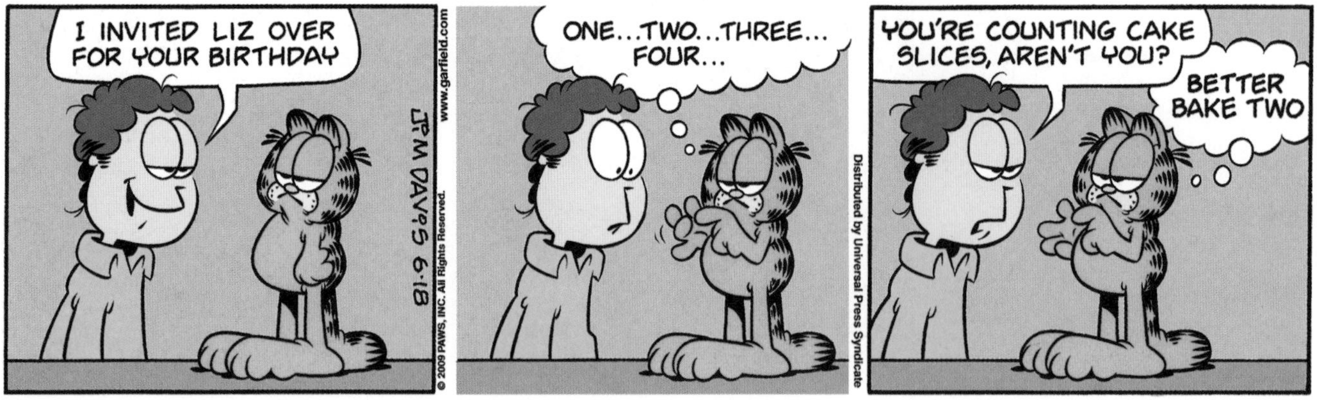
I INVITED LIZ OVER FOR YOUR BIRTHDAY
JPM DAVPS 6-18
www.garfield.com
© 2009 PAWS, INC. All Rights Reserved.
ONE...TWO...THREE... FOUR...
Distributed by Universal Press Syndicate
YOU'RE COUNTING CAKE SLICES, AREN'T YOU?
BETTER BAKE TWO

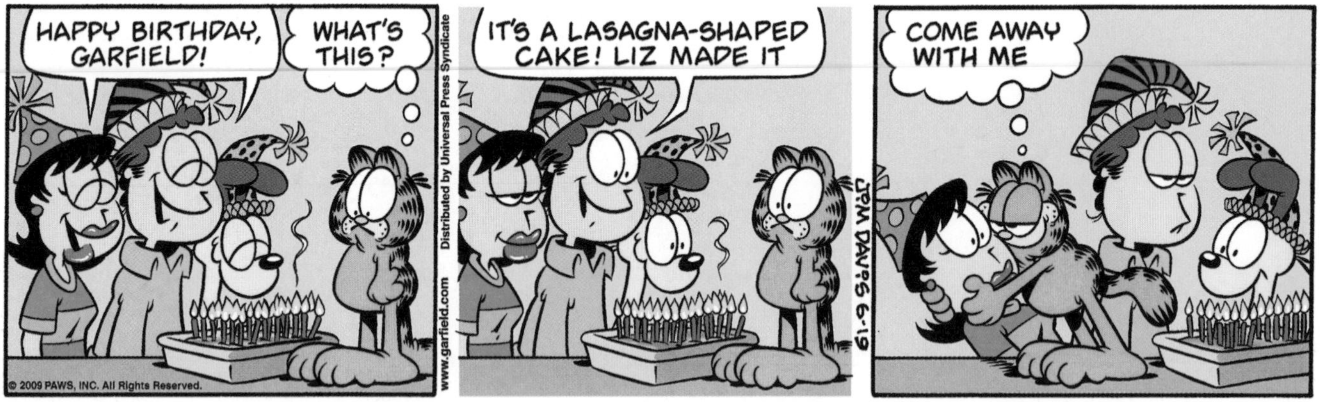
HAPPY BIRTHDAY, GARFIELD!
WHAT'S THIS?
© 2009 PAWS, INC. All Rights Reserved.
Distributed by Universal Press Syndicate
www.garfield.com
IT'S A LASAGNA-SHAPED CAKE! LIZ MADE IT
JPM DAVPS 6-19
COME AWAY WITH ME

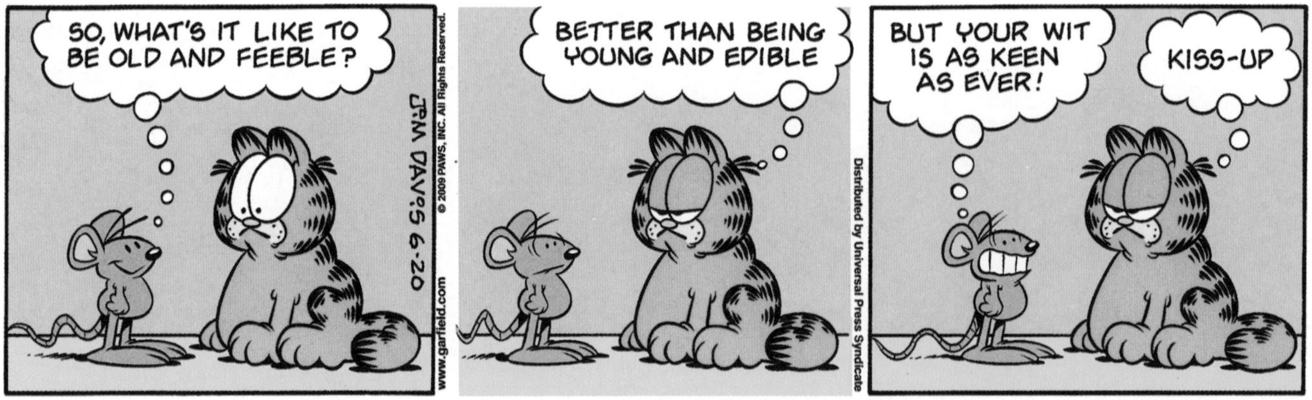
SO, WHAT'S IT LIKE TO BE OLD AND FEEBLE?
JPM DAVPS 6-20
© 2009 PAWS, INC. All Rights Reserved.
www.garfield.com
BETTER THAN BEING YOUNG AND EDIBLE
Distributed by Universal Press Syndicate
BUT YOUR WIT IS AS KEEN AS EVER!
KISS-UP

WORK ISN'T WORKING

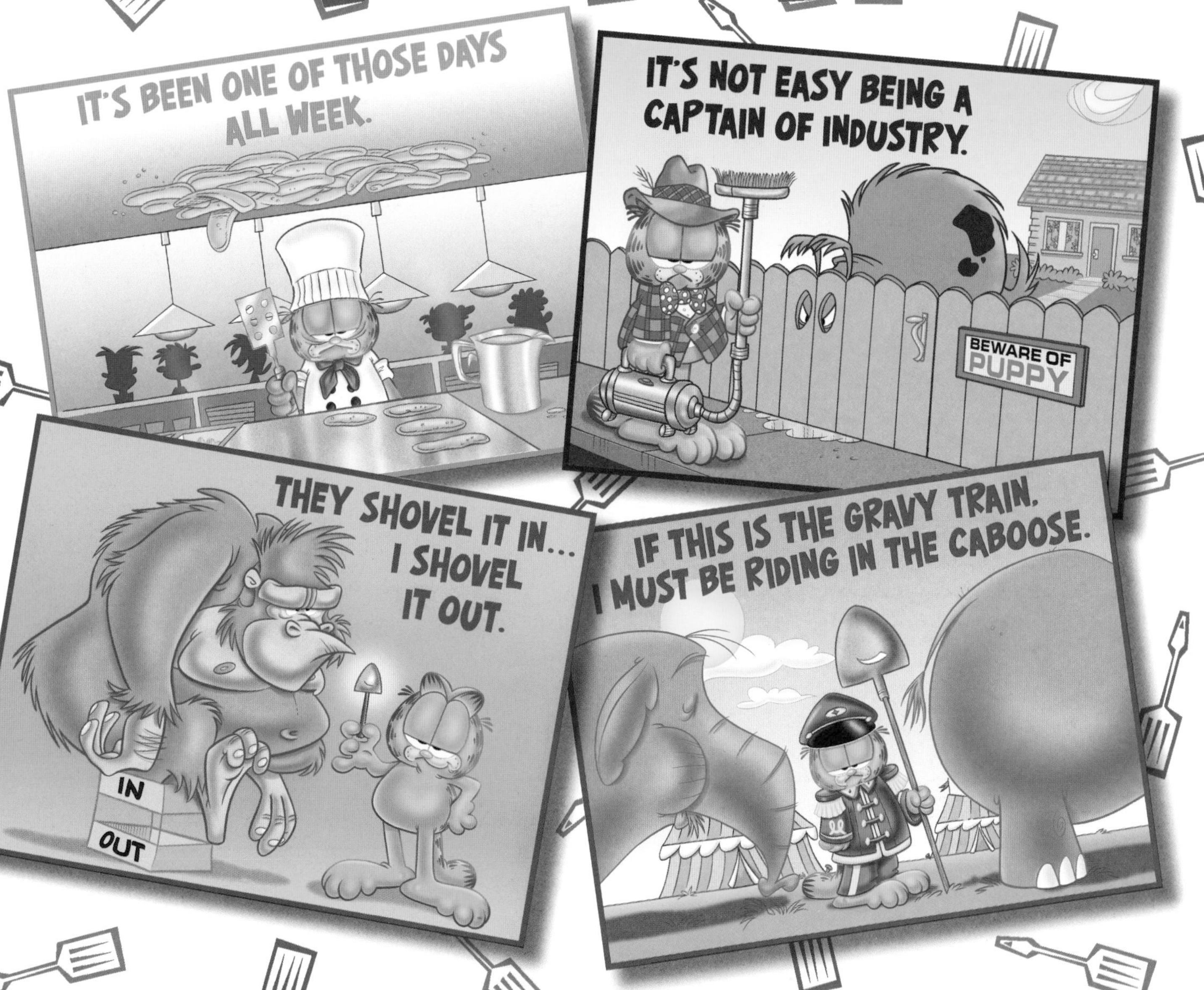

IT'S BEEN ONE OF THOSE DAYS ALL WEEK.
IT'S NOT EASY BEING A CAPTAIN OF INDUSTRY.
BEWARE OF PUPPY
THEY SHOVEL IT IN... I SHOVEL IT OUT.
IN
OUT
IF THIS IS THE GRAVY TRAIN, I MUST BE RIDING IN THE CABOOSE.

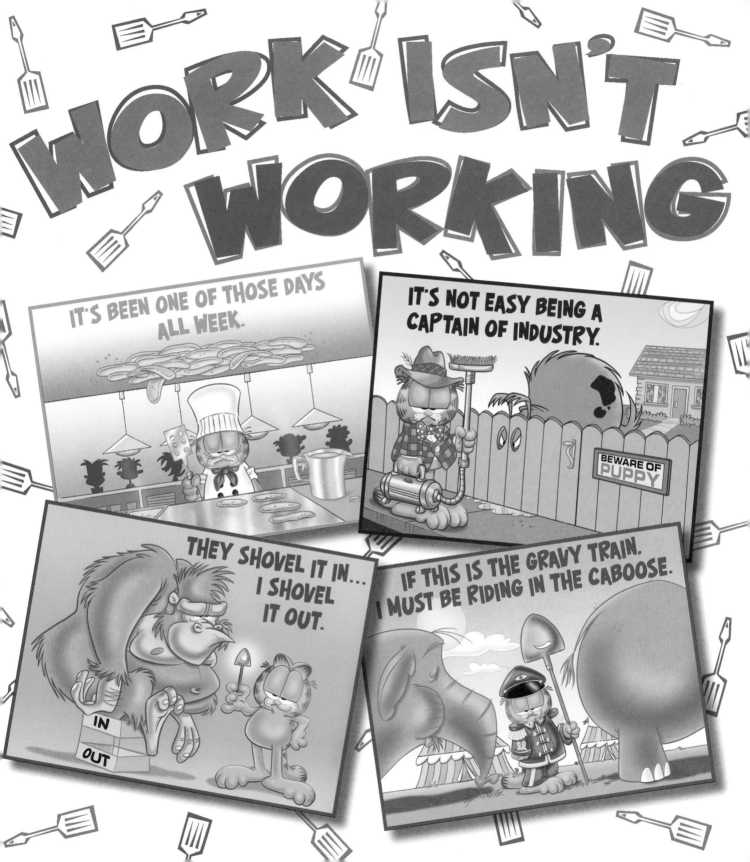

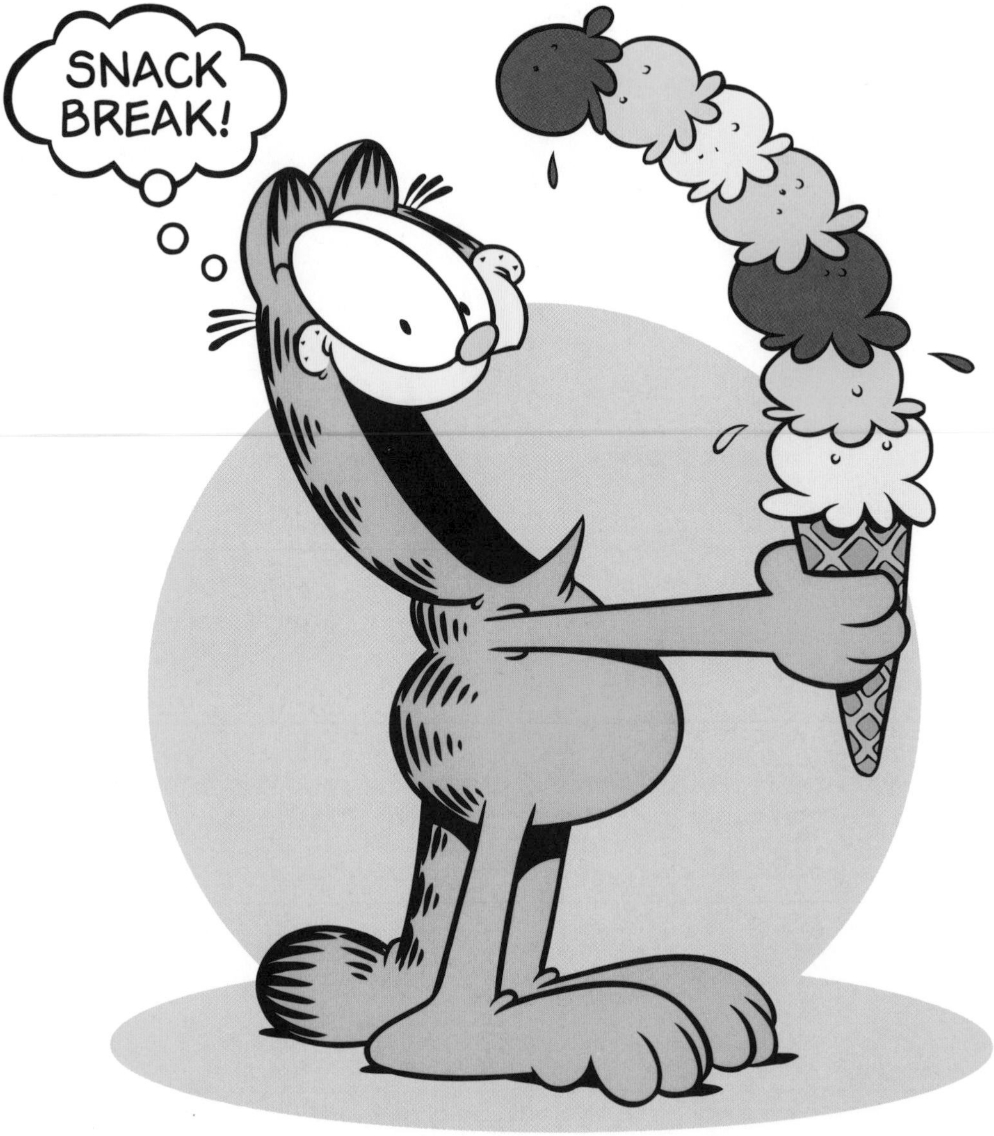
SNACK
BREAK!

Garfield
GETS IN A PICKLE

BY JIM DAVIS

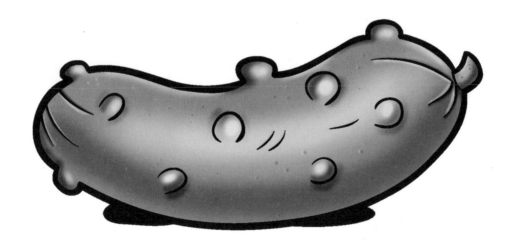

Ballantine Books • **New York**

The Geek Shall Inherit the Earth

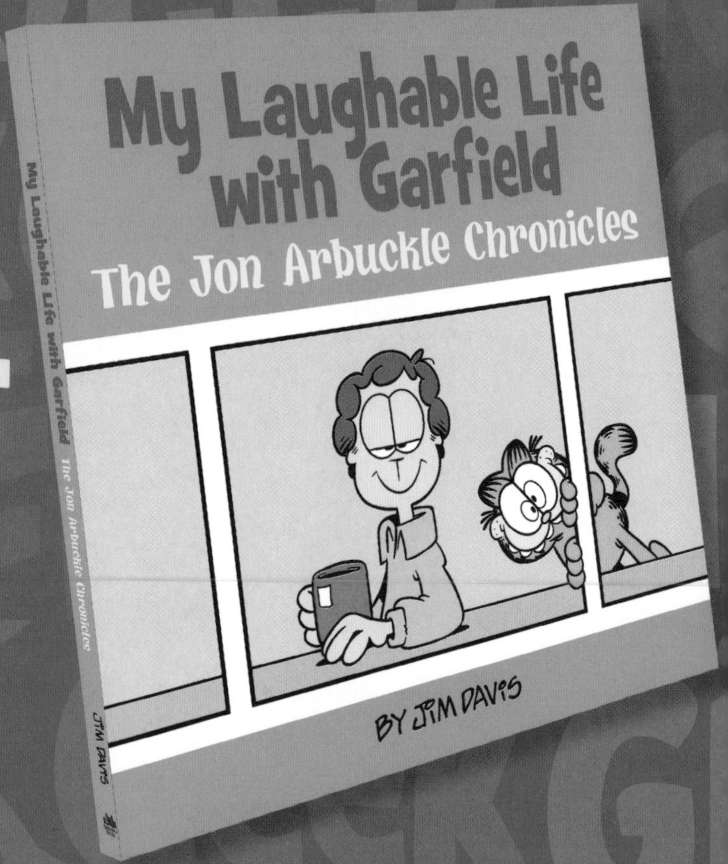
My Laughable Life with Garfield
The Jon Arbuckle Chronicles
BY JIM DAVIS
My Laughable Life with Garfield The Jon Arbuckle Chronicles
JIM DAVIS

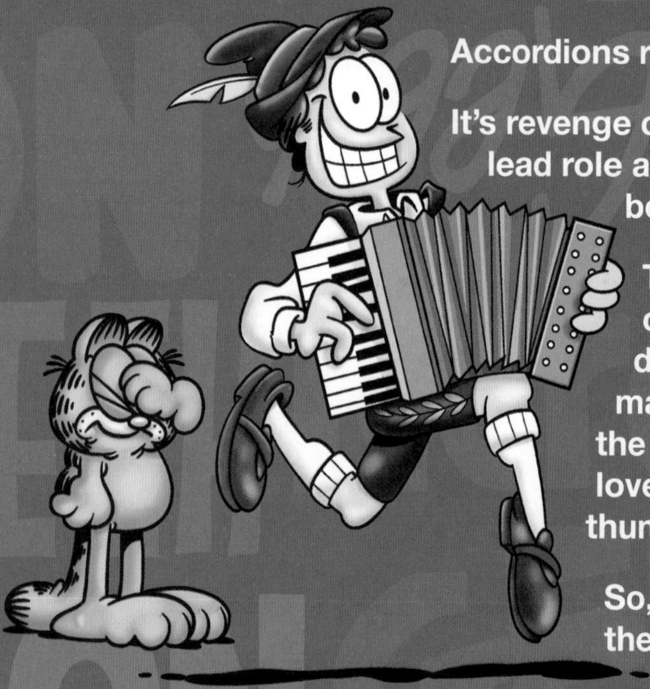

Accordions rule, and so—finally—does Jon Arbuckle!

It's revenge of the nerds when Jon grabs Garfield's traditional lead role and takes center stage with a delightfully dorky new book of his own.

Through classic comics, blog entries, and a wealth of other wacky new material, experience Jon's dating disasters, phone call faux pas, wardrobe malfunctions, and mirthful mishaps—and cheer the geek with a heart of gold as he finally finds true love with Liz, the veterinarian (who would've thunk it?).

So, rejoice, Jon fans, and enjoy the fun . . . the moment of *goof* has arrived!

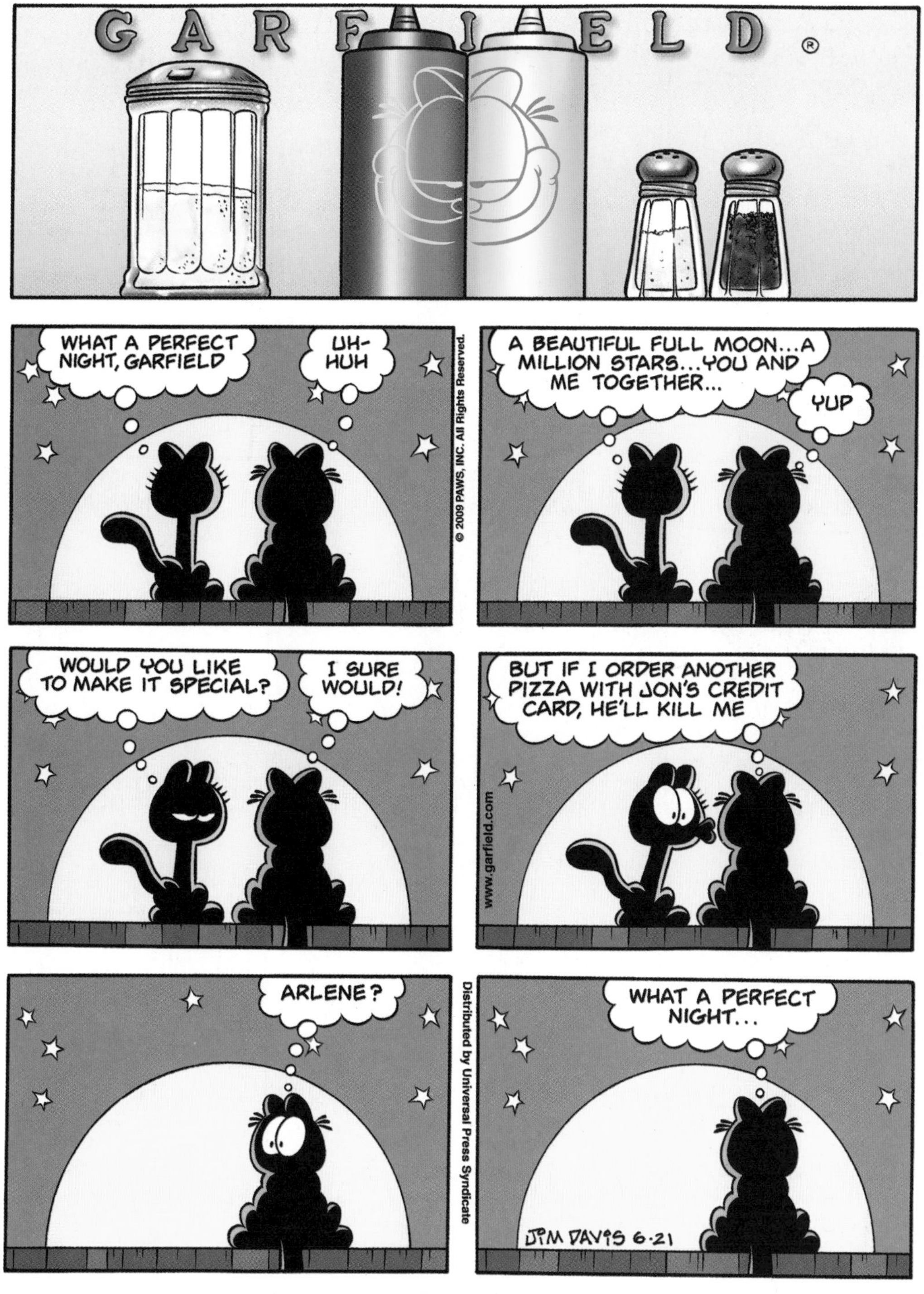
GARFIELD®
WHAT A PERFECT NIGHT, GARFIELD
UH-HUH
A BEAUTIFUL FULL MOON...A MILLION STARS...YOU AND ME TOGETHER...
YUP
WOULD YOU LIKE TO MAKE IT SPECIAL?
I SURE WOULD!
BUT IF I ORDER ANOTHER PIZZA WITH JON'S CREDIT CARD, HE'LL KILL ME
ARLENE?
WHAT A PERFECT NIGHT...
JIM DAVIS 6-21
© 2009 PAWS, INC. All Rights Reserved.
www.garfield.com
Distributed by Universal Press Syndicate

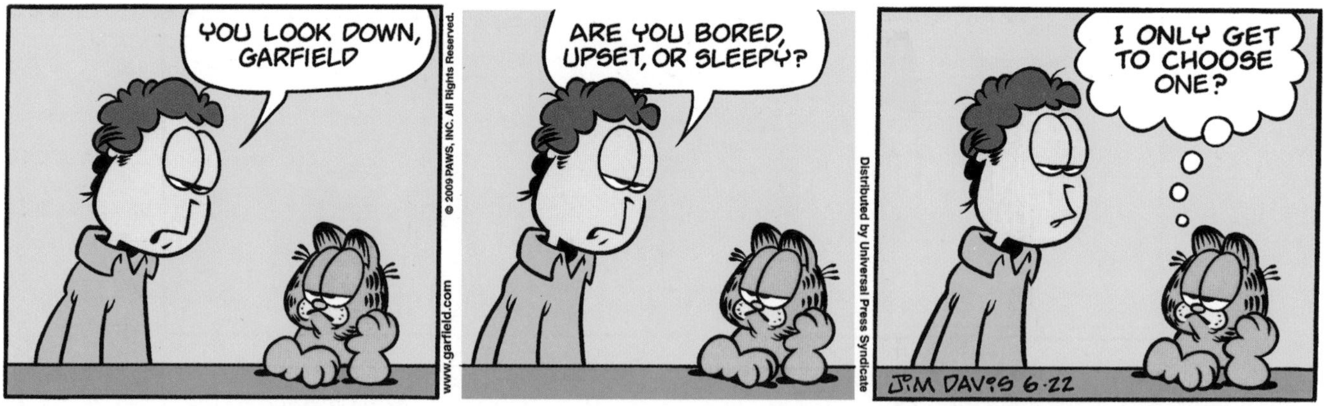
YOU LOOK DOWN, GARFIELD
ARE YOU BORED, UPSET, OR SLEEPY?
I ONLY GET TO CHOOSE ONE?
© 2009 PAWS, INC. All Rights Reserved.
www.garfield.com
Distributed by Universal Press Syndicate
JIM DAVIS 6-22

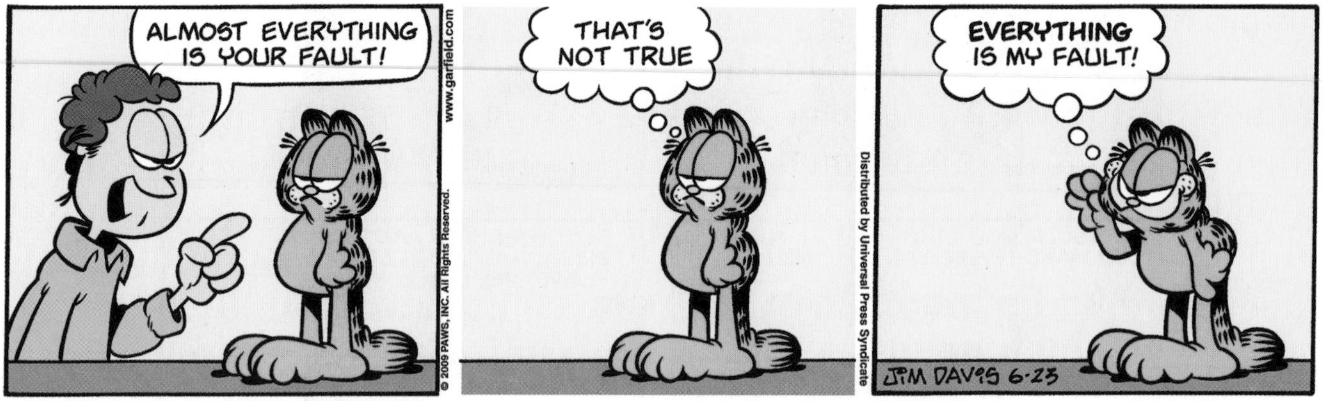
ALMOST EVERYTHING IS YOUR FAULT!
THAT'S NOT TRUE
EVERYTHING IS MY FAULT!
www.garfield.com
© 2009 PAWS, INC. All Rights Reserved.
Distributed by Universal Press Syndicate
JIM DAVIS 6-23

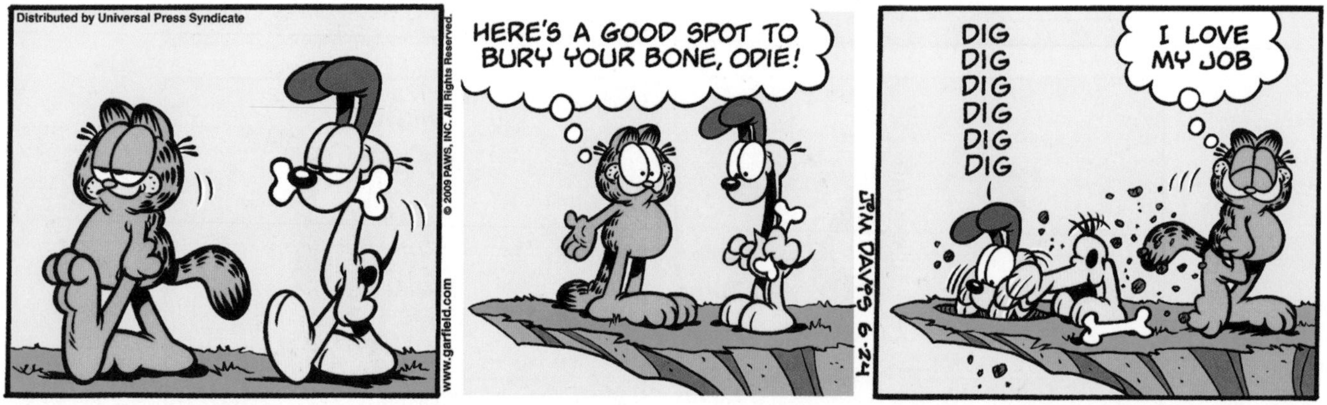
Distributed by Universal Press Syndicate
© 2009 PAWS, INC. All Rights Reserved.
www.garfield.com
HERE'S A GOOD SPOT TO BURY YOUR BONE, ODIE!
JIM DAVIS 6-24
DIG DIG DIG DIG DIG DIG
I LOVE MY JOB

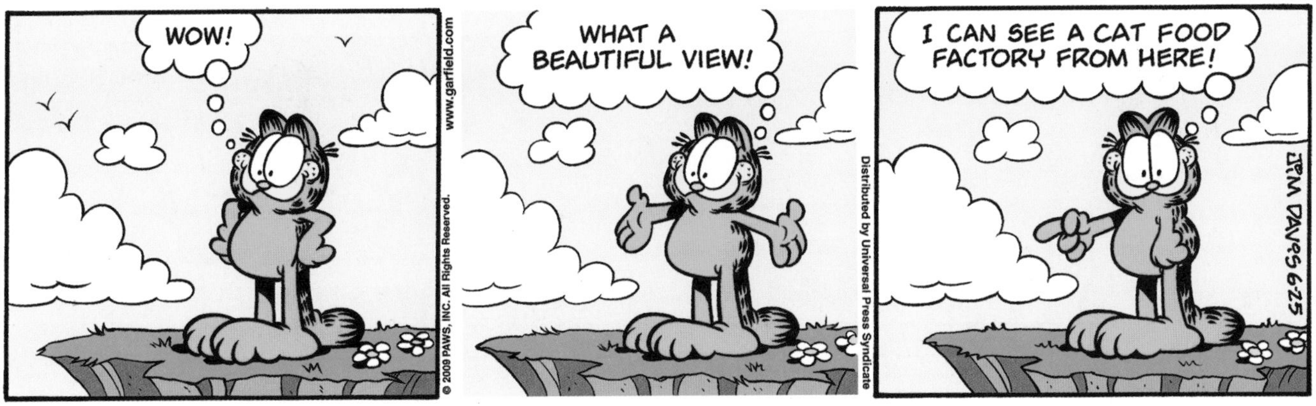
WOW!
WHAT A BEAUTIFUL VIEW!
I CAN SEE A CAT FOOD FACTORY FROM HERE!
JIM DAVIS 6-25
© 2009 PAWS, INC. All Rights Reserved.
www.garfield.com
Distributed by Universal Press Syndicate

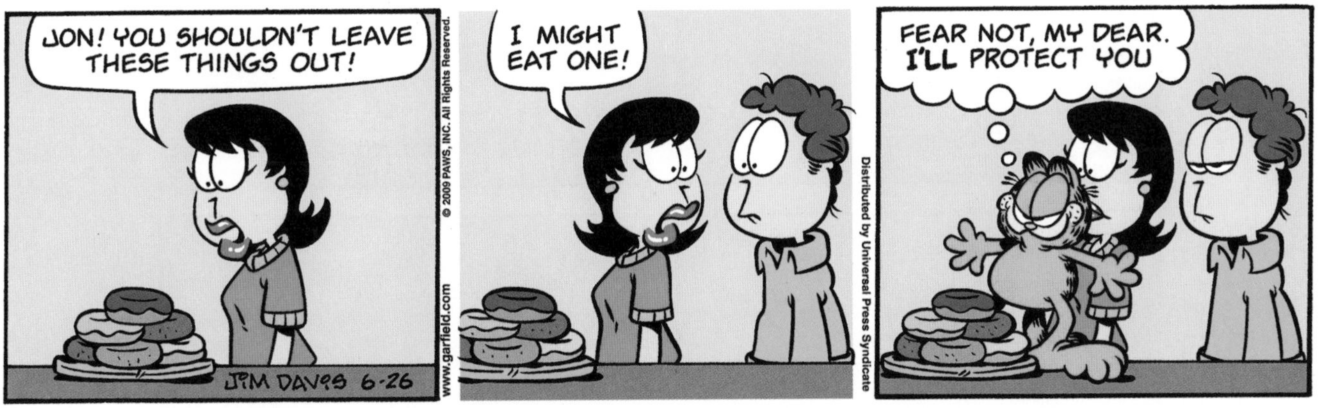
JON! YOU SHOULDN'T LEAVE THESE THINGS OUT!
JIM DAVIS 6-26
I MIGHT EAT ONE!
FEAR NOT, MY DEAR. I'LL PROTECT YOU
© 2009 PAWS, INC. All Rights Reserved.
www.garfield.com
Distributed by Universal Press Syndicate

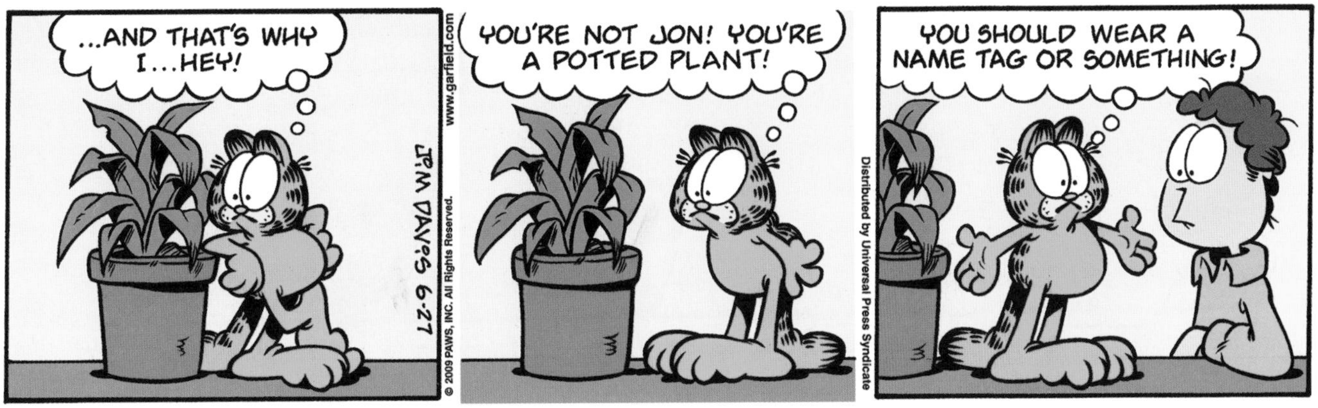
...AND THAT'S WHY I...HEY!
JIM DAVIS 6-27
YOU'RE NOT JON! YOU'RE A POTTED PLANT!
YOU SHOULD WEAR A NAME TAG OR SOMETHING!
© 2009 PAWS, INC. All Rights Reserved.
www.garfield.com
Distributed by Universal Press Syndicate

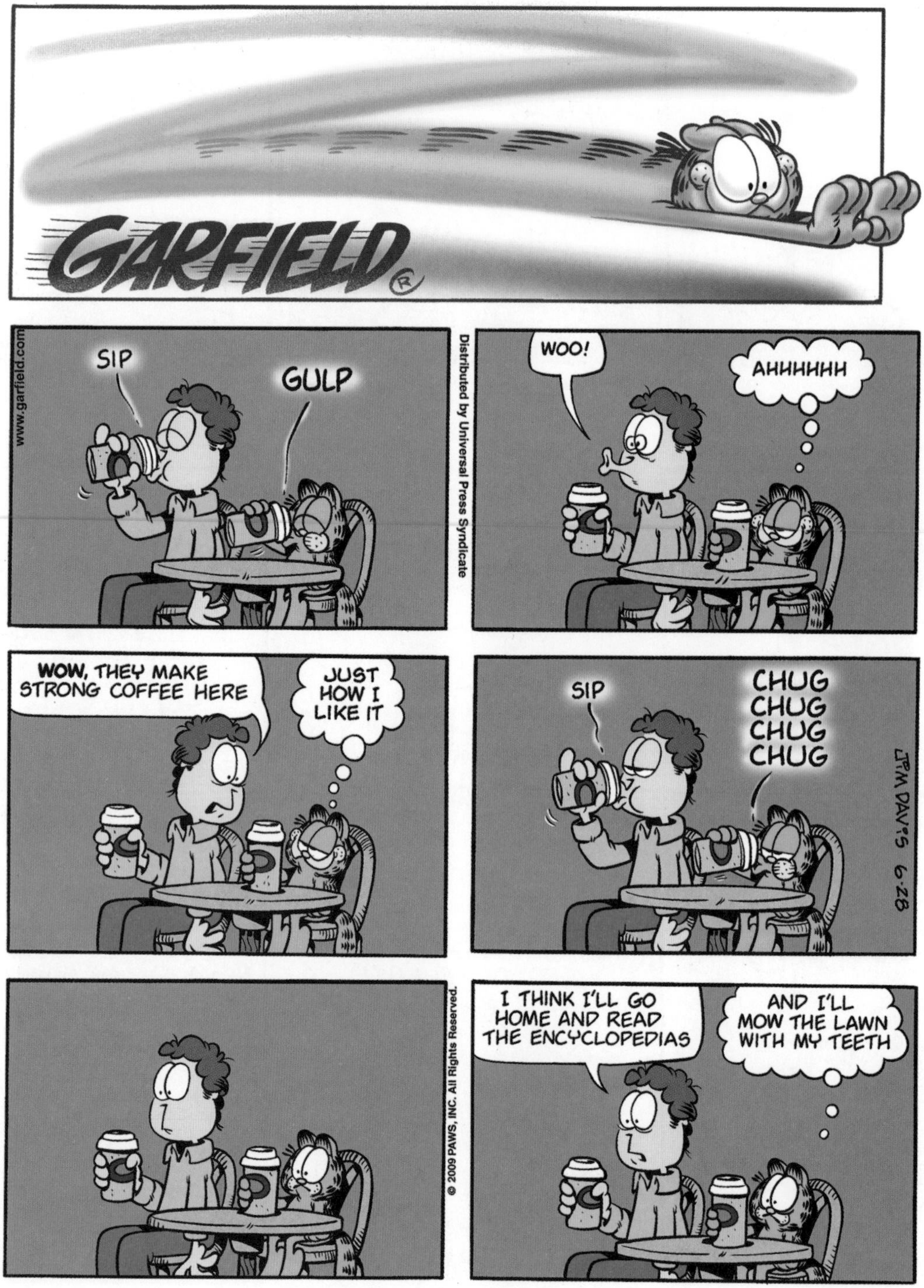
GARFIELD®
www.garfield.com
SIP
GULP
Distributed by Universal Press Syndicate
WOO!
AHHHHHH
WOW, THEY MAKE STRONG COFFEE HERE
JUST HOW I LIKE IT
SIP
CHUG CHUG CHUG CHUG
JIM DAVIS 6-28
© 2009 PAWS, INC. All Rights Reserved.
I THINK I'LL GO HOME AND READ THE ENCYCLOPEDIAS
AND I'LL MOW THE LAWN WITH MY TEETH

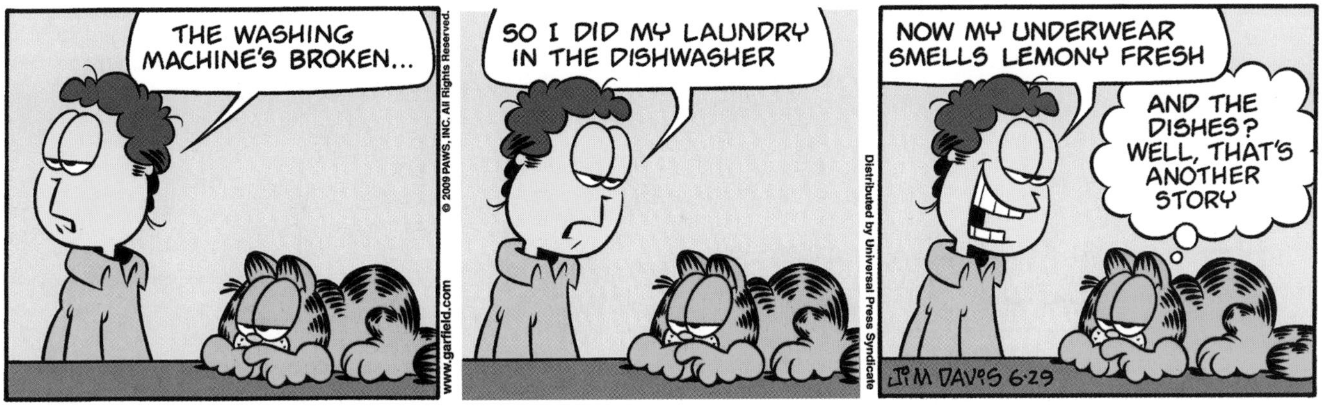
THE WASHING MACHINE'S BROKEN...
SO I DID MY LAUNDRY IN THE DISHWASHER
NOW MY UNDERWEAR SMELLS LEMONY FRESH
AND THE DISHES? WELL, THAT'S ANOTHER STORY
JIM DAVIS 6-29
© 2009 PAWS, INC. All Rights Reserved.
www.garfield.com
Distributed by Universal Press Syndicate

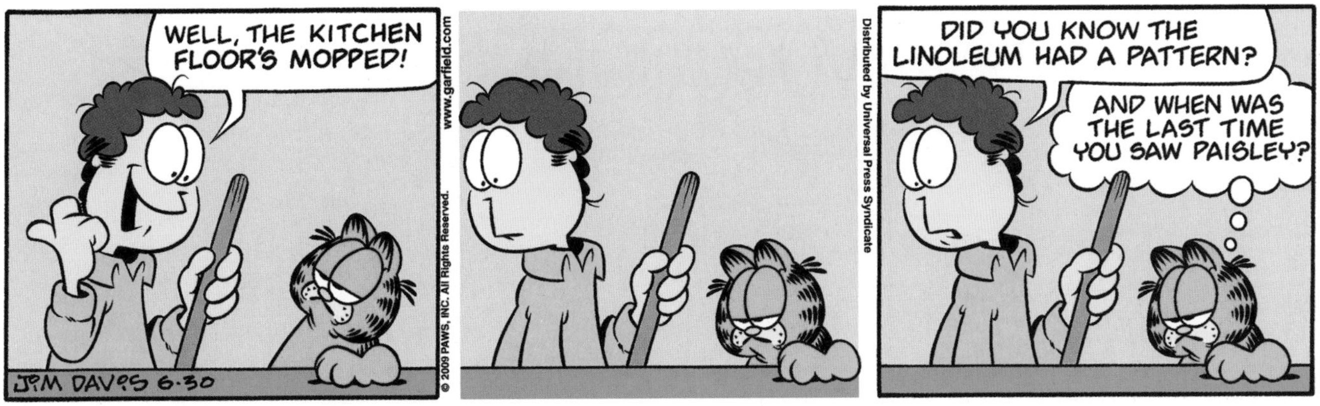
WELL, THE KITCHEN FLOOR'S MOPPED!
DID YOU KNOW THE LINOLEUM HAD A PATTERN?
AND WHEN WAS THE LAST TIME YOU SAW PAISLEY?
JIM DAVIS 6-30
www.garfield.com
© 2009 PAWS, INC. All Rights Reserved.
Distributed by Universal Press Syndicate

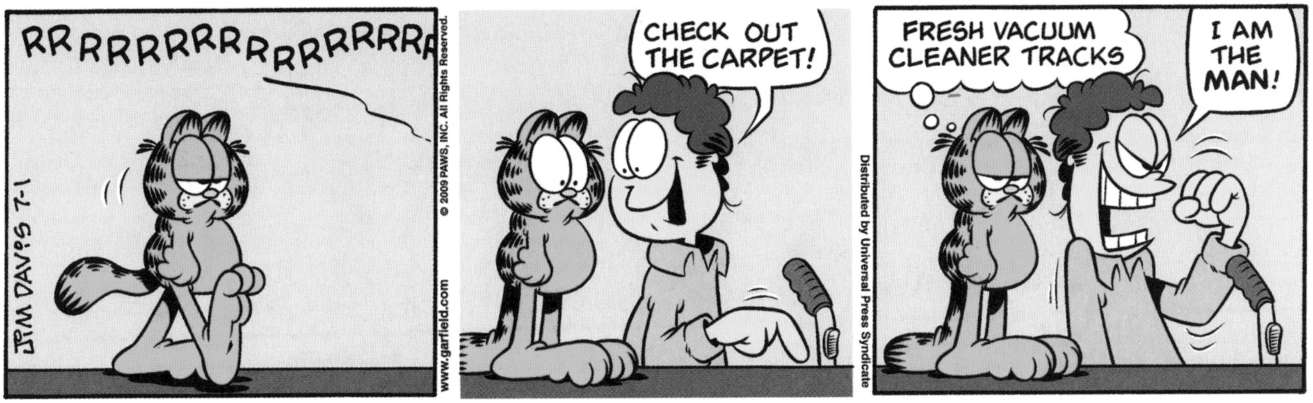
RRRRRRRRRRRRRRRR
CHECK OUT THE CARPET!
FRESH VACUUM CLEANER TRACKS
I AM THE MAN!
JIM DAVIS 7-1
© 2009 PAWS, INC. All Rights Reserved.
www.garfield.com
Distributed by Universal Press Syndicate

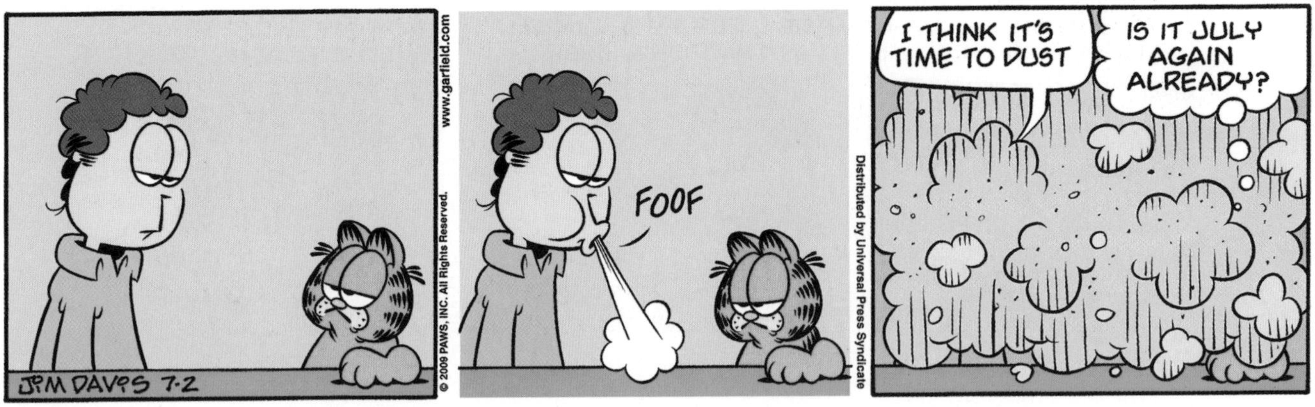
JIM DAVIS 7-2
© 2009 PAWS, INC. All Rights Reserved.
www.garfield.com
FOOF
Distributed by Universal Press Syndicate
I THINK IT'S TIME TO DUST
IS IT JULY AGAIN ALREADY?

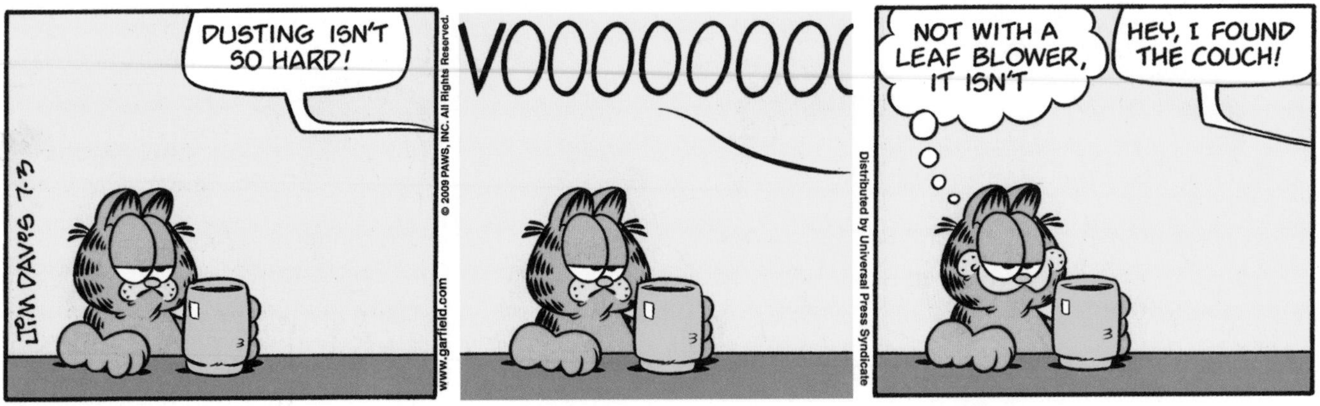
JIM DAVIS 7-3
DUSTING ISN'T SO HARD!
© 2009 PAWS, INC. All Rights Reserved.
www.garfield.com
VOOOOOOOOO
Distributed by Universal Press Syndicate
NOT WITH A LEAF BLOWER, IT ISN'T
HEY, I FOUND THE COUCH!

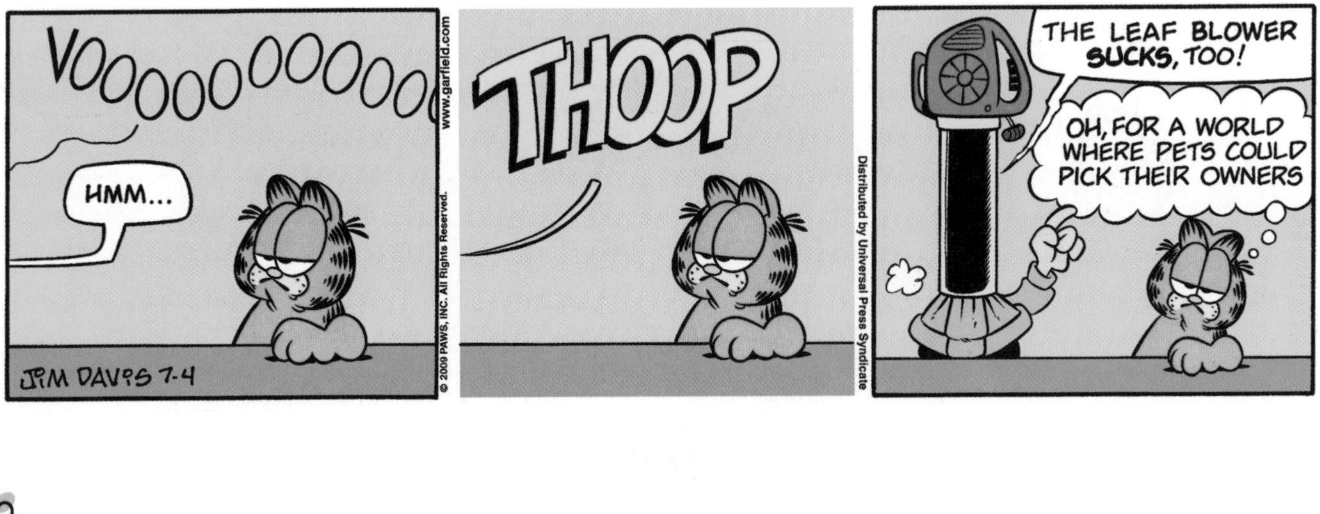
VOOOOOOOOOOOOOO
HMM...
JIM DAVIS 7-4
© 2009 PAWS, INC. All Rights Reserved.
www.garfield.com
THOOP
Distributed by Universal Press Syndicate
THE LEAF BLOWER **SUCKS**, TOO!
OH, FOR A WORLD WHERE PETS COULD PICK THEIR OWNERS

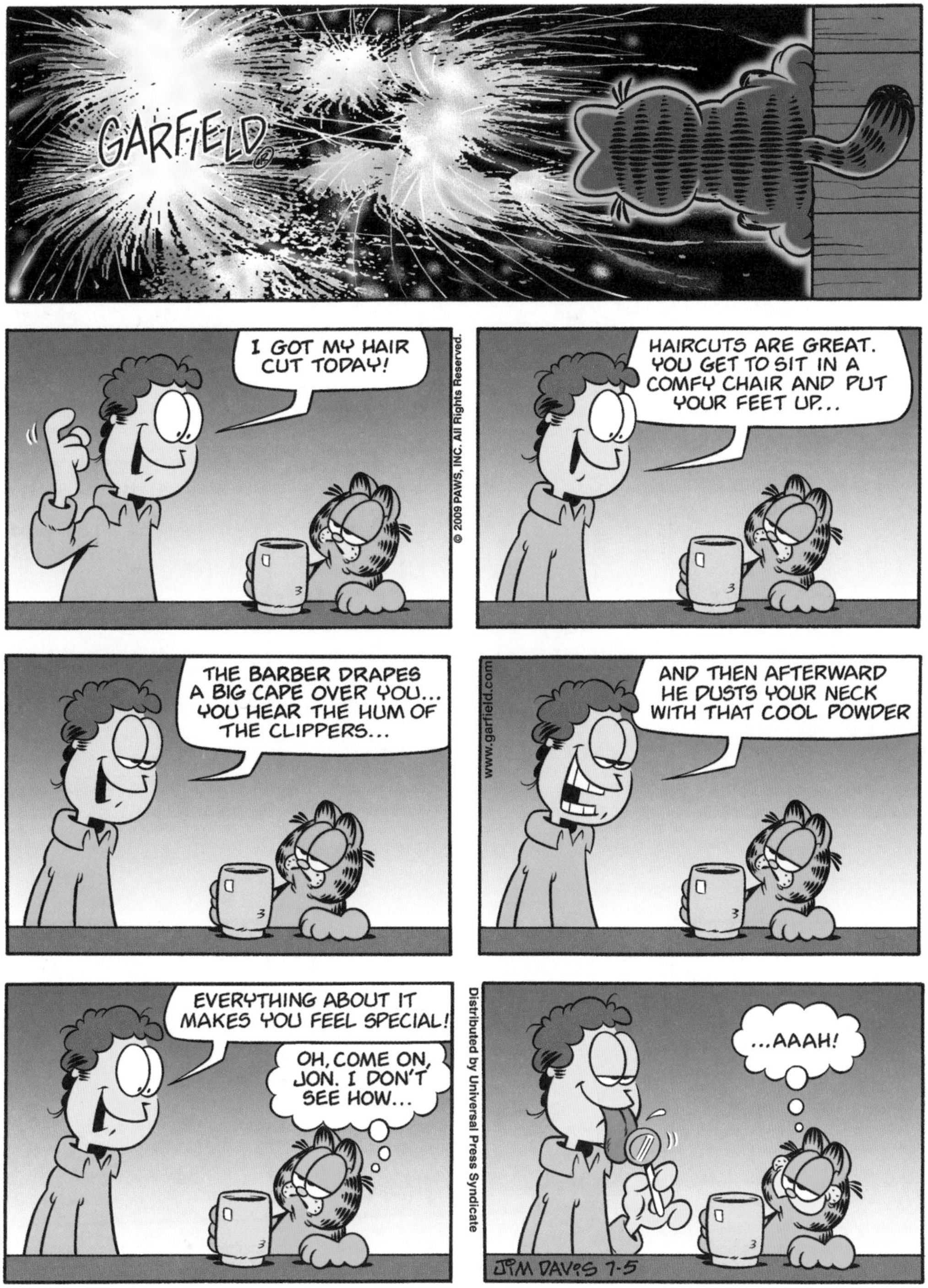
GARFIELD®
I GOT MY HAIR CUT TODAY!
© 2009 PAWS, INC. All Rights Reserved.
HAIRCUTS ARE GREAT. YOU GET TO SIT IN A COMFY CHAIR AND PUT YOUR FEET UP...
THE BARBER DRAPES A BIG CAPE OVER YOU... YOU HEAR THE HUM OF THE CLIPPERS...
www.garfield.com
AND THEN AFTERWARD HE DUSTS YOUR NECK WITH THAT COOL POWDER
EVERYTHING ABOUT IT MAKES YOU FEEL SPECIAL!
OH, COME ON, JON. I DON'T SEE HOW...
Distributed by Universal Press Syndicate
...AAAH!
JIM DAVIS 7-5

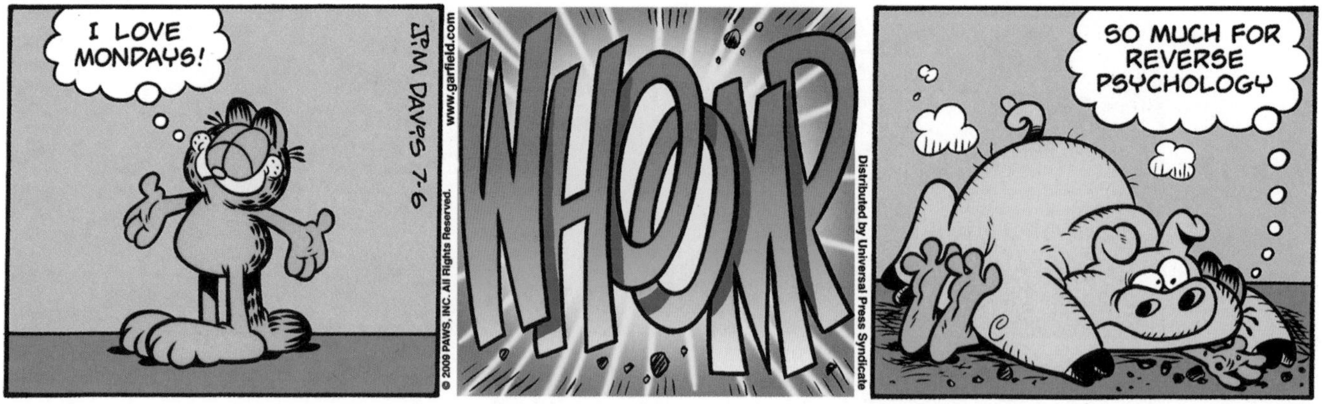
I LOVE MONDAYS!
JIM DAVIS 7-6
www.garfield.com
© 2009 PAWS, INC. All Rights Reserved.
WHOOMP
Distributed by Universal Press Syndicate
SO MUCH FOR REVERSE PSYCHOLOGY

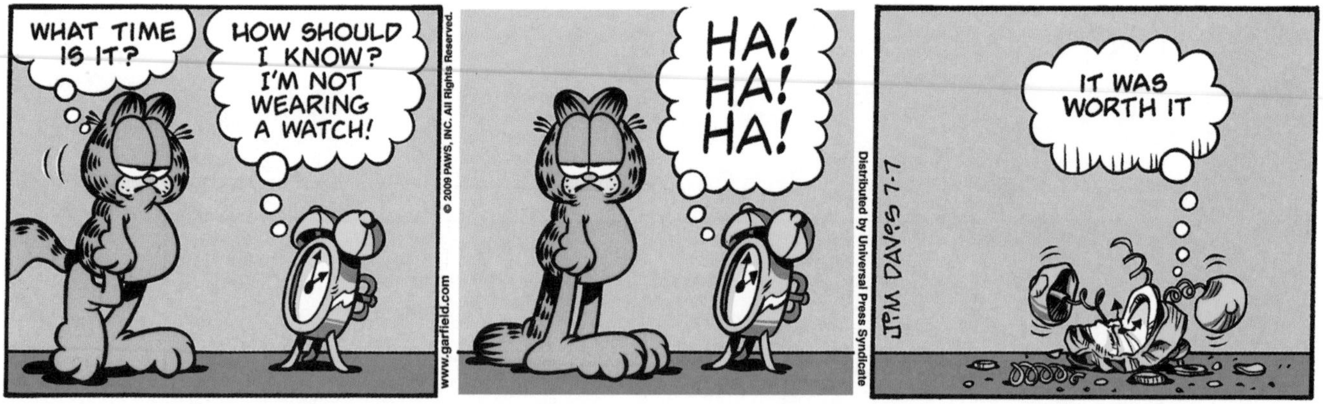
WHAT TIME IS IT?
HOW SHOULD I KNOW? I'M NOT WEARING A WATCH!
© 2009 PAWS, INC. All Rights Reserved.
www.garfield.com
HA! HA! HA!
Distributed by Universal Press Syndicate
JIM DAVIS 7-7
IT WAS WORTH IT

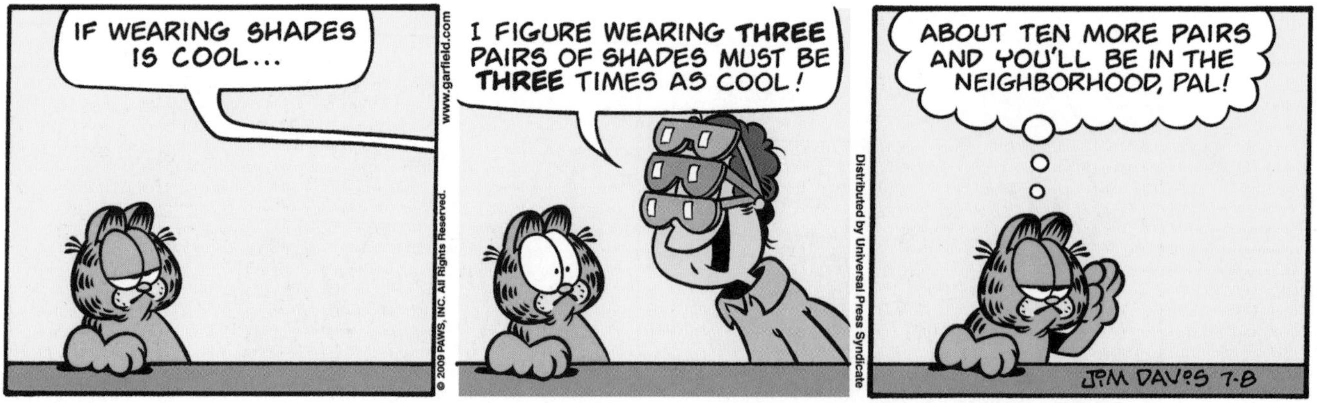
IF WEARING SHADES IS COOL...
www.garfield.com
© 2009 PAWS, INC. All Rights Reserved.
I FIGURE WEARING THREE PAIRS OF SHADES MUST BE THREE TIMES AS COOL!
Distributed by Universal Press Syndicate
ABOUT TEN MORE PAIRS AND YOU'LL BE IN THE NEIGHBORHOOD, PAL!
JIM DAVIS 7-8

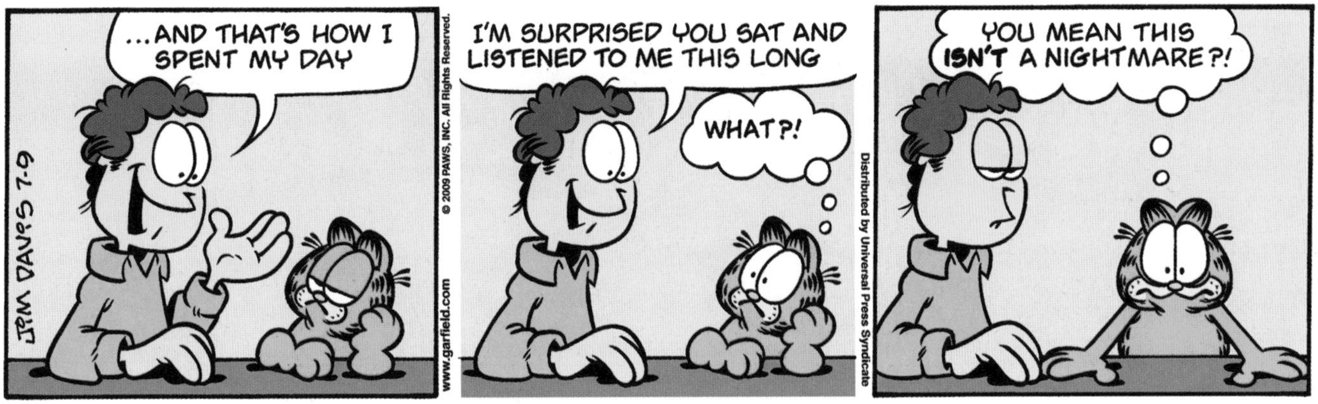
...AND THAT'S HOW I SPENT MY DAY
JIM DAVIS 7-9
© 2009 PAWS, INC. All Rights Reserved.
www.garfield.com
I'M SURPRISED YOU SAT AND LISTENED TO ME THIS LONG
WHAT?!
Distributed by Universal Press Syndicate
YOU MEAN THIS **ISN'T** A NIGHTMARE?!

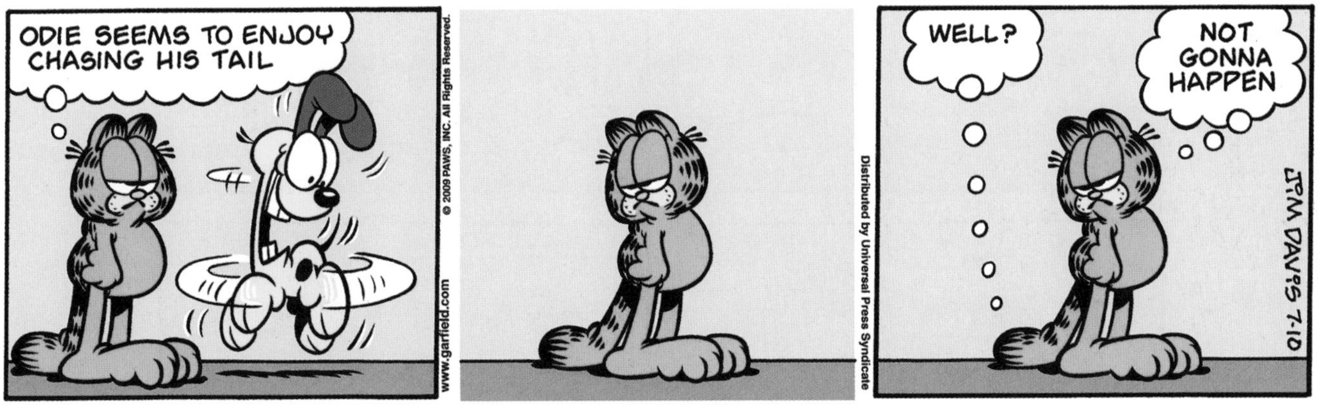
ODIE SEEMS TO ENJOY CHASING HIS TAIL
© 2009 PAWS, INC. All Rights Reserved.
www.garfield.com
Distributed by Universal Press Syndicate
WELL?
NOT GONNA HAPPEN
JIM DAVIS 7-10

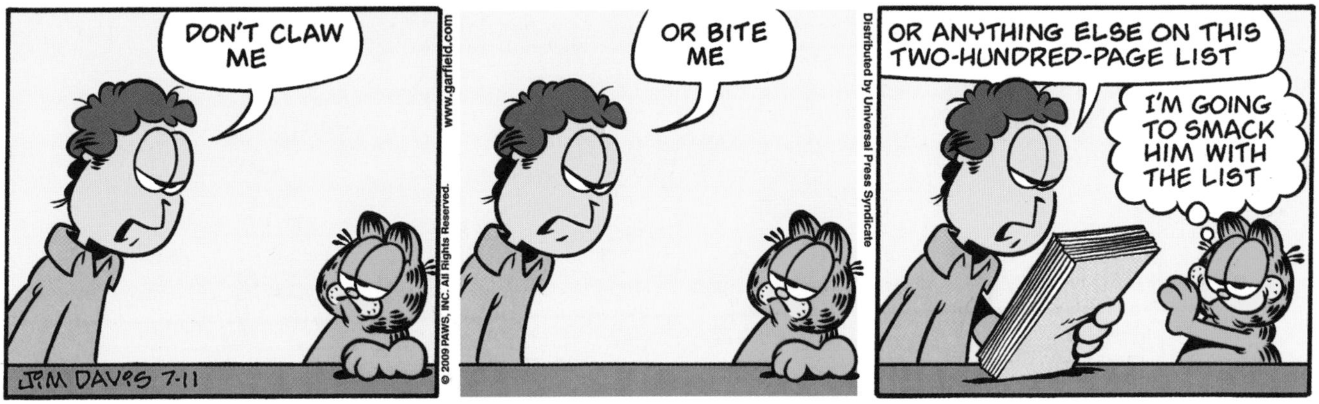
DON'T CLAW ME
JIM DAVIS 7-11
© 2009 PAWS, INC. All Rights Reserved.
www.garfield.com
OR BITE ME
Distributed by Universal Press Syndicate
OR ANYTHING ELSE ON THIS TWO-HUNDRED-PAGE LIST
I'M GOING TO SMACK HIM WITH THE LIST

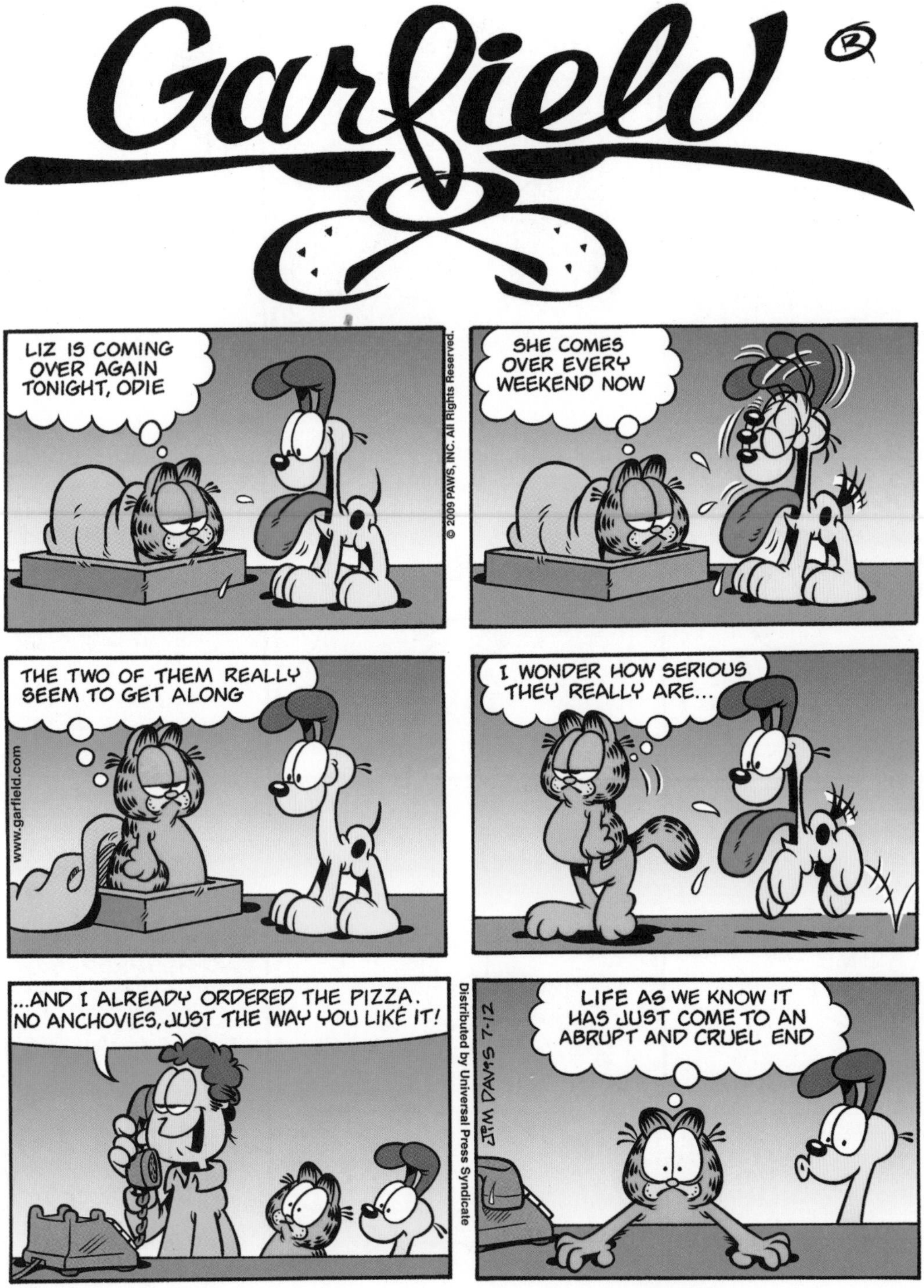
Garfield®
LIZ IS COMING OVER AGAIN TONIGHT, ODIE
© 2009 PAWS, INC. All Rights Reserved.
SHE COMES OVER EVERY WEEKEND NOW
THE TWO OF THEM REALLY SEEM TO GET ALONG
www.garfield.com
I WONDER HOW SERIOUS THEY REALLY ARE...
...AND I ALREADY ORDERED THE PIZZA. NO ANCHOVIES, JUST THE WAY YOU LIKE IT!
Distributed by Universal Press Syndicate
JPM DAVIS 7-12
LIFE AS WE KNOW IT HAS JUST COME TO AN ABRUPT AND CRUEL END

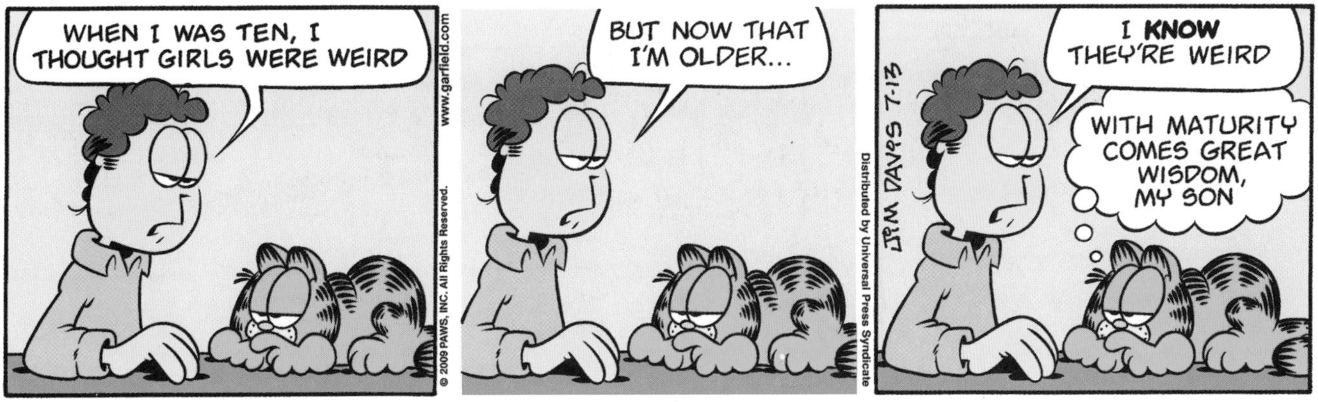
WHEN I WAS TEN, I THOUGHT GIRLS WERE WEIRD
BUT NOW THAT I'M OLDER...
I **KNOW** THEY'RE WEIRD
WITH MATURITY COMES GREAT WISDOM, MY SON
JIM DAVIS 7-13
© 2009 PAWS, INC. All Rights Reserved. www.garfield.com
Distributed by Universal Press Syndicate

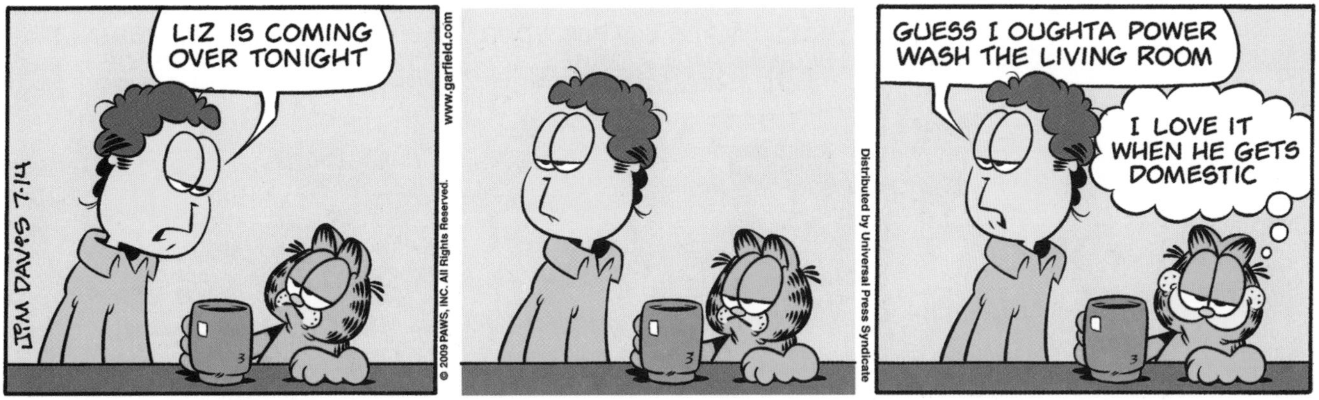
LIZ IS COMING OVER TONIGHT
GUESS I OUGHTA POWER WASH THE LIVING ROOM
I LOVE IT WHEN HE GETS DOMESTIC
JIM DAVIS 7-14
© 2009 PAWS, INC. All Rights Reserved. www.garfield.com
Distributed by Universal Press Syndicate

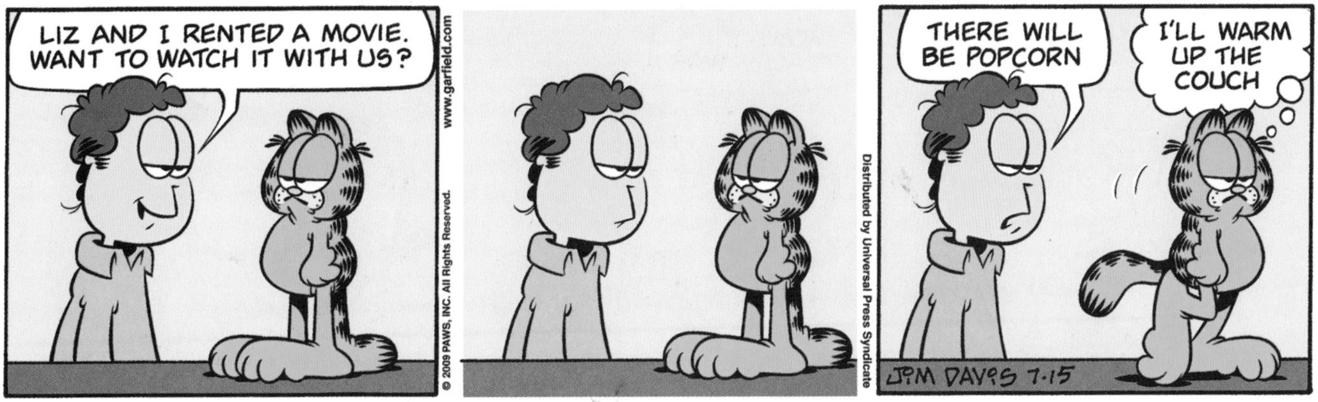
LIZ AND I RENTED A MOVIE. WANT TO WATCH IT WITH US?
THERE WILL BE POPCORN
I'LL WARM UP THE COUCH
JIM DAVIS 7-15
© 2009 PAWS, INC. All Rights Reserved. www.garfield.com
Distributed by Universal Press Syndicate

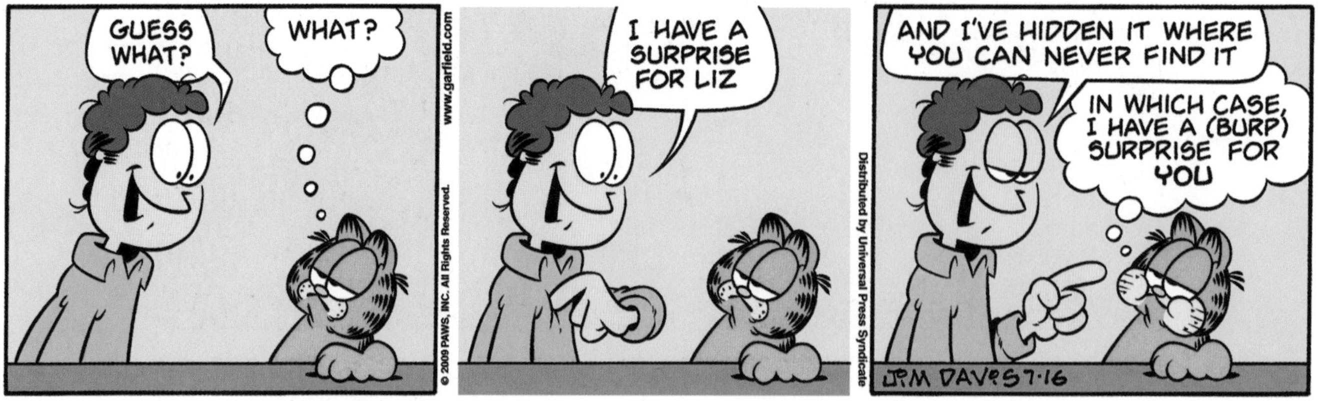
GUESS WHAT?
WHAT?
© 2009 PAWS, INC. All Rights Reserved.
www.garfield.com
I HAVE A SURPRISE FOR LIZ
Distributed by Universal Press Syndicate
AND I'VE HIDDEN IT WHERE YOU CAN NEVER FIND IT
IN WHICH CASE, I HAVE A (BURP) SURPRISE FOR YOU
JIM DAVIS 7-16

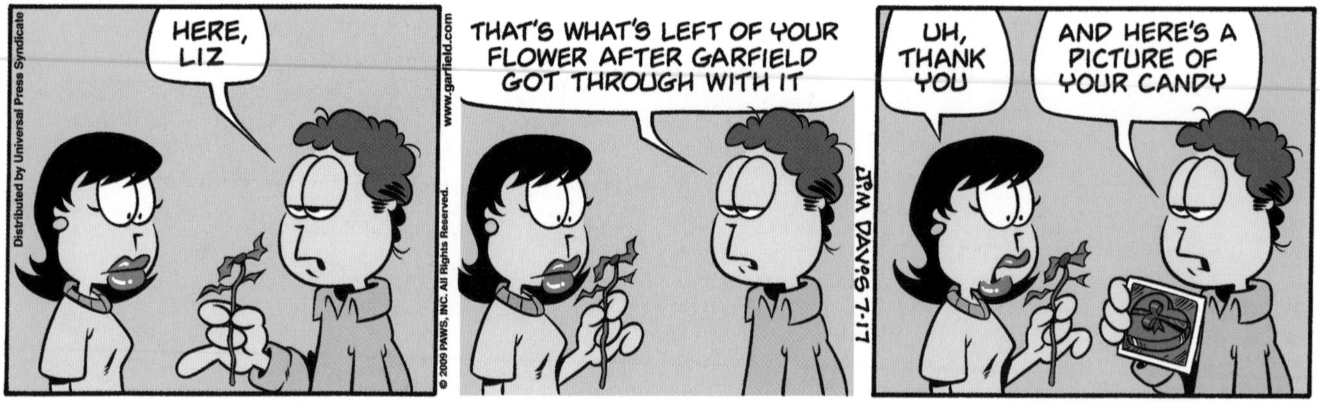
Distributed by Universal Press Syndicate
HERE, LIZ
© 2009 PAWS, INC. All Rights Reserved.
www.garfield.com
THAT'S WHAT'S LEFT OF YOUR FLOWER AFTER GARFIELD GOT THROUGH WITH IT
JIM DAVIS 7-17
UH, THANK YOU
AND HERE'S A PICTURE OF YOUR CANDY

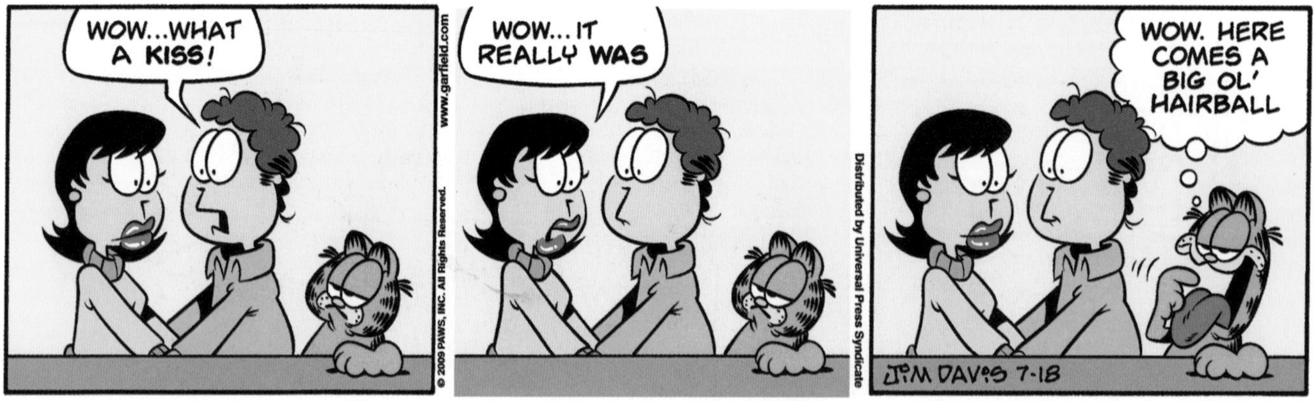
WOW...WHAT A KISS!
© 2009 PAWS, INC. All Rights Reserved.
www.garfield.com
WOW... IT REALLY WAS
Distributed by Universal Press Syndicate
WOW. HERE COMES A BIG OL' HAIRBALL
JIM DAVIS 7-18

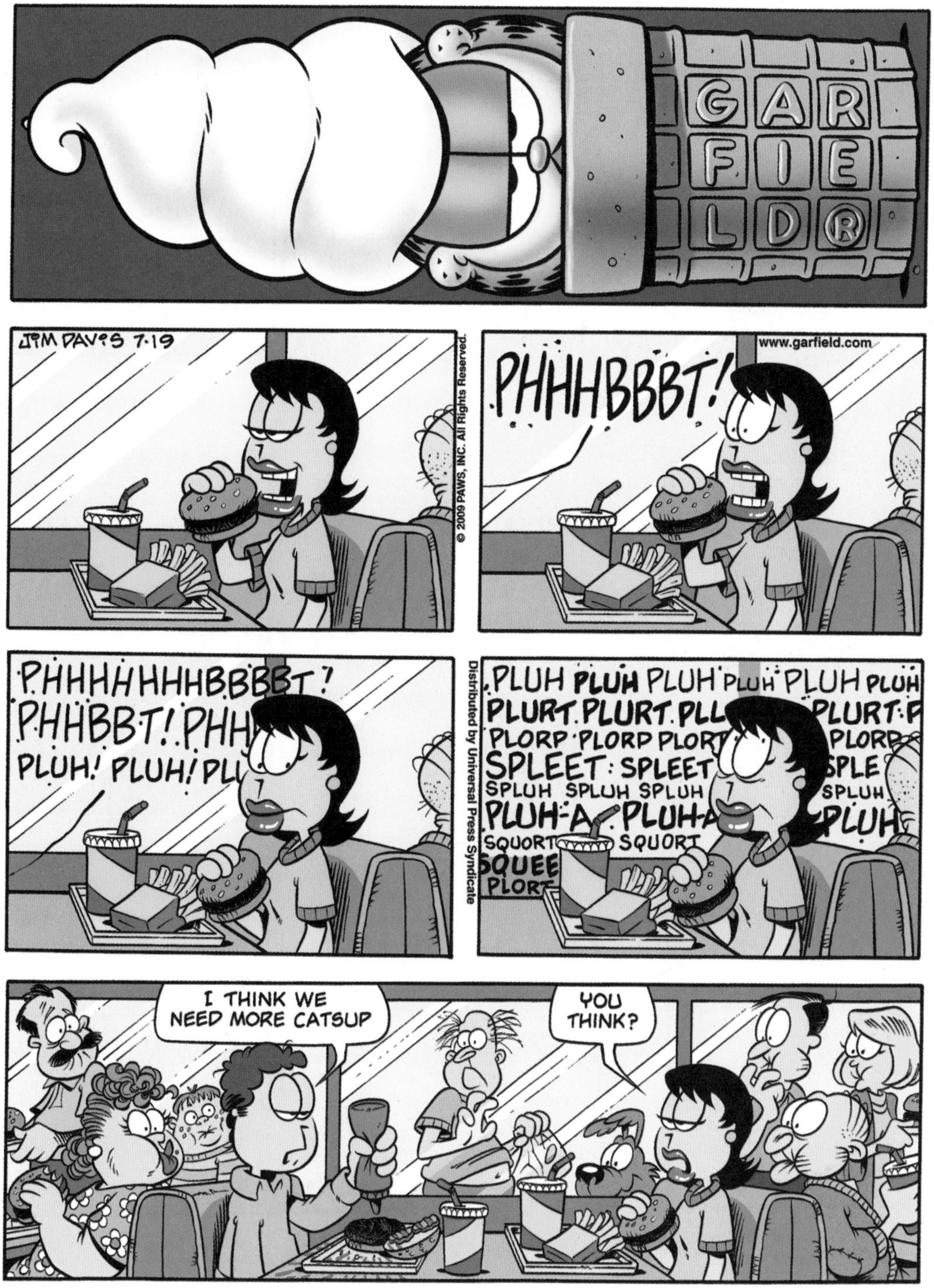

GAR
FIE
LD®
JIM DAVIS 7-19
© 2009 PAWS, INC. All Rights Reserved.
www.garfield.com
PHHHBBBT!
PHHHHHHHBBBBT!
PHHBBT! PHH
PLUH! PLUH! PL
Distributed by Universal Press Syndicate
PLUH PLUH PLUH PLUH PLUH PLUH
PLURT PLURT PLL PLURT P
PLORP PLORP PLORP PLORP
SPLEET SPLEET SPLE
SPLUH SPLUH SPLUH SPLUH
PLUH-A PLUH-A PLUH
SQUORT SQUORT
SQUEE
PLORT
I THINK WE NEED MORE CATSUP
YOU THINK?

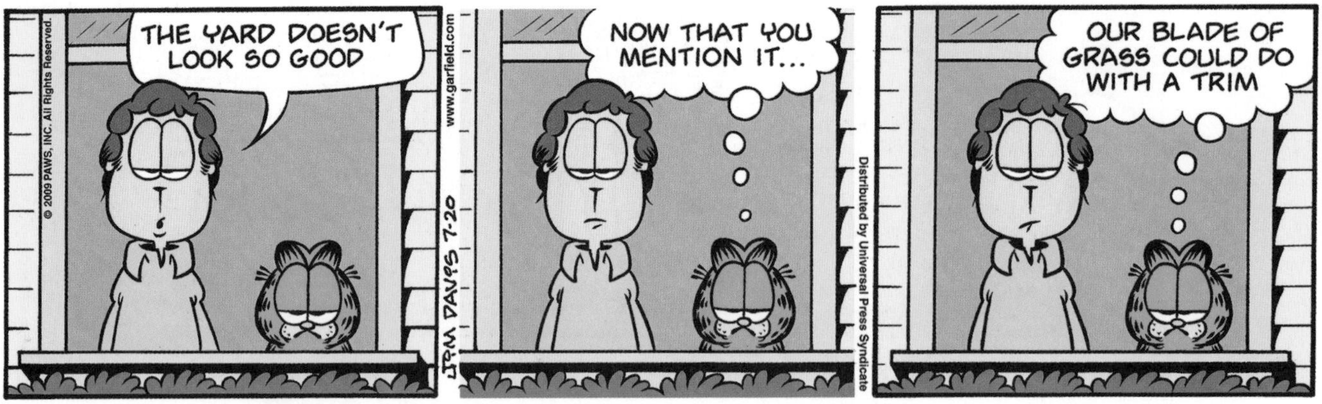
THE YARD DOESN'T LOOK SO GOOD
NOW THAT YOU MENTION IT...
OUR BLADE OF GRASS COULD DO WITH A TRIM
© 2009 PAWS, INC. All Rights Reserved.
www.garfield.com
JIM DAVIS 7-20
Distributed by Universal Press Syndicate

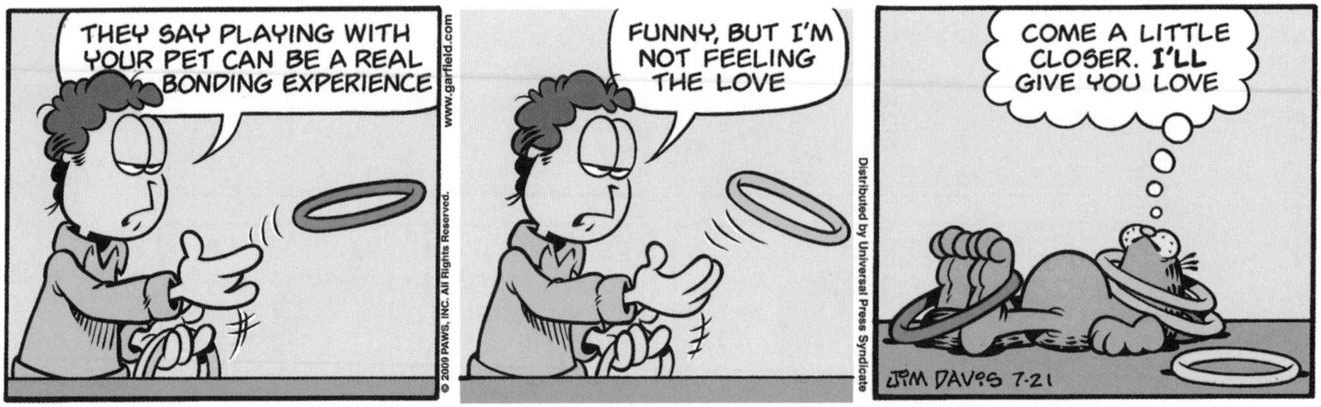
THEY SAY PLAYING WITH YOUR PET CAN BE A REAL BONDING EXPERIENCE
FUNNY, BUT I'M NOT FEELING THE LOVE
COME A LITTLE CLOSER. **I'LL** GIVE YOU LOVE
© 2009 PAWS, INC. All Rights Reserved.
www.garfield.com
Distributed by Universal Press Syndicate
JIM DAVIS 7-21

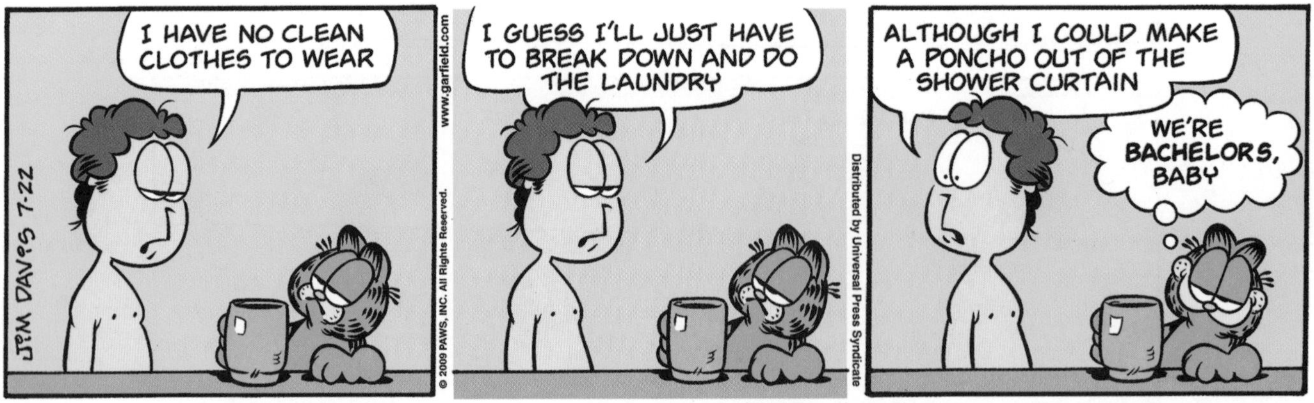
I HAVE NO CLEAN CLOTHES TO WEAR
I GUESS I'LL JUST HAVE TO BREAK DOWN AND DO THE LAUNDRY
ALTHOUGH I COULD MAKE A PONCHO OUT OF THE SHOWER CURTAIN
WE'RE **BACHELORS,** BABY
JIM DAVIS 7-22
© 2009 PAWS, INC. All Rights Reserved.
www.garfield.com
Distributed by Universal Press Syndicate

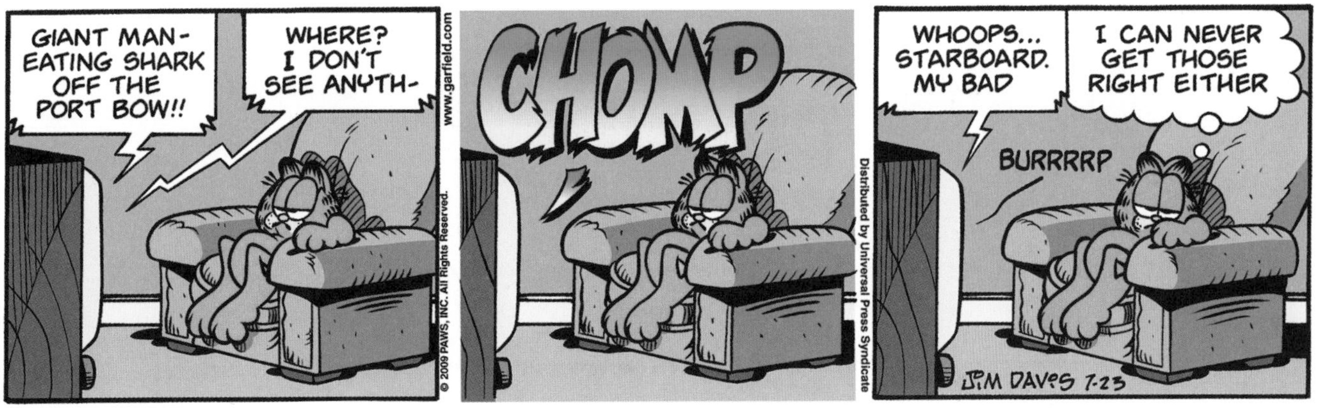
GIANT MAN-EATING SHARK OFF THE PORT BOW!!
WHERE? I DON'T SEE ANYTH-
www.garfield.com
© 2009 PAWS, INC. All Rights Reserved.
CHOMP
Distributed by Universal Press Syndicate
WHOOPS... STARBOARD. MY BAD
I CAN NEVER GET THOSE RIGHT EITHER
BURRRRP
JIM DAVIS 7-23

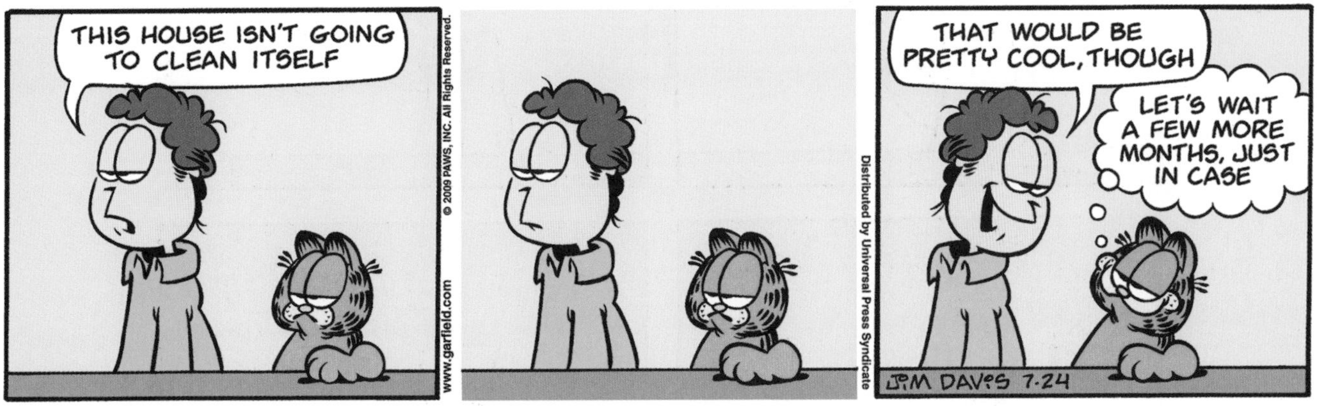
THIS HOUSE ISN'T GOING TO CLEAN ITSELF
www.garfield.com
© 2009 PAWS, INC. All Rights Reserved.
Distributed by Universal Press Syndicate
THAT WOULD BE PRETTY COOL, THOUGH
LET'S WAIT A FEW MORE MONTHS, JUST IN CASE
JIM DAVIS 7-24

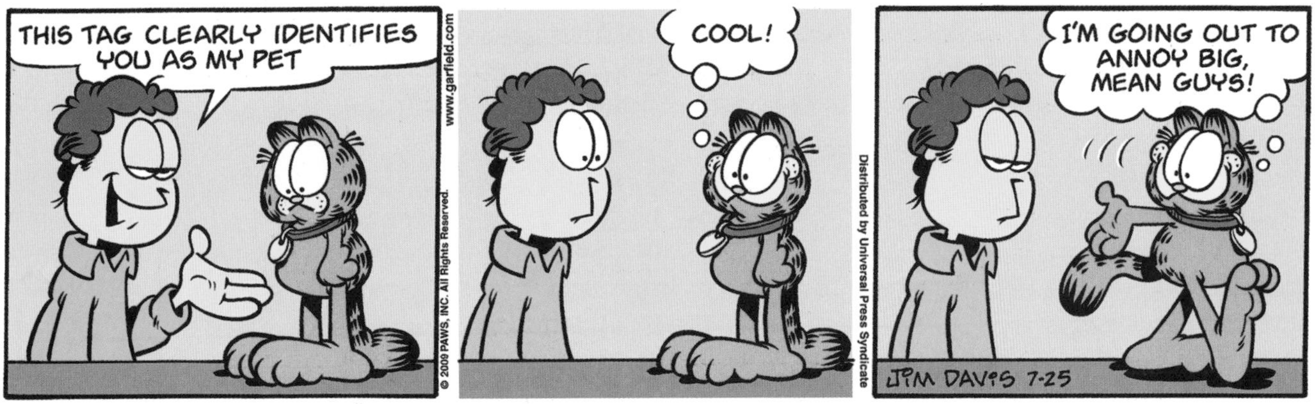
THIS TAG CLEARLY IDENTIFIES YOU AS MY PET
www.garfield.com
© 2009 PAWS, INC. All Rights Reserved.
COOL!
Distributed by Universal Press Syndicate
I'M GOING OUT TO ANNOY BIG, MEAN GUYS!
JIM DAVIS 7-25

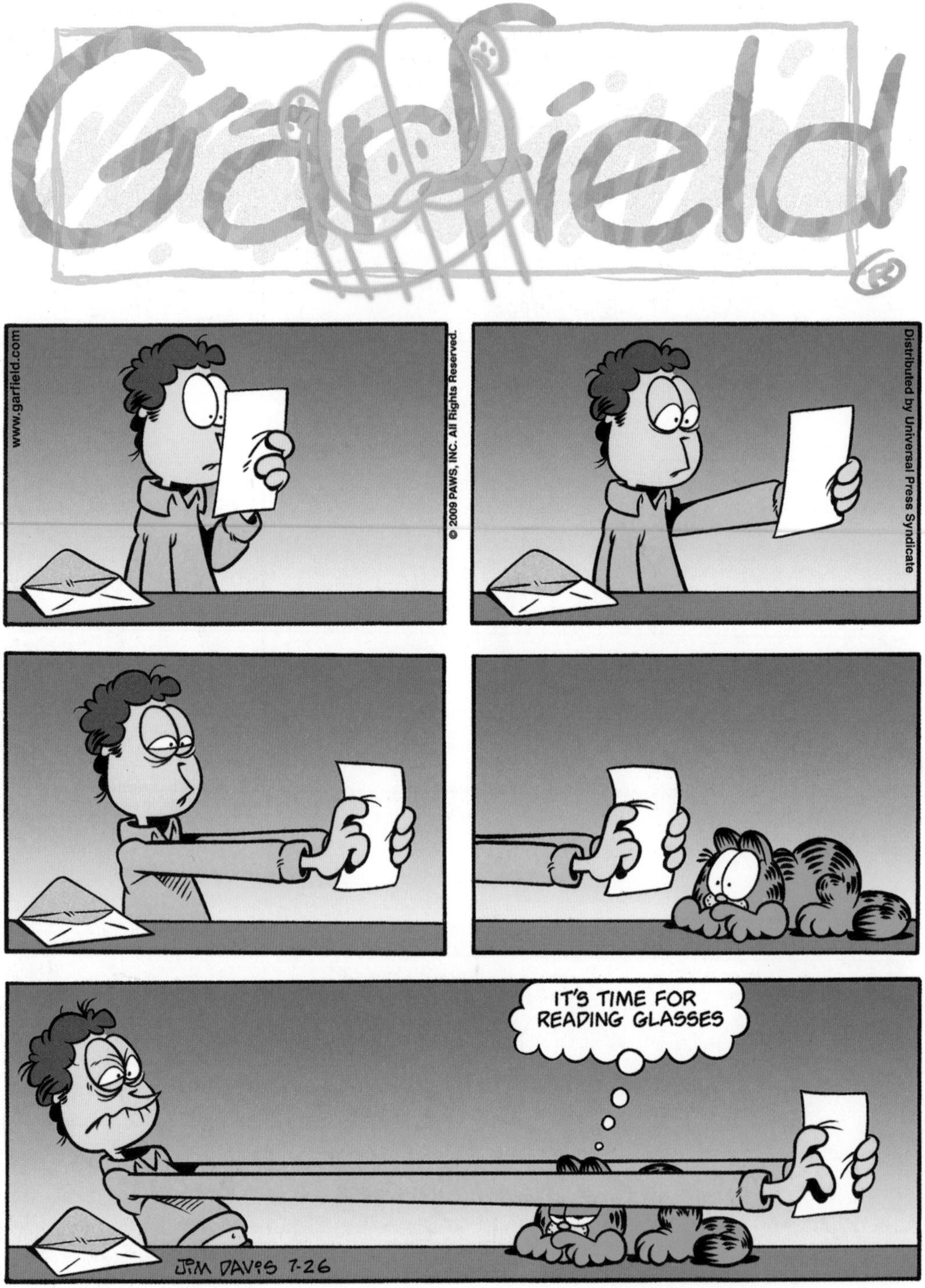
Garfield®
www.garfield.com
© 2009 PAWS, INC. All Rights Reserved.
Distributed by Universal Press Syndicate
IT'S TIME FOR READING GLASSES
JIM DAVIS 7-26

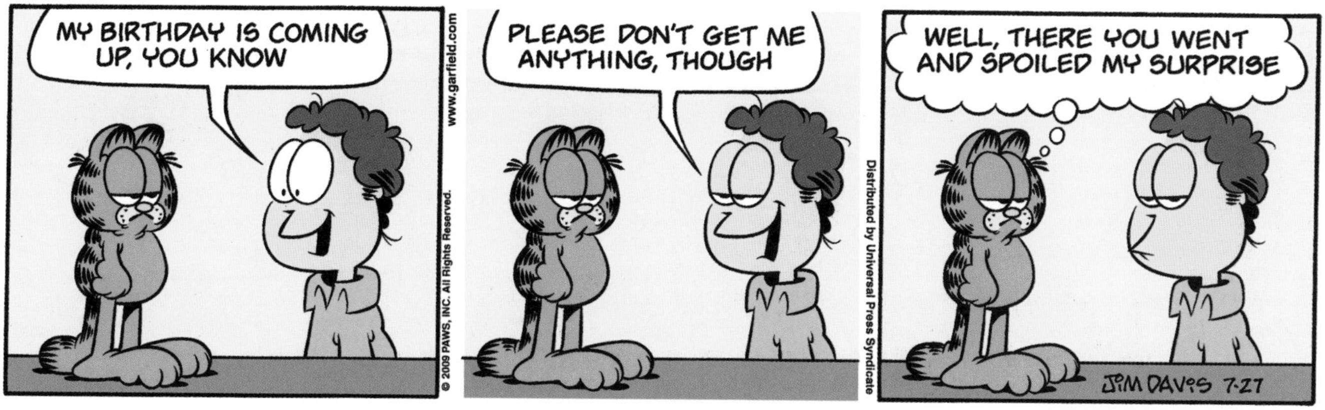
MY BIRTHDAY IS COMING UP, YOU KNOW
PLEASE DON'T GET ME ANYTHING, THOUGH
WELL, THERE YOU WENT AND SPOILED MY SURPRISE
JIM DAVIS 7-27

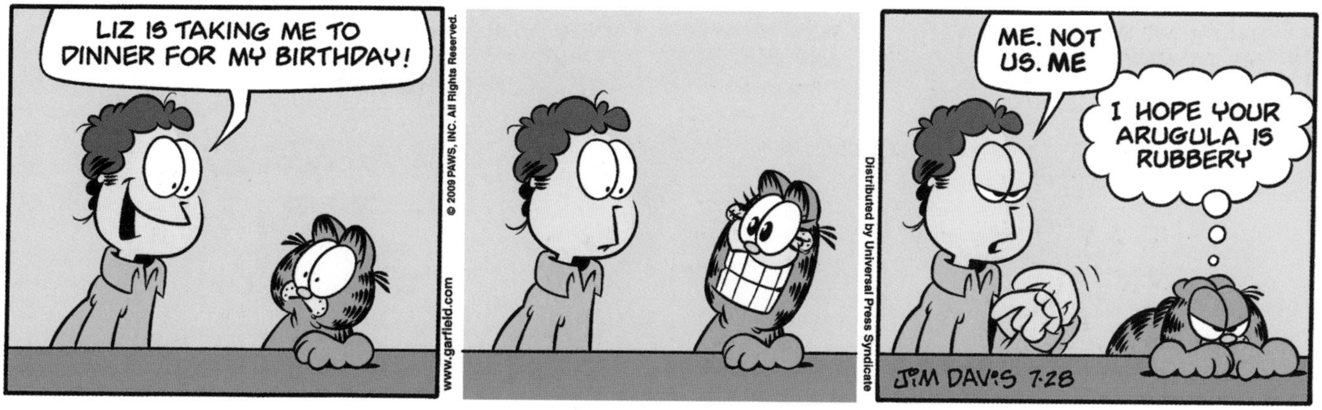
LIZ IS TAKING ME TO DINNER FOR MY BIRTHDAY!
ME. NOT US. ME
I HOPE YOUR ARUGULA IS RUBBERY
JIM DAVIS 7-28

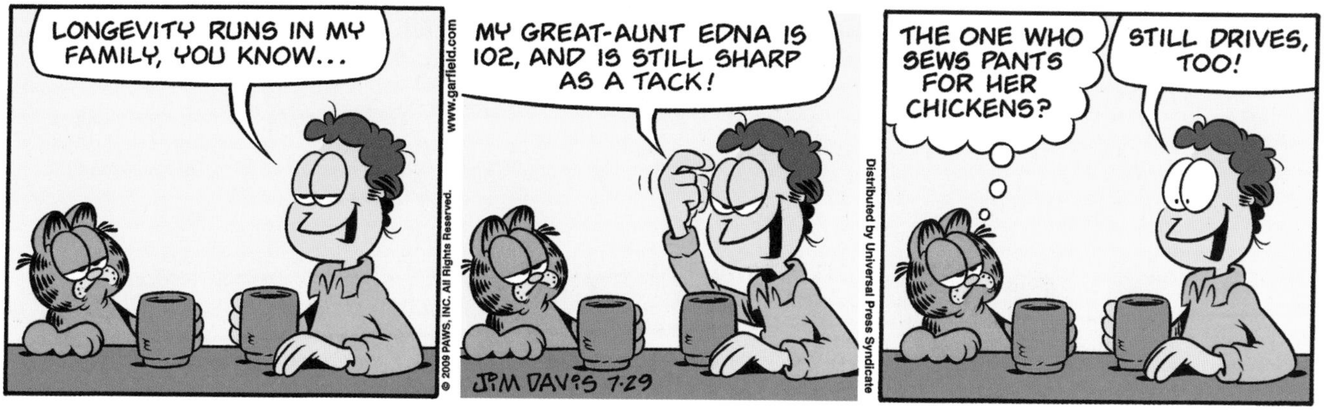
LONGEVITY RUNS IN MY FAMILY, YOU KNOW...
MY GREAT-AUNT EDNA IS 102, AND IS STILL SHARP AS A TACK!
THE ONE WHO SEWS PANTS FOR HER CHICKENS?
STILL DRIVES, TOO!
JIM DAVIS 7-29

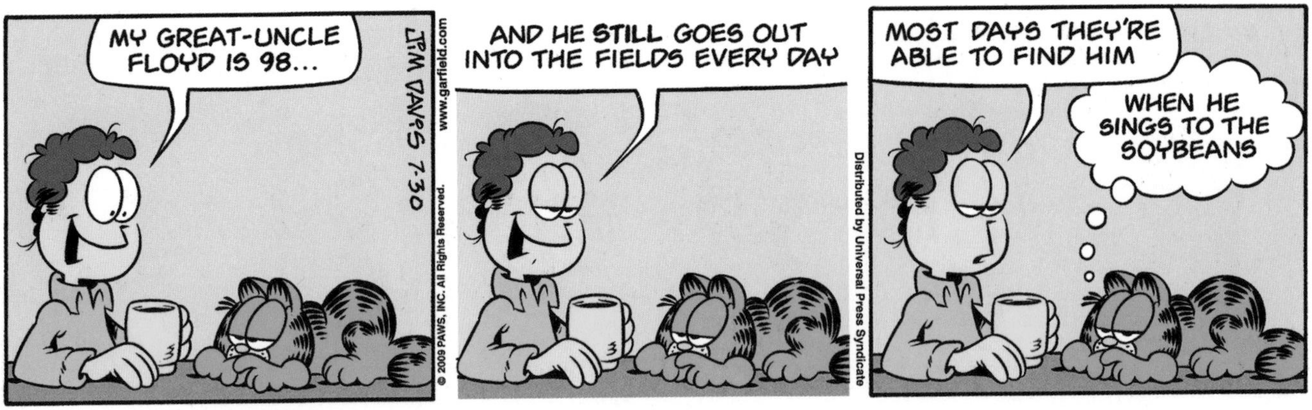
MY GREAT-UNCLE FLOYD IS 98...
JIM DAVIS 7-30
© 2009 PAWS, INC. All Rights Reserved. www.garfield.com
AND HE STILL GOES OUT INTO THE FIELDS EVERY DAY
Distributed by Universal Press Syndicate
MOST DAYS THEY'RE ABLE TO FIND HIM
WHEN HE SINGS TO THE SOYBEANS

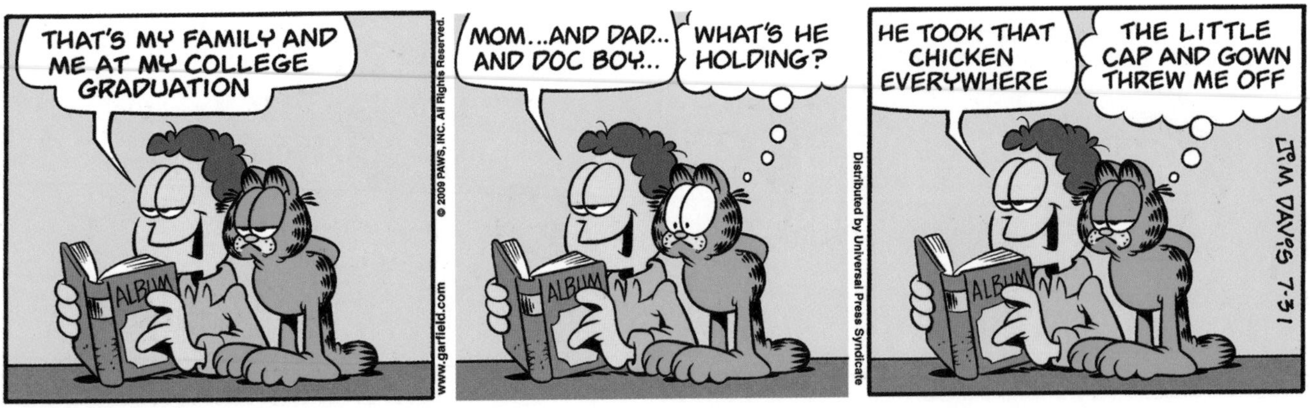
THAT'S MY FAMILY AND ME AT MY COLLEGE GRADUATION
© 2009 PAWS, INC. All Rights Reserved. www.garfield.com
MOM...AND DAD... AND DOC BOY...
WHAT'S HE HOLDING?
Distributed by Universal Press Syndicate
HE TOOK THAT CHICKEN EVERYWHERE
THE LITTLE CAP AND GOWN THREW ME OFF
JIM DAVIS 7-31

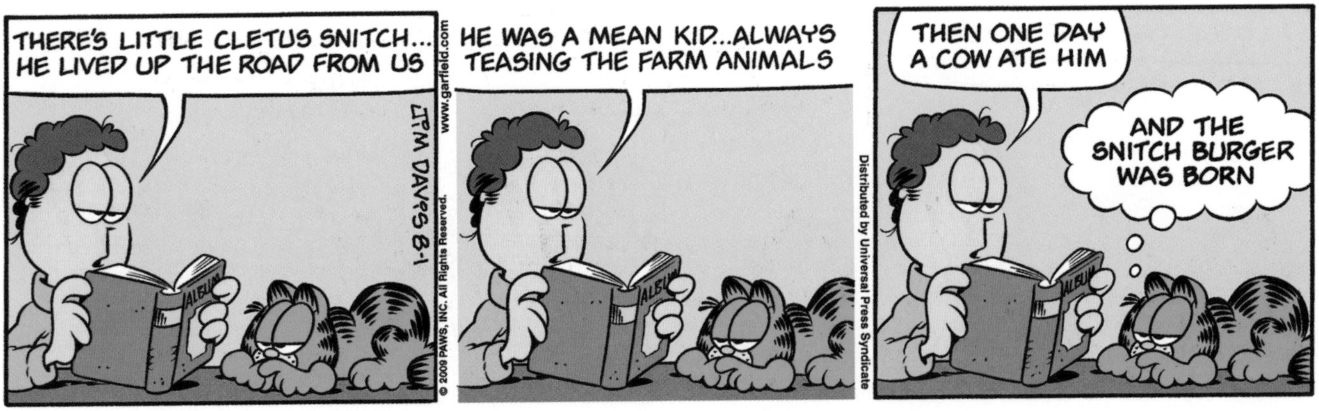
THERE'S LITTLE CLETUS SNITCH... HE LIVED UP THE ROAD FROM US
JIM DAVIS 8-1
© 2009 PAWS, INC. All Rights Reserved. www.garfield.com
HE WAS A MEAN KID...ALWAYS TEASING THE FARM ANIMALS
Distributed by Universal Press Syndicate
THEN ONE DAY A COW ATE HIM
AND THE SNITCH BURGER WAS BORN

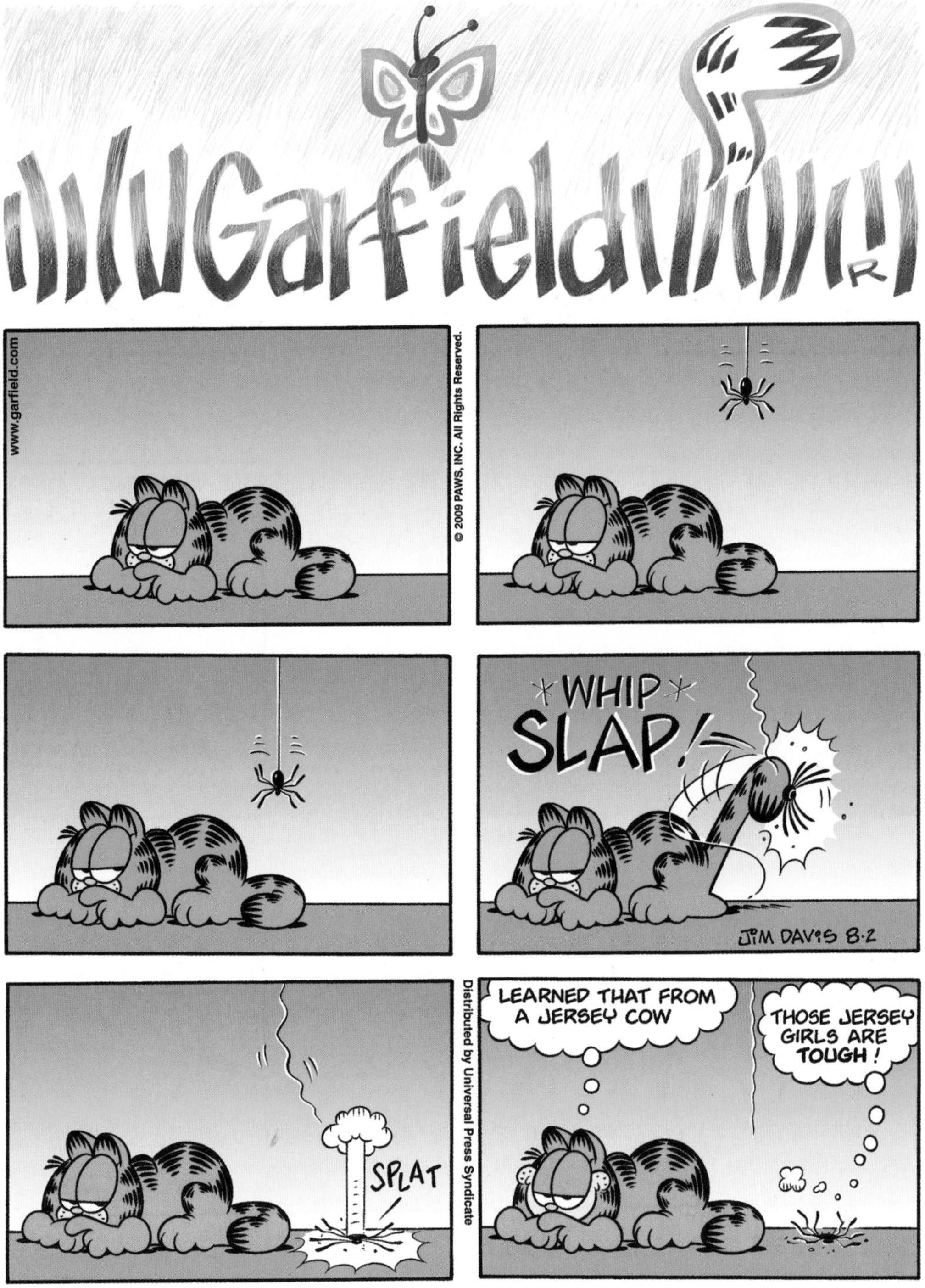
Garfield
www.garfield.com
© 2009 PAWS, INC. All Rights Reserved.
WHIP
SLAP!
JIM DAVIS 8-2
Distributed by Universal Press Syndicate
SPLAT
LEARNED THAT FROM A JERSEY COW
THOSE JERSEY GIRLS ARE TOUGH!

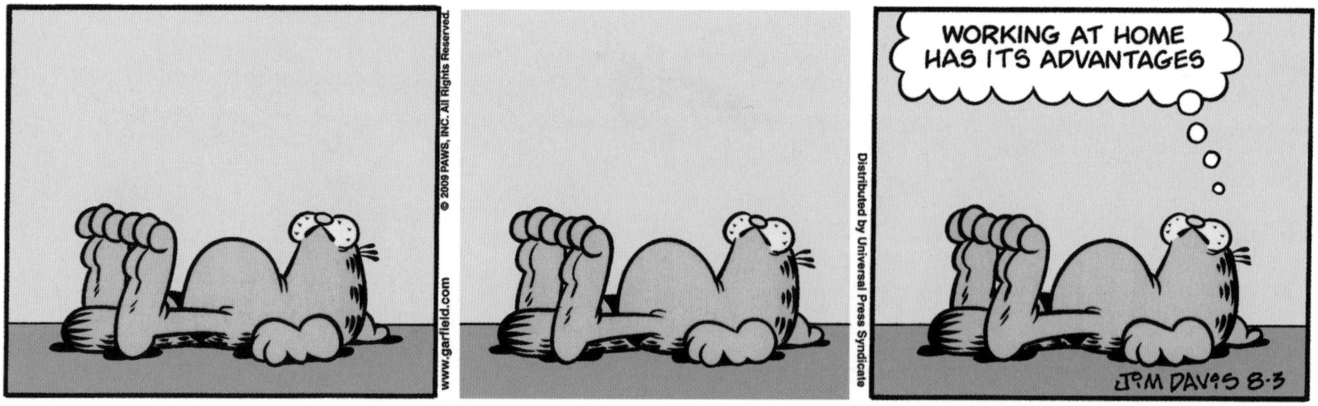
© 2009 PAWS, INC. All Rights Reserved.
www.garfield.com
Distributed by Universal Press Syndicate
WORKING AT HOME HAS ITS ADVANTAGES
JIM DAVIS 8-3

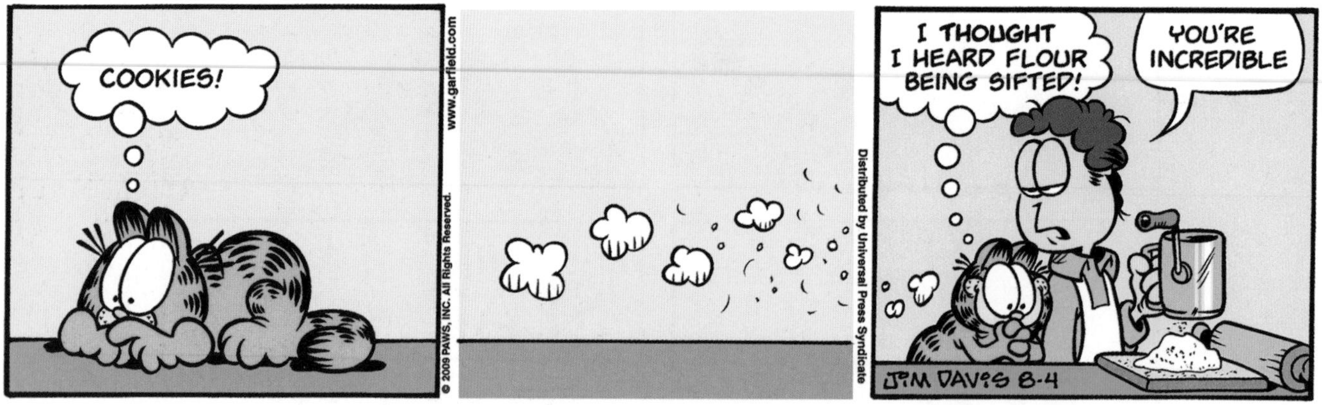
COOKIES!
www.garfield.com
© 2009 PAWS, INC. All Rights Reserved.
Distributed by Universal Press Syndicate
I THOUGHT I HEARD FLOUR BEING SIFTED!
YOU'RE INCREDIBLE
JIM DAVIS 8-4

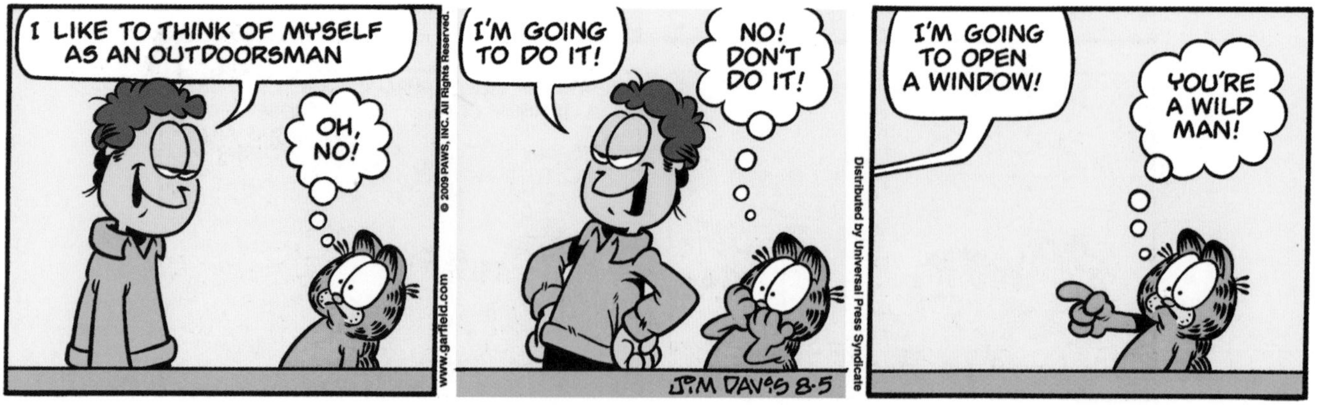
I LIKE TO THINK OF MYSELF AS AN OUTDOORSMAN
OH, NO!
© 2009 PAWS, INC. All Rights Reserved.
www.garfield.com
I'M GOING TO DO IT!
NO! DON'T DO IT!
JIM DAVIS 8-5
Distributed by Universal Press Syndicate
I'M GOING TO OPEN A WINDOW!
YOU'RE A WILD MAN!

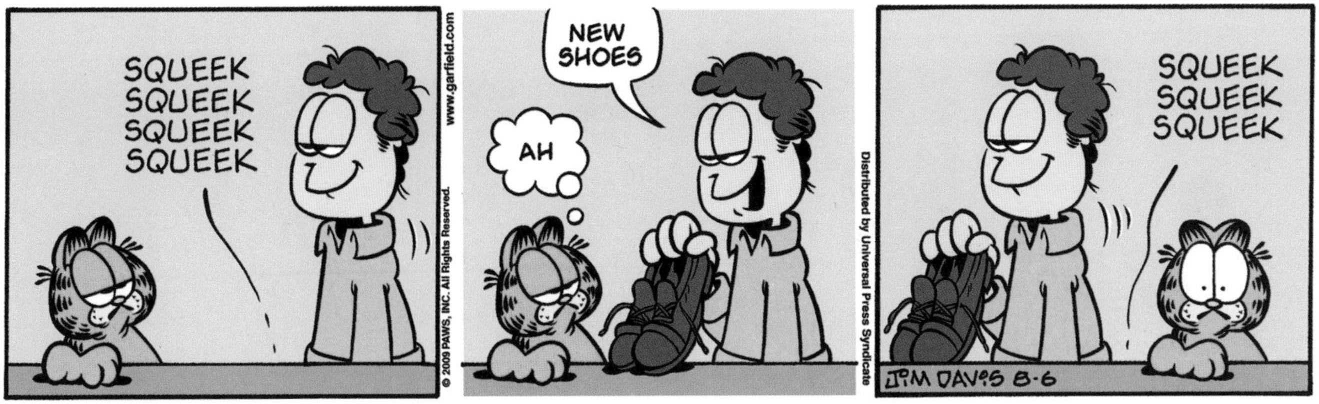
SQUEEK SQUEEK SQUEEK SQUEEK
NEW SHOES
AH
SQUEEK SQUEEK SQUEEK
JIM DAVIS 8-6

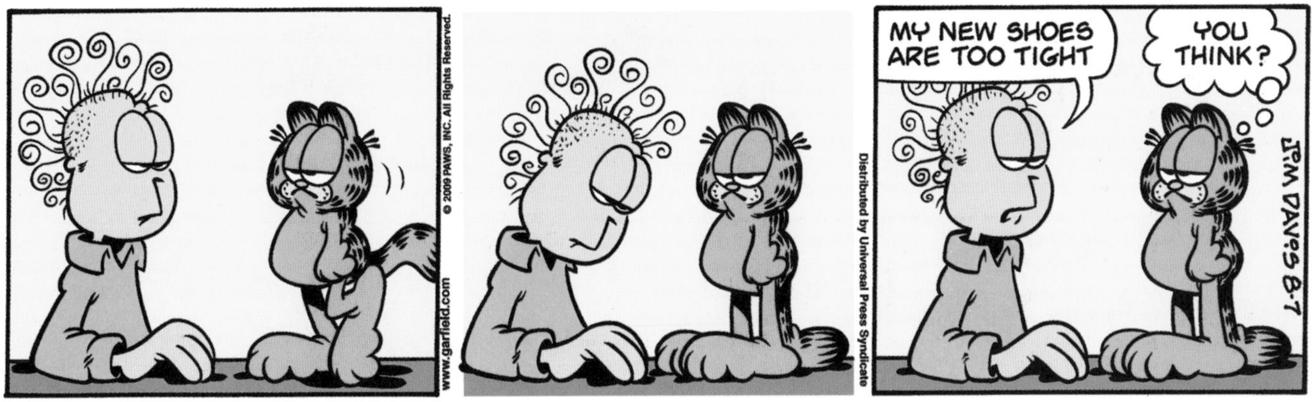
MY NEW SHOES ARE TOO TIGHT
YOU THINK?
JIM DAVIS 8-7

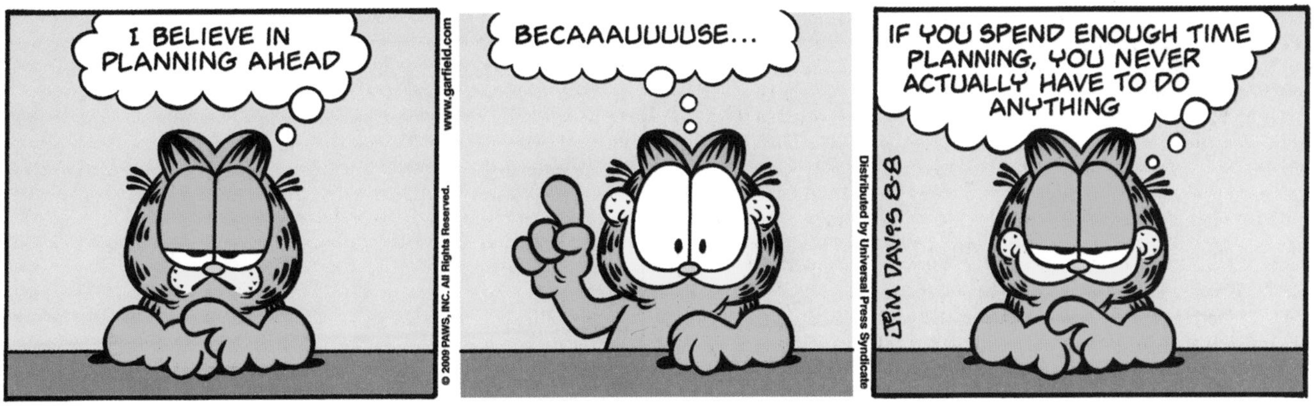
I BELIEVE IN PLANNING AHEAD
BECAAAUUUUSE...
IF YOU SPEND ENOUGH TIME PLANNING, YOU NEVER ACTUALLY HAVE TO DO ANYTHING
JIM DAVIS 8-8

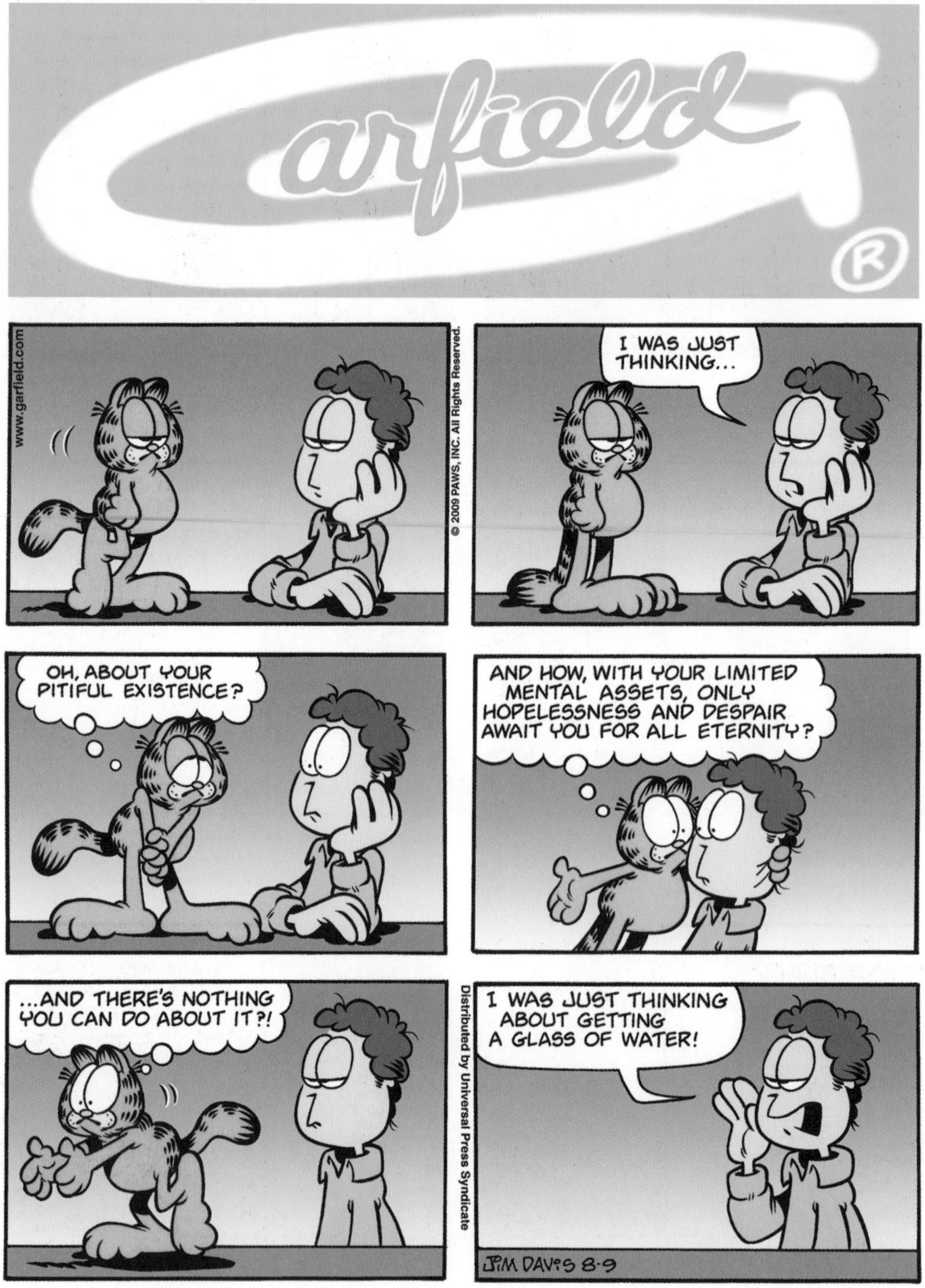
Garfield®
www.garfield.com
© 2009 PAWS, INC. All Rights Reserved.
I WAS JUST THINKING...
OH, ABOUT YOUR PITIFUL EXISTENCE?
AND HOW, WITH YOUR LIMITED MENTAL ASSETS, ONLY HOPELESSNESS AND DESPAIR AWAIT YOU FOR ALL ETERNITY?
...AND THERE'S NOTHING YOU CAN DO ABOUT IT?!
Distributed by Universal Press Syndicate
I WAS JUST THINKING ABOUT GETTING A GLASS OF WATER!
JIM DAVIS 8-9

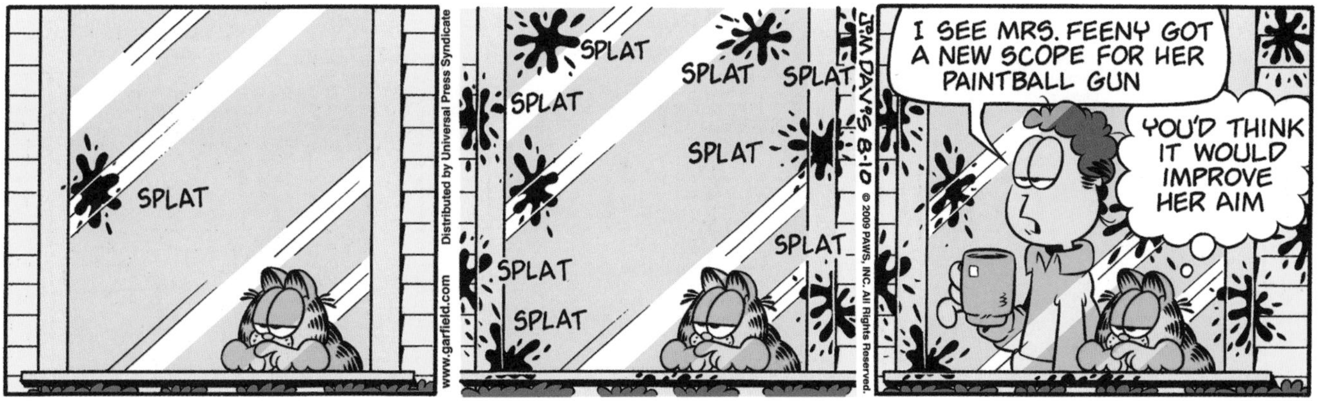
SPLAT
SPLAT
SPLAT
SPLAT
SPLAT
SPLAT
SPLAT
SPLAT
I SEE MRS. FEENY GOT A NEW SCOPE FOR HER PAINTBALL GUN
YOU'D THINK IT WOULD IMPROVE HER AIM
JIM DAVIS 8-10
www.garfield.com
Distributed by Universal Press Syndicate
© 2009 PAWS, INC. All Rights Reserved.

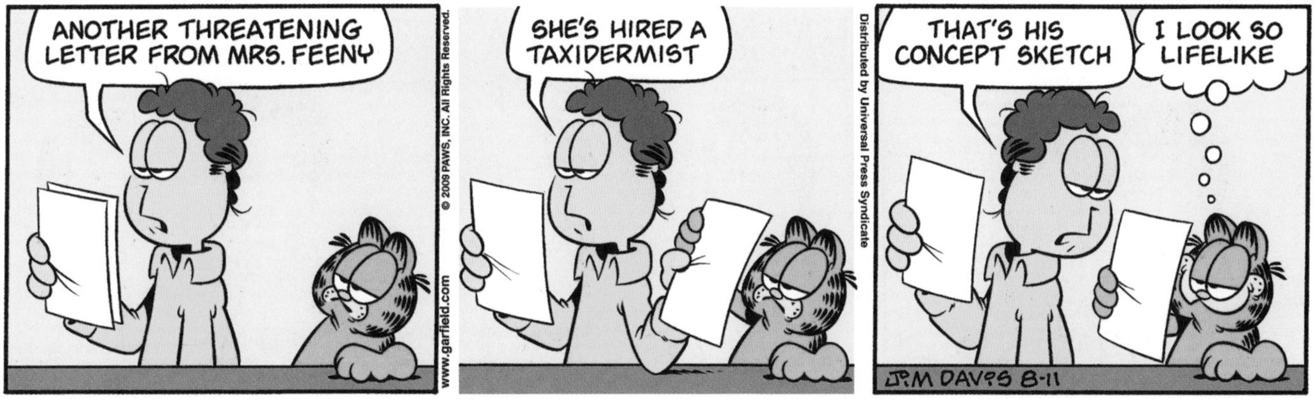
ANOTHER THREATENING LETTER FROM MRS. FEENY
SHE'S HIRED A TAXIDERMIST
THAT'S HIS CONCEPT SKETCH
I LOOK SO LIFELIKE
JIM DAVIS 8-11
www.garfield.com
© 2009 PAWS, INC. All Rights Reserved.
Distributed by Universal Press Syndicate

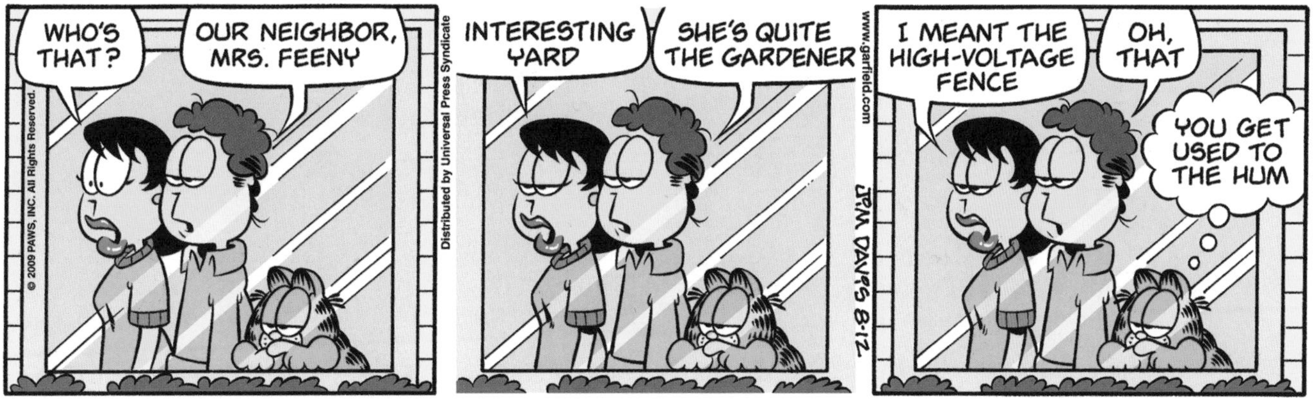
WHO'S THAT?
OUR NEIGHBOR, MRS. FEENY
INTERESTING YARD
SHE'S QUITE THE GARDENER
I MEANT THE HIGH-VOLTAGE FENCE
OH, THAT
YOU GET USED TO THE HUM
JIM DAVIS 8-12
© 2009 PAWS, INC. All Rights Reserved.
Distributed by Universal Press Syndicate
www.garfield.com

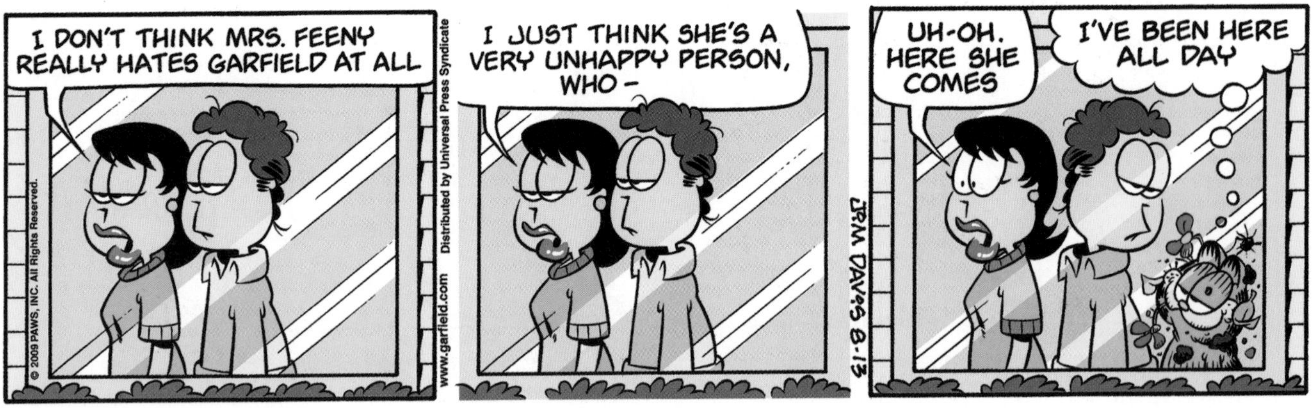
I DON'T THINK MRS. FEENY REALLY HATES GARFIELD AT ALL
I JUST THINK SHE'S A VERY UNHAPPY PERSON, WHO –
UH-OH. HERE SHE COMES
I'VE BEEN HERE ALL DAY
JIM DAVIS 8-13
© 2009 PAWS, INC. All Rights Reserved.
www.garfield.com Distributed by Universal Press Syndicate

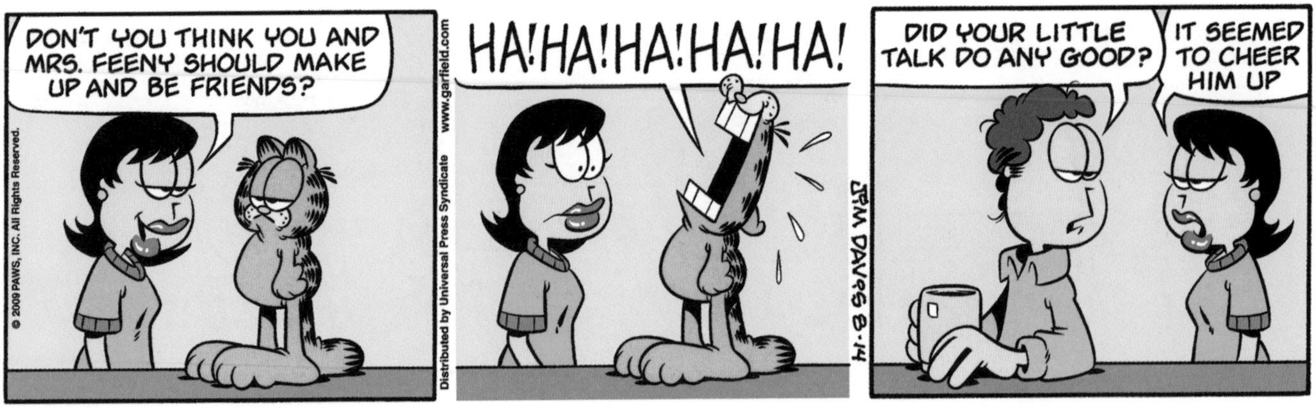
DON'T YOU THINK YOU AND MRS. FEENY SHOULD MAKE UP AND BE FRIENDS?
HA! HA! HA! HA! HA!
DID YOUR LITTLE TALK DO ANY GOOD?
IT SEEMED TO CHEER HIM UP
JIM DAVIS 8-14
© 2009 PAWS, INC. All Rights Reserved.
www.garfield.com Distributed by Universal Press Syndicate

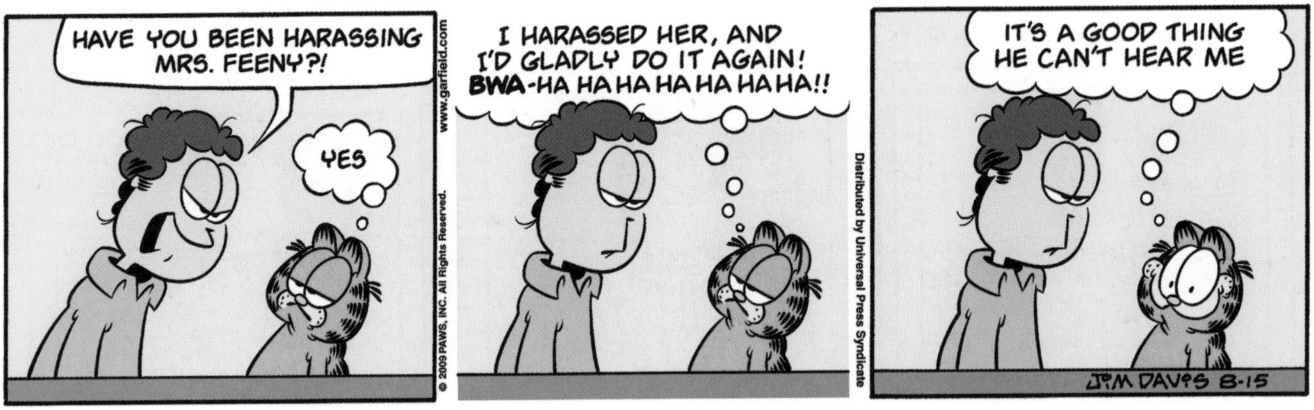
HAVE YOU BEEN HARASSING MRS. FEENY?!
YES
I HARASSED HER, AND I'D GLADLY DO IT AGAIN! **BWA**-HA HA HA HA HA HA HA HA!!
IT'S A GOOD THING HE CAN'T HEAR ME
JIM DAVIS 8-15
© 2009 PAWS, INC. All Rights Reserved. www.garfield.com
Distributed by Universal Press Syndicate

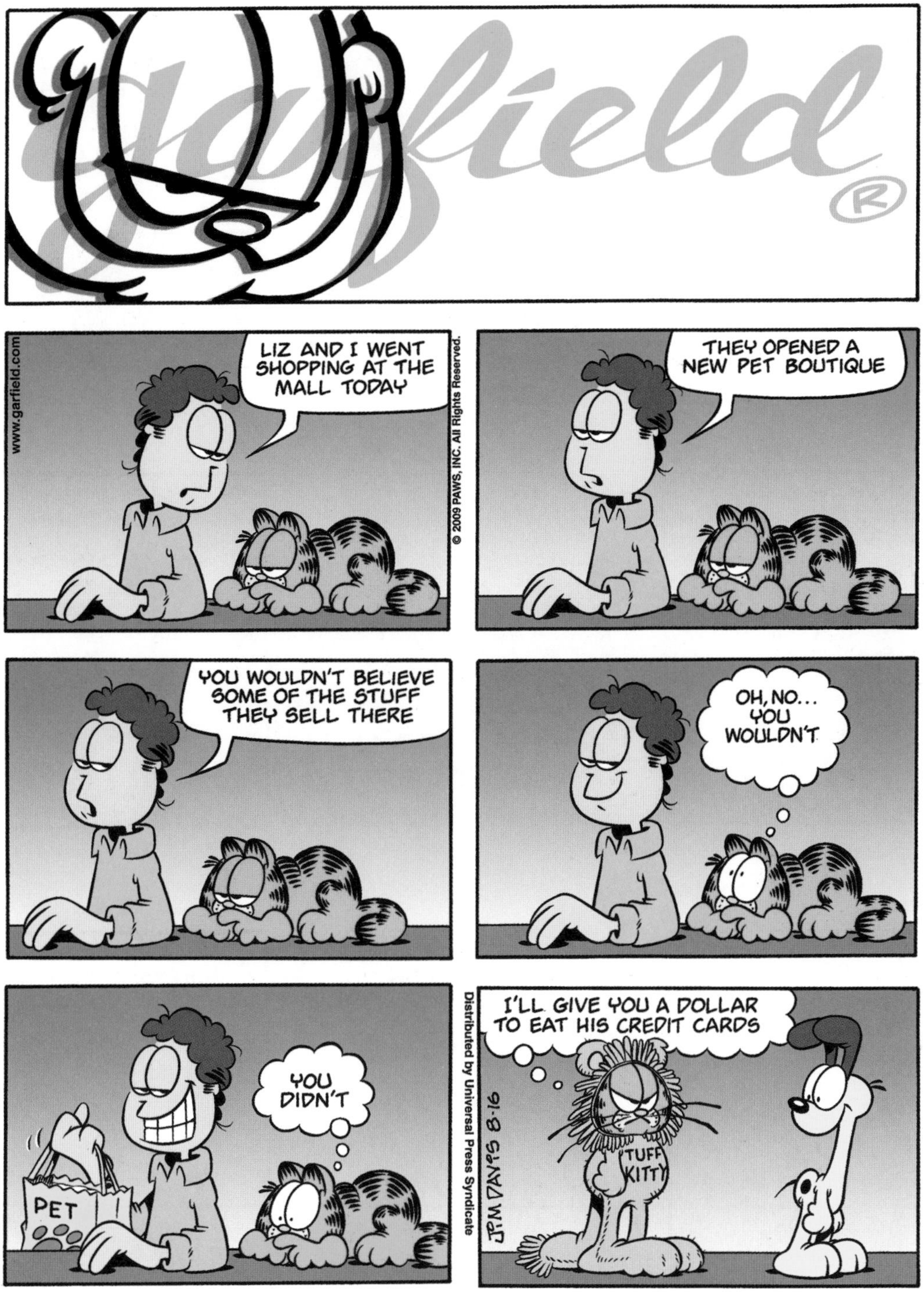
garfield®
www.garfield.com
LIZ AND I WENT SHOPPING AT THE MALL TODAY
© 2009 PAWS, INC. All Rights Reserved.
THEY OPENED A NEW PET BOUTIQUE
YOU WOULDN'T BELIEVE SOME OF THE STUFF THEY SELL THERE
OH, NO... YOU WOULDN'T
PET
YOU DIDN'T
Distributed by Universal Press Syndicate
JPM DAVIS 8-16
I'LL GIVE YOU A DOLLAR TO EAT HIS CREDIT CARDS
TUFF KITTY

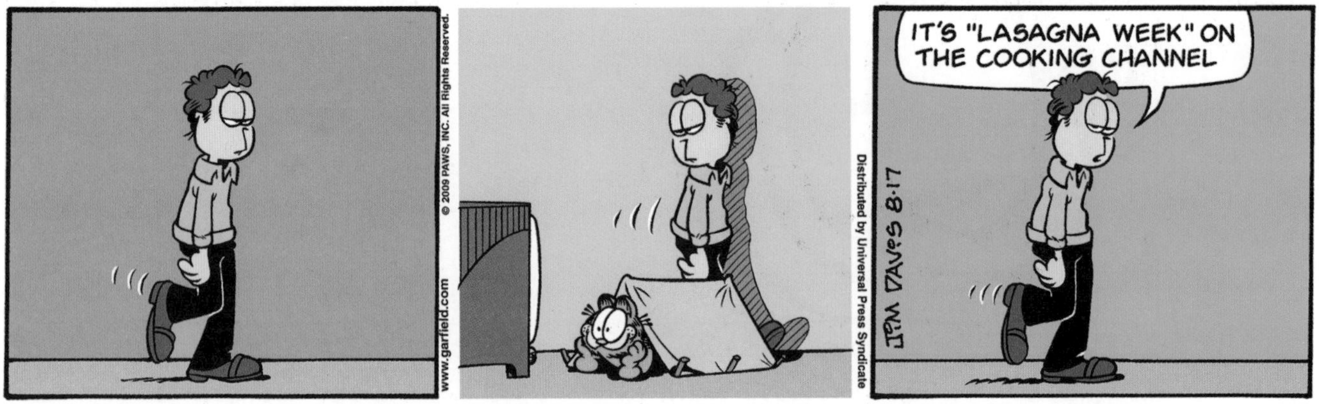
IT'S "LASAGNA WEEK" ON THE COOKING CHANNEL
JIM DAVIS 8-17

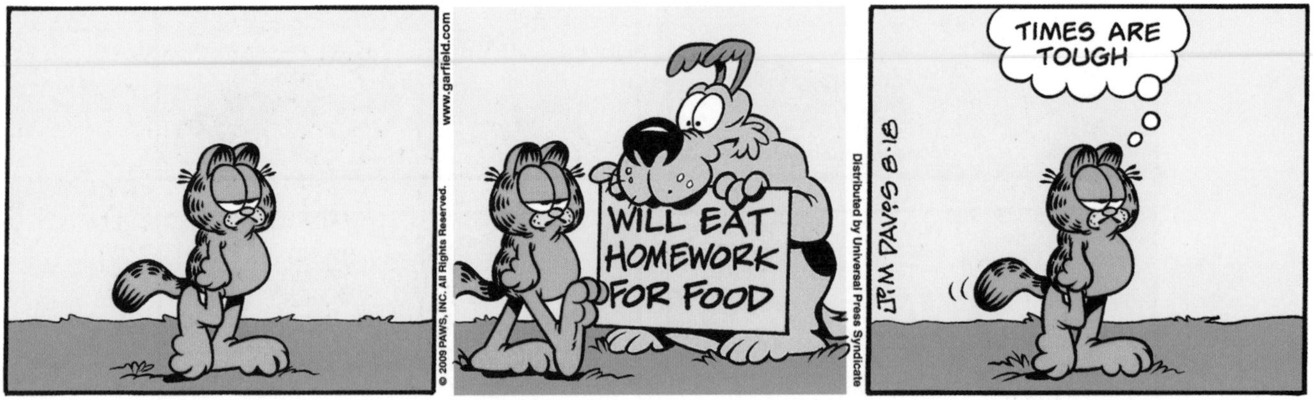
WILL EAT HOMEWORK FOR FOOD
TIMES ARE TOUGH
JIM DAVIS 8-18

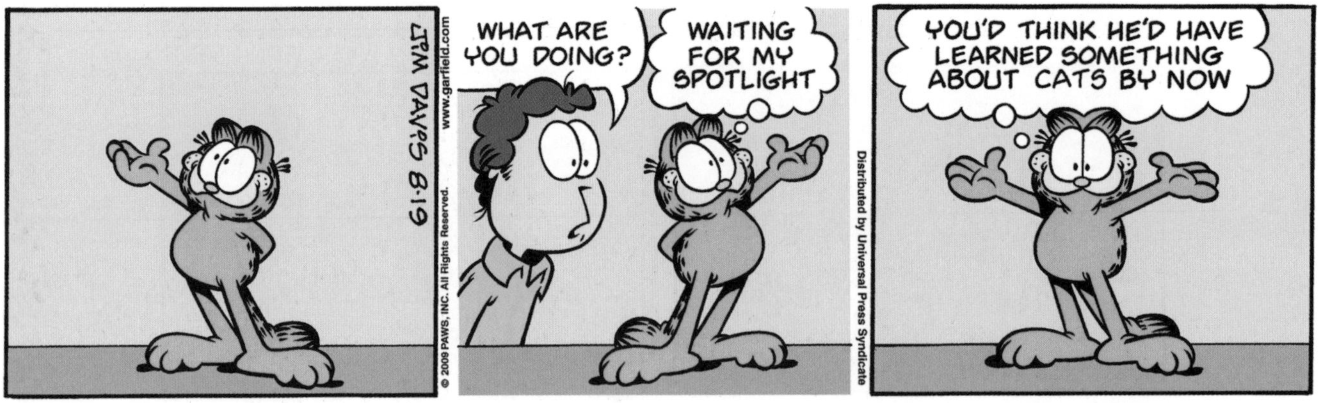
WHAT ARE YOU DOING?
WAITING FOR MY SPOTLIGHT
YOU'D THINK HE'D HAVE LEARNED SOMETHING ABOUT CATS BY NOW
JIM DAVIS 8-19

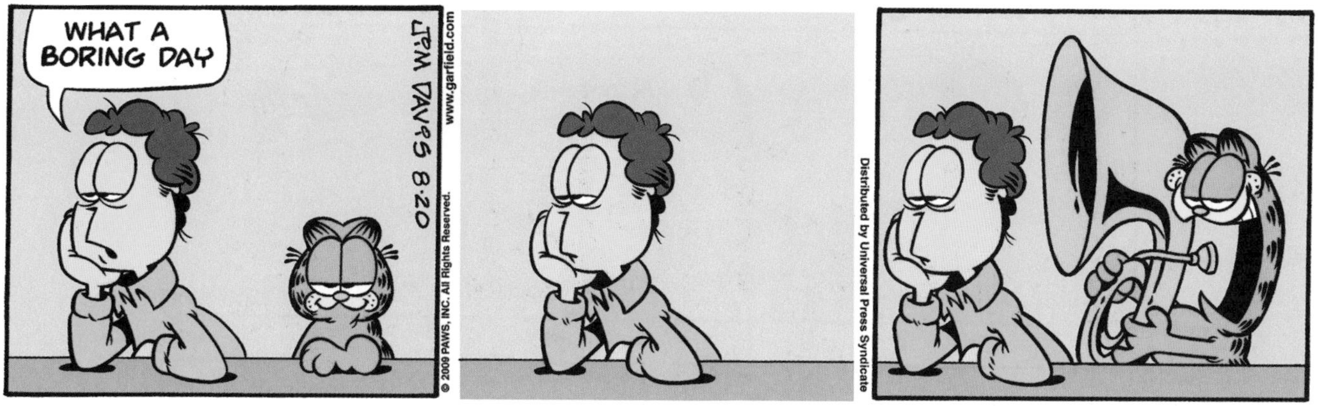
WHAT A BORING DAY
JIM DAVIS 8-20
www.garfield.com
© 2009 PAWS, INC. All Rights Reserved.
Distributed by Universal Press Syndicate

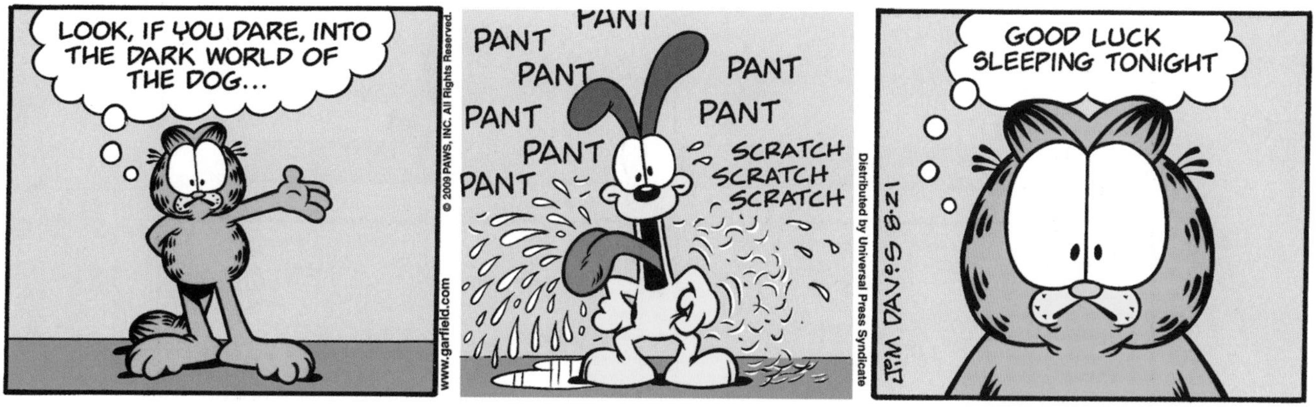
LOOK, IF YOU DARE, INTO THE DARK WORLD OF THE DOG...
© 2009 PAWS, INC. All Rights Reserved.
www.garfield.com
PANT
PANT
PANT
PANT
PANT
PANT
PANT
PANT
SCRATCH
SCRATCH
SCRATCH
Distributed by Universal Press Syndicate
JIM DAVIS 8-21
GOOD LUCK SLEEPING TONIGHT

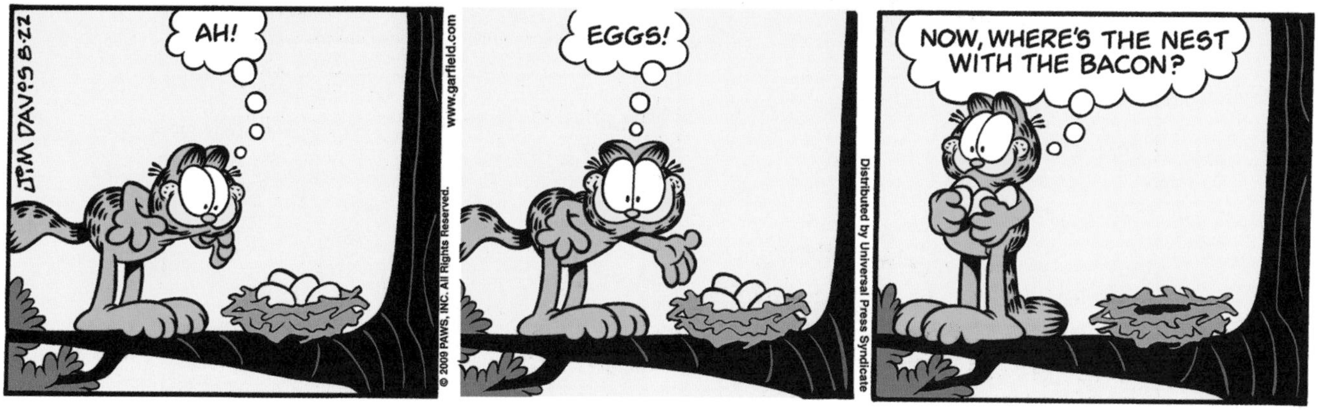
JIM DAVIS 8-22
AH!
www.garfield.com
© 2009 PAWS, INC. All Rights Reserved.
EGGS!
Distributed by Universal Press Syndicate
NOW, WHERE'S THE NEST WITH THE BACON?

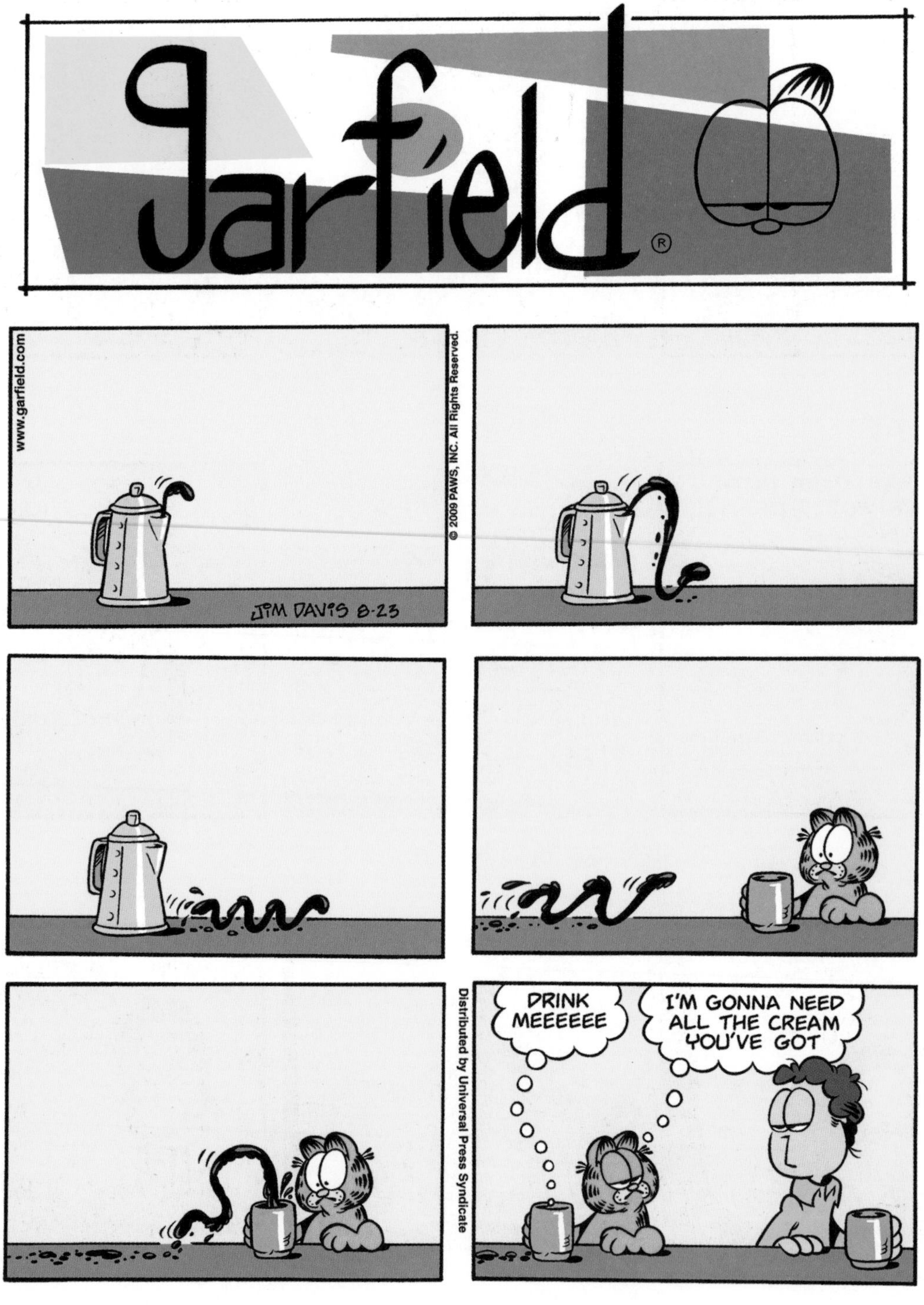
garfield
www.garfield.com
© 2009 PAWS, INC. All Rights Reserved.
JIM DAVIS 8-23
Distributed by Universal Press Syndicate
DRINK MEEEEEE
I'M GONNA NEED ALL THE CREAM YOU'VE GOT

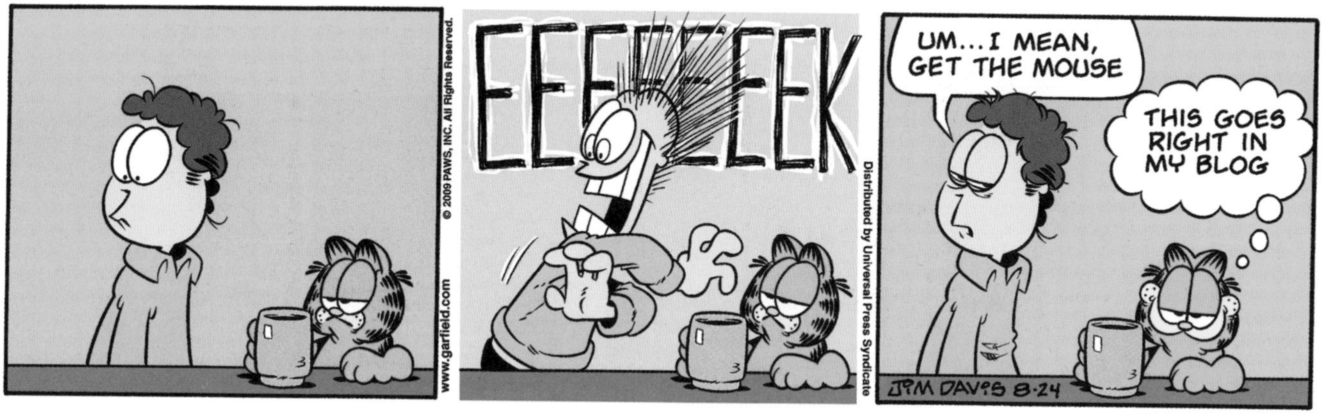
EEEEEEEEK
UM... I MEAN, GET THE MOUSE
THIS GOES RIGHT IN MY BLOG
JIM DAVIS 8-24

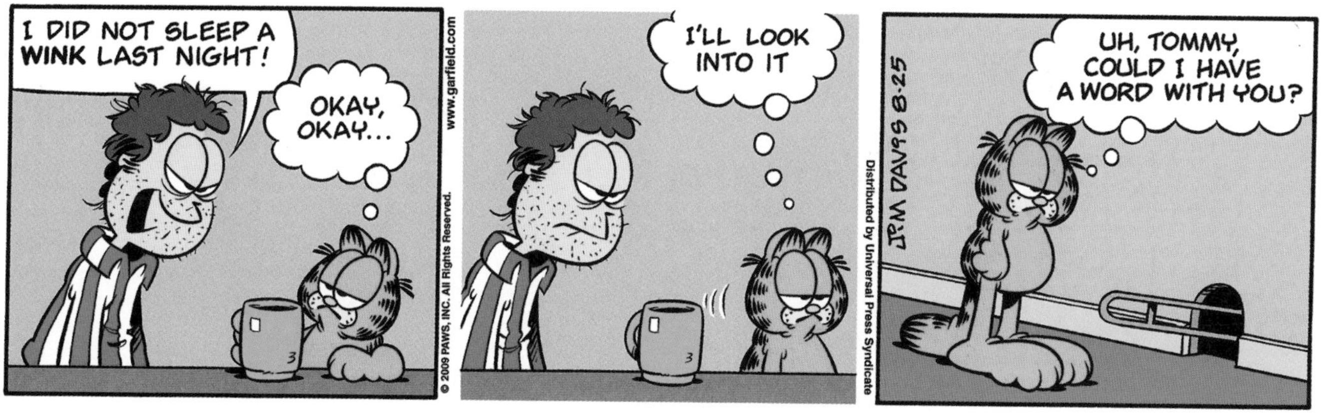
I DID NOT SLEEP A WINK LAST NIGHT!
OKAY, OKAY...
I'LL LOOK INTO IT
UH, TOMMY, COULD I HAVE A WORD WITH YOU?
JIM DAVIS 8-25

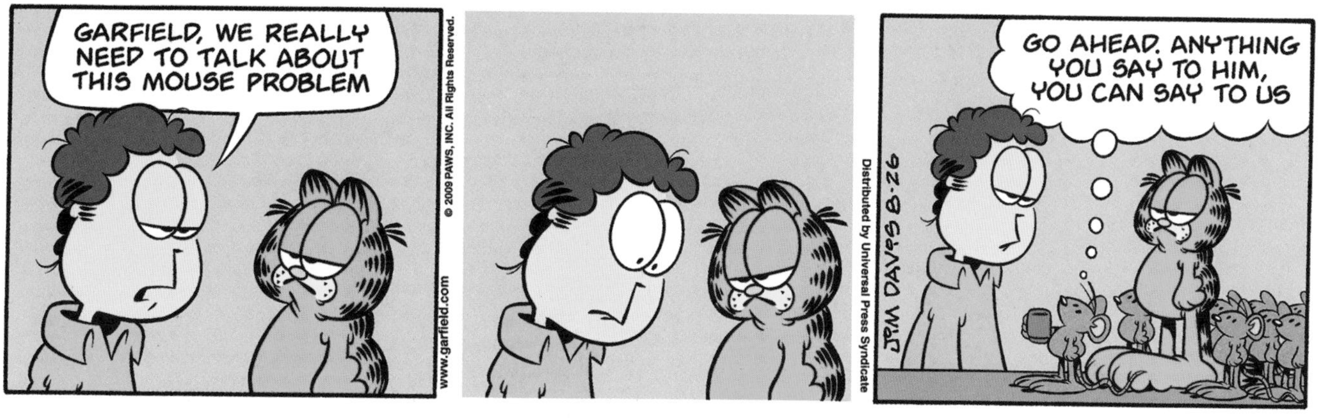
GARFIELD, WE REALLY NEED TO TALK ABOUT THIS MOUSE PROBLEM
GO AHEAD. ANYTHING YOU SAY TO HIM, YOU CAN SAY TO US
JIM DAVIS 8-26

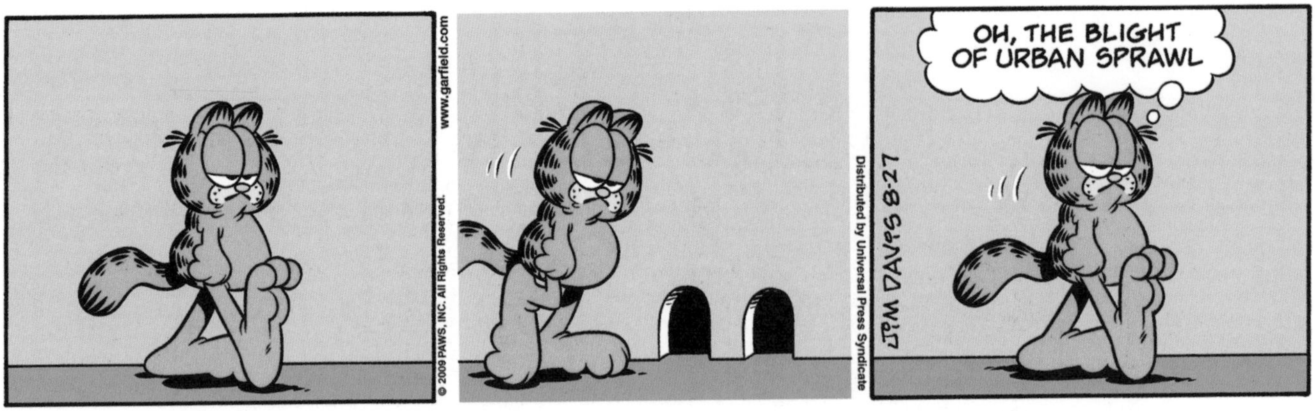
www.garfield.com
© 2009 PAWS, INC. All Rights Reserved.
Distributed by Universal Press Syndicate
JIM DAVIS 8-27
OH, THE BLIGHT OF URBAN SPRAWL

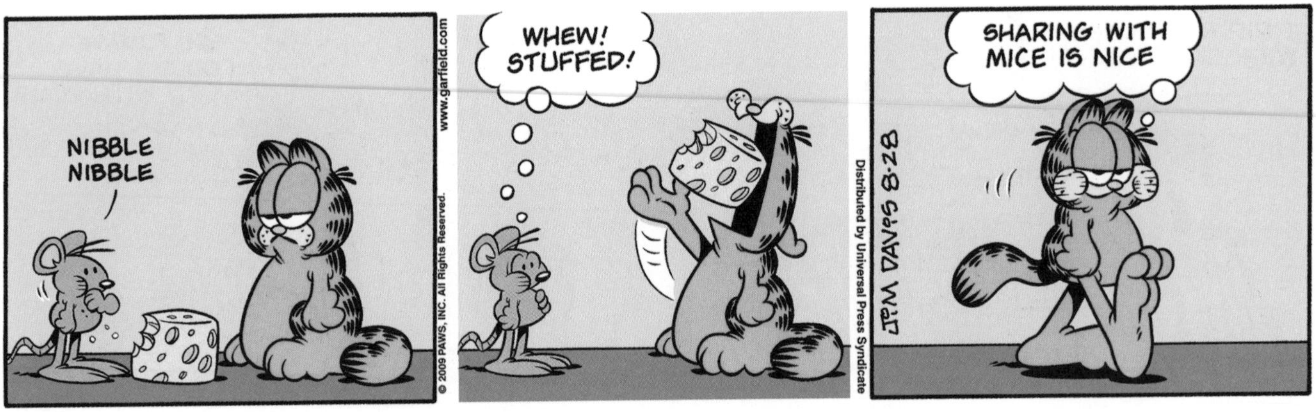
NIBBLE NIBBLE
www.garfield.com
© 2009 PAWS, INC. All Rights Reserved.
WHEW! STUFFED!
Distributed by Universal Press Syndicate
JIM DAVIS 8-28
SHARING WITH MICE IS NICE

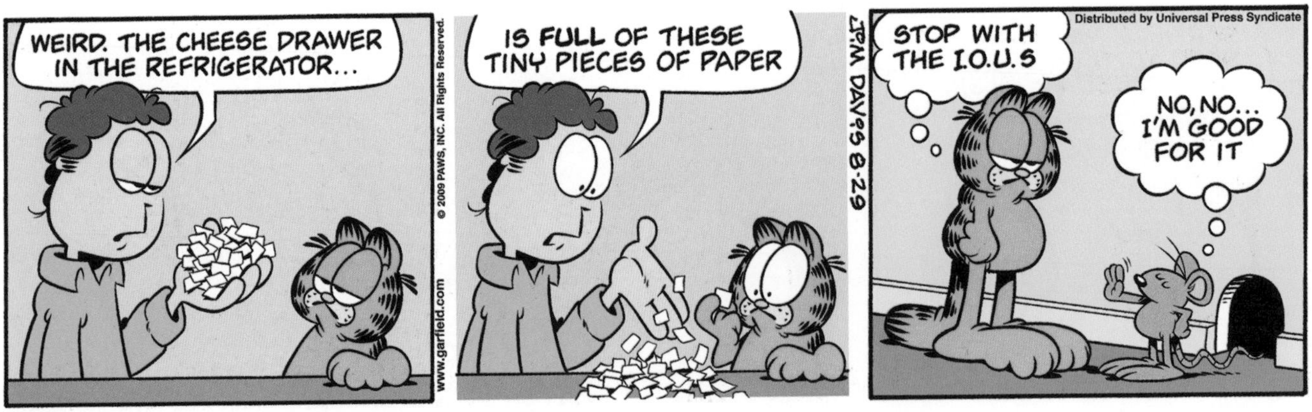
WEIRD. THE CHEESE DRAWER IN THE REFRIGERATOR...
© 2009 PAWS, INC. All Rights Reserved.
www.garfield.com
IS FULL OF THESE TINY PIECES OF PAPER
JIM DAVIS 8-29
Distributed by Universal Press Syndicate
STOP WITH THE I.O.U.S
NO, NO... I'M GOOD FOR IT

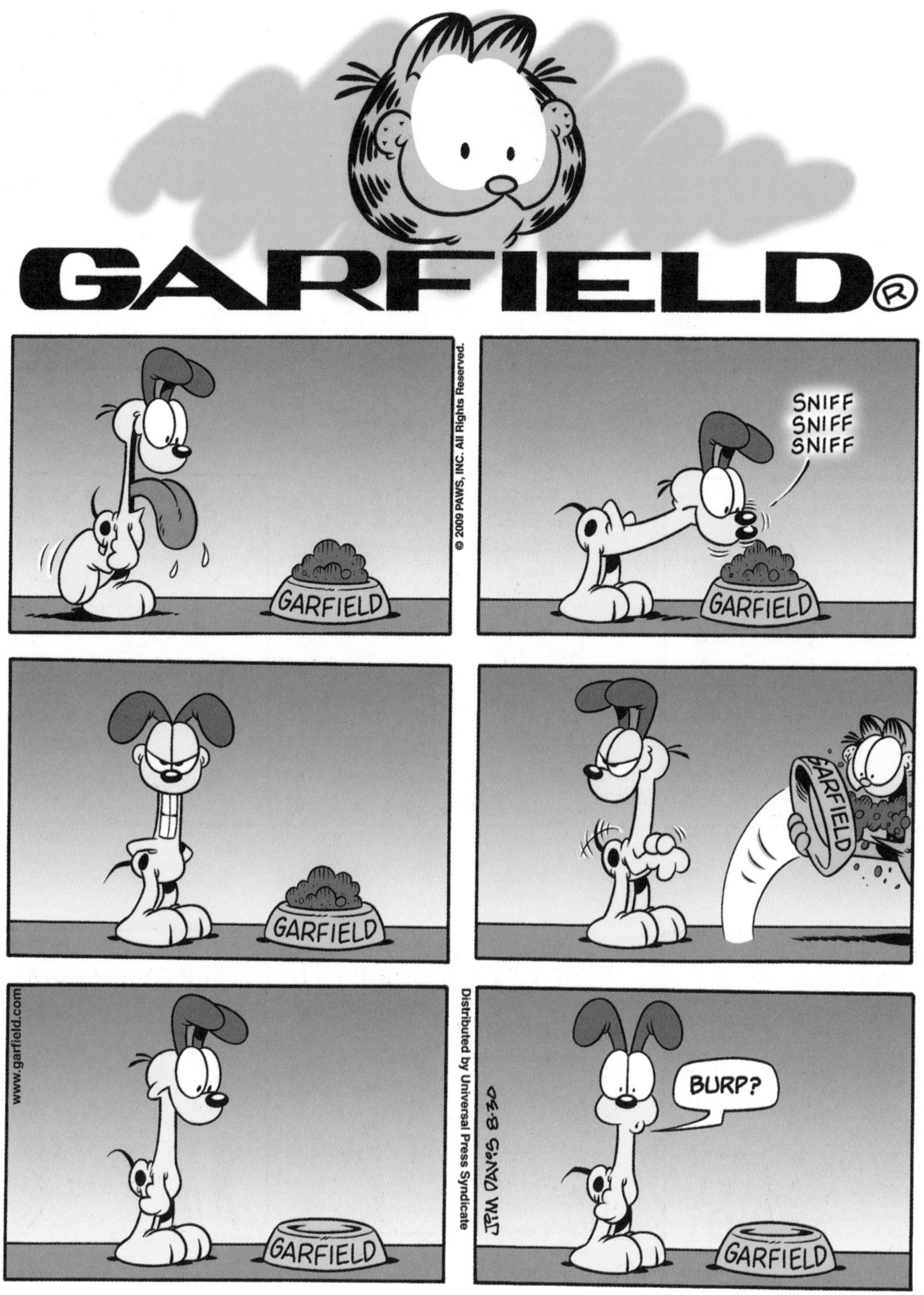
GARFIELD®
© 2009 PAWS, INC. All Rights Reserved.
GARFIELD
SNIFF
SNIFF
SNIFF
GARFIELD
GARFIELD
GARFIELD
www.garfield.com
Distributed by Universal Press Syndicate
JPM DAVIS 8-30
GARFIELD
BURP?
GARFIELD

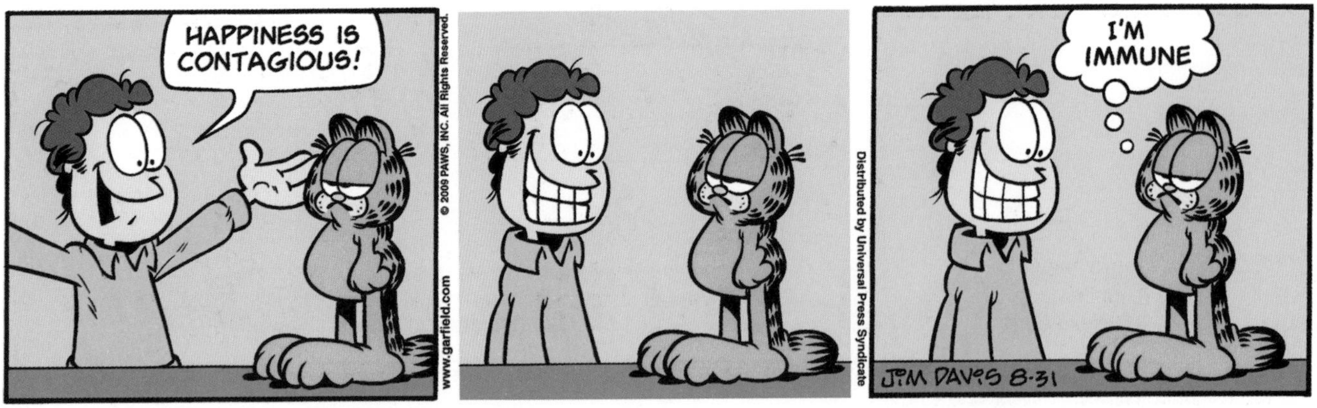
HAPPINESS IS CONTAGIOUS!
I'M IMMUNE
© 2009 PAWS, INC. All Rights Reserved.
www.garfield.com
Distributed by Universal Press Syndicate
JIM DAVIS 8-31

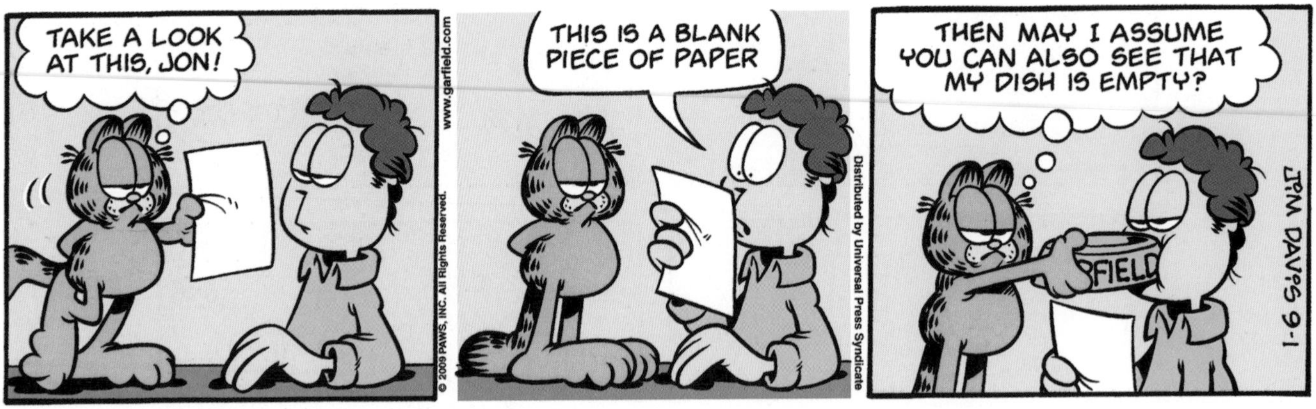
TAKE A LOOK AT THIS, JON!
THIS IS A BLANK PIECE OF PAPER
THEN MAY I ASSUME YOU CAN ALSO SEE THAT MY DISH IS EMPTY?
RFIELD
www.garfield.com
© 2009 PAWS, INC. All Rights Reserved.
Distributed by Universal Press Syndicate
JIM DAVIS 9-1

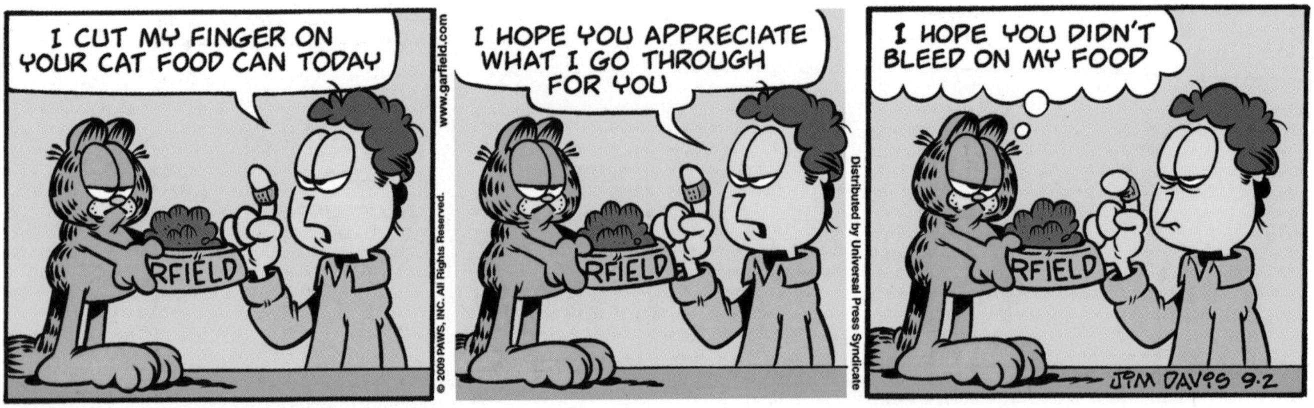
I CUT MY FINGER ON YOUR CAT FOOD CAN TODAY
I HOPE YOU APPRECIATE WHAT I GO THROUGH FOR YOU
I HOPE YOU DIDN'T BLEED ON MY FOOD
RFIELD
www.garfield.com
© 2009 PAWS, INC. All Rights Reserved.
Distributed by Universal Press Syndicate
JIM DAVIS 9-2

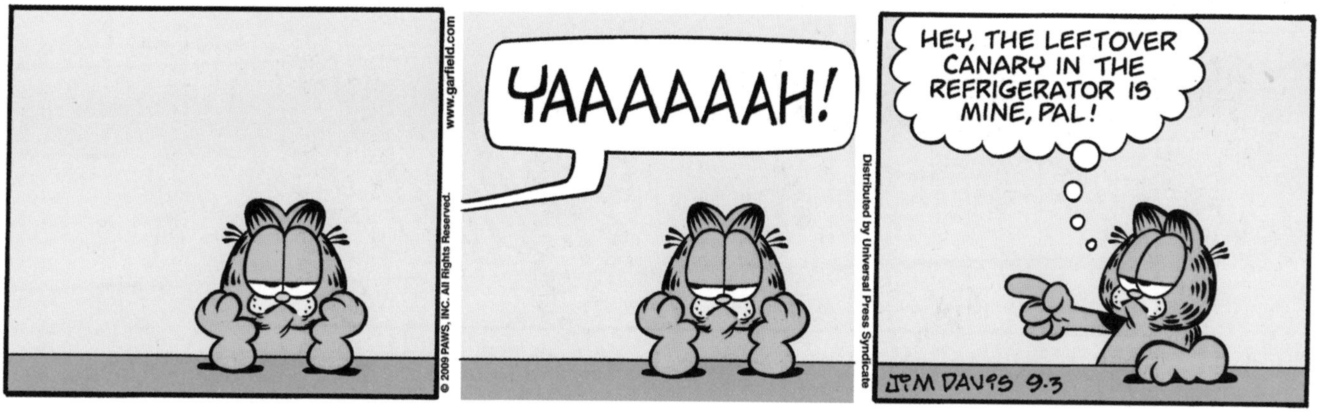
YAAAAAAH!
HEY, THE LEFTOVER CANARY IN THE REFRIGERATOR IS MINE, PAL!
www.garfield.com
© 2009 PAWS, INC. All Rights Reserved.
Distributed by Universal Press Syndicate
JIM DAVIS 9-3

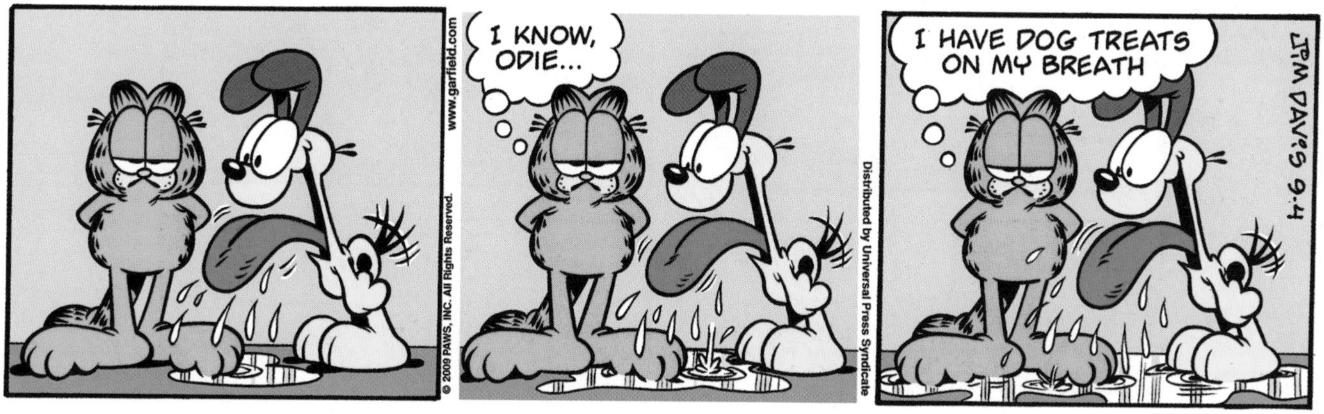
I KNOW, ODIE...
I HAVE DOG TREATS ON MY BREATH
www.garfield.com
© 2009 PAWS, INC. All Rights Reserved.
Distributed by Universal Press Syndicate
JIM DAVIS 9-4

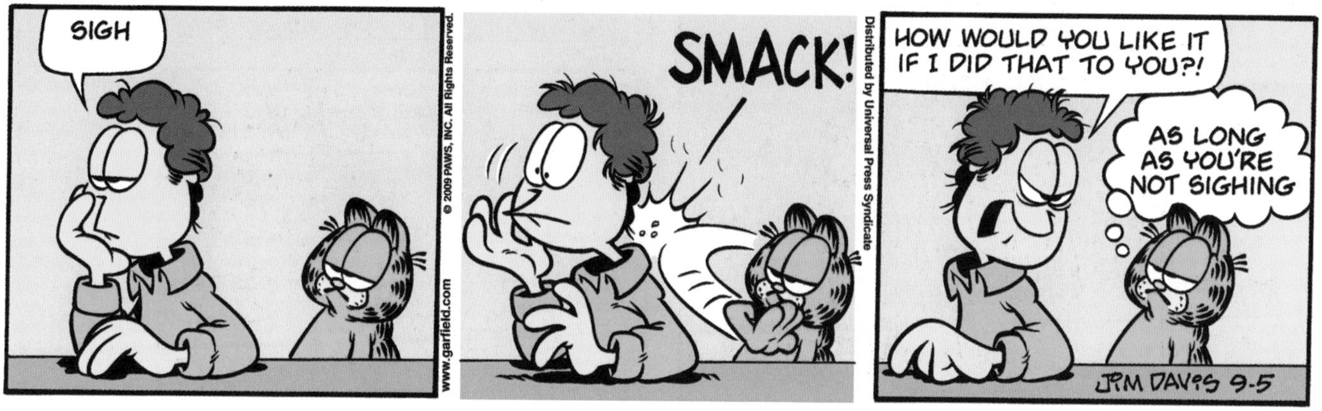
SIGH
SMACK!
HOW WOULD YOU LIKE IT IF I DID THAT TO YOU?!
AS LONG AS YOU'RE NOT SIGHING
© 2009 PAWS, INC. All Rights Reserved.
www.garfield.com
Distributed by Universal Press Syndicate
JIM DAVIS 9-5

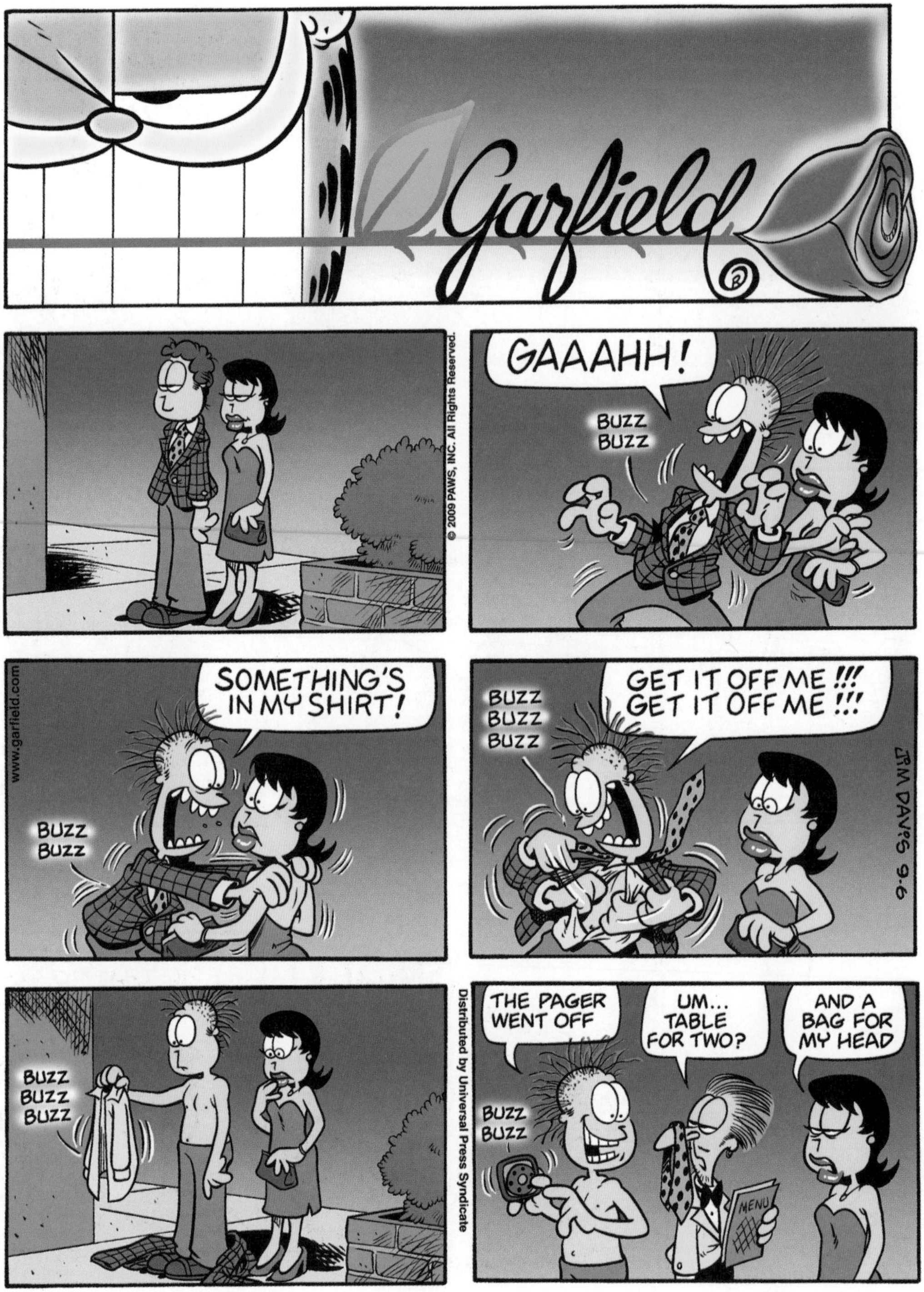
Garfield
© 2009 PAWS, INC. All Rights Reserved.
GAAAHH!
BUZZ BUZZ
www.garfield.com
SOMETHING'S IN MY SHIRT!
BUZZ BUZZ
GET IT OFF ME!!! GET IT OFF ME!!!
BUZZ BUZZ BUZZ
JIM DAVIS 9-6
BUZZ BUZZ BUZZ
Distributed by Universal Press Syndicate
THE PAGER WENT OFF
BUZZ BUZZ
UM... TABLE FOR TWO?
MENU
AND A BAG FOR MY HEAD

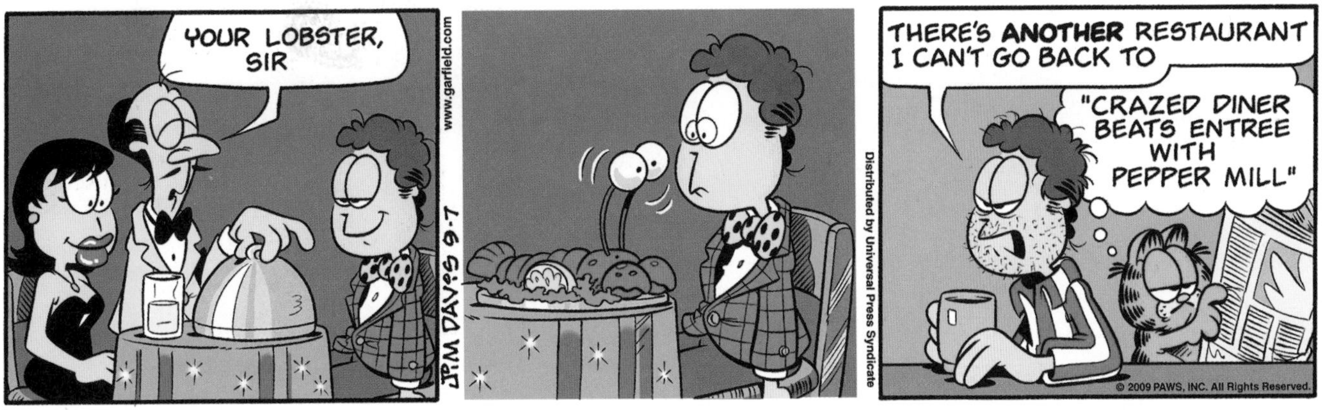
YOUR LOBSTER, SIR
www.garfield.com
JIM DAVIS 9-7
Distributed by Universal Press Syndicate
THERE'S **ANOTHER** RESTAURANT I CAN'T GO BACK TO
"CRAZED DINER BEATS ENTREE WITH PEPPER MILL"
© 2009 PAWS, INC. All Rights Reserved.

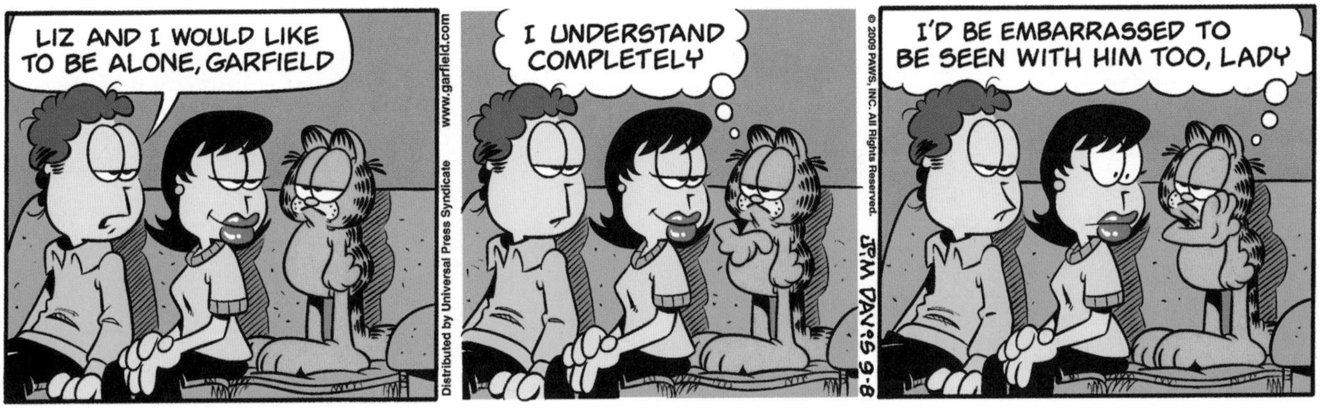
LIZ AND I WOULD LIKE TO BE ALONE, GARFIELD
www.garfield.com
Distributed by Universal Press Syndicate
I UNDERSTAND COMPLETELY
© 2009 PAWS, INC. All Rights Reserved.
JIM DAVIS 9-8
I'D BE EMBARRASSED TO BE SEEN WITH HIM TOO, LADY

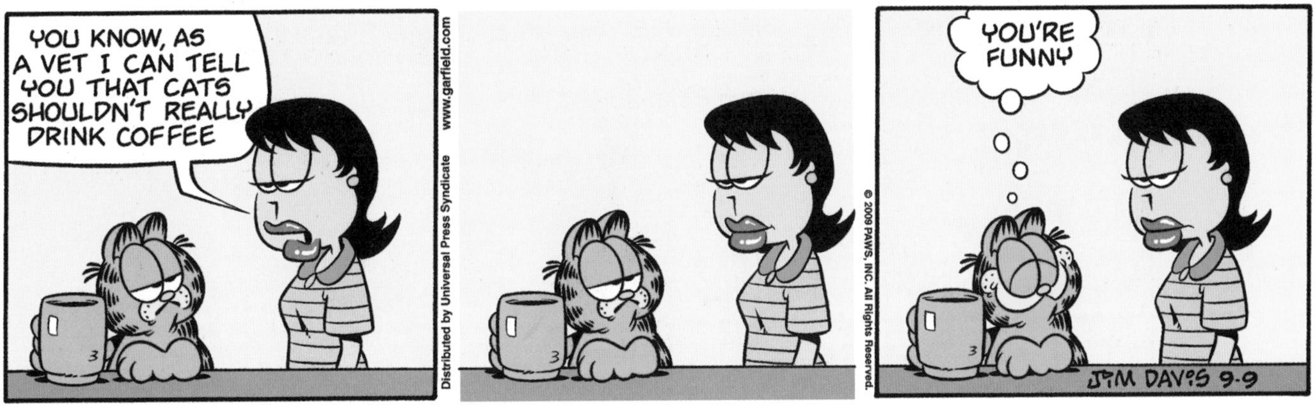
YOU KNOW, AS A VET I CAN TELL YOU THAT CATS SHOULDN'T REALLY DRINK COFFEE
www.garfield.com
Distributed by Universal Press Syndicate
© 2009 PAWS, INC. All Rights Reserved.
YOU'RE FUNNY
JIM DAVIS 9-9

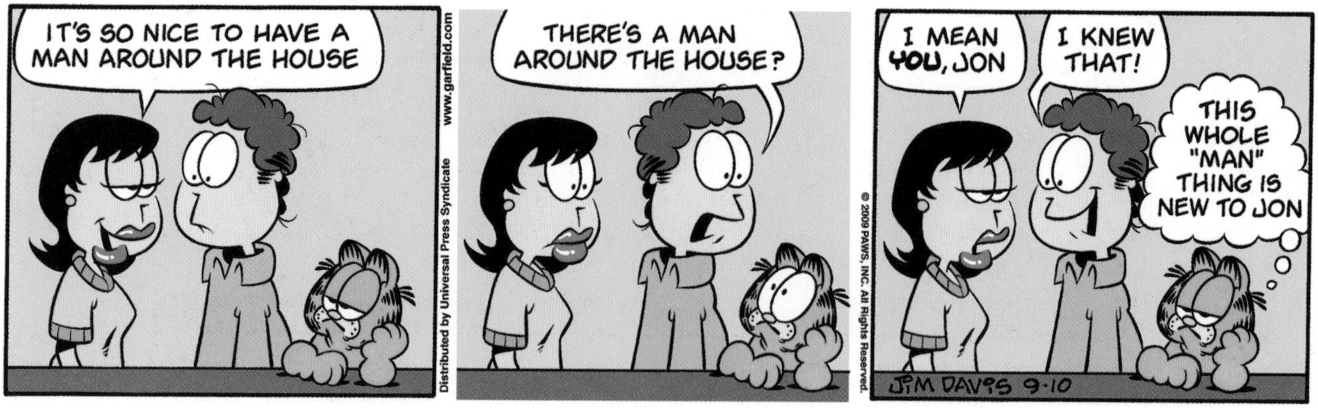
IT'S SO NICE TO HAVE A MAN AROUND THE HOUSE
www.garfield.com
Distributed by Universal Press Syndicate
THERE'S A MAN AROUND THE HOUSE?
© 2009 PAWS, INC. All Rights Reserved.
I MEAN YOU, JON
I KNEW THAT!
THIS WHOLE "MAN" THING IS NEW TO JON
JIM DAVIS 9-10

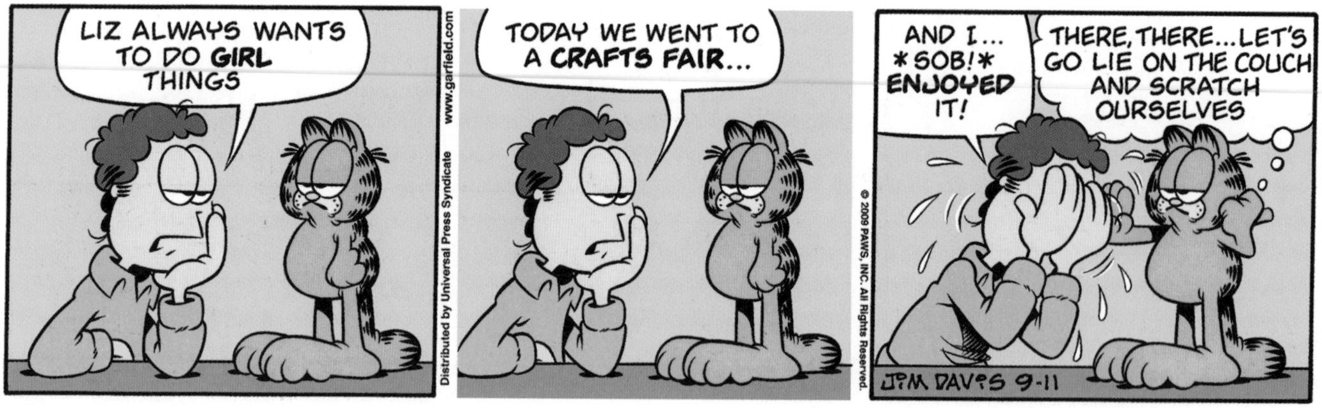
LIZ ALWAYS WANTS TO DO GIRL THINGS
www.garfield.com
Distributed by Universal Press Syndicate
TODAY WE WENT TO A CRAFTS FAIR...
© 2009 PAWS, INC. All Rights Reserved.
AND I... *SOB!* ENJOYED IT!
THERE, THERE...LET'S GO LIE ON THE COUCH AND SCRATCH OURSELVES
JIM DAVIS 9-11

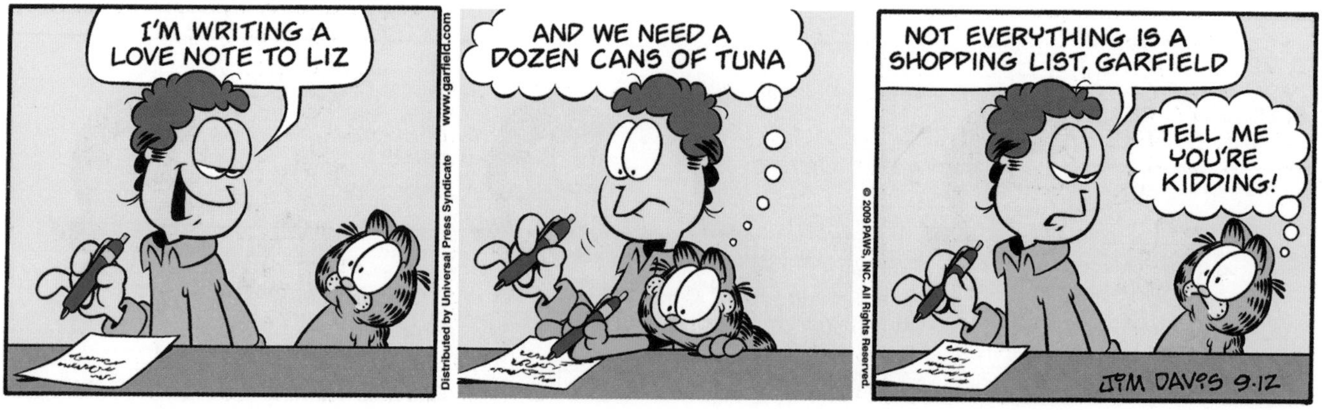
I'M WRITING A LOVE NOTE TO LIZ
www.garfield.com
Distributed by Universal Press Syndicate
AND WE NEED A DOZEN CANS OF TUNA
© 2009 PAWS, INC. All Rights Reserved.
NOT EVERYTHING IS A SHOPPING LIST, GARFIELD
TELL ME YOU'RE KIDDING!
JIM DAVIS 9-12

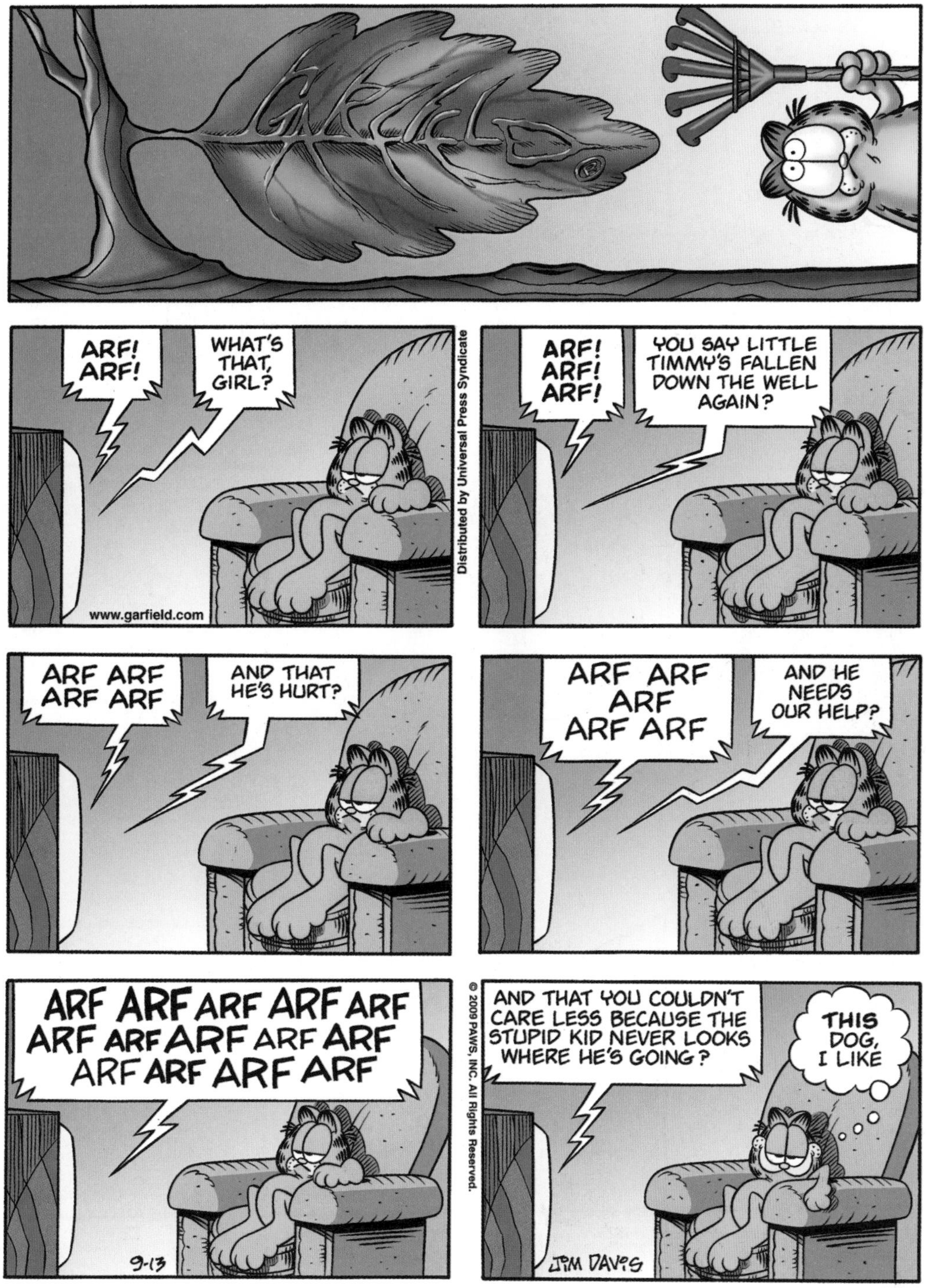
GARFIELD®
ARF! ARF!
WHAT'S THAT, GIRL?
www.garfield.com
Distributed by Universal Press Syndicate
ARF! ARF! ARF!
YOU SAY LITTLE TIMMY'S FALLEN DOWN THE WELL AGAIN?
ARF ARF ARF ARF
AND THAT HE'S HURT?
ARF ARF ARF ARF ARF
AND HE NEEDS OUR HELP?
ARF ARF ARF ARF ARF ARF ARF ARF ARF ARF ARF ARF ARF ARF
9-13
© 2009 PAWS, INC. All Rights Reserved.
AND THAT YOU COULDN'T CARE LESS BECAUSE THE STUPID KID NEVER LOOKS WHERE HE'S GOING?
THIS DOG, I LIKE
JIM DAVIS

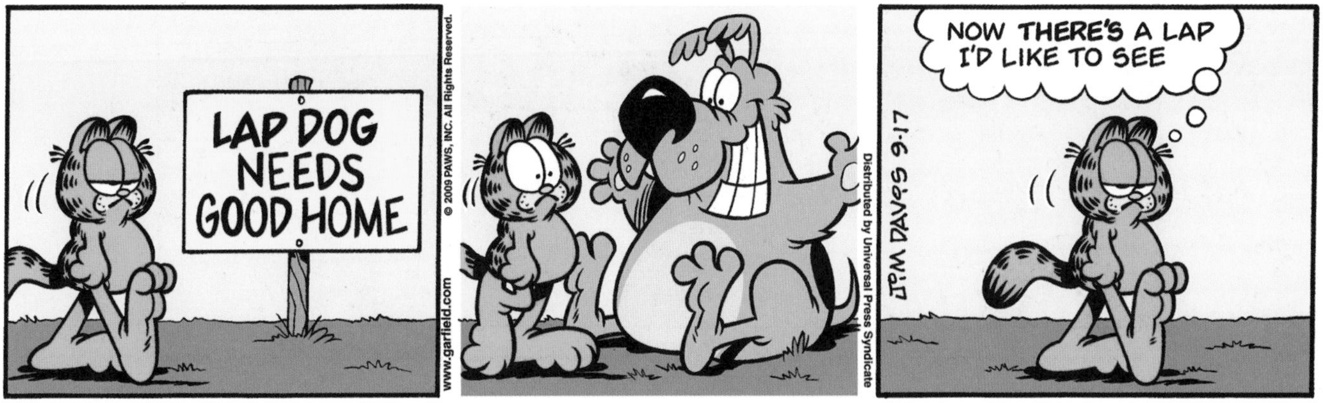
LAP DOG
NEEDS
GOOD HOME
© 2009 PAWS, INC. All Rights Reserved.
www.garfield.com
Distributed by Universal Press Syndicate
JPM DAVPS 9-17
NOW THERE'S A LAP
I'D LIKE TO SEE

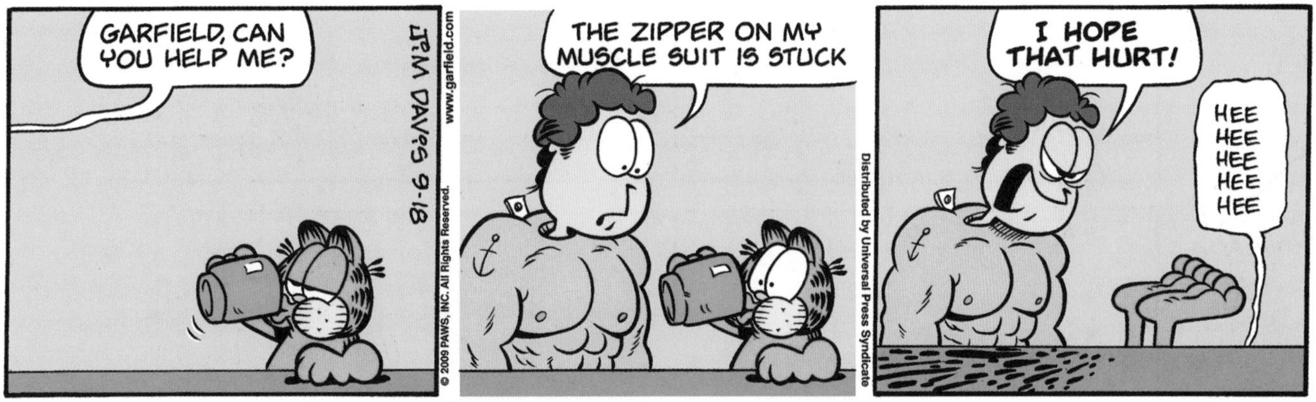
GARFIELD, CAN
YOU HELP ME?
JPM DAVPS 9-18
www.garfield.com
© 2009 PAWS, INC. All Rights Reserved.
THE ZIPPER ON MY
MUSCLE SUIT IS STUCK
Distributed by Universal Press Syndicate
I HOPE
THAT HURT!
HEE
HEE
HEE
HEE
HEE

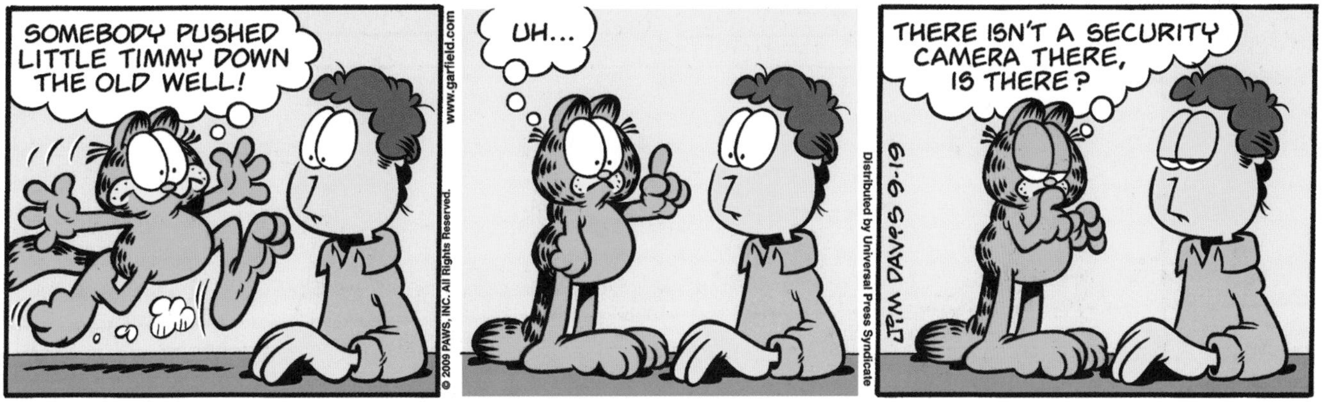
SOMEBODY PUSHED
LITTLE TIMMY DOWN
THE OLD WELL!
www.garfield.com
© 2009 PAWS, INC. All Rights Reserved.
UH...
Distributed by Universal Press Syndicate
JPM DAVPS 9-19
THERE ISN'T A SECURITY
CAMERA THERE,
IS THERE?

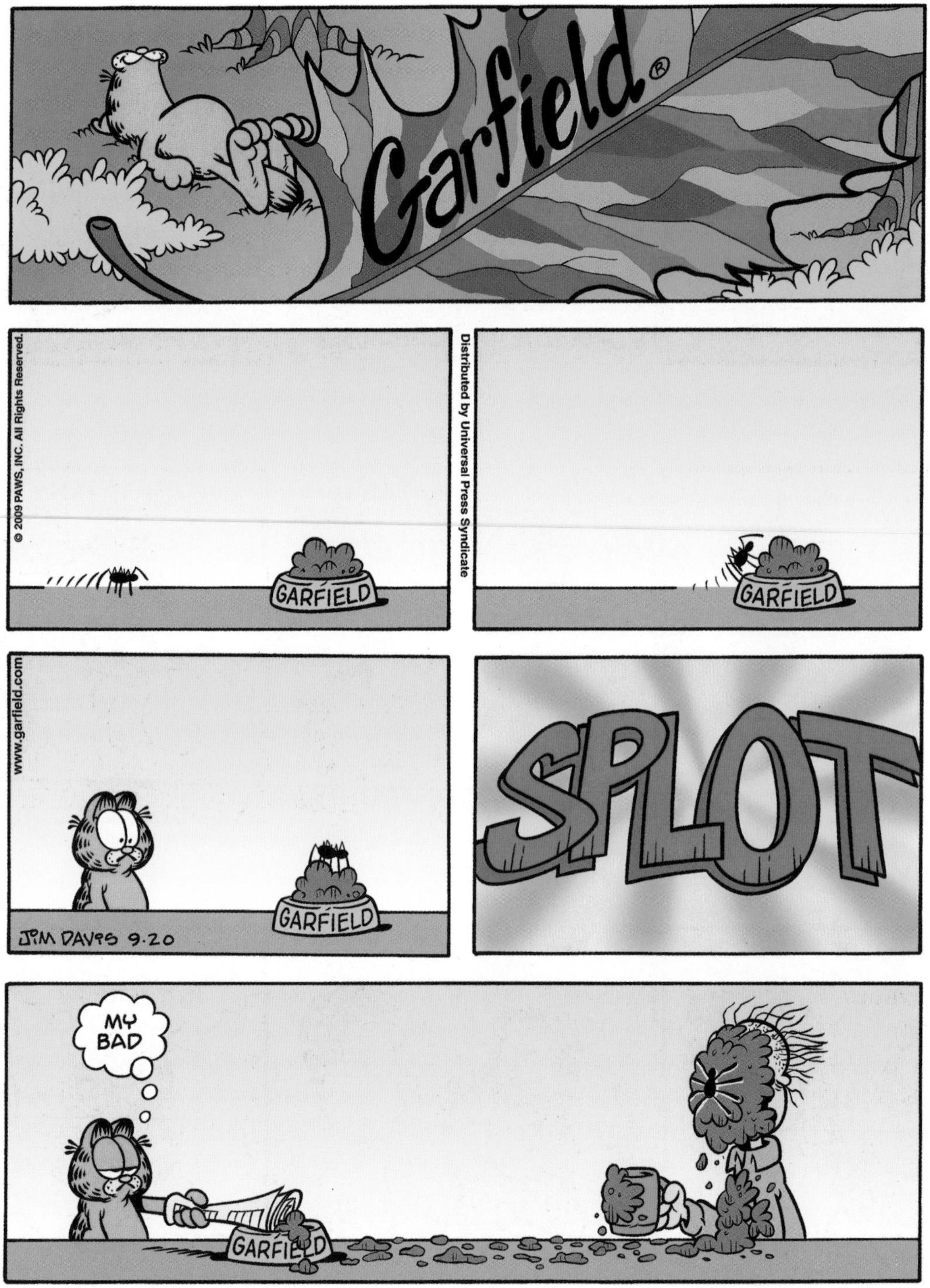

Garfield®
© 2009 PAWS, INC. All Rights Reserved.
Distributed by Universal Press Syndicate
GARFIELD
GARFIELD
www.garfield.com
GARFIELD
JIM DAVIS 9.20
SPLOT
MY BAD
GARFIELD

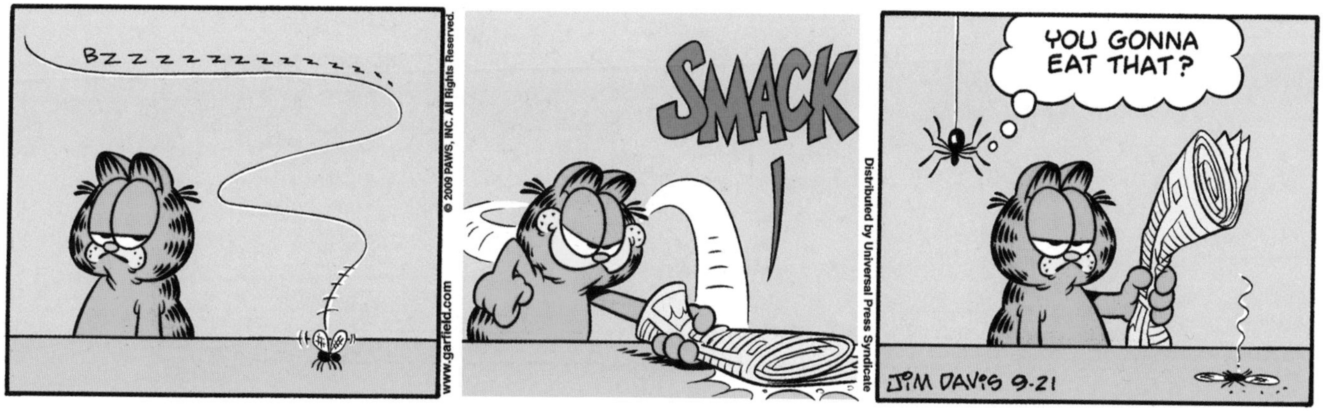
BZZZZZZZZZZZZZZ
© 2009 PAWS, INC. All Rights Reserved.
www.garfield.com
SMACK
Distributed by Universal Press Syndicate
YOU GONNA EAT THAT?
JIM DAVIS 9·21

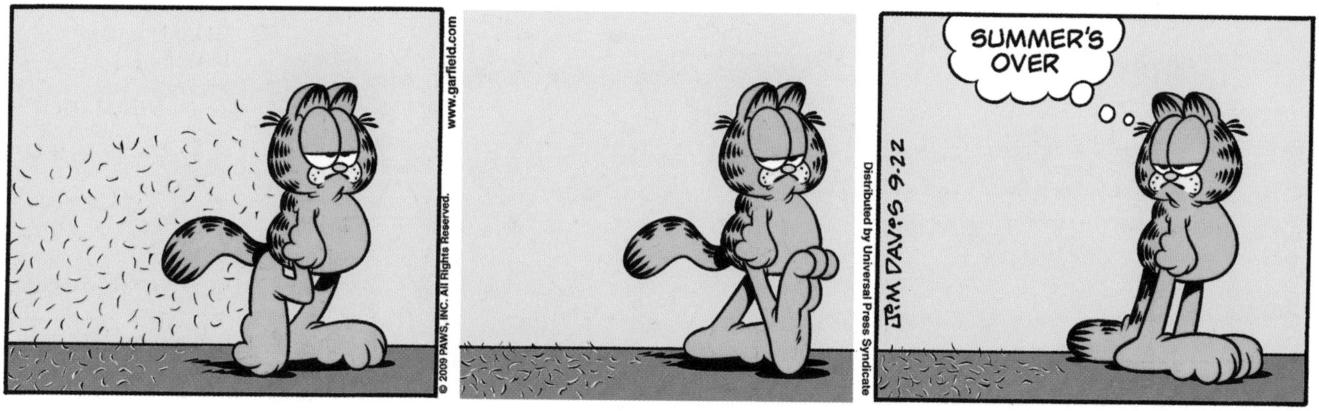
www.garfield.com
© 2009 PAWS, INC. All Rights Reserved.
Distributed by Universal Press Syndicate
JIM DAVIS 9·22
SUMMER'S OVER

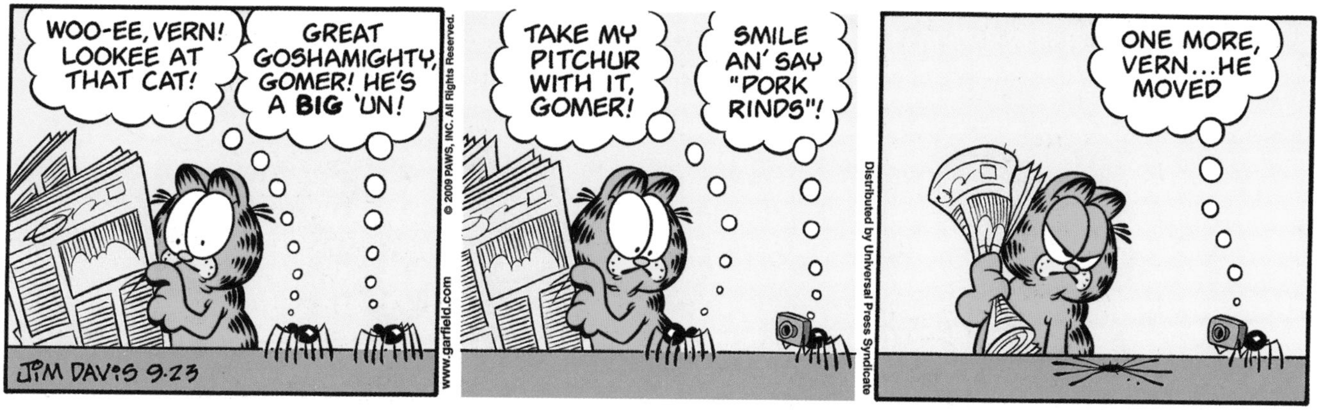
WOO-EE, VERN! LOOKEE AT THAT CAT!
GREAT GOSHAMIGHTY, GOMER! HE'S A BIG 'UN!
JIM DAVIS 9·23
© 2009 PAWS, INC. All Rights Reserved.
www.garfield.com
TAKE MY PITCHUR WITH IT, GOMER!
SMILE AN' SAY "PORK RINDS"!
Distributed by Universal Press Syndicate
ONE MORE, VERN...HE MOVED

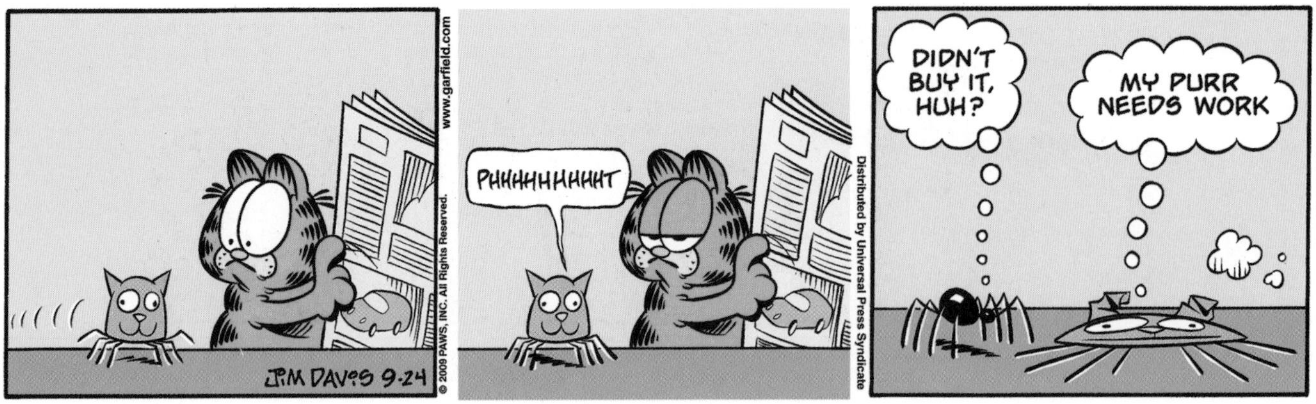
JIM DAVIS 9-24
© 2009 PAWS, INC. All Rights Reserved. www.garfield.com
PHHHHHHHHHT
Distributed by Universal Press Syndicate
DIDN'T BUY IT, HUH?
MY PURR NEEDS WORK

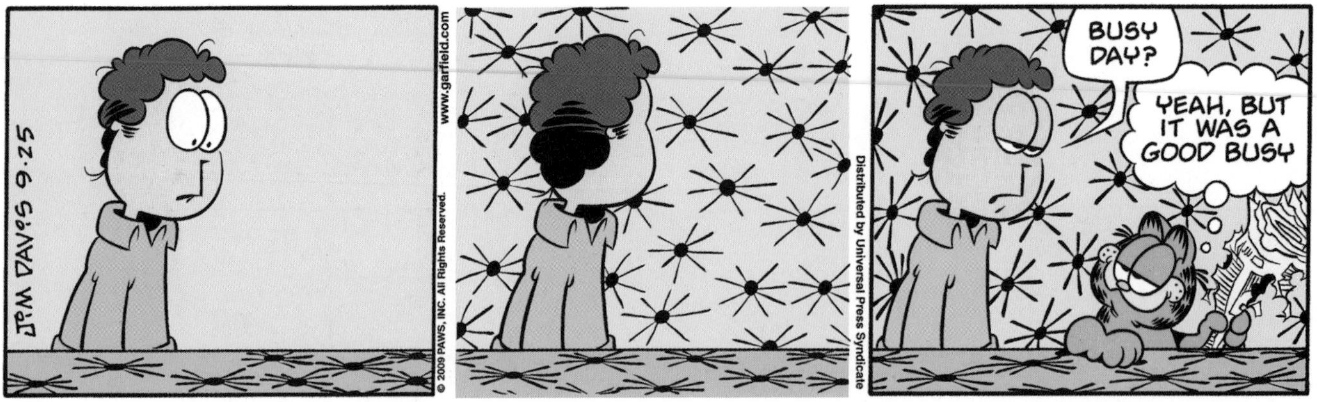
JIM DAVIS 9-25
© 2009 PAWS, INC. All Rights Reserved. www.garfield.com
Distributed by Universal Press Syndicate
BUSY DAY?
YEAH, BUT IT WAS A GOOD BUSY

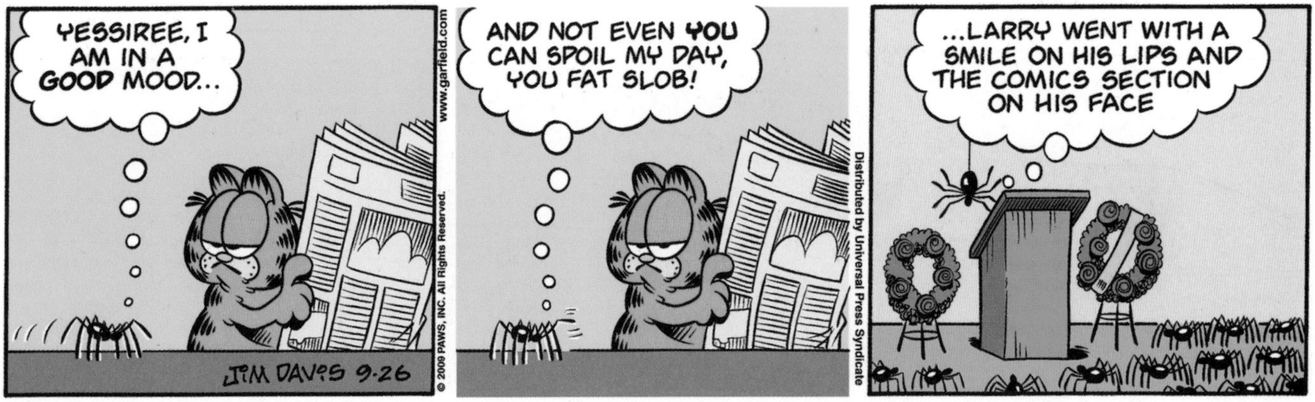
YESSIREE, I AM IN A GOOD MOOD...
JIM DAVIS 9-26
© 2009 PAWS, INC. All Rights Reserved. www.garfield.com
AND NOT EVEN YOU CAN SPOIL MY DAY, YOU FAT SLOB!
Distributed by Universal Press Syndicate
...LARRY WENT WITH A SMILE ON HIS LIPS AND THE COMICS SECTION ON HIS FACE

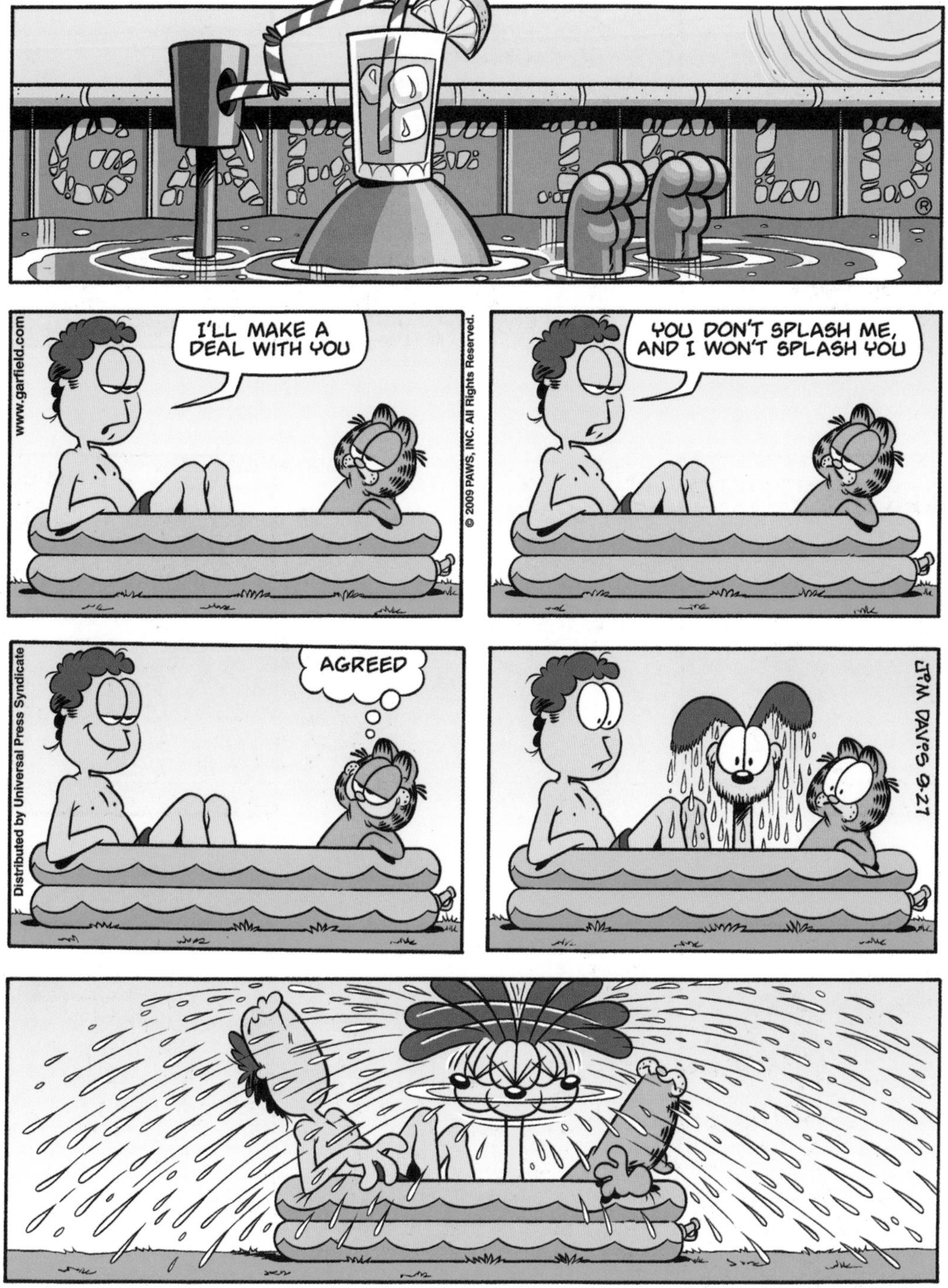
GARFIELD®
www.garfield.com
I'LL MAKE A DEAL WITH YOU
© 2009 PAWS, INC. All Rights Reserved.
YOU DON'T SPLASH ME, AND I WON'T SPLASH YOU
Distributed by Universal Press Syndicate
AGREED
JIM DAVIS 9-27

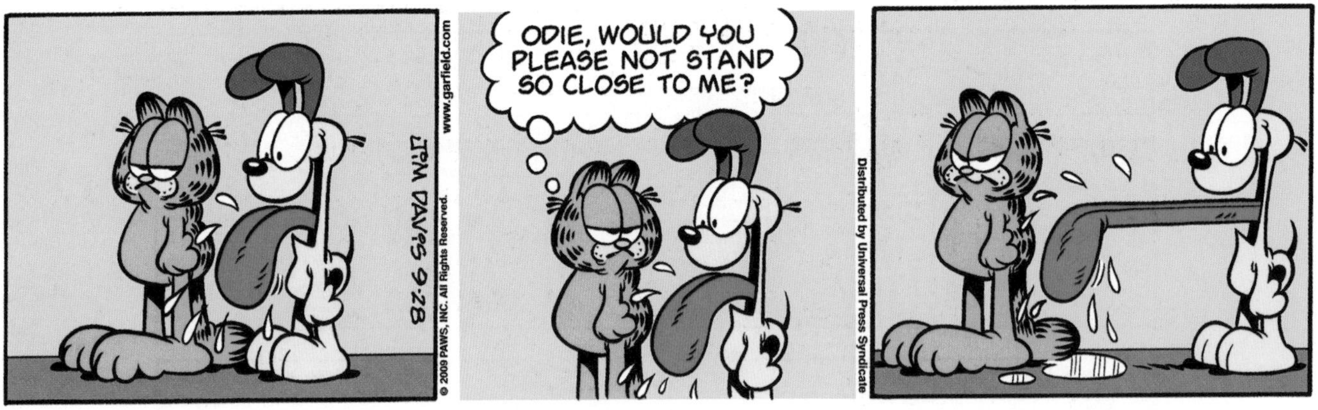
JIM DAVIS 9-28
© 2009 PAWS, INC. All Rights Reserved.
www.garfield.com
ODIE, WOULD YOU PLEASE NOT STAND SO CLOSE TO ME?
Distributed by Universal Press Syndicate

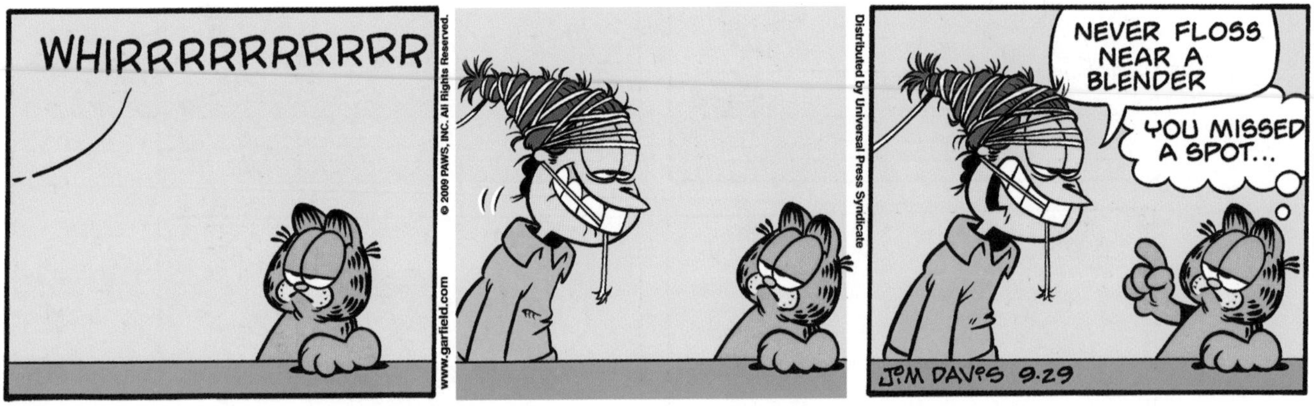
WHIRRRRRRRRRR
© 2009 PAWS, INC. All Rights Reserved.
www.garfield.com
Distributed by Universal Press Syndicate
NEVER FLOSS NEAR A BLENDER
YOU MISSED A SPOT...
JIM DAVIS 9-29

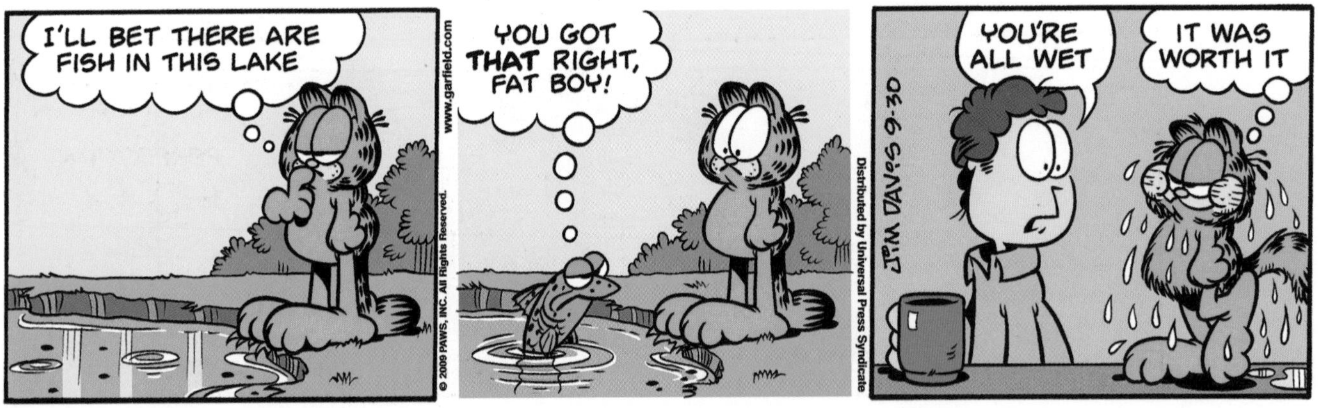
I'LL BET THERE ARE FISH IN THIS LAKE
© 2009 PAWS, INC. All Rights Reserved.
www.garfield.com
YOU GOT **THAT** RIGHT, FAT BOY!
Distributed by Universal Press Syndicate
JIM DAVIS 9-30
YOU'RE ALL WET
IT WAS WORTH IT

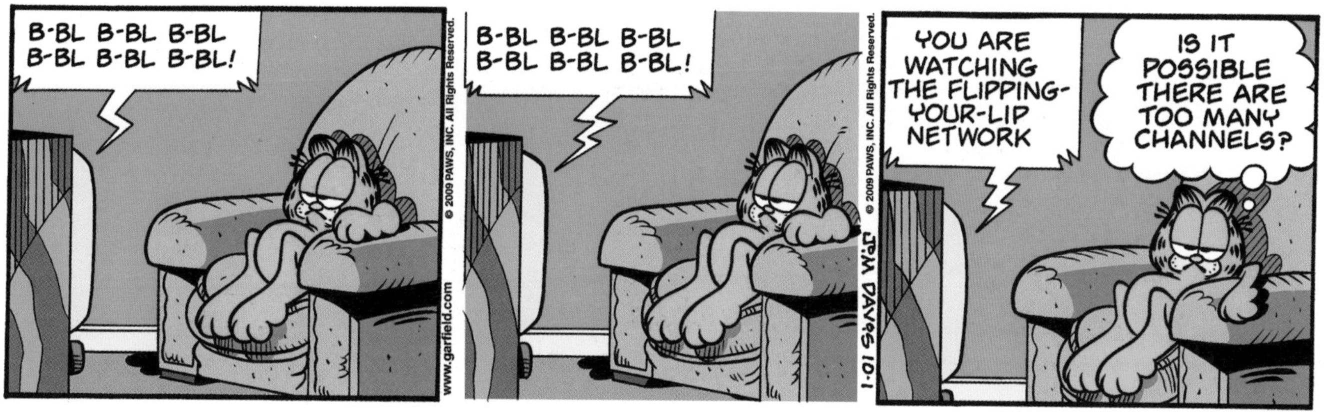
B-BL B-BL B-BL
B-BL B-BL B-BL!
© 2009 PAWS, INC. All Rights Reserved.
www.garfield.com
B-BL B-BL B-BL
B-BL B-BL B-BL!
© 2009 PAWS, INC. All Rights Reserved.
JIM DAVIS 10-1
YOU ARE WATCHING THE FLIPPING-YOUR-LIP NETWORK
IS IT POSSIBLE THERE ARE TOO MANY CHANNELS?

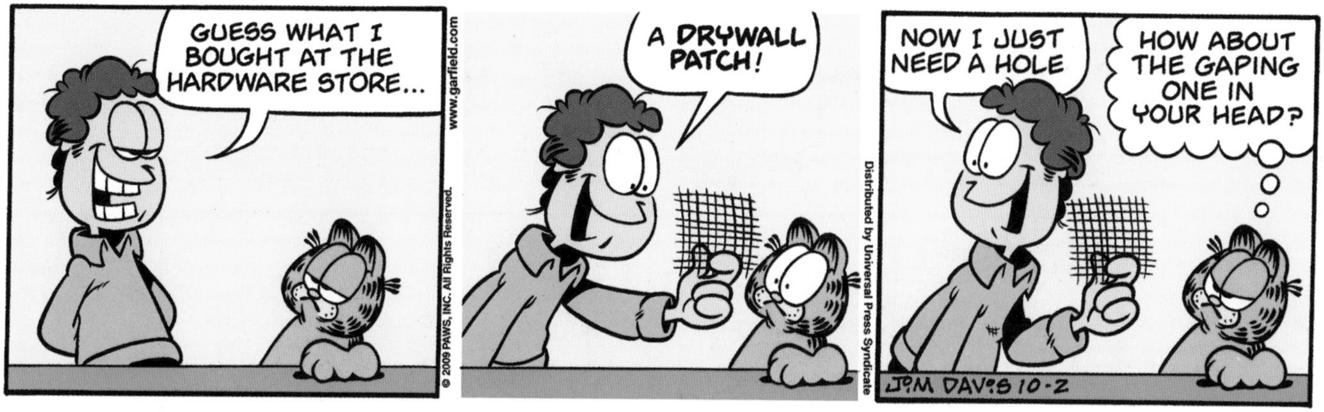
GUESS WHAT I BOUGHT AT THE HARDWARE STORE...
www.garfield.com
© 2009 PAWS, INC. All Rights Reserved.
A DRYWALL PATCH!
Distributed by Universal Press Syndicate
NOW I JUST NEED A HOLE
HOW ABOUT THE GAPING ONE IN YOUR HEAD?
JIM DAVIS 10-2

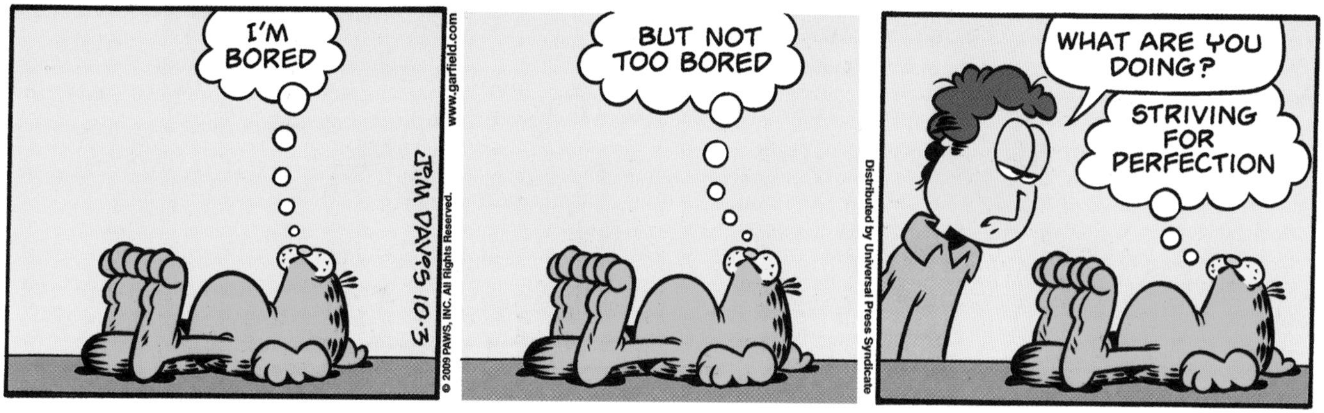
I'M BORED
JIM DAVIS 10-3
www.garfield.com
© 2009 PAWS, INC. All Rights Reserved.
BUT NOT TOO BORED
Distributed by Universal Press Syndicate
WHAT ARE YOU DOING?
STRIVING FOR PERFECTION

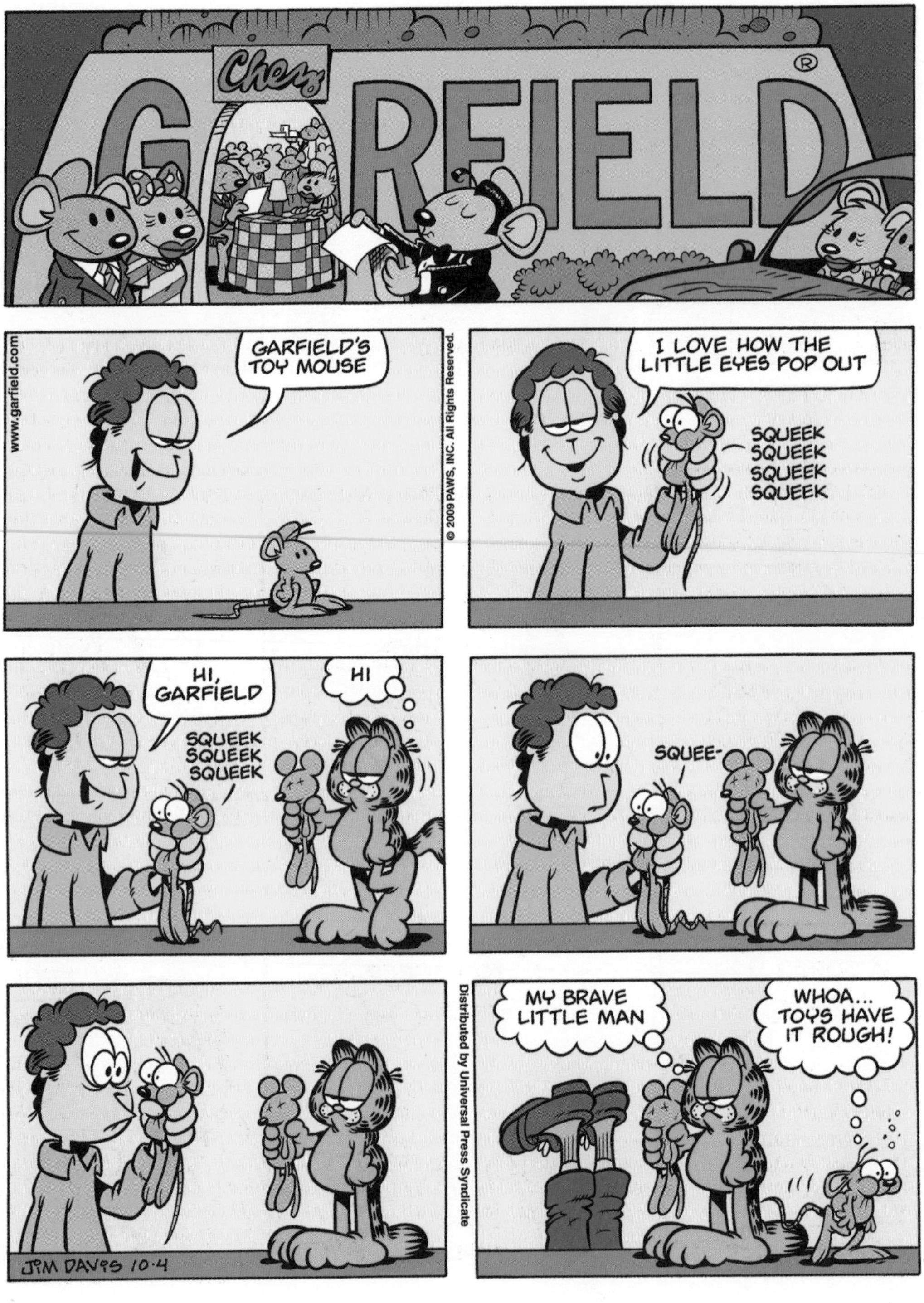
Chez
GARFIELD®
www.garfield.com
© 2009 PAWS, INC. All Rights Reserved.
GARFIELD'S TOY MOUSE
I LOVE HOW THE LITTLE EYES POP OUT
SQUEEK SQUEEK SQUEEK SQUEEK
HI, GARFIELD
HI
SQUEEK SQUEEK SQUEEK
SQUEE-
Distributed by Universal Press Syndicate
MY BRAVE LITTLE MAN
WHOA... TOYS HAVE IT ROUGH!
JIM DAVIS 10·4

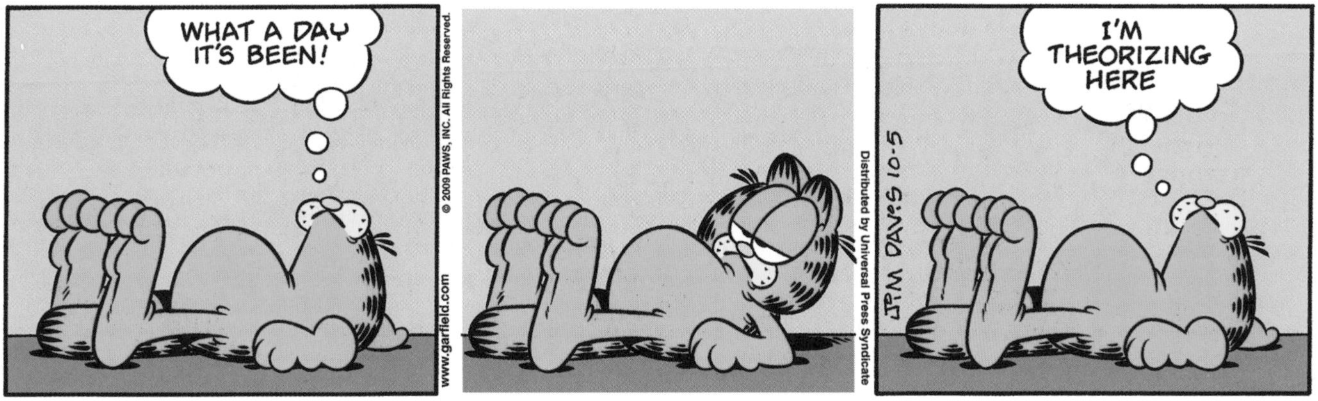
WHAT A DAY IT'S BEEN!
I'M THEORIZING HERE
© 2009 PAWS, INC. All Rights Reserved.
www.garfield.com
Distributed by Universal Press Syndicate
JPM DAVIS 10-5

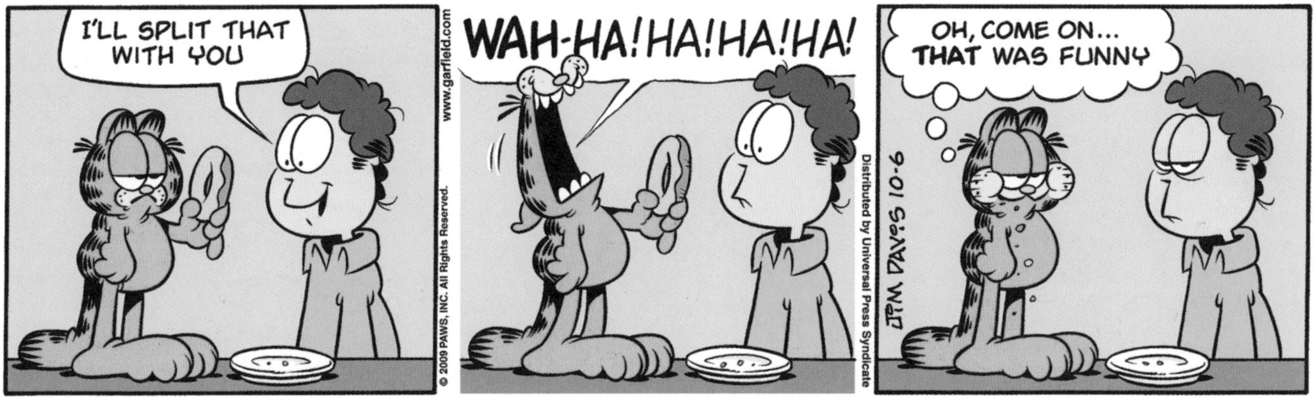
I'LL SPLIT THAT WITH YOU
WAH-HA!HA!HA!HA!
OH, COME ON... THAT WAS FUNNY
© 2009 PAWS, INC. All Rights Reserved.
www.garfield.com
Distributed by Universal Press Syndicate
JPM DAVIS 10-6

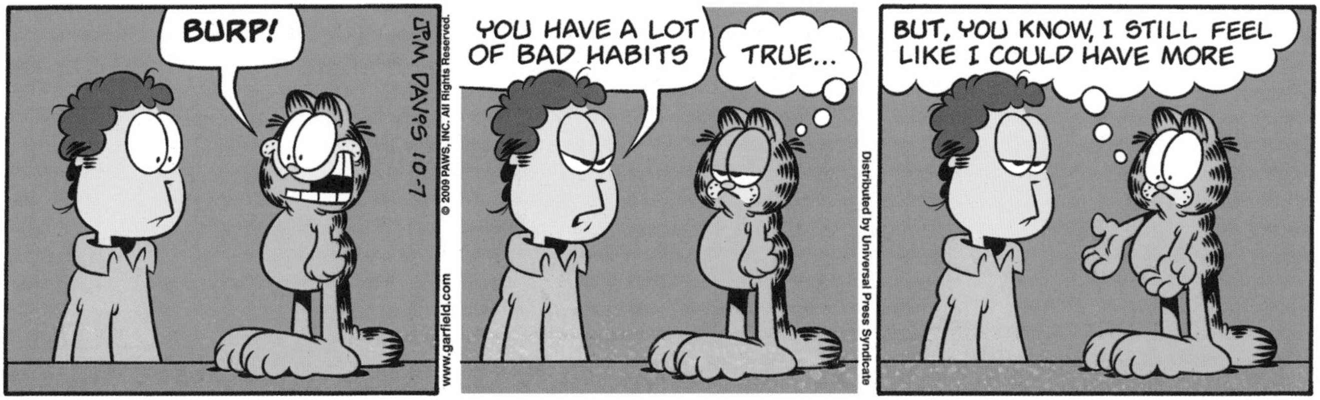
BURP!
YOU HAVE A LOT OF BAD HABITS
TRUE...
BUT, YOU KNOW, I STILL FEEL LIKE I COULD HAVE MORE
© 2009 PAWS, INC. All Rights Reserved.
www.garfield.com
Distributed by Universal Press Syndicate
JPM DAVIS 10-7

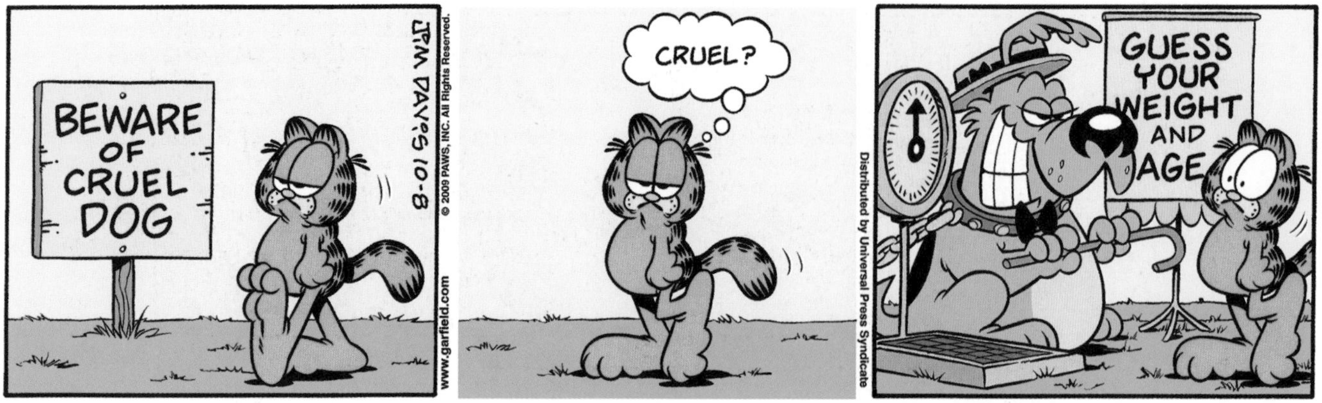
BEWARE OF CRUEL DOG
CRUEL?
GUESS YOUR WEIGHT AND AGE

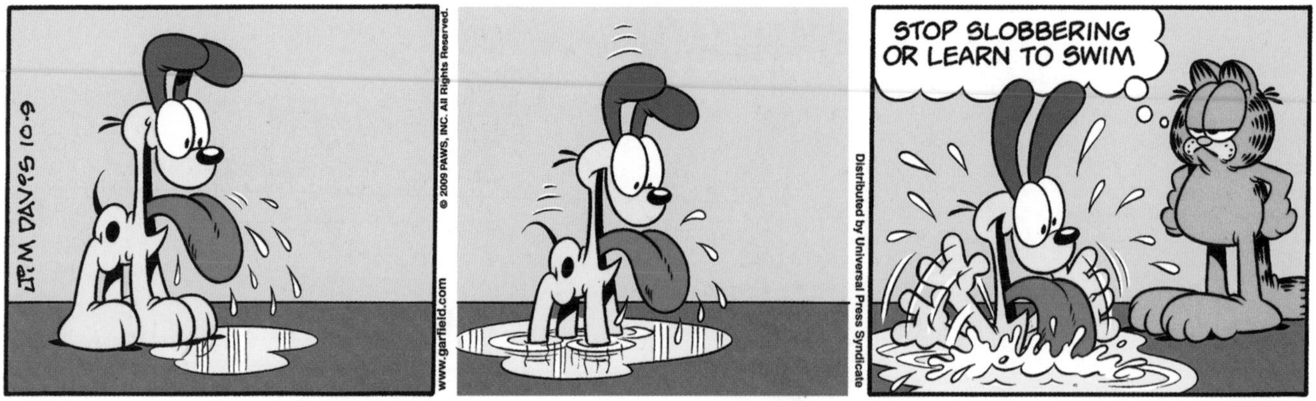
STOP SLOBBERING OR LEARN TO SWIM

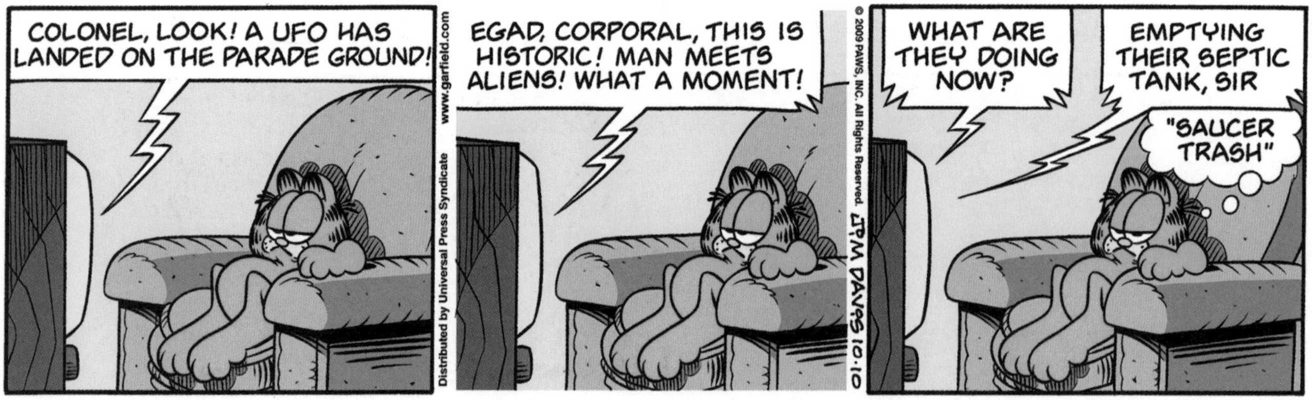
COLONEL, LOOK! A UFO HAS LANDED ON THE PARADE GROUND!
EGAD, CORPORAL, THIS IS HISTORIC! MAN MEETS ALIENS! WHAT A MOMENT!
WHAT ARE THEY DOING NOW?
EMPTYING THEIR SEPTIC TANK, SIR
"SAUCER TRASH"

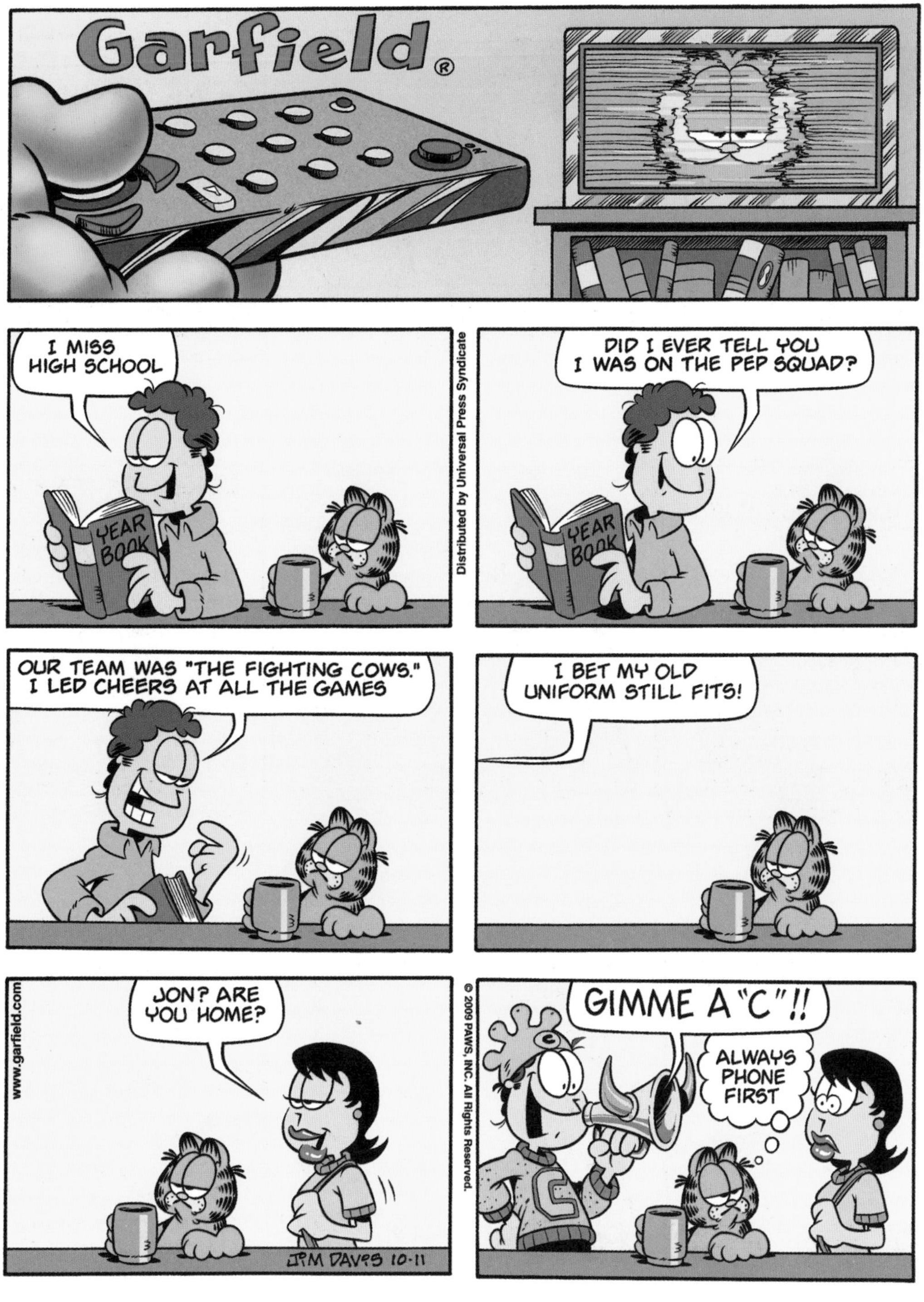
Garfield
I MISS HIGH SCHOOL
YEAR BOOK
Distributed by Universal Press Syndicate
DID I EVER TELL YOU I WAS ON THE PEP SQUAD?
OUR TEAM WAS "THE FIGHTING COWS." I LED CHEERS AT ALL THE GAMES
I BET MY OLD UNIFORM STILL FITS!
www.garfield.com
JON? ARE YOU HOME?
JIM DAVIS 10-11
© 2009 PAWS, INC. All Rights Reserved.
GIMME A "C"!!
ALWAYS PHONE FIRST

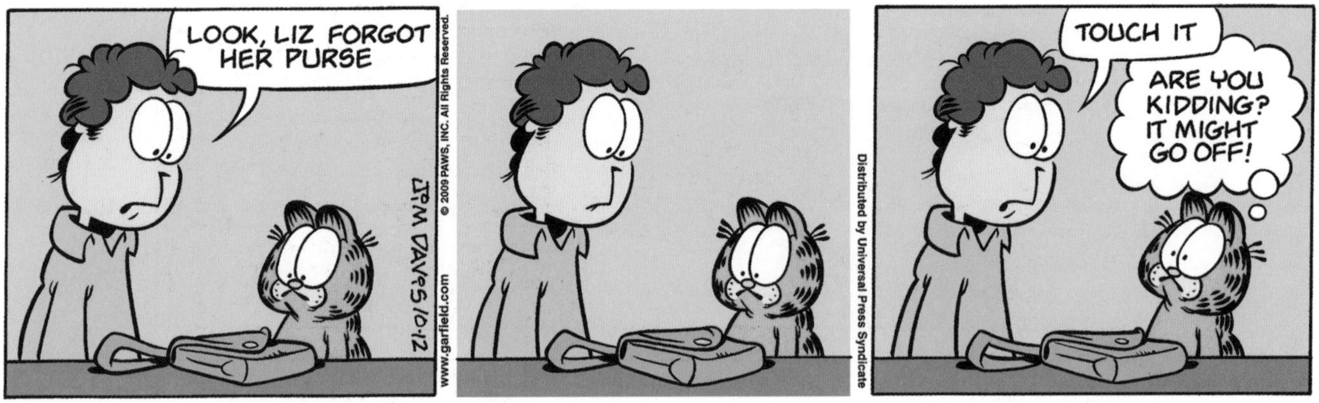
LOOK, LIZ FORGOT HER PURSE
JIM DAVIS 10-12
© 2009 PAWS, INC. All Rights Reserved.
www.garfield.com
TOUCH IT
ARE YOU KIDDING? IT MIGHT GO OFF!
Distributed by Universal Press Syndicate

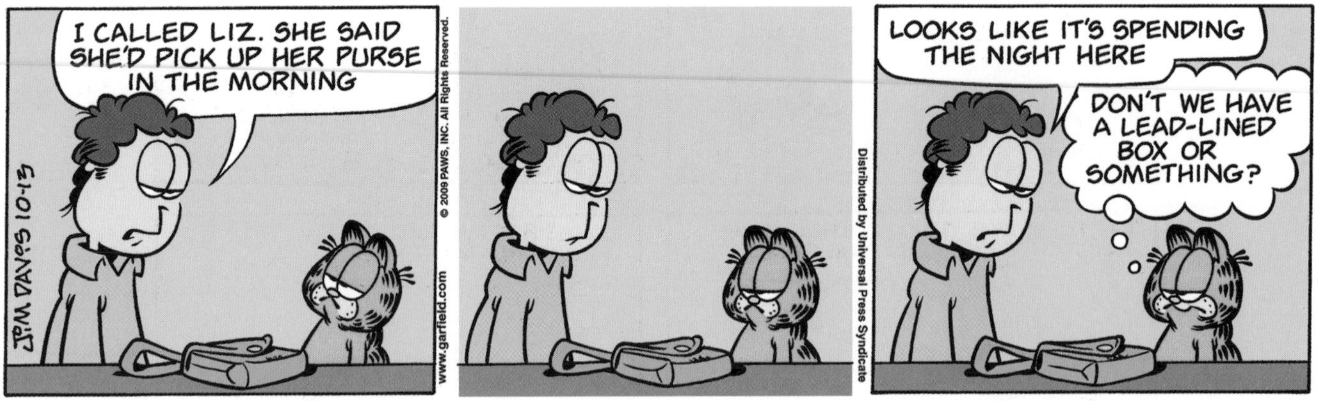
I CALLED LIZ. SHE SAID SHE'D PICK UP HER PURSE IN THE MORNING
JIM DAVIS 10-13
© 2009 PAWS, INC. All Rights Reserved.
www.garfield.com
LOOKS LIKE IT'S SPENDING THE NIGHT HERE
DON'T WE HAVE A LEAD-LINED BOX OR SOMETHING?
Distributed by Universal Press Syndicate

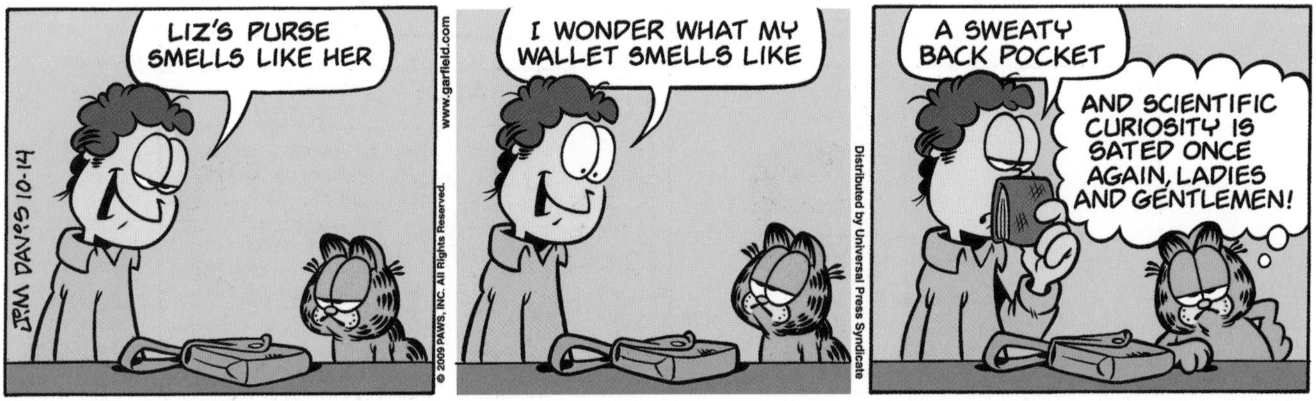
LIZ'S PURSE SMELLS LIKE HER
JIM DAVIS 10-14
© 2009 PAWS, INC. All Rights Reserved.
www.garfield.com
I WONDER WHAT MY WALLET SMELLS LIKE
A SWEATY BACK POCKET
AND SCIENTIFIC CURIOSITY IS SATED ONCE AGAIN, LADIES AND GENTLEMEN!
Distributed by Universal Press Syndicate

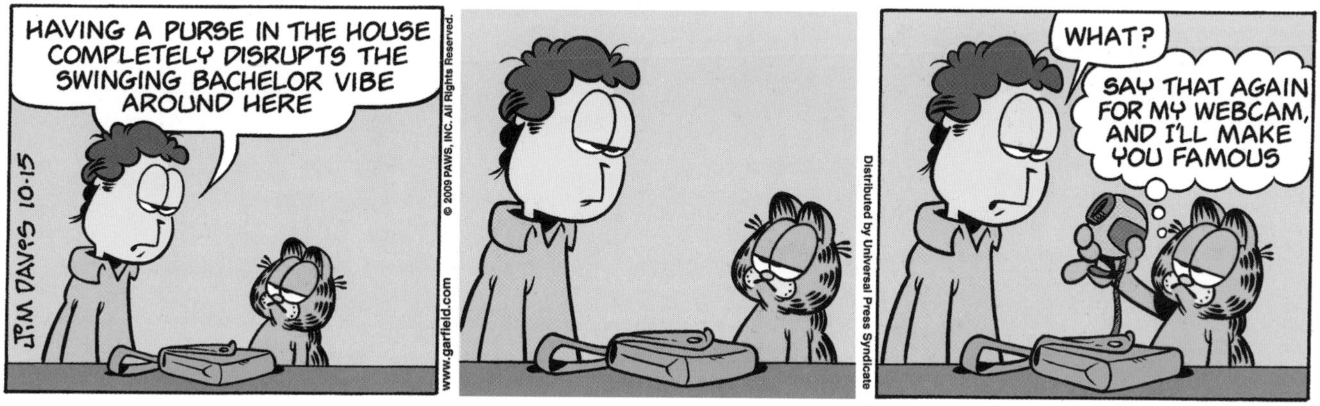
HAVING A PURSE IN THE HOUSE COMPLETELY DISRUPTS THE SWINGING BACHELOR VIBE AROUND HERE
JIM DAVIS 10-15
© 2009 PAWS, INC. All Rights Reserved.
www.garfield.com
Distributed by Universal Press Syndicate
WHAT?
SAY THAT AGAIN FOR MY WEBCAM, AND I'LL MAKE YOU FAMOUS

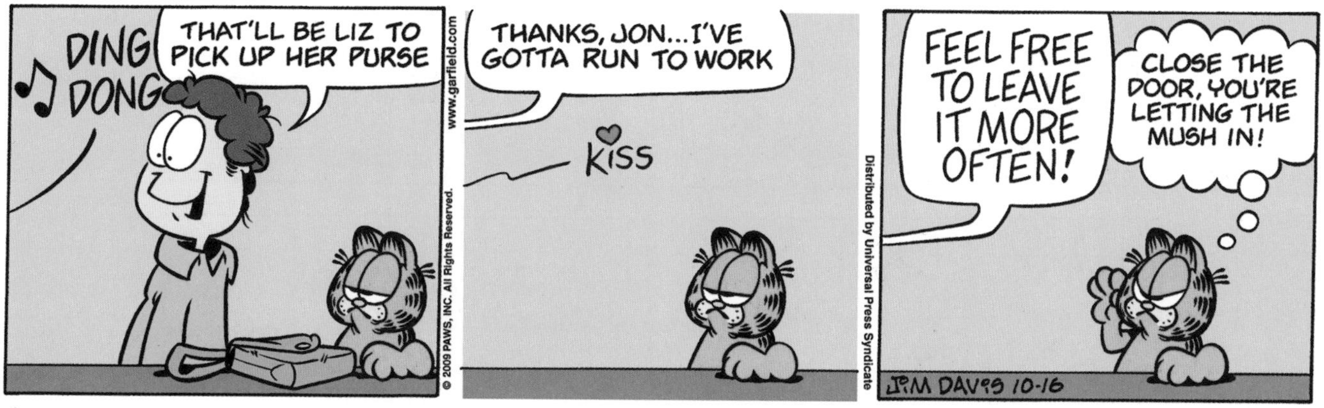
DING DONG
THAT'LL BE LIZ TO PICK UP HER PURSE
www.garfield.com
© 2009 PAWS, INC. All Rights Reserved.
THANKS, JON... I'VE GOTTA RUN TO WORK
KISS
Distributed by Universal Press Syndicate
FEEL FREE TO LEAVE IT MORE OFTEN!
CLOSE THE DOOR, YOU'RE LETTING THE MUSH IN!
JIM DAVIS 10-16

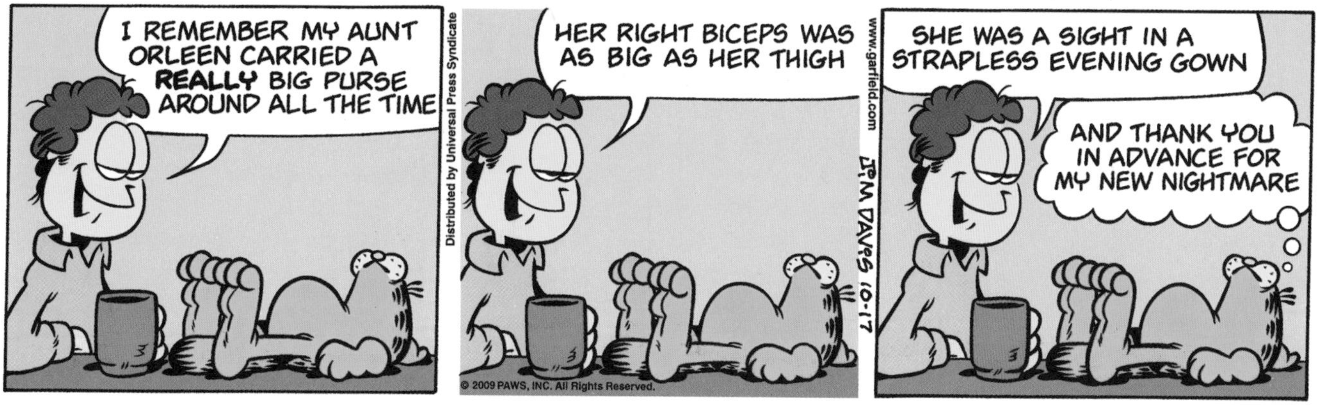
I REMEMBER MY AUNT ORLEEN CARRIED A **REALLY** BIG PURSE AROUND ALL THE TIME
Distributed by Universal Press Syndicate
HER RIGHT BICEPS WAS AS BIG AS HER THIGH
© 2009 PAWS, INC. All Rights Reserved.
www.garfield.com
JIM DAVIS 10-17
SHE WAS A SIGHT IN A STRAPLESS EVENING GOWN
AND THANK YOU IN ADVANCE FOR MY NEW NIGHTMARE

GARFIELD
Distributed by Universal Press Syndicate
BARK
BARK BARK
BARK
RRRRRR
RRRRRRR
www.garfield.com
© 2009 PAWS, INC. All Rights Reserved.
JIM DAVIS 10-18

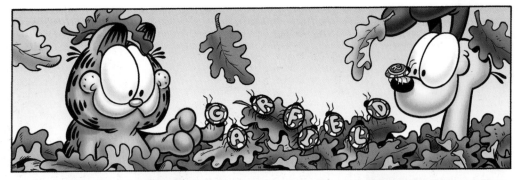

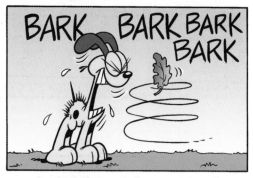

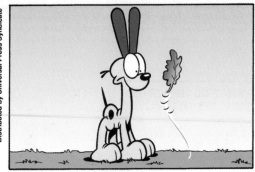

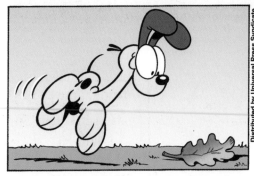

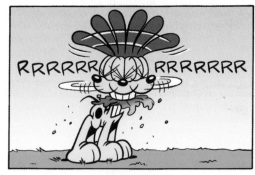

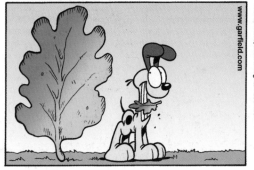

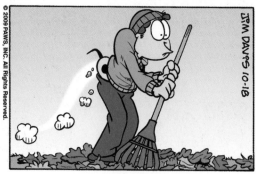

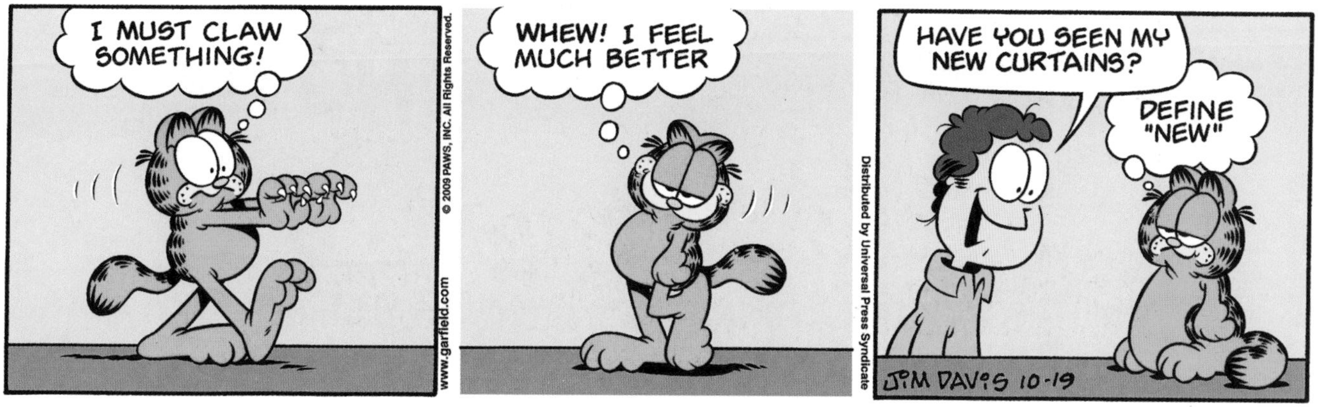
I MUST CLAW SOMETHING!
© 2009 PAWS, INC. All Rights Reserved.
www.garfield.com
WHEW! I FEEL MUCH BETTER
Distributed by Universal Press Syndicate
HAVE YOU SEEN MY NEW CURTAINS?
DEFINE "NEW"
JIM DAVIS 10-19

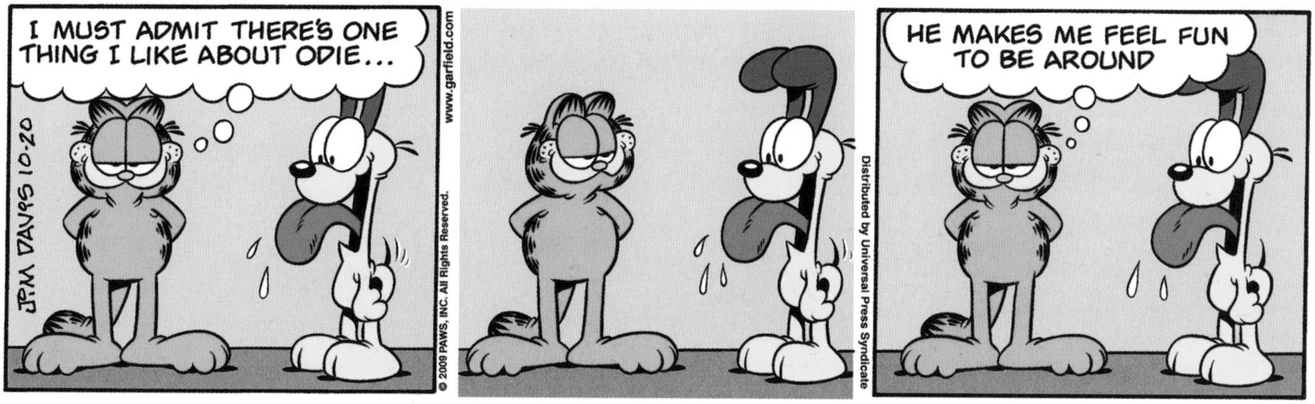
I MUST ADMIT THERE'S ONE THING I LIKE ABOUT ODIE...
JIM DAVIS 10-20
www.garfield.com
© 2009 PAWS, INC. All Rights Reserved.
Distributed by Universal Press Syndicate
HE MAKES ME FEEL FUN TO BE AROUND

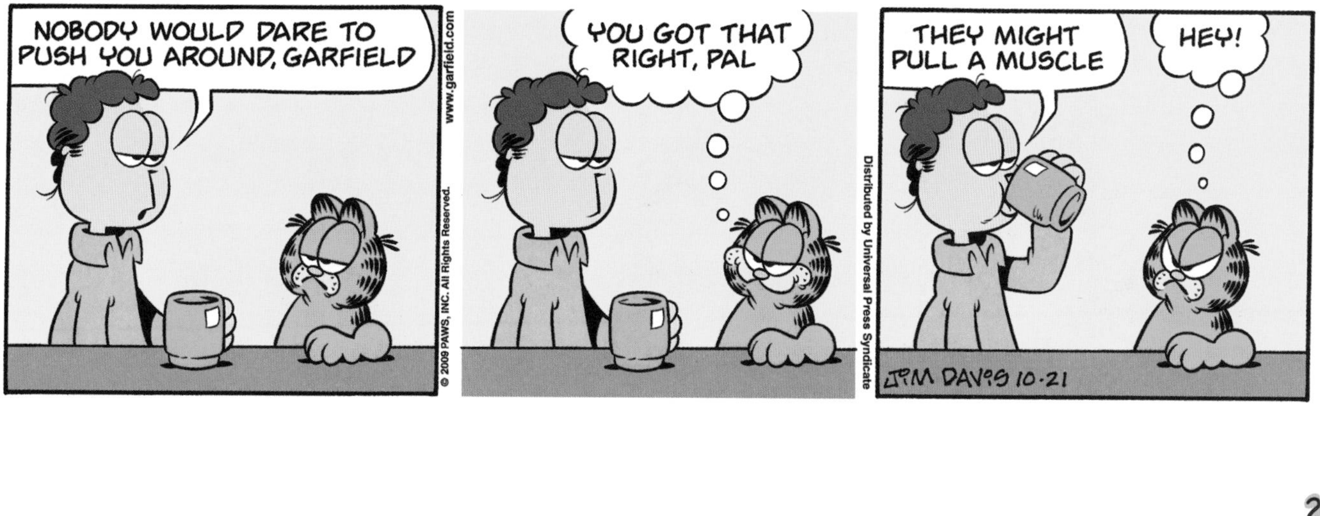
NOBODY WOULD DARE TO PUSH YOU AROUND, GARFIELD
www.garfield.com
© 2009 PAWS, INC. All Rights Reserved.
YOU GOT THAT RIGHT, PAL
Distributed by Universal Press Syndicate
THEY MIGHT PULL A MUSCLE
HEY!
JIM DAVIS 10-21

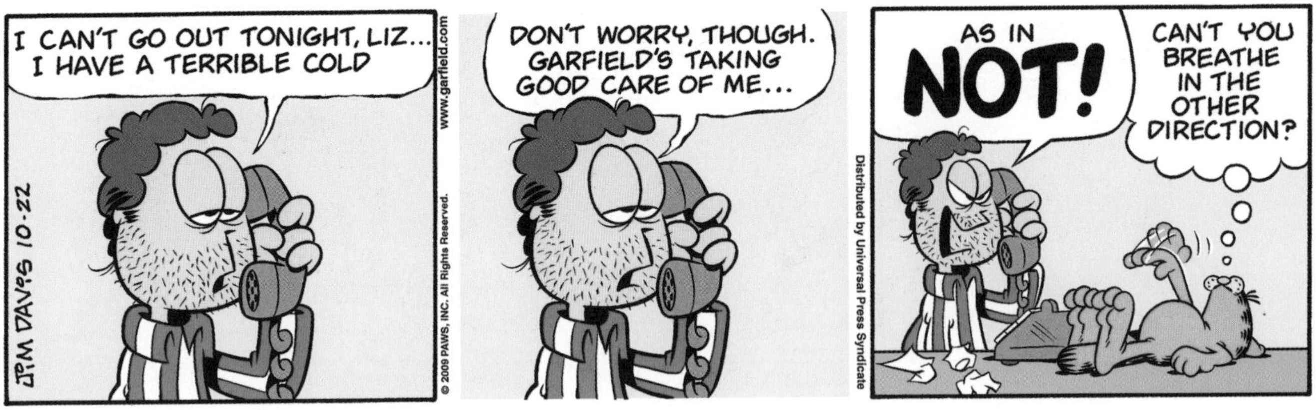
JIM DAVIS 10-22
I CAN'T GO OUT TONIGHT, LIZ... I HAVE A TERRIBLE COLD
© 2009 PAWS, INC. All Rights Reserved. www.garfield.com
DON'T WORRY, THOUGH. GARFIELD'S TAKING GOOD CARE OF ME...
Distributed by Universal Press Syndicate
AS IN NOT!
CAN'T YOU BREATHE IN THE OTHER DIRECTION?

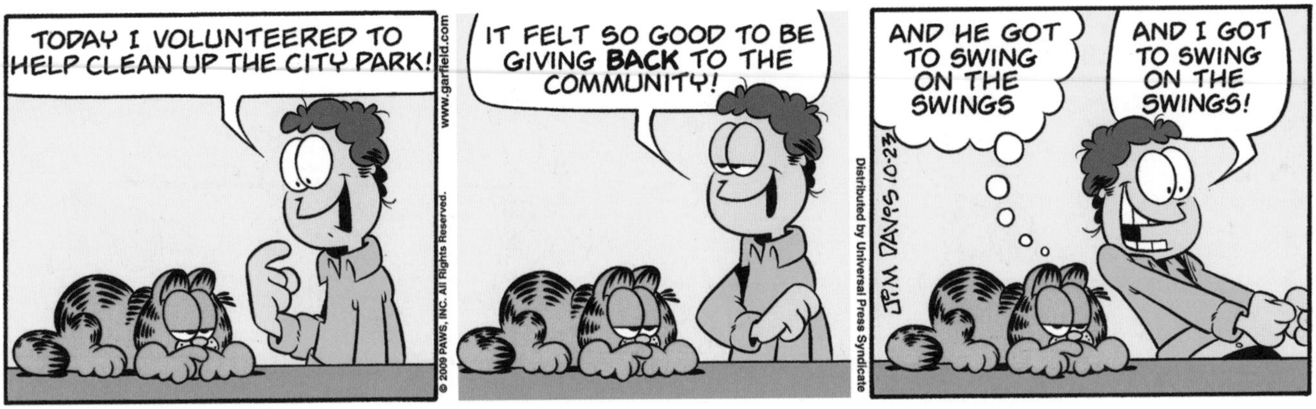
TODAY I VOLUNTEERED TO HELP CLEAN UP THE CITY PARK!
© 2009 PAWS, INC. All Rights Reserved. www.garfield.com
IT FELT SO GOOD TO BE GIVING **BACK** TO THE COMMUNITY!
Distributed by Universal Press Syndicate
JIM DAVIS 10-23
AND HE GOT TO SWING ON THE SWINGS
AND I GOT TO SWING ON THE SWINGS!

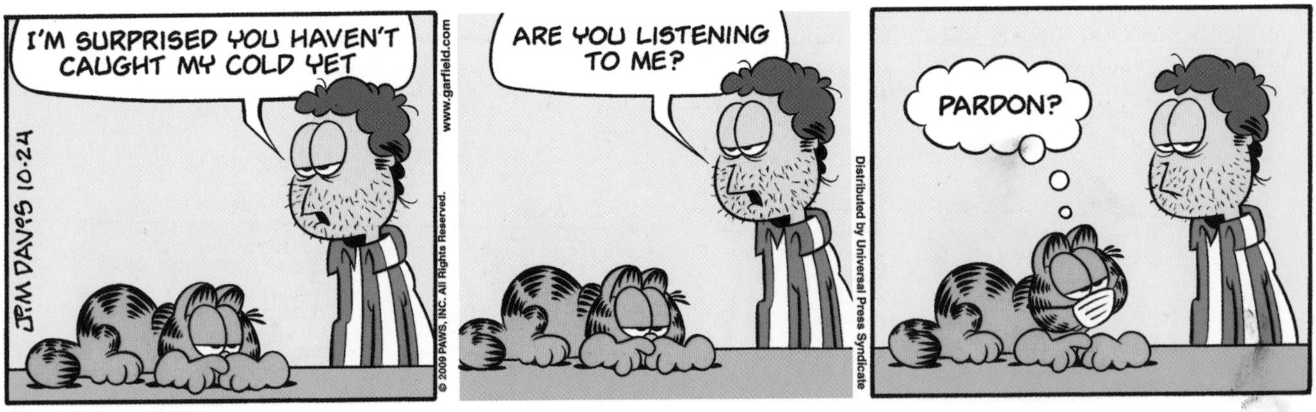
JIM DAVIS 10-24
I'M SURPRISED YOU HAVEN'T CAUGHT MY COLD YET
© 2009 PAWS, INC. All Rights Reserved. www.garfield.com
ARE YOU LISTENING TO ME?
Distributed by Universal Press Syndicate
PARDON?

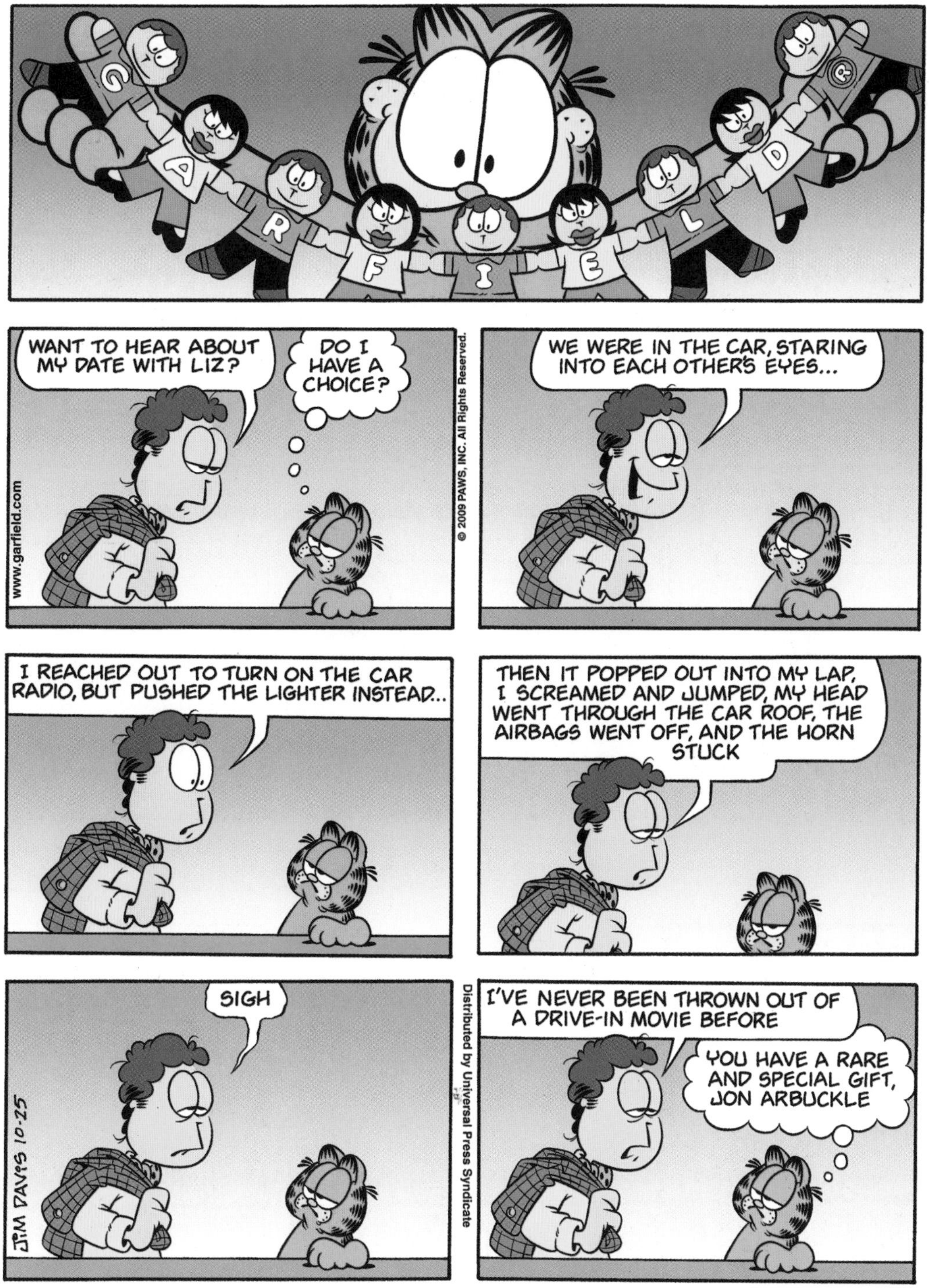
GARFIELD
WANT TO HEAR ABOUT MY DATE WITH LIZ?
DO I HAVE A CHOICE?
www.garfield.com
© 2009 PAWS, INC. All Rights Reserved.
WE WERE IN THE CAR, STARING INTO EACH OTHER'S EYES...
I REACHED OUT TO TURN ON THE CAR RADIO, BUT PUSHED THE LIGHTER INSTEAD...
THEN IT POPPED OUT INTO MY LAP, I SCREAMED AND JUMPED, MY HEAD WENT THROUGH THE CAR ROOF, THE AIRBAGS WENT OFF, AND THE HORN STUCK
SIGH
JIM DAVIS 10-25
Distributed by Universal Press Syndicate
I'VE NEVER BEEN THROWN OUT OF A DRIVE-IN MOVIE BEFORE
YOU HAVE A RARE AND SPECIAL GIFT, JON ARBUCKLE

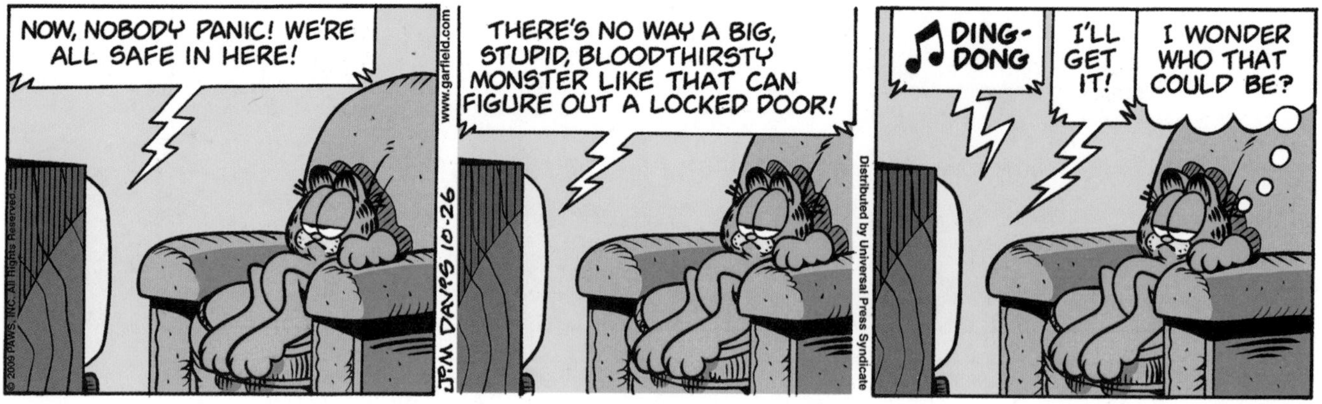
NOW, NOBODY PANIC! WE'RE ALL SAFE IN HERE!
THERE'S NO WAY A BIG, STUPID, BLOODTHIRSTY MONSTER LIKE THAT CAN FIGURE OUT A LOCKED DOOR!
DING-DONG
I'LL GET IT!
I WONDER WHO THAT COULD BE?
© 2009 PAWS, INC. All Rights Reserved.
www.garfield.com
JPM DAVPS 10-26
Distributed by Universal Press Syndicate

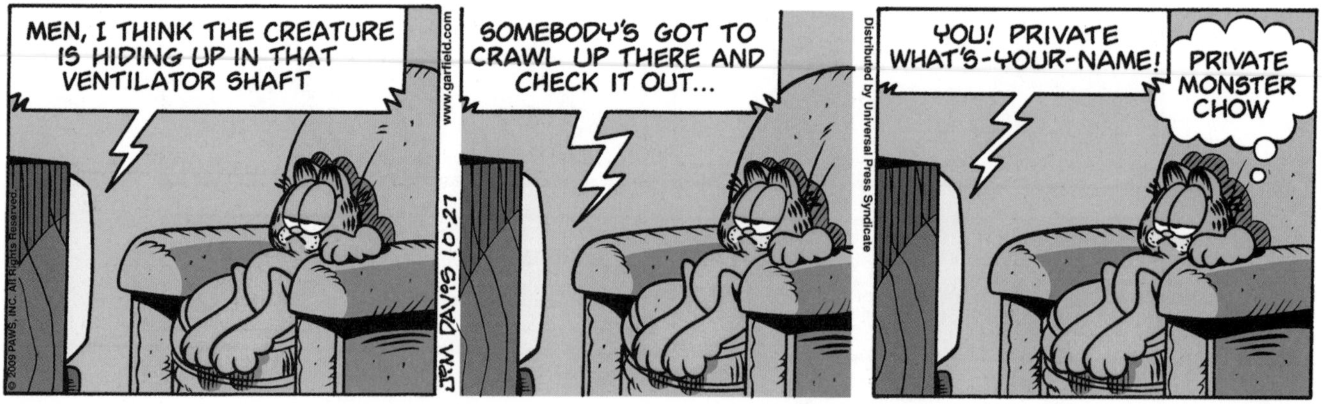
MEN, I THINK THE CREATURE IS HIDING UP IN THAT VENTILATOR SHAFT
SOMEBODY'S GOT TO CRAWL UP THERE AND CHECK IT OUT...
YOU! PRIVATE WHAT'S-YOUR-NAME!
PRIVATE MONSTER CHOW
© 2009 PAWS, INC. All Rights Reserved.
www.garfield.com
JPM DAVPS 10-27
Distributed by Universal Press Syndicate

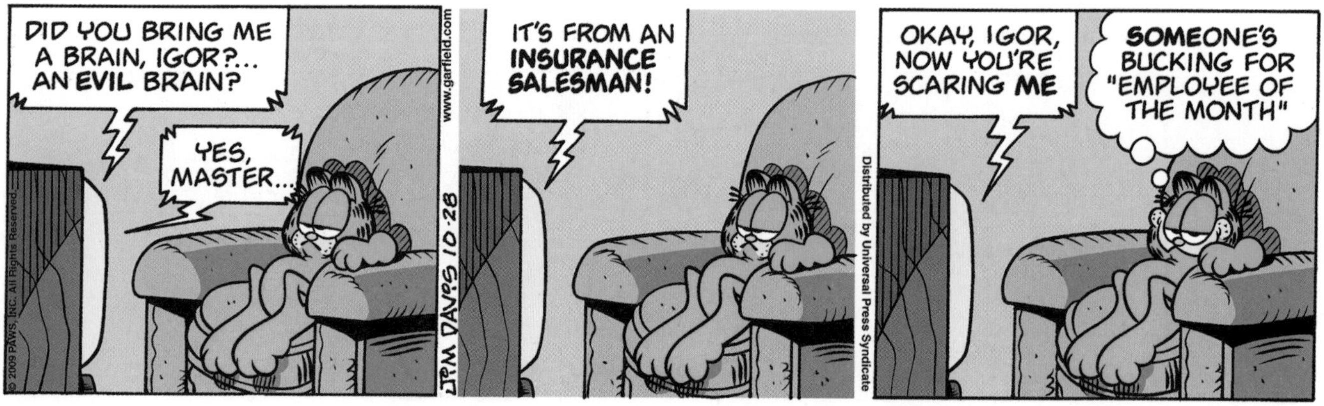
DID YOU BRING ME A BRAIN, IGOR?... AN EVIL BRAIN?
YES, MASTER...
IT'S FROM AN INSURANCE SALESMAN!
OKAY, IGOR, NOW YOU'RE SCARING ME
SOMEONE'S BUCKING FOR "EMPLOYEE OF THE MONTH"
© 2009 PAWS, INC. All Rights Reserved.
www.garfield.com
JPM DAVPS 10-28
Distributed by Universal Press Syndicate

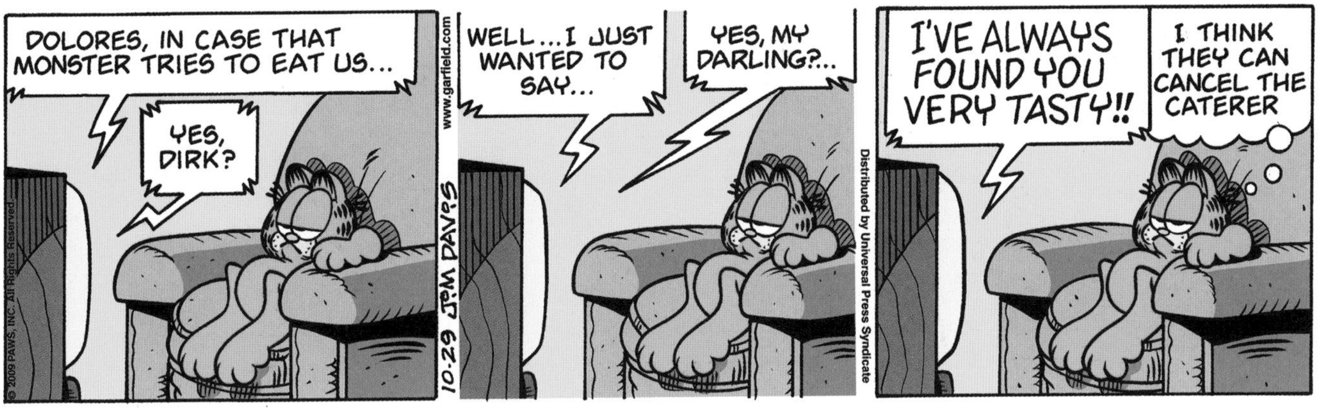
© 2009 PAWS, INC. All Rights Reserved.
DOLORES, IN CASE THAT MONSTER TRIES TO EAT US...
YES, DIRK?
10-29 JIM DAVIS
www.garfield.com
WELL... I JUST WANTED TO SAY...
YES, MY DARLING?...
Distributed by Universal Press Syndicate
I'VE ALWAYS FOUND YOU VERY TASTY!!
I THINK THEY CAN CANCEL THE CATERER

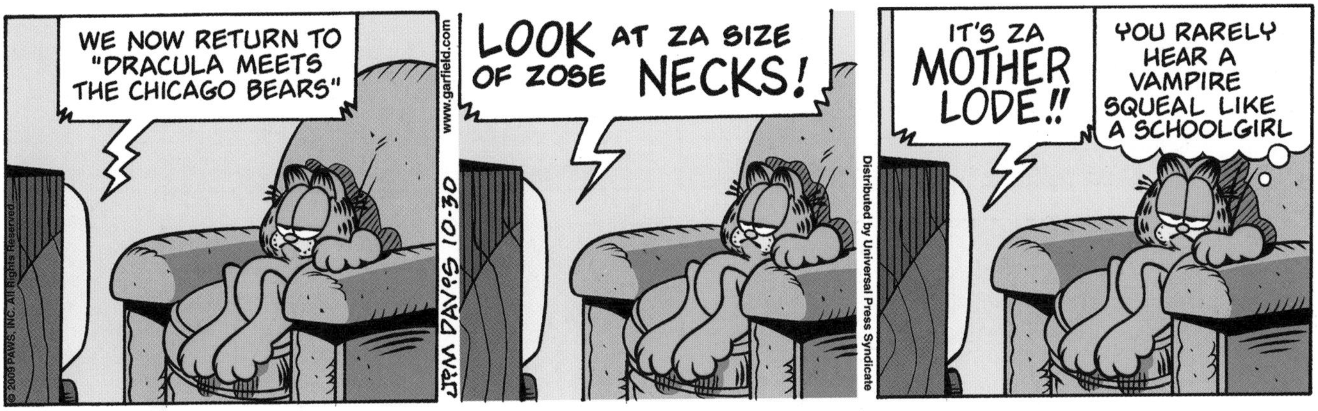
© 2009 PAWS, INC. All Rights Reserved.
WE NOW RETURN TO "DRACULA MEETS THE CHICAGO BEARS"
JIM DAVIS 10-30
www.garfield.com
LOOK AT ZA SIZE OF ZOSE NECKS!
Distributed by Universal Press Syndicate
IT'S ZA MOTHER LODE!!
YOU RARELY HEAR A VAMPIRE SQUEAL LIKE A SCHOOLGIRL

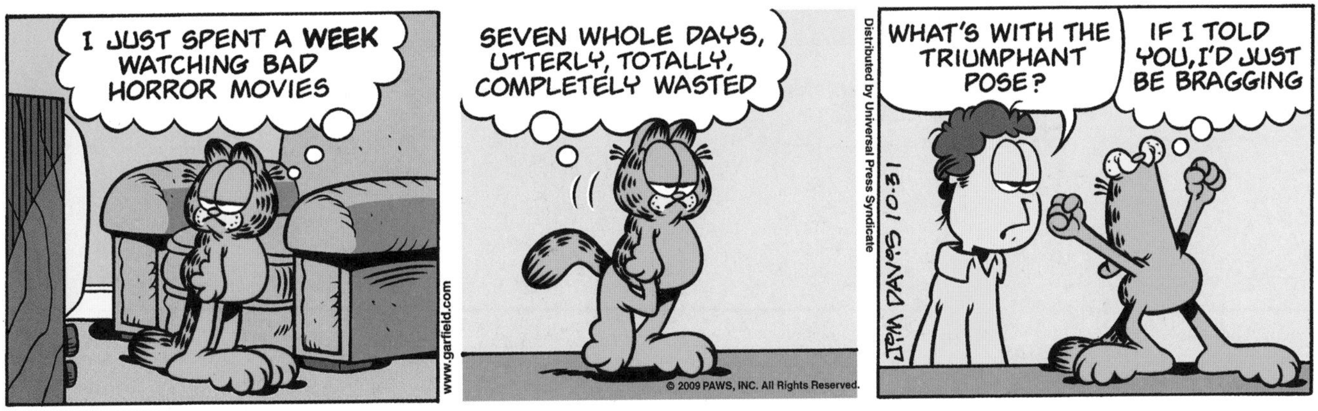
I JUST SPENT A WEEK WATCHING BAD HORROR MOVIES
www.garfield.com
SEVEN WHOLE DAYS, UTTERLY, TOTALLY, COMPLETELY WASTED
© 2009 PAWS, INC. All Rights Reserved.
Distributed by Universal Press Syndicate
WHAT'S WITH THE TRIUMPHANT POSE?
IF I TOLD YOU, I'D JUST BE BRAGGING
JIM DAVIS 10-31

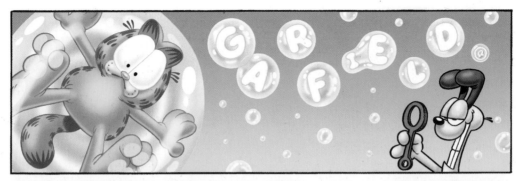

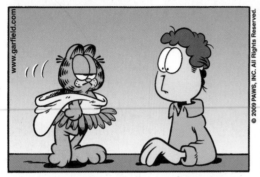

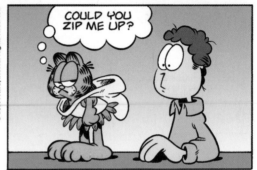

GARFIELD®
www.garfield.com
© 2009 PAWS, INC. All Rights Reserved.
COULD YOU ZIP ME UP?
ZIP
THE NEST IS A NICE TOUCH
THANK YOU
ISN'T HE THE CUTEST THI-
Distributed by Universal Press Syndicate
HEY!
HEEEERE, BIRDY, BIRDY, BIRDY...
JIM DAVIS 11-1

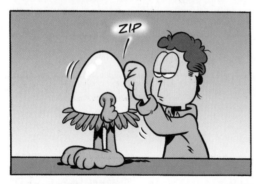

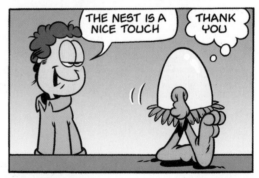

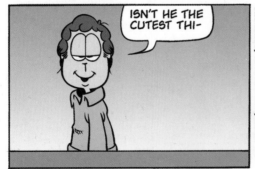

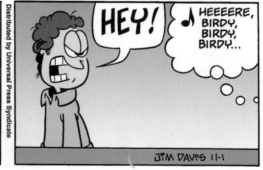

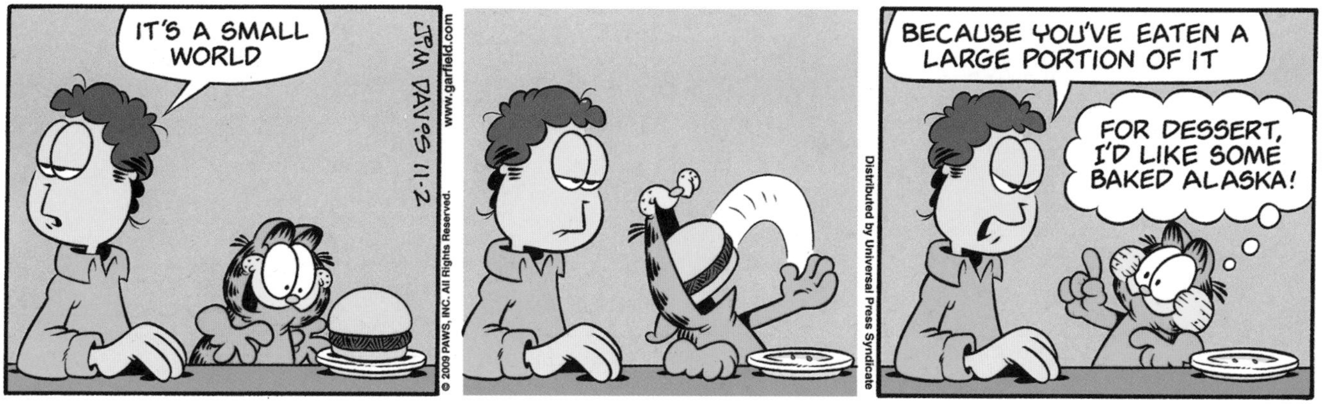
IT'S A SMALL WORLD
JIM DAVIS 11-2
BECAUSE YOU'VE EATEN A LARGE PORTION OF IT
FOR DESSERT, I'D LIKE SOME BAKED ALASKA!

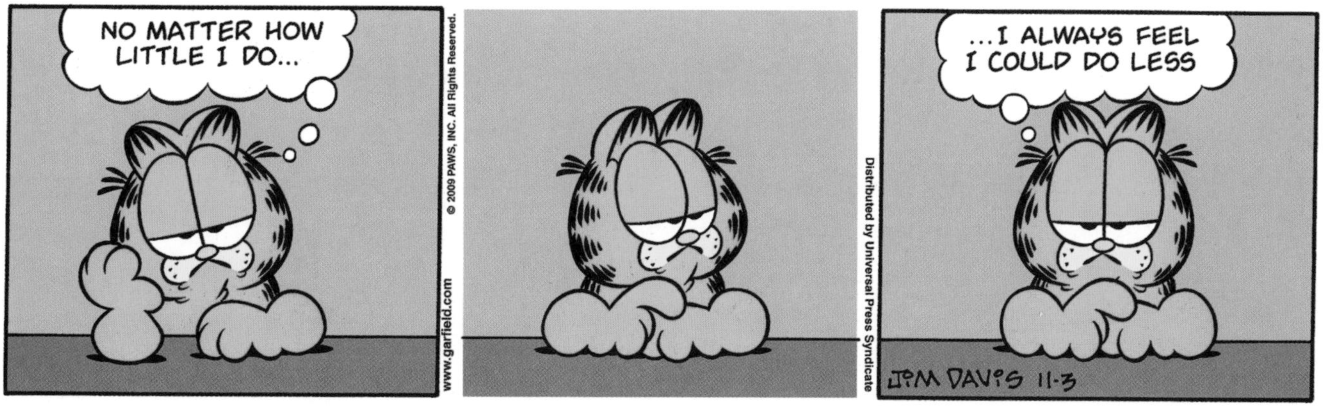
NO MATTER HOW LITTLE I DO...
...I ALWAYS FEEL I COULD DO LESS
JIM DAVIS 11-3

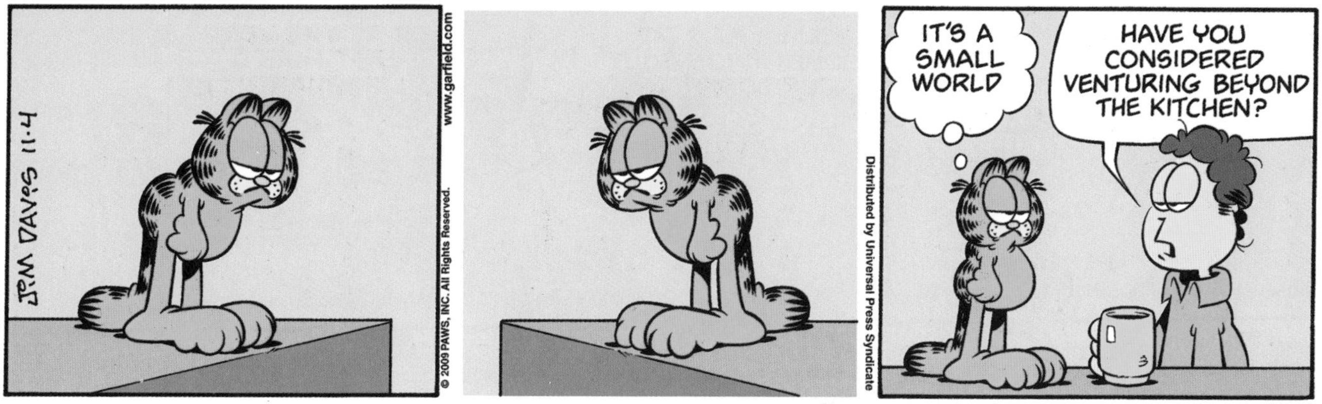
JIM DAVIS 11-4
IT'S A SMALL WORLD
HAVE YOU CONSIDERED VENTURING BEYOND THE KITCHEN?

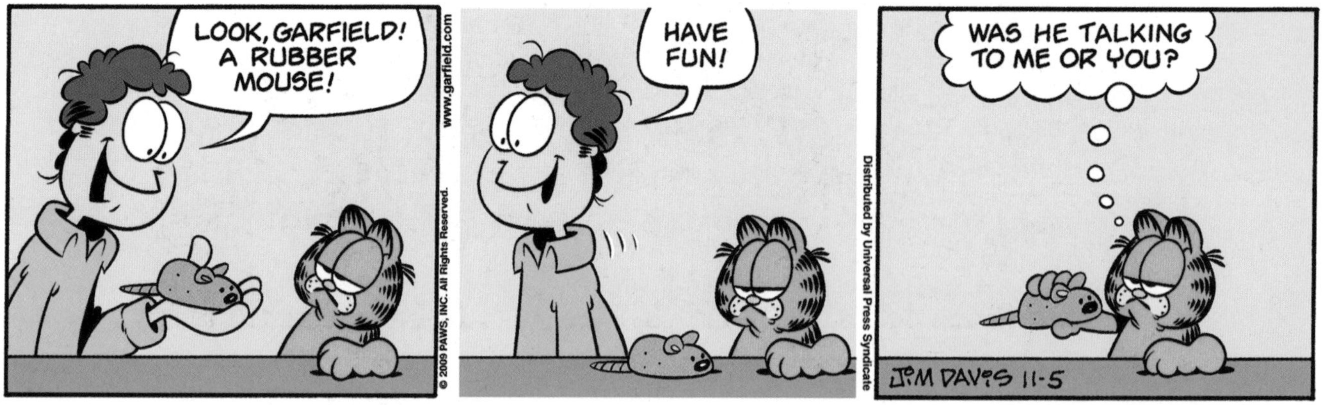
LOOK, GARFIELD! A RUBBER MOUSE!
HAVE FUN!
WAS HE TALKING TO ME OR YOU?
JIM DAVIS 11-5
© 2009 PAWS, INC. All Rights Reserved. www.garfield.com
Distributed by Universal Press Syndicate

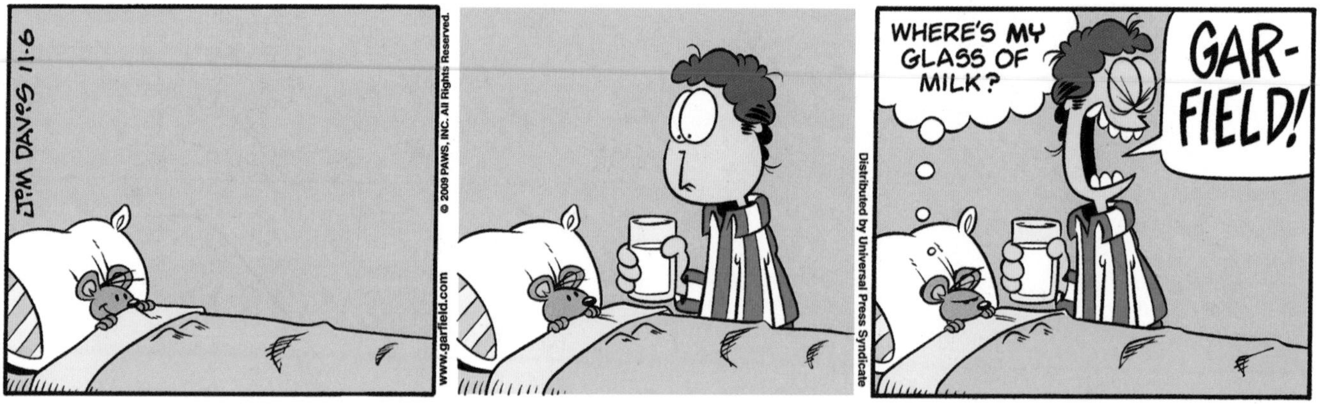
JIM DAVIS 11-6
WHERE'S MY GLASS OF MILK?
GAR-FIELD!
© 2009 PAWS, INC. All Rights Reserved. www.garfield.com
Distributed by Universal Press Syndicate

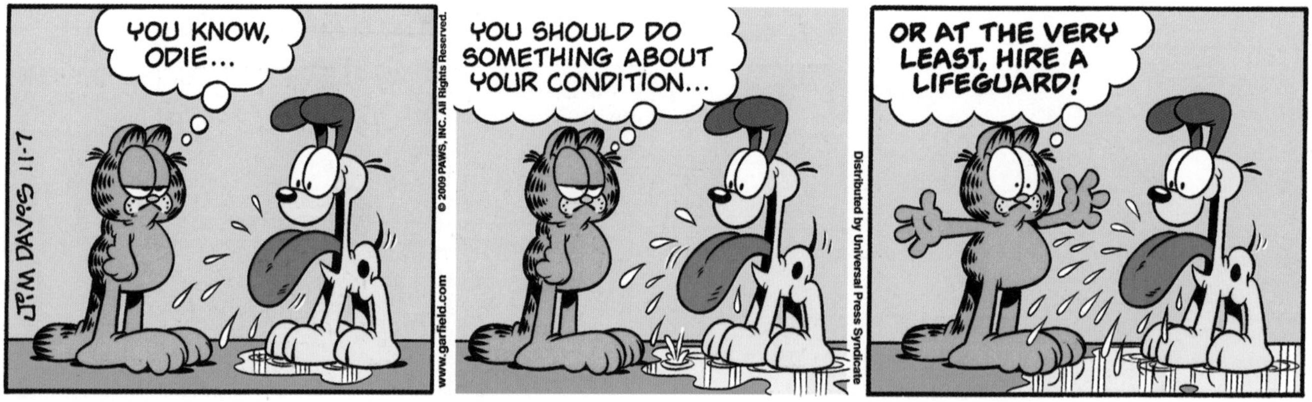
JIM DAVIS 11-7
YOU KNOW, ODIE...
YOU SHOULD DO SOMETHING ABOUT YOUR CONDITION...
OR AT THE VERY LEAST, HIRE A LIFEGUARD!
© 2009 PAWS, INC. All Rights Reserved. www.garfield.com
Distributed by Universal Press Syndicate

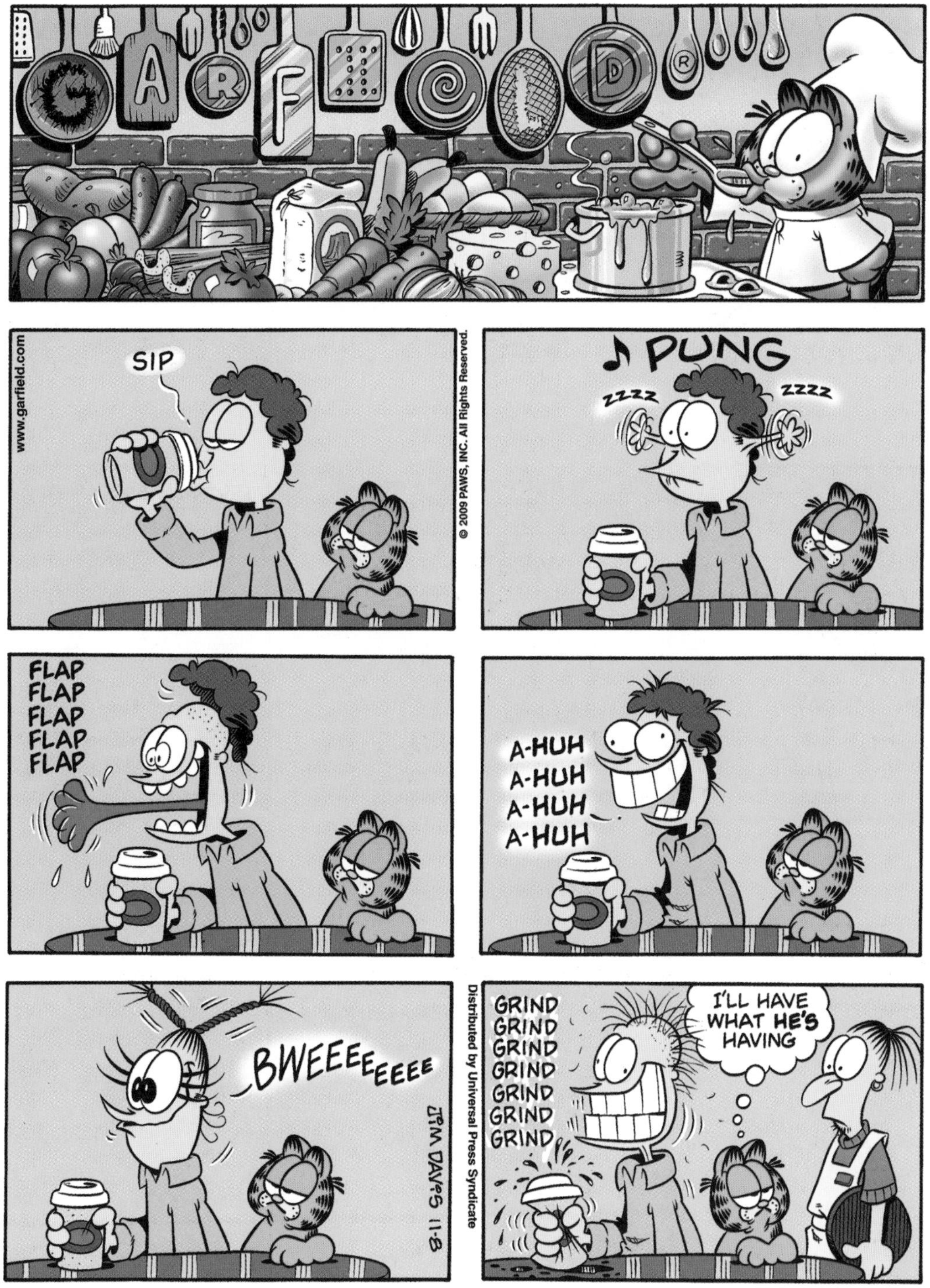
GARFIELD®
www.garfield.com
SIP
© 2009 PAWS, INC. All Rights Reserved.
♪ PUNG
ZZZZ
ZZZZ
FLAP FLAP FLAP FLAP FLAP
A-HUH A-HUH A-HUH A-HUH
BWEEEEEEEE
JIM DAVIS 11-8
Distributed by Universal Press Syndicate
GRIND GRIND GRIND GRIND GRIND GRIND GRIND
I'LL HAVE WHAT HE'S HAVING

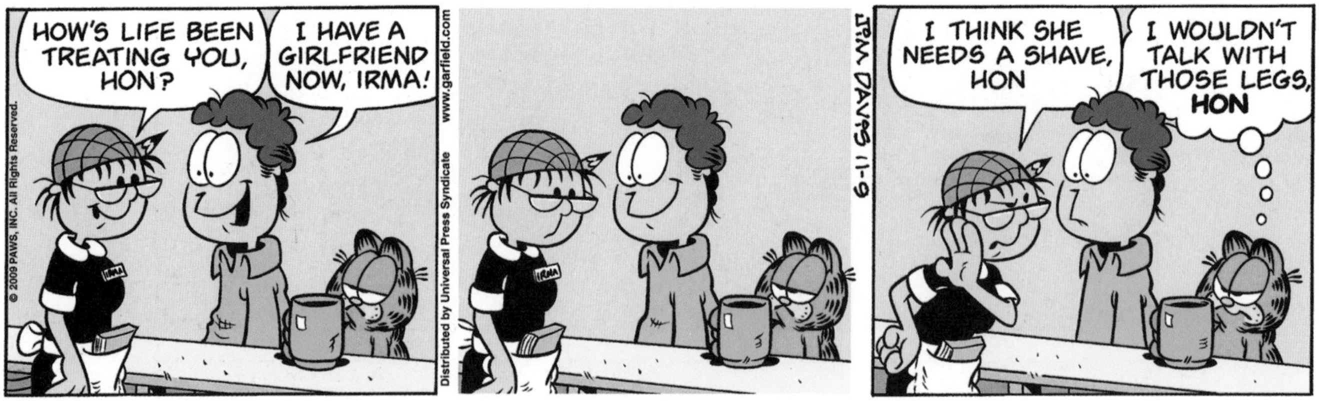
HOW'S LIFE BEEN TREATING YOU, HON?
I HAVE A GIRLFRIEND NOW, IRMA!
I THINK SHE NEEDS A SHAVE, HON
I WOULDN'T TALK WITH THOSE LEGS, **HON**
© 2009 PAWS, INC. All Rights Reserved.
www.garfield.com
Distributed by Universal Press Syndicate
JPM DAVIS 11-9

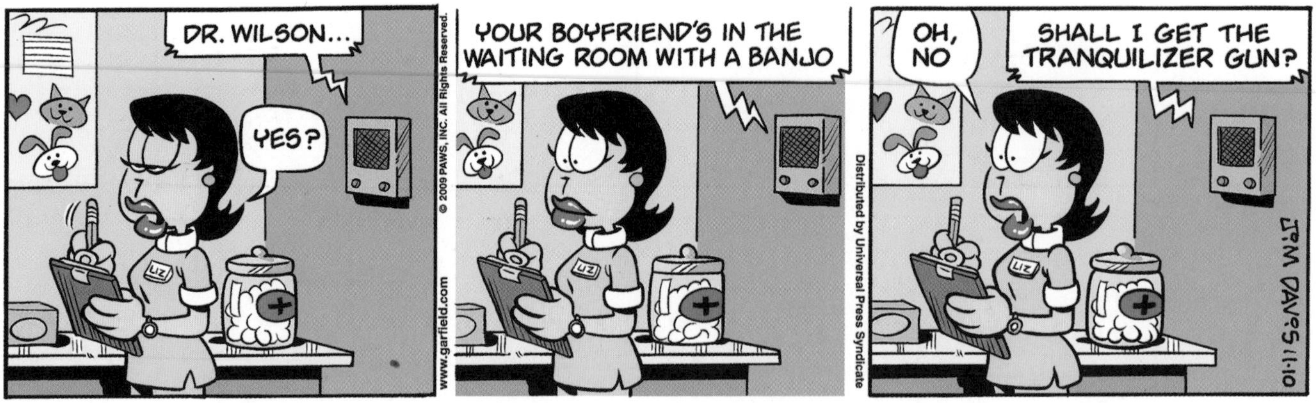
DR. WILSON...
YES?
YOUR BOYFRIEND'S IN THE WAITING ROOM WITH A BANJO
OH, NO
SHALL I GET THE TRANQUILIZER GUN?
© 2009 PAWS, INC. All Rights Reserved.
www.garfield.com
Distributed by Universal Press Syndicate
JPM DAVIS 11-10

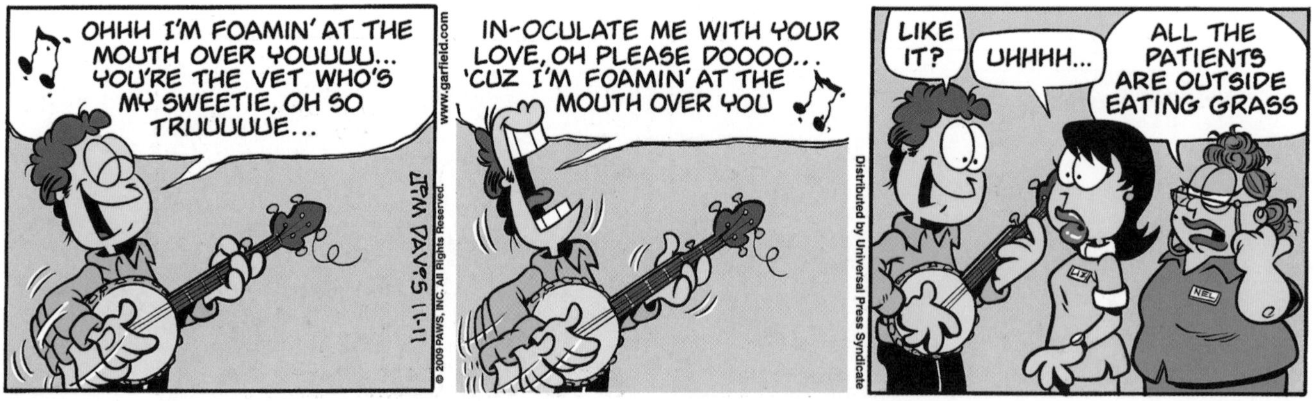
OHHH I'M FOAMIN' AT THE MOUTH OVER YOUUUU... YOU'RE THE VET WHO'S MY SWEETIE, OH SO TRUUUUUE...
IN-OCULATE ME WITH YOUR LOVE, OH PLEASE DOOOO... 'CUZ I'M FOAMIN' AT THE MOUTH OVER YOU
LIKE IT?
UHHHH...
ALL THE PATIENTS ARE OUTSIDE EATING GRASS
© 2009 PAWS, INC. All Rights Reserved.
www.garfield.com
Distributed by Universal Press Syndicate
JPM DAVIS 11-11

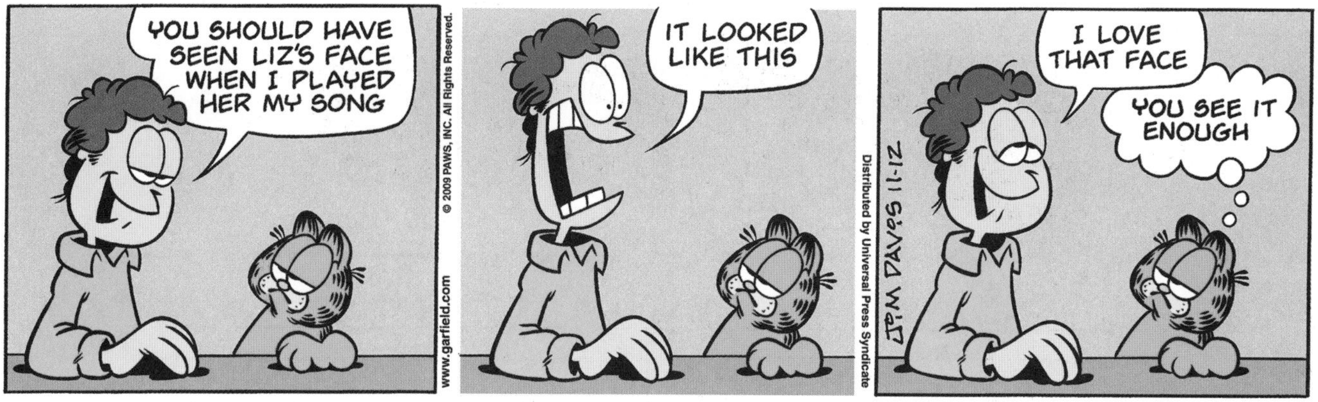
YOU SHOULD HAVE SEEN LIZ'S FACE WHEN I PLAYED HER MY SONG
IT LOOKED LIKE THIS
I LOVE THAT FACE
YOU SEE IT ENOUGH
JPM DAVPS 11-12
© 2009 PAWS, INC. All Rights Reserved.
www.garfield.com
Distributed by Universal Press Syndicate

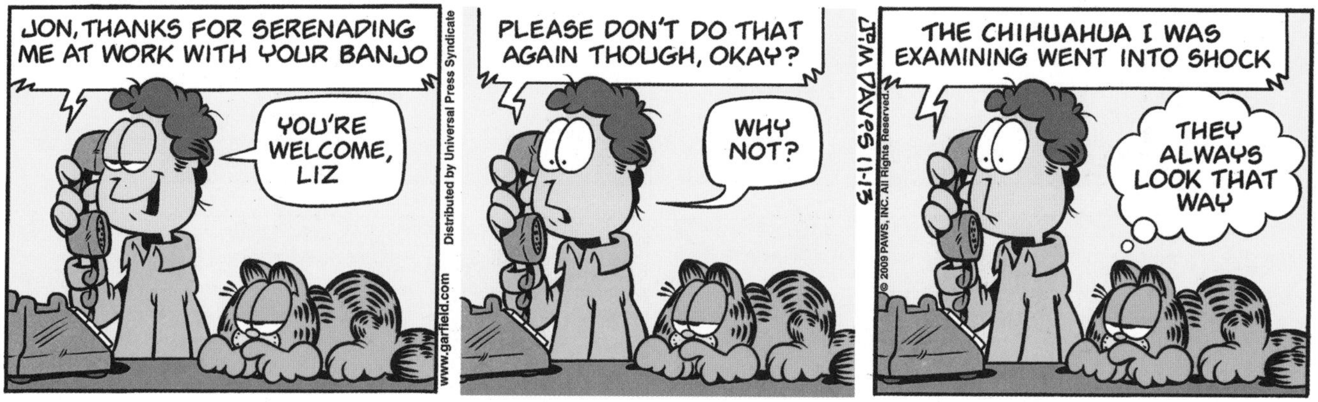
JON, THANKS FOR SERENADING ME AT WORK WITH YOUR BANJO
YOU'RE WELCOME, LIZ
PLEASE DON'T DO THAT AGAIN THOUGH, OKAY?
WHY NOT?
THE CHIHUAHUA I WAS EXAMINING WENT INTO SHOCK
THEY ALWAYS LOOK THAT WAY
JPM DAVPS 11-13
Distributed by Universal Press Syndicate
www.garfield.com
© 2009 PAWS, INC. All Rights Reserved.

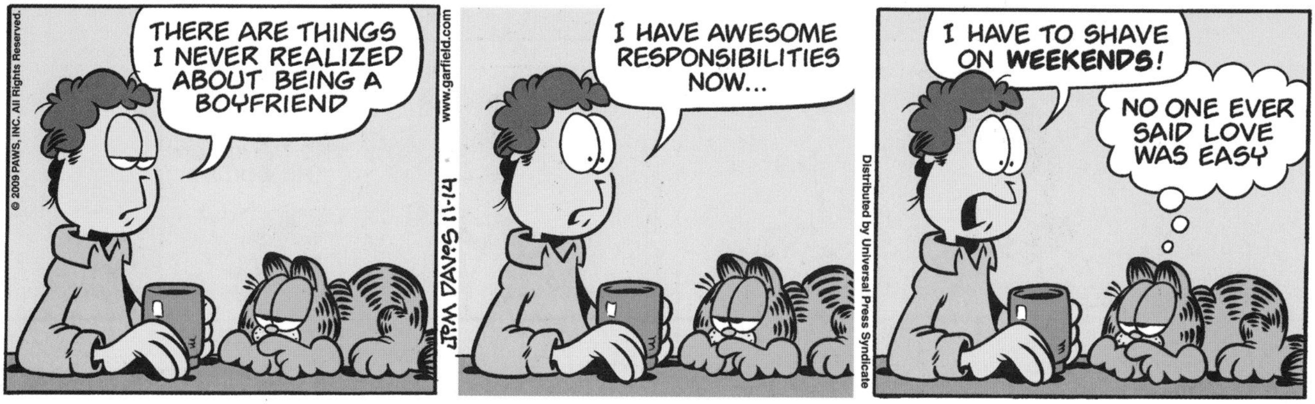
THERE ARE THINGS I NEVER REALIZED ABOUT BEING A BOYFRIEND
I HAVE AWESOME RESPONSIBILITIES NOW...
I HAVE TO SHAVE ON **WEEKENDS**!
NO ONE EVER SAID LOVE WAS EASY
JPM DAVPS 11-14
© 2009 PAWS, INC. All Rights Reserved.
www.garfield.com
Distributed by Universal Press Syndicate

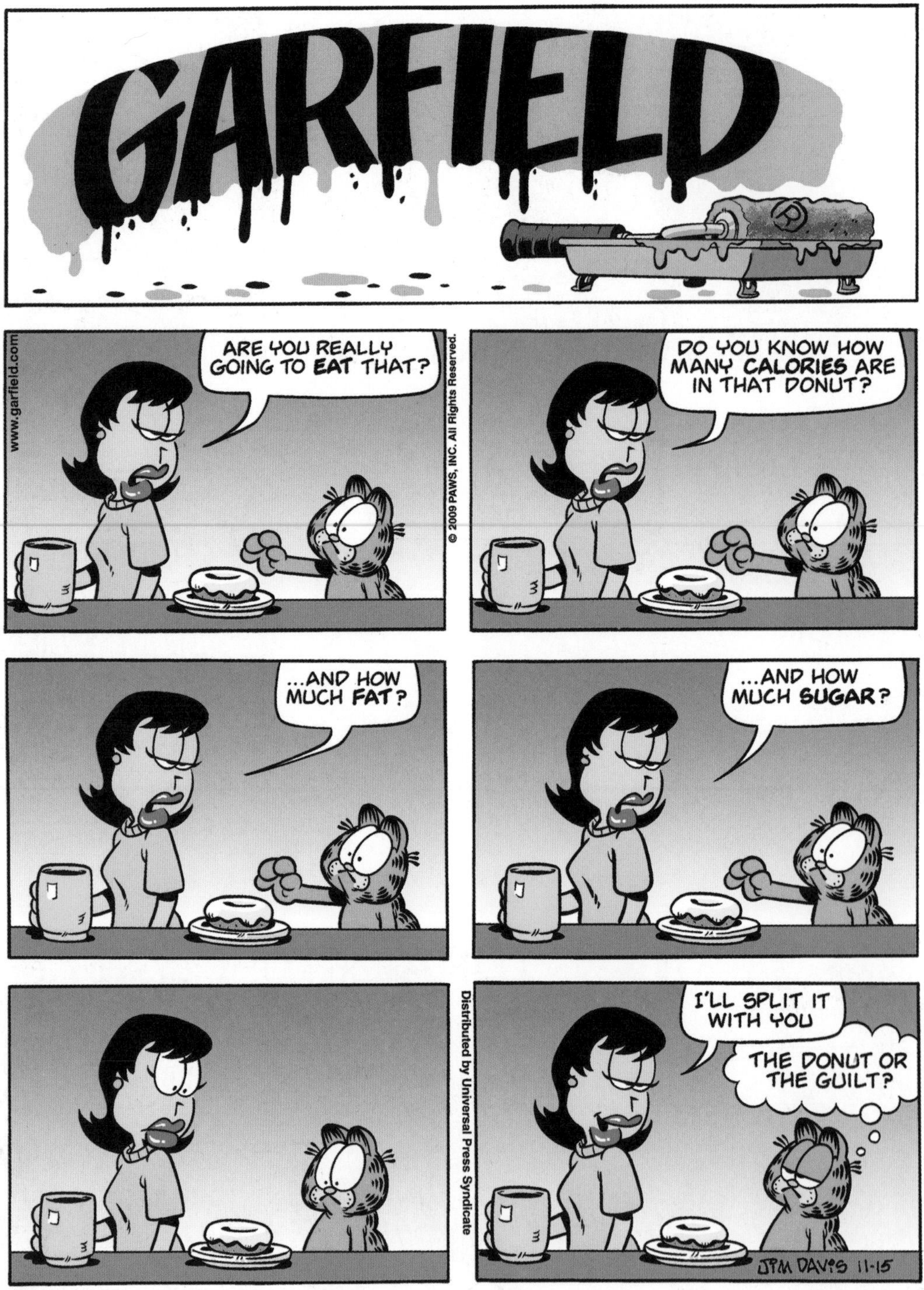
GARFIELD
www.garfield.com
© 2009 PAWS, INC. All Rights Reserved.
ARE YOU REALLY GOING TO EAT THAT?
DO YOU KNOW HOW MANY CALORIES ARE IN THAT DONUT?
...AND HOW MUCH FAT?
...AND HOW MUCH SUGAR?
Distributed by Universal Press Syndicate
I'LL SPLIT IT WITH YOU
THE DONUT OR THE GUILT?
JIM DAVIS 11-15

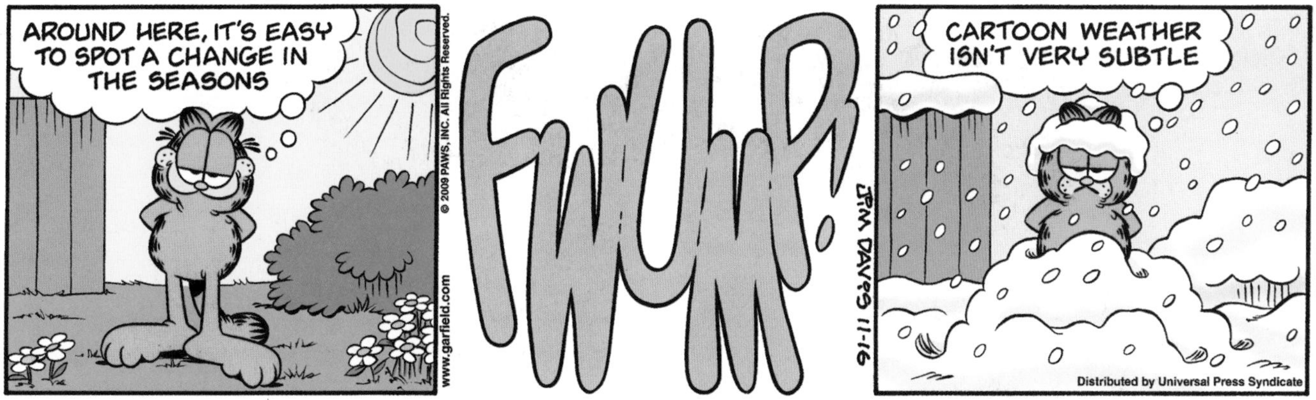
AROUND HERE, IT'S EASY TO SPOT A CHANGE IN THE SEASONS
FWUMP!
CARTOON WEATHER ISN'T VERY SUBTLE
© 2009 PAWS, INC. All Rights Reserved.
www.garfield.com
JIM DAVIS 11-16
Distributed by Universal Press Syndicate

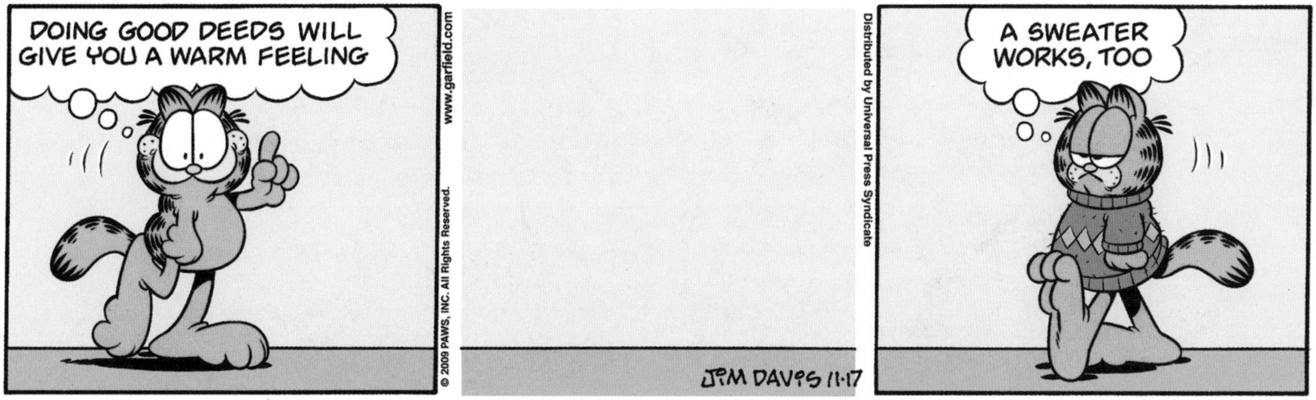
DOING GOOD DEEDS WILL GIVE YOU A WARM FEELING
A SWEATER WORKS, TOO
© 2009 PAWS, INC. All Rights Reserved.
www.garfield.com
JIM DAVIS 11-17
Distributed by Universal Press Syndicate

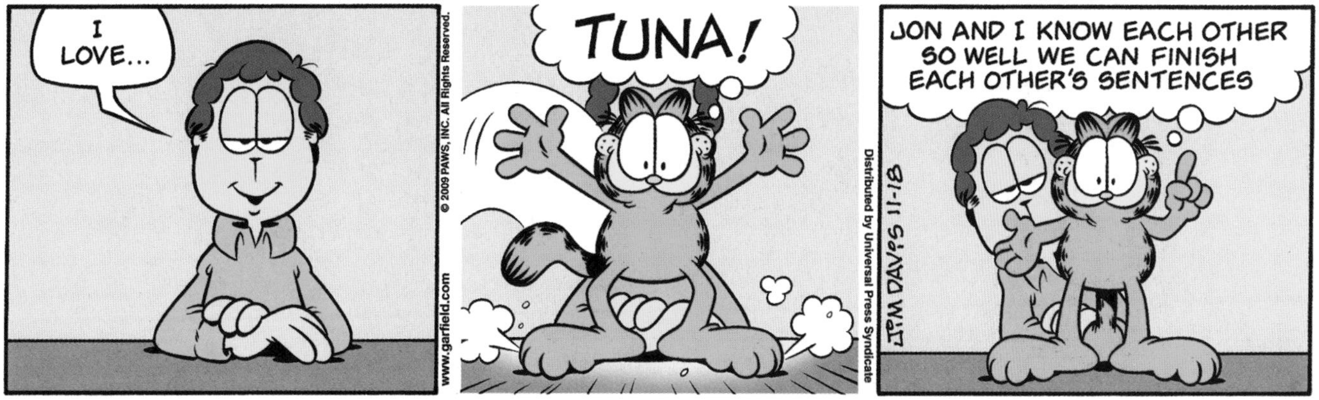
I LOVE...
TUNA!
JON AND I KNOW EACH OTHER SO WELL WE CAN FINISH EACH OTHER'S SENTENCES
© 2009 PAWS, INC. All Rights Reserved.
www.garfield.com
JIM DAVIS 11-18
Distributed by Universal Press Syndicate

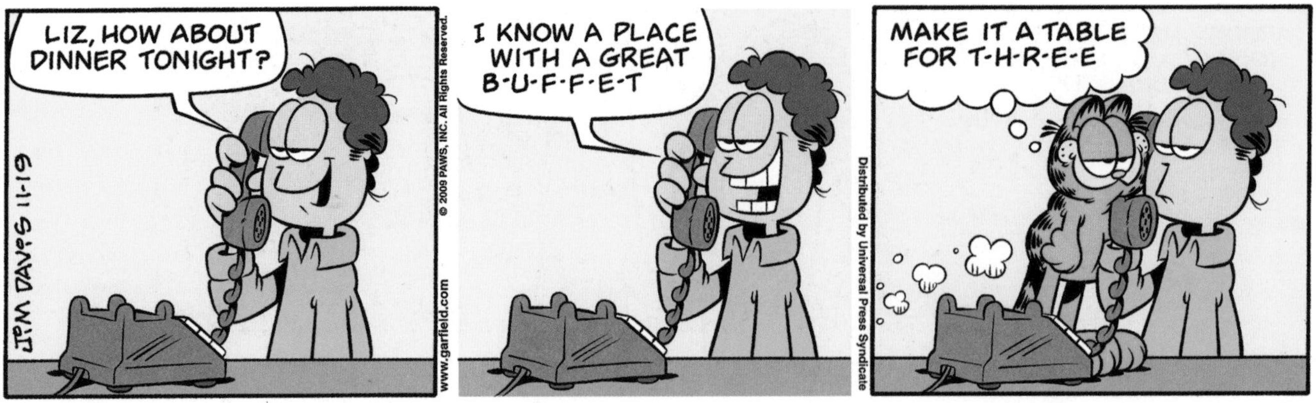
LIZ, HOW ABOUT DINNER TONIGHT?
I KNOW A PLACE WITH A GREAT B-U-F-F-E-T
MAKE IT A TABLE FOR T-H-R-E-E

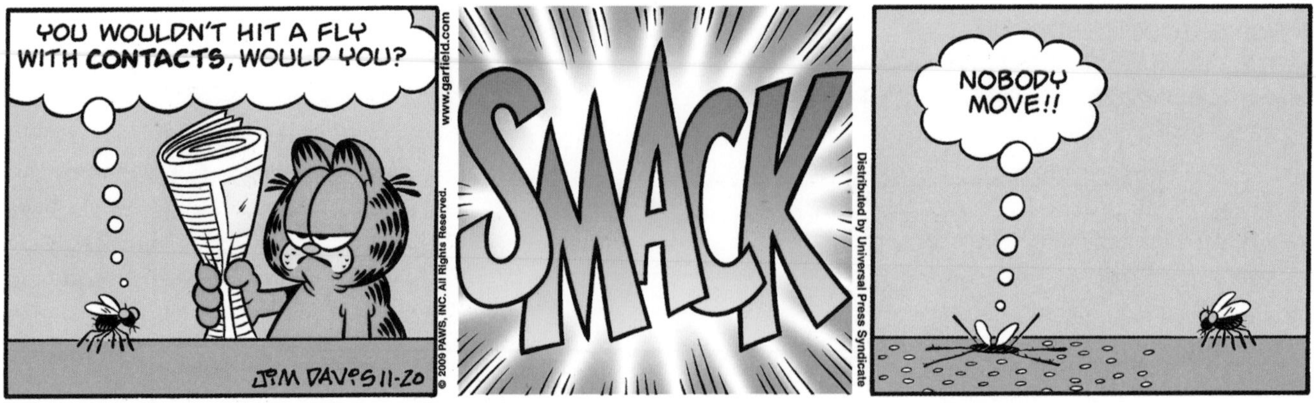
YOU WOULDN'T HIT A FLY WITH **CONTACTS**, WOULD YOU?
SMACK
NOBODY MOVE!!

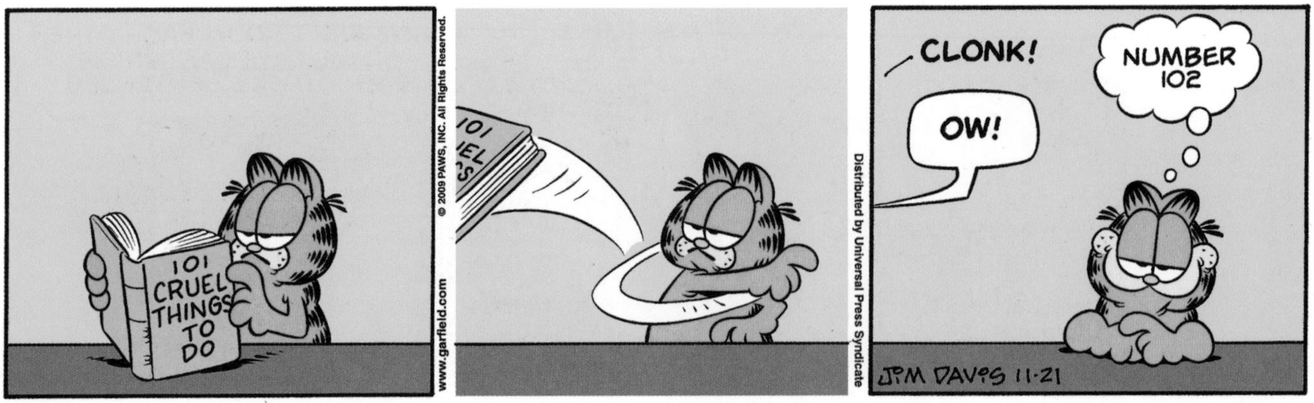
101 CRUEL THINGS TO DO
CLONK!
OW!
NUMBER 102

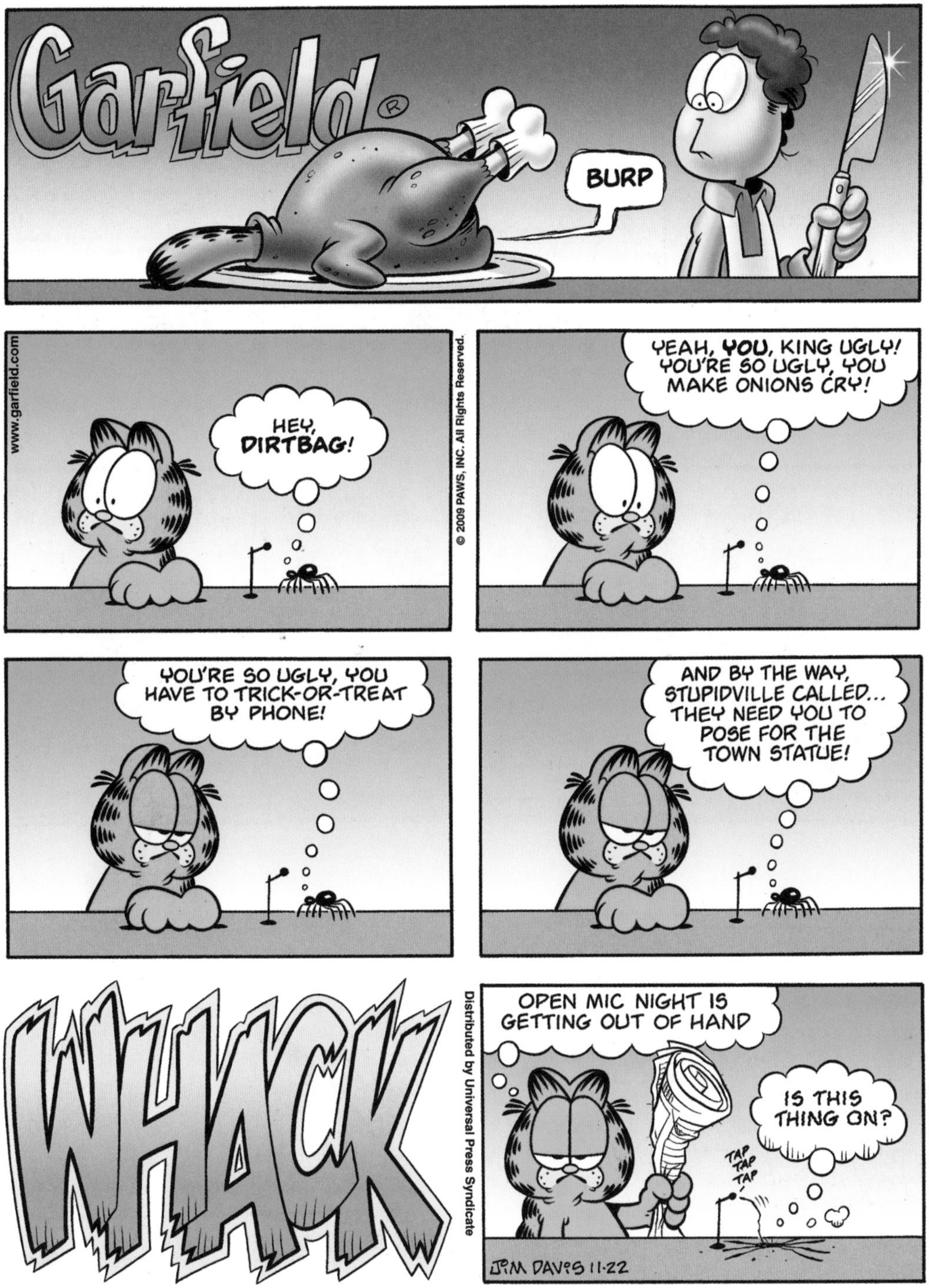
Garfield®
BURP
www.garfield.com
HEY, DIRTBAG!
© 2009 PAWS, INC. All Rights Reserved.
YEAH, YOU, KING UGLY! YOU'RE SO UGLY, YOU MAKE ONIONS CRY!
YOU'RE SO UGLY, YOU HAVE TO TRICK-OR-TREAT BY PHONE!
AND BY THE WAY, STUPIDVILLE CALLED... THEY NEED YOU TO POSE FOR THE TOWN STATUE!
WHACK
Distributed by Universal Press Syndicate
OPEN MIC NIGHT IS GETTING OUT OF HAND
TAP TAP TAP
IS THIS THING ON?
JIM DAVIS 11·22

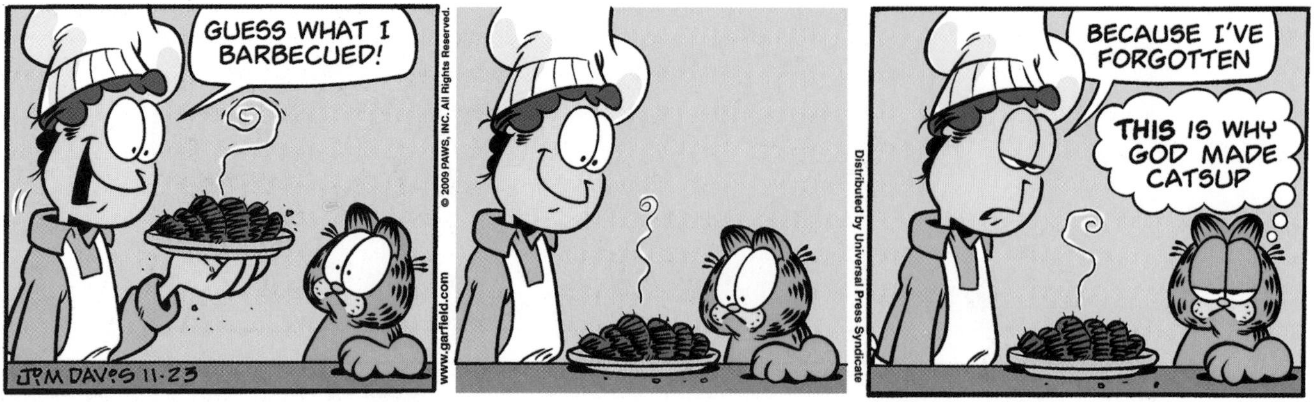
GUESS WHAT I BARBECUED!
JIM DAVIS 11-23
© 2009 PAWS, INC. All Rights Reserved.
www.garfield.com
BECAUSE I'VE FORGOTTEN
THIS IS WHY GOD MADE CATSUP
Distributed by Universal Press Syndicate

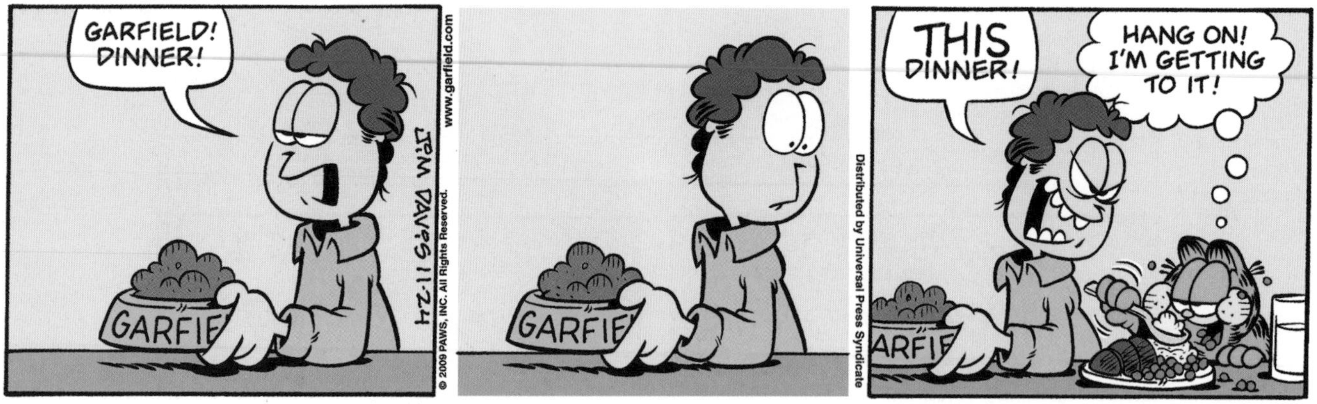
GARFIELD! DINNER!
GARFIE
JIM DAVIS 11-24
© 2009 PAWS, INC. All Rights Reserved.
www.garfield.com
GARFIE
THIS DINNER!
HANG ON! I'M GETTING TO IT!
ARFIE
Distributed by Universal Press Syndicate

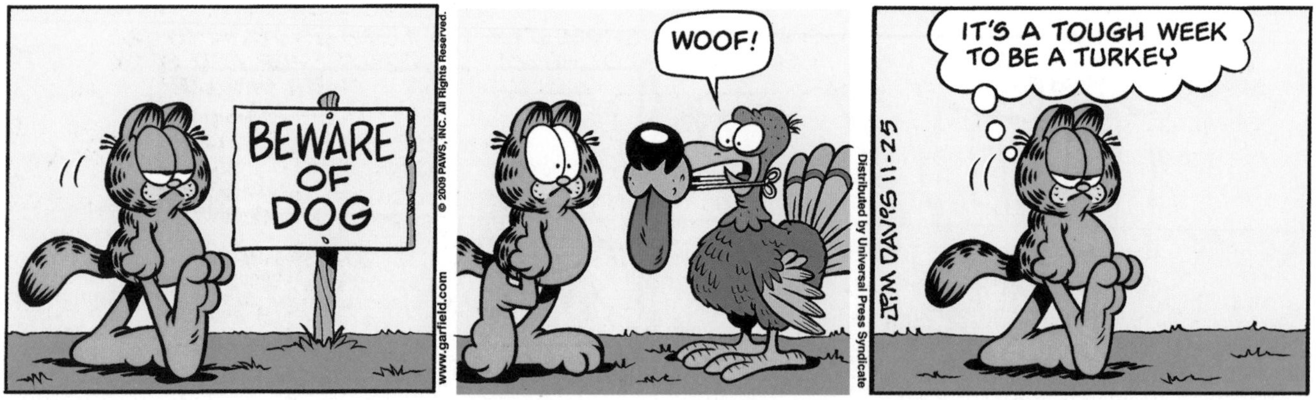
BEWARE OF DOG
© 2009 PAWS, INC. All Rights Reserved.
www.garfield.com
WOOF!
Distributed by Universal Press Syndicate
JIM DAVIS 11-25
IT'S A TOUGH WEEK TO BE A TURKEY

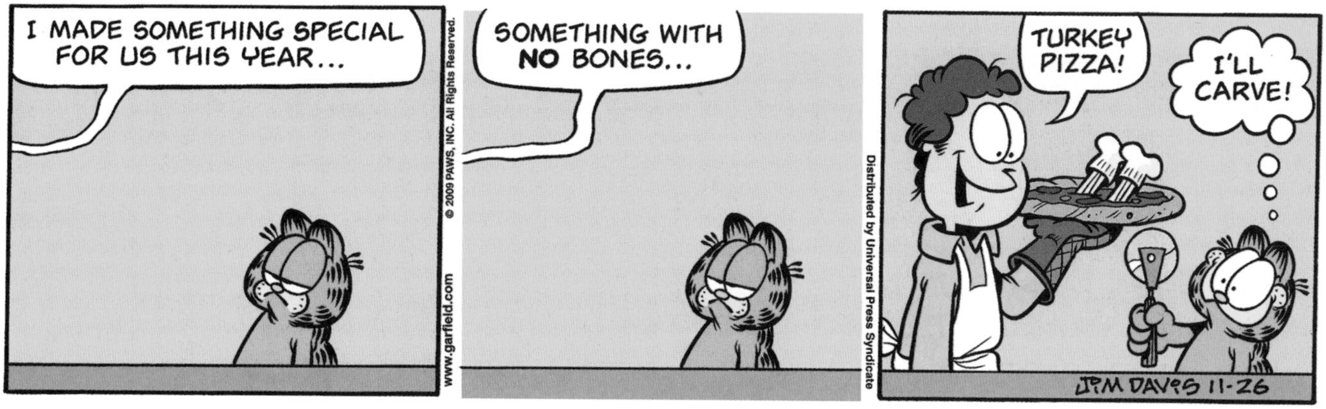
I MADE SOMETHING SPECIAL FOR US THIS YEAR...
SOMETHING WITH NO BONES...
TURKEY PIZZA!
I'LL CARVE!
JIM DAVIS 11-26
© 2009 PAWS, INC. All Rights Reserved. www.garfield.com
Distributed by Universal Press Syndicate

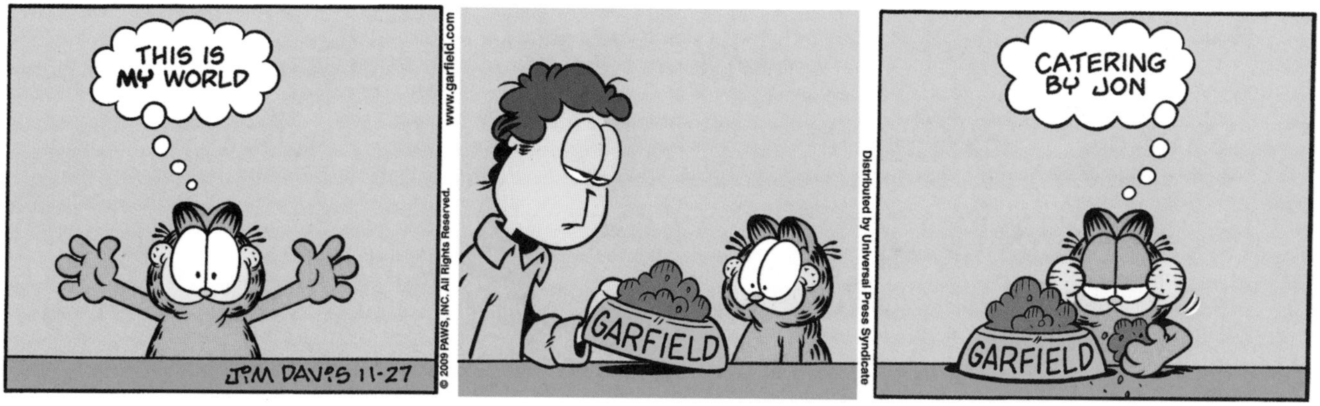
THIS IS MY WORLD
JIM DAVIS 11-27
GARFIELD
CATERING BY JON
GARFIELD
© 2009 PAWS, INC. All Rights Reserved. www.garfield.com
Distributed by Universal Press Syndicate

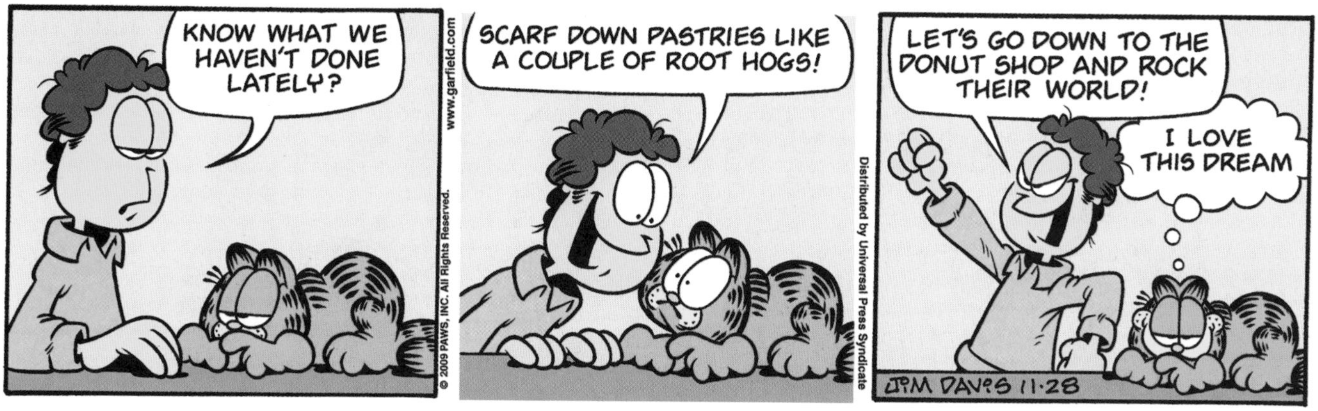
KNOW WHAT WE HAVEN'T DONE LATELY?
SCARF DOWN PASTRIES LIKE A COUPLE OF ROOT HOGS!
LET'S GO DOWN TO THE DONUT SHOP AND ROCK THEIR WORLD!
I LOVE THIS DREAM
JIM DAVIS 11-28
© 2009 PAWS, INC. All Rights Reserved. www.garfield.com
Distributed by Universal Press Syndicate

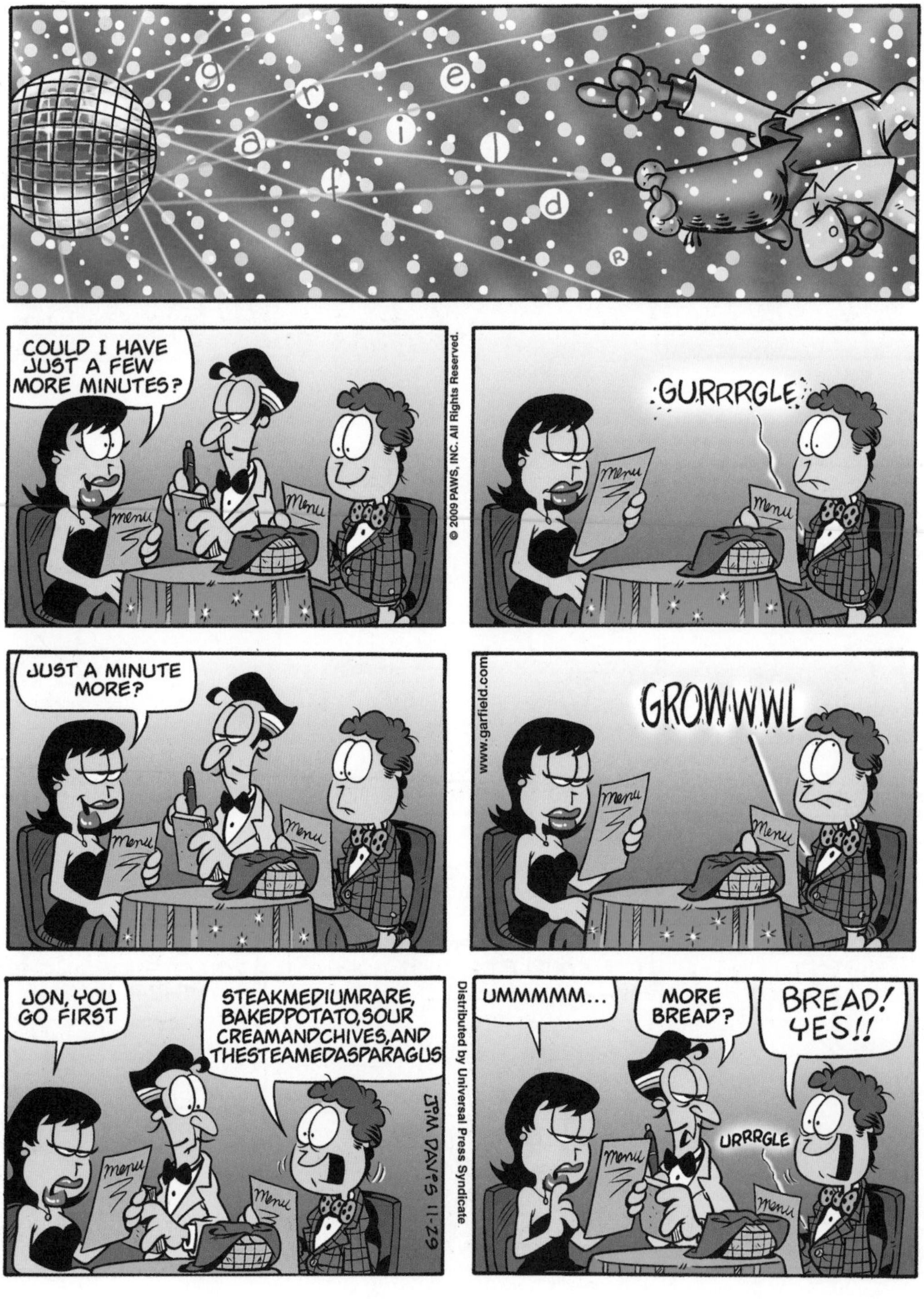
garfield
COULD I HAVE JUST A FEW MORE MINUTES?
© 2009 PAWS, INC. All Rights Reserved.
GURRRGLE
JUST A MINUTE MORE?
www.garfield.com
GROWWWL
JON, YOU GO FIRST
STEAKMEDIUMRARE, BAKEDPOTATO,SOUR CREAMANDCHIVES,AND THESTEAMEDASPARAGUS
JIM DAVIS 11-29
Distributed by Universal Press Syndicate
UMMMMM...
MORE BREAD?
URRRGLE
BREAD! YES!!

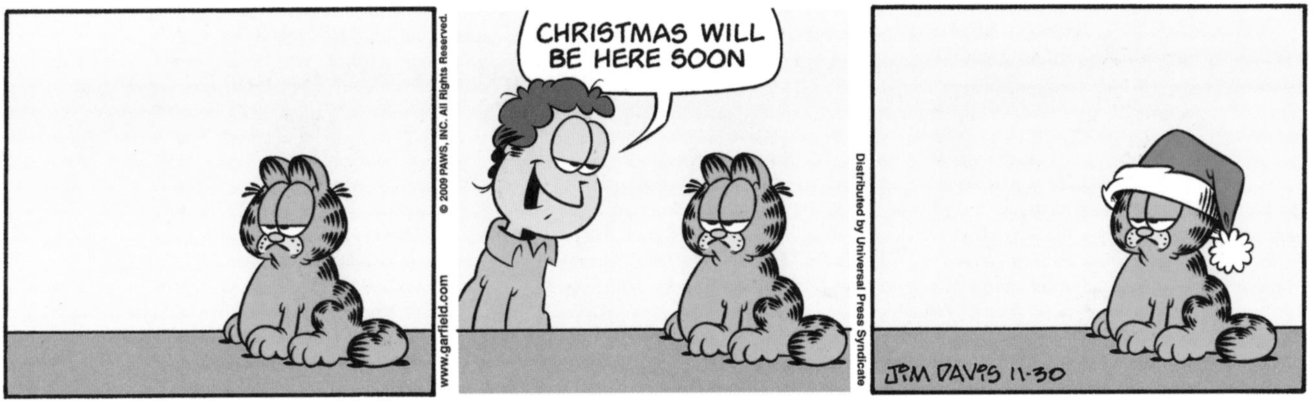
© 2009 PAWS, INC. All Rights Reserved.
www.garfield.com
CHRISTMAS WILL BE HERE SOON
Distributed by Universal Press Syndicate
JIM DAVIS 11-30

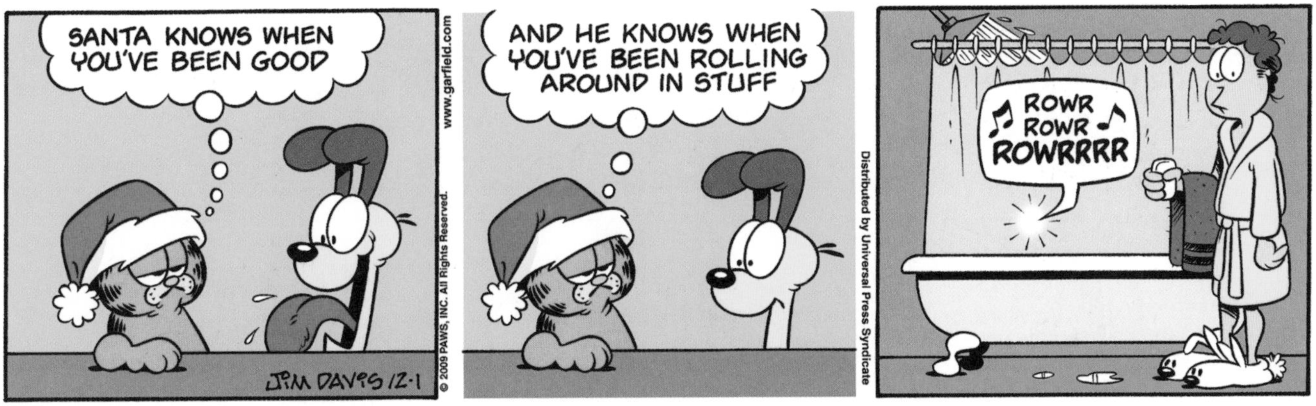
SANTA KNOWS WHEN YOU'VE BEEN GOOD
JIM DAVIS 12-1
www.garfield.com
© 2009 PAWS, INC. All Rights Reserved.
AND HE KNOWS WHEN YOU'VE BEEN ROLLING AROUND IN STUFF
Distributed by Universal Press Syndicate
ROWR ROWR ROWRRRR

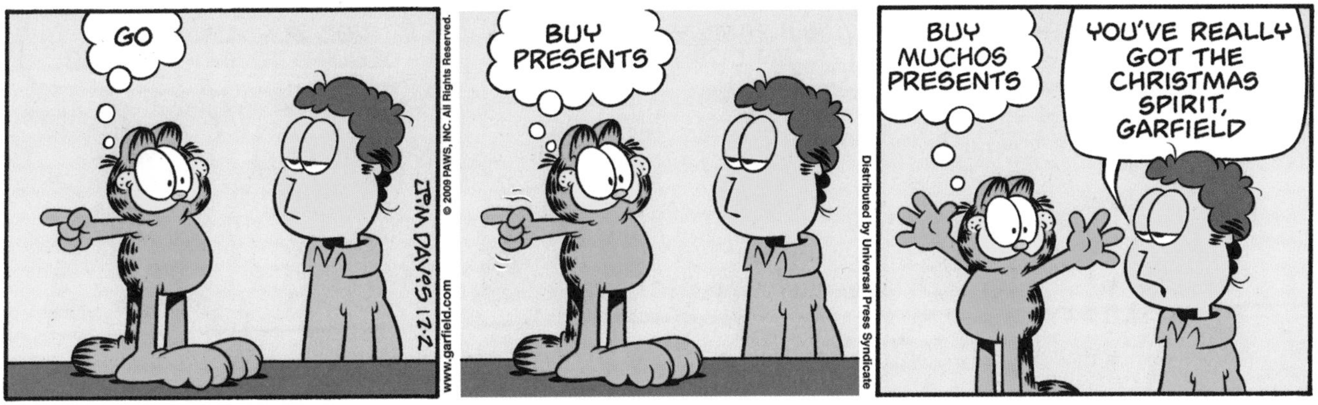
GO
© 2009 PAWS, INC. All Rights Reserved.
www.garfield.com
JIM DAVIS 12-2
BUY PRESENTS
Distributed by Universal Press Syndicate
BUY MUCHOS PRESENTS
YOU'VE REALLY GOT THE CHRISTMAS SPIRIT, GARFIELD

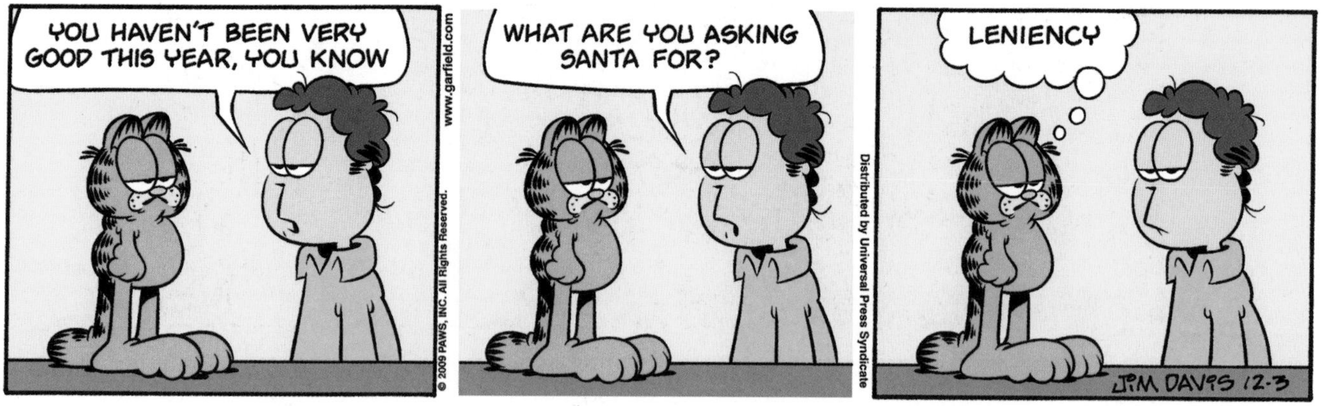
YOU HAVEN'T BEEN VERY GOOD THIS YEAR, YOU KNOW
WHAT ARE YOU ASKING SANTA FOR?
LENIENCY
JIM DAVIS 12-3
www.garfield.com
© 2009 PAWS, INC. All Rights Reserved.
Distributed by Universal Press Syndicate

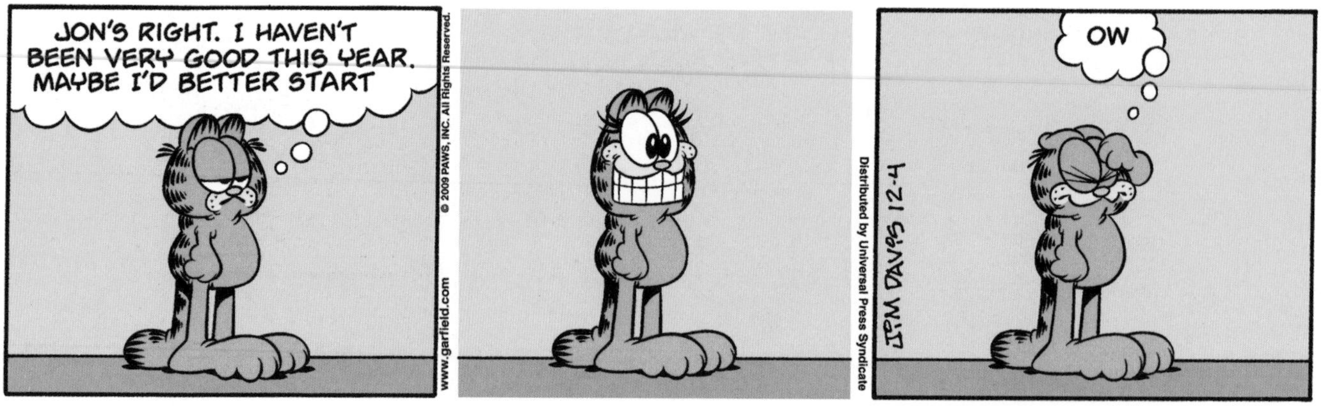
JON'S RIGHT. I HAVEN'T BEEN VERY GOOD THIS YEAR. MAYBE I'D BETTER START
OW
JIM DAVIS 12-4
www.garfield.com
© 2009 PAWS, INC. All Rights Reserved.
Distributed by Universal Press Syndicate

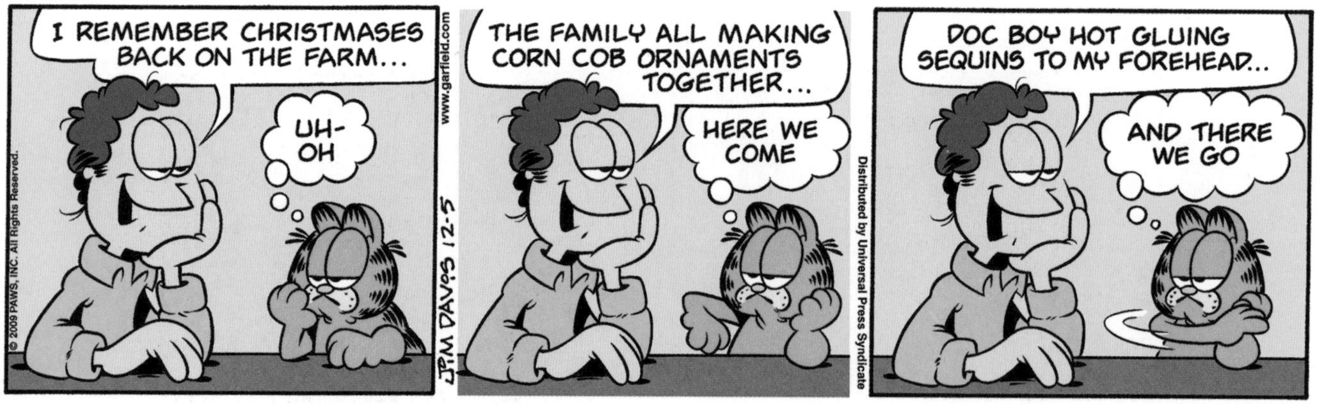
I REMEMBER CHRISTMASES BACK ON THE FARM...
UH-OH
THE FAMILY ALL MAKING CORN COB ORNAMENTS TOGETHER...
HERE WE COME
DOC BOY HOT GLUING SEQUINS TO MY FOREHEAD...
AND THERE WE GO
JIM DAVIS 12-5
www.garfield.com
© 2009 PAWS, INC. All Rights Reserved.
Distributed by Universal Press Syndicate

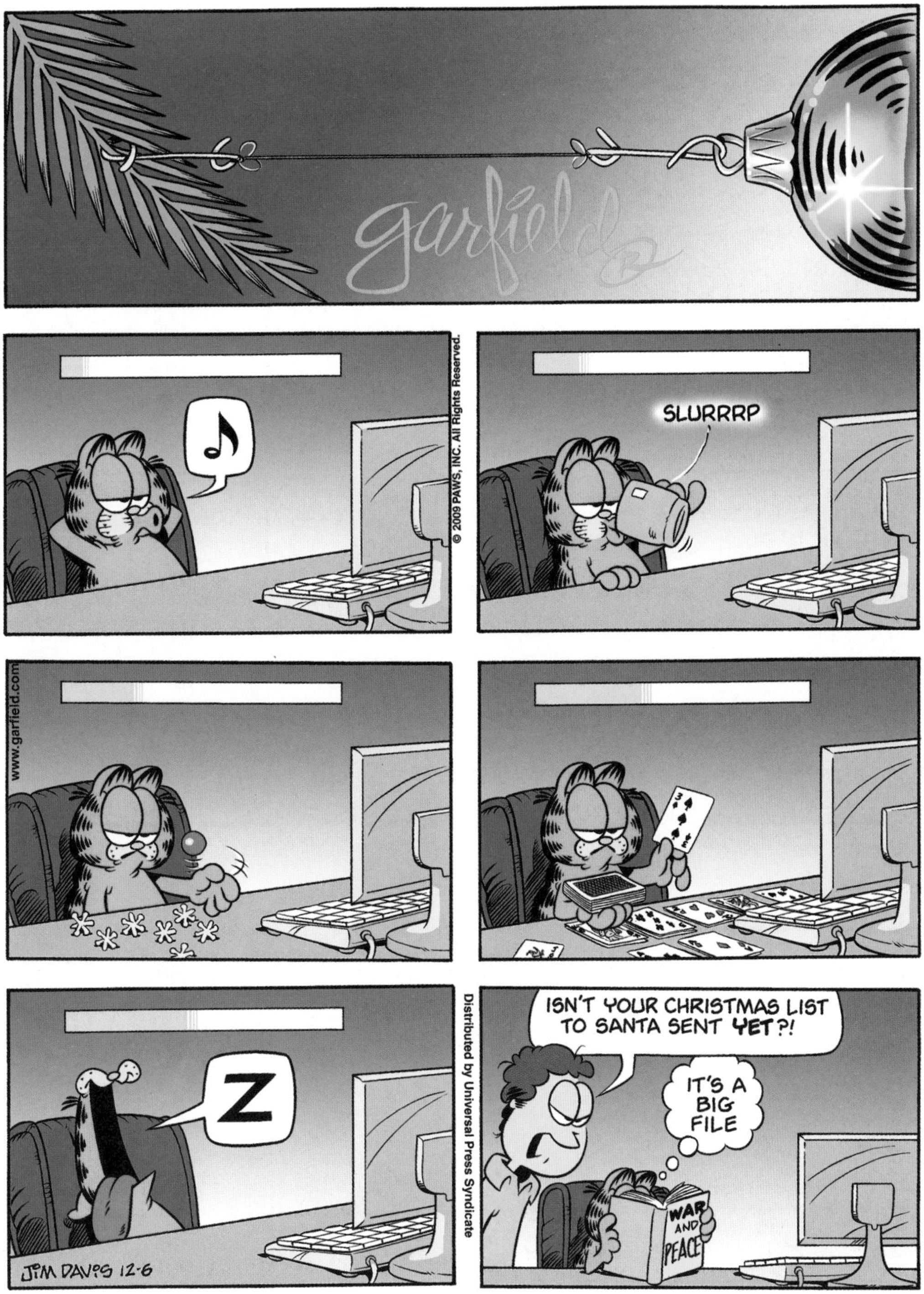
garfield
© 2009 PAWS, INC. All Rights Reserved.
♪
SLURRRP
www.garfield.com
Z
JIM DAVIS 12-6
Distributed by Universal Press Syndicate
ISN'T YOUR CHRISTMAS LIST TO SANTA SENT **YET**?!
IT'S A BIG FILE
WAR AND PEACE

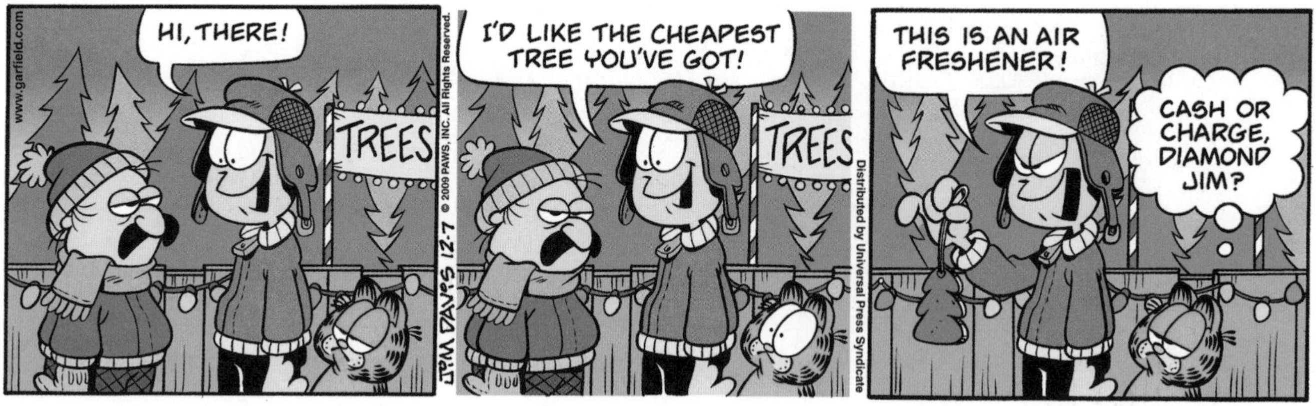

HI, THERE!
I'D LIKE THE CHEAPEST TREE YOU'VE GOT!
THIS IS AN AIR FRESHENER!
CASH OR CHARGE, DIAMOND JIM?
TREES
JPM DAVPS 12-7
www.garfield.com
© 2009 PAWS, INC. All Rights Reserved.
Distributed by Universal Press Syndicate

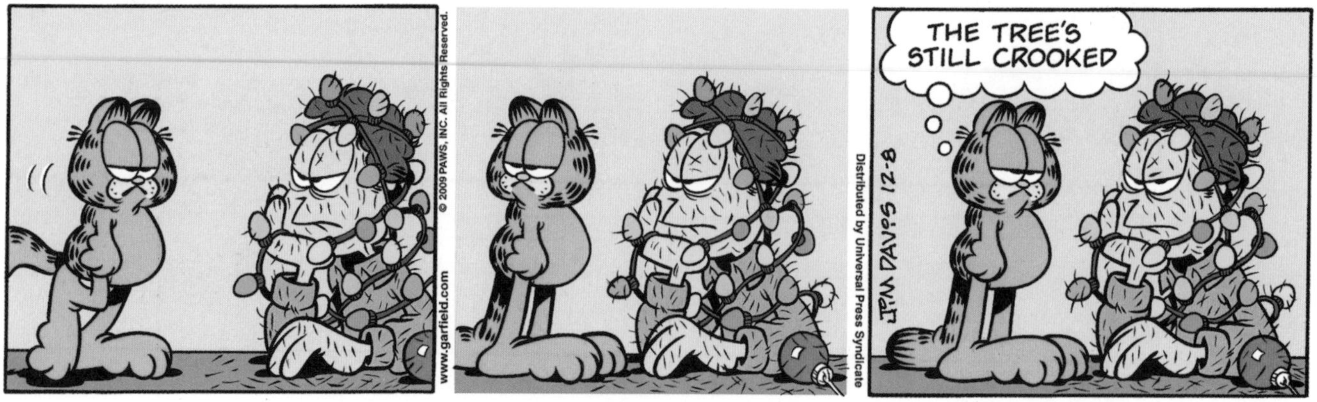

THE TREE'S STILL CROOKED
JPM DAVPS 12-8
© 2009 PAWS, INC. All Rights Reserved.
www.garfield.com
Distributed by Universal Press Syndicate

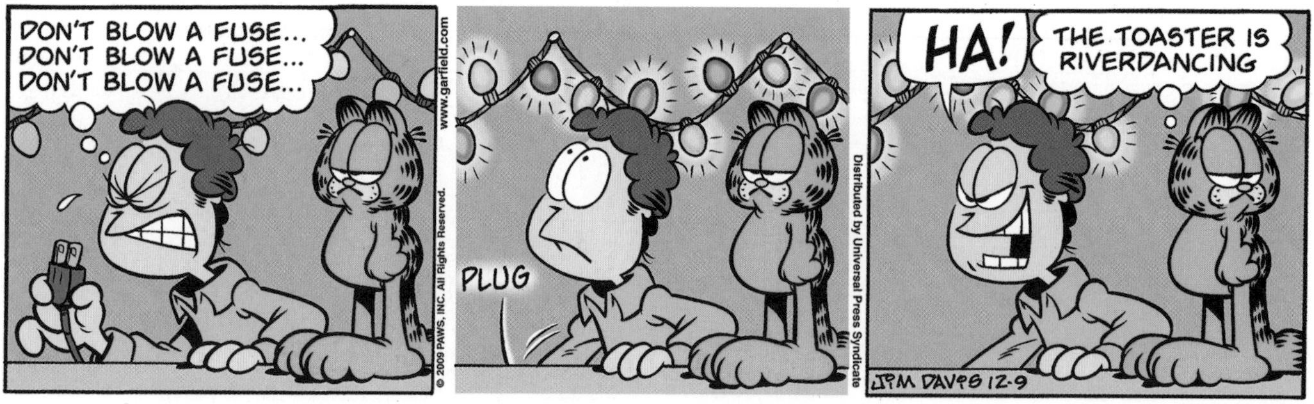

DON'T BLOW A FUSE...
DON'T BLOW A FUSE...
DON'T BLOW A FUSE...
PLUG
HA!
THE TOASTER IS RIVERDANCING
JPM DAVPS 12-9
www.garfield.com
© 2009 PAWS, INC. All Rights Reserved.
Distributed by Universal Press Syndicate

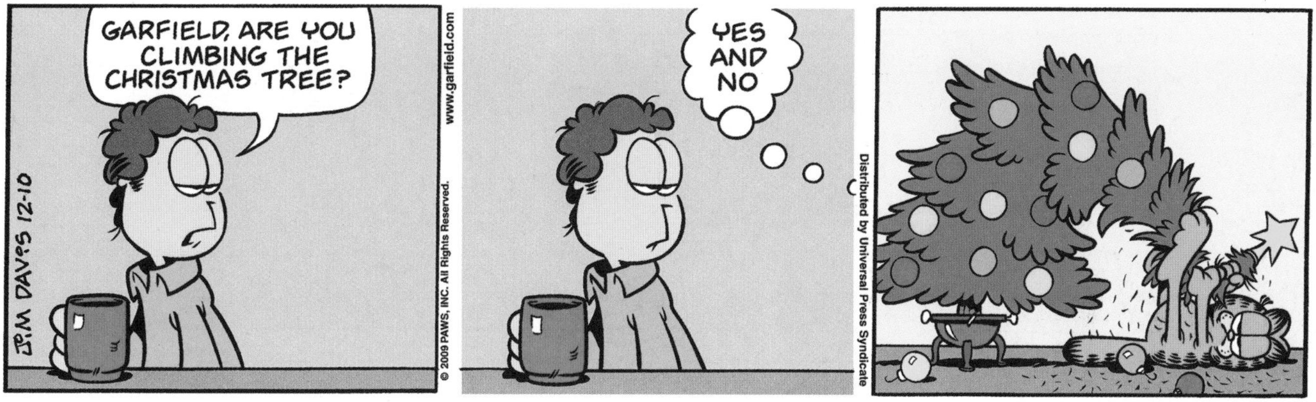
GARFIELD, ARE YOU CLIMBING THE CHRISTMAS TREE?
JIM DAVIS 12-10
© 2009 PAWS, INC. All Rights Reserved. www.garfield.com
YES AND NO
Distributed by Universal Press Syndicate

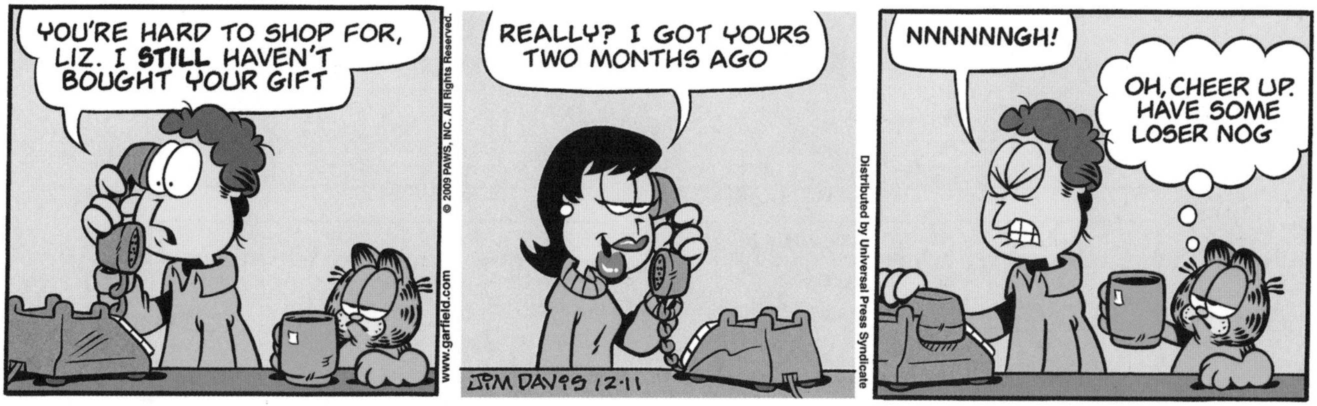
YOU'RE HARD TO SHOP FOR, LIZ. I STILL HAVEN'T BOUGHT YOUR GIFT
© 2009 PAWS, INC. All Rights Reserved. www.garfield.com
REALLY? I GOT YOURS TWO MONTHS AGO
JIM DAVIS 12-11
Distributed by Universal Press Syndicate
NNNNNNGH!
OH, CHEER UP. HAVE SOME LOSER NOG

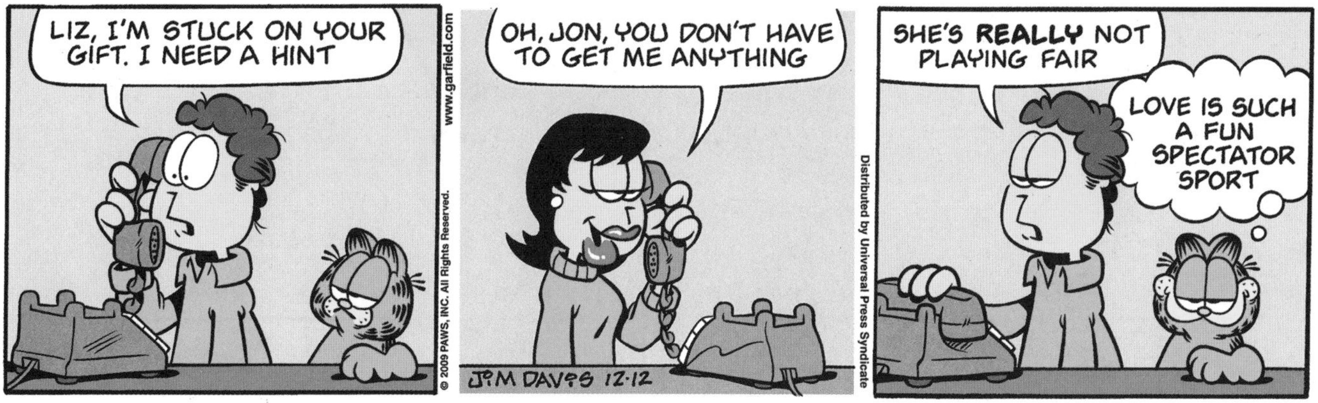
LIZ, I'M STUCK ON YOUR GIFT. I NEED A HINT
© 2009 PAWS, INC. All Rights Reserved. www.garfield.com
OH, JON, YOU DON'T HAVE TO GET ME ANYTHING
JIM DAVIS 12-12
Distributed by Universal Press Syndicate
SHE'S REALLY NOT PLAYING FAIR
LOVE IS SUCH A FUN SPECTATOR SPORT

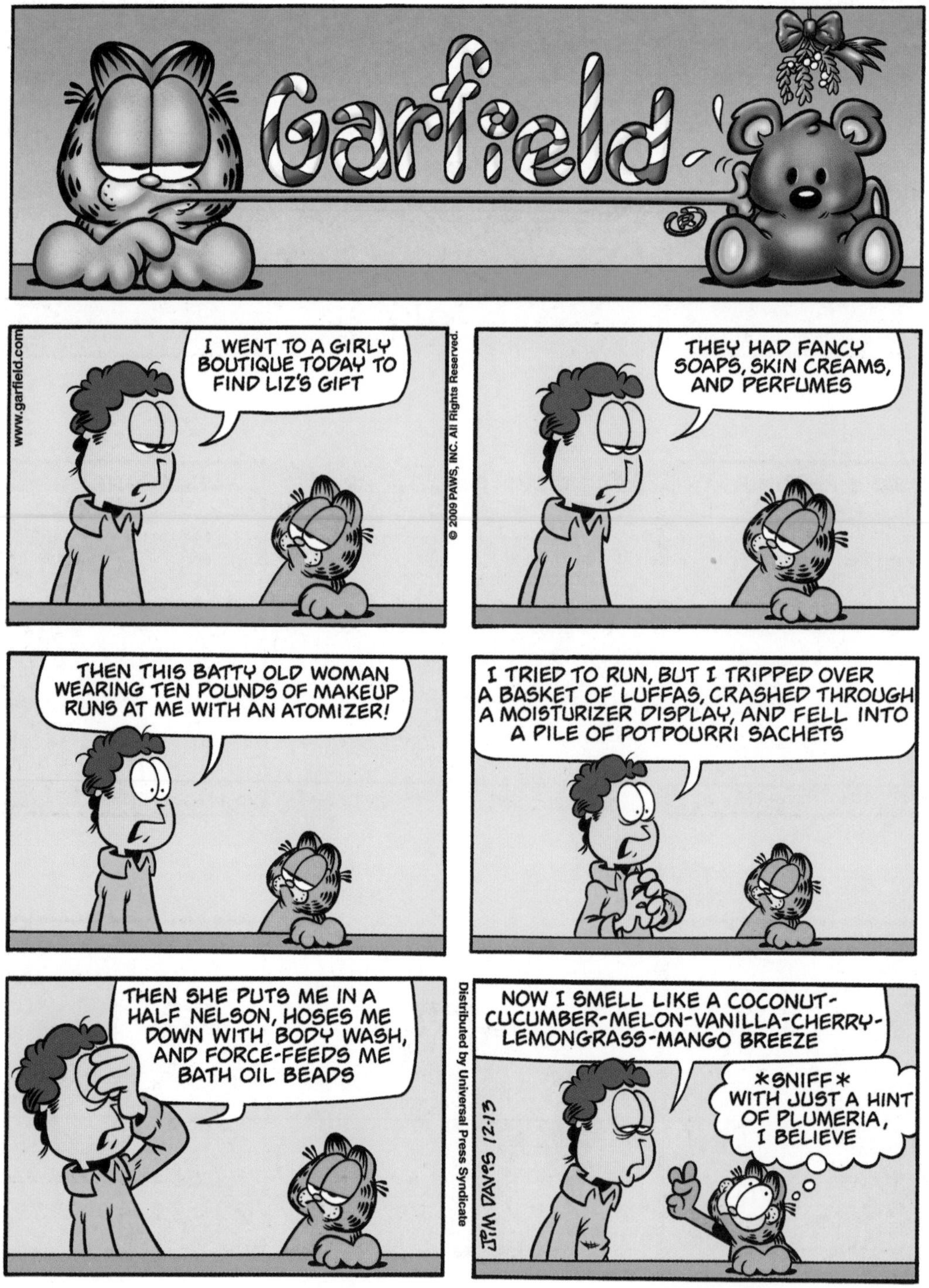
Garfield
www.garfield.com
© 2009 PAWS, INC. All Rights Reserved.
I WENT TO A GIRLY BOUTIQUE TODAY TO FIND LIZ'S GIFT
THEY HAD FANCY SOAPS, SKIN CREAMS, AND PERFUMES
THEN THIS BATTY OLD WOMAN WEARING TEN POUNDS OF MAKEUP RUNS AT ME WITH AN ATOMIZER!
I TRIED TO RUN, BUT I TRIPPED OVER A BASKET OF LUFFAS, CRASHED THROUGH A MOISTURIZER DISPLAY, AND FELL INTO A PILE OF POTPOURRI SACHETS
THEN SHE PUTS ME IN A HALF NELSON, HOSES ME DOWN WITH BODY WASH, AND FORCE-FEEDS ME BATH OIL BEADS
Distributed by Universal Press Syndicate
JIM DAVIS 12-13
NOW I SMELL LIKE A COCONUT-CUCUMBER-MELON-VANILLA-CHERRY-LEMONGRASS-MANGO BREEZE
SNIFF WITH JUST A HINT OF PLUMERIA, I BELIEVE

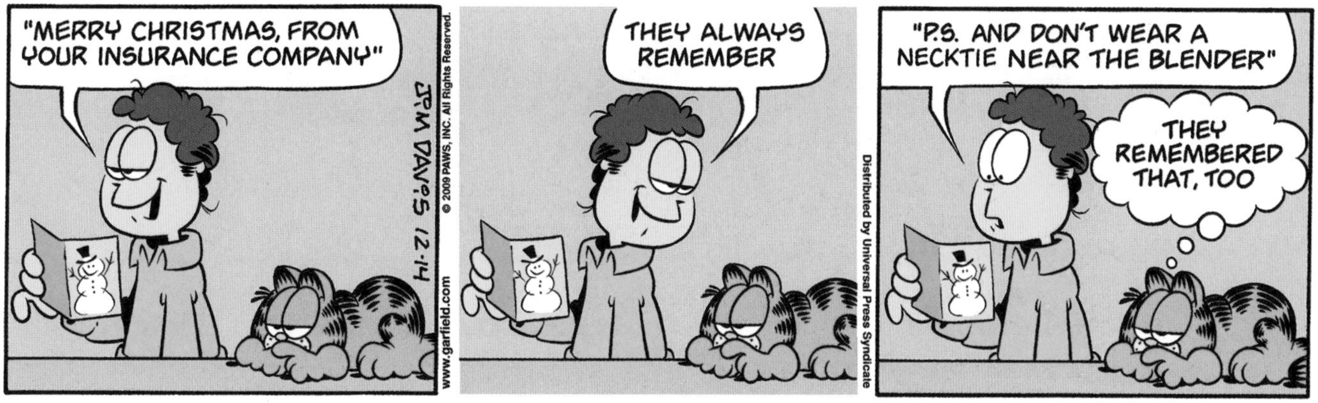
"MERRY CHRISTMAS, FROM YOUR INSURANCE COMPANY"
JIM DAVIS 12-14
© 2009 PAWS, INC. All Rights Reserved.
www.garfield.com
THEY ALWAYS REMEMBER
Distributed by Universal Press Syndicate
"P.S. AND DON'T WEAR A NECKTIE NEAR THE BLENDER"
THEY REMEMBERED THAT, TOO

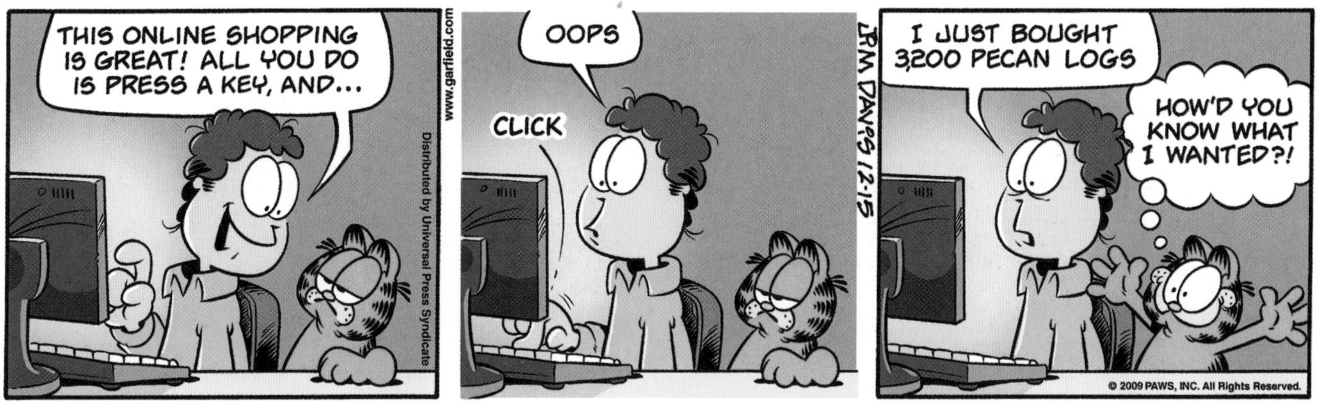
THIS ONLINE SHOPPING IS GREAT! ALL YOU DO IS PRESS A KEY, AND...
www.garfield.com
Distributed by Universal Press Syndicate
OOPS
CLICK
JIM DAVIS 12-15
I JUST BOUGHT 3,200 PECAN LOGS
HOW'D YOU KNOW WHAT I WANTED?!
© 2009 PAWS, INC. All Rights Reserved.

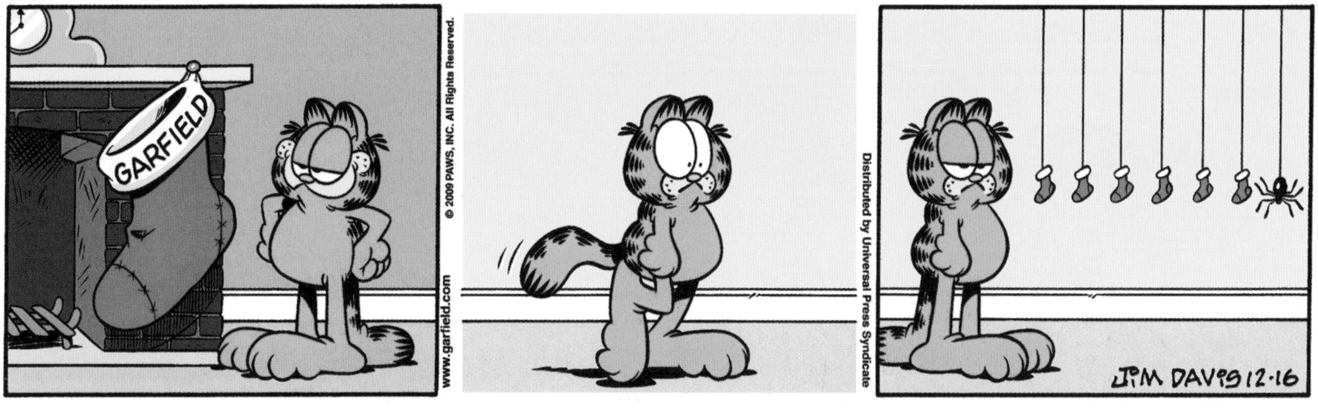
GARFIELD
© 2009 PAWS, INC. All Rights Reserved.
www.garfield.com
Distributed by Universal Press Syndicate
JIM DAVIS 12-16

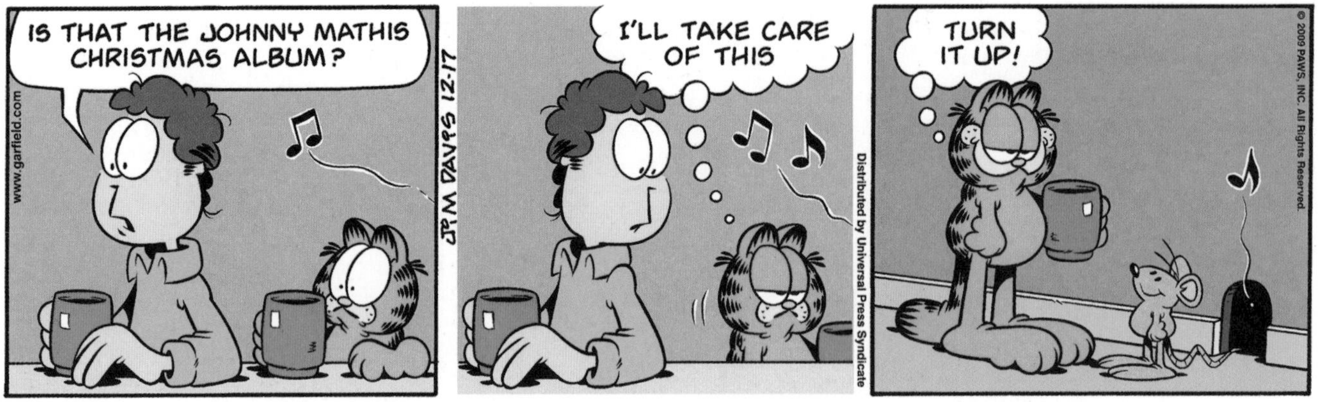
IS THAT THE JOHNNY MATHIS CHRISTMAS ALBUM?
I'LL TAKE CARE OF THIS
TURN IT UP!
JIM DAVIS 12-17
www.garfield.com
Distributed by Universal Press Syndicate
© 2009 PAWS, INC. All Rights Reserved.

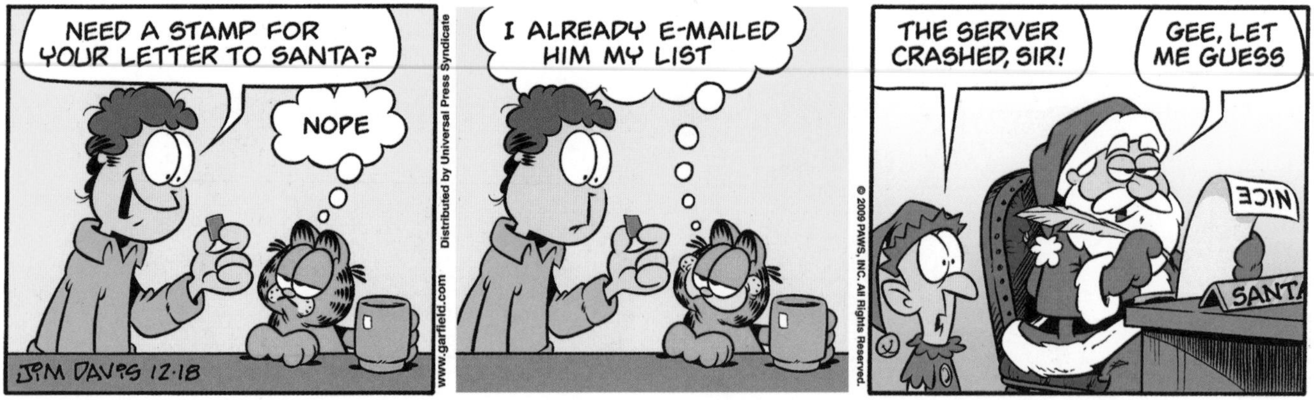
NEED A STAMP FOR YOUR LETTER TO SANTA?
NOPE
I ALREADY E-MAILED HIM MY LIST
THE SERVER CRASHED, SIR!
GEE, LET ME GUESS
NICE
SANTA
JIM DAVIS 12-18
Distributed by Universal Press Syndicate
www.garfield.com
© 2009 PAWS, INC. All Rights Reserved.

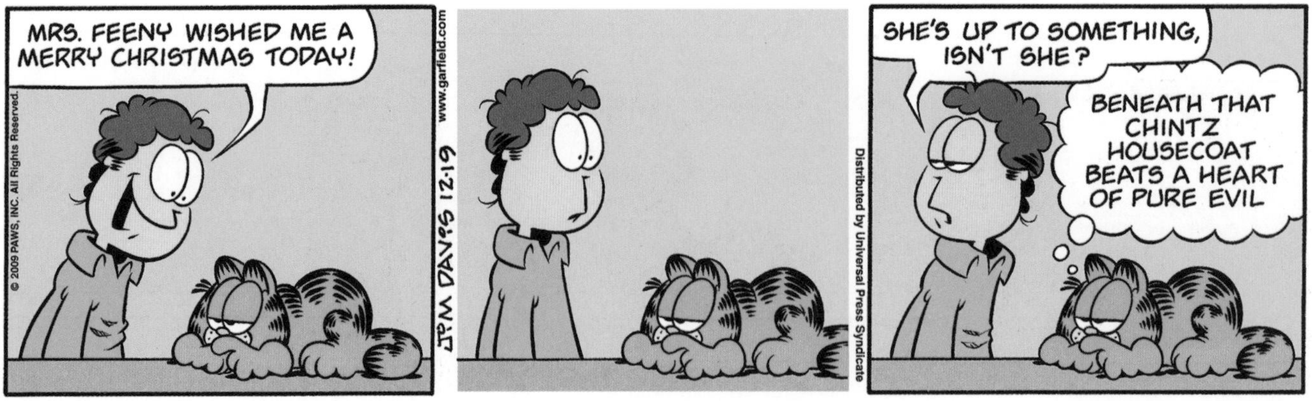
MRS. FEENY WISHED ME A MERRY CHRISTMAS TODAY!
SHE'S UP TO SOMETHING, ISN'T SHE?
BENEATH THAT CHINTZ HOUSECOAT BEATS A HEART OF PURE EVIL
JIM DAVIS 12-19
www.garfield.com
© 2009 PAWS, INC. All Rights Reserved.
Distributed by Universal Press Syndicate

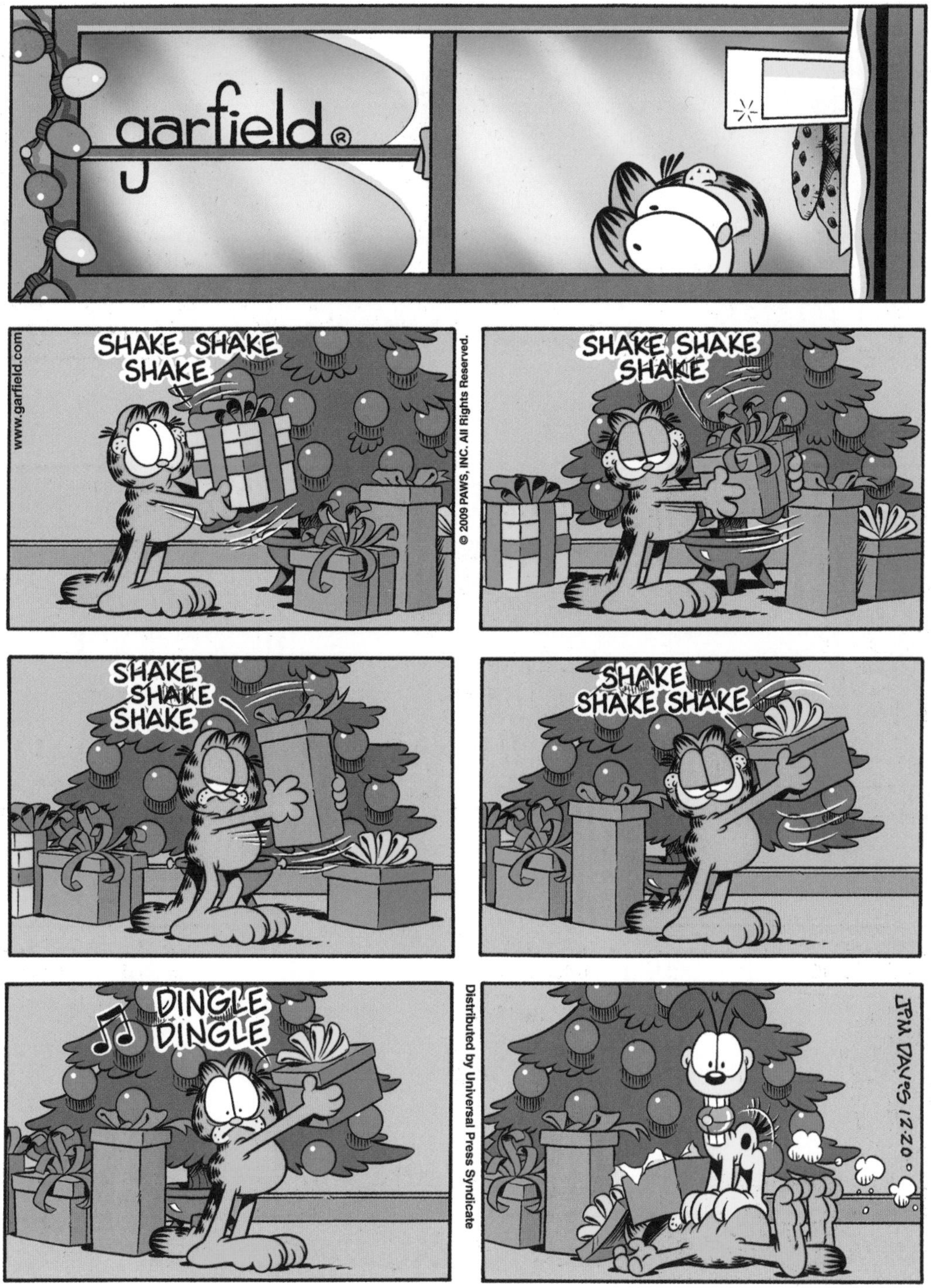
garfield®
www.garfield.com
SHAKE SHAKE SHAKE
© 2009 PAWS, INC. All Rights Reserved.
SHAKE SHAKE SHAKE
SHAKE SHAKE SHAKE
SHAKE SHAKE SHAKE
DINGLE DINGLE
Distributed by Universal Press Syndicate
JIM DAVIS 12-20

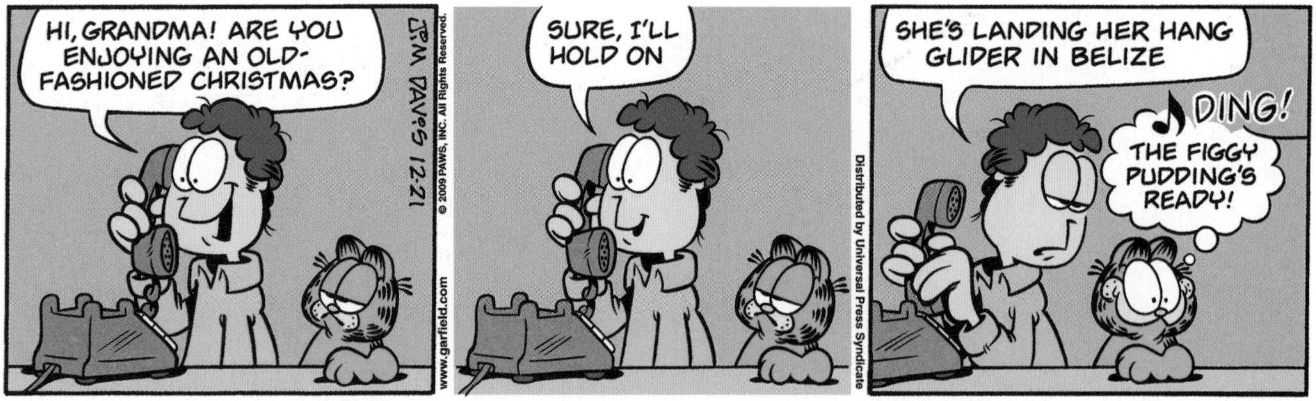
HI, GRANDMA! ARE YOU ENJOYING AN OLD-FASHIONED CHRISTMAS?
JIM DAVIS 12-21
© 2009 PAWS, INC. All Rights Reserved.
www.garfield.com
SURE, I'LL HOLD ON
Distributed by Universal Press Syndicate
SHE'S LANDING HER HANG GLIDER IN BELIZE
DING!
THE FIGGY PUDDING'S READY!

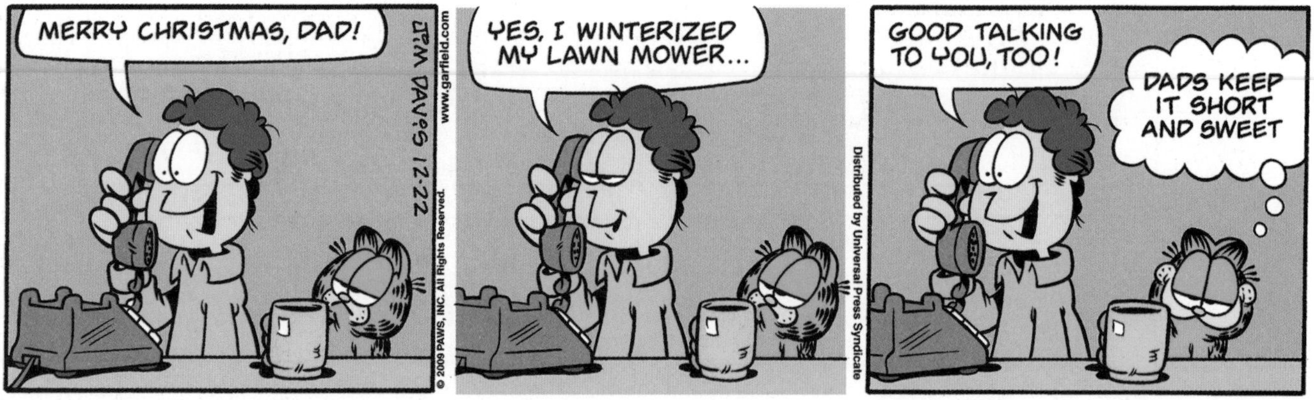
MERRY CHRISTMAS, DAD!
JIM DAVIS 12-22
www.garfield.com
© 2009 PAWS, INC. All Rights Reserved.
YES, I WINTERIZED MY LAWN MOWER...
Distributed by Universal Press Syndicate
GOOD TALKING TO YOU, TOO!
DADS KEEP IT SHORT AND SWEET

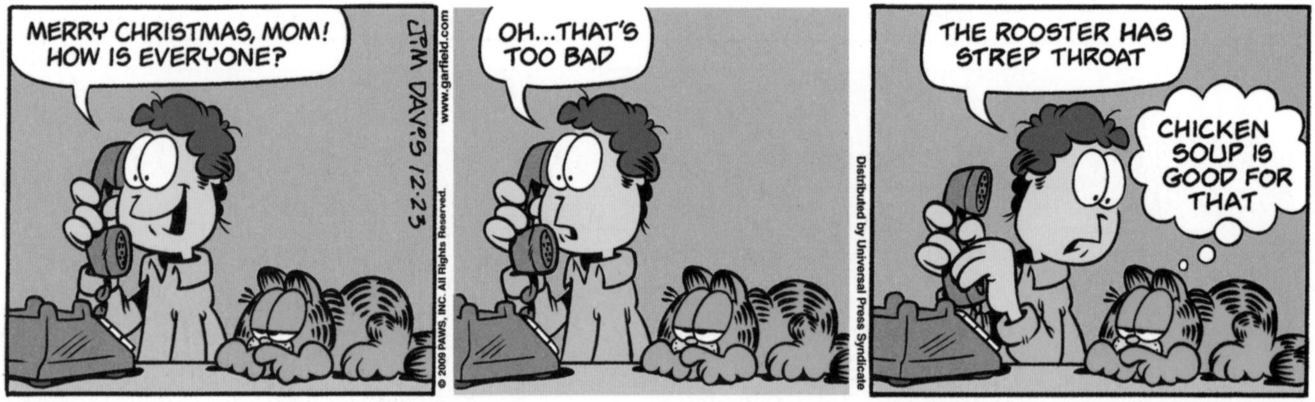
MERRY CHRISTMAS, MOM! HOW IS EVERYONE?
JIM DAVIS 12-23
www.garfield.com
© 2009 PAWS, INC. All Rights Reserved.
OH...THAT'S TOO BAD
Distributed by Universal Press Syndicate
THE ROOSTER HAS STREP THROAT
CHICKEN SOUP IS GOOD FOR THAT

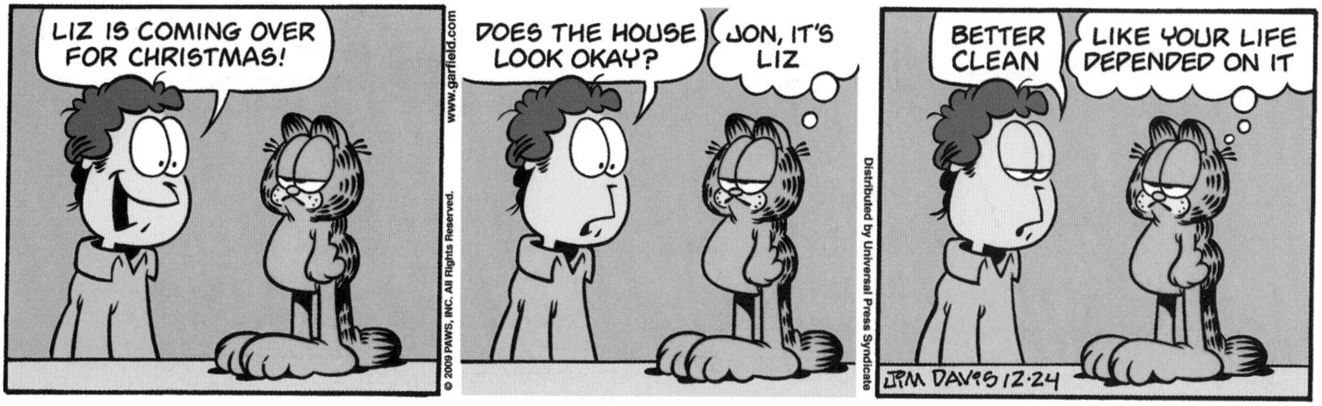
LIZ IS COMING OVER FOR CHRISTMAS!
DOES THE HOUSE LOOK OKAY?
JON, IT'S LIZ
BETTER CLEAN
LIKE YOUR LIFE DEPENDED ON IT
JPM DAVIS 12-24
© 2009 PAWS, INC. All Rights Reserved.
www.garfield.com
Distributed by Universal Press Syndicate

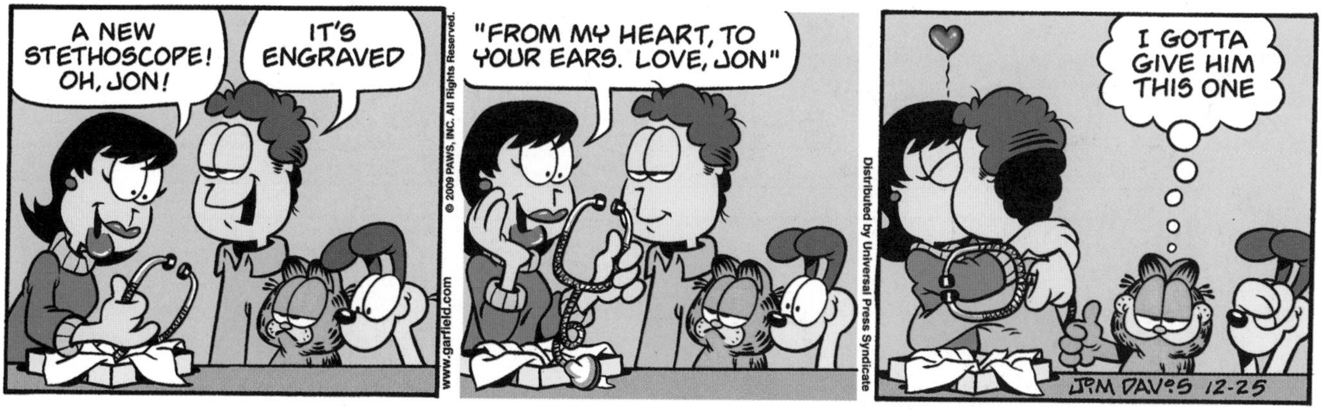
A NEW STETHOSCOPE! OH, JON!
IT'S ENGRAVED
"FROM MY HEART, TO YOUR EARS. LOVE, JON"
I GOTTA GIVE HIM THIS ONE
JPM DAVIS 12-25
© 2009 PAWS, INC. All Rights Reserved.
www.garfield.com
Distributed by Universal Press Syndicate

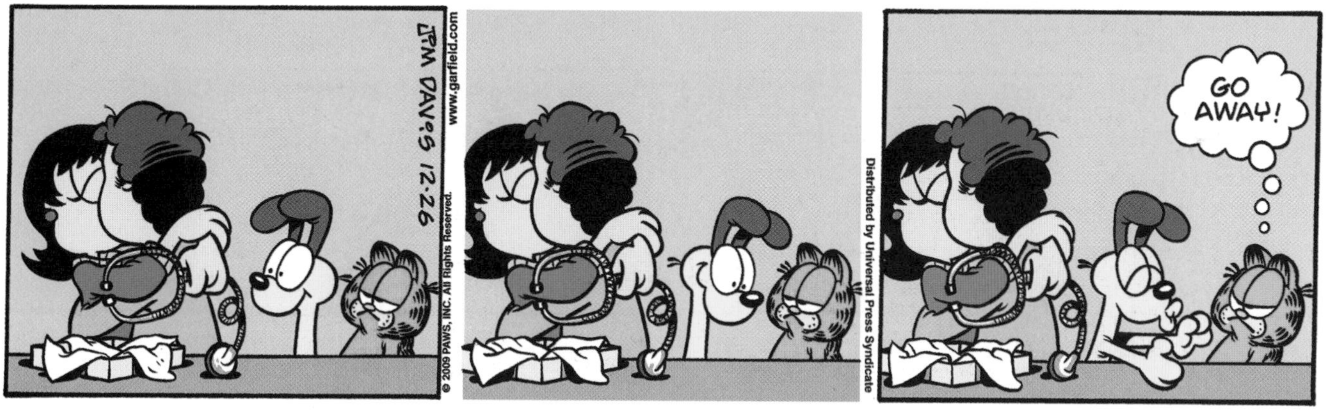
JPM DAVIS 12-26
www.garfield.com
© 2009 PAWS, INC. All Rights Reserved.
GO AWAY!
Distributed by Universal Press Syndicate

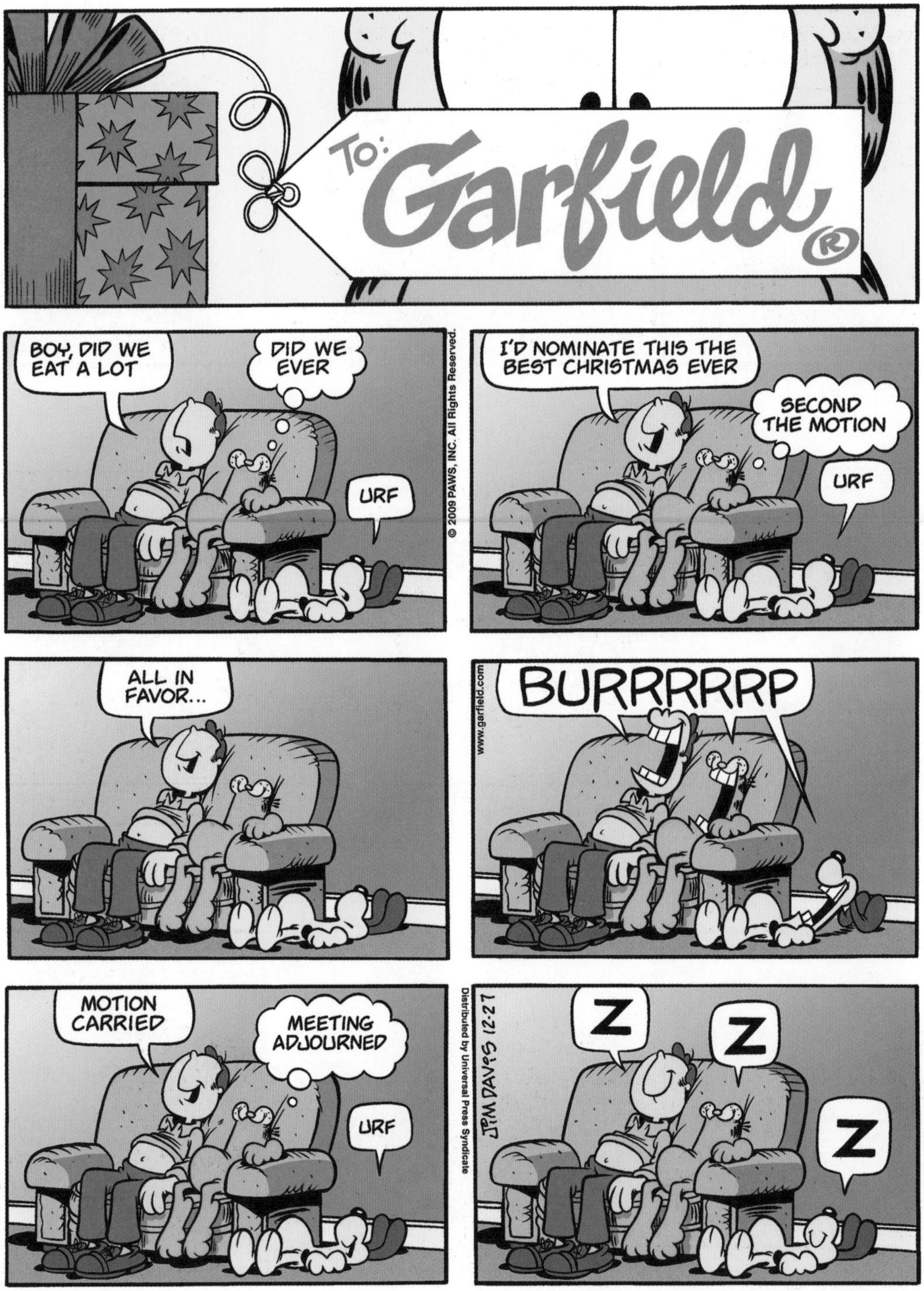
TO: Garfield®
BOY, DID WE EAT A LOT
DID WE EVER
URF
© 2009 PAWS, INC. All Rights Reserved.
I'D NOMINATE THIS THE BEST CHRISTMAS EVER
SECOND THE MOTION
URF
ALL IN FAVOR...
www.garfield.com
BURRRRRP
MOTION CARRIED
MEETING ADJOURNED
URF
Distributed by Universal Press Syndicate
JPM DAVPS 12-27
Z
Z
Z

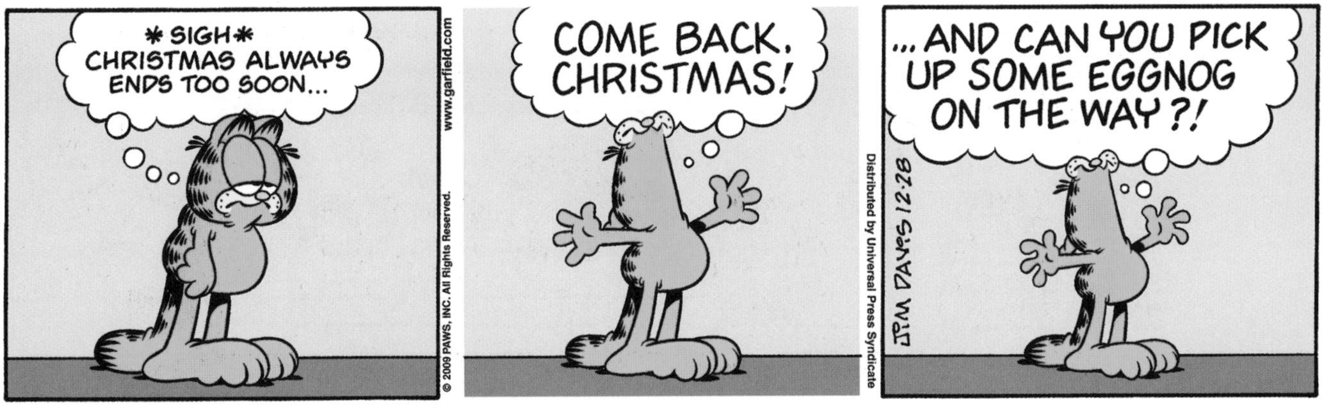
SIGH
CHRISTMAS ALWAYS ENDS TOO SOON...
COME BACK, CHRISTMAS!
...AND CAN YOU PICK UP SOME EGGNOG ON THE WAY?!
JIM DAVIS 12-28

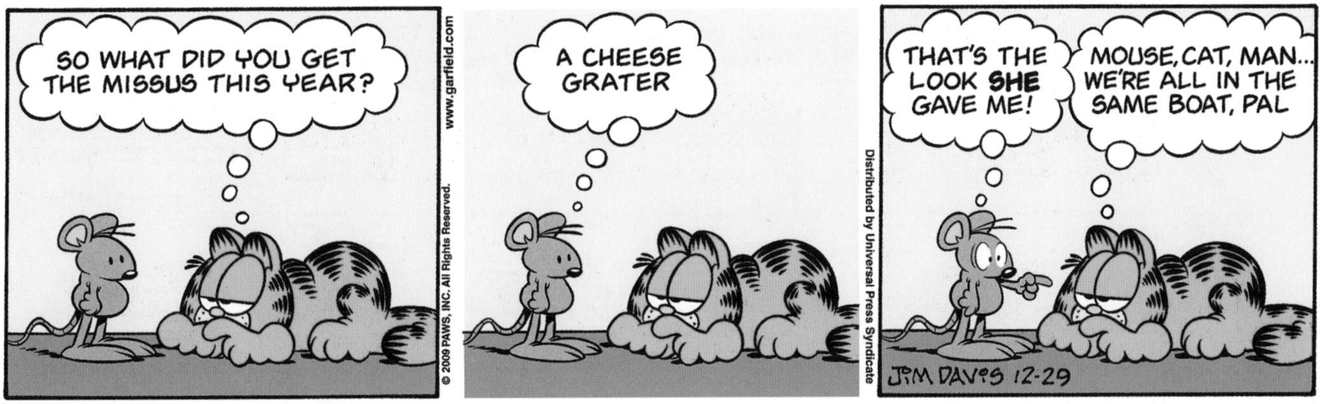
SO WHAT DID YOU GET THE MISSUS THIS YEAR?
A CHEESE GRATER
THAT'S THE LOOK SHE GAVE ME!
MOUSE, CAT, MAN... WE'RE ALL IN THE SAME BOAT, PAL
JIM DAVIS 12-29

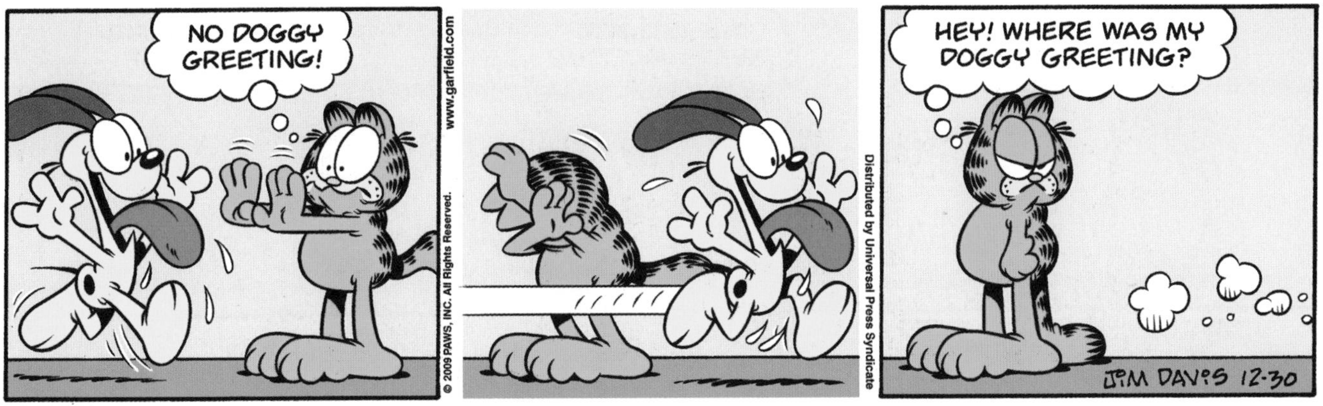
NO DOGGY GREETING!
HEY! WHERE WAS MY DOGGY GREETING?
JIM DAVIS 12-30

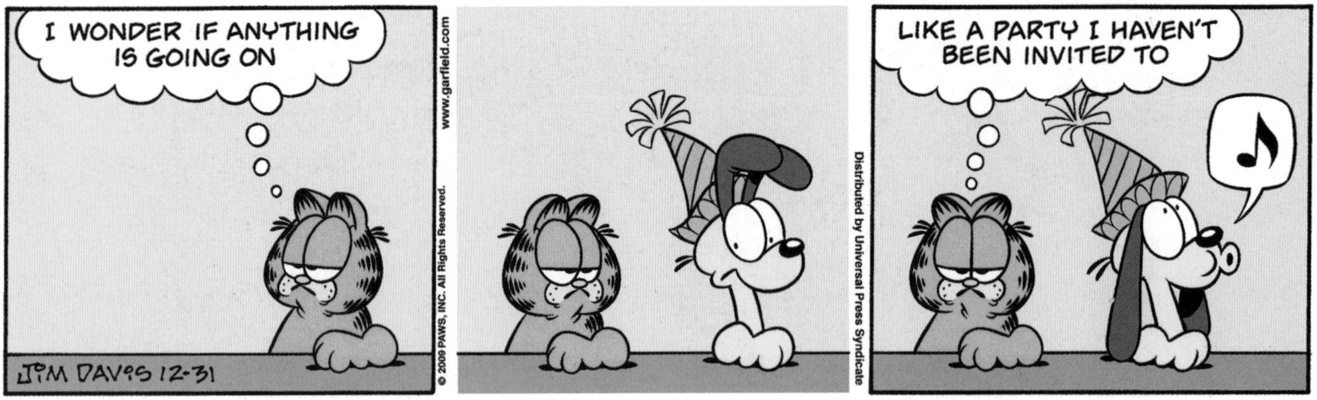
I WONDER IF ANYTHING IS GOING ON
LIKE A PARTY I HAVEN'T BEEN INVITED TO
♪
JIM DAVIS 12-31
© 2009 PAWS, INC. All Rights Reserved. www.garfield.com
Distributed by Universal Press Syndicate

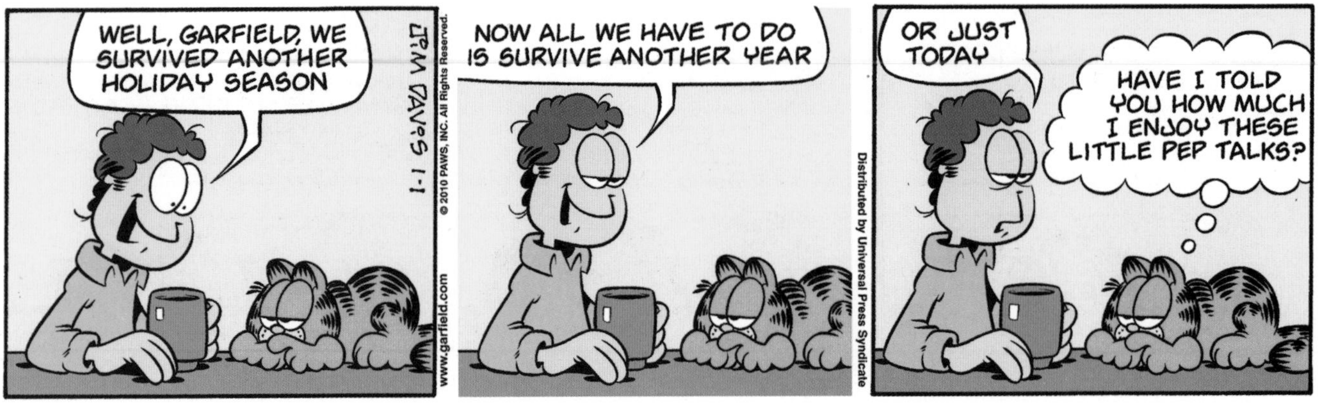
WELL, GARFIELD, WE SURVIVED ANOTHER HOLIDAY SEASON
NOW ALL WE HAVE TO DO IS SURVIVE ANOTHER YEAR
OR JUST TODAY
HAVE I TOLD YOU HOW MUCH I ENJOY THESE LITTLE PEP TALKS?
JIM DAVIS 1-1
© 2010 PAWS, INC. All Rights Reserved. www.garfield.com
Distributed by Universal Press Syndicate

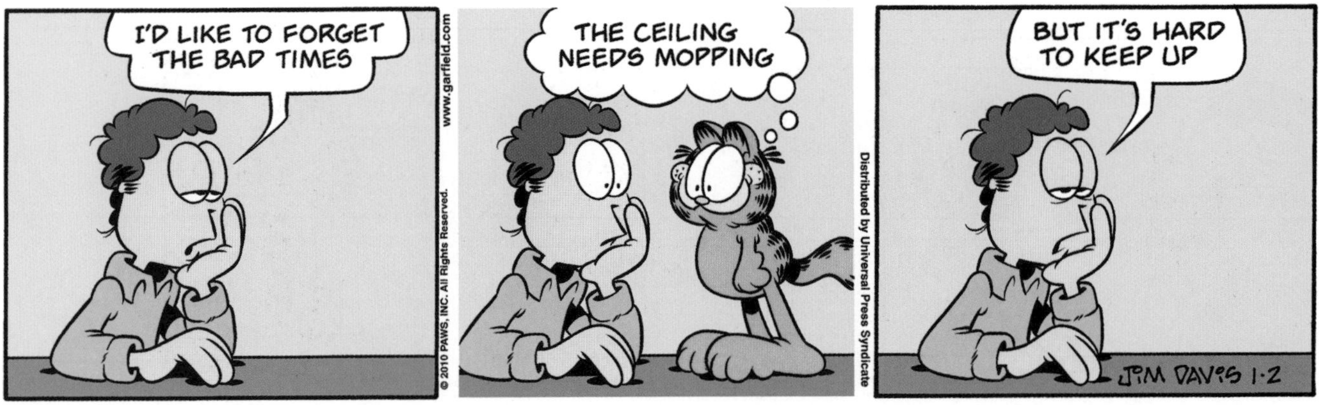
I'D LIKE TO FORGET THE BAD TIMES
THE CEILING NEEDS MOPPING
BUT IT'S HARD TO KEEP UP
JIM DAVIS 1-2
© 2010 PAWS, INC. All Rights Reserved. www.garfield.com
Distributed by Universal Press Syndicate

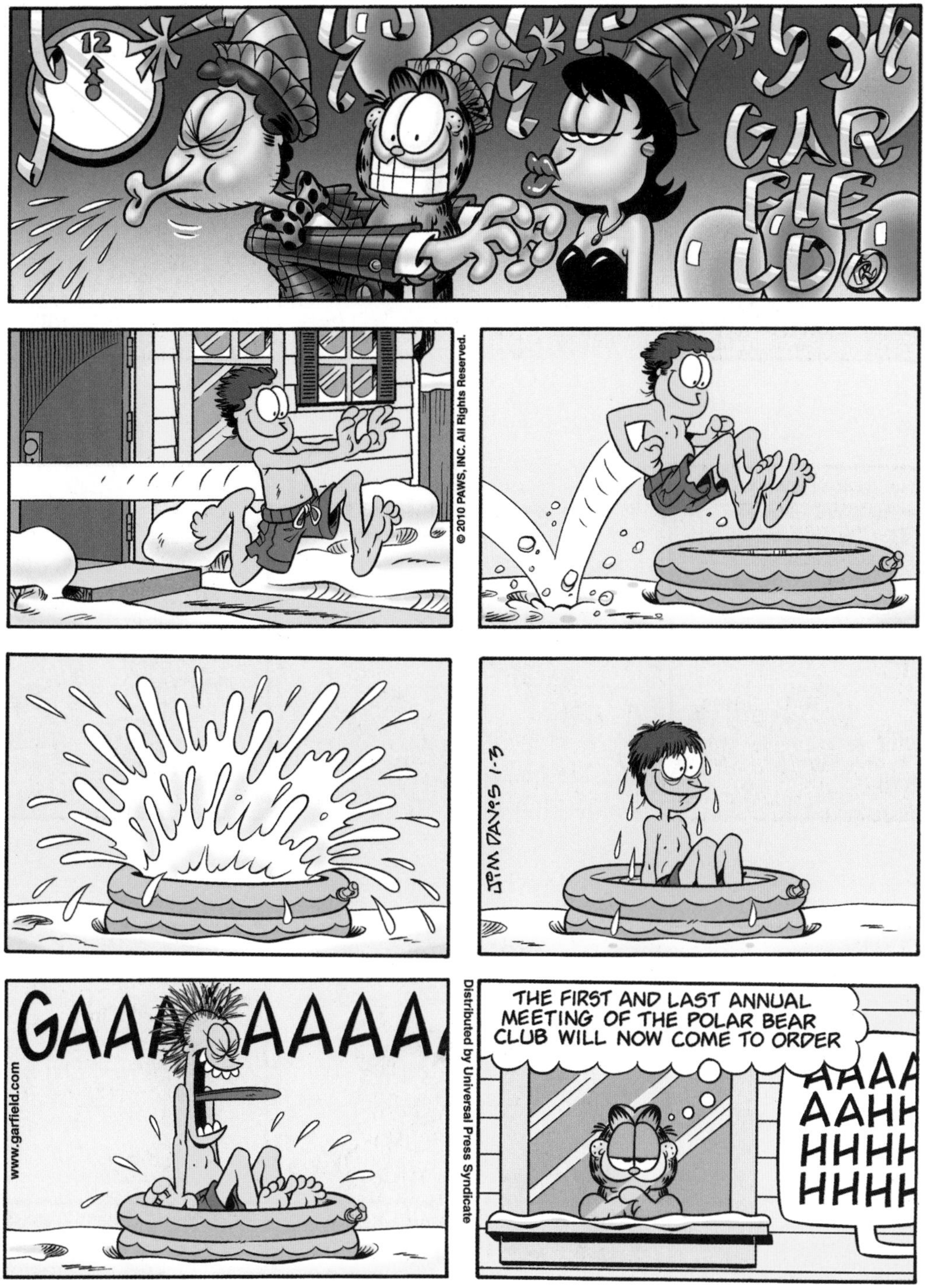
12
GARFIELD
© 2010 PAWS, INC. All Rights Reserved.
JIM DAVIS 1-3
GAAAAAAAA
www.garfield.com
Distributed by Universal Press Syndicate
THE FIRST AND LAST ANNUAL MEETING OF THE POLAR BEAR CLUB WILL NOW COME TO ORDER
AAAAAAHHHHHHHHHH

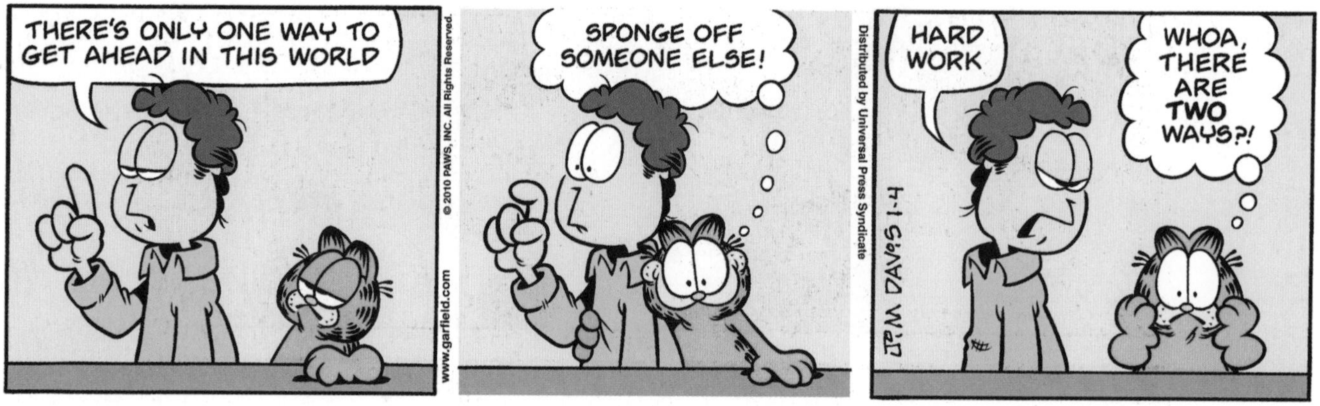
THERE'S ONLY ONE WAY TO GET AHEAD IN THIS WORLD
© 2010 PAWS, INC. All Rights Reserved.
www.garfield.com
SPONGE OFF SOMEONE ELSE!
Distributed by Universal Press Syndicate
HARD WORK
WHOA, THERE ARE **TWO** WAYS?!
JPM DAVPS 1-4

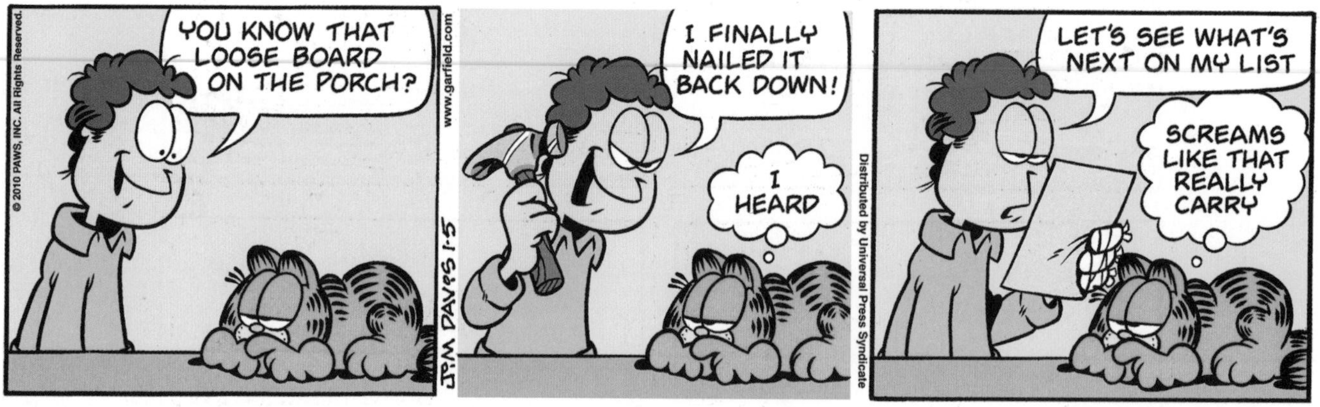
© 2010 PAWS, INC. All Rights Reserved.
YOU KNOW THAT LOOSE BOARD ON THE PORCH?
www.garfield.com
JPM DAVPS 1-5
I FINALLY NAILED IT BACK DOWN!
I HEARD
Distributed by Universal Press Syndicate
LET'S SEE WHAT'S NEXT ON MY LIST
SCREAMS LIKE THAT REALLY CARRY

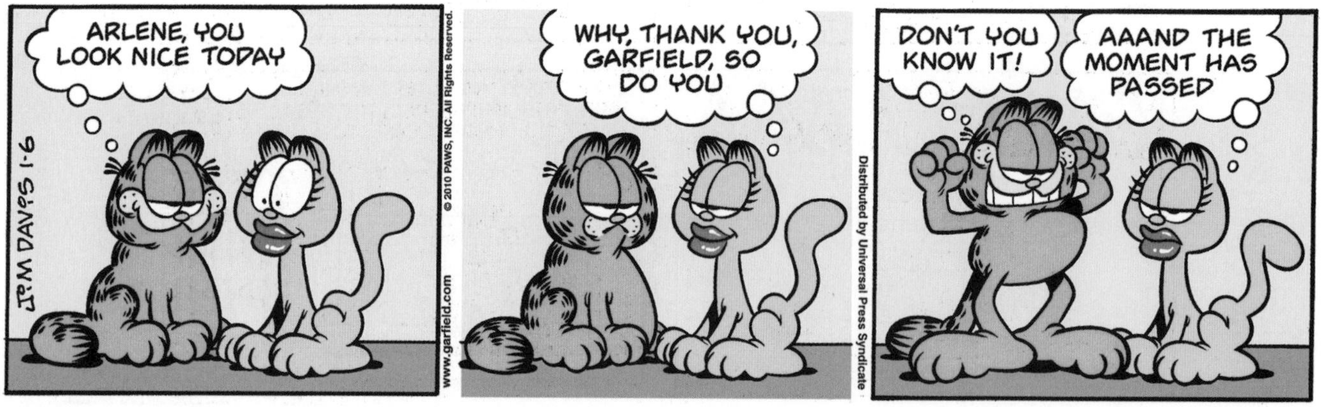
ARLENE, YOU LOOK NICE TODAY
JPM DAVPS 1-6
© 2010 PAWS, INC. All Rights Reserved.
www.garfield.com
WHY, THANK YOU, GARFIELD, SO DO YOU
Distributed by Universal Press Syndicate
DON'T YOU KNOW IT!
AAAND THE MOMENT HAS PASSED

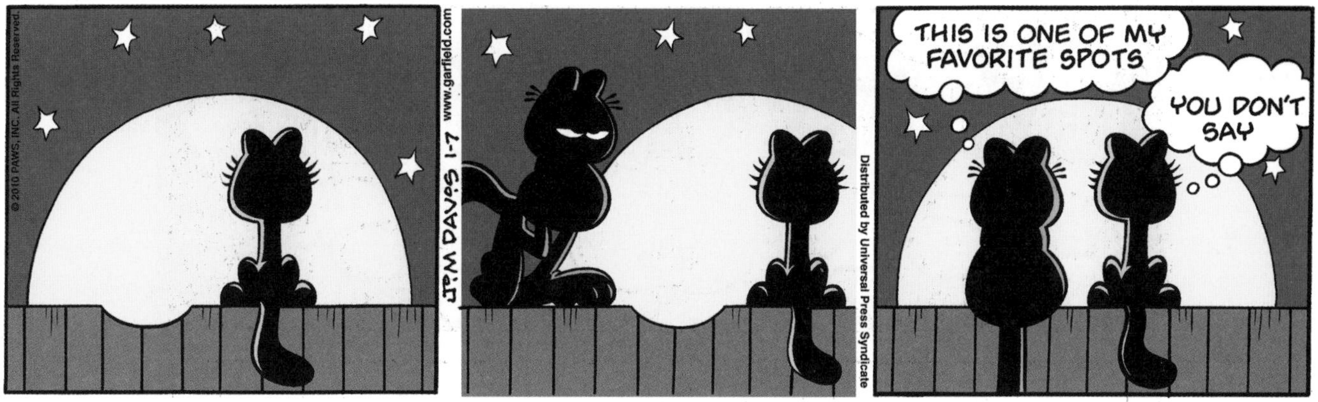
© 2010 PAWS, INC. All Rights Reserved.
www.garfield.com
JPM DAVPS 1-7
Distributed by Universal Press Syndicate
THIS IS ONE OF MY FAVORITE SPOTS
YOU DON'T SAY

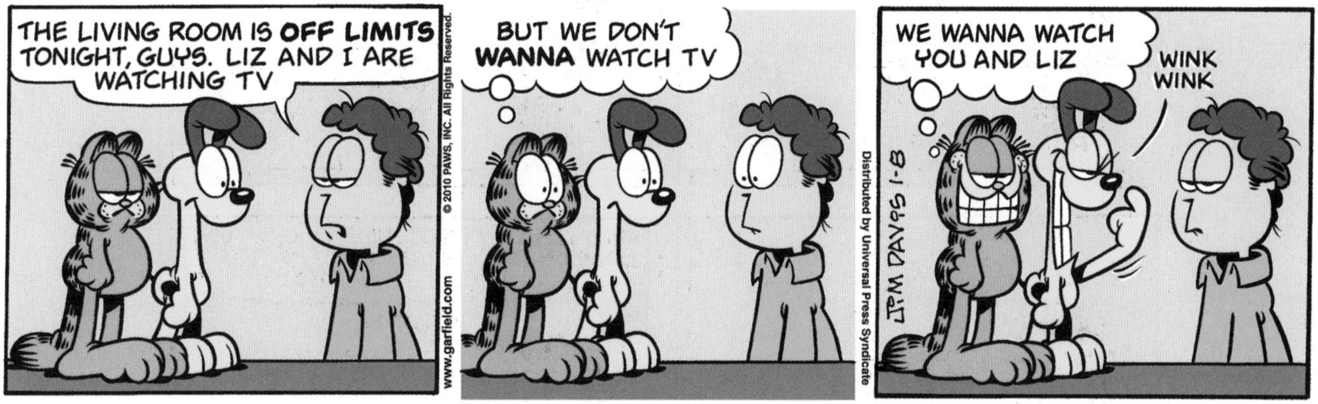
THE LIVING ROOM IS **OFF LIMITS** TONIGHT, GUYS. LIZ AND I ARE WATCHING TV
© 2010 PAWS, INC. All Rights Reserved.
www.garfield.com
BUT WE DON'T **WANNA** WATCH TV
Distributed by Universal Press Syndicate
JPM DAVPS 1-8
WE WANNA WATCH YOU AND LIZ
WINK WINK

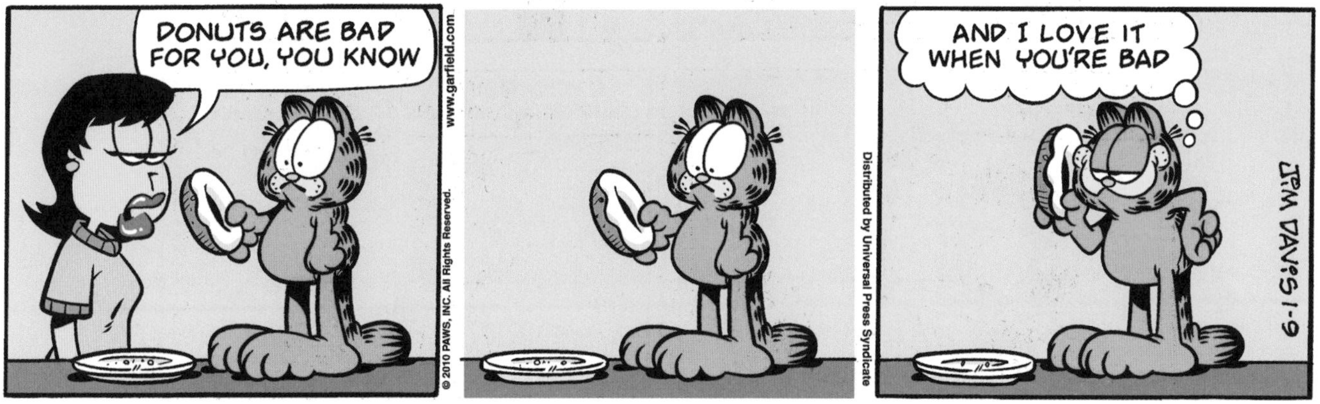
DONUTS ARE BAD FOR YOU, YOU KNOW
www.garfield.com
© 2010 PAWS, INC. All Rights Reserved.
Distributed by Universal Press Syndicate
AND I LOVE IT WHEN YOU'RE BAD
JPM DAVPS 1-9

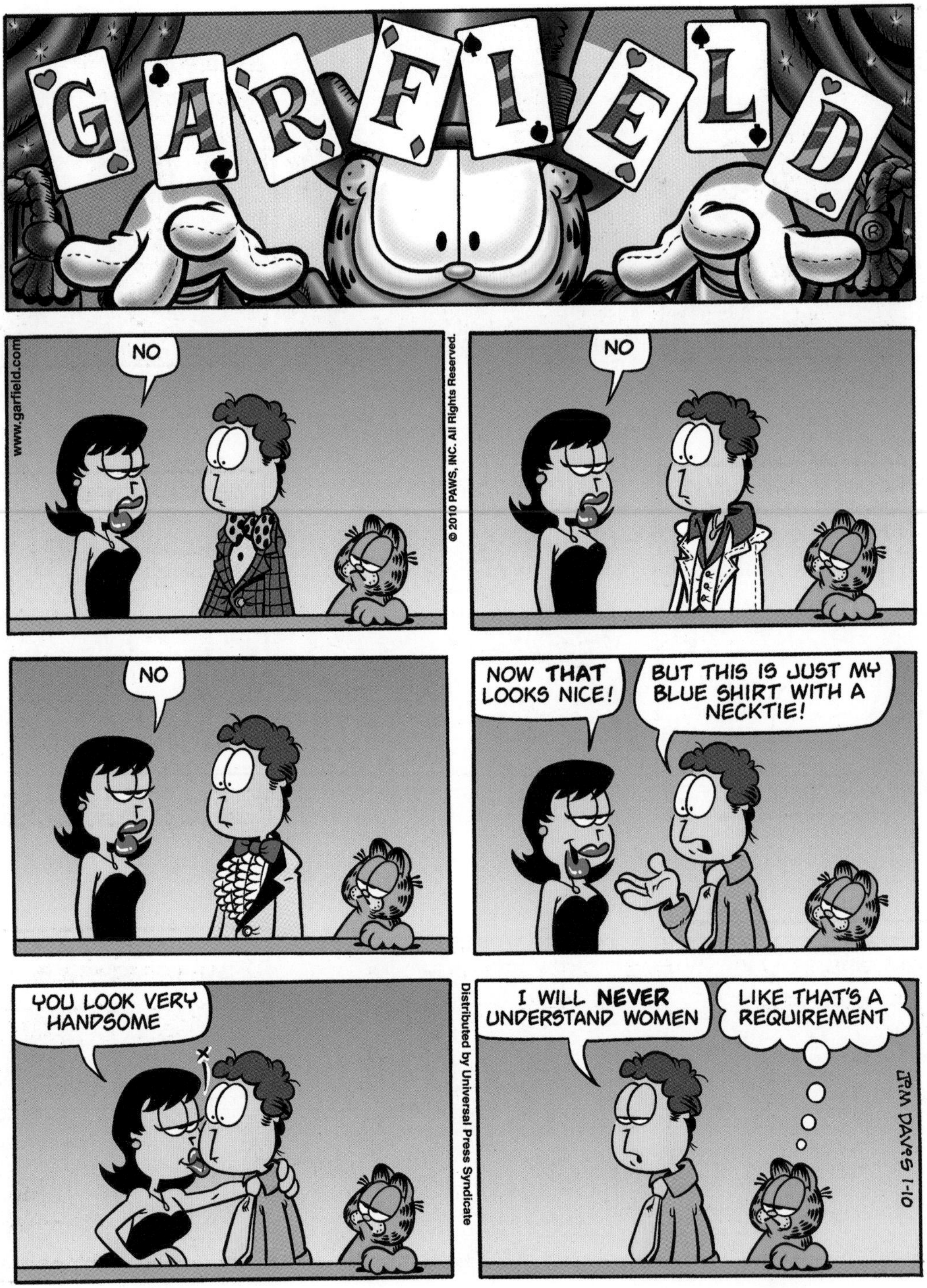
GARFIELD
www.garfield.com
© 2010 PAWS, INC. All Rights Reserved.
NO
NO
NO
NOW **THAT** LOOKS NICE!
BUT THIS IS JUST MY BLUE SHIRT WITH A NECKTIE!
YOU LOOK VERY HANDSOME
Distributed by Universal Press Syndicate
I WILL **NEVER** UNDERSTAND WOMEN
LIKE THAT'S A REQUIREMENT
JIM DAVIS 1-10

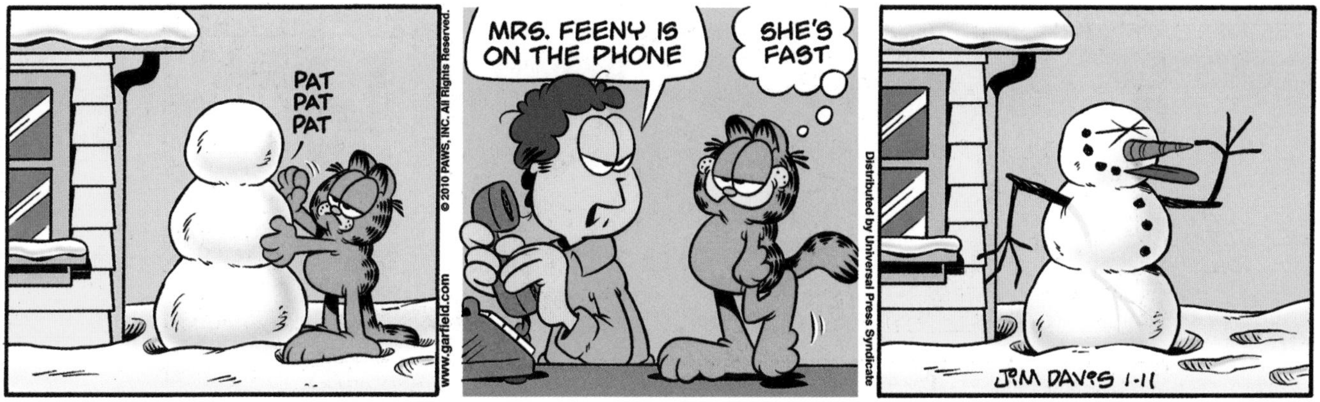
PAT
PAT
PAT
www.garfield.com
© 2010 PAWS, INC. All Rights Reserved.
MRS. FEENY IS ON THE PHONE
SHE'S FAST
Distributed by Universal Press Syndicate
JIM DAVIS 1-11

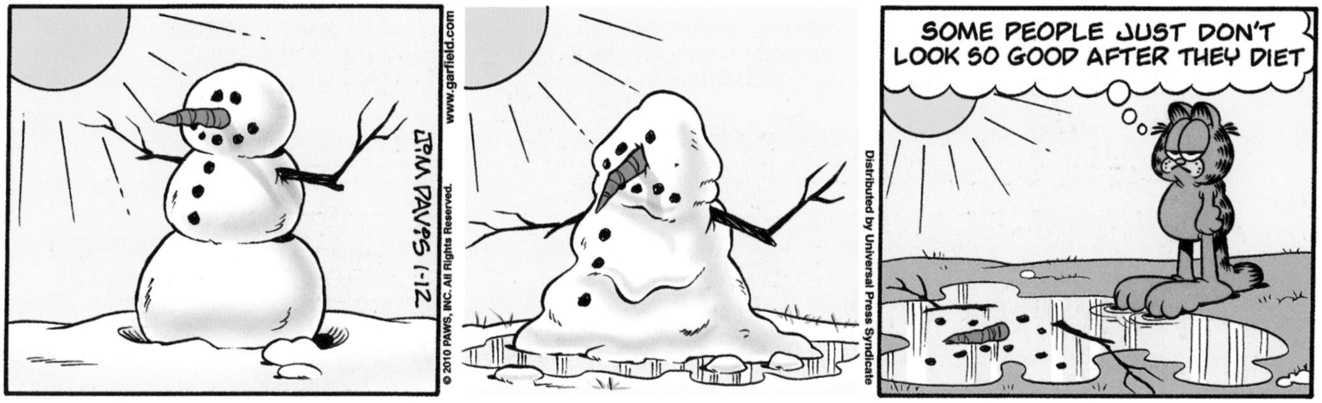
JIM DAVIS 1-12
www.garfield.com
© 2010 PAWS, INC. All Rights Reserved.
Distributed by Universal Press Syndicate
SOME PEOPLE JUST DON'T LOOK SO GOOD AFTER THEY DIET

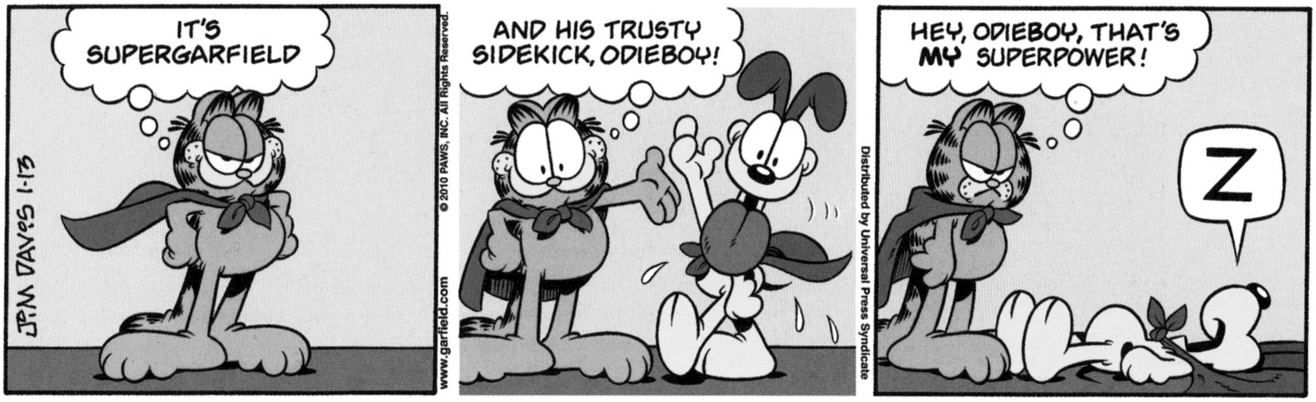
IT'S SUPERGARFIELD
JIM DAVIS 1-13
www.garfield.com
© 2010 PAWS, INC. All Rights Reserved.
AND HIS TRUSTY SIDEKICK, ODIEBOY!
Distributed by Universal Press Syndicate
HEY, ODIEBOY, THAT'S MY SUPERPOWER!
Z

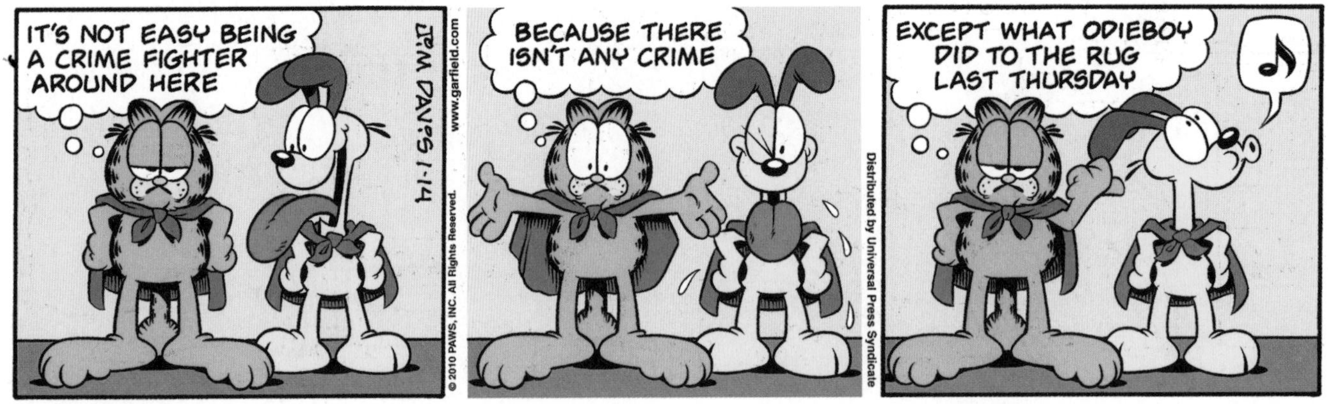
IT'S NOT EASY BEING A CRIME FIGHTER AROUND HERE
JPM DAVPS 1-14
© 2010 PAWS, INC. All Rights Reserved. www.garfield.com
BECAUSE THERE ISN'T ANY CRIME
Distributed by Universal Press Syndicate
EXCEPT WHAT ODIEBOY DID TO THE RUG LAST THURSDAY
♪

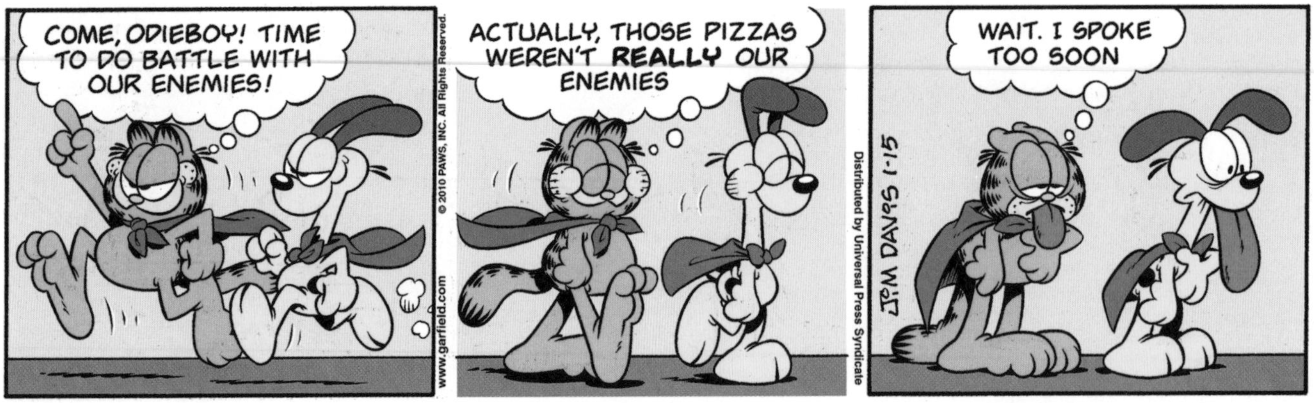
COME, ODIEBOY! TIME TO DO BATTLE WITH OUR ENEMIES!
© 2010 PAWS, INC. All Rights Reserved. www.garfield.com
ACTUALLY, THOSE PIZZAS WEREN'T **REALLY** OUR ENEMIES
Distributed by Universal Press Syndicate
WAIT. I SPOKE TOO SOON
JPM DAVPS 1-15

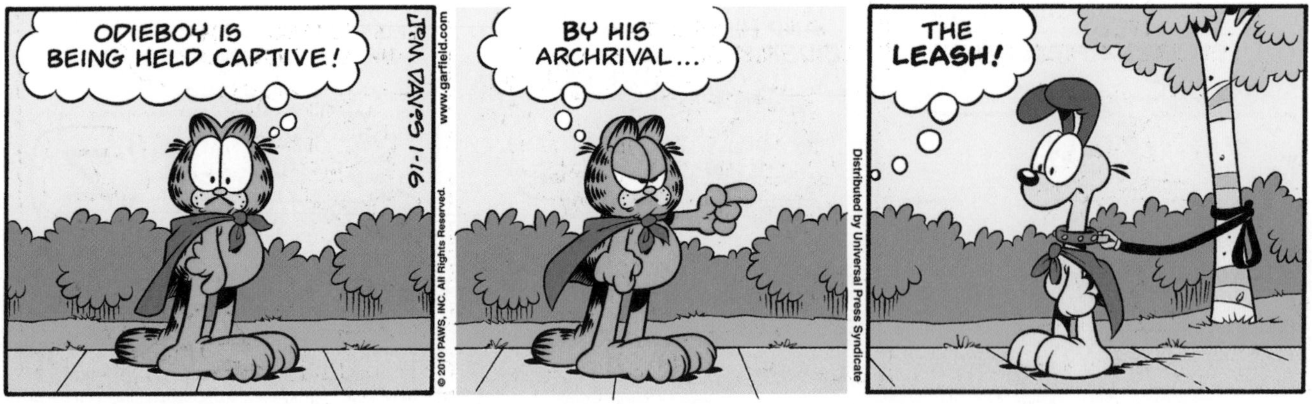
ODIEBOY IS BEING HELD CAPTIVE!
JPM DAVPS 1-16
© 2010 PAWS, INC. All Rights Reserved. www.garfield.com
BY HIS ARCHRIVAL...
Distributed by Universal Press Syndicate
THE **LEASH**!

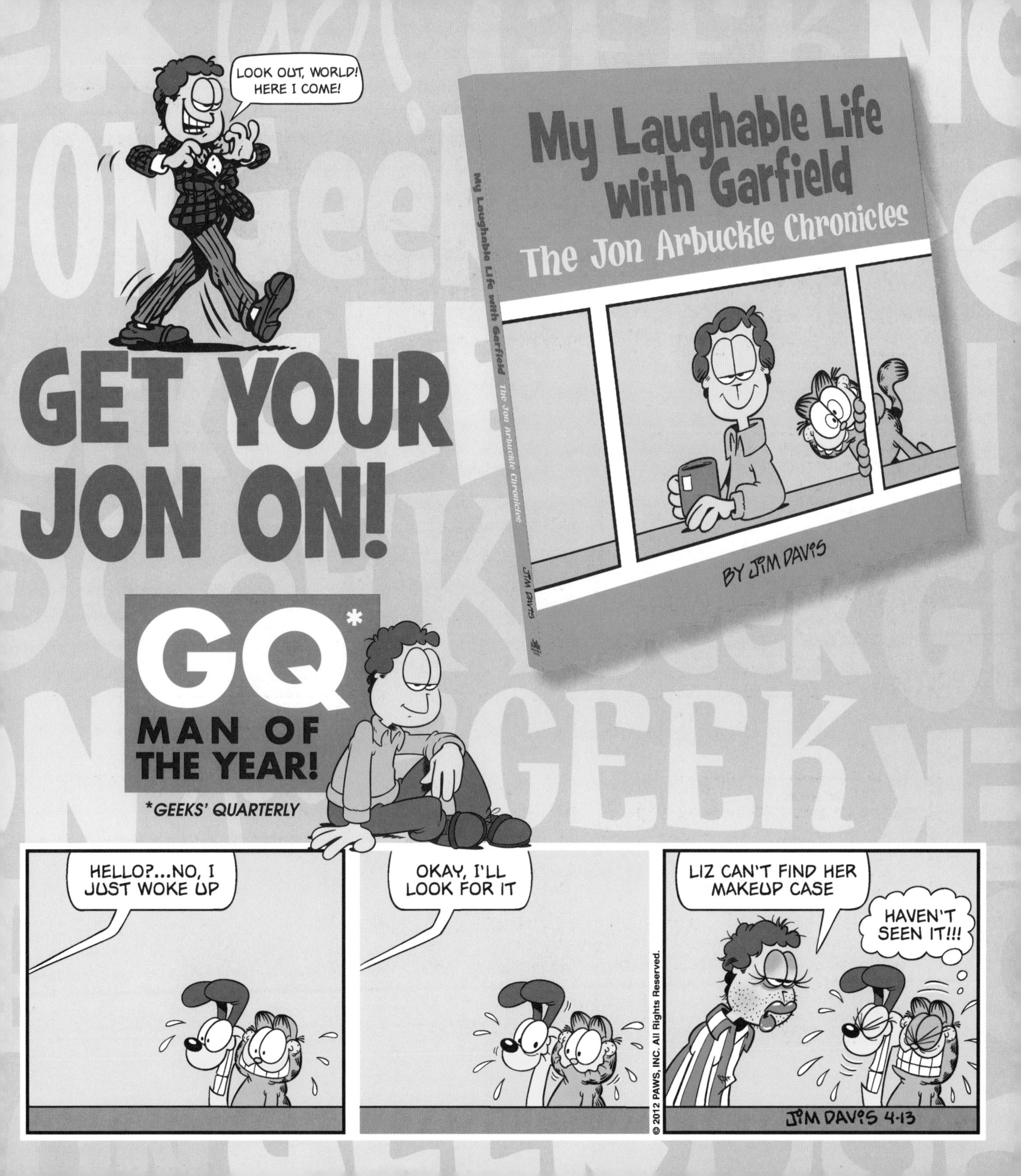
LOOK OUT, WORLD! HERE I COME!
GET YOUR JON ON!
My Laughable Life with Garfield
The Jon Arbuckle Chronicles
BY JIM DAVIS
GQ* MAN OF THE YEAR!
*GEEKS' QUARTERLY
HELLO?...NO, I JUST WOKE UP
OKAY, I'LL LOOK FOR IT
LIZ CAN'T FIND HER MAKEUP CASE
HAVEN'T SEEN IT!!!
JIM DAVIS 4-13
© 2012 PAWS, INC. All Rights Reserved.

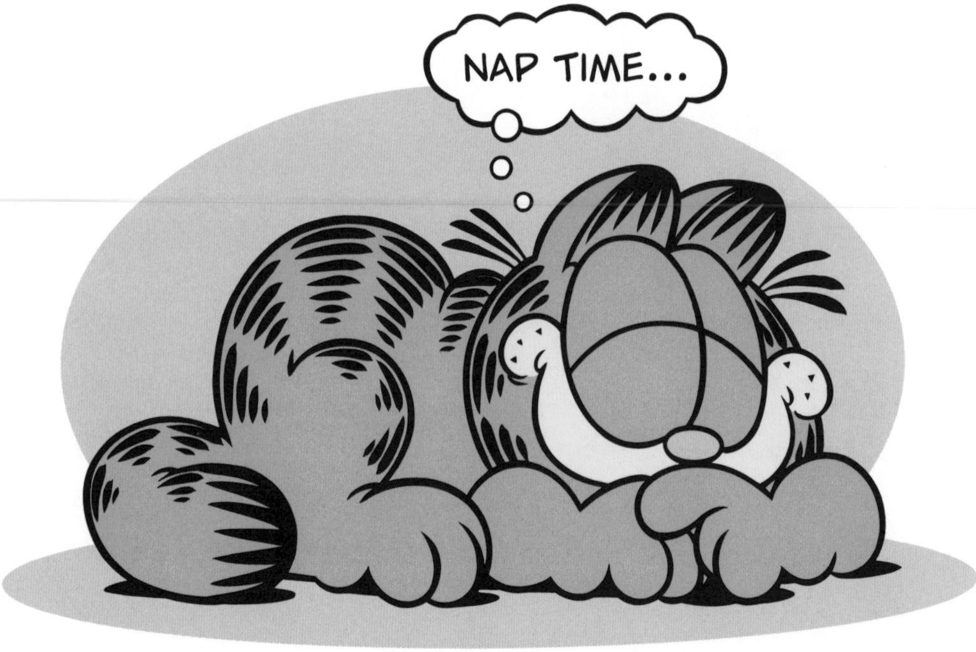
NAP TIME...